Defending the Music

Defending the Music

Michael Steinberg at the Boston Globe, 1964–1976

Conceived by

JORJA FLEEZANIS

Edited by

SUSAN FEDER, JACOB JAHIEL, AND MARC MANDEL

OXFORD
UNIVERSITY PRESS

OXFORD
UNIVERSITY PRESS

Oxford University Press is a department of the University of Oxford.
It furthers the University's objective of excellence in research, scholarship,
and education by publishing worldwide. Oxford is a registered trade mark of
Oxford University Press in the UK and certain other countries.

Published in the United States of America by Oxford University Press
198 Madison Avenue, New York, NY 10016, United States of America.

Library of Congress Cataloging-in-Publication Data
Names: Steinberg, Michael, 1928–2009 author | Feder, Susan (Arts administrator) editor | Jahiel, Jacob editor | Mandel, Marc editor | Globe Newspaper Co. contributor
Title: Defending the music : Michael Steinberg at the Boston Globe, 1964–1976 / conceived by Jorja Fleezanis ; edited by Susan Feder, Jacob Jahiel, and Marc Mandel.
Description: [1]. | New York : Oxford University Press, 2026.
Identifiers: LCCN 2025036127 (print) | LCCN 2025036128 (ebook) |
ISBN 9780197810217 hardback | ISBN 9780197810248 | ISBN 9780197810224 epub
Subjects: LCSH: Steinberg, Michael, 1928-2009 |
Musical criticism—Massachusetts—Boston | LCGFT: Music criticism and reviews
Classification: LCC ML423.S848 A25 2026 (print) | LCC ML423.S848 (ebook) |
DDC 070.4/4978—dc23/eng/20251212
LC record available at https://lccn.loc.gov/2025036127
LC ebook record available at https://lccn.loc.gov/2025036128

DOI: 10.1093/oso/9780197810217.001.0001

Printed by Sheridan Books, Inc., United States of America

The manufacturer's authorized representative in the EU for product safety is
Oxford University Press España S.A. of Parque Empresarial San Fernando de Henares,
Avenida de Castilla, 2 – 28830 Madrid (www.oup.es/en or product.safety@oup.com).
OUP España S.A. also acts as importer into Spain of products made by the manufacturer.

"I have done my best to fulfill my intense commitment to music itself, a commitment that comes right from the center of me."

—Michael Steinberg

"Connecting to music requires opening up, to identifying with the inner world of the composer so deeply that you are willing to devote your entire life energy to express it."

—Jorja Fleezanis

Dedicated to the memory of Michael Steinberg and Jorja Fleezanis

An undated photo (c.1992) of Michael Steinberg and Jorja Fleezanis. (Fleezanis personal collection; used with permission.)

Contents

Introduction xix
Note from the Editors xxxv

1964 1

Bernstein's *Kaddish* in Premiere Here 1
Glenn Gould, Pianist—Also a Critic of Music Worth Paying Heed To 3
Munch Conducts Berlioz—*Fantastique* 4
New Faces, Remarkable Symphony—Mahler Ninth Superb in New York Concert 6
Late Beethoven Sonata Heard in Special Perspective 8
Performing Composer—A Treat to Hear 9
I puritani—Opera a Triumph, Sutherland Great 11
Brendel—Outstanding Performance for Valorous Audience 13
Renaissance Music by the Camerata 14
Gina Bachauer—Pianist Commanding in Mussorgsky Work 15
Stokowski, BSO Share Afternoon of Glamour 17
Sawallisch—Viennese Outstanding in Bruckner Symphony 18
Philomel—New Babbitt Work Lyric Triumph 20
Elliott Carter—Prausnitz Gives Boston Premiere of Variations 22
On Segregation—Musicians, Politics, and Responsibilities 23
Brahms Concerto With Some Bold Retouches 25
La Bohème Has Its High, Low Spots 27
Our Unserious Public—What Does It Hear? 28
Musicians and Scholars—Must There Be War? 30
Composer-Performers—What Can They Teach Us? 32
Marian Anderson—South Better Now 34
Erich Leinsdorf Stresses Broader Musical View 35
Pierre Monteux, 1875–1964 37
Rudolf Kolisch—Music and Webern, and "Beautiful Tone" 39
From Price, Von Karajan Spectacular *Carmen* 41
Schoenberg—Thoughts on the Birthday of an Extraordinary Man 43
Boston Symphony Opens 84th Season 45
Virtuosity—Beautiful Sounds or Beautiful Music? 46
Barbirolli Conducts Music of England 48
Boston Symphony Chamber Group Disappointing in Debut 50
Handel and Haydn Society Gives Annual *Messiah* 51

1965 54

On Criticism—An Open Letter in Reply to Henry B. Cabot 54
Scissors and Paste Are Bad Composers 56
Ernst Haefliger's Beautiful Debut 58
Nono's *Intolleranza* Debuts Despite Delays 60
An Exciting Concert—*Groups*, *Circle*, and Beethoven 62
Not Such Very New Music—Schoenberg's Violin Concerto and Joseph Silverstein 64
Schoenberg Concerto and Joseph Silverstein 66
First Performance—Ives Symphony No. 4 Played at Carnegie 67
But No Green Paint—Fiedler Given Great Ovation as Pops Returns to Symphony 69
Composer-Conductor—Music Not Philanthropy for Pierre Boulez 71
Zukofsky and Kalish Play Ives Sonatas 72
The Beatles, the Pulitzer, and Other Related Topics 73
Frager Plays Mozart as Festival Opens 75
Claude Frank Superb in Beethoven Work 76
Lohengrin Splendid Finale 78
Help! Loud, Inaudible, and Evidently Sexy 80
Opera in Concert—A Valid Undertaking for Symphony Groups 81
Organist Like Conductor—Powerless, Responsible 84
Britten Premiere With Rostropovich 86
Rostropovich Speaks—Mainly About Britten 88
Moscow Philharmonic—Kondrashin Conducts, Vishnevskaya Sings 91
Carter Double Concerto in Boston Premiere 93
Serkin Masterful Beethoven Player 94
Handel's *Messiah*: For One Shaw From Another—One Serious Performance 96
More Mahler—Bernstein, Philharmonic Give Last Three Symphonies 99
Vishnevskaya Sings, Rostropovich Plays 103

1966 105

Beethoven—His Last Piano Sonata, Opus 111, Reconsidered 105
Martinon Conducts BSO in Beautiful *Eroica* 108
Beautiful Playing by a Legendary Pianist 109
Globe Critic Recommends [Stravinsky's *Rite of Spring*] 111
Neglected Masterpiece—Schumann's Interpretation of Goethe's *Faust* Tragedy 112
Schumann *Faust-Scenes* Are Sublime Experience 114
Webern and Isaac—Club 47 Concert Turns to Classics 116
At Old Opera House Farewell—Few Stars Among Met's "Ensemble of Stars" 118
Globe Critic Recommends [Mahler Symphony No. 4] 120

The Oratorio—Music for Voice 120
Goldberg by Leonhardt 121
Berlin and Broadway—Lotte Lenya Reminisces About Weill and Brecht 123
Guarneri Quartet: A Promising Group—But Doubts Remain 126
Clarity No Replacement for Color or Contrasts 128
Boult Opens Tanglewood Auspiciously 129
Guarneri String Quartet—Superb Ensemble, Peerless Virtuosity 130
Sir Adrian Boult—English Conductor, 77, Reminisces at Tanglewood 132
Guarneri Quartet a Quintet for Brahms 134
Even Mrs. Stravinsky Boos—NY Philharmonic Wrecks *Oedipus* 135
Stravinsky Conducts Philharmonic—Inspiring Performance With His Own Music 137
Major and Minor—Schoenberg for the Man Who Likes Webern 140
Composers Quartet Attains Distinction at Lenox 143
Handel's Opera *Giulio Cesare* Suffers from Tampering 145
Webern Festival—Fine Songs and Quartet in Posthumous Premieres 147
Moses and Aron—A Great Work Creditably Done 150
Brendel's Luminous Enchantment Dazzles 152
Vienna's Alfred Brendel—Pianist With Sense of Humor 153

1967 159
Carter's Concerto in Dramatic Debut 159
St. John Passion—A Stunning Version 161
Kubelik Conducts Great Mahler Ninth 162
Irving Fine on Record, Thanks to Brandeis 164
A Beautiful *Winterreise* 165
Extraordinary Mahler 166
Kubelik Chooses Exile to Privileges 168
Gertrude Schoenberg, 1898–1967—A Memoir 170
His Dedication Was Selfless—A Century of Toscanini 173
Stravinsky's *Rake's Progress*—Sarah Remembers With Affection 175
Mod *Rake* Bold, Fantastic 178
Cliburn—Great, but Could Do Better 180
Gustav Holst India Opera Remarkably Original Piece 181
Handel and Haydn's New Boss—Thomas Dunn, the Purist 183
Roland Hayes Verges on 80—Real Meaning of Great Man's Birthday 185
Roland Hayes Looks Back—"People Tell Me I Don't Realize What I Give" 188
Discovered: Wealth of Talent—Rewarding Day With Russian Music 190
Menuhin Uniquely Beautiful at Tanglewood 192
A Natural Sounding *Tristan und Isolde* 193
Tribute to Monteverdi 195
Rosen's Debussy Bright 197

Beethoven's Original *Fidelio* Tanglewood Delight 197
Crisp Handel by Mann 199
Pears and Britten—A Vigorous Schubert 200
French Charm Pervades Bernac, Poulenc's Album 202
Guarneri String Quartet—From Skillful to Marvelous 204
BSO's Leinsdorf Explains—Why Others Have Orchestra Problems 205
Leinsdorf Has a Good Point, Says Steinberg 207
Exciting *Messiah* Via Mozart 211

1968 215
The Music Guild Quartet—A Reader Writes, a Critic Answers 215
A Kind of Executive Partner—Role of the Accompanist 217
Bigger the Bang—The Art of Applauding 220
Emperor Given a Fresh Airing 222
For the Opera Company an Unexciting Season 223
Romantic Piano Style Lost? 226
Happy Maestro Steinberg Scoffs at "Interim" Talk 227
Harvard Student's Mozart Completion "Amazing" 230
Choice of Funeral Music Was Masterly 232
You Can't Have It Both Ways—Accept Approval, Reject Disapproval? 233
"Tempo" and "Character"—Are Beethoven, Others Heard Properly? 236
Is Beethoven's Tempo Too Fast? 238
Debussy—A Contemporary View 240
Original Beethoven Hardly Recognizable 242
Schumann "Premiere" by Frager, BSO First-Rate 245
Baker-Barbirolli, a Fine Partnership 246
Davis Conducts BSO Superbly 247
Leonhardt Harpsichord Master 249
Copland at His Best 251
History Aids Bach 252
Two Good Performances—The Year of Schoenberg 253
Beethoven in Puerto Rico—A Fellow Lecturer Sings Brendel's Praises 256
The Works of Elliott Carter—Where Drama and Music Intersect 258
An A-plus for Columbia 260
Superb! That's Sills 261

1969 265
Sherman's Piano Concert Stimulating 265
The New Fares Better Than Old 266
NY Philharmonic's 125th—The Pitfalls of a Complex Babbitt 268
Miss Sills Brilliant in Boston's *Lucia* 270
Babbitt's Music Requires Special Audience 272
Schnabel and Cone—Good Talks and Advice about Music 274
Berlioz—Outstanding Release 276

Hub Treated to Early Beethoven 278
Whoom-pahs and Goosebumps—the Untraditional 280
Schubertiades Recalled 282
Henry Lewis's Credo—"For Music, Not Myself" 284
Schoenberg Drama Awesomely Performed 286
Peter Serkin at 21—Exceptionally Gifted Pianist 288
Newton Memorial Concert Takes Ancient Theme for Youthful Piece 289
Had Refused the Job—Boulez to Philharmonic 290
Americans Ignored—Why Import Conductors? 293
Textbook from Bach 296
Tanglewood's *Otello* Saved by Cassilly 297
Superb Chamber Music 299
Dartmouth Delight—Sessions Old and New a Heady Mix 300
A Growing Symphonic Skill 303
Aspen's Music Festival—An Accompaniment of Real Thunder 304
Wishing Him the Best—Leinsdorf's Farewell 307
Britten Knows His "Repeats" 310
Not Enough New—What Symphony Lacks 311
The Ladies Left Too Soon—Elgar Needs More Patience 313
Reforming the BSO 314
Thomas in Dazzling BSO Debut 317
Public Concert Defended—More Than Meets Ear 318
Ormandy Does Mantovani Job 321
Horowitz—Boring, Marvelous, and Exciting 322
Pears, Britten—A Voyage of Discovery 323
Giulini and BSO With Brahms More Like Borge 324
Philharmonic Dilemma—New Hall Still Wanting 325
Pablo Casals—"What a Musician" 328

1970 334

Real Music Will Survive 334
New Memoirs Translation Revives Genius of Berlioz 336
André Previn in Hub Concert 338
The Moscow Philharmonic Performs 340
Carter Concerto Premiered 341
Schuller Leads BSO in His *Spectra* 343
Britten's *Brandenburgs* Exceptional Recording 345
Gifted Soprano Fills Gardner with Color 346
Composers String Quartet Plays Elliott Carter Works 347
Pianist André Watts Performs at Symphony Hall 349
Thomas Conducts BSO in Mahler's Ninth Symphony 350
New *Kreislerianas* 352
Problems of Big, Amateur Choruses 353
Monteverdi's *L'Orfeo* Impressively Produced 355

Steinberg on Steinberg 357
Schwann's Wonderful Catalogue 359
The Boston Musica Viva 362
Thomas Leads Symphony in Piston, Schuman Program 363
In Israel, Omit the Ratchet, Maestro 364
Harrison's Canticle No. 3 Fine, Sometimes Surprising 367
String Quartet Opens Series at MIT 368
BSO Plays Copland's *Short Symphony* 369
Steinberg Conducts BSO in Mahler's Seventh 371

1971 373
Thomas's Theater Sense Enlivens BSO 373
Camerata Early Music Series Sells Out 374
Horenstein Rare Conductor Who Grasps Mahler's Intent 376
Abbado . . . Davis . . . Kubelik . . . Ozawa?—Who'll Succeed Steinberg as BSO Conductor? 378
Haitink Even Better in the Flesh 380
Frank's Beethoven Sonata Series Best Buy 381
Cantata Singers Perform Bach and John Harbison 383
What to Do With Your Eyes While the Orchestra Plays 384
Bernstein—*Missa solemnis* at Tanglewood 386
Thomas and Berkshire Excel With the *Rhenish* 387
Aventures Brilliantly Staged 389
Ozawa's *Faust* 390
Bernstein's *Mass* at JFK Center 392
Fine Simplicity Marks Fleisher 394
When Twelve Music Critics Meet All Is Not Perfect Harmony 395

1972 399
The Inevitable Future of Michael Tilson Thomas—Where Is This Brilliant Young Musician Going? 399
Rubinstein Plays With BSO 406
BSO—An Impressive Concert 407
Met's New *Pelléas* More Lucid Than Most 408
Watts's Recital Brilliant in Part 411
Beethoven's Triple Concerto—Two Versions 412
Rosen's Sonata Album a Distinguished Work 414
Dunn Leads Bach at Symphony Hall 416
"Greatest Living Composer"? 417
Steinberg Conducts *Romeo and Juliet* 419
Brahms Concerto Well Done 420
. . . and Bing's Successor Plans His *Carmen* 421
Fine Arts Quartet Plays Fine, Babbitt 424
Gentele—Man of Many Parts 426

The Stanislaw Method 427
Bernstein at Tanglewood 430
A Moving Mahler 432
Levine's Mahler Rich, Clear 433
Soprano Almost Sensation 434
Thomas Conducts BSO's 92nd Opening Concert 436
Boston Symphony Taps Rich Era 437
Heifetz—In a Class by Himself 439
Berlioz's *Nuits d'été* Rare Treat 441
Oxford Issues Paperback of Tovey's Music Essays 442
Bernstein Conducts Boston Symphony 444
Saturday's *Oedipus Rex* an Event of Another Order 445
The Posthumous Success of Wilhelm Furtwängler 447
Franz Brüggen Magnetizes Atmosphere at Jordan Hall 449
Furtwängler Revisited 451

1973 455
Sherman to Perform All Twelve Liszt Etudes 455
Sherman the Best Yet 457
BSO's Strauss Worth a Rainy Trip 459
Abbado, Cleveland Orchestra 460
Elliott Carter's String Quartet No. 3 461
Ohlsson Right All Way 464
Pianist Returns to Classroom 465
Carter's Complexities Evoke Simple Ovation, Curiosity 466
Steinberg, Singers, Players Provide Treat at Symphony 468
Eight Songs for a Mad King 469
Lorin Maazel Impressive Conducting Boston Symphony 471
Isaac Stern and Friends "Rehearse" 472
After Hearing *Lily*—Leon Kirchner Should Compose More Often 473
Zander's "Fifth" Was a Mind Bender 474
Putting Reviews in Their Place 475
Rag Spells Cash 476
Klemperer Fame Forged in Pain 478
Cleveland, Tokyo Quartets Are the Real Thing 479
Orchestra Gave All Ozawa Asked 481
Casals and His Playing—"Unique Synthesis of Material and Spiritual Beauty" 482
Bernstein Winds Up a Brilliant Norton Lecture Series 484

1974 488
Splendid Bruckner Seventh by Steinberg and BSO 488
Palestrina Recorded, at Last 489
Oliver Knussen Readies Symphony for Premiere by BSO 491

Works-in-Progress at Spectrum 494
Cleveland Performs Bruckner Fifth 495
Tippett's Symphony No. 3—Excitement of a Decade 496
Callas—A Career in Four Stages 498
Shifrin, Schuller Quartets Have Boston Premieres 500
Callas Struggles in Hub, but Adds to Operatic Legend 501
Brendel—Full of Tension, Never Tense 503
Bruckner's Second—First Time in Boston 504
The Mirror of Music 505
1925 *Rosenkavalier* Movie Seen for First Time in US 507
Tourist's Report from Kresge Auditorium 510
Record Industry Starts a Korngold Revival 511
The Power of Critics 514
Monteverdi and Words of Love at the Aston Magna Festival 516
Koussevitzky—The Legend Still Lives 517
A Memorable Tribute to Koussevitzky at Tanglewood 520
Schoenberg—A Passionate Intensity from the Heart 522
Leipzig's Gewandhaus Orchestra Delights Symphony Audience 525
"Pied Piper" Peter Pears 526
Serkin's Perilous Risk Illuminates Beethoven 529
Pears-Perahia Concert Unforgettable 530
Tennstedt's BSO Debut Breathes Life into Brahms 531
Chicago Symphony, Solti Impressive 532
Bruckner, Tennstedt, BSO—Once-in-a-Lifetime Music 534

1975–76 536

Observing Ozawa: The Many Sides of the Maestro of the Boston Symphony Orchestra 536
BSO Bassist Wolfe Impressive as a Soloist 542
Richard Tucker Was All Tenor 543
Schuller Helps Students Succeed With Mahler 546
A Lovely Party for Mozart 547
Turangalîla Tiresomely Gorgeous 549
Luigi Dallapiccola, 1904–75 550
Once, in Concord, I Heard John Kirkpatrick Play the *Concord* Sonata 553
Sessions Cantata to Have East Coast Premiere Here Tomorrow 555
Walt Whitman's Poem-Turned-Into-a-Cantata 557
Sills Smash at Met Debut 558
Steve Reich's *Drumming* Should Also Be Filed Under Magic 560
Von Karajan Remarkable, a Conductor of Immense Resources 562
Violin-Harpsichord Concert 565
The Fortepiano Revolution 566
Harvard Summer Series Opens 568
Happy Birthday, Rudolf Kolisch 569

The Maestro Finally Comes to Tanglewood 572
A Poignant Roar at Tanglewood 575
Harvard Series Ends Memorably 576
La Scala Scores Triumph in *La Cenerentola* 577
Israel Philharmonic an Event 579
Michael Steinberg's Twelve Years of Music in Boston 580

Coda 585
The Appetitosissimi Cookbook of Ada Boni—A Fond Tribute to the Author of *Il Talismano della Felicità* 585

Acknowledgments 589
About the Editors 591
Index 593

An undated photo of Michael Steinberg from the period in which he was writing for the *Boston Globe*. (Photo credit: Larry N. Bolch; Fleezanis personal collection; used with permission.)

Introduction

> To write about Michael Steinberg, a friend and critic who has so consistently and warmly praised me, is not the easiest thing to do. After expressing my gratitude I should point out that his merits were many: the fluency and clarity of his prose, the sympathy for 20th-century composers, his knowledge of the scores, the unconditional conviction of his insights, and, next to some stern judgments, his genuine love of music. The glory of his era at the *Boston Globe* deserves not to be forgotten.
>
> —Alfred Brendel[1]

This book brings together, for the first time, selections from the more than 2,000 reviews, essays, and features written by the eminent musicologist and critic Michael Steinberg during his dozen years—from 1964 to 1976—as music critic of the *Boston Globe*. Steinberg possessed a special gift in his ability to make complex aspects of music easy to understand without being either condescending or esoteric. Writing with wit, elegance, and passion, he had an astonishing command of the Western secular and sacred repertoire, inspiring to both amateurs and professionals.

Born in Breslau, Germany (now Wrocław, Poland), on October 4, 1928, Steinberg escaped his homeland in 1939 as one of the 10,000 Jewish children who survived via the Kindertransport. He spent the early years of World War II in England before moving with his mother in 1943 to Saint Louis, Missouri, home to his 30-year-old brother, Franz. Steinberg attended Princeton University, where as an undergraduate he wrote a senior thesis in 1949 entitled "Religion and Music." He then obtained a master's degree in musicology in 1951, studying history with Oliver Strunk, theory and harmony with Edward T. Cone, and contemporary music with Milton Babbitt. At Princeton, he befriended and roomed with the pianist (and later writer) Charles Rosen,[2] with whom he "read piles of

1 Email to Jorja Fleezanis, May 2022.

2 An account of Steinberg's and Rosen's 1949 class with visiting faculty member Bohuslav Martinů may be found in Steinberg, *The Symphony: A Listener's Guide* (New York: Oxford University Press, 1995), 364–66. Steinberg describes the two of them as "a brilliant pianist who was actually a graduate student in Romance languages (Charles Rosen) and a musicology student with no talent for composition (myself)."

orchestra stuff in improvised, four-hand arrangements, and went through all of the organ literature, three-handedly. For me, Rosen was a major source of musical enlightenment."[3] Steinberg also grew frustrated at the sharp split between composers and musicologists, their seeming inability to support one another, and their distancing from the performing world.

Having secured a Fulbright Scholarship to Italy, ostensibly to study medieval music, Steinberg instead "experienced a consolidation of something that had started in my last Princeton years—a vital interest in contemporary music." He met the composers Luigi Dallapiccola and Goffredo Petrassi, as well as several young Americans who were in Italy on Fulbrights, and older Americans who were at the American Academy in Rome, among them Elliott Carter and Alexei Haieff. While in Italy, Steinberg began submitting pieces on music for monthly publication in the Sunday *New York Times*. He next taught briefly at the Manhattan School of Music, before being drafted in 1955 into the US Army. Stationed in Germany, Steinberg served as an administrator for the Seventh Army Orchestra, whose conductors at the time included Kenneth Schermerhorn and Henry Lewis.

Upon returning to the United States, Steinberg became head of the nascent music history department at the Manhattan School of Music, challenging himself "to see if I could present [history] in a lively fashion and yet stay musical enough to persuade [performers] that maybe they weren't wasting their time." Primarily he gave listening assignments to provide his students direct contact with music and some sense of different musical personalities. He also contributed reviews to *Saturday Review* and *High Fidelity*. (A doctoral dissertation for Princeton on Spontini went unfinished during this period.) In 1964 Steinberg moved to the Boston suburb of Newton with his wife, Jane,[4] and their sons, Sebastian and Adam, lured there to join the staff of the *Boston Globe* by its managing editor, Thomas Winship.[5]

[3] Unless otherwise noted, this quotation and the ones that follow come from interviews Steinberg gave in 1974 and 1975 printed originally in *The Musical Newsletter* 6, no. 4 (Fall 1976) and reprinted in *The Music Makers*, ed. Deena and Bernard Rosenberg (New York: Columbia University Press, 1979), 434–54.

[4] Steinberg met his first wife, Jane Bonacker, at a Fulbright orientation in Perugia; the Florida-born Wellesley College art history major was herself a Fulbright Scholar at the Università di Roma. In addition to homemaking and raising two sons, Jane Steinberg trained as a craft dyer and for decades had a business in hand-dyed silk fashions and accessories. An indispensable partner to Michael during the *Globe* years, she also wrote art criticism and did occasional editing.

[5] Thomas Winship (1925–2002) would succeed his father, Laurence, as the *Globe*'s editor in 1965 but was already aggressively hiring young journalists, including the columnists Diane White and Ellen Goodman and a team of sports and politics writers. Winship's wife Elizabeth was the granddaughter of the music patron Elizabeth Sprague Coolidge (1864–1953); the Coolidge family urged him to improve the *Globe*'s arts coverage and it was his sister-in-law, Melba Coolidge, who brought Steinberg to his attention. During Steinberg's tenure, Winship was notably supportive of him at critical junctures.

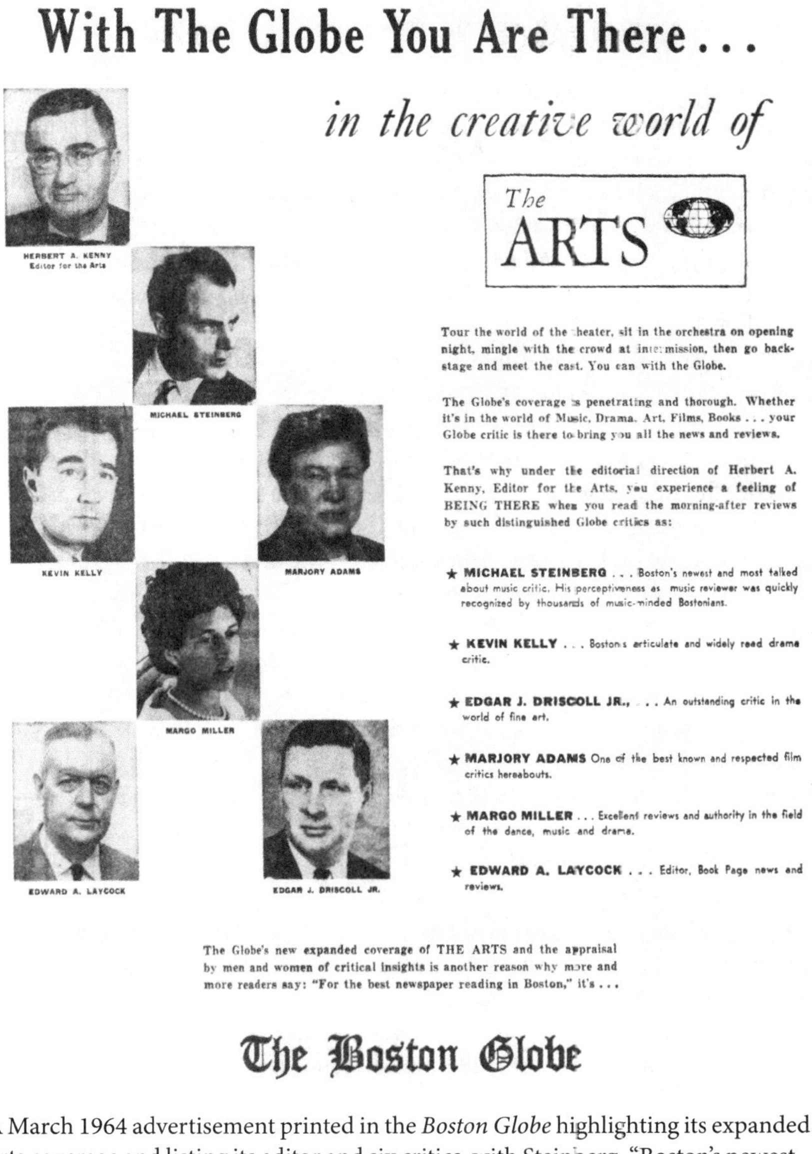

A March 1964 advertisement printed in the *Boston Globe* highlighting its expanded arts coverage and listing its editor and six critics, with Steinberg, "Boston's newest and most talked about music critic," listed first. (Used with permission.)

Eloquent and highly entertaining, Steinberg's *Globe* writings inspired admiration and controversy for their exacting standards. In retrospect, his long-form *Globe* articles anticipated the essays he would later write as program annotator for the Boston Symphony Orchestra (BSO) from 1976 to 1979; as publications director, and also artistic adviser, for the next decade at the San Francisco Symphony (to whose program book he continued contributing until his death, and where his responsibilities as artistic adviser gave him influence on both repertory and artistic policy); and as program annotator for the New York Philharmonic from 1995 to 2000. In San Francisco he met his second wife, the violinist Jorja Fleezanis, following her to Minnesota in 1989, when she began her twenty-year tenure as one of the first women concertmasters of a major American orchestra. There, already an acclaimed annotator and pre-concert speaker, Steinberg further enhanced his reputation and impact as a commentator on music, also serving as an artistic adviser for the Minnesota Orchestra's annual Sommerfest.

Steinberg's charm, graciousness, and nurturing generosity distinguished his coaching of young musicians at the Music@Menlo (CA) festival and the International Festival-Institute at Round Top (TX), as well as his mentorship of many early-career arts writers, critics, and administrators. He also regularly held public poetry sessions, believing that performers could learn more about musical phrasing and rhythm by reading poetry aloud. His writings also included dozens of entries in *The New Grove Dictionary of Music and Musicians* (1980), articles for a variety of music journals and magazines, and notes for such seminal recordings as John Adams's on Nonesuch Records and Claude Frank's complete Beethoven sonata cycle on RCA (the first such cycle by an American pianist). He provided detailed notes on Beethoven's string quartets for *The Beethoven Quartet Companion* (University of California Press, 1994) and compiled four volumes of his program notes and essays for Oxford University Press (OUP) in the 1990s and early 2000s.[6]

The profound respect Steinberg engendered in friends and colleagues was reflected in the numerous obituaries that followed his death on July 26, 2009. As Anthony Tommasini wrote in the *New York Times* (July 29, 2009): "His reviews were erudite and readable, his interests wide-ranging. He stood up for intellectually formidable composers at a time when a postmodernist backlash was taking root and also encouraged the early-music movement, which thrived in Boston during this period." A National Public Radio (NPR) obituary (July 27,

[6] Steinberg had hoped to follow up his three OUP program note compilations with a fourth, including a selection of miscellaneous program notes that did not fall conveniently under a single heading like "symphonies," "concertos," or "choral masterworks"—a project that unfortunately never came to fruition.

2009) quoted Tim Page's review of Steinberg's *Choral Masterworks: A Listener's Guide* (2005): "What sets Steinberg's writing apart is its appealing mix of impregnable authority (he *knows* this music) and purely personal asides (by the end of the book, we know this man)."[7] David Cairns, writing in *The Guardian* (September 29, 2009), noted "the sharpness of his criticism, which could draw blood,"[8] continuing:

> But if he was an unsparing critic, he was also a profoundly positive one. His consuming passion for the music he loved made him hostile to performers who, he felt, betrayed it. . . . For him music was the centre of life: "[I]ts capacity to give is as near to infinite as anything in this world. . . . [T]he only thing that matters is what happens privately between you and the music." That was his faith, and it lit up his life's work.[9]

*****

Long in the works, this volume had its inception shortly after Steinberg's death in July 2009. Fleezanis had recently left the Minnesota Orchestra to assume a teaching post at the Jacobs School of Music, Indiana University (IU), Bloomington, where she was to coach the university's five orchestras and maintain a small studio of private students. Steinberg, ill with the cancer that would take his life, was to have had no formal role at IU, but it was anticipated that his wit, wisdom, and experience would benefit all in their orbit. As Fleezanis's former student Jacob Jahiel recalls, she would speak of him often, share favorite recordings, and lend freely from his library of poetry. At least two large-scale initiatives at IU—"Behind the Score" lecture-performances and a series of chamber music recitals around the Second Viennese School—were inspired by their shared belief that performers should be thoroughly informed, and by their staunch advocacy for the music of Schoenberg, Berg, and Webern (two throughlines that also emerge within this collection). Like Steinberg, Fleezanis could tolerate a degree of technical deficiency but loathed playing that was casual, lazy, and uncritical. To miss a note was a minor matter. To be oblivious to the score beyond one's own part, or not to know the specific meaning of a text or

7 Tim Page, "Amid an Onslaught of the Familiar, Some Authors Hit High, New Notes," *Washington Post*, August 7, 2005.

8 For that matter, Steinberg could come across as downright nasty. Take, for example, his initial, harsh criticism of the Guarneri Quartet cellist David Soyer (May 27, 1966); his cruelly belittling put-down of the *New Yorker* critic Winthrop Sargeant (June 29, 1965); and his shockingly harsh review, discussed later in this introduction, of conductor Carlo Maria Giulini's November 1969 BSO Brahms Fourth. The *Globe* was not shy about publishing many letters to the editor attacking Steinberg's assertions.

9 Cairns here extracts two quotations from Steinberg's essay, "How I Fell in Love with Music," in *For the Love of Music* by Michael Steinberg and Larry Rothe (Oxford University Press, 2006), 10.

expressive marking—these were grievous offenses. Yet her critiques were never personal, mean-spirited, or tainted with ego; they were informed only by her conviction that performing great music was the highest privilege.

After her husband's death, Fleezanis sought to honor his memory more formally by establishing the Michael Steinberg & Jorja Fleezanis Fund, whose twofold mission was (1) to commission emerging composers to write works for narrator and small chamber ensemble, using poems that were meaningful to them both; and (2) to create a collection of Steinberg's *Boston Globe* reviews and essays as a companion volume to OUP's existing compilations of his work. Fleezanis viewed the *Globe* material not only as Steinberg's first major public platform, "where he established his love of music, and his deep knowledge of it, through his unique writing voice, one that spoke with the strongest of intentions to defend the composer and the artist's role in confronting the demands they ask," but also as "the bedrock that he drew from" later as a program annotator, coach, and mentor.[10]

In the initial stage of the book's conception, Fleezanis took sole responsibility for whittling down Steinberg's *Globe* contributions. Concurrently, in pursuit of her vision, she engaged in innumerable intense discussions with musician and scholar Patricia Lewy, her lifelong and closest friend. Given her extensive teaching responsibilities and performing schedule, it was only after Fleezanis's retirement from IU in 2020 that she finalized an initial selection that she felt was particularly representative of Steinberg's writing, philosophy, and attitudes, likening it to "a masterclass in listening." In early 2022 she sought comments from four other close friends and colleagues: Marc Mandel, whom Steinberg had hired as his assistant at the Boston Symphony in 1978; Susan Feder, whom he had hired as his assistant at the San Francisco Symphony in 1979; the historic preservationist and author Robert Guter; and the novelist Charles Baxter. At the time of her sudden death in September 2022, she was actively incorporating suggestions from her readers for additions, deletions, and editorial emendations.

Shortly thereafter, the present editors—Feder, Mandel, and Jahiel, Fleezanis's former Indiana University student who, since 2017, had assisted her in compiling and transcribing the *Globe* material—contacted OUP and were encouraged to submit a formal proposal. OUP initially wanted a book roughly half the length of Fleezanis's original compilation. However, the favorable response of OUP's peer reviewers resulted in a manuscript approximating the original length but with rebalanced contents, now including about forty record reviews (a category originally omitted by Fleezanis), as well as an additional selection of feature articles, interviews, and obituaries. In its final form, the book includes some 300 entries, weighted on the side of Steinberg's advocacy and praise-giving essays while not

10 Jorja Fleezanis personal papers.

stinting on examples of what he took issue with or frowned upon, however controversial. The selection also provides readers a wide-ranging, though inevitably not comprehensive, overview of the musical life of the period.

*****

The best criticism combines reporting the facts—who, what, where, when, why—with personal observation, insight, and analysis in a way that makes it not only a contemporary record but meaningful beyond its time. For Steinberg, serving as classical music critic of the *Boston Globe* meant not only being a part of the musical community in which he worked, but also applying standards that grew from his own love and passion for music. As a critic he saw himself simultaneously as teacher ("I started out as a teacher, and I can't ever quite let that go"), advocate, and—as he characterized one of his own early influences, the critic B. H. Haggin—a conscious moral force. Another figure of particular importance to him was the early 20th-century conductor-teacher-annotator Donald Francis Tovey, whose program notes Steinberg first encountered as a teenager and frequently quoted in his own writings. It is therefore not surprising that Steinberg likened his own critical stance as "counsel for the defense"[11]—referenced frequently in Fleezanis's correspondence about her plans and vision for this volume—to Tovey's.

Upon becoming a full-time critic, Steinberg quickly

> learned that there is a big difference between lecturing and reviewing. In a classroom, you can teach very effectively, without using a single technical term, because you can instantly illustrate everything. . . . In a newspaper article, where you still want to avoid being technical . . . [y]ou have to invent metaphors for everything, with no space to do it at all adequately. The result is a crazy *tour de force*, or, you might say, a crazy obstacle course, through which you maneuver as you write. You can't do what's most essential to the educational process—demonstrate.

To his surprise, as soon as he arrived at the *Globe*, Steinberg leapt from being a private citizen to a public figure; his presence on the *Globe* staff was advertised as a reason to subscribe to the paper, and, from his very first reviews, readers wrote impassioned letters to the editor, pro and con. Steinberg exercised considerable freedom in choosing which events he wanted to review, and also made a point of attending performances he did not review. Determined to broaden the *Globe*'s coverage, he personally selected a number of freelance "stringers," some of whom would

[11] Tovey uses the phrase in the introduction to his multivolume *Essays in Musical Analysis* (London: Oxford University Press, 1935), 1.

themselves gain distinction as writers or performers. Collectively, they reported not just on the concerts of such long-lived musical institutions as the Boston Symphony Orchestra and the Handel and Haydn Society, but also on Sarah Caldwell's groundbreaking Opera Company of Boston and the many smaller, sometimes up-and-coming choral and instrumental ensembles that would become a crucial part of Boston's thriving and wide-ranging musical community—among them the Boston Camerata, Boston Musica Viva, Cantata Singers, Cecilia Society, Collage New Music, and Emmanuel Music. Steinberg advocated for the improvement and continuing existence of these groups to the benefit not only of the organizations themselves but their audiences as well. His early, controversial reviews of the Handel and Haydn Society and Boston Camerata led to crucial changes in their musical leadership—namely the appointment of conductor Thomas Dunn to the helm of the former and of Joel Cohen as music director of the latter—that affected their performances for decades to come. Steinberg also strongly supported Emmanuel Music's activities under the direction of Craig Smith.

Steinberg was prescient about many trends that became important in composition and performance, especially with regard to emerging talent, even if his enthusiasm for mid-20th-century modernists is now measured more through respect than through regular performances. He made a point of championing noteworthy artists still at the start of their careers, such as the pianists Robert Levin, Garrick Ohlsson, Peter Serkin, and André Watts; conductors James Levine and Michael Tilson Thomas; soprano Jessye Norman; and composers Oliver Knussen, Peter Lieberson, and Steve Reich. He also regularly spotlighted such intellectually formidable composers and performers as Milton Babbitt, Alfred Brendel, Elliott Carter, Charles Rosen, Arnold Schoenberg, and Russell Sherman; attended rehearsals, score in hand, for new works he would be reviewing; and covered musical events at a wide variety of educational institutions and venues[12] when repertoire he deemed important, or local artists with more than local significance, warranted attention. And this was in addition to reviewing the well-known orchestras, solo artists, and chamber ensembles making appearances as part of the Celebrity Series of Boston, not to mention events farther afield when circumstances allowed, whether at the New York Philharmonic, Metropolitan Opera, New York City Opera, or other venues in the United States and Europe, as when he accompanied the BSO on tour—though most of that material proved beyond the scope and space limitations of this book.

[12] These included Boston University, Harvard University, the Longy School of Music in Cambridge, Kresge Auditorium at the Massachusetts Institute of Technology, New England Conservatory of Music (not limited to performances at NEC's Jordan Hall), Sanders Theatre in Cambridge, and even the suburban Newton South High School.

To facilitate his immersion in Boston's musical community, Jane and Michael Steinberg regularly hosted musical soirées at their Newton home, developing friendships with composers and performers he might find himself socializing with or interviewing one week and then reviewing the next, a practice that would not typically have been condoned at other papers. Steinberg recognized this as controversial:

> I hang around with composers and performers and musicologists and would be starved and deprived and a much worse critic if I didn't. . . . Friendship can be a problem, but it needn't imply wholesale endorsement of everything my friends do—or that I do. . . . Since I came to music criticism so late in my career, I'd already accumulated many friends elsewhere in the musical profession. . . . About none of my friends have I written only positively or favorably.

In that regard, he was "at the opposite pole from [his] colleague Harold Schonberg at the *New York Times*, who believe[d] that a critic should live in total isolation from the rest of the musical profession." He saw a parallel between critics and performers: "Basically, critics are born. They need to have the critical temperament, which is a counterpart of the performer's temperament. To excel, the public performer and the critic need musicianship, dexterity, projection, and a certain kind of magic."

A good part of Steinberg's "magic" derives from the extraordinary scope, unimaginable in present-day journalism, of subject matter and perspective preserved in his writing for the *Globe*. This breadth of coverage includes:

- **Close analyses of varied musical works** ("Beethoven—His Last Piano Sonata, Opus 111, Reconsidered," January 2, 1966; "Neglected Masterpiece: Schumann's Interpretation of Goethe's *Faust* Tragedy," January 20, 1966; "Two Good Performances—The Year of Schoenberg," November 17, 1968; "Elliott Carter's String Quartet No. 3," February 11, 1973).
- **Essays on performance-related questions** ("Virtuosity—Beautiful Sounds or Beautiful Music?," October 11, 1964; "'Tempo' and 'Character'—Are Beethoven, Others Heard Properly?," July 14, 1968; "Britten Knows His 'Repeats,'" September 7, 1969).
- **Responsibility to the art, the audience, and oneself as performer or composer** ("*I puritani*—Opera a Triumph; Sutherland Great," February 13, 1964; "Cliburn—Great, but Could Do Better," April 3, 1967; "Record Industry Starts a Korngold Revival," April 21, 1974").

- <u>The role and possible influence of the critic</u> ("When Twelve Music Critics Meet All Is Not Perfect Harmony," December 19, 1971; "Putting Reviews in Their Place," June 21, 1973; "The Power of Critics," April 21, 1974).
- <u>Aspects of audience behavior</u> ("Our Unserious Public—What Does It Hear?," May 10, 1964; "Bigger the Bang—The Art of Applauding," March 3, 1968; "Babbitt's Music Requires Special Audience," February 2, 1969; "What to Do With Your Eyes While the Orchestra Plays," July 11, 1971).
- <u>Noteworthy books and lectures</u> ("Schnabel and Cone—Good Talks and Advice About Music," February 23, 1969; "New Memoirs Translation Revives Genius of Berlioz," January 11, 1970; "Oxford Issues Paperback of Tovey's Music Essays," November 22, 1972; "Bernstein Winds Up a Brilliant Norton Lecture Series," November 25, 1973).
- <u>Subjects both adventurous and surprising</u> ("Tourist's Report from Kresge Auditorium," April 9, 1974, documenting his own voyage of discovery reviewing an evening of Indian music; and "*Help!* Loud, Inaudible, and Evidently Sexy," August 26, 1965, a foray into unexpected territory).

In one possibly unique instance, Steinberg chose to write a second review of a BSO program he had already covered, in which Leonard Bernstein conducted Stravinsky's opera-oratorio *Oedipus Rex* ("Bernstein Conducts Boston Symphony," December 9, 1972; "Stravinsky's *Oedipus Rex* an Event of Another Order," December 15, 1972). Steinberg's response on second hearing was so very different from his first that he felt it warranted a second review.

According to his *Globe* successor Richard Dyer, Steinberg's reviews were predominantly written with a strict 12:30 A.M. deadline and appeared in the paper later that same morning. Everything in that pre-computer era had to be typed out, at the *Globe*, with no room for second thoughts or revisions. Nor did Steinberg have any control over the length of a review: when he arrived at the *Globe* after a concert, he was told how many "twls" ("typewritten lines") the review had to be, as determined by the placement of the movie ads on the page. If an article had to be cut or expanded, Steinberg saw to it there. In Dyer's words: "What never ceased to amaze me was how much Michael was able to achieve when he was given very little room," as, for example, when he covered the local premiere at Harvard of Sessions's *When Lilacs Last in the Dooryard Bloom'd* (reviewed March 25, 1975): "I think he had something like 40 twls to work with yet produced something thoughtful, perceptive, appropriate, and substantial."

*****

When Steinberg's criticism turns harsh, one can understand and even accept it as relevant to the central position of music in his own life and worldview, that is, his expressed moral obligation to the subject at hand. But what made him such a convincing and formidable critic was equally and inherently tied not just to his vast musical knowledge, but also to the stylistic niceties, subtleties of approach, and consummately meaningful and absorbing use of language that permeate his writing, including the many sudden, startling barbs that can catch the reader by surprise.

To quote Dyer again:

> I think Michael thought of writing as performance art—and he was a performer. What made him flourish at the *Globe* was another part of his personality that was an outlaw, an Eulenspiegel, a scamp—in the sense that Shakespeare's fools were truth-tellers. . . . He was always listening to performances rather than reputations. . . . Michael's gift to the *Globe* and to music during that period was not limited to music lovers and concertgoers. The mythical "general reader" also read many of his pieces partly because of the controversies he generated (he liked to say he never said anything controversial—it was all only common sense to him) and partly because they were fun to read.[13]

*****

In his *Guardian* obituary, David Cairns observed that at the *Globe* Steinberg "became notorious as a feared and fearless critic, attacking sacred cows . . . and provoking angry calls for his dismissal. But his wit, his polished, easy writing, and above all his knowledge won him respect." On two occasions chronicled in this book, Steinberg's reviews provoked particularly forceful public responses:

The first came in the form of a letter to the *Globe* from BSO board president Henry B. Cabot—responding to Steinberg's strongly negative reviews of the BSO's September 1964 season-opening Beethoven *Pastoral* Symphony under Erich Leinsdorf's direction (September 26, 1964) and of the Handel and Haydn Society's annual *Messiah* that December (December 24, 1964)—to which Steinberg responded in print.[14]

The second was in response to Steinberg's scathing, now infamous review of a November 1969 BSO performance of Brahms's Fourth Symphony led by Carlo Maria Giulini (November 8, 1969). This review prompted not only numerous letters to the *Globe* from its readers (both pro and con) and attention from the national press (including *Time* magazine), but also a telegram from the Boston Symphony Orchestra Members Association to BSO management, asking them "not to welcome Mr. Michael Steinberg to our concerts until he publicly apologizes for his insulting and unethical assaults which have gone far

[13] Email to editors, December 23, 2023.
[14] See article of January 3, 1965.

beyond the scope of musical criticism."[15] Since tickets for the BSO's upcoming concerts were already in the *Globe*'s possession, this proved moot. More tellingly, Steinberg continued to cover the BSO, reflecting the consistent support of Winship and *Globe* management.

As it happened, another controversy was already brewing behind the scenes.[16] On October 24, 1969, the Philadelphia Orchestra led by Eugene Ormandy had played a program of Piston, Hindemith, and Mahler at Symphony Hall—a concert strongly criticized not only by Steinberg in the *Boston Globe* (October 27, 1969) but also by the newly hired young critic of the *Boston Herald Traveler*, George Gelles,[17] a former student of his who wrote for the *Globe* between 1965 and 1968. On November 24, a *Herald* review by Gelles was unflinchingly critical of a guest appearance by Seiji Ozawa with the BSO. A letter coincidentally written that same day by the Philadelphia Orchestra's board chairman to the BSO's president informed the latter that, in light of the preceding month's negative reviews, the Philadelphia Orchestra had "decided to omit Boston in planning our future travels" until the situation was rectified. In addition, Ormandy canceled a planned guest appearance with the BSO for the following season. Within a few days, Gelles was removed from his position as classical music critic of the *Herald*, in turn prompting a letter from Steinberg decrying the situation to colleagues across the country, drawing national attention. Ultimately, a BSO-initiated behind-the-scenes meeting that December, including Steinberg, the managing and arts editors of the *Globe*, and several BSO board members and players, brought the matter to a close, avoiding further unwanted public controversy. At Symphony Hall, however, there remained severe animosity on the part of some BSO players who continued to resent Steinberg's presence and attempted, unsuccessfully, to have him barred from accompanying the orchestra on its April 1971 tour of Europe.

Ironically, some years later, in a turn of events described by Nicolas Slonimsky in the 1978 edition of *Baker's Biographical Dictionary of Musicians* as "a spectacular peripeteia," the BSO administration, looking to restore and rethink its program book for the 1976–77 season, invited Steinberg to become its director of publications and program annotator. (For the 1975–76 season, as a cost-saving

[15] Telegram dated November 10, 1969, preserved in the Boston Symphony Orchestra Archives.

[16] The following account is based upon documentation preserved in the BSO Archives, including a detailed memorandum from the BSO's board president to the orchestra's trustees; the letter sent by the Philadelphia Orchestra's board chairman to the BSO's president; and a folder of material labeled "Boston Globe/Michael Steinberg imbroglio, 1969–1971." Further corroboration can be found in an unsigned *Globe* article of December 5, 1969 ("The BSO and Its Critics"); an editorial of December 13, 1969 ("Music Critics and Their Critics"); and a subsequent column of March 25, 1972 ("Critics at Last," by Louis M. Lyons) on the coverage of criticism at the *Globe* over the past decade, highlighting Steinberg's hiring and the 1969 controversy.

[17] In an October 25 *Herald* review headlined "Philadelphians Drab at Symphony Hall."

measure—and to general condemnation—the BSO had entirely eliminated its program book, substituting a tri-fold, single-sheet handout.) As it happened, Steinberg had taken a sabbatical from the *Globe* in 1975–76 to research a book on Elliott Carter, a project that never came to fruition.[18]

As then-BSO manager Thomas W. Morris recalls,[19] Steinberg had returned from his sabbatical eager to do more long-form writing away from the stress of daily deadlines and recent management changes at the *Globe*. "It was," Morris stated, "a 'win-win' situation for us both," thereby sparing the orchestra future criticism from Steinberg by bringing him onto the BSO staff. Steinberg joined the administration of the Boston Symphony Orchestra on October 1, 1976, thereby launching the next stage of his career. In Fleezanis's words, "Jumping ship when he did to head the publications department at the BSO allowed him to assimilate those twelve years of breakneck-pace writing of reviews, equipped with a voluminous body of experience and a profound moral conviction to defend music."

*****

In the article entitled "Putting Reviews in Their Place" (June 21, 1973), Michael Steinberg wrote:

> I am not proposing an end to criticism. A reader of criticism, I love good talk about books, plays, films, dances, paintings, and also about music and its performance. Such "talk," whether it comes literally as talk with a friend immediately after the experience, or whether you read it in the newspaper a couple of days later or in the magazine a few weeks later, or in a book dozens or hundreds of years later, informs, delights, clarifies, and stimulates. It makes you think, it leaves you hearing and seeing more clearly than before. It needs no defense.

The art of music criticism has a long and distinguished history that continues in our time, despite the disappearance of many newspapers and the relegation of music criticism to the general classification of entertainment. The publication of Steinberg's *Boston Globe* material follows in the tradition of collections by Virgil Thomson from the *New York Herald Tribune* (four volumes between 1945 and 1967, collected in 2014); B. H. Haggin from *The Nation* and other publications (three volumes between 1949 and 1973); Andrew Porter from *The New Yorker* (four volumes between 1974 and 1989); and, more recently, Tim Page's *On Music: Views and Reviews* (2002), Paul Griffiths's *The Substance of Things Heard: Writings about Music* (2005), Kyle Gann's *Music Downtown: Writings*

[18] The relatively frequent inclusion in this collection of Steinberg's Carter-related coverage suggests something of what that book might have been.

[19] Telephone interview, November 22, 2023.

from the Village Voice (2006), Edward Said's posthumously published *Music at the Limits* (2008), and Alex Ross's *Listen to This* (2010).

We were particularly mindful that this book could become a valuable artifact of reception history, for example, of how pieces of music, whether familiar, unfamiliar, or newly created, were interpreted by artists and received by audiences and critics. As Richard Dyer observed,

> Michael could not have accomplished what he did in any other American city at the time. Boston was then in ferment. The early music revival had begun here thanks to Nadia Boulanger at Longy during World War II, Frank Hubbard, Friedrich von Huene, Charles Fisk, etc., and Gunther Schuller was awakening New England Conservatory from its long winter's nap. NEC, Boston University, Longy, Harvard, and Brandeis were all in golden periods of superb faculty who attracted countless young and gifted musicians, many of whom (like Craig Smith or Joel Cohen or, from Yale, Martin Pearlman and Daniel Stepner) remained here and changed the texture and content of musical life. There were two great periods of opera in Boston, the second of which, Sarah Caldwell's, started in Michael's time. The resident community of performing musicians at the Boston Symphony and elsewhere was inexhaustible, and there were a very distinguished number and variety of composers and new music groups. Michael created some of that ferment (Thomas Dunn was at Handel and Haydn because of Michael) but also profited from it—it gave him important things to write about.[20]

In making final choices, we sought to present a book of maximal use to those studying the 20th century through the lens of music: the selections function as witnesses to some of the most important music and music-making of the time while being of equal interest to a wide variety of concertgoers, music aficionados, record collectors, and students. In addition, we hope that some of Steinberg's enthusiasms for underappreciated repertoire might engender a revival of interest among enterprising programmers.[21]

Regarding the title of the book, we fastened on Fleezanis's frequent references, in surviving correspondence about her plans and vision for this volume, to Steinberg's self-described stance as "counsel for the defense," that is, as an advocate for music and all things relevant to it. Finally, as a coda to the book, we

20 Email to editors, December 10, 2023.

21 Potential candidates include Carter's Variations for Orchestra (March 20, 1964), Schoenberg's Violin Concerto (March 21 and 27, 1965), Britten's Symphony for Cello and Orchestra (October 23, 1965), Schumann's *Faust-Szenen* (February 20 and 26, 1966), Holst's opera *Savitri* (April 5, 1967), Sessions's cantata *When Lilacs Last in the Dooryard Bloom'd* (March 23 and 25, 1975), and even such (to Steinberg's mind) undervalued pieces as the early Tchaikovsky symphonies (August 3, 1969) and Beethoven's *Consecration of the House* Overture (November 22, 1972).

couldn't resist sharing Steinberg's adventures in Italian cooking courtesy of Ada Boni ("The Appetitosissimi Cookbook of Ada Boni—A Food Tribute to the Author of *Il Talismano della Felicità*," September 2, 1973).

On June 12, 1966, early in his *Globe* tenure, Steinberg received an honorary doctorate from the New England Conservatory and gave the commencement address. The *Globe* printed excerpts the following day; Steinberg's original typescript, quoted here, remains among his personal papers. Perhaps at no other time did his credo as a music critic come across more clearly and effectively:

> Most of you being graduated today are performers and teachers. Your tasks and mine as a critic are not so dissimilar. We act in responsibility toward something more important than ourselves. To teach a subject is to make its meaning clear to your students. To play or sing or conduct a piece is done to show the listener how it goes. To criticize means to evaluate, but first to discover, describe, and explain the nature of the critical object, composition, performance, book, whatever it is. And we all share the duty of not getting in the way.
>
> I hope, too, we share the asking of questions. After all, to give a performance, a good performance, is to have grappled with many, many questions. The great pieces of music, our love for which has set most of us on the various roads that cross in this hall this afternoon, are terribly complicated organisms each of which poses more problems than can be solved in any one interpretation. Such a piece can never be just the same twice, and this is one of the ways in which they so wonderfully renew themselves all the time.

This philosophy, which permeated, enlivened, and emboldened Michael Steinberg's work, is reflected and preserved in the pages that follow.

—Susan Feder, Jacob Jahiel, Marc Mandel
March 2025

Note from the Editors

As conceived by Jorja Fleezanis, this volume of selections from Steinberg's writings for the *Boston Globe* was intended as a companion volume to his previously issued OUP collections of program notes and essays, being geared toward the same varied readership to which those earlier volumes appealed: an informed and responsive readership encompassing a general audience of music enthusiasts as well as such specialists as music historians, music critics, performers, and teachers. Following Fleezanis's death, we chose to respect her original intent, a crucial aspect of which was to let Steinberg's writings speak for themselves, as they did upon their original publication, avoiding, to the extent possible, extensive elaboration or detailed scholarly apparatus, which would have meant a book entirely different from and well beyond the scope of this project.

This in turn meant considering a number of questions, not least the question of how much background or explanatory material should be included to amplify, or provide context for, Steinberg's own words. Ultimately we decided to craft an introduction providing basic biographical information about Steinberg himself, a general sense of the contemporary musical scene in Boston, and some specific aspects of his work at the *Globe*. With this in mind, we sought input from, and showed early drafts of the Introduction to, a number of Steinberg's colleagues and friends who were themselves present in Boston during the period of his *Globe* tenure, and are credited in the Introduction and Acknowledgments.

In terms of organizing each chapter, we decided to organize by calendar year (1964, 1965, etc.) rather than what might typically be viewed as a musical season (1963–64, 1964–65, etc.) because Steinberg's very first *Globe* review appeared in February 1964, and because his coverage of summertime events did not always fall conveniently into a preceding or following season.

Given the ready accessibility of online information, we decided to include footnotes only where they seemed absolutely necessary, for example, in instances where a reference might be so obscure as to puzzle general readers; and for the purpose of cross-referencing other reviews or features by Steinberg that bore immediate relevance to the subject at hand. Over the course of his *Globe* tenure, Steinberg's writing became more self-contained, with fewer external references, consequently reducing the need for footnotes in later chapters. To account for inflation, we have also included footnotes providing 2025 dollar amounts for monetary items specified by Steinberg.

It was a given that many of the performer names mentioned by Steinberg, though perhaps or even likely recognizable to those familiar with the Boston musical scene of the 1960s and '70s, would be unfamiliar to most current readers, who could presumably be counted on simply to accept the presence of those names in the broader context of Steinberg's journalistic style. Some of these performers would later achieve wider recognition, others simply would not—a matter of fascination to Steinberg himself, who, decades later, stated to Marc Mandel that it was of specific interest to him to see which of many locally heralded performers would go on to develop meaningful careers beyond the Boston area. Had we chosen to elucidate the biographies of those performers, or the histories of various performing organizations Steinberg wrote about, there would have been no reasonable stopping point.

*****

The *Boston Globe*'s use of hot-metal typesetting in the 1960s and '70s resulted in numerous misspellings, word omissions, transposed lines, ink blots, and a variety of ambiguities, which also made it impossible to utilize image-to-text software—for which reason Jacob Jahiel painstakingly transcribed each article.[1] We were able to correct simple, obvious errors, but where educated guesses had to be made, these, as well as our occasional insertions of first names, are given in square brackets. The *Globe*'s original morning-edition headlines have been retained, even though they were clearly not Steinberg's own and were sometimes changed in later editions. Informal liberties have been taken—without being indicated—in occasionally removing the *Globe*'s subheadings; eliding or breaking up paragraphs; deleting tangential references to other local events; or, in Steinberg's record reviews, omitting additional subject matter not germane to the subject at hand.

As tempting as it was to remove the occasional outdated nomenclature or sexist comment, we chose to reflect the time and place in which it was penned. Other editorial changes follow OUP's house style. Seeming discrepancies in the placement and/or use of commas, colons, and semi-colons reflect not only Steinberg's own, often idiosyncratic use of punctuation, but our intent to retain the immediacy, particularities, and occasional peculiarities of his personal writing style as it appeared originally in the pages of the *Boston Globe*. Instances of the latter include, for example, occasional British words and spellings, and inconsistencies in the formulation of such titles as *Moses und Aron* vs. *Moses and Aron*.

*****

[1] These can be found in the *Globe*'s archives, accessible to subscribers via the paper's website.

In March 1965, a year after the start of his *Globe* tenure, Michael Steinberg was the featured speaker at a Boston Symphony–sponsored luncheon.[2] On that occasion, he outlined the critic's task: "knowledge and explanation are the object of the critic in his summary judgment conditioned by the time and space at his disposal, and not a personal rendering of 'what I went through.'" Steinberg further observed that one of the critic's major jobs is to "create a lively climate for the art of his time," also noting that, except for such time-honored figures as Hector Berlioz and George Bernard Shaw, critics are "not for posterity."

And yet . . .

[2] "*Globe* Critic Steinberg Charms BSO Lunchers," by Marjorie W. Sherman, as reported in the *Globe* on March 6, 1965.

Boston Globe advertisement introducing its new music critic, Michael Steinberg, placed in the Boston Symphony's program book in January/February 1964 at the start of his *Globe* tenure. (Used with permission.)

1964

Bernstein's *Kaddish* in Premiere Here

February 1, 1964

There is something enviable about the utter lack of inhibition with which Leonard Bernstein carries on. His Symphony No. 3 (*Kaddish*) is a piece, in part, of such unashamed vulgarity, and it is so strongly derivative, that the hearing of it becomes as much as anything a strain on one's credulity. Can the narrator really have said "Do I have your attention, Majestic Father?" and did she declare to her God, "We are in this thing together now, you and I"?

But yes, there it was, along with, at the end, the familiar figure of the composer himself, fetched from the wings by his wife (who had narrated), and bowing to the cheers and to the applause amid a veritable extravaganza of bear-hugs and kisses.

Kaddish was commissioned by the Boston Symphony and the Koussevitzky Music Foundation for the orchestra's 75th-anniversary season, 1955–56. The composer responded with an ambitious work, laid out on a large scale. At its center stands the Hebrew Kaddish, the prayer of sanctification, traditionally used as a prayer for the dead, though its text speaks not of death, but of the praise of God and the hope of peace. Bernstein has troped the liturgical words with an English text of his own, one in which the speaker fights her way, Job-like, from despair to faith.

The idea is splendidly imaginative, and it is tempting to think of what a poet like Auden might have made of it. But Bernstein as a writer of words has only fluency at his command, and that fluency produces a lava-flow of clichés wherein a few cozy intimacies (speaker to God, "We'll make it a sort of holiday") are contrasted against the tinny rhetoric of Norman Corwin's radio plays from the '40s.

As a composer of music, Bernstein's bent is principally theatrical. He knows how to make an effect, and *Kaddish* is full of detail that really tells: the dense and anguished cadenza for chorus *a cappella* is an example, and so is the tremendous orchestral outburst, with trumpets shrilling on high C-flat, that starts the finale. The last ten bars of "Amen" are quite wonderful, not only for the magic of their sonority, but for the precision and skill of their harmonic preparation as well.

At such a moment, Bernstein shows that he can compose, and I just wish he would. Mostly, he seems to prefer the easier way of assembling a series of tricks. These tricks are mutually incompatible, and they are generally irrelevant to the task at hand. The program notes explain how atonal chromaticism is associated with despair and G-flat major with faith, but no symbolism can justify the musical illogic of the transition. The idea of such a symbol is perfectly plausible, but Bernstein just has not managed to compose it out properly.

Kaddish was in the final stages of scoring last November when circumstances commanded its dedication "to the beloved memory of John F. Kennedy."

Charles Munch, during whose directorship *Kaddish* was commissioned, conducted this, its American premiere, and he led a spirited and exciting approximation. There were many ragged attacks and not quite comprehensible rhythms. I suspect that balances perhaps suffered because crowded conditions on stage necessitated the exile of a number of violinists. The principal chorus was that of the New England Conservatory, impeccably prepared by Lorna Cooke deVaron, and superb in every way. The Columbus Boychoir, Donald Bryant, director, had a substantial part as well: pitch and tone are amazing, rhythm less so, and there is no diction to speak of. The narration was by Felicia Montealegre (Mrs. Bernstein), who for all of her intensity is not really an interesting performer, and who was made to sound metallically cold by the electronic amplification. Jennie Tourel sang the soprano solos, and she did so with utmost beauty and distinction.

The concert began with Handel's Concerto Grosso, Op. 6, No. 4, in a curious reading that demonstrated that it is possible to achieve a certain charm even with every imaginable feature of sonority, speed, articulation, dynamics quite wrong. There followed Bizet's youthful Symphony in C, so attractive in its evocation of the 17-year-old boy's playing of Schubert duets. Mr. Munch slammed through it rather roughly, and I am afraid both its performance and that of the Handel demonstrated how much rehearsal the Bernstein Symphony had required. I found it interesting that even Handel's and Bizet's relatively simple patterns of quarters and eighths came out pretty much all over the place, and I was the more braced, therefore, against the confusion caused by Bernstein's rather more complex metrical requirements.[1]

[1] This, Steinberg's first review for the *Boston Globe*, made an immediate impression. Reader reaction came quickly, with five letters to the editor, all congratulatory, published on February 8, another two on the 13th (one pro, one con), and another seven on the 17th, five positive and two negative, ranging from the delighted to the derisive.

Glenn Gould, Pianist—Also a Critic of Music Worth Paying Heed To

February 3, 1964

In the liner notes for his recording of Mozart's C minor Piano Concerto, Glenn Gould wrote that the development section would have come out better if Haydn had composed it after, of course, taking a few piano lessons from Mozart.

When I read that, I knew that we had in Mr. Gould one of the very few music critics of our time worth paying attention to. Accordingly, I looked forward eagerly to the first of two lecture-recitals on the history of the piano sonata at the Gardner Museum Sunday afternoon.

I was not disappointed either. The task Mr. Gould set himself, or was set, is monstrous, and he explained at the outset that he could deal with it only by approaching it from some special and limiting point of view.

He chose for his focus the crisis of the sonata style at the time of Beethoven, and the central point of reference to which he returned again and again was the E major Sonata, Op. 109.

He began by demonstrating from the scherzo that the work is composed partly with techniques that are quite archaic for their day, and he made the point that this Sonata as a whole is fascinatingly balanced between archaic and the modern.

His analysis—and it really was analysis rather than description—shed light on the tension, so typical for late Beethoven, between the dynamic sonata style and the more static variations, a tension that becomes constantly more prominent in the last sonatas and quartets.

Quite properly, Mr. Gould pinpointed harmonic architecture as the most significant constant factor of the sonata style, and his many examples, drawn from Johann Sebastian Bach, Scarlatti, Carl Philipp Emanuel Bach, and other Beethoven sonatas (Opp. 2, 1, and 101), demonstrated different solutions across a hundred-year period to a variety of harmonic, structural, and rhetorical problems.

Such a lecture is not easy to do, and it was not designed for facile listening either.

Mr. Gould's manner is nicely straightforward: words and thoughts come fast and wittily. He does his audience the honor of assuming on its part a real interest in music and an active and curious intelligence, something that enabled him to do justice to his subject.

He spoke and played without a break for 110 minutes, every one of them illuminatingly dedicated to the proposition that music fulfills, among other things, an urgent human need for a richly involved mental activity. It is almost as though he had said, "If we wanted things to be all simple, we wouldn't be composing music."

The second of Mr. Gould's lecture-recitals, in which he promises to discuss the unity of a sonata as a whole, and once again dwelling on Opus 109, will be given in the Gardner Museum March 8. It is an event keenly to be anticipated. And while I am on the subject of the Gardner concerts, let me urgently counsel the recital February 16 by the young Austrian Alfred Brendel who, with Glenn Gould, is easily the most interesting and impressive of the pianists to have appeared in the last decade.

Munch Conducts Berlioz—*Fantastique*

February 8, 1964

When I was living in New York in the '50s, I used to imagine Symphony Hall as the scene of a more or less perpetual performance of the Berlioz *Symphonie fantastique*, relieved now and again by *Daphnis and Chloé* and *La Mer*. A touch of the old days returned with the second week of Charles Munch's current engagement with the Boston Symphony when, on Friday, he once again gave us the *Fantastique*.

He gave it much as he always did, coarse in sonority, frenzied in temper. The Symphony begins with a measure in which a few woodwinds and a horn play *pianissimo*. In the second measure, they all cadence, triple-*piano* and *diminuendo*. Not a trace of becoming softer, therefore no sense of cadence, therefore no sense!

Fifteen measures later, Berlioz has the first violins weave a dainty filigree of rapid staccato scales, and he wants them to do it *pianissimo* and lightly, "with the points of the bow." A scale there was, yes, but somewhere near *mezzo forte*, and coarsely scraped near the frog.

Munch conveys the Symphony's continuity only superficially as he proceeds from one abruption and one exaggeration to the next. "Hold back very slightly," asks Berlioz, and Munch grinds to a near halt. "No ritard," and Munch speeds up. In the final two movements, Munch altogether misses the mood. The "March to the Scaffold" is too fast to be sinister, and the "Dream of a Witches' Sabbath" is too fast for anything at all.

I know it's too fast for me to hear, and it is also too fast for the orchestra to play, and toward the end I had the impression of desperate wind players scattering notes into any feasible point of the measures at all in an attempt to be rid of them before Munch arrived at the final cadence.

All in all, I found it abominable. However, for the benefit of the lady who wrote in last week to object to my failure to report that the audience had liked that which I had not, I append the information that twenty-seven persons shouted "Bravo" and that Munch had four recalls.

After the intermission, Mme. Nicole Henriot-Schweitzer played Ravel's Piano Concerto in G. That event, too, has been quite a fixture at Symphony Hall. Mme. Henriot-Schweitzer has appeared in eleven out of the past sixteen seasons, and she has played the Ravel four of those times. Perhaps it is naive of me to infer from the number of her engagements here that the Boston Symphony considers her nearly three times as interesting an artist as Firkušný, Graffman, Istomin, Janis, and Serkin (each of whom has played with the Symphony four times during the comparable period), or nearly four times as well worth hearing as Arrau and Fleisher (three engagements each), or eleven times more estimable than Curzon and Rubinstein.[2]

Mme. Henriot-Schweitzer is a moderately engaging player, possessed of considerable personal charm, and apt to perform with attractive vigor and élan. She and her Baldwin piano between them produced a greyly limited range of sounds, and she lacks the control with which to keep the long cantilena in the Adagio alive and breathing. As a result she took to fussing with it rather, though even then she lost our attention and had us all coughing, rustling, stirring restlessly. Munch's accompaniment was admirably "with it," and full of nicely realized details, especially by way of wind playing.

The concert ended with Albert Roussel's Symphony No. 3 in G minor. It was composed in 1930 for the Boston Symphony's 50th anniversary season, and while it is far from the best-known of that series of commissions,[3] it is one of the most attractive. It was a pleasure to have that boldly original, yet quite conservative, Symphony back, and a double pleasure to have it in so lively and handsomely played a rendition.

Among other things Friday's concert was a showcase for the distinguished artistry of Louis Speyer, the orchestra's English horn player, soon to retire at the end of forty-six (!) years' service.

With control of pitch and timbre unimpaired, he plays with the warmth and eloquence of a great singer. The slow movements of the Berlioz and Ravel works gave him glorious opportunities, and he was twice brought front and center for a bow, once—typically and delightfully—with reed in mouth, and looking happy as can be.

[2] Mme. Henriot-Schweitzer's husband, Vice-Admiral Jean-Jacques Schweitzer, was the nephew of Charles Munch.

[3] The ten anniversary commissions included Copland's Symphonic Ode, Hindemith's *Konzertmusik* for strings and brass, Prokofiev's Symphony No. 4, and, most notably, Stravinsky's *Symphony of Psalms*.

New Faces, Remarkable Symphony—Mahler Ninth Superb in New York Concert

February 9, 1964

NEW YORK—The Cleveland Orchestra is at this time unequaled, and the program I heard in Carnegie Hall last Monday might have been designed to demonstrate that.

George Szell conducted Mozart's *Marriage of Figaro* Overture and B-flat Piano Concerto, K.450 (Rudolf Firkušný soloist), and the Ninth Symphony of Gustav Mahler. I could write about the special virtuosity of every section or about each of the solo winds, but what is so impressive is that Szell has built a real orchestra.

To choose players of extraordinary individual accomplishment is not enough, and Szell seems alone among orchestra builders in his skill at selecting players for their mutual relevance and compatibility. We expect of a great singer that his or her voice sound like the same voice all the way up and down, without jarring changes of color with every move into a different register.

It is the same with orchestras, which always are less great, no matter how brilliant, if one of the players constantly stands out like a soloist, or if two men in a section sound as though they belong, or ought to belong, to quite different ensembles. It is because of its unanimity as an orchestra even more than for its surpassing virtuosity in other ways that I would call the Cleveland Orchestra uniquely great, or perhaps even uniquely an orchestra.

One takes for granted that such an ensemble be completely responsive to its conductor, but what George Szell wants impresses me less than his ability to get it. The Mozart on Monday was mostly dreadful. Bad on a very high level, to be sure, but bad just the same.

The *Figaro* Overture was amazing. Szell used something like sixty strings and made them sound lighter and more transparent than twenty. At the end of the seventh measure we all gasped, and quite understandably, and we did so a couple of dozen more times during this brief masterpiece. It was great fun hearing all those eighth-notes go by so fast, and not unlike watching the Rockettes, but I doubt that anyone heard the music at all.

The Concerto was in its outer movements too fast to be good, and certainly faster than Firkušný, a rather casual technician, could comfortably play it. The Andante was beautiful. It is the sort of movement to be captured by careful attention to texture and to ensemble, and that meant that both pianist and conductor, both good listeners, were able to give us their best.

Mahler's Symphony was remarkable. Szell is obviously a great believer in law and order, and that makes him good at following instructions. Mozart gives few explicit directions about the inflection of dynamics and speed, and that is why Szell's Mozart is generally so bad: when Mozart says nothing verbally, Szell either does nothing, or he does something brutally wrong because he has no imaginative insight into the nature of Mozart's expressive gestures.

But Mahler's scores are loaded with information, and Szell can conduct them much as though he were assembling an FM tuner from a kit. That doesn't sound like a good recipe for conducting the Mahler Ninth, but it is. At least, it is an approach that I find salutary and welcome.

One of the most perceptive of my colleagues, Benjamin Boretz of *The Nation*, pointed out to me after the concert that while Mahler's large forms tend to be derivative and heavily dependent upon repetition, his small forms are consistently remarkable. Mahler is a composer of wonderful details, and it always matters in his music precisely how a thing is done. And listening to Szell, you can really find out.

Not an accent, not a fleck of color is lost. Every touch tells: even first and second violins sound different (which is important in the first movement). It's like reading the score—though, of course, more enjoyable. I have been more immediately moved when I have heard the Ninth conducted by Mitropoulos and particularly by Barbirolli, but in the past, Szell's Mahler readings (*The Song of the Earth* in 1960 and the Fourth Symphony last year) have been the ones to stay with me the longest.

Mahler once said, "The most important part of music is not in the notes," but only by going through the notes can we get behind the notes. Barbirolli, Kubelik, Mitropoulos, are more profoundly understanding guides to the wonderful world that "is not in the notes," but they are less reliable about getting you there. By giving us the sound of Mahler, Szell lets us find our own way to the heart, and in Mahler the sound and the heart are one.

One special feature of the concert must not go unmentioned: in Myron Bloom, Mr. Szell has a principal hornist as unique in his own way as the Cleveland is as an orchestra. He is a less firmly aggressive player than many, not so dependable as James Chambers in the New York Philharmonic, nor does he have the melting lovely high register of James Stagliano in Boston. But more than any player since Dennis Brain, Bloom uses the resources of his instrument for musical purposes. Every detail of color and articulation shows us something about the life of the music. In moment after moment, whether in the declamatory style, the lyric, or the grotesque, Myron Bloom demonstrated that he is easily the most varied, resourceful, and artistic horn player before the public now.

It is not easy to find repertory that most exploits George Szell's abilities without exposing his limitations. When it happens, and it did in the Mahler Ninth the other night, we can witness performance history being made and in the process of becoming legend.

Late Beethoven Sonata Heard in Special Perspective

February 10, 1964

A week ago at the Gardner Museum, Glenn Gould talked about the crisis of the keyboard sonata during Beethoven's last years. On Sunday afternoon, also at the Gardner, Leonard Shure provided another, and most fascinating, view of the same problem when he played Beethoven's Sonata in A-flat, Op. 110, prefacing it with Weber's Sonata in A-flat, Op. 39, and following it with Schumann's Sonata in F minor, Op. 14.

Beethoven's A-flat Sonata is a work I have usually thought of as being the one among the composer's late works in which the Romantic spirit is most anticipated. In the light of Gould's remarks about the many archaisms in late Beethoven, I now heard it quite differently. It was also put into a rather special perspective by the Weber-Schumann frame so imaginatively provided by Shure's program.

Weber's Sonata, played first, is the oldest piece, and it dates from 1816. In it a Romantic expressive ideal is uneasily wedded to a pedantically regularized formal design and to a glittering piano technique. The dramatic changes of register and texture are for all their immediate effectiveness quite superficially grafted to the rather square musical thoughts.

Beethoven's Sonata, written only five years later, is from another world. Beethoven writes as though he had never met another piano sonata in his life.

It was daring to program in succession two sonatas in the same key, but from the first chord of Opus 110 I saw the point: by providing so obvious an area of common ground, the juxtaposition vividly dramatized the difference. And paradoxically, the most archaic features provide the most striking "modernisms." The most "romantically" eloquent climax in Beethoven occurs at the top of a fugue on a typically Baroque subject, and at that, the fugue subject is the inversion of one used a few minutes earlier for another fugue.

Schumann's piece—like Weber's it is properly entitled "Grand Sonata"—was originally called "Concerto Without Orchestra." That does not mean much: the work is not significantly *concertante* in texture, and invoking the world of the concerto hardly indicates more than a particularly swashbuckling manner.

Written in 1836, the Grand Sonata moves in an expressive atmosphere far removed from Beethoven. Far from Beethoven, too, is the uneasy relationship of form and content. Thematic invention is rich, but Schumann has not really figured out how to deploy and articulate his ideas. I kept thinking about Carl

Philipp Emanuel Bach, about whom Glenn Gould last week shook his head sadly, saying "He was a very confused man."

I have written so much about the music because Leonard Shure is the kind of pianist who lets one hear it. He is not a particularly glamorous player. Sometimes the tone becomes harsh, and he certainly lacks the feathery lightness I would imagine Weber's own playing to have had. He is, however, always in and with the music, always interesting, and there is no question that he has a first-rate mind.

Somehow I had anticipated that Shure's brain might be a little wasted on the Weber, but not so. Structurally the most naive thing played was Weber's rondo-finale, but only a player of Shure's insight could have made sense and charm out of those many literal repetitions.

First of all by making up a program that was really a program rather than a mere collection of pieces of about the right length, then by playing it with such intelligence and integrity, Leonard Shure gave his audience an altogether absorbing and rewarding afternoon.

Performing Composer—A Treat to Hear

February 11, 1964

When composers perform, always go to listen. That is always a good maxim, and Leon Kirchner gave handsome proof of it in his concert at Harvard's Sanders Theatre on Monday night.

With Luise Vosgerchian he played two of Schubert's most wonderful pieces for piano duet, conducted a group of Boston Symphony players in his own Concerto for Violin, Cello, Ten Winds, and Percussion, and at the end of the evening led the most exciting performance of Stravinsky's *Les Noces* I have ever heard.

Kirchner's own piece was given in Boston for the first time. Large and uninhibited in its gestures, densely chromatic in harmonic style, busy in texture, it gives one plenty to listen to. It is conceived as an old-fashioned virtuoso number, though in characteristically contemporary fashion; the immense demands in performing skills are made not merely upon the two real soloists, but on every member of the accompanying, or better, surrounding, ensemble as well.

Sanders is not kind to deep instruments, and the solo cello part, though most excellently played by Madeline Foley, carried less than the composer must have intended. Joseph Silverstein, substituting at drastically short notice for Robert Koff, who is ill, played his part songfully and with brilliance.

Schubert's four-hand miracles are not often heard in concert. Composing all that activity into one piano is technically a terribly difficult business: the first player's right hand is constantly forced into a dangerously glassy high register, and the second player's right hand, of necessity sometimes a melody barrier, is not in a favorable position for cutting through. And those are just the beginnings of the textural miseries the players must cope with.

Hearing the Vosgerchian-Kirchner duo, one would hardly suppose that there is anything in the least problematic about four-hand playing. Their Schubert readings were pianistically as beautiful as their clumpy little Baldwin allowed, and musically they were miraculous. Miss Vosgerchian has a most delicate hand with a melody, and Kirchner's bass lines, so loving but so secure in their tread, made just the right foundation for the whole sound.

The A-flat Variations with which they opened are full of glorious harmonic detail; the F minor Fantasy is, with all its indebtedness to Mozart's model in the same key, one of Schubert's grandest conceptions. Its slow movement was the one thing that did not quite work in performance: its magnificence can be conveyed only through the most magistral sort of rhythmic pose, and Kirchner's playing became here rather too nervously urgent.

No matter: his handling of the most elementary accompaniment figurations was thrillingly masterful, and the Fantasy's last return to its main theme was one of those moments when time itself seems suspended.

In *Les Noces*, the soloists were Beverly Sills, soprano, Eunice Alberts, mezzo-soprano, James Miller, tenor, and John Hing, bass, easily as capable a quartet as I have ever heard. Especially their diction was on an unusually high level. I have never heard so many of the words; indeed, in view of the nature of the words, eyebrows seemed to be departing from scalps all over Sanders. The chorus was bright, clear, enthusiastic, accurate. It even looked good: all the girls wore solid color dresses, no two of the same color, and they suggested the end of some mad Easter egg hunt.

Everything was just right for Stravinsky's joyous bedlam, except perhaps at the very end, where the Baldwin thump multiplied by four—*Les Noces* uses four pianos and a whole carnival of percussion—made a pretty dull facsimile of Russian wedding bells.

So all in all we had three "classic" masterpieces revealed as only a composer's understanding can reveal them, and we had a chance to hear a persuasive example of the composer's own and proper art. He is one of the best around now, and I look forward to writing more about his vigorous and intense music.

I puritani—Opera a Triumph, Sutherland Great

February 13, 1964

Sarah Caldwell's act of daring in bringing Bellini's *I puritani* to the stage again paid off in a magnificent and deserved triumph.[4]

The score is Bellini's last and greatest. The flow of lyric melody is astonishing, even by Bellini's standards, but in the last year of his absurdly short life, the composer had begun to learn and understand so much. The perfumes of Bellini's music are always delicate, but those gentle harmonic colorations are used with a most touching sense of situation and with a lovely precision.

The orchestra is no longer just a big guitar either. The apparatus remains simple and so does the basic conception of the nature and function of the operatic orchestra, but never before had Bellini known how to use those strings *tremolandi*, the twittering flutes in thirds and sixths, the romantic four-part horn chords, so tellingly and with such fragrance.

Even the structures themselves are always thought out afresh. The constant expansions of the third-act finale, above all the elaborate scene of Elvira's madness built around the famous "Qui la voca sua soave," these are very far from being matters of mere routine.

Most of all, *Puritani* is a singers' opera, and Joan Sutherland's first Elvira on any stage in this country was an eagerly awaited event. She is marvelous, and one could almost leave it at that. She has the technical equipment for Bellini's difficulties, and indeed more, for in the true tradition of the 1830s she embellishes her part with all manner of extra figurations and roulades. Her voice has grown ampler and more colorful.

The art of phrasing, everything that falls under the general heading of "musicianship," has matured so that she is now able to achieve greater effects by simpler means. She can turn a phrase without twisting it, and those swooning mannerisms that were disfiguring some of her performances as recently as a couple of years ago are now quite gone.

4 Sarah Caldwell (1924–2006), the Boston-based opera impresario, conductor, and stage director, singlehandedly changed the face of opera in Boston, presenting more than seventy-five operas, including US premieres and challenging 20th-century work, "unified," as Richard Dyer wrote in her *Globe* obituary of March 25, 2006, "by a profound and comprehensive vision of how opera could be relevant and vital in our time, and defined by a splendid theatricality. Her adventurousness was often ahead of its time . . . and her administrative practices often summed up everything an impresario should avoid, establishing a negative example as powerful as the positive example of her artistic work. There were many unpaid bills, postponements, cancellations, and strange substitutions. . . ." That the articles and reviews contained in this volume refer variously to the company as Opera Boston, Boston Opera Company, Boston Opera Group, and Boston Opera reflect some of the administrative chaos that led to periodic reorganizations. See especially the assessment Steinberg wrote at the end of Caldwell's 1967–68 season (March 31, 1968).

She has worked hard on what used to be the most severe problem that stood between her and greatness: her diction. Her Italian sounds less innocent than it did, but above all, there is diction in place of what formerly seemed to be a vaguely organized assortment of diphthongs and a very few consonants.

The dramatic involvement in the part is complete, intelligent, and passionate. She is very large and she looks tough, and that is quite a handicap in the roles into which her voice casts her. She handles herself magnificently. Face and body are used with precision, power, and an amazing delicacy. Her performance in short is a thing whole and entire. One of the men, Spiro Malas, came closest to matching Sutherland's brilliance. He has less spectacular things to do, of course, than the soprano, but the part of Sir Giorgio demands, and must have gotten from Lablache[5] in 1835, a rich and evenly developed bass voice of great range and frequency, and the ability to make something convincing of a warm-hearted and by no means dramatic character. Without being able to radiate Sutherland's "star quality," Malas nonetheless functioned on a musical and dramatic level close to hers. His portrayal was a considerable achievement, and beautiful.

Richard Cross was more uneven. He is not a master of the florid style, and so his elaborate aria in the first scene made little effect. It is, however, tough to open an opera in which everyone is waiting for Sutherland. In the more straightforward moments later on he did well, and in the one moment where he must compete with Sutherland on her own ground by echoing a phrase of "Qui la voce" he came through splendidly. He and Malas brought down the house with their stirring duet in military style that closes Act II, a duet that actually was a trio by virtue of the blazing trumpet solo by Roger Voisin that went along in unison with the two singers.

Charles Craig is a vigorous tenor rather than an elegant one. He sometimes requires a considerable wind-up in order to work his way into the beginning of a phrase, and he tends to deal woodenly with tunes. He did well in the more aggressive moments, and it was reported that he even took the incredible F above high C in the final scene's "Ella è tremante," and very listenably, too. He looks and acts like a tenor, but he compensates by clear and intelligent diction.[6]

Chester Watson and Dorothy Cole were good in their rather small roles, but James Stuart was largely inaudible in his.

[5] The renowned bass Luigi Lablache (1794–1858), who premiered the role of Giorgio at the Théâtre-Italien in Paris in 1835, was one of four singers who became known as the "*Puritani* quartet." The opera was so successful that it was seen the same season in London, and opened and closed the Théâtre's next seven seasons, each time with its original cast.

[6] The *Globe*'s 12:30 A.M. publication deadline periodically necessitated Steinberg's having to leave a long performance before its completion, leading here to a second-hand report. The tenor's range seldom exceeds high C; in Craig's time, the high F was almost always lowered to a D-flat, making this execution newsworthy.

And far from least, there is Richard Bonynge. No one knows and loves the Bellini style so well as he, and in this style he has no rival as a conductor. Fluidity, cohesion, grace, and vigor are all his to command. The whole performance was most elegantly shaped, and the orchestra gave some charming playing. One of the evening's most agreeable moments was Charles Yancich's horn solo just before "Il rival" in Act III.

To return finally to Joan Sutherland, but for whom... Not only is she phenomenally gifted, but she is aware of her gifts and of her responsibility to them. She is, of course, fortunate in being married to the kind of scholar, coach, and conductor Richard Bonynge is, and in a sense perhaps that means she is married to her artistic conscience as well. In her own area she is as great a singer as we have today, but really the best thing about her is that she is so obviously still someone on her way up.

Brendel—Outstanding Performance for Valorous Audience

February 17, 1964

In the middle of a Sunday-afternoon snowstorm, which made it difficult even to see the Gardner Museum, Alfred Brendel's piano recital drew a considerable audience and one that must have felt well rewarded for its valor.

Brendel, an Austrian pianist not far into his thirties, played Schubert's posthumous C minor Sonata, Liszt's *Fantasia quasi sonata—après une lecture du Dante*, and Beethoven's B-flat Sonata, Op. 106, the so-called *Hammerklavier*.

Schubert sonatas are not often played in concert. The three late and very great ones are long, and they are often so loosely structured as to make the greatest possible demands on the player's ability to organize their flood of inspired ideas. Furthermore, they are very much more difficult than they sound: the pianist works unbelievably hard, but to most of the audience it sounds as though he were doing childishly simple things.

Since the death of Artur Schnabel, who really owned those pieces, Brendel is their outstanding exponent. From the point of view of intelligence, sympathy, warmth, grace, technical command, his reading on Sunday afternoon of the magnificent C minor Sonata left nothing to be desired. Particularly the finale, which can sound merely like an interminable gallop with some rather eccentric details, was played with such understanding and bravura as to reveal it as a veritable madhouse of humor, and quite sophisticated and highly organized besides.

Now that the battle for Berlioz is won, Franz Liszt is the greatest neglected genius of the 19th century. His compositional ideas are so closely tied to the performer's crafts that his music hardly exists away from performance, and the right performance at that. Pianists like to play Liszt for his octaves and the rest of the pianistic razzle-dazzle: few of them really believe in him.

Brendel does. He lives in it, glories in it, much as a Callas or a Sutherland can sing into, and alone make a living thing, of the music of Bellini or Donizetti. To hear Brendel play Liszt's *Dante* Sonata is to understand why this music was written.

The Beethoven interpretation is more controversial. That lies in the piece. It was Schnabel who once said of Beethoven's late sonatas that they were greater than any possible performance of them. Beethoven's late music represents the beginning of the trend of writing, as it were, beyond the performer. No one reading can solve all the problems in any given piece.

Brendel chose clarity, and in the outer movements he achieved it through tempi rather on the slow side, which, at least for the first Allegro, means eliminating the brio implied by Beethoven's (admittedly quite mad) metronome mark of 138. Again, the slow movement seems a little fluent for an Adagio sostenuto. It was, just the same, very beautiful, and there is something compelling about the classical restraint with which he conveyed, and very tellingly, Beethoven's "*appassionato e con molto sentimento*."

And even with all the problematic aspects of Brendel's reading, one was truly brought into the presence of the *Hammerklavier* Sonata. Rudolf Serkin and Charles Rosen are the only pianists I know who are his peers in dealing with this tremendous work.

The recital was deeply exciting. Alfred Brendel is among the elect.

Renaissance Music by the Camerata

February 26, 1964

In very new music and in the very old we have very much relaxed performance standards, partly, no doubt, because we are so grateful to be allowed to hear it at all. This was evident at Tuesday evening's concert by the Camerata in the Lecture Hall at the Museum of Fine Arts, when a couple of hundred persons sat solemnly listening to, and at least in part enjoying, the performance of an ensemble whose limitations of technique and of temperament make it only in a limited way qualified for the task it had undertaken.

The music that was performed is as beautiful as any I know. Victor Mattfeld, the Camerata's director, is obviously a man not only of scholarship but of taste. The music was almost entirely drawn from Netherlandish repertory of the late 15th century and the very early years of the 16th. Hayne van Ghizeghem,

Antoine Busnois, Philippe Caron, Johannes Ockeghem, and Josquin des Prez were the masters represented most extensively.

From the range of styles and moods these men offer, Mattfeld put together an admirably constructed program that went from the sheer fun of Josquin's *El grillo* to the gravity of his *Nimphes, nappés* and of Caron's *Helas que pourra devenir*. The program ended with two of the great Renaissance "déplorations": Ockeghem's on the death of Binchois and, in touching juxtaposition, Josquin's on the death of Ockeghem.

Now and again some of this was actually brought to life by the ensemble of two singers and seven instrumentalists. Particularly the soprano Ellalou Dimmock did some fine work when, late in the evening, she had loosened up: especially the serious Josquin songs were conveyed with great expression (though the *Déploration* needs more singers for the imitations to make their full effect). Also, earlier, a couple of the Busnois pieces went well, and so did Dalza's Piva for two lutes and drum.

Most of the concert was like walking on eggs. There was a certain amount of sheer technical incompetence—at least two pieces sounded as though they were being read at sight—and the prevailing rhythmic flaccidity was crippling. Under the circumstances to try an out-and-out virtuoso number like Josquin's *Faulte d'argent* was to court disaster, nor can I say that this courtship went unrequited.

Even when matters were technically in reasonably good order, there was not one instant of the vivaciousness, the flair, that would have suggested we were in the presence of a lively music of charm and passion. The dominant mood was one of dullness, and there reigned over all a lack of confidence, and a depressing gaucheness that was so unfortunately symbolized by the pair of maroon socks one of the gentlemen was wearing with his dress suit.

Gina Bachauer—Pianist Commanding in Mussorgsky Work

March 2, 1964

To hear Gina Bachauer play Mussorgsky's *Pictures at an Exhibition* as she played it Sunday afternoon in Symphony Hall is thrilling.

The work has a strange history. Written for piano in 1874, it became really popular only with Ravel's orchestration, commissioned by Koussevitzky in 1922. When it was thoroughly established as a repertory piece, but an orchestral one, pianists began to look at it again. Now quite a few of them play *Pictures*, generally managing to suggest rather unhappily that they are playing a piano reduction of Ravel's orchestra piece.

One could not entertain any such idea on hearing Miss Bachauer's commanding way with this music. First of all, she rendered absurd the notion that *Pictures* is badly written for the piano. In fact, she went rather further than that, because she revealed that not only did Mussorgsky write competently, but that his specifically pianistic imagination is something quite out of the ordinary.

It is rare that a pianist works with such precision and imagination to discover the effect of every change of register, of each octave doubling, of all the wealth of detail that constitutes the ensemble of good composing and good piano writing.

Bachauer's pianistic self-knowledge was impressive in the way it enabled her, even after the unleashing of her virtuosity in "Limoges Market" and "Baba-Yaga's Hut," to hold in reserve still greater masses of sound for the climactic "Great Gate of Kiev." The "Great Gate" is a treacherous piece: it consists basically of ever more sonorous repetitions of an idea that is grandiose even on its first presentation. Even orchestras are apt to exhaust themselves before the final climax, and how much more dangerous it is for pianists with their more limited dynamic and coloristic gamut! But Bachauer led this finale from magnificence to magnificence in a way I should not have believed possible.

Two of the scenes did not quite come off pictorially. The "Ballet of the Unhatched Chicks" was too fast, not only for pianist's fingers, but from the aural viewpoint as well. In "Goldenberg and Schmuyle" the marvelous (though mean) portrait of the nervously clinging Schmuyle was reduced to a neat repeated-note etude. One could almost believe Miss Bachauer never to have seen a Jew in her life.

That the *Pictures* were on the whole so handsomely played came not only as a great pleasure but as a surprise as well because nothing that happened earlier in the afternoon had promised such accomplishments. Apart from her beautiful tone, one that never becomes harsh even in the most aggressive passages, Miss Bachauer's best asset is her phrasing of certain kinds of melodies.

That is also her undoing: she is primarily a "tune" pianist. If she were a conductor she would always be facing the first violins, and now and again the cellos. Rhythmic articulations, structurally vital basses, tend to escape. When rapid figurations appear, she lets them run away. Thus in Chopin's B minor Sonata, the Italianate arias in the first movement and in the Largo were lovely: her Chopin, by the way, is basically in the straightforward, non-*affettuoso* tradition. But no one, I am sure, could have sung the melody of the scherzo having had to learn it from the blur of the much too rapid notes Miss Bachauer played, nor did anything in the finale that came between the returns of the main theme make much sense either.

Beethoven's A major Sonata, Op. 101, is about as elusive a piece as even Beethoven ever wrote. Most of it escapes most pianists, but even so I have never heard all of it get away so completely as it did from Miss Bachauer. She seems emotionally out of sympathy with it. She suggested none of the moods Beethoven asks for (with deep, intimate feeling; in the character of a march; with longing; with decision; etc.) and her uninformed ideas about the sonata's rhythmic and textural balances and the tendency to run prevented her from performing even the moderately useful service of giving an accurate "factual" reading.

The concert also contained the G minor and C minor Preludes and Fugues from Book I of Bach's *Well-tempered Clavier*, and a group of three of the most popular Brahms intermezzi.

It would be a welcome part of the housekeeping arrangements at a concert were the program to have indicated the source of the Bach pieces instead of just saying "Two Preludes and Fugues" and giving the keys. And can we not be spared inanities like "This work (the Chopin) is free from the preoccupation with mortality which so colors the B-flat minor Sonata"?

Stokowski, BSO Share Afternoon of Glamour

March 7, 1964

Leopold Stokowski conducted the Boston Symphony for the first time on Friday, and during an afternoon not devoid of some dazzling moments, conveyed to a remarkable degree the glamour of the concert world.

He chose a program of music from the 16th, 18th, and 20th centuries. In the first half, there was a Canzona by Gabrieli, a Concerto of Vivaldi's, and the Wind Concertante by Mozart. After the intermission, there were short works by Ned Rorem and Alan Hovhaness, and the suite from Stravinsky's *Petrushka*.

The program seemed put together as though to show us what a good orchestra we have, and at the same time to demonstrate how readily Stokowski could make it sound like one of his own.

The Gabrieli was for winds only, three five-voiced choirs of them occupying the front corners and the rear center of the stage. The Vivaldi was for strings alone—it was the famous D minor from Opus 3 that Koussevitzky was so fond of—and it made sounds that Vivaldi, at least in so far as he was a connoisseur of string playing, would have been impressed by. And the Mozart brought to the fore the virtuosity and taste of a quartet of wind principals: Ralph Gomberg, oboe, Gino Cioffi, clarinet, Sherman Walt, bassoon, and James Stagliano, horn.

The contemporary works all used full orchestra, and few blindfolded listeners would have guessed "Boston" on hearing the raw, visceral sounds Stokowski evoked.

Modern music has always had a big place in Stokowski's program building, and he has conducted significant American premieres of music by Mahler, Berg,

Stravinsky, Schoenberg, Prokofiev, and others. There was another side to his pioneering, however, for he always had a taste for trivial exotica, Henry Eichheim and such people, and it is that side of his predilections that he has favored in recent years.

Ned Rorem's *Eagles*, after Whitman's "The Dalliance of the Eagles," has some evocative pictorialisms and just enough touches of freshness to make one regret their entombment among clichés well staled in Hollywood. The Prelude and Quadruple Fugue by Alan Hovhaness is of the composer's usual studied simplicity, this time clothed in cap and gown. It fulfills its modest ambitions with vigor and competence, and it earned Hovhaness, who was present, a big hand.

Stokowski as an interpreter of music is obviously a well-known quantity by now. He makes orchestras produce a wonderful sound that, for a few pieces, is just the right one. It's mostly right for the gaudy Shrovetide Fair atmosphere of *Petrushka* though the rhythmic edge is softer than that which Stravinsky himself applies to this music. And what would the composer's comment be on the tam-tam added to the Coachmen's Dance?

Stokowski makes his own pieces out of raw material by Gabrieli and Vivaldi. The pitches are right, so are most of the metrical relationships and some of the timbres. Their pieces were not displeasing to hear, but if you think you can find out from a Stokowski performance what sort of music Gabrieli and Vivaldi wrote, forget it!

In the Mozart *Sinfonia concertante*, the solo parts were beautifully played, especially in the second and third movements. Stokowski was least effective here. Since he was accompanying a solo quartet, he couldn't very well turn it into one of his own pieces, yet he hasn't the discipline to play it properly. As a result the performance mostly hovered in an air of inhibited academicism, interrupted now and again by a little swoon. It isn't one of Mozart's great pieces anyhow, its main quality being its truly extraordinary euphony, and its thirty-odd minutes were just a little tedious.

But *Petrushka* really blazed, the orchestra men even smiled as they gave out those wonderful tunes, and those fifteen minutes were by far the most excited and exciting music-making I have heard at Symphony Hall since arriving here.

Sawallisch—Viennese Outstanding in Bruckner Symphony

March 9, 1964

Wolfgang Sawallisch is a great conductor, and the orchestra he leads, the Vienna Symphony, a great orchestra. Their Sunday-afternoon concert in Symphony Hall was devoted to two symphonies, Mozart's *Jupiter* and the Bruckner Third.

As an encore, Sawallisch gave *The Blue Danube*. It was the least satisfactory thing he did—having it at all seemed a mistake and it seemed a bit self-consciously a "house specialty." But it was interesting in that it laid bare to the bone the twin sources of the conductor's excellence. When Sawallisch conducts, the music sings and it dances.

Sawallisch is a prosaic looking young man, but his conducting is beautiful to watch the way Toscanini's was and Hans Rosbaud's. Every gesture one sees, every facial expression, is accompanied by its correlative in sound. In his conducting there is no cause without effect. There is no extravagance, and there is no ostentatious economy either. The whole operation is moving, morally moving, in that peculiar way in which only the right thing in the right place can move.

From the first page of the *Jupiter* the exalted level of Sawallisch's musicianship was evident. His is not my ideal Mozart: it is a little cool and dry. It lacks sex appeal. Also he used rather more strings than Mozart bargained for. Sawallisch understands how this endangers the balance, and it was impressive that the winds were not covered. But he achieved it by having the strings hold back with the result that the dynamic frame was not quite filled. A biggish orchestra playing a little down is quite different from Mozart's own smaller group playing with full vigor, and so the *Jupiter* also sounded a little small, a little "Classical," not suggestive of maximum grandeur on its own scale.

Still, Sawallisch is a conductor who knows upbeats from downbeats, who recognizes bridges and understands where they lead, who knows that a Mozart symphony requires a dozen different kinds of upbeat, and at least that many sorts of attack, release, and accent. All that puts him in quite another league from the stupefied routiniers who run most of the world's orchestras, not to mention the famous Mozart experts, from whom heaven preserve us. Sawallisch's handling of the lead-back to the finale's recapitulation, or the weighting of the Andante's two final chords, just to pick two examples, these are not things one encounters every year.

The Bruckner performance, free as it was of the special hazards of Mozart conducting, was as complete and as fulfilling a realization as I can imagine of this clumsy, yet magnificent masterpiece.

The phrasing of melodies was always lovely. The right rhythmic touch is more rarely found. Sawallisch builds a scaffolding so unassailable as to withstand any amount of flexibility of detail. Good breathing is the secret, and whether in Mozart's most mercurial sequences or in Bruckner's largest monster breaths, Sawallisch is always there. He is one of the rare masters who can even let music continue across a silence. Bruckner's vast pauses left one in the very stream of rhythmic continuity, suspended in the anticipation of the beat to come.

In the Strauss encore he even made the music continue across the usually so disruptive hiccups of the Viennese waltz style. And having heard his Mozart minuet and the accompaniment of the "chorale" in the Bruckner finale (and what a beautiful thing his anticipatory upbeat was here!), we did not need to wait for the *Blue Danube* to learn the springiness of his dance rhythms.

The Vienna Symphony Orchestra itself is a wonder. There is nothing slick about it, none of the homogenized quality that represents an orchestral ideal for many. Instruments sound highly characteristic, very stringy, very woody. There is an exhilarating sense of the physical materials of music: a timpani roll conveys an almost palpable sense of the rhythmic beats, of membrane and felt.

The overall virtuosity is surpassing: particularly one will hardly meet more beautiful brass playing. Yet the orchestra calls no attention to itself. Its playing partakes of the moral beauty of its conductor's work: everything the orchestra did was submerged in something greater than itself by becoming an inseparable part of a symphony by Mozart and Bruckner.

The concert was profoundly refreshing and moving.

Philomel—New Babbitt Work Lyric Triumph

March 15, 1964

Philomel by Milton Babbitt is a monodrama for soprano, recorded soprano, and synthesized sound. It was performed by the soprano Bethany Beardslee, for whom it was commissioned by the Ford Foundation, at Amherst College February 13, and at the Metropolitan Museum of Art, New York City, February 21.

Tereus, King of Thrace, raped his sister-in-law, Philomel, and in order to silence her, cut out her tongue. She and her sister Procne, who had taken a hideous revenge on her husband by killing his son and serving him to the king, are pursued through the woods by the enraged Tereus. The Gods intervene by transforming Procne into the swallow, Tereus into the hoopoe, and Philomel into the nightingale, the bird who since that time has sung.

The poet John Hollander, who teaches at Yale, and Milton Babbitt, who teaches at Princeton, had for some time had in mind a work on this gruesome, yet musically so suggestive subject. The commission from the extraordinary Miss Beardslee turned plan into realization.

Hollander's poem is in three parts. The monodrama takes place at the moment of Philomel's metamorphosis, and with the restoration of her voice. The first part begins with just sounds, and gradually they become coherent and informed with meaning. The second part is an obeisance to that tradition of vocal genres, the echo song. The third section is a strophic aria really about singing, and bound by the refrain, "Now I range/thrashing through/the woods of Thrace."

The music is in three layers: the live soprano voice; a soprano voice recorded and, in part, distorted and in various ways metamorphosed in the recording; an "accompaniment" of sound that is electronically synthesized, i.e., not produced by the manipulation in any way of already existing sounds.

Babbitt's formidable reputation as a theorist and as a representative of highly complex compositional procedures has rather obscured his lyric and dramatic gifts. One of his most significant pieces is a setting for soprano and electronic accompaniment of Dylan Thomas's "Vision and Prayer," a setting accomplished through music as intense, eloquent, meaningful as that powerful poem itself.

If *Philomel* is in any way less impressive than *Vision and Prayer*, it is because of the difference between two poems. Thomas's is an impassioned meditation on something very important, and by comparison Hollander's seems little more than a mannered game. He starts with the vowel "e," set to music on the note E in an impulse Josquin, Monteverdi, or Bach would have understood. "E" evolves into fee, feel, fee, a million trees, trees, tears, Tereus, Philomel, melons, honey trees filled with mellowing felonious fame, and so on. Babbitt has responded to the musical suggestiveness of these sounds, yet the libretto, through two performances, remained for me a constant irritant.

Babbitt has never written more beautifully. Even the hazard of the Hammond organ sounds that are apt to be so annoying in legato passages of electronic music are reduced to an amazing minimum. The combination of the voice with its own electronic shadow is striking in concept, and with Bethany Beardslee's singing, ravishing in sound.

Philomel is something special considered just as a commission. Miss Beardslee is not just someone whose name appears on the title page; her voice is embedded in the composition's physical sound. The living soprano duets with the recorded. Actually, the recorded soprano is on one or two of the tape's four tracks: she could therefore be filtered out and the voice of another soprano substituted. In other words, if, for example, Susan Belink were to sing Philomel, she could sing duets with Beardslee, or she could record her own track. It remains to be seen whether such an effort would be worthwhile: that is, to what extent the essential expressive effect of Philomel resides in the duetting of two female voices, or if something very important is lost when the two voices are not twins. Certainly in Beardslee's performances, a dimension of something especially touching was added by this haunting identity, this confrontation of quick and embalmed.

What is sufficient that one can say in praise of Bethany Beardslee? I heard *Philomel* for the first time the night after hearing Joan Sutherland in a stupendous performance of *I puritani*,[7] and it struck me then how Beardslee breathes and lives the music of her time in the same miraculous way Sutherland is the *bel*

[7] See review of February 13, 1964.

canto spirit incarnate. Bellini wrote for Giulia Grisi, with the same musicality, the same intensity of feeling for that most moving of instruments, the human voice.

Philomel is a triumph of modern lyricism. To hear it, and in such a performance, is an assurance that, so much evidence to the contrary, to be in music today is wonderfully worthwhile.

Elliott Carter—Prausnitz Gives Boston Premiere of Variations

March 20, 1964

Elliott Carter's Variations for Orchestra, written 1954–55, were played for the first time in Boston at Thursday night's Jordan Hall concert of the New England Conservatory Symphony Orchestra, Frederik Prausnitz conducting.

During the afternoon, the composers Robert Cogan and Pozzi Escot gave a brilliantly clarifying lecture on the work, mainly for the benefit of Conservatory students. During that lecture they made what may to some have sounded like strong statements, but which were hardly more than plain home truths. They said that Carter is today the American composer most respected and admired in the musical world, and they said that his Variations are the most significant orchestral score produced in America during the past decade.

The Variations, commissioned and first played by the Louisville Orchestra, have a wretched performance history. Since the premiere, they have been done by only two orchestras in this country. I heard them played by an orchestra whose advertising bills it as "the world's greatest," and I can report that the performances were useless if one assumes the purpose of such an occasion to be a revelation of the work, rather than a mere mutual loan of prestige by composer and orchestra.

The Variations are beautiful and rich in so many ways that I cannot begin even to describe, let alone to assess. They are deeply conservative in the way their expressive gestures reach into a most basically humanistic root level. They are wholly modern in that every means by which Carter conveys the expressive content is original, not superficially, but profoundly.

Carter writes a multi-level music in a language whose principal building blocks are speeds and rhythms. That means he calls on us to exercise the greatest sensitivity and receptiveness in the very areas where our training is poorest, where the past couple of centuries of musical history have most benumbed us.

As the Variations are hard to hear, so are they hard to play. Their score is an astounding imaginative feat of virtuoso orchestral writing, and that is an aspect of the piece no previous performance in my experience had been able to reveal.

Inevitably in a student orchestra levels of skill will vary. So, to put this review into its proper perspective, let it be said there were a few roughnesses of execution, and that they were to be expected. But then let it be said that the performance as a whole amounted to something that the celebrated professional orchestras of the world only rarely provide in their occasional condescension to new and difficult music, and that is a statement of the work that truly revealed every essential quality in it.

Frederik Prausnitz knows the work completely, and he knows how to make an orchestra play it. The orchestra itself is full of talent (though it is plainly more in evidence in certain sections than in others), it is quick, alert, responsive, in every way well trained.

All this was clear from especially the second and third movements of Debussy's *La Mer*, which opened the concert and which in its own way is murderously difficult also. In Elliott Carter's Variations, Prausnitz and his New England Conservatory Orchestra gave us a really electrifying twenty-five minutes of music. I can most vividly express my feelings by saying that I wish Carter could have heard it!

On Segregation—Musicians, Politics, and Responsibilities

March 29, 1964

Leonard Bernstein, Arthur Fiedler, Gary Graffman, Vladimir Horowitz, Eugene Istomin, Erich Leinsdorf, and Artur Rubinstein are among the performers who in recent weeks have let the world know where they stand on racial integration.

All have declared that they will not appear before segregated audiences.

Hurok Attractions, Inc., which manages Istomin and Rubinstein, has for the last ten years as a matter of policy avoided booking its artists in segregated concert halls. Their connection with Hurok automatically involves, among others, Marian Anderson, Victoria de los Angeles, Van Cliburn, Jan Peerce, Andrés Segovia, and Isaac Stern in the southern boycott.

It was Graffman who set off the recent series of declarations when he cancelled a February date in Jackson, MS, when he learned of the earlier arrest of two Negroes there on attempting to enter a concert hall. Graffman's management had difficulty getting someone to replace him. David Bar-Illan was pressed into service by not being told why Graffman had cancelled, though as soon as he found out he joined his colleague. Eventually it became known that the series of dates that was beginning to become vacant was to be filled by the German pianist, Hans Richter-Haaser.

Richter-Haaser felt justified in accepting the engagements on the grounds that artists ought not to get themselves mixed up in politics.

His action is perhaps well evaluated in terms of a statement made by Erich Leinsdorf to John A. Morsell, assistant to the executive secretary of the National Association for the Advancement of Colored People: "Booking organizations, like most people looking for financial profit, will be convinced of the validity of an issue only when their financial revenue suffers. I have seen that some foreign artists, fearing more the wrath of commercial agents than any wrath from their own consciences, have willingly replaced those who have refused to perform."

Still, the notion that artists ought to stay out of politics is one we have all encountered before, and it is one of the most vexing of the issues of the ever urgent problem of the artist as citizen. He may stay aloof from politics, as may the butcher, the baker, and the candlestick-maker. On the other hand, the banker may not (and he probably won't want to), and nowadays the scientist can't either (though he might like to).

But "ought" is another story. It is more than anything a kind of Romantic survival from a period when it assumed that the artist was a child or a madman, unknowing, uncomprehending. We prefer to think now that artists are, no more than others, exempt from their extra-professional responsibilities. I am not sure that anyone still believes that artists are not part of the human race, though the notion still has just enough viability to serve occasionally as an excuse for the evasion of responsibility.

The present discussion about the musicians and the South has a familiar ring to anyone who remembers the headaches about the German musicians in the immediate post-war period, especially all that farcical denazification business. The cases of Furtwängler, Strauss, Gieseking, von Karajan, were among the more celebrated, and these musicians had displayed various degrees of weakness, confusion, or frank opportunism.

What these men, and some others, did, and what they failed to do, was disappointing. It became disgusting only when some chose to assume the cloak of Parsifal, and masquerade as The Pure Fool.

Is the problem of segregated concert halls a political one anyway, at least as it affects men like Graffman or Richter-Haaser? Obviously, there are endless political and economic ramifications to the matter, but is it not time to understand and to say clearly, loudly, that the nub of the obligation is moral?

Any man, any artist, has a right to take an amoral stand just as he may take an apolitical one. But is there really any maintaining of the position that as an artist, as a man dedicated to a pursuit where decision and choice is all, he may not stand up to be counted on the side of what he believes to be right?

Brahms Concerto With Some Bold Retouches

April 5, 1964

When Van Cliburn was soloist with the Boston Symphony last month in the Brahms D minor Piano Concerto, I noted that Erich Leinsdorf's conducting achieved in this notoriously difficult work a textural clarification rarely met with.

From the second measure it was obvious that the theme stood out with a boldness its craggy grandeur suggests, but never really achieves in performance. I had no score with me—this was at a rehearsal which I happened to visit for a few minutes more or less by chance—but I thought I recalled that the theme was scored for first violins and cellos in octaves, and now Leinsdorf was having the second violins play with the firsts, and the violas with the cellos.

A little later, around measure 21, when the strings' cascade of trills is answered by similar cascades from flutes, oboes, and bassoons, it was clear that the woodwinds were playing their part with a force and on a scale that brought them into a reasonable dynamic relation to the strings. Usually the effect is that of a feebly ineffectual echo; now it was a significant answer that could truly continue Brahms's thought. The reason was that Leinsdorf was using four of each woodwind instead of the two specified in the score. In other words, Leinsdorf was using what we call "doublings," having two players on a single line, not all the time, of course, but only in the weighty passages.

The D minor Concerto was first played, with Brahms himself at the piano, in Hanover in January 1859, and then a few days later in Leipzig. I don't know precisely the size of either orchestra at those concerts. I do know, though, that ten years previously, the Hanover orchestra had a complement of twenty-six strings; the Leipzig Gewandhaus Orchestra in 1839 had had thirty-one, and by 1865 it had fifty-two. The Boston Symphony today has sixty-six.

As German orchestras of the period went, fifty was an unusually large string group. We must assume, therefore, that Brahms was imagining a volume of string tone far more slender than that to which we are now accustomed. Eight winds can hold their own against, say, forty strings as they cannot against sixty. Something, somewhere, must give.

Two basic solutions present themselves. One is to cut back the number of strings, something conductors are understandably reluctant to do because the music of Brahms or Beethoven, to whom these problems also apply, then tends to sound small in the context of repertory that includes Strauss and Wagner. The alternative is to double the wind parts.

This is being done more and more frequently by conductors, though not yet nearly enough. Leinsdorf, by the way, used double wind to magnificent effect when he did the Beethoven Seventh some weeks ago. The scheme, here at least, is practical economics. Four flutes are on the payroll anyhow. Why not make them work?

In the particular instance of the Brahms D minor Concerto, one must also face the consequences of a very young composer's inexperience with the orchestra. He was 21 when he began to orchestrate the piece, 25 when after many changes it was finished. It was his first work for orchestra: the First Serenade was done the year the Concerto was completed (1858), the *Haydn* Variations and the First Symphony followed only fifteen and eighteen years later, respectively.

Brahms was anything but a composer of Mozartean or Mendelssohnian facility. Nothing came easily to him, and his orchestral mastery was hard won. It was to become the most elevated and assured sort of mastery: there isn't a more accomplished piece of composing for orchestra than the Fourth Symphony, but that was Opus 98, 1885, and another story altogether.

In the early '50s, Brahms lacked confidence as well as experience. He showed a sketch of the Concerto's opening to his violinist-conductor-composer friend Joachim. The big proclamatory theme was scored for brass. Perhaps it was clumsily done. At any rate, Joachim laughed, and Brahms retreated, but perhaps too far, to the version in the score now, whose sound never seems to live up to its rhetorical assumptions.

Leinsdorf's aim has been orchestrally to rethink Opus 15 in terms of the experience of the composer of Opus 98. It must sound like an ideal Brahms sound, not like Richard Strauss or Robert Russell Bennett. Leinsdorf has gone about his work boldly: about a quarter of the measures in the first movement, for example, are affected by his retouches.

I have now had the opportunity to hear the Leinsdorf edition four times, and it strikes me on the whole as a useful, well executed, successful piece of work. Yet is it the answer? Certain points, most of the woodwind doublings or the missing upbeat for clarinet in measure 399, are beyond argument.

But that opening—it is good to hear it big and bold, but is not the strain of just the first violins and cellos forcing to cut through, to sound like so much more than they are, is that not part of the expressive content? When in Leinsdorf's version it sounds so full-bodied and easy, has it somehow become another piece?

Whether of a composition or a person, the character is the sum of the defects as well as of the virtues. How hazardous a thing is the pursuit of interpretive loyalty. In accepting the challenge of the Brahms D minor Concerto, Leinsdorf has presented us all with a provocative and important challenge of his own.

La Bohème Has Its High, Low Spots

April 16, 1964

During the Metropolitan's performance of Puccini's *La bohème* Wednesday evening, my mind kept coming back to that horrible story about the crowd on the Albany sidewalk yelling "C'mon, jump!" at the young man on the 14th-story ledge. They are really Puccini's ideal customers: abetted by an extraordinary sense of stagecraft, and in complete abandonment to emotional cynicism, he caters with superlative and horrifying success to the most brutal, morbid voyeuristic impulses in human nature.

Puccini takes sadistic relish in the humiliation of his female leads, victims only of their own pitiful combination of passion and brainlessness. He indulges himself, and us, in the most painful drawing out of Mimì's death scene, and all for its own sake. Few of his musical devices really make much dramatic sense: the many allusions, reprises are hardly ever relevant. When he brings all the voices into a unison at the end of the third-act quartet, there isn't the slightest cause for it except self-indulgence in a pretty sound. Just compare how meaningful, for example, are Verdi's unisons in *Falstaff*!

Much of *Bohème* has the attraction of a certain youthful freshness. The actual quantity of music that is soggy or arch is smaller than in most of his mature works. Also, the situation allows him a beguiling display of high spirits, the start of the first act, or through the whole of the scene at the Café Momus (a clip-joint that serves beer steins only three quarters full, and most of that head). And the proto-Debussy "winter music" is very precisely atmospheric.

I did not find the performance altogether persuasive. Renata Tebaldi, last heard here in *Chénier* four years ago, sang Mimì. When she first began to be heard from in the late '40s, her voice was of an intoxicating warmth and loveliness, perhaps the most wonderful instrument of its kind then around. The bloom is now gone. What is left is serviceable and strong, but in high register and at great volume, there is forcing and harshness. The voice no longer carries me as irresistibly over her limitation as once it could.

She sacrifices diction to tone. She dislikes consonants and is capable of beginning her most famous aria as "Miyamano Mimì."[8] But a far more severe defect is that she sings with no rhythm, and that unarticulated flow of sound becomes as tedious as a diet only of honey. In any event, I am not sure Mimì ever was an ideal Tebaldi part. She looks too regal for it, and while she acts it with an alert sort of charm, her very grandeur of bearing makes the stickily coy aspects of the part harder than ever to take.

[8] The opening words of Mimì's aria are "Mi chiamano Mimì."

Richard Tucker sang Rodolfo with a voice admirably powerful and steady, but without much warmth, sometimes edged with a slight metallic buzz. He tends to over-declaim the part as though unaware that his job is to convey the words and sentiments through the tunes Puccini wrote. In general, he underscored details to a point where he hardly sang one directly musical phrase all evening long. I, at least, have not forgotten Bjoerling, and Tucker's way of solving everything with gasps seems a little facile.

Calvin Marsh was an excellent Marcello, and it is a pleasure to have that admirable singer given a substantial part. Laurel Hurley as Musetta, that sentimental shrew, was very good also, though more in an all-round sense than as a singer. Jerome Hines acted the part of Colline with humor and sentiment, but he showed little flair in his singing: "Vecchia zimarra" made little effect. Gerhard Pechner as Benoit and Andrea Velis as Alcindoro had the other significant parts, and each handled his with vivid theatrical skill.

Fausto Cleva conducted. I am not sure that he didn't lose some musical grip toward the end in letting things get a bit static, but altogether he achieved the right combination of control and flexibility. Far from the most glamorous and the most appreciated of the Met's conductors, he seems to me by miles the most capable of the permanent staff.

And how the orchestra plays for him! He commands precision, warmth, and delicacy, and he achieved a feat I had almost forgotten could be done, and that is to get a pizzicato chord played together!

Our Unserious Public—What Does It Hear?

May 10, 1964

Twice very recently I have been made acutely aware of the difference a good audience makes. Once was at the Harvard-Radcliffe Orchestra concert at Sanders Theatre, and once was at the Shubert for *King Lear*.

Cambridge audiences seem notably good anyhow. They seem to know why they are there. No particular social merit is attached to attendance at a Sanders Theatre concert. It is not a habit, one of a series of Friday afternoons automatically marked on the calendar at the beginning of the season.

Some people were undoubtedly in Sanders that night because they had friends in the orchestra or for other miscellaneous reasons, but in general, people seemed to be there because they wanted to hear Bartók's *Bluebeard's Castle* and the rest of the music on the program. They listened to the music attentively, and when it was over, they applauded.

The quality of the applause was striking, just as the quality of the listening had been. Dramatic works are, by their nature, apt to contain important silences. At Sanders, they were really silences, unfilled by conversation, coughs, the crackly unwrapping of devices for the prevention of coughs, dropped umbrellas, and so forth.

And the applause that followed was a genuinely and properly expressed gesture of appreciation for an absorbing performance. At the concert's end, it was just a few minutes before 11—and that, for a concert, is very late—and with a deadline to make I had to run, and run quite quickly. Even so it took perhaps half a minute before I had threaded my way through the labyrinths of the Sanders rows and aisles and actually achieved the exit. I looked behind me, and I was the only person in the auditorium on his feet. Everyone else was applauding and had not made a move to go. At Symphony Hall on Friday afternoons, no matter how speedily I leap up with the last chord, 87 women and 4 men have made it to the door ahead of me.

I find it odd, the way people just cannot seem to wait to get out. Watching and listening to the Royal Shakespeare *King Lear* was no holiday. The play began fairly promptly at 8, and the final curtain came down at 11:52. There had been one intermission, and it had come after a first act playing about two hours and a quarter.

Granted that the *Lear* production was remarkable, but I have been to concerts and operas in their way equally good, without, however, being able to count on an audience to listen for so long in such absorbed quiet. Concertgoers are apt to be like children who decided at some point they have had enough ice cream or whatever. They have had enough music—just like enough ice cream or enough martinis—and there comes the whispered, "Let's go, shall we?," the banged seat, the ritual and repeated "pardon me" ("excuse us" is recommended as being more sibilant), and the hell with Isolde and her Love-Death.

Most of the people at concerts hardly seem aware that compositions have ends that relate somehow to their beginnings, that pieces of music have a dialectic—a scenario even, if you will—that is to be followed from premises to a conclusion. They are content simply to bathe in attractive sonorities. They are not disposed, and no doubt unequipped, to try to come to terms with music whose interest is not in the first line sensuous.

The degree to which, for example, the Boston Symphony Orchestra audience is out of touch with the large musical world is dismaying. For a person, be he professional or not, to whom music is a means of urgent and immediate communication and not a mere casual pleasure among many others, contact with "music-lovers" who have literally hardly the first idea of what the art is all about, becomes an experience at first puzzling, eventually frightening.

If so few really care, so few really hear, what will become of the musical world? The Symphony audience's reaction to Gunther Schuller's *Klee* Studies and to Webern's Passacaglia (which is more than half a century old!) shows that part of the Boston public to have become incapable of dealing even with the least forbidding sides of contemporary music. Are these the inheritors of the public Dr. Koussevitzky educated and bullied for a quarter-century? Under the circumstances, I cannot find Mr. Leinsdorf's stated and implied willingness to indulge and flatter his audience much to cheer about.

Musicians and Scholars—Must There Be War?

May 24, 1964

To confuse composition and performance is a common critical error. New music suffers from it, and so does the rather old. A contemporary composition is performed: a listener does not like what he hears, and, of course, it is the composer's fault. It never occurs to the listener that the performance was perhaps on a level that would start a riot if, say, a Brahms symphony were so treated.

It happens with old music, too, this inability to distinguish the piece from its performance. The wildest example I know is a critic's remark that Bach's *Brandenburg* Concerti aren't really good, the Busch Chamber Players just made them so.

More often, and more seriously, the trouble is the other way around. I have read a complaint about the dullness of the Telemann overture the Boston Symphony played in March, and I have heard several about what a bore Purcell's *Fairy Queen* is. The reaction is understandable: in performances here, both were painfully tedious to sit through. The fault, however, lay not in the works but in the way they were done, and these two examples can stand for countless others in any season and in any town.

Composers strive to write down their music for the benefit of players and singers as accurately and as informatively as the notational conventions of their day permit and necessitate. Not everything can, or should, be written down.

If Chopin had attempted to write in exact rhythmic notation the rubato with which he played one of his nocturnes, the simplest measure would be hopelessly bewildering to the pianist's eye. And to fix the rubato, the elasticity of line, the breathing, is not the point anyway. Chopin doubtlessly never played the same melody in precisely the same way twice, and he would not have wanted other pianists to make quasi-phonographic reproductions of any one of his own interpretations. Provided the result remains within the limits of the implications of the compositional form, the freedom, the individual response is the thing.

Most music assumes some flexibility. The composer knows he cannot write down everything, and he supposes, and must in any event hope, that the performers are sufficiently trained, experienced, intelligent, musical, imaginative, to make the proper gestural response to whatever the written notation can convey or suggest.

The survivor of even the fewest music lessons probably remembers that a dot after a note lengthens that note by one-half its value. So, at least, one is taught, and it is fair enough for 19th- and 20th-century music. In a lot of 17th- and 18th-century music, however, the dot does not command a lengthening by any particular arithmetical ratio such as one-half. Often it means "lengthen by at least a half." In Baroque music, the intention in the so called "dotted rhythms"—the first two notes of "The Star-Spangled Banner" are an example of "dotted rhythm"—is to dramatize the difference between the long and the short notes, to lengthen the long, to shorten the short. If, in a passage where the composer intended such a "dramatic" interpretation of the dots, the modern player or conductor reads them according to the 19th-century literal "plus one-half" convention, he will quickly turn a series of snappy, exciting gestures into a foot-dragging shapeless bore.

Now, this is partly a matter of scholarship, but rather more it is a matter of musicianship. No one expects performers, who have enough troubles of their own, to be expert musicologists: it would not, however, hurt for them to be at least a little aware of the results of scholarship, where such results have bearing on their work. Even if every violinist, flutist, cellist, pianist, about to play a Bach sonata were to invest a dollar more or less in a paperback, Thurston Dart's *The Interpretation of Music*, the millennium would not be with us yet. That book, nor any other, does not supply all the answers, but let us at least make a beginning by knowing what the questions are.

But as for the so-called practical musician, what disturbs me much more than his occasional laziness, ignorance, presumption, cynicism ("even the experts don't agree, so why should I care?"), is the failure of his musicianship. Scholarship aside, he should hear that harmonic and rhythmic accents are not falling in the right places, that cadences (sentence and paragraph endings) are not being intelligibly articulated. With his own structural, rhetorical, above all rhythmic sensibilities in good order, he might even come to believe that the man worrying about things like double dots or cadential ornaments is not necessarily an ivory-imprisoned lunatic, but possibly, just possibly, a musician.

Composer-Performers—What Can They Teach Us?

June 14, 1964

How well does a composer know his own music? Stravinsky would answer that he knows it better than anyone else, and he is the first composer to leave behind at least an attempt at a systematic legacy of records of his own music so that future musicians may have a phonographic as well as a written documentation of his work.

A composer's performance of one of his own works is almost always apt to be a valuable point of reference, but it can bewilder as well as clarify. Stravinsky himself has provided an example as startling as any I know, or better, a pair of examples: his two recordings of his own Symphony in Three Movements, one made with the New York Philharmonic-Symphony about eighteen years ago when the piece was quite new (Columbia ML-4129), the other about three years ago with a recording orchestra in California (Columbia ML-5731/MS-6331).

Stravinsky has often commented on other conductors' performances of his music, not often kindly. His statements on the whole problem of performance, his praise of conductors like Monteux and (in the past) Ansermet for the objectiveness of their approach, suggests that for him the ideal performance is the one that gives the notes and the silences cleanly and accurately. Furthermore, his statements suggest that he believes that it can actually be done, i.e., that a given set of written symbols—indications for pitch, dynamics, duration, speed, etc.—should produce one particular objective result, and that everything else then becomes subjective interpretation.

If you listen to no more than even the first four bars of the Symphony in Three Movements conducted by Stravinsky—New York, 1946—and conducted by Stravinsky—Hollywood, 1961—it is clear that two different conductors are at work and that they have quite different views of the Symphony. Both men are extremely good, and both produce results that are clearly within the limits of what is prescribed—or is it suggested?—by a third Igor Stravinsky, the one who is the composer of the Symphony in Three Movements.

I think at this point of Artur Schnabel, who was once asked how he could reconcile his mastery as a player of Mozart, Beethoven, and Schubert, with the highly dissonant "modern" music he composed. "Either you were lying when you played Opus 111 just now," his questioner insisted, "or you were lying when you wrote your own piece." "Or perhaps both times," suggested Schnabel.

The people who write publicity for record companies are forever proclaiming the appearance of a definitive recording. Which Symphony in Three Movements is "definitive," and which the lie?

The question of the composer's interpretive authority is raised provocatively by a record of music by Elgar, conducted by the composer (Odeon ALP 1464). Elgar made quite a number of records of which the most treasurable is not now available in this country because of a trademark technicality, and that is the Violin Concerto, done in 1932 in which the 75-year-old composer had the 15-year-old Yehudi Menuhin as soloist.

What is available on the Odeon import is the *Enigma* Variations, made with the Royal Albert Hall Orchestra in 1926; the Serenade for Strings, with the London Philharmonic in August 1933; and the *Cockaigne* Overture, with the BBC Symphony in April 1933.

The theme of the *Enigma* Variations begins with six measures, each containing a quarter-rest, two quarter-notes, and two eighth-notes. The rest always falls on the downbeat, half the time the pair of eighths precedes the quarters, half the time the pair of quarters precedes the eighths. In the score, the eighths are always marked to be played each with a separate accent, while the pair of quarters is always slurred. Now, the most elementary analysis of the theme would suggest that this systematic motivic distinction between the slurred slow notes and the more detached fast ones is of primary importance. It would follow that the conductor's first duty is to clarify this motivic structure of the theme. Listen to Toscanini's recording, and you can hear this done in what is, in fact, the most beautiful phrasing of the theme that I know. Now turn to the composer's own recording and hear nothing of the sort: in each measure all four notes are slurred together, and the distinction between the two contrasting elements is not even hinted at. Which Elgar is telling us the truth, the one who wrote the phrasing into the score in 1899, or the one conducting a London orchestra in 1926?

Even though the orchestra is not first-rate, Elgar's own *Enigma* recording is full of beautiful and revealing things: the humor of the rowdy fourth variation is better realized here than in other performances I have heard, for example. Many conductors have something to learn from the way the eighth-notes flow in Var. V. The viola phrase in Var. VI is much more intelligently phrased than is usual, and I was struck by the way the final G-C pizzicato in the bass is used to give so cogent a summation to the whole episode.

The restraint of "Nimrod," the delicacy of "Dorabella," are lovely in effect, and in spite of technical advances since 1926, no other recording so well evokes the pictorial (Cunard) element of the Romanza.[9] Oddly enough though, Elgar's handling of the finale is not successful all the time; especially the return to the original theme is marred by a tempo dislocation that, however slight, is damaging to the flow.

9 The Romanza evokes an ocean voyage on a cruise liner, with the drums suggesting the ship's engines, Cunard being the most famous operator from the 1840s on.

The sound of the recording has been made glossy, a bit souped up in not very nice taste, but still the record has immense value as a document.

Marian Anderson—South Better Now

June 15, 1964

For a few hours on Sunday afternoon, Marian Anderson was in Boston in order to receive an honorary doctorate from the New England Conservatory. The occasion made her Dr. Anderson for the third time in four days—she had been honored by Fordham University on Thursday and by the University of Illinois, giving its first doctor of music degree, on Saturday.

"We hold the New England Conservatory in the highest regard"—Miss Anderson with great naturalness and seemingly perfect appropriateness likes to use the royal "we"—"and we had hoped to study there ourselves."

But on looking back over the years since lack of funds made it impossible for her to matriculate here, she is happy to settle for the honorary distinction in place of the earned degree she had once so much desired.

Then Boston had happy associations for the singer because it is the town of Roland Hayes.[10] She recalled the days when his annual concert at the Union Baptist Church in Philadelphia was "our concert season." One of the great moments of those years for her was the time she was allowed to appear on one of the Hayes concerts, "Not because of any merit on our part, but because it was thought that for those who couldn't understand the Italian, German, and French, Marian could sing in English."

Marian Anderson's stature as a human being has at times virtually overshadowed her fame as a musician.

How did she assess the importance of the role she had played in the public life of the country, her appointment as delegate to the UN, for example, or her stand on racial issues? "Many of our people would feel that we have not taken a sufficiently strong stand."

Miss Anderson believes that an artist works most effectively in his chosen medium, that she herself is a more effective spokesman as a singer for the causes in which she believes than as someone more explicitly active in politics.

How about concerts in the South? "For many years we stayed away from the South. It did not seem right that part of the people should be forced to sit all the way up in the peanut gallery."

[10] Steinberg profiles Roland Hayes in two articles included in this collection, May 28 and June 1, 1967.

And she mentioned a practice of, on occasion, making only the most expensive seats available to Negroes. "But last year we returned. We sang always before non-segregated audiences and we found that in every way conditions were much improved."

As for the artists' boycott of the South, Miss Anderson believes that more important than taking any specific stand on the racial or any other issue, it is essential for the artist to be true to himself. On the musician who chooses the amoral, apolitical stand, "We would not condemn him in any way." She returned to the "definite and good changes" she has observed in the South.

She is keenly aware of the problems of white persons' "bending over backwards." I cited a Negro musician who always maintained that after the initial and great handicaps, being Negro can actually be advantageous in the progression.

"Very true. The person who is put on one side as an exception is noticed later, but then he may be noticed the more because people feel that they have lost something by not having found this out a bit sooner."

Miss Anderson drew a parallel with non-Negro Americans whose successful entries into concert life here have to be made via Germany or London or Moscow.

We spoke of the Cliburn case,[11] the responsibilities of managements, and of her own beginnings, when Hurok, whom she has been unable to see at his office in New York, signed her up at once after happening upon a recital of hers in Paris. I wondered, and was left to wonder, if Mr. Hurok had learned anything from that experience. But by then it was in any event time for the singer to move on to Jordan Hall and become Doctor Anderson for the twenty-seventh time.

Erich Leinsdorf Stresses Broader Musical View

June 28, 1964

This afternoon the opening exercises of the Berkshire Music Center[12] at Tanglewood take place, and as is the custom, the music director will address students, faculty, and guests with an appropriate homily. In his talk, Erich

[11] Van Cliburn's triumphant win at the first International Tchaikovsky Competition in 1958, personally approved by the Soviet premier Nikita S. Khrushchev, thrust him immediately into international prominence both as a musician and as a cultural symbol representing a thaw in relations between the Cold War adversaries US and USSR.

[12] Founded by Serge Koussevitzky in 1940 as a summertime training academy for young musicians on the verge of professional careers, the Berkshire Music Center was officially renamed the Tanglewood Music Center in 1985, to clarify the connection between the Music Center and the BSO's summer home at Tanglewood.

Leinsdorf has many interesting and provocative—even sometimes provoking—things to say.

The separation of creative and performing musicians, the perception of greatness by contemporaries, the charge that performers do not champion contemporary music, the relation of musicology and performance, all these are among the topics that Leinsdorf touches on.

One point strikes me as something that students cannot have pounded into their heads too often, and here I should like to quote Leinsdorf in full:

> Studying a composer in depth is of great importance for your understanding. You may wonder how a clarinetist could benefit from knowing the poetry which Brahms chose for his songs, or how a singer might benefit from being acquainted with Brahms's chamber music. Your authority, your mastery of the expressive content and of the deeper meaning of any music can only manifest itself if you have a total knowledge of a composer's output and a complete understanding of the atmosphere in which he existed and from which he took his inspiration.

That is well said, though perhaps it comes dangerously close to the optimistic-inspirational language that is too familiar to the students from their college and conservatory catalogues. In other words, it may sound too familiar to warrant much attention. I hope, though, that they will pay attention, and that the teaching they are offered at Tanglewood and at their home schools will implement in practice and in close detail the important idea behind Leinsdorf's words.

Performers' interests are notoriously parochial: tuba players only go to the opera when Wagner is played, flutists only listen to wind quintets and *Afternoon of a Faun*, and many a violinist would accept the contention that Diabelli wrote the *Goldberg* Variations.

The performer's training leads him to allot say, four-fifths of his attention to making his instrument produce beautiful sounds. Anything that is left over goes to the music. To begin with, then, musical comprehension is apt to be shallow—it is deeply fallacious to suppose that either talent or experience at performing is a guarantee of an ability to understand music—and it will be the more shallow if the musical experience is limited to the performer's own active repertory.

The language of the most interesting composers is too involved in cross-references to support so narrow a view. The literature abounds in examples. Recently I heard a Rubinstein recording of Schubert's G-flat major Impromptu. It was in many respects entrancingly beautiful playing, but it was the kind of beauty that seemed an irrelevant, almost frivolous comment on the piece. Listening to performances by Edwin Fischer and Alfred Brendel helps me better to understand the nature of what Rubinstein was doing, and why it did not seem right. They played the melody in the simple, almost folk song-like manner of the greatest Lieder singing; Rubinstein's playing, elegantly restrained and free from vulgarity as it was, seemed suave and glossy. And I am willing to bet that Rubinstein's knowledge, esoteric and exoteric, of German Lieder cannot match that of Fischer and Brendel. The musical language of "Du bist die Ruh" and "Der Wegweiser" is not native to him, and that imposes distance between him and the piano Impromptu as well.

There are countless other instances. In Beethoven's *Hammerklavier* Sonata, Op. 106, a pianist will always play the third of the Adagio's themes, the one where the melody is in the deep bass, better if it is associated in his mind with the parallel place for cello in the *Archduke* Trio variations.

It is impossible for two pianists to make sense of the Andante in Mozart's great F major Sonata for piano duet unless they have in their ear the dialogues for violin and viola in the *Sinfonia concertante* and the C major Quintet. And then imaginative comprehension must embrace the knowledge that Mozart's conversations for strings, like most of his instrumental music, are themselves to be heard as operatic numbers. To the player with the Mask Trio in *Don Giovanni* firmly fixed in the heart, the gestures of Mozart's instrumental music will be familiar, they will be specifically and intensely communicative. He will, or at least he might, play the music the more beautifully because he will not be worrying about the phrasing or the dynamics per se; rather, he will make the right shapes and articulations because they are part of a language he understands and speaks.

And so it goes with Bach, Mahler, Stravinsky—name who you will. The point will be hard to establish because it assumes the supremacy of the music over the instrument, and that is a point of view to call forth the performer's most deep-seated resistances. I have the vision of the clarinet student at Tanglewood into whose hand Leinsdorf has just pressed a volume of Platen or Rückert. "Aw c'mon," says the student to his buddy, "let's go find a practice room."

Pierre Monteux, 1875–1964

July 5, 1964

When the papers of April 2 carried the news that Pierre Monteux had collapsed and fallen from the stage during a concert in Rome the night before, most of us experienced a pang of something like a sobering fright. To be sure, he was able to finish the concert twenty minutes later and the account spoke of sightseeing around Rome and an impending trip to Assisi, but still, it was hard to pass lightly over the sentence which mentioned that Monteux, on April 4, would be 89 years old.

Later, we heard that his two concerts at Tanglewood had been canceled. The optimism of the account was characteristic: it was stressed that Monteux would omit the concerts only because he wished to reserve his strength for his classes at "Le Domain" at Hancock, ME, and for his many engagements during the coming winter.

In Boston there were rumors of a special Pension Fund Performance of the Beethoven Ninth to be conducted by Monteux on his 90th birthday. Many recalled how his 80th and 85th birthday had been celebrated here in glory by what the passing of years had turned once again into his orchestra. But 90 has a different ring from 80. There is a point when the numbers attached to birthdays mix fear into jubilee. There was the knowledge, inescapable now, that some day the news from Hancock would be graver.

Now that news has come. We must learn to live with the idea that some part of Beethoven, of Schumann, Brahms, Debussy, Strauss, Stravinsky has died with Pierre Monteux, whose figure, so unforgettable an amalgam of dignity and humor, we shall not see again.

The grand figures among the conductors of his generation are almost all gone now. He stood apart from his contemporaries because his era was one essentially of eccentrics, often inspired ones. It was an age of a distinctly idiosyncratic approach to performance: Stokowski, Koussevitzky, Mengelberg are the archetypes. Pierre Monteux gave the music straight, as straight, at least, as he knew how. That, to many, was his limitation, but to many it was his glory.

It took me a long time to understand Monteux. My inclination always ran toward the conductor who did some violence to music, Toscanini for many years, and later Furtwängler. I do not know when I came to be able to hear what Monteux was doing, but I know that now there are some pieces about which I almost feel that I shall never really hear them again. *Death and Transfiguration* is one that comes to mind, and the *Tragic* Overture. I think I have never spoken with anyone about Monteux without hearing about one of these unsurpassed performances, a Ninth Symphony at Tanglewood, *Mathis der Maler* in Philadelphia, the *Enigma* Variations in Symphony Hall. There are not many performers to whom we could render the tribute of saying about even one interpretation, "this was the best I ever heard." But by sheer directness and honesty Monteux could sometimes lead us to the essence of a piece so that it stood revealed, it seemed, as never before nor since. Stravinsky, not a man given to sympathy for performers, once wrote, "Let me say here that Monteux, almost alone among conductors, never cheapened *Le Sacre* or looked for his own glory in it, and that he continued to play it all his life with the greatest fidelity."

The refusal to look for his own glory made slow Monteux's rise to the eminence he enjoyed at the end of his career. Someone has said that longevity is genius. For Monteux it was at least a blessing that enough years were granted him to overcome the discouragement of some of his American experiences in the '20s. The reunion with Boston, which had treated him shabbily after more than ordinary services rendered by him to its orchestra between 1918 and 1924, was an especially happy thing.[13]

Monteux was fond of attributing the course of his career to indolence. He switched from violin to viola, he insisted, because it was easier, and the violist became a conductor for the same reason. And what was he planning to do when he retired from conducting? "Music criticism, of course." I am glad it never came to that point. It was, after all, so good to have Monteux conducting.

Rudolf Kolisch—Music and Webern, and "Beautiful Tone"

August 20, 1964

MARLBORO, VT—The fact that Rudolf Kolisch was preparing Schoenberg's Chamber Symphony seems a good reason for the summer's second trip to Marlboro. I had hoped also for a chance to talk with Kolisch. He is, after all, a man of extraordinary background and unusual experience, and he was especially interesting to me for his association with Arnold Schoenberg.

The association was personal—he was the great composer's brother-in-law—but Kolisch had also studied with Schoenberg, and had participated in the premieres of the Third and Fourth string quartets, the Serenade, the Septet, and the arrangement of the Handel Concerto Grosso. During those same years, the Kolisch Quartet had also given the first performances of Berg's *Lyric Suite*, Webern's Trio Quartet, and the Third and Fifth quartets of Bartók.

We spoke first about the work in hand. The Chamber Symphony, though for only fifteen players, is usually conducted. Had Schoenberg ever suggested it be led chamber style from the first violin chair? "No, not at all. But I am convinced it must be done."

Kolisch has played it and he has conducted it, but he had never felt such pleasure in the preparation as here at Marlboro.

Players, he insists, give their best when they are not conducted. If they are playing chamber music, they take far greater pains over the details in their part. Oh, yes, they resisted at first; but they were now enjoying the flexibility of a chamber performance. "It's important not to have all those downbeats," he added, thinking of the conductor's baton.

13 Following his music directorship, Monteux was not invited back to conduct the BSO until 1951, only after Munch had succeeded Koussevitzky as music director.

Flexibility and spontaneity are of tremendous importance, and to instrumentalists who during the year make their living in orchestras Marlboro offers an occasion to recapture some of that. Kolisch pointed out, however, that even though the players involved in the Schoenberg were technically superbly equipped and of outstanding musical intelligence, they had to be taught the kind of chamber-musical freedom he was looking for. "And all the time they have to be taught to listen, and not to play so loud."

I asked him if he had ever played in an orchestra himself. "Never, thank Heaven." He showed me his left hand where the first joint of the middle finger is missing, destroyed in a childhood accident. "That saved me." He had been playing for about a year when his finger was injured; he relearned to bow with his left and finger with his right—and he has been playing that way ever since.

Listening is a most important clause of the Kolisch credo: his one disappointment at Marlboro where he was otherwise marvelously happy, was that his Schoenberg instrumentalists were playing from individual parts. "That is something I normally do not allow. Everyone must play from the full score."

Miniature scores are dismembered, and the pages pasted onto large cardboard sheets. It had not been possible here—though at rehearsals each player had a score in his lap—but it is essential to Kolisch so that the individual instrumentalist will think of himself as playing a string quartet or whatever, rather than a viola part.

In 1922 Kolisch founded his own quartet whose other violinist was Felix Khuner, the violist, Eugene Lehner (now of the Boston Symphony), the cellist, Benar Heifetz. The Kolisch Quartet played its entire repertory from memory. That, too, for Kolisch, is a necessity if real ensemble, real listening is to be achieved. The Quartet disbanded when its members were caught in America as war broke out—"there was a sort of panic."

A quarter-century later Kolisch still seems to feel as strongly the bitterness of losing what had become for him the realization of an ideal of music-making.

I asked about Anton Webern as conductor. Suddenly there was real happiness in the face as Kolisch remembered performances of Webern's own music, Schoenberg's Mahler,[14] Schubert, Mozart, unequalled for their elasticity, expressive songfulness, and tonal beauty. "He was the greatest of all." What about Schoenberg? "An incomparable musician, of course, but physically clumsy in his movements, and not always an effective conductor."

[14] This presumably refers to Webern's conducting of reduced orchestrations of Mahler's music made by Schoenberg for performance by the Verein für musikalische Privataufführungen (Society for Private Musical Performances), which was founded by Schoenberg in the fall of 1918 and whose "performance directors" (*Vortragsmeister*), besides Schoenberg himself, included, among others, Webern, Alban Berg, Rudolf Kolisch, and Eduard Steuermann. Such arrangements included Mahler's *Das Lied von der Erde*, Fourth Symphony, and *Songs of a Wayfarer*; Debussy's *Prélude à l'après-midi d'un faune*; and works by numerous other contemporary composers.

Kolisch had much to say about the way instrument and music are balanced in the performer's mind. The instruments are made for the music, but too many use the music to show off the instrument and the playing. The obsession with "beautiful tone" angers him especially. The *appropriate* tone is a beautiful tone—strings must not always be played with the same lush legato bowings and fast vibrato.

"Nowhere in music has something been written for beautiful tone!"

Besides his teaching at the University of Wisconsin, Kolisch still plays some concerts. He is off to Europe to play the Beethoven Concerto, which he has thoroughly restudied. He sang a few bars of the Larghetto to demonstrate the correct rhythm and tempo. "It will make such a scandal," he said—not at all unhappily.

From Price, Von Karajan Spectacular *Carmen* [Record Review]

September 3, 1964

"Are you all right?," inquired my wife a bit anxiously as Leontyne Price was smoldering her way through the Habanera. Well might one ask. The performance is of a kind calculated to make men crawl.

But let me not suggest that the only values of the Price *Carmen* are those of its torrid sexuality. That we have had before—the throaty growls and all the rest of it. The remarkable thing about the Price interpretation is how all of that is integrated into a musical performance of rhythmic and timbral continuity, verbal and dramatic clarity, and unfailing vocal beauty.

Essentially Price sings the low, mezzo version of the role, though now and again it gives her pleasure to sing a few of the high notes in the soprano version which a mezzo could not reach.

Price is here superbly resourceful in the use of her voice. She uses far fewer tricks than most Carmens, but the dynamic and coloristic gamut is astounding, from the "*Ta ra ta ta*" of the castanet scene to the whispering "*En chemin te pousserai*" in the first finale.

Also, Price is exciting because she is so strong rhythmically. "*L'amour!*" in the Habanera is a whole lesson in the meaning of rubato, luxurious freedom projected always against the most rigorous metric framework. The long arches of the Seguidilla are another such lesson.

And best of all is the passage that for me has always been the most touchingly beautiful in the opera, the scene for Carmen and Don José just after the Flower Song: never have I heard "*Là-bas, là-bas dans la montagne*" done with such freedom and so movingly realized for its essential melancholy.

Price as Carmen would be good anyway, but she can do so exceptional a performance partly because of the context Herbert von Karajan creates for her singing and acting. His *Carmen*, too, is an achievement of beauty and distinction.

In some respects von Karajan's performance is a little mannered, and it certainly is rather slow (without, however, being absurd like Beecham's). He inclines sometimes to over-refinement, something that has produced unfortunate results in Beethoven and Brahms, but which does *Carmen* no end of good.

There is nothing effete or restrained about the Prélude, for example, but right from the start there is evidence of the operation of a rather special ear simply because the music sounds brilliant and rhythmic rather than noisy and thumpy. And von Karajan realizes wonderfully the imaginative orchestral delicacy of the opening chorus with those amazing low flutes at the reprise, the children's military scene, the Seguidilla, and the Card Scene.[15]

Also, von Karajan has a highly developed sense of drama. Accents are gentle and the motion suave, but that increases immensely the force of the moments of dramatic emphasis. I am sure no conductor has ever propelled Carmen onto the stage more compellingly than von Karajan with the rubato that he imposes on the 16th-notes at her entrance, "*La voilà!*" And the same rhythmic distension, a kind of built-in fermata effect, is used brilliantly for the first up-and-downbeat of the Toreador Song.

Again, within a framework of rather continent dynamics, the force of the pit orchestra's *crescendos* during the stabbing of Carmen is terrifying.

With von Karajan in charge, the other singers outdo themselves, but they cannot overcome their ultimate limitations. I have never heard Corelli sing so nearly agreeably and musically, but even here he remains a yelling tenor of not the highest taste and intelligence. Merrill as Escamillo has a far easier role. He sings it fairly well, but it seems to be beyond the persuasive or the disciplinary powers even of von Karajan to get him to sing "*Toréador, en garde!*" lightly and softly as Bizet asks—and as apparently no baritone would dream of doing.

From a musical point of view, Mirella Freni sings very beautifully as Micaela. Her performance is, however, distractingly flawed by her bad French. Both she and Corelli are quite uncivilized in this respect and they tend to sing French as most German opera singers sing Italian: that is, without seeming even to try to get it right.

The many vivid minor roles, all blessedly taken by French singers, are excellently done. The choruses and the orchestra do their job beautifully. The stereo recording has splendid sound and a good—which means among other things unobtrusive—dramatic presence. One side-break is very bad, the one that

[15] The performing forces in this recording included the Vienna Philharmonic and Vienna State Opera Chorus.

separates Carmen's castanet song from José's outburst, "*Ah! J'étais vraiment trop bête!*" Also, the surfaces on my review copy are noisy.

In spite, then, of a less than ideal Escamillo and Micaela and a barely acceptable José, for the extraordinary achievement of Leontyne Price and Herbert von Karajan I recommend the new RCA Victor *Carmen* most warmly.

Schoenberg—Thoughts on the Birthday of an Extraordinary Man

September 13, 1964

Arnold Schoenberg would be 90 years old today. He was almost 77 when he died, but he died in his prime. Last May I heard a beautiful performance of the String Trio he had written for Harvard in 1946. It sounded so fresh, so adventurous, that I think I realized then for the first time how the death of Schoenberg, well into his 70s, could be a tragedy of unfulfillment like the death of Schubert at not quite 32.

When Schoenberg died, his name had been well known for forty years. What hurt was that the name was so much better known than the music. What hurt as much—and it was infinitely more damaging—was that insofar as the music entered the picture at all, people knew things about the music rather than the music itself.

Not that people in any proper sense really knew anything about Schoenberg's music, but they had read about things concerning the number twelve, and they had been told such things as well. There was just enough hazy misinformation, imprecisely stated and improperly interpreted, to give the public the idea that here was a man indulging in purely mechanical speculation and altogether removed from artistic creation as that had been traditionally understood.

Hindsight has suggested that it was a mistake for Schoenberg and his circle ever to publicize anything at all about the new methods of organizing compositional materials that he began to use in the early 1920s. Modern communication being what it is, the day was probably past when such a thing could be kept a professional secret as seems to have been done with the isometric techniques of the medieval motet composers.

At any rate, Schoenberg could only turn his greatest scorn on "those who look in my music only for the twelve notes."

It was not just the public either. Rarely has a musician been so betrayed from within the profession. The talk and the writing about the music—some of it informed by malice, more of it by ignorance and stupidity—was just part of it.

Schoenberg pointed with great precision at another injustice when he once said: "My music isn't modern: it's just badly performed." After the first performance in 1930 of his opera *Von Heute auf Morgen*, Schoenberg had just one remark to make to the orchestra: "Gentlemen, out of the difference between what I wrote and what you played, I could make a whole new opera." And that was not the only time he felt that way. A letter to Fritz Reiner, describing Koussevitzky's performance of the Orchestra Variations, Op. 43b, is a sobering document, worth reading.[16]

All his life a grimly humorous man, Schoenberg became with the years a bitter one also. But his passion, his sense of engagement and commitment were often turned in directions other than scorn. His correspondence with Kandinsky is of searing agony over a lost friendship as it then seemed. And I know nothing more warmly appreciative than a letter to the conductor Hans Rosbaud thanking him for a beautifully made performance of the Orchestra Variations, Op. 31.

Schoenberg knew exactly who he was. He did not arrogate when he indicated to the city of Los Angeles that his first public recognition there should come in some form other than an invitation to serve as a mere extra at a testimonial dinner for Otto Klemperer.

His cruelly publicized quarrel with Thomas Mann about *Doktor Faustus* was in all ways pathetic and unfortunate. When Mann finally conceded to the extent of adding to his novel a note that the compositional techniques of his hero were really the intellectual property of Arnold Schoenberg, "a contemporary composer and theorist," the Schoenberg anger and scorn were evoked once more. "We shall see who was whose contemporary," he wrote in reply.

In a radio lecture about the Variations, Op. 31, Schoenberg described a certain orchestral detail as "a sound which I hope will one day be considered beautiful." The hope is more plausible now than in 1951 when Schoenberg died, and much more so than when the Variations were written in 1928.

But much needs to be done. We need a good critical study of the music. The correspondence should be made available in a good edition in English. More than anything, we need good performances so that the appearance on concert programs of works more than twenty and thirty years old no longer maintain their status of esoteric and problematic novelties.

Once when Goethe was a very old man he received a visitor, a young man who began to complain to the poet about the inaccessibility of much of what he had written. It was, he said, like building an ark on the top of a high mountain. Goethe spoke: "The water will rise, the water will rise."

[16] Schoenberg's letter to Fritz Reiner of October 29, 1944, as well as the subsequently referenced letter to Hans Rosbaud of April 15, 1931, may be found in the online archives of the Arnold Schönberg Center at https://archive.schoenberg.at/letters.

Boston Symphony Opens 84th Season

September 26, 1964

The 84th season of Boston Symphony concerts began greyly Friday afternoon, with Erich Leinsdorf conducting. The program consisted of the Brahms *Academic Festival* Overture, the Symphony No. 1 by Shostakovich, and Beethoven's *Pastoral* Symphony—all of it played to an audience that gave Mr. Leinsdorf about an 85 percent standing greeting, but which was otherwise cold even by Friday-matinee standards.

Ever since 1925 when Shostakovich wrote his First Symphony, our relations with the Soviet Union have been continuously interesting, with the result that our perceptions and our criticism of art produced in Russia have always been politically colored. It is good now to forget some of the more embarrassing nonsense written about Shostakovich during the war years, but we are faced at every turn with the legend that his was a great talent destroyed, or at least hampered, by political oppression.

A hearing of the First Symphony, written at nineteen, makes it perfectly clear that there is no reason to have expected Shostakovich to become a better composer than the one he in fact became. The First Symphony is a work of considerable talent, with much resourceful imitation of Mahler and Prokofiev among others—and there is even a touch sometimes of original invention.

It shows little feeling for architecture. The first movement is ably, in some ways even interestingly, put together. After that, however, there is a succession of ideas Shostakovich was evidently incompetent to compose: the whimsical but unsuccessful coda of the scherzo, for example, and almost everything about the chaotic finale. That he could have solved the problem better as an older man is doubtful in view of the devastating evidence of the long-winded later symphonies.

As the music is structurally uncontrolled so it is also undisciplined expressively. When it is serious, it is merely gross. Its derivative mockeries cheapen and degrade that of which they seek to make fun, so that the total effect is one of painfully ugly vulgarity.

It was a pleasure afterwards to be able to hear Beethoven's *Pastoral.* It is original in its every sound and silence; above all it is astoundingly modern in the way so much of its discourse is expressed through the subtle manipulation of texture, a process that imparts life to the music even when there is no theme in the conventional sense, and when the harmonies have come to a stand-still.

Neither it nor the Brahms Overture was at all well performed, and for the reasons that often hamper Leinsdorf in the German classics. In the face of the expressive demands of certain kinds of music he becomes extremely inhibited—and he seems to fight off the inhibition with an irresistible desire to interfere with the natural flow of things.

He will ram his way ruthlessly through the first half-dozen pages of the Beethoven, and then suddenly introduce a touch of synthetic articulation by a pointless little hiccup just before the new theme arrives in measure 67. He will start the "Scene by the Brook" at a well-considered tempo and with nicely phrased accompaniment, but then let much of the Symphony's most remarkable movement go for nothing because of the monotonous and uninflected sound that permitted, among other things, the blotting out of the broken chords for flute and later for violas in the development, which then are so beautifully extended and fulfilled when the recapitulation begins.

Nor did the "Storm" have any poetic force. There was not a proper *pianissimo* for those evocative raindrops at the beginning; there was, in fact, not even the technical virtue of precision, because of Mr. Leinsdorf's nervous habit of foreshortening passages that contain only *tremolando* bass notes, passages he evidently thinks of as those in which nothing is happening.

I would put under the heading of technical as well as musical carelessness the many undigested trumpet blasts in which this movement abounded. Granted Beethoven's instrumentation is awkward, but other conductors and other trumpeters have solved the problem.

And what produced all this, produced a performance of the *Academic Festival* Overture that drove so tensely from one event to the next that nothing had time to breathe or to make its point. The "Gaudeamus" was booted into the hall with unbelievable lack of ceremony. Surely there is something here more relevant than the absence of a specific direction to prepare its glorious arrival!

Virtuosity—Beautiful Sounds or Beautiful Music?

October 11, 1964

Virtuosity is admirable. There is a remark by W. H. Auden: "Every high C accurately struck demolishes the theory that we are the irresponsible puppets of fate or chance."

The public hardly needs to be told that virtuosity is admirable. It admires and loves and revels in every accurately struck high C, the fabulous finish on the sound of a great orchestra, the pianist's flying octaves, and the whole bag of string players' pyrotechnics.

That is natural enough. In fact, the one odd thing about it is that the admiration of the public is not confined by any means to "every high C accurately struck." If the soprano is sufficiently famous and her name hypnotic enough, the public will settle for a B-and-a-half. And there will be a storm of bravos also for the pianist whose flying left hand happens down onto the wrong keys, and for the violinist whose octaves are sevenths.

It appears, then, that what the public really cares about is the grand virtuosic gesture rather than its really precise execution, which it is not always equipped to recognize. By the same token, there is a limited recognition of what technique, and its virtuosic command, means.

One can read often enough that Artur Schnabel was not a great technician. It is true that he avoided repertory in which the display of technical mastery is a primary aim. It is also true that on occasion his fingers could go to pieces, famously so in his recording of the first movement of Beethoven's *Hammerklavier* Sonata. Yet there appears to be ample technique for the finale. But what is still more important is that it took real mastery of the piano, as distinct from the musical mastery, to produce the voicing and balance of the chords at the beginning of the slow movement, where the mere hitting of the notes is no problem at all, and that it took an extraordinary control of the fingers, as well as an imaginative and intellectual control of the music, to produce the inimitable Schnabel *cantabile* style.

There are the snobs who affect to despise virtuosity and technical achievement. But they should remember what Erich Leinsdorf once summed up in the statement that "no performance was ever improved by being imprecise." The music is in the notes, and the performer practices in order to be able to play the notes he wants when he wants them and the way he wants them.

Actually, the snob position is the unthinking distortion of a point that is extremely important: technical command is one thing, and the intellectual and expressive grasp of music is another, and it is rare for the two to be found in one person.

The two are not equivalent in any way: there is more to playing a Beethoven sonata than the physical ability to negotiate its notes. Also, if a person is gifted with a beautiful voice, or the powers of coordination to command the fingers, arms, lips, breath, and so on, it does not necessarily follow that he will also be gifted with musical understanding or with taste.

On two successive days last weekend I had the opportunity of witnessing two performances, each at a high pitch of virtuosity, that seem to illustrate the point. One—outside my profession, but not at all outside my interests—the evening of Dickens readings by Emlyn Williams; the other was the concert by Jean Martinon and the Chicago Symphony Orchestra.

I have rarely encountered the virtuosic and the interpretive elements in so elegant a state of equipoise as in the Williams performance. There was a dazzling display of technique, thoroughly enjoyed both by performer and audience, but altogether at the service of the material being performed. The judiciousness with which Williams, as it were, played off Williams and Dickens against one another, the very elegance of the balance between the two sides of the performer's art, itself became an element of virtuosity to be admired.

The Chicago Symphony plays with tremendous power and superb finish. It does so partly because Martinon's predecessors have trained it that way, but it does so also because Martinon's qualifications for his post of musical director include the ability to make the orchestra continue to play beautifully.

But the beautiful sounds of the Chicago orchestra do not constitute a performance of the Brahms Third Symphony. For that it takes the organization of these sounds into a coherent sequence, a sequence for which the score, by direct instruction or by implication, provides the master plan. Martinon chose, however, to proceed according to a plan of his own, and one, moreover, that demonstrated at every point Brahms's superiority to Martinon as a composer.

Martinon is, in fact, a composer, and that led me to await his performances with some eagerness. I was, as it turned out, too naive in assuming that his own involvement in the compositional process might give him special insight into the creations of others.

But I found myself very much interested in the critical performances, and it was evident that the technical razzle-dazzle deluded some reviewers, as well as much of the public into thinking the beautiful orchestral playing they heard was also a valid statement of the music of Schumann and Brahms. Neither for the first nor for the last time.

Barbirolli Conducts Music of England

November 7, 1964

For his second week with the Boston Symphony, Sir John Barbirolli chose a program of music associated with England. First, there was a suite from the dramatic music of Henry Purcell arranged by Barbirolli, then the symphony [No. 92] Haydn conducted at Oxford when he received an honorary doctorate there, and Symphony No. 2 in E-flat by Elgar.

Given Sir John's strengths and limitations, it meant that the concert began badly and ended well. The Purcell suite departs from the good intention of acquainting modern audiences with some vivid music, but the plan is frustrated by the stylistic ignorance and the tastelessness that characterizes both the arrangement and the performance.

Except for the fairly lively playing of the finale, Haydn's *Oxford* Symphony was given a performance that was drab, uninflected, unwitty, if not outright witless. It was the kind of performance that explained Haydn's 19th-century reputation as a composer who had some charm but whose music was essentially rather trivial.

But after the deadly miseries of these excursions into what Sir John turned into dusty history, everything came grandly to life with the Elgar symphony. Completed early in 1911, it is really one of the last of the 19th-century symphonies in the big, affirmative manner. Intended as a tribute to King Edward VII, it was dedicated eventually to his memory, and it is perhaps the most complete embodiment of that side of Elgar's art that is expressive of the spacious comforts and the grand illusions of the Edwardian era.

It is full of themes marked "*nobilmente*" and climaxes marked "*grandioso*." There are hugely sonorous passages for brass, lush multiple divisions of strings. The form is expansive with ample repetitions and elaborate sequences.

Elgar's musical language is a kind of amalgam of Brahms and Wagner, and many of the rhetorical gestures, the harmonies, even the sounds themselves, are reminiscent of those two masters. To draw on both Brahms and Wagner was not so common then, and I was surprised to be reminded occasionally of another and very different piece that acknowledges the same double ancestry, namely Schoenberg's *Gurre-Lieder*.

Though all this is true, Elgar speaks with an individual and unmistakable voice. No one else could have written the opening measures, for example, and he manages to be original even when he is most obviously derivative. The really striking and personal passage in the finale is also one of those closest to their models.

And the scherzo is a surprise altogether. Mercurial in mood, adventurous in its treatment of harmony, of rhythm at least in detail, and of orchestration, it reveals an unsuspected mood in the composer much as the Trio in the Bruckner Ninth does in that work.

In general, the themes are not distinguished, and occasionally some of the crucial dramatic points misfire, for instance the lead-back to the first movement's recapitulation. But when Elgar is not so concerned with the grand rhetoric, he composes some breathtakingly beautiful music. That is what happens in the scherzo, and it happens most beautifully in the first movement's quiet development, with those mysterious sequences in which the bass moves by tritones.

Not least, Elgar composed a successful finale, something that few authors of symphonies in that period managed. This one is nicely poised, free from strain, and it settles with perfect timing into a lovely and tranquil coda.

There are conductors which emphasize a certain Brahmsian inhibition in Elgar's music, who give what might be described as a very English performance. Sir Adrian Boult, who led this piece at a Boston Symphony concert in 1935, is a distinguished example. Barbirolli's approach is different. He plays with emphasis on flexibility of pace, and on the brightness and richness as well as the magnificence of the scoring. He brings out an element of sensuality that is a definite, unrepressed, part of Elgar's music. The price for this is an occasional vulgarity, and clarity may be sacrificed for it. But the approach is effective, it is certainly legitimate, and on these terms Barbirolli's performance was a tremendous and beautiful achievement. Once again, Sir John was warmly greeted by the audience, and there was an almost ostentatious demonstration of enthusiasm from the orchestra.

Boston Symphony Chamber Group Disappointing in Debut

November 9, 1964

A friendly audience filled Sanders Theatre on Sunday evening for the inaugural concert by the Boston Symphony Chamber Players, an organization of twelve of the orchestra's principals. The participants this time were Joseph Silverstein, violin, Burton Fine, viola, Jules Eskin, cello, Georges Moleux, bass, Doriot Anthony Dwyer, flute, Ralph Gomberg, oboe, Gino Cioffi, clarinet, Sherman Walt, bassoon, and James Stagliano, horn. And that leaves the Messrs. Voisin, Gibson, and Firth yet to be unveiled.[17]

It is natural for orchestral musicians to feel the need to make music without a conductor before them, and in the natural course of things they were apt to frequently get together to play chamber music for their own pleasure. The uniqueness of the situation here rests in the fact that the Boston Symphony is the only major orchestra in the country officially to sponsor such an activity for solo players.

The desire to play chamber music and an interest in it do not necessarily guarantee excellent results. While Sunday night's concert showed once again that our Symphony soloists are in many respects highly accomplished players, it was on the whole a bland and disappointing affair.

The choice of program was partly at fault. The music played was Beethoven's Serenade, Op. 25, for flute, violin, and viola; Mozart's Oboe Quartet; and the Beethoven Septet. The composers' names are formidable, but this music is not. The two Beethoven pieces are genial and agreeable to be sure, but they are so slight as to make their presence in the repertory highly unlikely were it not for the composer's name. The Mozart is on a higher level, but still miles below his most beautiful chamber music.

[17] Roger Voisin, trumpet; William Gibson, trombone; and Everett Firth, percussion.

In other words, it was all music that one does not mind hearing—though I am sure that at best the Beethoven pieces are more amusing to the players than to listeners—but one missed having something really substantial on the program.

The players make beautiful sounds together. Throughout the evening there was ample evidence of impressive technical resources, even though neither Mr. Gomberg nor Mr. Stagliano was from this point of view at his excellent best. The players are also skilled enough to have achieved a generally satisfactory ensemble.

It is, however, of the essence in chamber music to expect more than having the participants arrive at the same place simultaneously. That something more was consistently lacking. In places where the utmost calm and poise are necessary, for example, the last two movements of Beethoven's Serenade, nerves began to dominate, and the playing became tense, breathless, rushed.

In both Beethoven pieces the interpretation was one of uneventful neutrality. Rhythmic and phraseological solutions were not wrong, but they were not especially right either. They were not illuminating and they were almost invariably obvious, unsettled, unvaried. The Septet was the more successful in performance: it had some pleasant moments of relaxed and lively playing, and in Mr. Eskin's solo in the scherzo, there was the only really enlivening phrasing heard during the evening.

The Mozart performance was in a different style. Here the three string players provided an unobtrusively neutral background against which Mr. Gomberg projected an extravaganza of tricky and tasteless over-phrasing.

A rich repertory awaits these twelve gifted musicians. I hope they will come into that inheritance, and that at their future concerts they will give pleasures barely hinted at in their debut.

Handel and Haydn Society Gives Annual *Messiah*

December 14, 1964

Late in the summer of 1741, Handel wrote a sacred oratorio called *Messiah*. Since then, some devastating things have happened to it, and one of them certainly was the performance in Symphony Hall on Sunday afternoon. The chorus and orchestra were those of the Handel and Haydn Society; the soloists were Francesca Roberto, soprano, June Genovese, contralto, Joseph Sopher, tenor, and Chester Watson, bass. Dr. Edward Gilday conducted.

What was performed was not strictly speaking Handel's *Messiah*, for the work had undergone changes—each one a disfigurement—at the hands of persons as various as Mozart and Ebenezer Prout, and also of two impersonal evil demons called Ignorance and Tradition. It is of course Dr. Gilday's privilege to consider Prout superior to Handel himself as a composer of Handel's music. The point is perhaps arguable, but even if, for the sake of argument, we accept the Handel-Mozart-Prout-Gilday *Messiah* as a legitimate work of art, it must still be said that Dr. Gilday conducted it quite amazingly badly.

The question of different versions of *Messiah*, legitimate and illegitimate, is so complex that discussion of it is best left until my next Sunday article.[18] This must be largely limited to appraising how this performance realized its own assumptions of what *Messiah* is.

On the whole, the chorus is good, though the tenors become strident around G and the altos are weak in the low register (Handel's boys and male falsettos would have given a more penetrating sound). There is no question of Gilday's skill at getting them to sing with good pitch, reasonable diction, and much enthusiasm.

Among the soloists, Miss Roberto, the soprano, stood out not only for the ample brilliance of her voice, but because she was alone in putting some passion, a certain creative intelligence, and even rhythm, into her recitatives and arias. Mr. Watson, the bass, sings with force, if with no particular musical sophistication. Miss Genovese and Mr. Sopher are competent professionals in the dreariest sense of what that phrase suggests.

A few of the numbers were played in Handel's own scoring, and a couple in Mozart's diverting, though wildly inappropriate, orchestration. Most of the time, the orchestra played the arrangement by Prout (1902), which is imbecilic in conception and brutal in execution. Prout's great mud-puddle is not flattering to an orchestra anyway, but one should, in Boston, be able to hope for something better than the out-of-tune woodwinds and amateurish fiddlers that were so painfully in evidence when they were not drowned out by the chorus that outnumbered them something like four to one.

About the conducting: most of all *Messiah* suffered from impossible tempi. Gilday created far more slow movements than Handel intended, and many numbers were as a result grotesquely misconceived in character: the Sinfonia, "Comfort ye," "But who may abide," the Pifa, "He was despised," "Thou art gone up on high," "I know that my Redeemer liveth," and twice again as many. A few tempi were rushed beyond any possibility for Handel to make sense and beyond the performers' technical abilities: "O thou, that tellest good tidings" (which actually had enough different tempi to please almost any taste) and "His yoke is easy" among them.

[18] Although that "next Sunday article" is not included in this book, a fuller discussion of the different versions may be found in Steinberg's essay on *Messiah*, in his *Choral Masterworks: A Listener's Guide* (New York: Oxford University Press, 2005), 138ff.

For one example considered in detail, take "He was despised and rejected." Its middle section, "He gave His back to the smiters . . . " was about twice as fast as the first part, which would have been about right for the whole aria. This created an absurd disproportion of form by making the middle much too short in relation to the principal part. The one time when Dr. Gilday and I really saw eye to eye about things came when he himself could not face the tedium of going through "He was despised" again at his tempo, and he cut out the repeat Handel wanted.

There was no rhythmic life in the performance. That is partly because Gilday feels no rhythm: if he did, he would not tolerate the misreadings of rhythmic values in, among others, "The Lord gave the word" and "The trumpet shall sound." However, what rhythm he feels, he is incompetent to communicate. The stick wavers, he cannot be counted upon to get anything started together, and hardly ever did a number settle into its eventual tempo until it had been under way for quite a few measures.

A large audience enjoyed the concert, and, indeed, a couple of choruses including "And the glory of the Lord" and "He trusted in God" went in a straightforward way that did make them enjoyable to listen to. But these moments were just a few oases in a long, long afternoon that was primarily a disfigurement of a beautiful composition, and in the second place a demonstration that by temperament, scholarship, musicianship, and technique, Dr. Gilday is not qualified to conduct Handel's *Messiah*.

1965

On Criticism—An Open Letter in Reply to Henry B. Cabot

January 3, 1965

Mr. Henry B. Cabot, President
Boston Symphony Orchestra, Inc.
Symphony Hall
Boston, Massachusetts

Dear Mr. Cabot:

Your letter to the Editor, published in the *Globe* of December 26, calls for reply.

You say that "nobody in the field of musical criticism has a right to assume that he alone knows what is right and what is wrong." I object to your implication that I have assumed that about myself. In both reviews you mention, that of the recent *Messiah* and the one of Leinsdorf's performance of the Beethoven Sixth, I explained my reservations in terms of what I read Handel's and Beethoven's intentions to be.[1] While I attempted thus to justify my opinion, I neither stated nor implied that no other view was possible.

You say "Steinberg seems to assume that what he likes is good and what he doesn't like is awful." When I give a detailed opinion on a performance as I did with the recent *Messiah*, what I say is based on my knowledge both of the music and of whatever seems to me relevant about the music also. It is a considered statement on the music, even as a performance is, the one being articulated in words, the other in musical sounds. I found the *Messiah* performance and the one of the Beethoven Sixth unsatisfactory for reasons stated, and because they were unsatisfactory I did not like them, not the other way around. Let me then reverse your statement: when something seems good to me, I like it; when something seems bad, I do not like it.

You write about the possible "damage Steinberg can do to the musical situation here in Boston." You and I share deep concern for the musical welfare of the city that has been your home for such a long time and mine for only eleven months.

[1] See reviews of September 26 and December 14, 1964.

Last September, we both attended a dinner given for Erich Leinsdorf at Temple Ohabei Shalom in Brookline. You made a speech in which you said something to the effect that since you did not wish to brag by claiming that the Boston Symphony was the best orchestra in the country, you would limit yourself to saying that there was none better.

Now any musician would like to live in a city that has the best orchestra in the country, and I am no exception. But I do not believe we can have the best orchestra in the country simply by saying that we do. In fact, such complacency, such an unexamined taking-for-granted of superiority, is a sure way to let standards slip.

There was a time, under Koussevitzky, when Boston orchestral playing represented, along with that in Philadelphia and New York, the best in America. That is no longer so. Leaving questions of musical interpretation aside altogether and staying strictly with matters of orchestral virtuosity, flexibility, precision, intonation, and tone, I would say that the orchestras in Chicago, Cleveland, and Philadelphia, fairly consistently play better than the Boston Symphony. I very much want Boston to regain the place it once held, but it is not likely to if no one points out what sometimes is wrong and if the only public statements are those which assume that our orchestra is the best around.

You say that my comments on the conductor of the Handel and Haydn Society "will discourage the whole organization." It is the responsibility of the Board of Government of that Society to engage a conductor who will not merely enable his singers to enjoy themselves and get them to sing well, which Dr. Gilday does, but who can also competently perform *Messiah*. The Society must take the consequences of being found out in musical practices of the sort that are documented in my *Messiah* review and in my Sunday article of December 20. My job is to be on Handel's side.

You accuse me of carping, that is, of criticizing unreasonably. Is it unreasonable criticism to point out defects which I can identify and describe? Does it not occur to you that if I point out bad performances and complain about them, it may be that I do so, not out of a perverse desire to damage the musical life of the city where I have chosen to live, but because the performances are actually bad?

You rise to the defense of the Boston Symphony Orchestra, which is an understandable action on the part of its president. You rise to the defense of the Handel and Haydn Society, which, since it is this month giving concerts with the Boston Symphony, is understandable also. Last spring, in a letter to me as well as in a conversation at your office, you objected to what I had written about Charles Munch. Your concern was that such criticism might deprive the Boston Symphony of his services as guest conductor. My concern was that his appearance had been the occasion for misrepresenting the music of Berlioz and others. That appeared to be of little consequence to you, just as now the misrepresentation of Handel is of less consequence to you than my alleged discouraging of the Handel and Haydn Society.

Understandably it is your position to defend the Establishment, which includes defending performers for whose eminence and influence you are, in part, responsible. Naturally you deplore critical activity that is not directly helpful to you in this. But it is not my job to engage in public relations work on behalf of the Boston Symphony or any other organization. I cannot afford a parochial point of view.

It is my belief that the *Boston Globe* has engaged me to use whatever resources I have in taste and education to comment on the musical situation in Boston, without fear, without prejudice, from the broadest point of view and with the highest ideals in mind.

Yours faithfully,
Michael Steinberg
Music Critic

Scissors and Paste Are Bad Composers

January 24, 1965

Some weeks ago, Erich Leinsdorf conducted Dvořák's Symphony in E-flat, No. 3. I hadn't heard it before, but I had read it and I had noted that the finale seemed long and a bit scatterbrained, though no more so than many other movements by Dvořák. Leinsdorf evidently thought so, too; anyway, I was not surprised to be told there would be some cuts.

In reviewing the concert I wrote that the finale would, after all, have been quite agreeable to hear uncut, and that I regretted especially the absence of a certain E major episode in the middle of the movement. This produced a letter from a woman who was cross because I questioned Leinsdorf's decision to make cuts. She wrote: "If the E major episode referred to were of any importance Mr. Leinsdorf would not have left it out." How important, I wondered, did poor Dvořák think it was?

The effect, that is the possible benefit or damage, of cutting varies according to the size of what is omitted, but even more according to the shape of what is left. The recent Boston Opera Group production of Mozart's *Abduction* left out two arias, Blonde's first one, and the one with which Belmonte begins Act II.[2]

[2] Context suggests that Caldwell split the opera into two acts rather than the customary three. Blonde's first aria, "Durch Zärtlichkeit und Schmeicheln," ordinarily begins Act II. Caldwell's "Act II" may have begun with Belmonte's "Wenn der Freude Tränen fliessen," given its placement roughly halfway through *Abduction*.

I thought the omissions a pity. Blonde was left stranded somehow because this way she was around a long time before she had a chance to establish her character vocally, and that is, after all, how operatic characters have to do it. While Belmonte's aria is not one of the stronger numbers in the score, there was a loss in the destruction of a certain formal symmetry with Act I, in which action is also preceded by an aria for Belmonte, and in the elimination of the stylistic formality that frames action within pure music. In extenuation one can point out that these omissions left behind no bleeding gashes.

The cuts that Leinsdorf made in his recent performance of Haydn's *Seasons* did not exactly create the effect of "bleeding chunks" either—Tovey's term for the customary Wagner concert excerpts—but they did suggest hideously stunted growth. From the Storm chorus near the end of "Summer," Leinsdorf eliminated about one-third (something like sixty measures), giving us, among other things, the absurdity of a Storm with most of the storm left out. I would estimate the time saved to be a minute-and-a-half.

The great final Trio with Double Chorus was treated worse than that. Its music at first is in a rather broken style: there is a bass solo, then a bass-tenor duet, then the solo trio has a dialogue in short phrases with alternative halves of the chorus. During all this the C major tonality is colored and darkened by foreign notes, many borrowed from C minor. At last (measure 60, "*Ein ew'ger Frühling herrscht*"), after a majestic upbeat, the music broadens out into a firm, clear C major, and more spacious in its motion than anything so far.

This also turns out to be preparatory, and it leads into a choral fugue (same tempo, but with more quick notes predominating). This fugue mirrors the comparative harmonic complexity of the beginning of this movement. Haydn now reaches a climax of great intensity: musical events succeed one another rapidly, the fugue's polyphony gives way to chordal writing again, and at last the tension of all this is released in another great arrival on C major (measures 116–18, "*Dann singen wir*"). Again in the most spacious manner, and with the harmonic magnificence of the turn toward F major, the music moves with concision to its conclusion in about a dozen measures.

Leinsdorf's way of saving two minutes was to skip from the first C major outburst directly to the second. Thus, he left out nearly half the piece. In omitting the fugue, he not only threw out what is in itself beautiful and effective music, but also eliminated a necessary and marvelous contrast in texture and pace. And when the climax of measure 118 arrived where measure 61 should have been, it arrived, so to speak, unearned.

In place—in the place Haydn assigned it, that is—that climax is as moving as anything I know in music. In the place assigned it by Erich Leinsdorf, who with all respect is not so good a composer as Haydn, the effect was scrappy. It was disconcerting, even ugly, to have a movement come to an end so brusquely after all the preparations for something obviously much broader.

This is the effect also of Leinsdorf's orchestral essays on the Wagner music dramas. In his recent performance of a *Götterdämmerung* potpourri, preparations and preliminaries seemed to lead always to further preparations and preliminaries. The interlude before Act I, scene 3, is wonderful music, but it needs the intently listening Brünnhilde and the arrival of Waltraute to complete its meaning. The kind of continuity that led Leinsdorf instead to the Act II Prelude, which in turn needs the sinister Alberich-Hagen scene to complete its meaning, is the arbitrary patchwork of a cheap pun.

Worse at least because more insidious is the cutting in the first-act interlude of a single measure containing only a soft timpani roll, a similar measure a moment later, and two such measures a little farther on. True, there was nothing of thematic content. The lay listener could be excused for thinking of such a measure as one in which nothing is going on; not, I think, the music director of the Boston Symphony Orchestra.

There is beautiful music in the rhythm of those measures, that is, in the breathing spaces those measures provide between the expressive phrases of the violins and woodwinds. Is Leinsdorf to such a degree insensitive to pace, continuity, the need of music to breathe? Does he think those measures a mistake of Wagner's?—and in this context I am reminded of his arbitrary omission of a measure's silence in the Haydn Symphony No. 96 a couple of years ago. And I cannot believe he was just concerned with shortening the concert by twenty seconds!

Would the public really not have sat through the extra twenty minutes of Haydn's *Seasons*? There are people in the Symphony audience whose inner clocks propel them from the hall at a given hour, no matter what. If the program had said that the concert would last until 4:45 Friday, 11:15 Saturday, would there have been mass outrage?

The Handel and Haydn Society commands a public that sits attentively through *Messiah* for much longer than that. Must the Boston Symphony assume less love for music and less *Sitzfleisch* from its patrons?

Ernst Haefliger's Beautiful Debut

February 14, 1965

The Lieder recital which the Swiss tenor Ernst Haefliger and the pianist Paul Ulanowsky gave in Sanders Theatre on Friday night turned out to be not merely the musical event of the day, but one of the most beautiful concerts likely to come along in many seasons.

The pleasures of Haefliger's singing begin with his being a tenor. There have been, and are, great Lieder singers with high voices, but in recent decades most of the most famous ones have been baritones (Schlusnus and Hüsch of an earlier generation, Fischer-Dieskau, Souzay, Prey more recently).

Most of the great Lieder literature happens to have been written for high voice. This was determined less by esthetic theory than by practical reasons—Schubert's friend Vogl, for example, was a tenor. A large part of the repertory is easily transposed for lower voices, but some of it suffers.

Lighthearted songs become dark, pathos turns into tragedy. And, as Gerald Moore pointed out in one of his books, the piano parts not only become thicker from the downward transposition, they actually become more difficult to play gracefully because of the adjustments in fingering that have to be made.

It was most pleasant to have the relatively rare experience of hearing the group of ten Schubert Lieder sung at the pitch where their composer imagined, and to hear Schumann's *Dichterliebe* cycle—though baritones often sing it in the original key—given a lighter coloration than usual.

Haefliger, who made his Boston debut on this occasion, has a beautiful tenor voice, easily produced even in high registers at light volume, and amply solid for the low notes needed in songs like "Aufenthalt." Still more important is that Haefliger uses it superbly. His voice is not naturally an outstandingly colorful or glamorous instrument, but he achieves miracles of subtle variety with his creative and nice sense of pitch, and with his exact and imaginative coloration of vowels. Though the physical equipment is quite different, in this respect the singing reminded me of what I had heard on records by the young Julius Patzak, and at least one word—the "*verlangen*" that ends the first song of *Dichterliebe*—could have come right out of Patzak's mouth.

It was obvious as well that Haefliger is a singer of special poetic sensibilities and that he is a musician of noble taste. Even at moments of the greatest pathetic intensity, there was a controlling measure that is absent from the work of, say, Fischer-Dieskau.

A singer does not give a Lieder recital in a vacuum, and every sung phrase was enhanced by Ulanowsky's playing. He is a great craftsman, and ensemble and balance were flawless. He phrases melodies a little more smoothly than I like, but he never allows them to become bland. His playing has a great rhythmic impetus, and the musicianship that emerges, for example in the way he negotiates key changes, is impressive and beautifully revealing.

The two men together gave an evening of songs that will, I am sure, be unforgettable to me for its aristocratic musicianship and for the intensity of its emotional communication. And when they had finished Schumann's "Mondnacht"—an encore—I realized with some sense of shock that it might be very many years before I would be lucky enough to hear such singing and playing again.

Nono's *Intolleranza* Debuts Despite Delays

February 22, 1965

Luigi Nono's opera, *Intolleranza 1960,* was given its first American production by the Boston Opera on Sunday afternoon.[3]

It seems incredible. Most of the opera public still regards *Wozzeck* as an alarming novelty. We are accustomed to the most enormous time lags before we have a chance to see operas in the contemporary idiom of *Intolleranza 1960,* yet here it was, just three-and-a-half years after its stormy Venetian premiere.

Things had been anything but easy until the curtain rose. The composer's arrival had been delayed for a crucial two weeks by visa difficulties. Badly needed rehearsal time was lost. Then the tenor originally scheduled to sing the principal role of The Refugee became ill and had to be replaced at the last moment by Lawrence White, an American tenor who had sung the part in Germany. These factors together brought about the postponement of the premiere from Friday evening to Sunday afternoon.

A single picket, representing Polish Freedom Fighters, Inc., bearing a sign labeling the composer as a "Red Fascist"—this surely strikes a new level in political sophistication!—marched under the theater marquee. Inside, the audience watched and listened attentively (one imbecile chose to let out a shrill whistle just before the final scene), and afterwards applause grew slowly, but grew in warmth and went on at length. When Nono appeared on stage with Sarah Caldwell and the conductor, Bruno Maderna, there were a few boos, and much cheering.

Intolleranza 1960 made an impact. It is an effective theater piece. Its loosely constructed scenario follows the fortunes of a political refugee who decides to return to his own country. After an experience in a concentration camp he meets his death in a flood, realizing that this time he may not run and again become a refugee. Slides are used to portray scenes of intolerance and war, the evils against which the composer cries out. The music often has the function of a soundtrack.

[3] The cast of this production, not all of whom are clearly identified in Steinberg's review, included tenor Lawrence White (The Refugee), mezzo-soprano Margaret Roggero (The Woman), baritone Ercole Bertolini (The Algerian), bass Guus Hoekman (The Tortured Man), and soprano Beverly Sills (The Refugee's Companion).

It is a means of intensifying the visual impact of the Hiroshima desolation or of Southern lynchings.

With his intense cluster of dissonance, shot-like explosions of sound, *crescendos* for massed percussion, Nono manages this superbly. He is a composer with extraordinary imaginative powers. The orchestra is brilliantly used, not only for its powers of theatric emphasis, but as sheer musical accentuation, in the way, for example, that a closely spaced violin chord will seem to catch the echo of high soprano notes. The chorus, whose music is pre-taped, and whose text is made from quotations (Ripellino, Fučik, Brecht, etc.) is very important, and Nono has written for it some of his most expressive music.

And one of the very best musical inventions of all is one whose impact must have been largely lost on the audience. It is a scene entitled "The Absurdities of Everyday Life," used to open Act II, and it consists of an ingenious sound montage of madly jabbered bureaucratic jargon, assembled with bitterness and wit. And every bit of it is in Italian!

Which brings up the language problem. The choruses were in Italian, with some of their texts projected on a screen now helpfully, more often distractingly. There were also some untranslated spoken pronouncements in Italian (quotations from Alleg and Sartre). The five principals sang in English, but even knowing the libretto and score at least somewhat, I understood nearly nothing. The English words almost completely resisted the alien rhythms and contours into which they were forced. Nono's vocal writing has peculiarities that hardly helped. He writes B and C for tenor and soprano as nonchalantly as Verdi wrote G and A, and at those altitudes most vowels become hopelessly distorted.

Much of the score is monotonous, partly because so much of it consists of slow music. However effective the music could be when the eye had something to look at, it was not strong enough to hold the attention during the scenes when the singers with their unintelligible texts were on their own, for example, the scene in which The Refugee and The Algerian make their escape from the concentration camp, and the long monologue for The Refugee's Companion at the beginning of Act II.

Intolleranza 1960 is an opera carried more by its subject matter and its dramaturgic techniques than by its musical power. That is, the existing resources of music are used effectively for background, but the music itself is, I think, inventive and meaningful only in the choruses and in the sound-juggling of the "absurdities." Star of the performance was the completely masterful Bruno Maderna, who has also conducted all the European productions of the work. The excellent orchestra played for him with power and finesse. The lately enlisted Lawrence White managed credibly. But for diction, Miss Sills and Miss Roggero would have been completely effective. Bertolini has good stage presence, he is accurate and secure, but his vibrato obscures pitch, and there seemed to be no words at all. The finest performance was the brief one by Guus Hoekman as a dying tortured prisoner. Words were clear, there was a sense of musical line, and he was the one singer with the personal force to fill the stage with meaning even without uttering a sound.

Sarah Caldwell, in staging *Intolleranza 1960*, was more the executrix of the composer's ideas than, as is more usual for her, the inventor of a concept of her own. No plot summary was provided, but evidently the audience found the work forceful as an entity, even if doubtless confusing in detail. But even with its imperfections, what the Boston Opera offered was a real performance. And the most important thing of all is that an American audience had the opportunity to see a significant modern opera.

An Exciting Concert—*Groups*, *Circle*, and Beethoven

March 5, 1965

Thursday night's orchestra concert at the New England Conservatory was exciting. It began in Brown Hall with the first American performance of Karlheinz Stockhausen's *Groups* for Three Orchestras, William Stein, Fredrik Prausnitz, and Diamantis Diamantopoulos conducting. Then, in Jordan Hall, came the Beethoven Eighth, Prausnitz conducting. It was followed by another American premiere, Ernst Krenek's *Circle, Chain, and Mirror*, which the composer led. The evening ended where it had begun, in Brown Hall, with a second playing of the Stockhausen.

Groups uses three orchestras, each of thirty-some players, deployed about three sides of a room. The makeup of each orchestra is basically normal, though brass, and especially percussion, are reinforced.

In the Scherzo of Mahler's Fifth Symphony, there is a wonderful moment of orchestral drama when all the horns, one after another, blast out the same note, so that it travels across the stage from right to left. That is the kind of stereophony Stockhausen has in mind. His multiple orchestras have nothing in common with the ping-pong antiphonies of the old Venetians like Gabrieli. Much orchestral writing since Mahler has made the orchestra shimmer and spring to life in unexpected quarters. Space has become part of music, and you can find this technique of traveling sounds used beautifully even in scores as unshowy as the symphonies of Roger Sessions.

What Stockhausen has done is to exploit this idea to a previously unprecedented extent. He has also made it a fundamental structural principle in *Groups*.

He has an imaginative ear for sound and an impressive sense of large form, and with these gifts, combined with his sense of theater, he has made *Groups* an exciting and often a beautiful piece to listen to.

The details are sometimes puzzling, if not out and out inconsistent. That is particularly true of the elements that have most to do with pure, and clearly audible pitch, and least with color. *Groups* is a long work, but on both hearings it seemed to fill its twenty-five-minute span grandly. Above all, though, the treatment of sound in space, its brass *crescendos* (as a matter of fact very like the Mahler piece mentioned above), and its spectacular percussion climax, make *Groups* a really interesting piece.

To go from Stockhausen to Krenek was like a return to the classics, and it was a real pleasure, after the expansive and even undisciplined dramatic gestures of *Groups*, to hear so controlled a music as Krenek writes. The serial manipulations of *Circle, Chain, and Mirror* move according to an intricate and fascinating design, and one that in effect predetermines the pitch successions. The other aspects of the music such as rhythm, timbre, dynamics, are freely invented.

Krenek has in recent years been much interested in music that shows such a combination of restraints and freedom, music where much is predetermined and where, as he has written, "the surprises are built in." The tone-row in its various manifestations is here so clear that *Circle, Chain, and Mirror* might almost have been written as an ear-training exercise in serial hearing. In fact, it seemed so clear, so over-explicit, that before long that aspect of the composition became predictable and a little dull. The rest, however, the sense of overall movement and particularly the fastidious scoring for the small orchestra, is finely and freshly inventive. The composer produced a sharply defined and beautifully transparent performance, and he was recalled many times and much applauded and cheered.

The Beethoven Eighth made excellent company for Krenek and Stockhausen. With its propensity toward epigram, ellipsis, compression, rhythmic displacement, it is after all a perpetually astounding modern piece. For that matter it even goes in for all sorts of quasi-stereophonic pileups (the first movement fermata and all over the Menuet).

There was some rhythmic shakiness through the first movement, but in its larger dimensions the performance was superbly thought out and most of the playing was really impressive. Beethoven had benefited from the kind of drilling Stockhausen and Krenek had required. Warm applause here also, and long rounds of applause for the orchestra and all three conductors after the Stockhausen, and well deserved it was, too.

Not Such Very New Music—Schoenberg's Violin Concerto and Joseph Silverstein

March 21, 1965

Arnold Schoenberg wrote his Violin Concerto in 1936 and dedicated it to Webern. Louis Krasner was the first violinist to play it: that was with the Philadelphia Orchestra, Stokowski conducting, on December 6, 1940. Now Joseph Silverstein will introduce it to Boston at performances this Friday and Saturday, March 26 and 27.[4]

Every student of contemporary music knows Schoenberg's Concerto, but very few violinists do, and, in spite of three recordings, few listeners. To Silverstein's and my combined knowledge, only six violinists have, or have had, it in their repertory. There is Krasner, who introduced it and was the first to record it, and the German Wolfgang Marschner and the American Israel Baker who have made more recent records. The others are Tibor Varga, Zvi Zeitlin (of whose performance Bruno Maderna spoke with enthusiasm), and now Silverstein.

Plans for this performance began with Erich Leinsdorf's suggestion some years ago that Silverstein play the Alban Berg Concerto with the Symphony. Silverstein made the counter-suggestion of the Schoenberg. "The Berg is not my cup of tea. It's not my world. I'm not a Mahler man." Schoenberg's Concerto, however, he regards as "one of the great classical works, spare and precise." Incidentally, Silverstein took great satisfaction in the subsequent Berg performance by George Zazofsky: "He has the feeling for it, and he played it much better than I ever could."

Friday's performance of the Schoenberg will have been carefully prepared. This refers not only to the ten hours of rehearsal with orchestra that are planned for this week, but to Silverstein's own long study of the music. He began learning the music two-and-a-half years ago, and he estimates there will have been perhaps a thousand hours of practice time. "But," he adds, "don't forget all the time I worked on the piece before I was ready to begin practicing." Wanting to feel that he knew about every note just what it was doing there, he made a thorough analysis of the music.

Later, both for violinistic and musical reasons, insofar as the two can be separated at all here, Silverstein had what he described as "several very rewarding sessions" with Krasner. While preparing the premiere, Krasner had gone over the piece with Schoenberg, and was therefore peculiarly fitted to help Silverstein read between the lines of the score. And besides Krasner's specific affinity to Schoenberg's Concerto, there was his general expertness with modern

[4] See next article.

music (the concertos by Berg and Sessions are among the works Krasner was the first to play).

While it is still difficult enough, Schoenberg's Concerto is not as terrifying as it must have seemed in 1940. Still, it is necessary, Silverstein points out, to develop one's pedagogy in order to master it. He began by writing out the twelve-note sequence on which the Concerto is based in its ordinary form, in retrograde, in inversion, in a combination of the last two, and each of these at every possible level of transposition. That makes forty-eight ways in all, "and these became my daily scales."

Silverstein plans to write a book of exercises based on Schoenberg's Concerto, on the fugue in Bartók's Sonata for Violin Solo, and on the violin part in the Berg Chamber Concerto. He is much concerned with the absence of such music from the standard violin teaching curriculum:

> Instead of teaching two Vieuxtemps concertos, we ought to be able to get to the point where we teach one Vieuxtemps and the Berg. There is some improvement now in violinists' standards of musicianship as more pupils by the enlightened teachers like Krasner, Joseph Knitzer, and Josef Gingold, get into circulation.
>
> The sphere of reference for this music is somehow very young for me still. I can't remember a time when I didn't know the Beethoven Concerto, but even now the Schoenberg is another language, though it isn't such very new music. . . . The situation places an unfair burden on the music. If I play the Beethoven unconvincingly people will know it's me and not Beethoven. Here, if there's a sense of struggle in the performance, they'll blame Schoenberg.

Silverstein thinks that even what are now the standard concertos bear traces of the idiosyncrasies of their first interpreters, that the Mendelssohn and the Brahms, for example, contain, as it were, bits of David and Joachim that are not organically related to the design.

Silverstein takes great delight in Schoenberg's Concerto, and he pointed out many examples of beautiful melodic phrases, witty structural touches, and the magic sound. "It's a normal orchestral complement, but it's used as though in chamber music, just one string section against a single woodwind, violin double stops with two bassoons, things like that."

For sheer sound, Silverstein's favorite place is one near the beginning of the finale when snare drum and military drum beat a tattoo with low strings beaten with the bows' wooden backs. "This started out for me as an intellectual and a physical challenge, but as I have lived with the music it has come to mean very much more than that to me. It is very communicative and beautiful music for me, and I play it with a strong sense of personal and emotional commitment."

Finally, for those who might have pleasure getting into their ears the musical source from which, in a sense, both Schoenberg and Silverstein began their tasks, here is the twelve-note series on which the Violin Concerto is based: A–B-flat–E-flat–B–E–F-sharp–C–C-sharp–G–A-flat–D–F.[5]

Schoenberg Concerto and Joseph Silverstein

March 27, 1965

Almost 29 years old, and more than twenty-four years after its first performance, Arnold Schoenberg's Violin Concerto has at last come to Boston. Joseph Silverstein played it at Friday's Symphony concert, which, conducted by Erich Leinsdorf, also included Weber's *Oberon* Overture and some Richard Strauss operatic excerpts sung by Leontyne Price.

Schoenberg's is a remarkably beautiful violin concerto, perhaps the most beautiful since the Brahms. The pre-compositional material from which the themes, figurations, and harmonies are drawn, yield for Schoenberg a richly varied music. The melodies are full of expressive semitones, sometimes inverted into sevenths or stretched into ninths; the intense sevenths are often heard in the harmony as well, but so are warm thirds. And all of this is already prefigured in the opening two measures.

The orchestration is miraculous. Schoenberg avoids doubling notes in different octaves: in other words, if middle C occurs in a chord, there will be no lower or higher C present in the same chord. It has the effect of giving to each single sound and to every simultaneous stack of sounds an extraordinary clarity and sharpness of profile.

The problem that arises when there are no octave doublings is how to keep the orchestra busy, because in conventional orchestration most of the instruments are engaged in precisely such doublings. Some composers escaped into a chamber-orchestral style. Schoenberg, however, by a most stupendous feat of imagination and of dazzling technique, forged a completely original style that is unmistakably full-orchestral.

It is, moreover, completely successful, even when measured against the exacting standards of Schoenberg's own earlier masterful orchestra scores like the Variations and the opera *Moses and Aron*. Fascinating as it is, Schoenberg's way with instruments is not a self-sufficient virtuosic activity. It is completely organic, inseparable from the rest of the act of composition. This integrity is in evidence even when the instrumentation is minimal, that is, in the cadenzas

[5] The notation in the printed score is A–B-flat–*D-sharp*–B–E–F-sharp–C–*D-flat*–G–A-flat–D–F.

for unaccompanied violin, when the different "orchestrations" (harmonics, pizzicatos, *tremolandos*, etc.) are brilliantly and wittily used to clarify the material and to separate the different and simultaneous layers of activity.

Silverstein must be one of the very few violinists who can play this music with a sense of ease. His imposing mastery of the violin was especially useful in the complex technical and analytical task of separating the strands of polyphony implied in Schoenberg's difficult multiple stops. Silverstein's idea of the piece is clear, soundly based, and he played the work very well.

Still more to the point is that he will come to play it even better. It is too rare and too hard a piece to be let go in the three performances it is getting now. It should become a fairly frequent repertory item for Silverstein and Leinsdorf, and early next season would not be too soon for its next performance.

The orchestral task is extremely difficult also. Again it is partly a matter of non-doublings, which means that the conducting was not always ideal, but it was never less than adequate, and many passages were extremely well achieved. That, too, will become better as Leinsdorf and the players come to feel more at home in the piece.

The Schoenberg Concerto was, however, unhappily programmed. Partly it was the consequence of Leontyne Price's illness that had prevented her appearance earlier in the season. Still, it did not seem unavoidable to follow the Schoenberg immediately with an excerpt from Strauss's *Ägyptische Helena*. That could nicely have gone into the second half of the program, but what actually happened was regrettably consistent with some bad ideas of Leinsdorf's earlier in the year, such as following the *Gurre-Lieder* excerpt with Respighi and Menotti, and Berg's *Le Vin* with Kodály.

Oddly, the *Helena* excerpt was called "The Awakening of Helen." That is the name of the first-act finale, but what was actually performed was the opening of Act II, "Zweite Brautnacht!," in which Helen is wide awake from the start (though the composer seems not to have been). By any name, it is stale rubbish.

Not so the *Salome* finale, which is composed with great verve and invention. It was preceded, with not especially good effect, by the interlude that follows Jochanaan's exit, and Salome's Dance was also played. Leontyne Price was in most magnificent voice and sang splendidly.

First Performance—Ives Symphony No. 4 Played at Carnegie

April 27, 1965

NEW YORK—The Symphony No. 4 by Charles Ives received its first performance at a Carnegie Hall concert Monday night. Leopold Stokowski conducted the American Symphony Orchestra, with David Katz and José Serebrier as assistant conductors, and with members of the Schola Cantorum of New York, Hugh Ross, director.

The historical facts contribute to making this a remarkable event. Ives died eleven years ago at the age of 80, he had not composed since 1928, and the Fourth Symphony was finished in 1916. Actually, in various ways, some of the music had been heard before. Eugene Goossens conducted the first two movements, though in simplified versions, in 1927, the first public performance, by the way, of any orchestral piece by Ives. The third movement is an arrangement of the first movement of the "Revival Meeting" [First] string quartet, and it had been heard not only in its original form, but also in an orchestral setting by Bernard Herrmann, the first radio performance of anything by Ives.

To get the finale into performable order was a labor of about a decade, undertaken first by the musicologist Joseph Braunstein; later by Theodore Seder of the Fleisher Library in Philadelphia with his assistant Romulus Franceschini; by Kurt Stone, then editor-in-chief of Associated Music Publishers, and his assistant, Ronald Herder; by Oliver Daniel of the American Composers Alliance; and above all by the composer Henry Cowell, Ives's biographer and literary executor.

The Fourth Symphony has extramusical meaning. Ives himself wrote: "The esthetic program of the work is that of the searching questions of *What?* and *Why?* which the spirit of man asks of life. This is particularly the sense of the prelude. The three succeeding movements are the diverse answers in which existence replies."

The prelude is built about a vocal setting of the hymn, "Watchman, Tell Us of the Night," the favorite of Ives used in the First Violin Sonata also. But, as happens often in Ives, the movement as a whole lessens trust in hymnology, and contains quotations from many other hymns also, prominently, "Nearer, My God, to Thee." The scherzo is derived from the "Hawthorne" of the *Concord* Sonata. The third movement is a solemn and simply diatonic double fugue on two more hymns, "From Greenland's Icy Mountains" and "All Hail the Power of Jesus' Name." The slow finale is almost entirely based on "Nearer My God," "Jesus, Lover of My Soul" also being used prominently.

For anyone familiar with the *Concord* Sonata, the Violin Sonata, and *Three Places in New England*, there is nothing new in kind in the Fourth Symphony. It is, however, an uncommonly impressive example of what those pieces represent. Besides the regular orchestra, which is large, and chorus, there is a small distant ensemble of five violins, viola, and harp; in the finale, the percussion section is also made into an independent body.

The music is altogether an extraordinary extension of the idea of polyphony. Ives deals not merely with the simultaneity of melodies, nor even of textures. He's concerned with bringing together greatly diverse rhythms, and beyond that, he seems even to make polyphonies of entire pieces. His notions of what can go with what, either as juxtaposition or as simultaneity, call into question every previous idea of composition.

The result is not always successful. The music sometimes seems madly overwritten, and the ear longs for something transparent and consistent. But there is here no touch of Dada, nothing merely silly. Even as it exasperates it fascinates, and it often goes beyond that to move powerfully. The complex texture is itself strongly expressive, and especially the textures generated by the vast rhythmic multiplicity create an exciting hurricane of fresh air.

But No Green Paint—Fiedler Given Great Ovation as Pops Returns to Symphony

April 28, 1965

In weather more appropriate to the *Christmas Oratorio*, spring officially came to Boston's musical world: the Pops opened in Symphony Hall Tuesday night. This is the 80th season of the concerts, and it is thirty-five years since Arthur Fiedler began to conduct them.

The program contained some anniversary tokens. It began with the *Tannhäuser* March,[6] played at the first "Promenade" concert in 1885, and it continued with Nicolai's *Merry Wives of Windsor* Overture, which was on the first Pops program in which Fiedler participated as a violinist in 1916. Later came Ravel's *Boléro*, which Fiedler introduced into the Pops repertory at his first concert as permanent conductor in 1930.

Just after *Boléro*, Francis W. Hatch appeared on stage, and introduced himself as "an anticlimactic trustee," and with grace and humor on behalf of all musical Boston congratulated Fiedler on his half-century's professional activity here. He also introduced Mrs. Fiedler, who was applauded for being so nice about "allowing Arthur so many nights out." The affection in which Fiedler is held

[6] This was the "Entrance of the Guests" (minus the vocal parts) from Act II of *Tannhäuser*, which remained a staple of the Boston Pops repertoire well into the 20th century.

by his public is as warm as ever. The audience let out a great yell when he first appeared on stage, and many stood to greet him. Later, at the time of Hatch's citation, Fiedler was given a prolonged standing ovation. At one point there was a serious note, unusual for Pops. The death last week of the impresario Aaron Richmond was commemorated by the playing of the Bach-Wilhelmj Air for the G String.

Symphony Hall looks a little different this year. It is not wearing the customary coat of Pops green. Some member of the Hall's maintenance staff evidently attacked the wall with some sort of weapon and drew forth a kind of geologic sample that revealed paint strata of about an inch-and-a-half's thickness from the annual green paintings and maroon re-paintings. And it was decreed that the 1900 plaster could not be expected to withstand the strain of further superimpositions.

Everything looks cheerful just the same. There is the customary large spray of flowers in front of the podium, and green plants on the sides. The back of the floor is brightly lit, and there are large quantities of handsome white flowers there.

Other than the pieces already mentioned, the program included the Vaughan Williams *Greensleeves* Fantasy, its flute solo radiantly played by James Pappoutsakis; the *Emperor Waltzes*; and the first of Elgar's *Pomp and Circumstance* marches.

Soloist at this year's opening was Susan Starr, who played Mendelssohn's G minor Piano Concerto, a piece, incidentally, whose first recording was made by the Pops and Fiedler, with [Jésus María] Sanromá as soloist. Miss Starr is 20 years old, small except for a heap of dark brown hair, and quite pretty.

Her approach to the piano is rather aggressive. In loud passages she made jangly sounds, but in some of the quieter moments in the second and third movements she suggested at least some of the grace and elegance the Concerto demands.

In the last portion of the evening, Fiedler conducted selections from *Fiddler on the Roof*, "Chim-Chim-Cheree" from *Mary Poppins*, and also a "TV Triptych" that included the theme from *The Man from U.N.C.L.E.*, the "Tab" commercial [listed in the printed program as "Big Beat Baroque (Tab)"], and the theme from *The Munsters*. I don't know what Tab is, but its energetic and attractive music suggested one of these kinetic commercials all about dirty shirt collars. Anyway, it all suggested that television employs more amusing and inventive composers than Broadway and Hollywood. And, best of all, there was THE Beatle[s] song.[7]

[7] According to the cue-sheet in the BSO Archives this was "I wanna hold your hand," in 1964 the first Beatles song to reach the top of the *Billboard* charts. It was played as an encore, so not printed in the program.

Composer-Conductor—Music Not Philanthropy for Pierre Boulez

May 2, 1965

NEW LONDON, CT—Pierre Boulez is perhaps the most interesting of the post-war European composers, and in that capacity at least his name is well-known here, if not much of his work. And now part of the American public is having a chance to find out something about the 40-year-old composer's reputation, growing almost to be legendary, as a conductor.

During the season now ending, Boulez conducted a chamber ensemble in Los Angeles at the opening of the Museum Auditorium and he was a guest conductor for a week each with the Cleveland Orchestra and the Pittsburgh Symphony. Last Tuesday he arrived in this country again to conduct the BBC Symphony Orchestra in five concerts of its current American tour.

Boulez spent a morning rehearsing at Palmer Auditorium of the Connecticut College for Women. The music was Debussy's *Images*, Webern's Six Pieces, Stravinsky's Symphonies of Winds, and Beethoven's *Emperor* Concerto (the only piece in the entire tour repertory written before 1900, and being given just this one performance).

Boulez and the orchestra seemed pleased to see each other. At the rehearsal for their Boston concert, several players had said, "But you must come to one of our concerts with Boulez," and now there were smiles and applause when he stepped onto the podium. Boulez looked around, and at once said, "These curtains must go. I can already tell that from the sound of my voice." Then he called for Debussy's *Rondes de printemps*, saying to the orchestra, "I just want to see how you are." Later he commented: "I like this orchestra very much. They are very quick and intelligent, they work hard, and we get on very well."

Boulez spoke warmly of the Cleveland Orchestra: "Such discipline! We made very good concerts. I think it is the best orchestra I have had."

He got his start as a conductor under very different conditions, namely as house conductor for the theatrical troupe of Jean-Louis Barrault and Madeleine Renaud, and so it was that he made his New York debut leading a pit orchestra in the late '50s. He began being active as a concert conductor in 1957, and that activity became very intense about 1959.

Now Boulez is enormously in demand as a conductor. Remembering that he is first a composer, he allots only a few months each year to concerts, and on that basis he is solidly booked for at least the next three seasons. He makes extraordinary demands for rehearsal time, something that has also become a means for politely refusing engagements. He now finds, though, that orchestras are more and more willing to admit his conditions. "I could make more money and conduct more programs, but there is not time to study the scores as they ought to be studied and to rehearse them as they ought to be rehearsed. It is important for me now that I will make my first New York concerts with programs that have been really prepared."

Boulez considers most conductors to be "the laziest beasts on earth." He refers not only to the willingness of most of them to conduct programs that he would not consider "really prepared," but also to their negligence in introducing their audiences to important but not obviously popular repertory.

Zukofsky and Kalish Play Ives Sonatas

May 25, 1965

Sunday afternoon's Gardner Museum concert consisted of the Second, Third, and Fourth sonatas for violin and piano by Charles Ives, given magnificent performances by the violinist Paul Zukofsky and the pianist Gilbert Kalish.

The numbering of the sonatas indicates their order of completion, but actually all four of them were written more or less simultaneously during the period of 1902–16. The connection between them goes beyond contemporaneity to a great stylistic closeness. To a certain extent they share thematic material, particularly the hymn tunes that appear, as it were, between quotation marks, and this in turn relates the sonatas to still other pieces by Ives.

To some degree, then, the sonatas illuminate and complement each other, and to give three of them together was a good idea. Four would have been better still, but the format of the Gardner concerts does not permit such a long program.

The inventiveness of this music with its extraordinary juxtapositions, simultaneities, abruptions, and disruptions, is impressive. But while Ives was almost always inventive and original, he was often less successful at ordering, that is composing his material. The violin sonatas are gratifying to listen to as well as stimulating because to what was for Ives an unusual degree, they are really composed.

The Second and Third sonatas are large pieces, the more familiar Fourth, *Children's Day at the Camp Meeting*, is by comparison a miniature and perhaps not quite so interesting. And if the Second is the most impressive as a whole, the finest single movement is the long, slow one that opens the Third, an enormous kind of chorale-fantasy on the hymn, "Beulah Land."

A characteristically Ivesian thing happens in the middle movement of the Second Sonata, a barn dance. Here the pianist's page turner seems suddenly to go berserk and begins thundering out wild rhythmic patterns in thick note-clusters at the bottom of the keyboard. This part was played most forcefully by Elinor Preble.

The intelligent, thinking performer in America today is in the youngest generation represented at his most impressive by Paul Zukofsky. In the most familiar and traditional sense of what virtuosity means, he has no superior among living string players. In intelligence, intellectual penetration, and musicianship, Zukofsky, who is barely into his 20s, goes far in his accomplishments beyond those of most of the big-name players.

Kalish is an intelligent musician and a highly competent pianist, but his playing is not the marvelously forceful and beautiful thing Zukofsky's is. It is, however, well attuned to his and the two make an impressive ensemble.

This might be the occasion also for reviewing the two records (Folkways 3346-7) on which Zukofsky and Kalish play all four of the Ives sonatas. It is necessary to say only that the music is interesting and often startlingly beautiful, that the performances are first-rate, and that the records, which come with a helpful introductory essay by Samuel Charters, are very highly recommended.

The Beatles, the Pulitzer, and Other Related Topics

June 20, 1965

In England they do things right. It was a pleasure to find the Beatles on the queen's recent Birthday Honours list. The four Liverpudlians earned their MBE as much for the grace and stylishness of their conduct as for their lively and diverting music.

Over here things have not looked so good in the world of honors and prizes. The latest cause for dismay among musicians was the choice of Ned Rorem and Robert Whitney to represent American music at the recent culture marathon in the White House.

No one was astonished that conservative music was chosen, though to have been surprised in one's certainty that it would be so would have been most agreeable. Still, even with conservatism evidently a prime *desideratum*, was it necessary to assume that blandness had to be part of the package as well? Was it necessary to descend to quite so dismal a level of non-distinction?

Earlier we had the row over the Pulitzer prizes in which, last month, the music award was omitted for the second successive year on the grounds that there was nothing good enough.

The absurdity of that contention, both in an absolute sense and in view of past awards, has probably been sufficiently discussed. After all, even the *New York Times* was shocked![8]

Usually the membership of the Pulitzer juries is kept secret, and the most interesting by-product of last month's ruckus was that the names of the jury members were published. Two belonged to nonentities,[9] the third to Winthrop Sargeant of the *New Yorker*, who is far worse than a nonentity.

Sargeant's taste is not impressive and neither is his intellectual probity. He hates—and from the evidences of his writing he cannot properly hear—contemporary music. He goes mainly to the opera and to the concerts by the big orchestras, which itself is an effective way of staying out of touch with most of the significant new things.

There are persons of competence whose interest leads them to awareness of what is going on in the world of new music. What did the Pulitzer committee that picked the jury think it was doing? The lack of sympathy for their task displayed by the jury members was deplorable, but it is their ignorance, and the irresponsibility of the Pulitzer people in loosing this ignorance onto the public, that is inexcusable.

Last Monday it was announced that the Music Critics Circle of New York would give no award for the past season. The special citation to the Ives Fourth Symphony, given its premiere in April,[10] was at least face-saving.

The list of works eligible for the prize had 269 items on it, and according to the report in the *Times*, "not enough of the Circle's 27 members had heard any single work on the list to allow for a set of awards that would be fair to both composer and public and that would equitably represent the Circle's majority opinion."

The honesty of the decision is commendable however regrettable the non-award may be in its way of misrepresenting the quality of musical life in New York during the past year. Both this and the Pulitzer story suggest that current methods of prize-giving are hopelessly inadequate.

The news about the Critics Circle appeared on the same day as the report of William Schuman's commencement speech at Brandeis.[11] Schuman spoke about the Pulitzer scandal and quite properly he raised the question of how the jury can "discharge its obligations under the present haphazard system by which new works are brought to the attention of the jury."

[8] "Reviewing the Pulitzers" [editorial], *New York Times*, May 9, 1965.

[9] The so-called "nonentities" were Ronald Eyer, music critic of *Newsday*, and Thomas Scherman, music critic of the *St. Louis Post-Dispatch*.

[10] See review of April 27, 1965.

[11] "Schuman Scores Pulitzer Awards," *New York Times*, June 14, 1965. At the time Schuman was president of Lincoln Center.

When Schuman said that "no other award for music is so highly regarded in this country as the Pulitzer," he was right in the sense that there is no other prize for composition that most of the public has ever heard of. At the same time, Pulitzer prestige is variable. It is generally considered that the journalistic awards represent genuinely distinguished and valuable achievement, but more and more people are coming to be aware that this is not so for the awards in fiction, poetry, drama, and music.

There are exceptions to this, of course: the poetry award to John Berryman was one. The music award to Elliott Carter for his Second String Quartet in 1960 was another. I still recall my own shock at reading about that one in the paper. At the first opportunity I stopped to phone the news to a friend. My friend's reply came swiftly: "He isn't going to accept, is he?"

With the names of Stravinsky, Sessions, and Varèse, among others, still absent from the Pulitzer list, it may be that the Pulitzer will attain status as the prize not to win. Ives was recently quoted as having dismissed prizes as badges of mediocrity, and it may be that he was right.

All this brings to mind that in Boston we just had a news release that suggests still another possible area of honor-by-omission, and that is the list of next year's guest conductors for the Boston Symphony.

Frager Plays Mozart as Festival Opens

July 3, 1965

LENOX—The twenty-eighth Berkshire Festival at Tanglewood opened Friday night with a Mozart program played by the Boston Symphony, conducted by Erich Leinsdorf and with Malcolm Frager as piano soloist. Frager played the very unjustly neglected C major Concerto, K.415, an uncommonly spacious, inventive, and in every way extraordinarily beautiful work. "Extraordinarily beautiful" is also the appropriate phrase with which to characterize Frager's remarkable playing.

His playing is marvelously Mozartean, alive, that is, to the ever-amazing amalgam of wit, pathos, and ear, that makes Mozart's music what it is. Everything that happens is a surprise, a surprise produced by an unexpected darkening of the harmony, a rhythmic elision, the entrance of a new instrument in the orchestra, a change of hand position in the piano, or something of that sort. And Frager, with the clear articulation of his playing, its forward-pressing variety, the care with which he matches and modulates his tone according to what is happening, shows his awareness of all these miracles. His performance of the Concerto was a great one, because it made it possible for the audience to be aware of them as well, as in spirit he virtually taught the work to us.

The most treasurable aspect of Frager's playing is the vocal quality behind his passionate, yet unfailingly elegant, phrasing or lyric melody. Another is the imaginative and therefore always functional handling of the cadenza and fantasia-like sides of the music. But this was merely the most obvious externalization of Frager's feeling for the sense of adventure and exploration in Mozart's music.

There were in Frager's playing a few less fortunate moments, some unhappy experiments in phrasing and some rushed rhythms, but these blemishes were quite insignificant in the context of his impressively mature and musical conception and the virtuosity that is at its service.

The orchestral portion was sometimes disconcertingly sloppy, and at no point was it really well integrated with the solo playing. It was, to be sure, the sort of playing that would be adequate under most circumstances, but as framework for the remarkable things Frager was doing it was mostly disappointing.

Frager's point-to-point perceptiveness about Mozart's way of composing was in great contrast to the undeveloping and extremely tedious playing of the notes that the Boston Symphony produced for Leinsdorf in the lovely B-flat Symphony, K.319. And for that matter the smooth uninflected playing was in itself in striking contrast to the personal extravagances in Leinsdorf's corybantic pantomime and ecstatic mugging.

The concert ended with the *Prague* Symphony, K.504, like the B-flat, a repeat from the winter season. The attendance at this first concert was 4,317.

Claude Frank Superb in Beethoven Work

July 5, 1965

LENOX—On Sunday afternoon the music of Haydn and Beethoven was added to that of Mozart during the Boston Symphony's first Tanglewood weekend of the current season. It was Beethoven who got what was easily the weekend's best performance, when Claude Frank played the C major Piano Concerto.

Certainly it was the pianists who lent the weekend its musical distinction. Malcolm Frager, who had played Mozart's C major Concerto, K.415, very beautifully on Friday reappeared Saturday with one of its companion pieces, the more familiar A major, K.414.

Once again Frager was remarkably impressive, intensely musical, and often very moving. If the experience was not so transporting as his Friday performance had been, the difference lies partly in the two works, for the A major work is most of the time the smoother, the more "normal" of the two. Frager responds particularly to the fantastic side of these works, and the A major offers him a little less to respond to. Still, he gave a subtle and responsive performance, and it was again obvious that he is one of the very best Mozart players around.

Claude Frank's playing is completely different from the flexible and extraordinary detailed lyricism of Frager's. The melodic line seems straighter, less fancifully vocal. It is also of a marvelously sustained tensile strength.

Frank's playing is highly architectural, being founded on a powerfully inflected and revealingly directional bass line. The sense of the large paragraph is strong, whether in the lyricism of the Largo, the wit of the rondo theme, or the tour de force of the long and great first-movement cadenza.

The pianistic skill as such is something one doesn't think about at all, so organic is it and so completely absorbed into his musical purposes. Frank's finger work is, in fact, not the astonishingly impeccable thing Frager's is, but he plays with great variety of tonal resources, from the hushed delicacy of the scales that begin to prepare the first movement's retransition to the enormous sound in the cadenza.

In its simplicity, penetrating intelligence, and in the huge spans covered by the thought and imagination, Frank's playing becomes absorbing and exciting to a degree almost unbelievable in view of how unobvious and unpretentious the whole performance is. I have not for many years heard a piano concerto so marvelously played, and it is a pleasure to report that the audience's response—prolonged applause after the first movement, a standing ovation at the end—suggested that people really knew what they were hearing.

Sunday's program consisted otherwise of Haydn's fascinating Concertante for violin, cello, oboe, and bassoon and Mozart's Concertante for violin and viola. The Haydn benefited from Leinsdorf's best conducting of the weekend. Among the soloists, Jules Eskin, the cellist, stood rather more than head and shoulders above his colleagues, the Messrs. Silverstein, Gomberg, and Walt, in every essential of good musicianship. The Mozart soloists were Joseph Silverstein and Burton Fine, with Fine considerably the more in touch with Mozart's intentions.

Friday's all-Mozart program also contained the B-flat Divertimento, K.287, and the Symphony No. 39 in E-flat. The Divertimento was passable in those passages where the compositional continuity is obvious. Much of it, however, was so beside the point, stiff, and unmusical that it came as a real shock to learn from the Symphony that Mozart could be played still worse. Moreover, the woodwind and horn playing in the Symphony was disgraceful with its bad phrasing, bad intonation, and harsh tone.

After Sunday's concert, a bronze tablet in the Music Shed was dedicated to the memory of Henry Hadley (1871–1937), composer and conductor who conceived and led the first Berkshire Festival in August 1934. The tablet was put up by the National Association for American Composers and Conductors.

Lohengrin Splendid Finale

August 23, 1965

LENOX—The final Tanglewood weekend was given over to a complete concert performance of Wagner's *Lohengrin*, spread, one act at a time, over Friday and Saturday evenings and Sunday afternoon. Public response picked up as the weekend went on, and the size of the audience grew from under 6,000 Friday to just about 8,000 Sunday.

The project was well worth doing and it was mostly done very well. Erich Leinsdorf conducted the Boston Symphony and the Chorus Pro Musica, Alfred Nash Patterson, director, and the principal singers were Sándor Kónya as Lohengrin, Lucine Amara as Elsa, William Dooley as Telramund, Rita Gorr as Ortrud, Jerome Hines as King Henry, and Calvin Marsh as the Herald. William Dupree, John Glenn Paton, William Ledbetter, and Eugene Thamon were the four nobles. Helene Farras, Barbara Smith Conrad, Judith Keller, and Batyah Godfrey were the quartet of pages.

Lohengrin is uneven, but the best of it is remarkable. Some of the best includes that which is normally cut in the theater, and it was a pleasure to have a chance for once to hear a live performance of the entire score, and to hear and enjoy it all with the welcome elimination of fatigue which is one of the benefits of the one-act-at-a-time method.

Leinsdorf even went so far as to restore a passage cut by Wagner himself, possibly even before the first performance. The place in question consists of fifty-six measures that form something like a second stanza to Lohengrin's grail narrative. Record buffs may know it from a disc made by Franz Völker in the 1930s, but it can't be found even in most of the printed scores. It's a fine place, too. It has no urgent dramatic necessity, but it does benefit the musical shape and I shall probably miss it next time I hear the standard version.

This *Lohengrin* offered the most intelligent solution to the problem of opera in concert that I have encountered. Three small spaces were cleared amid the massed choristers, just enough to give an illusion of the spatial relationships that would obtain on stage. Singers made entrances and exits, and since access to their little platforms was from below, they could do so with impressive dramatic effect when appropriate. There was one naive but effective and in-tune touch of visual symbolism. The villains, Telramund and Ortrud, were dressed in black, in contrast to everyone else's festive summer whites.

Leinsdorf paced the opera superbly and most of the performance had a tremendous vitality. The orchestra played beautifully except for a tendency to let some very soft passages coarsen out into *mezzo-forte*. The Chorus Pro Musica did itself proud, too, though sometimes the women were hard to hear through the enormous numbers of men *Lohengrin* requires. The opera also makes extraordinary demands on extra brass on and behind the stage. There were trumpeters everywhere, and the Tanglewood topography makes some really miraculous and exciting spatial effects possible.

The cast was mostly strong, with Kónya as Lohengrin as its one significant weakness. He has a good tenor voice. He can also sing beautifully, but mostly he doesn't bother. He is capable of effectively forthright declamation and sometimes of a well-phrased bit of lyric singing. Once he was extremely impressive, and that was in the scene with the king and the crowd just before the grail narrative. But "In fernem Land" brought back the other Kónya, the one who was heard in most of the performance, and that is a man given to sentimental half-voice, to sobs and chokes, and with no sense of rhythm so that phrases trail off and slide into one another vaguely.

Lucine Amara's voice is more fragile than what we usually expect from an Elsa, but it was ample for the physical demands of the part. Her performance was touching, and, even if it is not yet an interpretation with a thoroughly developed profile, getting her to sing Elsa was good casting.

Gorr and Dooley were both marvelous. Gorr has vocal limitations. The high notes are difficult for her and she tilts at them rather violently. Her brief appearance in the third act demands mostly what she does least well, but her second act was a hair-raising achievement. She has a strong musical intelligence and a sense of rhythm and of declamation that are altogether out of the ordinary.

Dooley was a partner worthy of her. He has a young and powerful voice, one with more metal than velvet. It serves a fine musical and dramatic intelligence, too, and he gave a brilliant performance. The Ortrud-Telramund scene that begins the second act is not only the best thing in the score. It was the climactic achievement of the performance as well.

Jerome Hines as the king, which is a stupid stuffed-shirt part, was undistinguished. The voice was small and colorless, the declamation drab. Calvin Marsh as the Herald was excellent as it seems one can always depend on him to be.

Lohengrin was a splendid end to the season. Leinsdorf is to be thanked for thinking of it and congratulated for achieving it so well.

Help! Loud, Inaudible, and Evidently Sexy

August 26, 1965

For the next few weeks Loew's Orpheum will sound like the bird house at the zoo with the volume turned up. The Beatles' new movie, *Help!*, has just opened there. I am not sure that anything beyond the Beatles' being in it is relevant.[12]

There is a very slender story line, and it remains intelligible even under conditions where the dialogue cannot be heard. Ringo wears a huge ring—there has been nothing like it since Edith Sitwell—and some thugs in the service of an Eastern religion and a pair of nutty scientists try to get it from him. Why is not clear and not especially important either.

This gets the boys into a number of interesting locations, starting from London and including a ski resort in the Alps, Salisbury Plains, where military maneuvers are going on, and the Bahamas. Basically, *Help!* is a zany chase.

Some of it is very funny. The director, Richard Lester, who did their earlier film and that recent comic delight, *The Knack*, is an inventive man even when he is not really trying terribly hard. There are good gags, an agreeable sense of the pleasures of non-sequitur, and especially the near-surrealist montage that accompanies the seven songs in the picture is very charming.

The dialogue appears to be good. Most of it is inaudible through the shrieking audience, but some of it is sophisticated enough as to not pose a threat to the little dears' minds, and they let that be heard.

As for the music, I couldn't say. I had no time to hear the Capitol record before seeing the film, and that would be my only source of information. When a Beatle appears on the screen everybody screams, and when they sing a song everyone yells for four full minutes.

There is a scene in which Ringo is trapped with a hungry tiger, though it turns out the tiger can be pacified by having Beethoven's Ninth sung to him. Everybody does that, and I was pleased to observe that just as they do to the bona fide Beatles songs, they yell like mad, clap in rhythm, and obviously Beethoven did manage to invent a song with really universal appeal just as he intended.

Performances are OK. Leo McKern is a simple but effective villain. Eleanor Bron is a high priestess who is really on the heroes' side—she winks broadly at the audience every now and then—and gives quite a funny performance wearing

[12] That Steinberg should be writing on the Beatles at all, let alone in a movie review, seems an anomaly. Yet according to an unsigned notice in the *Globe* on September 12, 1964, he had been scheduled to review a Beatles concert the following Saturday at the Boston Garden "to bring you a first-hand report of the frenzied doings. Look for his amusing article." That report never appeared. However, in a subsequent essay on awards (see article of June 20, 1965), he opened with a brief positive assessment of the Fab Four, who had recently been named to the Queen's Honours list.

a series of costumes that make her look like the ambitious and not-quite-in-touch fashion editor of a provincial newspaper. Victor Spinetti and Roy Kinnear do very well with their juicy parts as the two scientists. One of them claims to have been bid for by MIT to help them rule the world; the other remarks wistfully while in perpetual difficulties with his transistors, "Animals trust me; I should have gone into vivisection."

The Beatles themselves, for that matter, have a certain style, especially Ringo, who drops his nuggets of dialogue rather effectively into space.

But it's all sex, really. Visual symbols are uninhibitedly explicit.

None of it gets by the kids either. There is a lot of humor and fantasy mixed in with the noise and the rubbish, though whether you can survive a room full of hysterical little girls is, of course, another matter.

Opera in Concert—A Valid Undertaking for Symphony Groups

September 19, 1965

The *New York Times* and the *New York Herald-Tribune* were displeased with the performance of Wagner's *Lohengrin* with which the 1965 Berkshire Festival ended,[13] and the displeasure was not merely with this or that about the music or the performance, but with the very fact of the performance.

Part of the indignation had to do with the link between the orchestra and the company for which it records and that the project was RCA's as much as the Boston Symphony's.

Those critics would not, however, object if the Boston Symphony were to perform, say, the Brahms Fourth to coincide with RCA's desire for a new recording. The complaint was clearly directed at the fact that an opera was performed and at Erich Leinsdorf's decision to spread that opera, one act per concert, over the whole weekend.

It is no secret that the recording contract an orchestra has affects its operations in matters especially of repertory and choice of guest soloists. There is good reason to believe, for that matter, that the *Lohengrin* cast heard at Tanglewood represented a compromise between Leinsdorf's wishes and recording necessities. Altogether though, the relations between orchestras and their recording companies is so complex a subject that it is best left untouched here.

Performing operas in concert is, I believe, a peculiarly American practice. It reflects the failure of our opera companies to provide us with an adequate

[13] See review of August 23, 1965.

operatic life. To be sure, concert performances are generally something done *faute de mieux*; stage works belong on the stage.

Still, concert performances have made it possible for a considerable public that is not content with learning everything from records, but wants live music, to become acquainted with a valuable repertory it could otherwise never come to know.

The American Opera Society and the Little Orchestra Society, for example, have given performances of things like Busoni's *Doktor Faustus*, Rossini's *Guillaume Tell*, Stravinsky's *Rake's Progress*, many Italian works from the bel canto period, operas by Gluck and Handel, that have been actually, or at least to all intents and purposes, unavailable in the theater. Quality of performance has ranged from superb to wretched, but even the poor performances have had some value.

Sometimes the concert versions provide the necessary impetus for someone to get the work onto the stage. This must be to some extent true of the Boston Opera's productions of *Puritani* and *Semiramide*.

I doubt that the New York City Opera would have staged Berg's *Wozzeck* in 1952, not to mention the Metropolitan six years later, had it not been for the excitement stirred up by the concert performance Mitropoulos gave with the New York Philharmonic in 1951.

Yes, but what about *Lohengrin*, which is not a masterpiece of the very first order, and not so very rare? The justification that I imagine Leinsdorf would wish to offer is the possibility of a performance musically superior to that available in most theaters. Whether or not he succeeded is, of course, as debatable as the quality of any other performance.

I disliked Sándor Kónya in the title role, but otherwise the performance as a whole seemed to me remarkably successful, and certainly incomparably better than any I have seen at or heard from the Metropolitan in twenty years. The last eighteen words are a regrettably small compliment to Leinsdorf and his forces.

Leaving aside differences of opinion about this or that singer, it must still be said that the Tanglewood *Lohengrin* achieved a discipline and precision rarely encountered in the theater. They are qualities sacrificed to the problems related to the stage and that is a price most theater-goers gladly pay, even if theatricality is not a very lively issue in *Lohengrin*. Still I found it good once to have a really clear view of the music.

But the greatest source of clarity came from the absence of cuts. *Lohengrin* is not long by Wagnerian standards. The first and third acts run about sixty-four minutes each, the second about eighty. Except at Bayreuth, you probably cannot see it uncut in any theater in the world. It is long, it is not uniformly interesting, but it is better uncut.

Wagner's possible miscalculations about form are preferable to some conductor's. Also, you cannot right miscalculations by cutting. All that does is to shorten the period during which you can have to face them.

What is usually cut from *Lohengrin* is a large amount of choral music. Its restoration gives the opera quite a different character. Much of this music was very exciting in itself, especially the superb male chorus writing, but the more significant point is that it seemed as though one had never heard Wagner's *Lohengrin* before, nor had any idea of what sort of work it really was.

That leaves one at liberty not to care—as it turned out Harold Schonberg did not care—but if the object of giving performances is to reveal the nature of the work performed, what more justification is wanted?

That brings me finally to Leinsdorf's controversial splitting of *Lohengrin* over three concerts. It is a plan that does not fit well into the habits of most of the Tanglewood public. That, and the comparative unpopularity now of early Wagner, accounts for the fairly small audience the performance drew.

Nonetheless, it was a good idea, and without it the performance would not have been possible. When the *Lohengrin* project was first announced, I wondered about several things, including the choice of the work itself and some of the casting. One thing it did not occur to me to wonder about was the one-act-per-concert idea.

The reason is that the most valuable event of my own Wagnerian education was a concert performance of the entire *Ring* conducted by Furtwängler for the Rome Radio early in 1954. There were two concerts a week, each consisting of one act only, so that the cycle was spread over a little more than a month.

I suppose there was a certain disadvantage in that it disabled me from thinking about anything else for five weeks. On the other hand, I quickly learned, and have never forgotten, what was to be gained from investing one's whole store of attention to a first act without worrying about the hours lying ahead, or of coming to a third act completely fresh. Reduced to a more normal time scale it was a pleasure to be repeated at the Tanglewood *Lohengrin*.

This is not a proposal to close the theaters or to turn the Boston Symphony into an opera orchestra. *Lohengrin* is something for which the Boston Symphony has the resources, and it appears that no organization in America has better resources. It is therefore a legitimate and a valuable project for the Symphony to have undertaken.

There are wonderful possibilities: *Götterdämmerung*, *Meistersinger*, *Tristan*, *Don Carlo*, *Les Troyens*, *Pique Dame*. I very much hope that *Lohengrin* was only the beginning.

Organist Like Conductor—Powerless, Responsible

October 17, 1965

The organ world is one of the most special and certainly among the more isolated of the worlds within worlds that make up the musical community.

Anton Heiller's really extraordinary recital at Kresge Auditorium about a week ago[14] reminded me of this vividly, and not least by the fact that Heiller is one of the few players of this instrument to have broken out of the organists' mold.

There was, to begin with, the audience. Except, naturally, for organists I know, it was quite unfamiliar, and someone who goes to as many concerts as I do comes to recognize audiences and to distinguish among them, specific faces as well as general types.

It was as quiet and devoted an audience as I have sat with, there on time, intent while there, reluctant to leave afterwards. Clearly no one was there other than on purpose. These were real aficionados, like standees at the opera only not so exuberant.

But what a strange beast the organ is! On the old tracker instruments the organist still was in direct physical contact with the music. The modern organist, even playing on an instrument as good as the Holtkamp in Kresge, is an operator of machinery that interposes immense mechanical distance between himself and the music.

Only an orchestra conductor is as powerless to exert a direct effect on the physical sounds for which he is nonetheless responsible, and conductors at least have magic, if not witchcraft, working with them.

The organ does not breathe, or rather, it does not need to. Other instruments are faced with the need of constant renewal of the sound. Breaths must be taken; a bow runs out and must change direction. At least articulation is in the nature of these instruments, however the players may misuse it or try to disguise it. The organist could play an unbroken, unarticulated legato forever. Many do.

The organ is an instrument of inflexible dynamics. Its changes of timbre and volume occur in jumps. True, they have shutters for making gradual *crescendos*, but they are pitiful gadgets. What they effect is not like the living dynamics of a singer's breath or a cellist's bow arm: it sounds like someone twiddling an amplifier knob.

[14] Steinberg's review, published October 11, 1965, is not included in this collection. Heiller's October 9 program consisted of the E minor Prelude and Fugue by Nicholas Bruhns; Variations on a Passamezzo by Samuel Scheidt; three pieces from J. S. Bach's *Little Organ Book* as well as the G minor Fantasy and Fugue; the Second Sonata by Paul Hindemith; and Max Reger's D minor Fantasy and Fugue, Opus 135.

That is why it is so hard to make convincing rubato on the organ. Listen to rubato on a violin or even on a piano (and that is pretty much a machine, too), and you hear that the elasticity is not confined to the placement of the notes in time. The curve of tension and relaxation, of hurrying and retarding, is illuminated by a corresponding flexibility of loudness. The organist cannot do it, and neither, unless on the old tracker instruments, can he vary the modes of attack that contribute to the rubato of a Schnabel or a Szigeti.

Then, simply by pulling out stops, the organist can double whatever he is playing at an octave above or below or, for that matter, two octaves in either direction. It is an important tool for building sheer weight of sound or for throwing a line into a particular dynamic or textural relief. Because it is so easily done, it is one of the most abused of the organists' devices.

In modern music octave placement is a very important element. In other words, whether a D is the one in the middle of the bass staff or the one near the top of the treble staff is almost as important a part of its message as the fact that it is a D rather than a G.

The cultivated mid-20th-century ear is apt, I am sure, to pay much more attention to such matters than its counterpart 100 years ago, and it is apt to be especially disturbed by most organists' recklessness with octaves and the whole business of taking a voice that Bach has placed into the middle of a texture and making it scream out across the top line like massed piccolos in the *Stars and Stripes.*

Organists themselves are apt to be an odd lot, too. In part this must have to do with the fact that all but a very few like Biggs lead professional lives centered about the church. I would not presume to speculate on the effect this has on their personalities, but I have a clear idea of the struggle it must be for a musician to maintain his artistry in an environment where artistic standards are as dismaying as they generally are in our religious institutions. On quite another level there is the valid point to be made that church acoustics do not contribute notably to the preservation, let alone the development, of a fastidious ear.

Not least, the organ has in a crucial sense been a nearly dead instrument for 200 years. Since the death of Bach, its literature has been insufficiently refreshed and renewed. There are a few significant and beautiful compositions by Liszt, Franck, Brahms, Reger.

Today there is Messiaen, but other major figures have been apt to ignore the organ altogether (Bartók, Stravinsky) or to make few and minor contributions (Schoenberg)—perhaps even the three very pleasant sonatas of Hindemith belong in this last category. Karg-Elerg, Vierne, Widor, all this is preposterous music and on a dismal level that would make inconceivable its admission into the serious repertory of most other instrumentalists. (Yes, I know Heifetz plays the Miklós Rózsa Concerto, but probably out of boredom or friendship rather than from necessity.)

There is a lot of wonderful organ music, and because of what the instrument is and has become and because of what it has made of those who play it, it is often hard to find out from listening how it really goes. To enter the organ world involves a more than ordinary suspension of disbelief.

A few players have made valuable contributions toward bringing the organ into the civilized musical community. E. Power Biggs has been one, partly by the mere vastness of his repertory (what an education those Sunday-morning broadcasts were when this music was not yet on records), also by dramatizing the true nature of the instrument that Bach and his predecessors knew as opposed to what the organ became in the 19th century.

And now a more recent generation has produced some organists whose educated and virtuosic playing ranks among the best being done by any instrumentalists today, notably the Italian Luigi Ferdinando Tagliavini, the Dutchman Gustav Leonhardt, and the Viennese Anton Heiller whose recent concert here proved to be so restorative and musical an experience.

Britten Premiere With Rostropovich

October 23, 1965

It was, I believe, the philosopher Lichtenberg who said that we call men geniuses for the same lazy reason that we call a centipede a centipede. We are indeed lazy, and lax, with superlatives.

Luckily, every so often there comes someone to set our standards straight. Among its musical performers, this generation of listeners has the Russian cellist Mstislav Rostropovich as a stirring reminder of what great playing really is.

Rostropovich appeared with the Boston Symphony on Friday afternoon and played three concertos to an audience that applauded him long and loud and that offered him a standing ovation at the end. He began with Haydn's recently unearthed C major Concerto, gave the American premiere of Britten's Symphony for Cello and Orchestra, and ended with the Dvořák.

Britten wrote his Symphony in 1963 for Rostropovich, the inspiration also for the slightly earlier Cello Sonata and for an unaccompanied cello suite which the Russian will introduce to America at his Carnegie Hall recital in December. Britten has called the work a Symphony because the relationship between solo and orchestra is that of two partners equal in dialogue. It is, in other words, a Sonata for cello and orchestra, and Britten has deferred to the custom by which we call an orchestral sonata a symphony.

There are four movements. The first is a massive sonata structure, somber, rich in vividly characterized themes. Then comes a spooky scherzo, swift and nervous, almost all quiet. The third movement is song-like, built about a magnificently eloquent, large-spanning melody. A cadenza, which is in effect a second development for this Adagio, leads into the finale. This is a set of variations which, like that in the *Eroica* finale, uses both a ground and a tune.

The Symphony is difficult to hear. It is large, dense, and perhaps the most thoroughly and rigorously composed piece the composer has yet written. It is tonal, of course, and it uses key relationships with a strength, sense, and expressive effect virtually unknown to the '60s. The distribution of themes among the participants—the dialogue, in a word—recalls the sophistication of the great Mozart concertos that Britten the pianist plays so gloriously.

Rostropovich speaks of the Symphony's "poly-mood." Thoroughly instrumental in conception, the Symphony still has something anthropomorphic about it—again like Mozart—a rhetoric that is becoming to a composer who has been so involved with poetry and the voice. The juxtapositions and simultaneities of mood are complex and interesting. They are not always easy to understand, and after considerable time spent with the Symphony I am just beginning to sense the rightness of its optimistic finale. And this movement has details whose suggestions of Copland and even Sibelius still sound a little odd to me.

Writing for cello and orchestra is notoriously difficult, but one would not know it from Britten's Symphony. The very difficulty has inspired him to an excitingly fresh and unfailingly clear texture.

Rostropovich's performance was indistinguishable from the music itself. He now plays it with still more invention and freedom than on his superb record. In Erich Leinsdorf and the Boston Symphony he found a virtuosic partner.

Rostropovich's playing is the most inflected I have ever heard. Its variety, the sense of life being renewed in every note, the powerful coherence seem unique today, and to convey all this, Rostropovich has developed a degree of technical control in itself hardly to be believed.

Actually, he takes considerable liberties with the Dvořák Concerto. Mostly I like Dvořák's ideas even better, but the point is that while an extra-fine *pianissimo* or a great broadening of the pace may be a fussy and unnecessary addition to the work, there is never anything that contradicts the music. Even when his playing touches the Romantic virtuosic tradition with its permissiveness about personal extravagance, and in the Dvořák it undoubtedly does, the man obviously cannot play a bad phrase.

Leinsdorf's accompaniment in the Dvořák was not always chamber-musically sympathetic, though there were the rewards of fine wind solos from Cioffi and Gomberg and especially from Pappoutsakis. The orchestral part of the delightful "new" Haydn was fairly animated. Leinsdorf conducted seated at the harpsichord with which he toyed in a rather irresponsible now-you-hear-it-now-you-don't way.

Friday, incidentally, was exactly the Symphony's 85th birthday, and the concert was a fine celebration. Rostropovich is a marvel and if you can possibly contrive to hear the Saturday concert, don't miss it. I could imagine holding up the box office at gunpoint myself.

Rostropovich Speaks—Mainly About Britten

October 31, 1965

Mstislav Rostropovich was delighted to learn that his first appearance with the Boston Symphony a couple of Fridays ago[15] was to fall precisely on the 85th anniversary of the orchestra's debut concert. The Russian cellist is a man who likes anniversaries and all sorts of gestures and events that link seemingly remote things. For Rostropovich, the Boston Symphony, which he heard in Russia in 1956 and in New York two years ago, is "the greatest of all orchestras."[16]

And he has long known Koussevitzky's recording of the Prokofiev Fifth: "It was his favorite recording of his own music. We often heard it together, and he gave me his copy shortly before he died." Then Rostropovich went on to recall that Benjamin Britten, whose new Cello Symphony he was about to play in America for the first time, also had close associations with Koussevitzky and the Boston Symphony, for it was the conductor who helped set the composer on the road to success by commissioning the opera *Peter Grimes.*

Rostropovich was speaking to a few members of the press in the Ancient Instruments Room at Symphony Hall. Some photos of the BSO's Russian tour were on display. Suddenly he stopped before one of them, a shot of a banquet table in which Charles Munch, Richard Burgin, and Dimitri Kabalevsky were clearly identified. At the far end of the table was a beautiful, dark-haired woman. "My wife!" he exclaimed, adding, by way of explanation, "*Meine Frau.*" And then, pointing with delight to perhaps a half-millimeter of bald head visible behind the lady, he said, "*Und das ist ich.*"

Languages are evidently not a strong point with Rostropovich, and both then and in a later conversation, he preferred to speak in Russian, using the Symphony's violinist Victor Manusevitch as interpreter. He has a few words of English and a

[15] See previous article.

[16] That BSO tour, led by Munch in September 1956, marked the first appearance by an American orchestra in the Soviet Union.

little more German, and he sometimes mixes them engagingly. For example, the answer to one question came out: "My... wife... English.......Noch... worse."

"My wife" is a distinguished performer also, the soprano Galina Vishnevskaya, who sings here tomorrow with the Moscow Philharmonic.[17] There are two daughters, 9 and 6, currently being taken care of by their grandmother Rostropovich. "Fortunately they look like their mother," was Father's comment.

Rostropovich, while undeniably less pretty than Madame Vishnevskaya, is a pleasing-looking man. On stage he looks a little older than his 38 years; close to, he makes a distinctly youthful impression. He rather resembles Prokofiev, something that is first suggested by the baldness and the metal-rimmed eyeglasses, though the similarity continues almost astonishingly about the nose and ears. The jutting lower lip is the cellist's own.

I would guess that the resemblance to Prokofiev pleases Rostropovich. He counts the composer as perhaps the greatest influence on his life. He acknowledges three teachers, Prokofiev, Dimitri Shostakovich, and Benjamin Britten.

"Prokofiev made me change from a cellist to a musician. When I was a conservatory student, Shostakovich wanted me to switch from cellist to composer, but he was wrong. I am a very bad composer. Cellists, you know, are mostly very bad musicians, very primitive. They are too much concerned with stupid music, Popper, Vieuxtemps, things like that. Prokofiev was the one who made me aware of all the great music that I would never play on the cello."

"Now," Rostropovich continued, "I am very lucky to have Britten. We are very close friends, but for me he is also a teacher, a great teacher. He is a musical genius, as composer, as pianist, as conductor, a total musical genius. To work with him is to be in heaven."

Their friendship began in 1961 when Rostropovich was in London to play the Shostakovich Concerto. Afterwards, Britten appeared backstage, introduced himself, and told the astounded cellist that he would like to write a sonata they could play together.

The association has had remarkable results. Britten always has liked to write with a particular performer in mind, and it is likely that Rostropovich is responsible for his recent renewed interest in large instrumental forms. So far, Britten has composed for Rostropovich a Sonata for Cello and Piano, the Symphony for Cello and Orchestra, the cadenzas for the recently resurrected Haydn C major Concerto which he played here, and a ten-movement suite for unaccompanied cello, which will be given its first American performance at Rostropovich's Carnegie Hall recital December 17.

[17] See next article.

Britten meant the soprano solo of his *War Requiem* for Galina Vishnevskaya. The most recent Britten contribution goes to both wife and husband, a song cycle on poems by Pushkin. Rostropovich is an excellent pianist, and the new Pushkin-Britten cycle will be given its American premiere at Philharmonic Hall, New York, December 19, when Rostropovich will accompany Vishnevskaya in a program otherwise devoted to songs of Mussorgsky and Tchaikovsky.[18] As for the unaccompanied cello suite, both player and composer hope that it is just the first in a set of six.

At Carnegie Hall, Rostropovich will play Schubert's *Arpeggione* Sonata. "It is the first time I play it without Britten. We have performed it five times, but oddly enough I had never played it before." Of all Britten's firsts as a performer, Rostropovich regards his Schubert playing as the most beautiful," the "most unreplaceable," recalling besides his own performances of the *Arpeggione*, those of the great song cycles with Peter Pears and those of the great piano duet works with Sviatoslav Richter.

Rostropovich hopes to record the *Arpeggione* with Britten soon after his return to Europe, and one reason for the Carnegie performance is "to be a little in practice."

Rostropovich is very happy with "his" Cello Symphony. "Britten's technical skill is amazing," he said. "Britten and Shostakovich are the only two composers in whose music I have never had to change a note. I got from Britten a perfectly written part, completely bowed and articulated, and even all the double and triple and quadruple stops fit. Marvelous!"

So far, Rostropovich is the only person to have performed the Cello Symphony. That is not, however, by design.

"Britten asked me if I wanted exclusive performance rights for a certain period, and I told him, yes, for the first thirty-five minutes. And as soon as the premiere is over, I hope a thousand cellists will learn it."

He sat at the piano and offered a guided tour of the work, pointing out features like the gradual acceleration built into the variation finale, the cadenza at the end of the slow movement, both for the details of its writing and its place in the Symphony as a whole; points of orchestration, especially the many ways in which the cello is thrown into combination with solo instruments in the orchestra.

Mostly, though, Rostropovich spoke about character, atmosphere, gesture, and mood. It was a crystallization almost of what I had already observed in a rehearsal of the Haydn Concerto when by means of a constant play of facial expression and bodily posture he had sought to convey that work's changing temper as it was being played.

[18] See review of December 21, 1965, for Steinberg's account of the song cycle's Boston premiere.

"Yes, it is important to understand what is being said as well as how it is said. The Britten is a difficult work. The poly-harmony, the polyrhythms, yes, these are perhaps obvious, but the poly-mood, that is difficult. And now I realize that I did not fully understand the work myself the first four or five times I performed it."

That is the sort of thing that makes Rostropovich worry about critics: "I should have known that work better than anyone except Ben, but there were things I didn't know. A critic will write very authoritatively after just one hearing. Generally, I don't care what they say about my playing. But the worst is when they say I play well but the work is bad. Then I feel guilty for the work."

Rostropovich had just had that experience in New York after playing a concerto by a young Russian, Boris Tchaikovsky. "Both Britten and Shostakovich think it is a masterful work." And returning to criticism, "Sometimes what they write is true, but not interesting; very occasionally it is interesting, but not necessarily true."

Both Rostropovich and Vishnevskaya have a very busy tour ahead of them during the next month-and-a-half, though their paths will at least cross occasionally. The next stop is England, specifically the Britten House at Aldeburgh. There the *lingua franca* is German. "Britten's German is very bad, but mine is much worse. When we speak together, no German would understand a word."

He looks forward to the visits with his teacher and to their music-making together. Rostropovich emphasized again, "It has been very important for me to work with composers, to be forced to become a musician. And perhaps lately it has helped my cello playing, too."

Moscow Philharmonic—Kondrashin Conducts, Vishnevskaya Sings

November 2, 1965

The Moscow Philharmonic gave us a wonderful concert in Symphony Hall on Monday night. Kiril Kondrashin conducted the Ninth symphonies of Shostakovich and Mahler; Galina Vishnevskaya sang the Letter Scene from Tchaikovsky's *Eugene Onegin*. Mstislav Rostropovich, the great cellist who had such a triumph with the Boston Symphony ten days earlier,[19] was in the audience to hear his wife sing. "Tonight," he said, "I am not Rostropovich; I am Mr. Vishnevsky."

Vishnevskaya had a vast success of her own. She sang Tchaikovsky's beautiful *scena* wonderfully. Her voice has, I believe, grown larger and richer since she

19 See again review of October 23, 1965.

sang the same music here with Kondrashin and the Moscow State Orchestra in 1960. But even more remarkable is her dramatic gift that enabled her to make orchestra and conductor seem invisible and to create, on the concert stage, the whole lovable character of Tatiana and her situation.

She is beautiful and she has extraordinary presence. Face, hands, arms, body, all became part of the performance, and she used gesture to a degree that perhaps no other singer could have brought off. She could have done anything at all—we would have believed it. It was a marvelous and lovely achievement of ripe and assured artistry.

Warmly applauded and cheered, Vishnevskaya gave an encore. Unaccompanied, she sang something wonderfully melancholy from Rimsky-Korsakov's *Czar's Bride*. Toward the end of it, her voice suddenly opened and warmed completely, taking on a glow not heard before.

Kondrashin's performance of the Mahler Ninth was strikingly different from any one is apt to hear in America. It was fast and tight, intensely dramatic. There were many points so well made and gestures so vividly realized that often it suggested that Kondrashin must be one of the best Mahlerians around. There were also exaggerations, sudden bursts of speed, and an unwillingness to allow breadth of statement and repose.

Perhaps the performance took many of its characteristics from the nature of the orchestra. Its sound is light in weight, with delicate woodwind playing, transparent horn tone, sweet and lyric trumpets. Its playing is impressive except for the percussion, which is crude by American standards.

The string tone has less body than that of any comparable American group, or, for that matter, the Leningrad Philharmonic. It was also the string playing that showed most clearly the Moscow Philharmonic's most arresting characteristic, namely the highly inflected variety of its playing.

There was not a dead note all evening, hardly ever two in a row that were identical in weight, shape, color, or mode of attack. Their playing, in fact, is very similar to what can be heard, raised to a special virtuosic level, in Rostropovich's solo work.

The Moscow Philharmonic is an amazingly musical orchestra. When the Cleveland Orchestra makes such an astounding continuity of inflection, one can also see Szell producing every bit of it. With the Moscow players, it just seems to happen spontaneously. They are not so virtuosic as their numbers in the Boston Symphony and are more liable to accidents. But their resources are fully used. The variety of sound is wonderful for Mahler: the startling succession of gestures in the music calls forth ever new sounds to illuminate where the composition is going.

Also the players listen to each other. Kondrashin, conducting sometimes a bit roughly, often produced a performance that was quite imprecise. But the texture remained clear, and nothing was ever covered. The playing of the incidental solos was extraordinarily musical, especially the oboe in the Tchaikovsky, the horn throughout, the trumpet in the third movement of the Mahler, and many others at many moments.

Both as orchestral playing and as Mahler interpretation it was an occasion of unorthodox and unexpected virtues and blessings. There were also peculiarities enough to have spelled disaster for many a performance. Here, the sweep and conviction of the whole was so grand that the oddities simply retreated and became eccentricities that had no essential bearing on what was happening.

Vishnevskaya, Kondrashin, and the Moscow Philharmonic gave us a remarkable concert indeed.

Carter Double Concerto in Boston Premiere

November 18, 1965

Elliott Carter's Double Concerto for Harpsichord and Piano with Two Chamber Orchestras was heard in Boston for the first time Wednesday. The soloists were Paul Jacobs, harpsichord, and Charles Rosen, piano. Frederik Prausnitz conducted members of the New England Conservatory Orchestra.

Carter is almost alone in having addressed himself to the problem of combining piano and harpsichord. In his Double Concerto the two instruments are widely separated on the stage, and each is surrounded by its own orchestral ensemble, harpsichord with flute, horn, trumpet, trombone, viola, bass, percussion and the piano with oboe, clarinet, bassoon, horn, violin, cello, and percussion.

As well as being thus characterized by timbre, each group works with materials that have special rhythmic and intervallic characteristics. The Double Concerto is "about" the interaction of these characteristics, a fanciful and often highly dramatic exploration of the possibilities of differentiation between them or of their synthesis.

As always, Carter is fascinated with the time element. Indeed, in his program note, he speaks of having tried to "present a musical analogue to the human experience of time both in brief moments and in the longer patterns of evolving events." The Double Concerto is almost always on the way from one speed to another, from one density to another. One consequence of this is that Carter is able to achieve his most dramatic moment in the central Adagio by abolishing this sense of flux and hemming the music into an ominously steady beat.

For its fusion of rhythmic and timbral sophistication, instrumental virtuosity, and not least, human experience, Carter's Double Concerto has been recognized since its first performance in 1961 as a milestone in the music of our time and by many as the greatest achievement in American music so far. It is a marvel indeed.[20]

Any reasonable performance of it would be an important event, but as a matter of fact Wednesday's performance was an outstanding one, and certainly the most effective of the several I have heard. Jacobs and Rosen, who represent what you might call the new American virtuosity at its best, have played the work often and they do it superbly.

Prausnitz displayed what is by now an expected mastery of the work, and he got from his players a performance that was extraordinarily clear in outline and marvelously gripping and vital as well. And what players! There were, to be sure, some unevennesses and some of the playing was less delicate than that I have heard from New York's best freelancers. But the playing Wednesday night by the Conservatory students was unfailingly competent and secure, and from many players, particularly the flute, clarinet, both horns, bassoon, and trumpet, it was often exceptionally beautiful.

Carter was present in Jordan Hall, and he shared quite an ovation with the performers.

The concert began with Schubert's Symphony No. 3 in D, which was nicely done and with some attractive wind playing. Stravinsky's Concerto in D for strings went well in the finale, but before that was pretty fuzzy. The strings are not the best part of the Conservatory Orchestra and the sort of sharp-edged music Stravinsky was writing in the '40s is not quite Prausnitz's forte either.

Charles Rosen also played Mozart's G major Concerto, K.453. It seemed underplayed and rather dispirited. Even with its lacks, it was clearly the work of a superior musician and pianist, but Rosen is not a Mozart player by the grace of God, and it seems somehow to take nothing less. There were some lovely things in the playing of the orchestral part, but the inadequacies of the second team of wind players were a bother, too. Disappointing on a high level, but disappointing just the same.

Serkin Masterful Beethoven Player

December 6, 1965

Opus 111, the last and greatest of the Beethoven piano sonatas is, in the words of Schnabel who in some ways was its finest interpreter in our times, better than any possible performance of it. There have been countless concert performances

[20] See also record review of December 22, 1968, and concert review of August 11, 1976.

and many recordings to demonstrate that for most pianists to touch it at all is an impertinence.

Rudolf Serkin, who included it in his Sunday-afternoon Symphony Hall recital, is one of the pianists who should play Opus 111. He is its master, and he played it most beautifully. I have not heard such a performance of the Sonata since Schnabel, nor, for that matter, can I remember ever hearing Serkin play so well. It was a performance in a straightforward, objective manner, and one that was completely communicative by virtue of the clarity of conception and the beauty of the playing itself.

The articulation was incisive and lucid, in the fury of the first movement, the precipitate third variation of the second, the filigree of the fourth variation and the coda. There was particular strength in the rhythm. This came through in the laying out of the introduction's mysterious harmonies, in the syncopated chords with their marvelous controlled *diminuendo* in the first-movement coda, in the subtle rhythmic speech of all the variations of long and short values in the second movement. Throughout it was a performance remarkable for the precisely conceived and telling effect with which the events of this stupendously rich music were played in their context.

The shape of the Sonata was excitingly revealed. Its climax came, not at a dynamic high-point, but, as it should, at the point of maximum intensity, that terrifying moment when after the long trill chains the two hands are most widely separated on their strange journeys. And of course from the beginning, Serkin had prepared this moment by his careful attention to Beethoven's imaginative use of registral changes. In a sense, I have known Opus 111 played well for a long time, but Serkin's performance was of the kind that made me feel I really had had no idea previously of how extraordinary this music was.

Serkin also did first-rate playing in a Busoni group after intermission. The borderland at the beginning of the 20th century is an exciting period, and Busoni was a remarkable and original inhabitant of it. Serkin played a Toccata written in 1921, consisting of a chordal Prelude, a recitative-like Fantasia, and a Chaconne; and also the "Berceuse," an arrangement of the orchestral *Berceuse élégiaque* Busoni wrote in 1909 in memory of his mother. Both pieces were masterfully imagined and played.

There were impressive things in the playing of Schumann's *Carnaval* also, notably the linear clarity of the conception that displayed the composer's fantastic variation technique so vividly. It was an astonishingly forward-looking performance—that Serkin was a Schoenberg pupil still tells—and it suggested that were it not for Beethoven, Schumann would really be the first modern composer.

Less fortunately, much of the poetry and humor of *Carnaval* were lost in playing whose surface was singularly harsh and aggressive. Bach's A minor

Fugue, BWV 944, which began the concert, was mostly a meaningless jangle. A pleasant, fairly early Haydn Sonata in D was done with placid lack of differentiation and character.

When Serkin played here last year, he was nowhere near his best. This time, particularly in the Beethoven, also in the Busoni, in some ways in the Schumann, he played as great artists play. There are few.

Handel's *Messiah*: For One Shaw From Another—One Serious Performance

December 12, 1965

CLEVELAND—In a passage that has been cited on this page before, Bernard Shaw wrote about the evident "impossibility of obtaining justice" for Handel's *Messiah* in a Christian country. He asked, "Why . . . does not somebody set up a thoroughly rehearsed and exhaustively studied performance of *The Messiah* . . . with a chorus of twenty capable artists? Most of us would be glad to hear the work seriously performed before we die."

I do not know if Shaw got his wish, though he lived almost sixty years longer. Now, fifteen years after Shaw's death, one need no longer speak of "impossibility." Even in Boston we could hear about two-fifths of it "exhaustively studied" when Daniel Pinkham conducted Part I in King's Chapel two Sundays ago. But to hear Handel's masterpiece—as I am coming to be convinced *Messiah* is—"seriously performed" still requires considerable diligence. I must report that I found a journey to Cleveland for Robert Shaw's December 2 performance deeply rewarding.

George Szell has given Cleveland a remarkable setup for choral music. He has attached a large, amateur chorus to the Cleveland Orchestra and he has for the last nine years had one of the world's outstanding choral men, Robert Shaw, as one of the orchestra's associate conductors. Shaw's responsibilities include, but are not limited to, preparing the chorus and conducting many of its performances. The Cleveland Orchestra Chorus has 243 voices. From this group Shaw has drawn the Cleveland Orchestra Chamber Chorus, thirty-seven voices, also all amateur, and those are the people who sang in the *Messiah* concerts.

Shaw used an orchestra of thirty-nine. There were twenty-six strings, four oboes, three bassoons, and a contrabassoon, doubling string and choral parts; two trumpets and timpani; organ and harpsichord. Handel himself usually had a half-dozen fewer strings and only about two-thirds as many singers, but the balance in Shaw's performance was, however inauthentic as to the arithmetic, convincing to the ear, right, and Handelian.

Shaw used the last version of *Messiah* prepared by Handel himself, that of the 1754 performances. It includes a few unusual things: "But who may abide" for soprano in G minor; the short form of the Pastoral Symphony; the short form of "Why do the nations" ending with the recitative setting of "The kings of the earth rise up." Shaw made a cut of his own by omitting the middle section and *da capo* of "The trumpet shall sound"; he also made a condensed *da capo* for "He was despised" and that worked out very badly. Score and parts were those of the Watkins Shaw edition (Novello); there are no parts available yet for the Alfred Mann edition (Rutgers), but Shaw used its score for reference.

There were five soloists. The first soprano was Janice Harsanyi (for the Nativity recitatives, "Rejoice greatly," "Come unto Him," "He was cut off" and "But Thou didst not leave," "How beautiful are the feet," and "I know that my redeemer liveth"), and she was superb. The second soprano, Lorna Haywood (for "But who may abide," "Thou art gone up," "If God be for us") is a very young singer with an unusually simple and beautiful voice, but she is an insecure technician and an indifferent musician. The alto was Florence Kopleff, who has probably the most sumptuous voice of its type and who is a superbly musical singer, but who is often a little placid and devotional for my taste.

The tenor was Seth McCoy, who has a more powerful voice than what we usually hear in *Messiah*, and who used it with skill in coloratura and an impressive intensity, taste, and vividness of diction. The bass was Thomas Paul, a fine musician who was in excellent voice and who gave a powerful performance.

I found my Cleveland *Messiah* experience, which included most of two rehearsals as well as one performance, exciting, musically fulfilling, and often intensely moving. It is in that context that I should like the account of my few reservations understood.

There was the musically undependable second soprano. Then, Shaw himself is sometimes a little glib, and he slides over some events too smoothly. The music might modulate: see, for instance, the tenors' quiet and magical turn to the subdominant in measures 38–39 of "All we like sheep," but for Shaw the gait and the inflection of phrase is not much affected by the sudden E-flats, and that is a loss.

In his desire to keep the piece moving, Shaw mostly revealed an admirable sense of continuity and pace. Sometimes the commendable and necessary desire to fight a bad tradition defeated him. Why, for example, rush from "And He shall purify" into "Behold, a Virgin shall conceive"? And while a Handel Largo is by no means an Adagio, I found some of them, especially "Worthy is the Lamb," lacking in breadth.

A question of vocal ornaments is, of course, completely controversial. Thinking not about historical knowledge, but wholly about taste, I found, for example, Pinkham's *Messiah* performance at King's Chapel excessively ornamented. I also found Shaw's a little naked. Shaw of course used the necessary minimum—after all, omitting cadential turns, for example, is not controversial but merely illiterate. There were the proper appoggiaturas, some musical and tasteful filling-out of skips, but few cadenzas or embellished repeats. What there was, was without exception beautifully done; what was omitted, nowhere by omission distorted Handel. It is a wholly personal matter; my ideal *Messiah* is a little more Italianate and Baroque than Shaw's.

But how wonderful this performance was for its life and rhythm! The warmth and tenderness of "Comfort ye," "He shall feed his flock," "How beautiful are the feet," the buoyancy of "And He shall purify," "For unto us a Child is born," "His yoke is easy," "Lift up your heads," "Hallelujah!," "Blessing and honour, glory and power," the intensity of "He gave his back to the smiters" (a great moment for Miss Kopleff), "Surely He hath borne our griefs," "Why do the nations," "Let us break their bonds"; the suggestiveness of "For behold, darkness shall cover the earth," "Glory to God," "Behold, and see," "Behold, I tell you a mystery"—all these were marvelously realized.

It was a tremendously impressive and beautiful *Messiah* performance, one made altogether with Handel's means. The conductor remarked in a program note: "I believe uncompromisingly that we cannot expect to discover Handel's 'spirit' without recreating insofar as possible the number, nature and disposition of his musical forces. . . . A composer's meaning is not to be separated from the sound he 'heard' in his inner ear and prescribed."

One of the unexamined assumptions customarily made in connection with the *Messiah* problem is that *Messiah* would be unacceptable to listeners today if performed close to the way in which Handel himself imagined and performed it. This argument, which seems to assume Handel's incompetence as a composer and which has brought together such strange bedfellows as Ernest Newman and Edward Gilday, seemed persuasive as long as it did not go unexamined, as for years it did. Now we have a growing body of evidence from places including London, New York, Cleveland, that *Messiah*, when well performed in Handel's own manner, is entirely persuasive to a modern audience.

The audience among whom I heard *Messiah* in Cleveland was the regular Thursday-night subscription audience for the Cleveland Orchestra concerts. It was described to me by a number of people as an audience which, while educated, is conservative and tradition-bound, Cleveland's nearest equivalent, socially and musically, to the Boston Symphony's Friday subscription audience. It was not alienated by what it heard. There was quiet and concentration, no early leavers (there were two-and-a-half hours of music), warm and long applause, and a standing ovation at the end.

The "it can't be done" argument must be ruled out of court from now on.

Which brings me finally to the amusing, and serious, episode of the "Hallelujah!" Chorus. Concerning this piece, Shaw wrote in his program note,

"If anyone stands up during its performance at these concerts out of deference to the tradition instituted by a remote monarch who mistook it for the national anthem, or who did not realize that an intermission followed directly, he can have his head back."

The general feeling in Severance Hall that morning was that Shaw would learn that people did not read notes attentively, or at least that the tradition was too well entrenched to be broken by humorous fiat. When "Hallelujah!" began, about eight people stood up, and so far as I could see, all but two immediately sat down again. Afterwards there was speculation about the two blue-haired, fur-coated women who remained on their feet. Were they wearing tennis shoes, one person wondered? Someone asked Klaus George Roy, director of publications for the Cleveland Orchestra, to what sect persons who have to stand for the "Hallelujah!" chorus belong. What do they believe in? Roy crisply replied, "The King of England."

More Mahler—Bernstein, Philharmonic Give Last Three Symphonies

December 19, 1965

NEW YORK—For some years now, New York has been the Mahler capital of the world. At the end of March 1966, when Barbirolli and the Houston Orchestra play the Fifth Symphony, New Yorkers, within a twelve-month period, will have been able to hear the last six symphonies and *Das Lied von der Erde.*

The Fifth also has been done by the Manhattan School of Music orchestra and Jonel Perlea, the Sixth by Leinsdorf with the Boston Symphony, and by Steinberg with the New York Philharmonic, *Das Lied* comes up in February with Ormandy, the problematic Tenth has been played under Arthur Bloom and Ormandy in two different editions, and most recently Bernstein gave his Philharmonic subscribers the Ninth, Seventh, and Eighth in three consecutive weeks and in that order.

Mahler himself played relatively little of his own music when he was at the Philharmonic; Mengelberg during the '20s did rather more. The activity in New York of Bruno Walter helped, of course, but the Mitropoulos years were more significant, especially because he went out of his way to give the little-known symphonies like the Third, the Sixth (which he introduced to America), and the Seventh. Now in Leonard Bernstein the Philharmonic has another convinced and able Mahler apostle.

Bernstein began his cycle with the Ninth, and I can imagine several reasons for the ordering of his performances. Having been away from the orchestra for some weeks he probably preferred to begin with something they know fairly well rather than with the unfamiliar and very difficult Seventh. And there was obvious reason for reserving the enormous Eighth, the so-called "Symphony of a Thousand," for the culmination of the series.

Still, when it was all over, I found myself wishing I could have heard the symphonies in their chronological order. The Ninth is so clearly the best of them. Leaving aside considerations of what Mahler's symphonies are about—and many people are unsympathetic to their content—the Ninth is that rare thing in Mahler, something that is achieved completely and with assurance. Its language is consistent, and it is economical because every one of its eighty or so minutes is dynamically used.

Bernstein's performance was impressive. His Mahler has been variable, going from a superb Third to an atrocious Fourth. The Ninth really worked well. When he took risks like the continually greater expansion of the upbeat in the first movement's main theme, they justified themselves. Only in the second movement did he begin, toward the end, to lose control of the tempi, and I was told he had not done so in the earlier performances (I heard the final one, in the Monday-night series).

The Burleske was first-rate, and it was especially impressive for the restraint with which all the *espressivo* in the middle section was managed, a restraint that allowed the mystery as well as the passion to come through. The Adagio was exceptionally well understood, though Bernstein succumbed to a slight impatience over the very long notes and the silences on the last page, something done better by the more literal-minded Szell.

The performance also demonstrated something that became increasingly evident in the other two symphonies, and that is the continuing and appalling deterioration of the Philharmonic. The playing was mostly loud, crude, and undifferentiated, and most of the solos were done with no distinction. The hoarse, unfocused noise that the violins offered on the last page in place of the *ppp* high A-flat that they could not even bother to try to find, spoke of the ultimate in demoralization. If one of Bernstein's missions when he was brought in after the de facto firing of Mitropoulos was to make the Philharmonic shipshape again, there is one area in which he has failed.

The concert was also the occasion for my first visit to Philharmonic Hall in its fourth edition, and while it is by no means the disaster it was at the beginning of its depressing history, it is a worse hall than anyone should have to put up with. It is now a sick caramel brown; the ceiling, which was always ugly, is now doubly irritating because the acoustic clouds are no longer functional; and the hall is no longer as comfortable to sit in since the installation of 182 additional seats, 118 of them in the orchestra.

The main thing, of course, is the continued acoustic failure. Players and conductors complain bitterly about not being able to hear on stage. As for the audience, while some of the worst problems like the total lack of bass response and the mysterious echoes have been eliminated, the music still sounds hollow, without bass solidity, with harsh treble, and hopelessly remote. It takes the loudest climaxes of the Mahler Eighth to achieve even a suggestion of music's physical impact.

Back to Mahler, then. The Seventh is the least familiar and the most problematic of the symphonies. It is also a particular favorite with many of those who take a Schoenberg's-eye-view of Mahler because in some ways it contains his most forward-looking music. It is, moreover, a work that caused Mahler particular trouble and one with which he seems to have remained dissatisfied.

It fills its great length less comfortably than the Ninth. Its five-movement structure resembles those of the Fifth and Tenth symphonies. The first movement is one of Mahler's marches, part funereal, part energetic, and it shows similarities to the first movement of the Sixth. The middle three movements form a block, a ghostly, quick scherzo surrounded by two "*Nachtmusiken*." The finale is an enormous rondo, something on the order of the finale in the Fifth, but somehow hypertrophied. It has swallowed too much *Meistersinger* for its own good, and I find its form bewildering and unconvincing.

I must add, however, that it made more sense in Bernstein's performance than it had when William Steinberg conducted it a few years ago and, as so often, attempted to solve the formal problem by leaving out a large part of the music.

The first movement is, however, an impressive design on a large scale, and the middle movements are probably Mahler's most adventurous music before the Tenth, with many entrancing ideas, breathtaking continuations, and fascinatingly scored. The attentive ear finds something arresting on every page, and the "night pieces" and scherzo are of unflawed mastery.

Bernstein conducted with magnificent sense of pace and design, with great verve, and also with restraint. The Philharmonic's playing was forceful and lively, but rough and badly lacking in refinement. Columbia will issue a recording.

Bernstein will record the Eighth also, but in London. For his New York performances, he used the Westminster Choir, the St. Kilian's Boychoir, and the following soloists: Saramae Endich as first soprano and Una poenitentium, Ella Lee as second soprano and Magna peccatrix, Ernestine Lazenby as Mater gloriosa, Jennie Tourel as first alto and Maria Aegyptiaca, Beverly Wolff as second alto and Mulier Samaritana, George Shirley as Doctor Marianus (tenor), John Boyden as Pater Ecstaticus (baritone), and Ezio Flagello as Pater Profundus (bass). Boyden was inadequate, though the singing of the extremely taxing parts was generally excellent, with Endich, Wolff, and Flagello especially fine.

To begin with one is impressed, and maybe overwhelmed also, by all the apparatus. The orchestration is lavish, too. Here Mahler comes closest to being the composer of massive effects that he has been wrongly reputed mainly to be, but even so the Symphony of a Thousand—actually about 400 at Bernstein's performances—is also a symphony of fastidiously crafted delicacy.

There are two movements, one a setting of the medieval "Veni creator spiritus," the other a setting of the last scene of Goethe's *Faust*, Part II, beginning after Mephistopheles' last lines with "*Waldung, sie schwankt heran*" ("Forests are swaying here").

Though there is an uninterrupted purely instrumental music only for a few minutes at the beginning of the second movement, one clearly hears the Eighth as a symphony, not as an oratorio, a pair of cantatas, or anything like that. The continuity, the motivic web, above all the astonishingly rich and daring harmonic design, all are entirely convincing and effective in the Eighth. The harmonic procedures often suggest those in the Seventh, in particular the wild slewing about from key to key, and given the failures in the earlier work and the successes in the later, I found it valuable to be able to hear both in close succession and in chronological order.

It is amazing, too, how uninhibited Mahler felt by the challenge of setting the end of *Faust*. The crucial places all work: the first choral entrance, the appearance of the Mater gloriosa, the hushed "*Alles Vergängliche*." The Maria Aegyptiaca passages have a special interest in the exactness with which they anticipate the orientalisms of *Das Lied von der Erde*, the jade pavilion movement in particular.

The whole *Faust* movement returns to the language of the finale of the Second, but with more control and freedom from strain. The immense gestures ring more true in the Eighth. And for all that much of the effect of the Eighth is not to be separated from its theatricality, the ultimate climax which, after all that has gone before, still sends you out of your skin, is something purely musical: the translation by the brass at the back of the hall of the E-flat–B-flat–A motive into E-flat–B-flat–C. From the first shout of "*Veni, veni*" in the second and third measures of the symphony, Mahler has worked for that moment, and the stretching of the upward seventh into a ninth is unbelievable in its power.

The Eighth, too, was excitingly done by Bernstein. It suffered from the hall, though, because obviously a lot of sound was being generated by singers and players (woodwinds and low strings especially) that just was not getting to row Q in the orchestra.

The whole experience of the three-week Mahler cycle was something to be profoundly grateful for. It was good to be able to hear the music at all, especially the rare Seventh and Eighth symphonies, good to hear it conducted with such musical intelligence and conviction, and especially good, even bearing in mind the hardship on an orchestra in far from first-rate condition, to get it on so concentrated a schedule.

Vishnevskaya Sings, Rostropovich Plays

December 21, 1965

The first half of the season ended in a blaze of glory Monday night when the Russian soprano Galina Vishnevskaya gave a Symphony Hall recital with her husband, Mstislav Rostropovich, at the piano. The program: eight Tchaikovsky songs, *The Poet's Echo* by Britten, and a Mussorgsky group with "Savishna, My Life" and the four *Songs and Dances of Death.*

Britten's cycle was written for Vishnevskaya and Rostropovich, and they introduced it to America only on Sunday afternoon in Philharmonic Hall, New York. It has six songs, all settings of Pushkin. In its musical vocabulary, especially in respect to a certain hardness in it, it suggested Britten's earlier Hardy cycle, *Winter Words.*

I do not know Russian, but Rostropovich has said that Britten's declamation of the poetry is perfect in aptness and sensibility. The program, incidentally, carried informative and evocative English translations by Peter Pears. The vocal part is sometimes lyrical, more often declamatory, and sometimes Purcellian in its use of special coloration, for example in the evocation of the nightingale's love song to the rose.

Britten's songs are unfailingly and imaginatively vocal, but half their life is in the piano part. The keyboard writing is texturally sparse, but the interplay of musical events and relationships created between it and the voice is complex. It is also beautifully suggestive in a pictorial sense, and while there is not a trick in it, the piano sound itself has been imagined with freshness and realized with virtuosic assurance.

It was a pleasure to hear Tchaikovsky's songs, all lovely, some very impressive indeed—"Why?," "If I had Known," and the more familiar "At a Noisy Ball" and "On Golden Cornfields"—though seven melancholy pieces in a row might be more effective if spread over the two halves of a program. The major key of the final and delightful "Serenade" at any rate came as a relief.

The performances were stunning. Vishnevskaya's ample soprano was lustrous, her phrasing and her ability to color the sound gave an extraordinary immediacy to everything she did. The performance was often dramatic as well as musical, most so in the great Mussorgsky cycle where the conviction behind what she evoked with face and body as well as with voice enabled her to take vast musical liberties, especially in distending tempi, and to make them completely persuasive.

Vishnevskaya is a beautiful woman, and when she is herself, acknowledging applause, she radiates glamour. She gives some songs as a pure poetic and musical experience, but she not only has an actress's personal power of projection, she has an actress's skill at seeming to change age, sex, shape of face, bodily structure, costume. She can use this to spectacular effect, as in the demonically seductive dance of Mussorgsky's "Trepak" or the insane swagger of "Field Marshal Death." She also uses it with marvelous quiet as the slow downward movement of the lifted arms and clasped hands continues "Lullaby" long after the music is over, just as she had done earlier with her special kind of physical illumination of the piano postlude of Tchaikovsky's "Why?"

1966

Beethoven—His Last Piano Sonata, Opus 111, Reconsidered

January 2, 1966

My mind keeps going back to Rudolf Serkin's beautiful playing four weeks ago, of Beethoven's last piano sonata, Opus 111.[1] In a way, I know the sonata well, and certainly I have spent much time with it, hearing performances, trying to play it myself, teaching it, reading it.

Not since Schnabel's performance about fifteen years ago at what I believe was his last New York recital have I felt so commanded to listen to it, neither has the experience revealed the work with such shocking clarity. More precisely, then, what my mind keeps returning to is Opus 111 itself.

Opus 111 was written in 1822 when Beethoven was 52. In the remaining five years of his life, he composed, among other things, the *Consecration of the House* Overture, the last piano Bagatelles, the *Diabelli* Variations, the Ninth Symphony, which had been in progress off and on since 1817, the *Missa solemnis*, in progress since 1818, and the five last string quartets. Beethoven died March 26, 1827.

For some time before Opus 111, Beethoven had tended to experiment with the formal externals of large-scale works. Trying to decide just when this began is bound to produce an arbitrary result. Even something as early as the G minor Cello Sonata of 1796 is quite unconventional, and one thinks, of course, of the smaller two-movement piano sonatas, Opus 54 in F (1804), Opus 78 in F-sharp (1809), Opus 90 in E minor (1814). Beginning with Opus 90 and with the two cello sonatas, Opus 102, completed the following year, special formal arrangements, with an unusual number of movements or an idiosyncratic ordering of them, become more frequent.

One thing, obviously, that troubled Beethoven was the problem of the finale, as indeed that was to be a difficulty for most 19th-century composers and for many in the 20th century as well. It was a problem, in a sense, of Beethoven's own creation because he really invented the idea of the finale-as-climax.

Traditionally, the center of gravity of a multi-movement piece had been in the first movement. The long and adventurous coda of the Second Symphony's

[1] See review of December 6, 1965.

finale shows at least a slight shift of balance, but even in the *Eroica* the old system is still essentially in force, though it is subjected to considerable strain by this vast finale and especially the triumphal "Poco Andante" variation.

It was the Fifth Symphony, with its spiritual progress "*per ardua ad astra*" from terse C minor battle to expansive C major victory, that changed the function and the meaning of the finale for good. Naturally, the kind of noisy public rhetoric of the finale in the Fifth would not do under all circumstances.

There is kinship between the Fifth Symphony and Opus 111. Both progress from C minor to C major. All Beethoven's C minor first movements have a certain pugnacious, fist-flailing mood in common, a mood that can yield great music as in both these works and which also can lead to something as cheap as the Violin Sonata, Op. 30, No. 2. And in the Piano Sonata as well as the Symphony, C major means victory—not without some crowing in the Symphony, and of sublime spiritual exaltation in the Sonata, and most reticently expressed there.

In Opus 111, the contrast between the externals of its two movements is extreme. In the first movement, from the initial downward plunge, E-flat to F-sharp, everything proceeds violently and by abruption. In the second, the events succeed one another in calm and order. Yet the second movement, an Arietta followed by three variations, a double variation, and a long coda, is by far the more adventurous and the sort of progression of thought whose conclusion is altogether unforeseeable from its beginnings.

Beethoven's composition of variations, that is, his discovery of the possibilities of the form, was an adventure that extended across his whole career. For Baroque composers, variations could be the vehicle for the most profound communication. In Haydn and Mozart, they are more often ornamental, an occasion, often, for all manner of loveliness, delight, or wit, but not the language of the deepest secrets.

Beethoven's own earlier variations continue the tradition of Haydn and Mozart, though there are stirrings, for example, in the piano variations on the "Prometheus" theme (1802) and in the set on the same theme in the *Eroica* the following year. Those in the E-flat String Quartet and the *Archduke* Trio (1811) represent further extensions. Then, beginning with the Piano Sonata in E major, Op. 109 (1820), Beethoven's exploring of variations becomes ever more remarkable. It becomes more frequent as well, and more and more something for him to rely on, in the Piano Sonata in A-flat, Opus 110, with its two arias and two fugues, in Opus 111, in the thirty-three *Diabelli* Variations, in the slow movements of the Ninth Symphony and of the string quartets in E-flat, Op. 127, A minor, Op. 132, C-sharp minor, Op. 131, F major, Op. 135, and in the "Great Fugue," Op. 133.

Among these, the second movement of Opus 111 is special because it is the variation set whose shell is the most rigid. The other series present a freer surface. Some use two themes (the Ninth and Opus 132), some have dramatic changes of pace and mood (Opus 109 and Opus 131), some plunge at length into remote keys (Opus 127).

Opus 111 is perhaps a special marvel among marvels because of its sense of flowering amid restraint. There is just one key change: in the tenth measure of the coda, the rapid figuration dissolves into a trill firmly on the dominant of C, but after two measures, E-flats and A-flats appear, until four simultaneous trills move the music onto the doorstep of E-flat. What happens here is in every way special: the chains of trills move the right hand higher and higher, then the left strikes in the extreme bass so that at the climax the two lone voices are separated by a gap of five-and-a-half octaves.

Then, as soon as the spacing becomes more normal, we hear a new kind of melody, a dialogue, rhythmically broken and a foreshadowing of the "*beklemmt*" ("straitened") episode in the Cavatina of Opus 130. And here Beethoven puts the first *espressivo* marking in the movement, in direct contrast to the "*molto semplice e cantabile*" at the beginning. And quickly, too, in less than a dozen bars, he returns to C major and to the kind of melody and figuration he had established as the norm for the movement.

Rhythmically, these variations are equally astonishing, and such variety of pace and tension is produced without any departure from the pulse of the original Arietta. In the first three variations, the principle is to get faster and faster, going from 8ths and 16ths to 32nds and 64ths—but in its effect what an advance over the old-fashioned "*doubles*" variations as we find them in the *Appassionata*. The fourth variation, with its syncopated chords over the throbbing bass, anticipates the "*espressivo*" passage in the coda. And later, there are the trill chains, the steady flow of 32nds, and at the very end the simple 8ths and 16ths of the opening.

Thomas Mann's discussion of Opus 111 in *Doctor Faustus* through the voice of the stuttering lecturer, Wendell Kretschmar, is at the very least debatable and in certain respects undeniably wrongheaded. It is also remarkably perceptive about Beethoven's relation to convention in his late music. Mann has Kretschmar say that:

> Beethoven had been far more "subjective," not to say far more "personal," in his middle period than in his last, far more bent on taking all the flourishes, formulas, and conventions, of which music is certainly full, and consuming them in the personal expression, melting them into the subjective dynamic. The relation of the later Beethoven to the conventional is . . . much more complaisant and easy-going. Untouched, untransformed by the subjective, convention often appeared in the late works, in a baldness, one might say exhaustiveness, an abandonment of self, with an effect more reckless and awful than any reckless plunge into the personal.

In Opus 111, the relation between the content of the music and the language used to express it is singularly direct. J. W. N. Sullivan in his *Beethoven, His Spiritual Development*, writes of the late piano sonatas as giving us "more than glimpses of a new state of being as revealed in a music utterly unlike any other music."

Part of its utter unlikeness in Opus 111 resides in the mysteriously sovereign relation Beethoven assumes toward the most conventional components of the musical language. His writing is a serenely exalted conquest of language, and it is the externalization of the music's inner content, the culmination of a spiritual development without parallel in the arts.

Martinon Conducts BSO in Beautiful *Eroica*

January 22, 1966

Jean Martinon's second program with the Boston Symphony, played in Symphony Hall on Friday afternoon, was thoroughly absorbing and successful. He conducted his own *Overture to the Greek Tragedy*, Hindemith's Concert Music for String Orchestra and Brass Instruments, and Beethoven's *Eroica* Symphony.

Martinon's Overture now leads an independent life as a concert piece, though it was originally composed in 1949 as the second-act prelude to his Euripides opera *Hecube*. It is a fluent piece of eclectic writing, reminiscent of Honegger, and with just a few things like the opening roar of the tam-tam that sounded a bit like a film score by Maurice Jarré. The performance seemed excellent.

Hindemith's Concert Music, commissioned by the Boston Symphony for its golden anniversary in 1930, is full of energy and life. Intended to display the flexibility and strength of a great orchestra, it did so as persuasively this week under Martinon as it must have under Koussevitzky thirty-five years ago.

Then came the *Eroica*. It started well, in that Martinon, by establishing the tempo immediately, actually made the first two chords part of the piece instead of setting them off as a pompous exordium. It was a good tempo—"allegro with fire," just as Beethoven asks—and here, as again in the scherzo and finale, it was a great pleasure to hear the music move at a real Allegro again instead of the heavy breathing Andantes that have become so prevalent.

Unlike Leinsdorf, who doubles the woodwinds in the Beethoven symphonies to match the weight of the modern large string band, Martinon used only the pairs of flutes, oboes, clarinets, and bassoons as actually specified in the score. Then he proceeded to scale down the string playing so as properly to match the slightened wind sounds. Balances were impeccable throughout, and at times, for example the lead-back to the first movement recapitulation and other places in the second and fourth movements, they were unprecedentedly clear and revealing.

The large and significant result was that it produced quite a new kind of *Eroica*, or rather, one that I imagine must come very close to that of 1805. At least, what came across to my ears was a composition of heroic gestures as that idea would have been understood at the threshold of the 19th century.

From the point of view of the time element, the *Eroica* is a very large and very grand work indeed. It is not, however, a very loud one, and its sonority, eleven winds with the addition of a third horn, is that of a classical symphony. By clarifying this so effectively, Martinon was able to make the dynamic climaxes uncommonly telling. Within such a framework, the climax in the C major section of the funeral march sounded like a bigger and more meaningful event than it often does when conductors try to blow it up to *Götterdämmerung* proportions, something that Beethoven's scoring simply resists. Again, the same thing was true of the highpoints reached by the finale's slower variations.

Sforzandi and other accents were never feeble, but they were always kept to the minimum weight at which they could be functional. The force of Martinon's performance came from its rhythm. It was always sharp and vital, giving tensile power to the phrasing of the melodies of the funeral march, producing an electric scherzo, and making the variations wonderfully buoyant.

Martinon, incidentally, is one of the few conductors who believes that measures 20 through 27 in the finale should be bowed by the strings rather than plucked, something I cannot find convincing in performance. I do not believe that we now stand in need of a great reform movement to bring in this style of Beethoven playing. Nevertheless, however much Beethoven's music looks forward to Brahms and Wagner, most of it was written in a language much closer to that of Haydn and Mozart, and it was fine to hear a performance that combined historic and musical perceptions so well. I learned much from Martinon's *Eroica* and found it fresh and exciting. It was a performance that was finely proportioned, thoroughly consistent within itself, and for these reasons beautiful.

Beautiful Playing by a Legendary Pianist

January 25, 1966

NEW YORK—Arturo Benedetti Michelangeli's Carnegie Hall recital last Friday showed why the press agents are right when they call him legendary.

There is, of course, no getting away from all the extramusical elements. Michelangeli rarely plays in public and there are very few recordings. Carnegie was sold out and had apparently become so practically by virtue of a single advertisement in the Sunday papers a couple of months ago.

There is his own vivid presence, tall enough to fill the vertical space of the stage door, all but gaunt, with long, lank, rust-colored hair. There is always a wait after the door opens before he appears, and another while, hands clasped in front of him, he coldly surveys the audience before bowing. There is, for that matter, the tuner who was on stage until about 8:45 (in shirt-sleeves) and again all during the long intermission (in a jacket).

When Michelangeli sits down to play, though, there is nothing egotistical. His performances are personal, even idiosyncratic, but when he is working, no part of the operation is intended to draw the attention from composer to performer. Except perhaps for Schnabel and Hess, I think I have never seen a pianist sit so still. Maybe four times during the course of the evening, a hand would rise to shoulder level, but most of the time, to look at him from the elbows up, one might have supposed him to be playing *Für Elise*.

What he actually played was Busoni's setting of the Bach Chaconne, Beethoven's C minor Sonata, Op. 111, both sets of Debussy's *Images*, and the Chopin *Berceuse* and B-flat minor Scherzo.

I have always supposed that when Busoni himself played the Chaconne it must have sounded like Bach. It does when Michelangeli plays it, though with other pianists this arrangement sounds like a meretricious inflation, a mindless orgy of octaves. It was Romantic Bach, to be sure, but noble, eloquent, coherent, and with Busoni's Liszt-plus piano writing clearly to be understood as a translation, both beautiful and faithful, of Bach's violin writing.

I would suppose Michelangeli's technique to be unparalleled today. He plays fewer wrong notes than other pianists, though that is not so important or interesting in itself. What does count is the control that makes it possible for him to play everything beautifully. The coloristic resource is astounding: the great D major moment in the Chaconne, for example, was marvelous for being introduced with a tone that was not just new within that particular performance, but which also gave the illusion of being one that one had never heard on a piano before at all.

Control of dynamics, of the weight of the notes within a chord, or of the successive notes in brilliant passage-work, these things are glorious. Octaves go beyond even one's best usual praise; they did not sound merely as easy and smooth, as elegantly phrased as single notes, they were like some sort of a dream of octaves.

Michelangeli's musical ideas are not necessarily convincing. His performance of Beethoven's Opus 111, for instance, is at once mysteriously cool and sentimentally pathetic. What he did on Friday was both more or less successful than what can be heard on his recent London record: details of phrasing were sometimes distended to the point of fussiness, but on the other hand, Variation II was now clearly integrated rather than disrupting the flow with a much slower tempo.

When the Debussy group began, I had the impression that like most pianists, Michelangeli was more concerned with atmosphere and texture than with line and rhythm, though with his own special skill and refinement. Then, with the last two pieces, the other dimension was added: "Et la lune descend sur le temple qui fut" was marvelously evocative and an extraordinarily complete performance in every way, and the playfulness and vitality of movement in "Poissons d'or" was enchanting.

His Chopin was extravagant, with tremendous rubato and some tricky dynamics. This was the music in which he took the greatest risks, as it were, but it was clear here as elsewhere that no matter what, his playing is always musical in that the stresses and proportions unfailingly remain right.

It is also unfailingly seductive, something that perhaps stems from a technique so extraordinary that it is in itself extraordinarily beautiful. The inability always to agree with him became irrelevant. The combination, in Michelangeli, of technique, taste, an active mind, compelling personal force, add up to something almost entirely new in my experience.

Michelangeli goes beyond merely playing better than other pianists. He has the magic that, in spite of any reservations, sets a Caruso, a Chaliapin, a Callas, a Fonteyn, a Nijinsky, a Nureyev, apart in their generations.

Globe Critic Recommends [Stravinsky's *Rite of Spring*]

February 13, 1966

Stravinsky's "Rite of Spring" as recorded by the French Orchestre National, Pierre Boulez conducting (Nonesuch 1093/71093).

The two concerts Boulez conducted with the BBC Symphony in New York last May, plus what one could learn in rehearsal about how the results were achieved, showed the 40-year-old composer to be the greatest of living conductors. His performance of the *Rite* is quite different from Stravinsky's own marvelous one (Columbia). It is not so massive, its impact is sharp rather than weighty, its movement is more supple (more Debussian?), and it seems swifter even though it actually takes about a minute longer. Its most astounding attribute is its transparence. Constantly one hears things never heard before. It is not fussy exposure of intrinsically unimportant detail: rather the extreme clarity of the texture and its changes brings the rhythm of the music into unprecedentedly sharp relief. That helps make Boulez's the most exciting performance of *Rite of Spring* ever recorded. The record is filled out by Stravinsky's Four Etudes, delightful transcriptions of the Three Pieces for String Quartet, and of the pianola piece, *Madrid*. Nonesuch is a low-price label, and in spite of a somewhat unspacious recorded sound, this record must be one of the best buys ever offered the American public.

Neglected Masterpiece—Schumann's Interpretation of Goethe's *Faust* Tragedy

February 20, 1966

For his wife Clara, Robert Schumann's *Scenes from Goethe's "Faust"* was a work that would "one day take its place among the very greatest of all." Liszt admired it. Bernard Shaw clamored for performance of it, and referred to Part II as a "summit of Schumann's achievement." Much of the popular Schumann literature, on the other hand, ignores or dismisses it. Listeners have had no chance to find out for themselves. A performance I heard Hans Rosbaud conduct thirteen years ago must have been one of the very few complete ones anywhere in my lifetime. Not a note is available on records. There is cause, therefore, to be grateful to Erich Leinsdorf for putting the *Scenes from Goethe's "Faust"* on the next Friday–Saturday pair of Boston Symphony concerts.[2]

Schumann first made some sketches for what he evidently meant as a *Faust* opera when he went with Clara on a concert tour of Russia from January to May, 1844. He was then about to become 34. In the next few years he was much plagued by physical ill health and by depression, and he composed little. In the spring and summer of 1847 he wrote what is now Part III of his *Faust-Scenes*. During the second half of 1848 and early in 1850 he added to his score, completing it with the Overture in the fall of 1853.

Schumann seems to have changed his mind quite early about the proper format for his *Faust* music. One of the things, interestingly enough, that interrupted its composition was *Genoveva*, the only operatic project he was ever to complete. The following is an outline of the *Scenes from Goethe's "Faust"* as they now stand:

An Overture and Part I, consisting of three scenes from Part I of Goethe's play: the Garden Scene between Faust and Margareta, including a few lines of farewell from the following Summer House scene; Margareta's soliloquy at the shrine of the Mater Dolorosa; Margareta and the Evil Spirit in the Cathedral.

Part II, also in three divisions: the opening scene with the sunrise from Part II of Goethe's play; the Midnight scene from Part II, Act V, with Faust and the four

[2] See next article.

hags, Want, Guilt, Need, and Sorrow; the next scene, Great Outer-Court of the Palace, with Faust's death.

Part III, divided into seven connected movements, consists of Goethe's final scene, Mountain-Gorges, Forest, Rock, Wilderness, beginning "*Waldung, sie schwankt heran*" ("Forests are waving here") and set in its entirety.

Schumann's scenario is strange in a number of ways. It has no complete continuity of its own. Rather, for the filling out of the selected scenes into a fully coherent scheme, the participation of the listener is required. Schumann's ideal listener, moreover, is one who has read *Faust* well, both parts.

Then, Schumann avoids Goethe's most obvious invitations to music. There is no Auerbach's Cellar with its "Song of the Flea," no "King in Thule" ballad, no "Gretchen at the Spinning-Wheel," no "Walpurgis Night's Dream," no floral pageant (Part II, Act 1, iii) with its choruses of gardeners and flower-girls.

Not least, Schumann's concern with Part II of Goethe's tragedy is itself noteworthy, especially in historical context. Goethe began *Faust* in 1773 as a young man of 24. He finished Part I, the Gretchen tragedy, in 1801, and published it in 1808, having added and altered a few things. In 1806, Goethe spoke of Part II as "not yet all written, but composed." By the end of 1831 it was at last "all written," though it was still being critically scrutinized by Goethe up to within weeks of his death in March 1832.

It is now one of our received ideas to regard *Faust* as one of the most exalted achievements in Western literature, and German readers in particular hold it in a kind reverence for which Anglo-American literary attitudes offer no parallel. When it was new, however, Part II was deemed unintelligible, an arbitrary and inorganic addition to the familiar and popular Part I, the oddly hermetic preoccupations of an old man, something to not be taken quite seriously. It is also worth remembering that when Schumann made his first *Faust* sketches, not quite twelve years had passed since the posthumous publication of Goethe's Part II, and the play had been only twenty-one years before the public when the composer finished his music. When Schumann set the great final scene with the Holy Anchorites, it was not an awesomely regarded classic: it was a highly controversial piece of contemporary poetry, newer than say Pound's *Pisan Cantos* are today, and at least as problematic.

In an essay called "Schumann as an Interpreter of Goethe's *Faust*" to which this article is much indebted, Donald Mintz points out how much the "vulnerability of the *Faust* music was heightened" by contemporary attitudes to Part II of the play. If, however, insistence on Part II created problems for the acceptance of this music, his quick realization of the musical possibilities in Goethe's work constitute a most audacious stroke of the imagination.

Much of Goethe's writing in *Faust* II is thoroughly operatic, deliberately so. He loved and admired Mozart's *Magic Flute*: it was the most performed opera during his year as theater director at Weimar. More important still, off and on during the 1790s he worked on a continuation of the *Magic Flute* libretto, abandoning it when he realized that neither Zelter nor anyone else was a Mozart who could adequately compose it, but rescuing some of the fragment for Act III of *Faust* II.

Schumann's calling was not for the theater, but he understood, and beautifully realized, the musical challenge in Goethe's finale. His setting, beginning with the unobtrusive processional quality in the quiet polyphony at the opening, is a glorious achievement. It is less vividly detailed than Mahler's in the Eighth Symphony, and at one point I feel that as a loss, namely when Schumann runs together into a simultaneously declaimed trio the verses of Magna Peccatrix, Mulier Samaritana, and Maria Aegyptiaca, while Mahler gives to each a solo variation that makes the three women as sharply characterized as Balanchine's muses in *Apollo*.

One of Schumann's finest moments, on the other hand, is his "*Wer immer strebend sich bemüht, Den können wir erlösen!*" ("For he whose strivings never cease/Is ours for his redeeming") with its solo voices detaching themselves in rising scales from the choral texture. Mahler omits the angelic chorus containing that passage, which is odd because for Goethe that was the passage "in which the key to Faust's salvation was contained." Also, Schumann's composition of the very last lines, quiet and becoming ever more spacious, is more profoundly satisfying than anyone else's.

In what precedes these moments there are beautiful examples of deep insight on Schumann's part and of marvelous musical imagination: the blinding sunrise, the ghostly entrance of the four hags, the clash of spades as the mocking Lemures prepare for Faust's burial.

Faust the play occupied its creator's far-ranging, well-stocked, and complicated mind, for sixty years, and from that the composer selected scenes in a way that was frankly subjective, even idiosyncratic, and "difficult." Schumann's scenes may not ever be destined for a very wide popularity, but it is high time that we look seriously at what is certainly one of the noblest moments in 19th-century music.

To conclude, I should like to endorse emphatically the recommendation repeatedly made in recent Boston Symphony program notes that you should read Goethe's whole *Faust* before listening to Schumann's.

Schumann *Faust-Scenes* Are Sublime Experience

February 26, 1966

Symphony Hall was nearly a third empty on Friday afternoon. The weather was difficult, and there is a certain Symphony-audience allergy to choral music and the unfamiliar. Those who stayed away missed something wonderful: a beautiful performance of Schumann's *Scenes from Goethe's "Faust."* Those who were there had no doubt about the nature of the occasion: it is rare to find such rapt attention during a Friday-afternoon concert and such prolonged and warm applause and cheering afterwards. Moreover, no one walked out. Here's to more snowstorms!!

Schumann's *Faust* music is a masterpiece, one of the 19th century's very great ones. If you look it up in the standard reference works, you find contempt, condemnation, condescension, stemming mostly from ignorance of the score and from writers' tendency to copy from each others' books.

It is a difficult work, one that demands attention and generously repays preparation. Schumann has set three scenes from Part I of Goethe's tragedy—the first Faust-Gretchen love scene, Gretchen before the Mater Dolorosa, the Cathedral scene—but concentrates on Part II, its opening, the scenes of Faust's blinding and of his death, the entire final scene.

Some of what Schumann does is puzzling. To succumb to a critical commonplace, he was not a born theater man. While in the Cathedral scene, for example, he used the language of the second *Don Giovanni* finale with skill, he also muffs the timing from Gretchen's final "*Nachbarin! Euer Fläschchen!*" and the lines from the Dies irae that follow. There are often instances of strange text setting, of a running together of lines that deprives them of effect and sometimes almost of intelligibility.

But it is Schumann's successes that remain in the memory: the lovely lyric writing in the Garden scene; the sinister fear so well expressed in the behind-the-attacks at the beginning of the Cathedral scene; more of the beautiful lyric writing for Ariel and the dazzling sunrise; the rushing about of muted violins and plucked low strings for the Midnight scene of the four hags, Care, Need, Want, Guilt; the sense of musical tempo in Faust's growing ecstasy before his death and the chorale-like postlude to that scene.

Goethe's greatest moment becomes Schumann's also: the final scene. Rhythms are handled surely and the melodies are inspired, the whole range of them from the folk song symmetries of the angelic choruses to the subtleties of the Chorus Mysticus.

Schumann had the quality of simplicity, and that made it possible for him to compose a great setting for this poetry. Mahler, too, conveys the mystery of the chorus that sets and describes the scene ("*Waldung, sie schwankt heran*"); only Schumann rises to that part of the poem that resides in the stunning simplicity of Goethe's words and images, such a thing, for instance, as the picture of the silent and friendly lions slinking about.

The editorial problems in the performance of any Schumann work with orchestra are complex and inevitably some of the solutions are debatable. Leinsdorf as editor tends to be bold. His loyalty is to Goethe and he does not shrink from the acts of minor re-composition called for in restoring the original "*Hier ist's getan*" in place of the corrupt and obviously inferior "*Hier ist es getan*," or from restoring a line into Ariel's song that Schumann forgot to set. There were considerable orchestral retouchings, mostly useful, though some produced a brightness Schumann might not have liked and there were some places that still had insufficient punch (the end of the Overture and of the Midnight scene). More significantly, I question Leinsdorf's judgment in placing the intermission between Midnight and Faust's death, rather than following Schumann's division that makes of the finale, Faust's Redemption, a discrete entity, a solution that would be more effective in the most superficial sense as well as in a more profound one. There were also rather arbitrary decisions that created the special effect of an *a cappella* chorus where Schumann had intended none and that, even more oddly, took the chorus out of a couple of pages, leaving only the orchestral doublings.

The performance was all-in-all splendid, and Leinsdorf paced it well and led it energetically. He had a superb cast of singers, including Hermann Prey as Faust (also Pater Seraphicus and Dr. Marianus), Thomas Paul as Mephistopheles (also Pater Profundus), and Beverly Sills as Gretchen. Excellent in smaller roles were Charles Bressler (Ariel, Pater Ecstaticus), Tatiana Troyanos (Need, Magna Peccatrix), Florence Kopleff (Want, Mulier Samaritana), and the gifted young Batyah Godfrey (Guilt, Maria Aegyptiaca), while Veronica Tyler (Care) seems to be having problems of technique that keep her from realizing the potential of her beautiful and her excellent musical and dramatic intentions.

There was good choral singing from the New England Conservatory Chorus, Lorna Cooke deVaron, director, the Harvard Glee Club and Radcliffe Choral Society, Elliot Forbes, director, and the impressive though dynamically inflexible St. Gabriel's Boychoir, Edward Boagni, director. Except for the out-of-tune solo strings in the Pater Ecstaticus area and too many bad oboe and clarinet solos, the orchestra played well.

Webern and Isaac—Club 47 Concert Turns to Classics

February 28, 1966

The concerts at Club 47 in Cambridge have usually been devoted to the most recent music, but this Sunday afternoon the directors turned to the classics, Anton Webern and Heinrich Isaac.

There is, of course, a connection between the two. As a young man, Webern earned his doctorate in musicology with a dissertation and also edited a volume of Isaac's music for the "Monuments of Music in Austria" series. If that were all, putting pieces by the Flemish Renaissance master on a Webern program would still be little more than an academic in-group gag. It is not all, though, because Webern's interest in the works of the great polyphonic era was musical as well as historical, and the juxtaposition of the two musics was intended to show one of the less familiar sources of Webern's style and technique.

The program was introduced by John Harbison, the director of the Club 47 concerts, and a young man who wears his learning and his seriousness with grace and humor. Harbison specifically pointed to the intricate relating of parts, the sparing use of material, the preference for non-dramatic formal design and for polyphony, especially canon, as characteristic of Webern's music as well as of Isaac's.

Three instrumental works by Isaac, played by four strings, were followed by Webern's String Quartet, Op. 28, and it did indeed turn out that the earlier pieces were ideal ear-sharpeners for the later ones. Webern's earlier quartet works, the Five Pieces and the Bagatelles, begin to assume the status of standard repertory; the Opus 28 Quartet, written in 1939, remains little known. Unlike those earlier works, it is by no means a character piece. Its beauty is that of perfect design and poise, infused with a delicacy that knows nothing of preciousness, and with charm.

The Three Pieces for Cello and Piano, Op. 11, go back to 1914, and they represent Webern at his most astonishingly compressed and intense. A highly dramatic expression is here subjected to an exciting control and discipline. By comparison the Four Pieces for Violin and Piano, Op. 7, written in 1910, seem lavishly expansive in the articulation of their poetic, often mysterious, content.

After this the program returned to the later, more abstract Webern of the Piano Variations, Op. 27 (1939). As in the Quartet, canon serves precision, precision serves poetry. Partly because of the clear perception underlying Martin Boykan's performance, but also because of the three-directional bearing we could now take on the piece—from Isaac, from early Webern, from a parallel piece of late Webern—listening to the Variations, often so perplexing, was this time an experience both rich and lucid.

And then the program returned to its beginnings, a different set of three especially fine Isaac pieces, and another and mostly finer performance of the String Quartet, it too clarified by the context so intelligently created for it.

Besides Martin Boykan, already mentioned, the following musicians were responsible for the perceptive, carefully prepared, and vivaciously executed performances: Rose Mary Harbison and Bentley Layton, violins, John Harbison, viola and piano, and Helen Harbison, cello.

At Old Opera House Farewell—Few Stars Among Met's "Ensemble of Stars"

April 24, 1966

It may be that music and singing were not really the issue at the Gala Farewell at the old Metropolitan Opera House on April 16. Glamour and sentiment played large roles that evening. Nevertheless, I was listening and I find I cannot stop thinking about what I heard.

If one had to confine one's comments to a single remark, it would be fair to say with Harold Schonberg of the *New York Times* that the display of the fifty-seven singers involved showed the general decline of the standards of singing.

Some performances gave real pleasure. Jon Vickers sang "Winterstürme" from *Walküre* lyrically and with warmth. Régine Crespin, in a ghastly duet from *Gioconda* that she sang with the excellent Biserka Cvejić, was impressive for the tremendous power, brilliance, and energy of what she did. Leontyne Price sang "D'amor sull'ali rosee" from *Trovatore* with vocal purity and aristocratic musicianship.

In a less well-bred way, Corelli—but especially Tebaldi—did a superbly effective performance of a duet from *Manon Lescaut.* Nilsson, I think, sang well in the *Götterdämmerung* finale, but a singer cannot carry it alone and she was hampered by [Joseph] Rosenstock's stodgy conducting. Judith Raskin sounded beautiful in the *Rosenkavalier* Trio, while Gabriella Tucci and Nicolai Gedda did their parts of the *Faust* Trio very well.

The dominant impression left by the evening was that here was a stage full of people who did not really know how to sing. I am not referring now to artistry, to taste and musicianship, but simply to the ability to produce sounds of pure and steady tone, evenly, on pitch, smoothly connected when appropriate, at whatever volume the singer decided, and with clearly audible words.

The concert began with the *Lucia* Sextet. It is dominated by three voices, and the baritone, William Walker, was certainly competent. The desperately and tensely shouting and quavery tenor's presence at the Met speaks only for the universal tenor shortage. But what really troubled me was the soprano Anna Moffo, unsteady, unfocused, with little carrying power. What I have heard of Moffo's new *Lucia* recording suggests that what I heard at the Met was not just the result of a temporary condition. Moreover, I remember Moffo's singing just a very few years ago as being vocally beautiful—on the Angel *Bohème* with Callas, for example—and she is only about 32.

Young singers in trouble are distressing. There was a vivid reminder in the presence as one of the honored guests at the Met gala of Patrice Munsel who quit the company in 1957 at age 33 with her voice a wreck.

Cesare Siepi and Giorgio Tozzi, both 43, sang with colorless and muffled voices of hoarse old men, and Siepi had to strain to stay in pitch in the upper register and even so did not always make it. Fernando Corena, a little younger than they, specializes in *buffo* roles that involve a little legato singing, but he too sounded painfully strained in the finale of Cornelius's *Der Barbier von Bagdad.*

These are people with inadequate techniques. There have been singers who have early damaged their voices, but who have managed to stop in time to do rehabilitative repair work.

When Tebaldi, then about 40, left the Met in mid-season a few seasons ago, there were fears she was finished. The luscious warmth that once gave her voice its unique sensuous beauty is gone and so, I gather, are the very high notes, but at the Gala her voice was under control, powerful, handsome in every way, and also perfectly on pitch, which is something the young Tebaldi had never managed. Not only that, Tebaldi looked marvelous, and it was pleasant to have proof that a singer who loses weight does not have to spoil her voice.

Price, now in her late 30s, was another singer in severe trouble a few years ago. The bloom that her young voice had is gone, but otherwise her work at the gala had every attribute of first-rate singing. I was also impressed with Corelli. When he first came to the Met in 1961 at 37, he always sounded as though on the point of bursting a blood vessel, but he no longer does.

Some of the older singers acquitted themselves well. Milanov at 60 sounded better than some younger colleagues, and on the whole she is no more undependable now than when I first heard her over twenty years ago. Peerce is close to 60, and while his voice is less robust than it was, it is true and steady. Tucker at 51 was, with Vickers, vocally the best tenor in the house. From the fairly recent past, I recall a beautiful Hans Sachs by the 65-year-old [Paul] Schoeffler, not to mention the clarity, brightness, and magnificence of Flagstad's voice at 58 and 60. Lotte Lehmann gave up opera at 57, but her voice was still outstandingly beautiful when she quit the recital stage at 62.

These were and are busy singers. It is true that the speed at which one can now zip around from New York to Vienna to Buenos Aires to Milan makes it easy to become too busy. It takes sense and foresight to resist vanity and greed. The same factors, combined with the shortage of good singers, push people into roles too heavy for them. Violettas sing Aida, Elsas sing Isolde. Such a development often takes place naturally, but it must do so at its own pace. Hurrying nature is bad—cf. one of those nasty, tasteless, hypodermically cured hams—and it works havoc with the singing voice.

In the so-called Golden Age, there were plenty of outstandingly successful singers with no sense and no taste, but most of them could sing. A crude shouter like Robert Merrill, with no soft tones and no command of legato, might have found work at the Met, but he is not likely to have been mistaken for a very good singer. In his speech at the Gala, Rudolf Bing called the Met company an "ensemble of stars." There were few stars.

The evening's most ambitious ensemble effort, the Triumphal Scene from *Aida*, displayed such mediocrities as [Mary] Curtis-Verna, [Jean] Madeira, and [Kurt] Baum; furthermore it seemed to be unrehearsed and nearly fell apart because the conductor, [Zubin] Mehta, was not only glamorous, but erratic, undisciplined, willful, and vain.

The Met, then, offers the good, the adequate, and the bad, all jumbled together, but claiming all of it is good. The public applauds, and it often applauds things more than they deserve. It was interesting, though, that at the Gala, when one could hear so many people—not merely [Sándor] Kónya but Kónya in the context of Vickers, for example—the public tended fairly consistently to discriminate in favor of the better performance.

Globe Critic Recommends [Mahler Symphony No. 4]

May 1, 1966

Mahler's Symphony No. 4 in G, as recorded by George Szell and the Cleveland Orchestra with Judith Raskin as soprano soloist (Columbia 6223/6833).

This is easily the finest recording of this gently humorous and lyric symphony, and with the exception of a broadcast with Britten conducting the London Symphony, it is the best performance of it I have ever heard. Szell's approach is deliberately anti-sentimental but the performance is marvelously songful, rhythmically alive, and with the fantastic play of textures realized not just precisely but with deep imaginative insight. As in any Szell performance in any kind of repertory, there are a couple of oddly arbitrary touches, an excessively pointed phrase here, a needlessly stressed articulation there, and a curious moment (III, m. 255) where he hurries in exactly the measure where Mahler says not to, but this time these are trivial details that hardly mar a conception of integrity and actual playing of exceptional beauty. In the song that is the symphony's finale, Raskin is beyond praise, for the vocal loveliness of her singing as well as for the unaffected rightness of style.

The Oratorio—Music for Voice

May 8, 1966

Oratorio has never been a really popular sort of indulgence here, and the audience in America for Elgar's *The Dream of Gerontius* is always going to be a special one: Anglophiles of a certain Edwardian stamp, choral enthusiasts (who are few), Elgar buffs (whose number is growing), and doubtless some who are attracted by the fragrance of Cardinal Newman's grand and occasionally clumsy poem about the journey of a soul from earth to purgatory.

Gerontius is a problem piece: there is a lot of slow music, holiness sometimes leads to stasis, the demons sound funny (I bet they did to a lot of people in 1900, too). It is not, then, a complete masterpiece like *Falstaff*, the First Symphony, the *Enigma* Variations, but flawed though it may be, *Gerontius* is a masterful and largely inspired work just the same.

Its very sound is magnificent, sumptuous, but never thick. It has glorious melodies, and certain of its passages place it surely among the greatest religious compositions: the death of Gerontius (from "I can no more" to the end of Part I), the song of the Angel of the Agony, the Angel's final "Softly and gently," are a few of them.

Angel now offers a new recording of the work, good, but not quite as good as its earlier one (3660, two records). Barbirolli's best conducting is eloquent, but he is given to overdoing things rather.

The Gerontius is Richard Lewis, a technically insecure singer, but so expressive that his performance is a great one just the same. Janet Baker, her voice a brighter sister of Ferrier's, is wonderful as the Angel. Kim Borg is dull, muffled, stiff as the Priest and the Angel of the Agony.

The Hallé Orchestra plays very well, and the singing of the Hallé Choir, the Sheffield Philharmonic Choir, and the Ambrosian Singers is beyond praise. If, however, you have the older recording (Sargent, Lewis, Thomas, Cameron), you have a superior one that you should not give up.

Goldberg by Leonhardt

May 15, 1966

One of the first recordings the Dutch harpsichordist Gustav Leonhardt made was of Bach's *Goldberg* Variations. He was very young then, and the record, still available on Vanguard, probably did much to hold back his reputation here, and he himself now describes it as "atrocious."

My own experience was that, when a friend urged me to go to hear Leonhardt play at the Union Theological Seminary in New York in the summer of 1961, I was not in the least bit interested because of the *Goldbergs* and some other records I had heard. I finally went anyway and realized at once that what Leonhardt was capable of by then was not merely harpsichord playing unlike any I had ever heard, but keyboard playing that was among the greatest being done.

I offer the preamble lest anyone who knows the early Leonhardt records is properly skeptical of my recommendation of Leonhardt's new recording of the *Goldberg* Variations as one of the greatest things ever put on a disc (Telefunken SAWT 9474-A). It is that, something altogether wonderful, and the only other *Goldberg* recording at all in the same class is the first one by Landowska (not available now and on no account to be confused with her later gigantesque caricature still available on RCA Victor).

The theme gives you a perfect example of Leonhardt's best playing: the broad architectures of melody (hear especially the four measures leading up to the double bar and the last eight measures), the fancifully realized ornaments, the powerful support given by the grandly sustained bass. Its flexibility is one of the great merits of Leonhardt's playing.

It was Landowska's merit to establish that Bach should not be stiff in performance, but the plasticity of her own early playing led to the spastic exaggerations of her own later work and its intolerable imitations by two subsequent generations of harpsichordists.

The flexibility one hears from Leonhardt, the breathing, singing, dancing it suggests is something else altogether. Nor is there ever any mere clatter in Leonhardt's playing. In most performances, Var. 28 with its trills and Var. 29 with its alternating triads in the two hands, usually make a horrible noise. Leonhardt always phrases, and there is no musical or technical negligence, nor any misunderstanding about the nature of virtuosity, to lead him into merely percussive playing.

Perhaps the most revealing detail of all is the alternating-hand triplet figuration in Var. 29, beginning at measure 9, again after the double bar, again in measure 27, where, instead of the usual dry toccata style, we hear sinuous Baroque curves of exciting grandeur. The chromatics in that variation (mm. 25–26) and in the preceding one (mm. 25–30) come out beautifully, too, because Leonhardt with his skill in articulation can make them expressive without disrupting the flow of the larger line.

It is not only that Leonhardt's musical understanding is superior: he plays the harpsichord better than other people. Virtuosity in the ordinary sense can be taken for granted, but his playing is so exciting because of the variety in touch and articulation. His registrations are restrained and elegant, yet this is much the most colorful *Goldberg* performance I know. The simple writing of Var. 19 is a good example and the double keyboard brilliance of Var. 20 a stunning one, and when it comes to playing sustained melody, Leonhardt's performance of Var. 13 is an unforgettable lesson in eloquent articulation.

Leonhardt has said that a superior player must be able to give a good recital even on a Pleyel; just the same, part of the pleasure in his new *Goldberg* record comes from the instrument. It is one built in 1962–63 by Martin Skowroneck of Bremen, the only one of the European builders to compare with the best Americans, and it is modeled on a 1745 harpsichord by the Antwerp builder J. D. Dulcken. It is a beautifully balanced instrument: bright yet sweet, clear, and with superb sustaining power in the bass, an important quality for the *Goldbergs* which are built from the bass up.

Leonhardt also heads an ensemble called the Quadro Amsterdam, whose other members are the flutist and recorder player Frans Brüggen, the violinist Jaap Schröder, and the cellist Anner Bylsma.

Together with the violinist Marie Leonhardt and the flutist Frans Vester they have recorded two of François Couperin's suites from the series he called *Les Nations*: No. 1, "La Française" and No. 3, "L'Impériale." They represent Couperin's essays at joining the Italian manner to the French by appending a series of French dance movements to a Corellian sonata. "L'Impériale" is an especially marvelous piece, and both works are given beautifully played, sensitive, imaginative, and somewhat low-pressure performances (Telefunken SAWT 9476-A).

Brüggen is the conductor, Schröder the concertmaster, and Leonhardt the continuo player, of the Concerto Amsterdam, a first-rate ensemble that has now completed the third and final installment of Telemann's *Musique de Table* (Telefunken SAWT 9453-4-A). *Musique de Table* III consists of a suite for oboes and strings, a quartet for flute, violin, cello, and continuo, a concerto for two horns, a trio for recorders and continuo, a sonata for oboe and continuo, and a furioso "Conclusion" that really is a finale to the big suite at the beginning.

Berlin and Broadway—Lotte Lenya Reminisces About Weill and Brecht

May 22, 1966

"I guess I represent an era," said Lotte Lenya to a staff member at WGBH-TV, where for a few days she worked on a show about herself and her first husband, Kurt Weill, the composer of *The Threepenny Opera*, *Mahagonny*, *The Seven Deadly Sins*, *One Touch of Venus*, *Lady in the Dark*, *Street Scene*, *Lost in the Stars*.

Lenya was very young when she married Weill in 1926—he was born with the century—and still very young when the *Threepenny Opera* made them both very famous in 1928. The Weills went into exile in Paris in 1933, and the production that year of *The Seven Deadly Sins*, the last collaboration of the composer with Bertolt Brecht, really marked the end of the first phase of Lenya's career as a performer.

New York became the Weills' home in 1935, and the composer died there in April 1950. The refugees from Berlin and some other big German cities remembered Lenya; there were those who owned, or who had heard, the hard-to-find Telefunken recording of excerpts from the *Threepenny Opera*; there must have been some who had seen the old *Threepenny* film. But the Lenya who participated in a Weill memorial concert in New York's Town Hall some months after her husband's death—a concert so successful that it had to be repeated twice—faced a largely new audience.

I was one who knew the recording—she sounds girlish and high-voiced on it and except for the magnetism not much like later Lenya—and while I had not been able to hear any of the New York concerts, I made the trip from New Jersey to Waltham to hear a concert performance of the *Threepenny Opera* at the first Brandeis Festival in June 1952.

I still remember how the performers walked out on the stage, and among them was a rather short, elegantly built woman. Her hair was flaming orange-red. The long face with the full, down-curving mouth, had something ravaged about it, and deeply pathetic. She wore a light pink sweater that was a little bit sleazy. She did not have to do a thing to prove she was dynamite though she shared the stage with such commanding personalities as Leonard Bernstein and Anita Ellis, one of the most amazingly beautiful creatures ever to work the nightclubs. Then she sang the song "Pirate Jenny"—more properly, she sang, she spoke, she negotiated a kind of *Sprechstimme*, all a smoky, almost hypnotically monotonous voice, her extremely American English tinged with Viennese intonations—and the audience went wild. Most of us, I imagine, came away hooked. After that came the *Threepenny* revival in New York and the many recordings.

Lenya, too, remembers that evening with pleasure, and especially Bernstein's conducting. "I think I have never heard it done more beautifully since that time, or perhaps before. All the instruments sang so. But he kept back, and he let us have the show. He was wonderful."

That was also the first *Threepenny* performance in the English translation of Marc Blitzstein, who was also the narrator that night. Lenya believes that it was largely the bad translation that made the work fail on Broadway in 1933. "We learned later that the singers almost made up their own. Weill was sent and offered so many English versions," but Blitzstein's was the first to approach the spirit of Brecht's play.

What about the criticism that Blitzstein had softened the effect of some of Brecht's lines? "I would like personally to strangle every one of those critics," Lenya broke in. "'*Und ein Schiff mit acht Segeln, und fünfzig Kanonen*'—*ach*, so what! I watched Wystan Auden struggle for days to find an image in English for that and he could not do it. Marc's black freighter, it cannot go better."

Weill, Lenya thinks, might have been surprised by the tremendous posthumous interest in his European theater pieces. "He was deeply wounded and he had forgotten all that. Sometimes I would hum a tune from, say *Mahogonny*, and he would look up and say 'What are you humming?' 'Wait, I hum it again,' but no idea. He really didn't remember them.

"He was tremendously adaptable. In Paris he composed a perfectly French music for *Marie Galante*, and then here he became perfectly American.

"He wanted it so," she continued, "he wanted to compose for Broadway, for the commercial theater and not for an elite audience. But he wanted to bring to Broadway his special craft. In every one of his musicals there is a long unbroken stretch of music unlike anything else on Broadway, the Bacchanale in *One Touch of Venus* for example. He wanted opera for Broadway, or at least semi-opera. So *Street Scene* was particularly close to him, and *Lost in the Stars* also represented the sort of thing he wanted to do. At the end he had begun a *Huckleberry Finn* opera. He was doing what he wanted, and he didn't long for what was earlier. I think he died happy. I think."

What were Lenya's recollections of Bertolt Brecht, especially from the last years? "When he left Hollywood in 1947, he visited us in New York and he wanted Weill to go back to Berlin with him, to the Theater am Schiffbauerdamm, where the *Threepenny Opera* had been played. But Weill did not want to. His work was in America and his career, and you know we had no contacts with the German refugee circles in New York, all our friends were Americans, mostly theater people.

"So Brecht went back to East Berlin, and you know his story. I saw him once more, in 1955, when I went to Germany to record the *Berlin Theater Songs* album for Columbia. I wanted to show him the list of songs we had chosen, and I was in Berlin and dressed up in a babushka and went over on the Stadtbahn." Brecht was asleep when Lenya arrived. His wife, the actress Helene Weigel, received her, and eventually the playwright and poet came downstairs. He looked at Lenya in long and silent astonishment. Finally he spoke, "*Wieso*?" ("Why?"). Lenya replied "*Darum*" ("Because").

Lenya is sure Brecht was uncomfortable and unhappy those last years. "He pretended," she said, "that he could do what he liked in the theater, but it was not so. He made only adaptations those last years, and those are his worst poems, and from a man who had never in his life written a bad poem."

I suggested that Brecht was a disappointment to many admirers who hoped to the last that some day he would rejoin the world, come back across the border. "And a disappointment to himself," Lenya added. "He was not so convinced politically actually. His wife, Weigel, was the fierce one—Ana Pauker[3]—even back

[3] Ana Pauker (1893–1960) was a Romanian Communist leader who served as the country's foreign minister between 1947 and 1952, becoming the first woman in the world to hold this position.

in 1927, always with the party card here," and she thumped her chest vigorously. She never saw Brecht again.

When she arrived in Hamburg for a recording some time later, she saw his photo and hers side by side on the front page of the newspaper—her arrival in the city and his obituary.

She recalled one other incident of her visit to Brecht. As a reminder of how they went, she sang him some of the songs she planned to record, "Surabaya Johnny" and others. "Suddenly I remembered how much he had changed. In the old days he had not had these theories about epic theater and so on. I thought perhaps I should sing them differently, standing apart, detached. I asked him, 'Brecht, shall I sing these in the style of epic theater?'

"He had been sunk low in his chair. He was a shy man in a way. He did not easily pat a woman. Of course he slept with women all the way through, that's not what I mean, and that is different. But now he walked over to me, and he patted me on the cheek, and he said, 'Lenya, anything you want to do is epic enough for me.'"

Guarneri Quartet: A Promising Group—But Doubts Remain

May 27, 1966

Not since the Juilliard Quartet began its career about twenty years ago has there been so much excitement over the birth of a new string quartet as recently over the Guarneri Quartet. Even Harold C. Schonberg and B. H. Haggin are in agreement.

The Guarneri Quartet is a product of Marlboro, Rudolf Serkin's Vermont institution which has quietly been metamorphosed from a place for study, recreation, and artistic refreshment into a major musical industry. The Guarneri Quartet has been in official existence a little less than two years, and it has played Sanders Theatre concerts during the summers of 1964 and 1965. Its members are Arnold Steinhardt and John Dalley, violins; Michael Tree, viola, and David Soyer, cello.

The group has a recording contract with RCA which has just issued their first two records. One (2888) has two Mozart quartets, in B-flat, K.589, and in F, K.590; the other (2887) the Smetana *From my life* and the Dvořák A-flat, Op. 105.

The Guarneri has marvelous technical equipment. Steinhardt, a Leventritt and Queen Elisabeth winner, is a most elegant violinist. Dalley is a first-rate player also, responsive, intelligent, flexible, just what one wants from a second. Tree, whose violin playing used to be marred by rough and unfocused tone, has found his métier as a violist, and while not a Rhodes or a Trampler, he is one of the best. Soyer is also a brilliant instrumentalist. When it comes to precision, justness of intonation, beauty of sound, vivid projection of rhythm, the Guarneri Quartet is, to my knowledge, unequaled today. There has been nothing like it since the great, and short-lived, New Music Quartet (Earle, Raimondi, Trampler, Adam) of the late '40s.

Now what about interpretations of music? I remember some of their Sanders performances with great pleasure, including some of the repertory now recorded, and especially their exciting performance of Berg's Opus 3 and an aristocratic one of the Mendelssohn A minor. Leon Kirchner was enthusiastic about their playing of one of his quartets, and there were unanimously good reports about their Bartók Fifth.

Yet there were doubts mixed with the pleasures, and hearing the group on records I feel those doubts again. They stem from two sources: Marlboro and the group's cellist, Soyer. There is a tendency at Marlboro toward a certain vehemence in performance, something that stems from Alexander Schneider and ultimately derived from Casals. Accents are apt to be extremely emphatic, upbeats sharply exaggerated, lines disrupted with violent upheavals of *crescendo* and *diminuendo*. Life is injected into the playing inorganically, by force from outside. The intemperance of enthusiastic sight-reading is frozen into the finished performance of virtuoso professionals.

The most typical example of all this is in the recent Marlboro recording of the Dvořák Piano Quintet in A (Vanguard 1148/71148), in which both Tree and Soyer of the Guarneris participate along with Schneider, Galimir, and Peter Serkin. The Guarneri's Dvořák Quartet is nothing like that bad, but it, too, suffers from the same tendency to overdo. Their simple playing is beautiful, and that makes their oversteppings hurt the more. The Smetana performance is similarly mixed, though on the whole, better.

Mostly one can trace the trouble to the cello. Soyer is a tasteless musician—his playing of the opening melody in the Dvořák Quintet involves some of the most comically grotesque misshaping of a phrase I have ever heard. And one can hear the same thing in his playing of the sinuous second theme in the first movement of Mozart's K.589; moreover, there is a devastating contrast between the vulgarity and total indiscipline of Soyer's playing of the phrase and Steinhardt's refined and sensitive variation of the same rubato seconds later.

And so it goes. When the music allows for tricks, tricks is what we get. The really fast Mozart movements are well done, though one notices another kind of immaturity in the lack of variation; repetitions and reoccurrences are often mechanical (cf. both Mozart minuets). In sum, the Guarneri Quartet, having already achieved much, has much to learn. I hope their development will consist of a consolidation of their remarkable qualities and an outgrowing of their silly ones. We badly need another first-rate quartet, and in two decades no one has held out such hopes as the Guarneris.[4]

Clarity No Replacement for Color or Contrasts

June 19, 1966

Stokowski gave Alban Berg's *Wozzeck* in Philadelphia and New York in 1931, but then it was somehow lost again until Mitropoulos stunned New York Philharmonic audiences with his concert performances in 1951. Parenthetically, Boston has not seen it yet, not even Büchner's play.

A recording of the opera combined from the Mitropoulos concerts was issued by Columbia. It is still available, and until fairly recently it was the only *Wozzeck* recording to be had.

The Mitropoulos *Wozzeck* was in many ways a great performance, but there were also ways in which it was inadequate. No *Wozzeck* performance before, and, I am sure, since, was put together with so little rehearsal. The orchestral playing was often approximate and some of the singing was wildcat. The essential gesture was there.

No one who heard those performances had any doubts about the stature and the force of *Wozzeck*, but still, there was a need for a performance that would let one hear in more detail and with greater clarity what Berg had actually written.

This has now been provided by Deutsche Grammophon (18991-2/138991-2), who have issued a performance conducted by Karl Böhm with the chorus and orchestra of the Berlin Opera, and a cast including Dietrich Fischer-Dieskau (Wozzeck), Evelyn Lear (Marie), Helmut Melchert (Drum Major), Fritz Wunderlich (Andres), Gerhard Stolze (Captain), Karl Christian Kohn (Doctor), Kurt Böhme (First Apprentice), and Robert Koffmane, Martin Vantin, Alice Oelke, and Walter Muggelberg.

Let us say at the outset that both performance and recording are remarkable achievements. Fischer-Dieskau's portrayal is imaginative, astonishingly resourceful, moving. Lear, though her somewhat hard soprano is not one everybody would care for, gives a completely realized performance as Marie. Wunderlich's Andres is marvelously sung and properly conveys a kind of wide-eyed innocence as well. Kohn is chilling, horrifying as the doctor, amazing in speech as well as in song, especially in the icy objectivity with which he observes Wozzeck's death... "*Stiller... jetzt ganz still.*" No part, indeed, is played with less than the highest competence.

[4] See also reviews of July 13 and 26, 1966, and October 16, 1967.

Böhm's conducting is careful, precise, poised, so clear in its realization of detail that listening to this recording becomes in a way much like looking at a full score. It is a completely honest effort to make the score as audible as possible, carried out with a skill and integrity that demand the greatest respect.

When Böhm conducted *Wozzeck* at the Metropolitan, his work was found a bit tame, especially by those who remembered the Mitropoulos performances or who had learned it from those. That was my feeling at the time also, but now, on hearing the Böhm records and on rehearing the Mitropoulos records, I realize that it is not the simple question of the presence or absence of dramatic temperament I had believed it to be.

For all its confusions and inaccuracies, the Mitropoulos picture of *Wozzeck* is clearer. The dynamic contrasts, the changes of color, the abruptions of motion, all the traits of language through which the dramatic atmosphere is conveyed, are sculpted by Mitropoulos with an extraordinary sense for the uniqueness, the special here-and-now-only character of each event. It is characteristic of Berg's style to be mercurial.

With Böhm it is smoothed out. It is as though he tried to find a common expressive and technical denominator all that time. The deliberately bewildering multi-dimensionality of the music becomes elegantly simplified into something approaching undimensionality, quite as though he were saying, "You see, it's not so difficult, not so modern after all. It's really just like *Rosenkavalier*." For all its literal truth, and far though it be from knowing meretriciousness, the Böhm *Wozzeck* is essentially a falsehood. It is, for sheer acoustic clarity, a useful, even an essential, supplement to the Mitropoulos recording, but it is not a replacement.

The Mitropoulos recording also had some fine people singing, notably Mack Harrell, whose Wozzeck is altogether in a class with Fischer-Dieskau's, the extraordinary loony Captain by Joseph Mordino (better, on the whole, than Stolze's), Frederick Jagel's Drum Major (definitely better than Melchert's), and David Lloyd's Andres, very good, even if not as beautifully sung as Wunderlich's.

Boult Opens Tanglewood Auspiciously

July 9, 1966

LENOX—The first concert of the season by the Berkshire Music Center Orchestra was given Thursday night in the Theatre-Concert Hall at Tanglewood, conducted, and evidently to the great pleasure of all concerned, by Sir Adrian Boult. The program consisted of Walton's *Portsmouth Point* Overture, the Horn Concerto No. 2 by Richard Strauss with William Lane as soloist, and the Vaughan Williams *London Symphony*.

The Strauss is a brilliantly imagined work, composed with dazzling technique, and graced with a singularly pretty and lyric slow movement. Nothing in it is terribly substantial. On the other hand it is pleasantly perilous for the soloist in a way that makes it an entertaining thing to hear. Lane is a superbly gifted young player.

I had the feeling that when it was over he could, now that he was thoroughly relaxed, have knocked the whole thing off impeccably and with ease. Even so, he managed a murderous test for a treacherous instrument impressively. He plays beautifully in tune and in rhythm, phrases musically, commands a fine legato, and has an especially lovely tone in quiet high register passages. The orchestral part was not merely precise but quite exceptionally delicate and well-integrated with the solo.

A London Symphony is a puzzling piece, diffuse, sometimes amateurish, but often poetically evocative and exploding into interesting and really original ideas. It is hard to hold together, but Boult did a brilliant job of the special sort of creative conducting that is needed in loosely worked pieces.

Boult, indeed, is in all ways a first-rate conductor. He has precisely thought through ideas about the music, which were also thoroughly appropriate ones. He has a clear, economical, and unostentatious technique that produces sharp rhythms, transparent textures, coherent and shapely phrases, and all that effortlessly—or so he makes it seem. He has the important gift of making it easy for the orchestra to play and, from what I could observe, a genuine pleasure as well. Boult's quiet and commanding performance was one of the most imposing and refreshing displays of sheer professionalism I have ever seen.

The playing of the orchestra was excellent. The group seems an especially fine one this year and particularly considering it was their first concert of the season, the neatness and the good, solid sound of this playing was especially notable.

Guarneri String Quartet—Superb Ensemble, Peerless Virtuosity

July 13, 1966

Monday evening the Guarneri String Quartet began its Harvard Summer School series of five concerts in Sanders Theatre by playing Beethoven's Quartet in E-flat, Op. 127, Webern's Five Pieces, Op. 5, and Schumann's Quintet in E-flat, Op. 44, the last with the pianist Leonard Shure.

It must have been brutally hard to play, and it was sometimes hard to listen, even to hear. Sanders with all windows open is noisy and it was ghastly hot inside just the same, so from the outside one got fire sirens, Vespas, and other delights of Cambridge nightlife, while inside there was a complex rhythmic counterpoint of fanning which, however it might have delighted Charles Ives, was no help to someone just wanting to cope with Beethoven.

Without doubt, though, the Guarneris—Arnold Steinhardt, John Dalley, Michael Tree, and David Soyer—are extraordinary. As string players what they do is virtuosic and finished in a manner unmatched by any other quartet that I know. Their ensemble is superb, and the more impressive for being achieved with a minimum of bodily motion.

Musically they are a superior and cultivated group also, though their interpretive skills are not always on the really awesome plane of their technical ones. I have, however, never heard them play music so well as they did on Monday.

Their Beethoven performance was the evening's weakest. It was the most difficult music they played and besides, the first work on the program is at a disadvantage. There were some unconvincingly vehement accents, and in the slow movement especially there was a tendency to give too much weight to the long notes and not enough to the short ones. That is the sort of over-simplification that sometimes characterizes their work. Another striking example of one-level thinking was the exact imitation every time by all instruments of Steinhardt's slide in the rising fifth of the finale's coda. On the other hand, the scherzo was exceptionally well done, and so was most of the finale, both benefiting from the group's good rhythm and its strong continuity across all manner of syncopations.

That pompous arch-boor among critics, Olin Downes, once sought to prove the unhealthiness of Webern's music by pointing out that it could not be played while the windows were open. While one can decline to accept that as criticism of Webern, there is no doubt that Monday much of the delicate filigree of the Five Pieces was simply inaudible, or at least not continuously enough to make complete sense. What I heard suggested that the Guarneri Quartet plays this music wonderfully.

Schumann's Quintet, on the other hand, is vigorous, even aggressive, in a way that defies interference. It lacks the poetry that is the most treasurable thing about Schumann. It is, however, an enjoyable work with the atmospheric interludes to the funeral march, the amusing tour de force of the scherzo built all on scales, and especially the finale with its audacious and spine-tingling architectural strokes.

A violinist friend used to dislike playing works like the Schumann because, he maintained, the piano was an imperialistic instrument. I suppose he could never have played with as good a listener as Leonard Shure. He is an exceptionally responsive and intelligent musician, and while certain details in the interpretation like the ritards in the first movement were not fully worked out and thus not fully convincing, it did all add up to a lively and imaginative performance.

Sir Adrian Boult—English Conductor, 77, Reminisces at Tanglewood

July 17, 1966

LENOX—"I had said before," Sir Adrian Boult was saying, "that at my advanced age I would not cross the Atlantic again except for a Vaughan Williams cycle, but then the chance to prepare his *London Symphony* with American students and in seven rehearsals proved a sufficient inducement."

The previous evening the 77-year-old conductor had led the Berkshire Music Center Orchestra in a concert including the Vaughan Williams. Afterwards he had been presented with a dedication scroll signed by all the players, and he had delighted them by saying that he was so pleased because it would match one very like it that he had already, that one being from the Vienna Philharmonic.

Now, as he sat at lunch in the Tanglewood cafeteria, students and members of the faculty and staff came by in a continuous stream with congratulations, some with pictures to be signed, most with obviously affectionate thanks.

I remarked on the evident pleasure with which the students had played for him—the same pleasure was to be evident on the faces and in the demeanor of the Boston Symphony when they had a concert with him two days later—and I suggested that he seemed to be a conductor who made it easy for an orchestra to play.

"Well, in 1912, you see, I went to Leipzig for a year, and there I could watch Arthur Nikisch in rehearsal nearly every day. By that point—he was close to 60 then—he had mastered entirely the technique of rehearsing almost altogether with the stick and nearly not at all with his mouth. The economy with which he worked was the greatest influence on my conducting career."

(Later I learned that Sir Adrian used to have a nightmare about coming to an orchestra for a first rehearsal, playing through the music, and finding there was absolutely nothing to say.)

Before the Nikisch experience, the great influence had been that of Hans Richter, who lived in Manchester as conductor of the Hallé Orchestra from 1897 to 1911. Boult's mother was an admirer of Richter's and he was a frequent visitor in the Boults' Liverpool home.

"From him I learned about musical architecture. Of course, they say architecture is frozen music, and I think it essential to think of music as molten architecture.[5] Shape is everything, and it has always been what I most particularly strive

[5] Recorded originally in *Conversations with Goethe* by the poet Johann Peter Eckermann, who was Goethe's personal secretary for the last nine years of Goethe's life, a typically encountered formulation of this idea is "Music is liquid architecture and architecture is frozen music."

to clarify, even if it means sacrificing some of the detail when, for example, there isn't quite enough time."

The difference between Nikisch and Richter? "Ah, that was put well by one of your colleagues in London when both men had conducted the *Flying Dutchman* Overture with the same orchestra in the same hall within a few days. 'With Nikisch,' he said, 'fate pursued you wherever you turned.'

"The other great conductor of that generation was Fritz Steinbach," Sir Adrian continued, "though you must understand I never heard Mahler. Steinbach was absolutely unparalleled as a Brahms conductor and in general perhaps somewhere between Nikisch and Richter, with something of the warmth and sensitivity of one and the magnificent grasp of the large of the other. Like Weingartner's work, which perhaps you know, it was extremely simple, but it had somehow more character. Later on I'm afraid he was rather a naughty old man with the girl students at the Cologne conservatory and so he disappeared from the scene a bit prematurely."

In many ways, Sir Adrian is a singularly modern conductor: He is, for example, almost alone in his generation in his respect for historical scholarship and in his understanding of its relevance to the activity of the performer.

In one area he is, however, an ardent champion of a conservative point of view, and that is in his retention of the old seating for orchestra that puts the second violins on the conductor's right, opposite the firsts. He insists—and his results with the Boston Symphony bore him out—that 18th- and most 19th-century music assumes such a division of violins and that is vital to the proper hearing of the music.

"I know the disadvantages for the seconds: they often play with the firsts and they bow together and they think together and it's a nuisance for them to be playing toward the back of the platform always, but one mustn't let an orchestral convenience become a criterion. The only important thing is to present music to the audience in the right way."

Conservatism brought us to the subject of recent music. "Oh, I'm afraid I'm quite an old fogey now and I don't really keep up any more. There are many gifted and interesting chaps among the younger Englishmen, but I don't know how to conduct the sort of music they write. I've conducted pieces by Malcolm Williamson: He writes stuff I can do.

"But I wish I could be like Vaughan Williams. At 85, he still took an interest in all the new music. He complained about lots of it, but his mind was open and he kept going to concerts every evening and one would see him there with an ear trumpet in each ear and sitting in the front row."

Sir Adrian's association with Vaughan Williams was long and close. From the first revision of the *London Symphony* to the posthumous performance of some Variations, he led seventeen Vaughan Williams premieres, recorded all nine symphonies, and conducted at the composer's funeral in Westminster Abbey. "He revised the *London Symphony* in my office, made cuts, took out what he called some horrid modern music. That was during the '14 war, and I was working in a sort of distant outcrop of the War Office spreading boots about, and he sat there among the samples and worked on the symphony.

"That certain awkwardness in the music is characteristic of him. A clumsy sort of beggar he was, really. Couldn't tie his boots properly so they wouldn't come undone. But it's completely personal music, and so vital. I'm so glad to have been able to do it with young American players and I hope some of them will do it on their own later on. And now I must write them a letter to thank them."

Guarneri Quartet a Quintet for Brahms

July 26, 1966

For its third Sanders Theatre concert in the Harvard Summer School series, the Guarneri String Quartet (Arnold Steinhardt, John Dalley, Michael Tree, David Soyer) played the Brahms Clarinet Quintet with Harold Wright, Stravinsky's Concertino, and Beethoven's Opus 131 in C-sharp minor.

Excepting what one might call the new clarinetists, Arthur Bloom, William O. Smith, and so forth, whose work really falls into a different and not comparable category, Wright, whose lot it is to play in the National Symphony Orchestra, is the finest we have in America today.[6] The instrument itself has its limitations, but his working around them, his control, his taming of its somewhat crudely atavistic and monotonous sound, all this is remarkable.

He is a fine chamber musician who listens, and the response on the part of all five players to Brahms's subtle integration of timbres was sensitive. The first movement was a bit ponderous. Surely Brahms means "Allegro" when he writes "Allegro" though tradition seems to have turned the piece into an "Andante con moto." The remainder, however, had flow and simplicity, and for once the gypsy rhapsodies in the Adagio, which look so obvious on paper, yet which almost never come off, made the proper effect. I have heard good performances in the past, but I generally wondered if the Quintet had not after all died with Mühlfeld for whom Brahms wrote it. Evidently not.

Stravinsky's Concertino is a short one-movement work he wrote for the Flonzaley Quartet. That was in 1920, which places it between the wit and gaiety of *Pulcinella* and the austere grandeur and intensity of the Symphonies of Wind

[6] Wright would become principal clarinet at the BSO in 1970, a post he held until his death in 1993.

Instruments. It prefigures some of the concentration of the latter, though its most arresting characteristic is a motoric energy and physical drive of Bartók's music from that period. As writing for string quartet it is delightful, not so wildly colorful as Bartók's, but inventive and pointed in a way altogether worthy of the master of *Agon* and *The Flood*. The Guarneri's playing of it was superb, though I had the feeling the audience did not care for it much, probably being jarred by and resenting the astringency after the warm and damp Brahms.

The Beethoven, too, was beautifully played in a way that confirmed my previous suspicion that some of the problems in their playing of Opus 127 and 130 at previous concerts arose from their placement at the beginning of the program.[7] This time they gave a performance that truly represented their idea of the piece.

And it was remarkable. Their polished technique made possible a brilliant scherzo, a tellingly characterized variation movement, an immensely powerful finale. It seemed more imaginative than their other Beethoven performances had been, and the bold flexibility of tempo in the fugue (for instance, the approach to the diminution) and especially in the finale was exceptionally strong as idea and as execution.

Some things in the interpretation were not convincing. As they had missed the implied "*attacca*" between Cavatina and finale in Opus 130 last week, so they missed the transition into the second movement of Opus 131 by playing the octave D's as though they had no connection with the octave C-sharps that end the fugue. The best answer here is still Wagner's, i.e., not really to hit the tempo of the second movement until after the fermata. Likewise the octave G-sharps between scherzo and Adagio failed their function as bridge because of mistiming of the fermatas on either side (too short before, too long after).

The Guarneri's work with music as demanding as late Beethoven is not yet matured. Even so, I have not heard Opus 131 more beautifully played, and it is by no means easy to think of a quartet that could reliably think it through more effectively.

Even Mrs. Stravinsky Boos—NY Philharmonic Wrecks *Oedipus*

July 27, 1966

NEW YORK—At the end of last Thursday's performance of his *Oedipus Rex* in Philharmonic Hall, Igor Stravinsky bowed briefly to the audience, made a few applauding motions toward the stage, and left his seat. Mrs. Stravinsky booed

[7] See review of July 13, 1966, regarding Opus 127.

loudly, but of course her displeasure, and that of the many who reacted the same way, was not directed at her husband's music, but at the performance it had just received.

This happened at the New York Philharmonic's recent Stravinsky Festival, and *Oedipus Rex* had been conducted by Lukas Foss, artistic director for the festival, played by the Philharmonic, sung by the Camerata Singers, prepared by Abraham Kaplan, with Jason Robards as narrator, and with soloists Ernst Haefliger (Oedipus), Shirley Verrett (Jocasta), Heinz Rehfuss (Creon, Messenger), Thomas Paul (Tiresias), and Richard Shadley (Shepherd). The visual presentation, which was certainly the most controversial contribution, though not more destructive than Foss's conducting or the Philharmonic's playing, was by the painter Larry Rivers.

Foss's program note included the statement: "In honoring Stravinsky we use Stravinsky." A note by Rivers said: "If I went against Stravinsky's recorded prescriptions it is only because . . . I wanted to be beside it on its own terms and on my own as well. Stravinsky made something in music . . . and with my work I hoped to become a part of it."

Foss and Rivers are gifted men, not least at drawing attention to themselves. This *Oedipus* was designed to get them talked about. "*Épater le bourgeois*" was their aim; the storm of booing that greeted their appearance (especially Rivers's) and the furious review in the *New York Times*, were sources of satisfaction to them.

The "visual presentation" included bleachers for the chorus with approximate human silhouettes drawn on them, and blue sky with white clouds. The orchestra, in shirtsleeves and suspenders, the latter not obligatory, sat on platforms that rose steeply toward the sides which were covered with orange paper. There were pennants on poles, various colors, with bugs prettily drawn like on comic valentines.

Costumes: undershirts, sunglasses, grey-green or red work gloves for the chorus. Oedipus a boxer, including violet and gold bathrobe, red-and-white striped socks, sparring mask, and hand bandages—no gloves, no sunglasses. Jocasta in a metallic-looking gown of four broad stripes, gold, pink, silver, gold, with sunglasses. Tiresias in clerical collar, but with tight pants unbecoming to the cloth, and sunglasses. The Messenger as a chauffeur with high peaked cap and goggles (dark) in a belted outfit. The Shepherd as Ben Casey. Jason Robards refused to wear his costume, which included a sweatshirt inscribed "O Rex," had on a business suit, but did consent to sunglasses. Lukas Foss was fully and normally dressed in white tie and tails, without sunglasses.

The staging was foolish. Tiresias was made to point at Oedipus when he sang "the assassin of a king is a king." Jocasta remained on stage with her back to the audience through the description of her suicide. Oedipus likewise simply stood there as his self-defenestration was described, though during the chorus's farewell to him he began to rise on a platform into whose front there were set lights that shone into the audience and at the same time managing to catch the conductor's try for a Bernsteinian profile.

They did these perverse things a lot in the '20s, especially in Germany, and it seems a waste and bore to go through all that again. Relevant though it is to the Foss-Rivers world, it is hard to see the point of reducing *Oedipus Rex* to a fable about the public relations business, the story of a leader who lost his usefulness when people found out he had been sleeping with his mother.

As for the musical performance, Haefliger and Verrett were marvelous, Paul and Shadley were excellent, and Rehfuss was effective though his voice was artificially amplified and raucous. The chorus was very good. Robards, in spite of his attack of sense about the sweatshirt, brutalized his reading so that it sounded like the roaring of a semi-literate stevedore. Foss, who seemed to know the score less well than is desirable for a conductor, provided uncertain and shapeless leadership. The Philharmonic, the world's most demoralized orchestra, made a coarse out-of-tune racket.

Stravinsky Conducts Philharmonic—Inspiring Performance With His Own Music

July 31, 1966

NEW YORK—The New York Philharmonic's recent Stravinsky Festival, invented, designed, and directed by Lukas Foss, ended gloriously with Stravinsky's own conducting of the *Symphony of Psalms*. Orchestra players like to say Stravinsky cannot conduct, yet they continue to produce for him distinctively rugged and steady performances of unique sharpness of accentuation. The *Psalms* in Philharmonic Hall July 22 showed that Stravinsky is not just an authentic, but a great conductor of his music.

As a matter of fact, this performance shed interesting light on the question of authenticity. It seemed extraordinarily slow, especially the final section of the tolling E-flat–B-flat–F ostinato, "*Laudate eum in cymbalis*"; yet as nearly as I can reconstruct it, it would have been little slower, if at all, than what is indicated by the metronome marks, 72 to the quarter for that particular section. We are, however, used to hearing it faster. On his own most recent recording, Stravinsky takes it slightly quicker than 80, and Robert Shaw, who comes closer with something like 76, gives a different and essentially alien effect by an elasticity that goes against the direction "*rigorosamente*" and against the spirit of the music as it emerges even from the composer's faster version.

It was the steadiness combined with the slow, and proper, tempo that gave Stravinsky's Philharmonic performance sustained grandeur, an intensity, a magnificence, that made it more moving than any singing and playing of the Psalms I have ever heard.

Possibly the most exciting detail of all was the six measures of rising lines for the oboes that lead to the final "Alleluia," and there was a similar, and in my experience unprecedented, power in the way the first movement moved to its climax from "*Quoniam advena ego sum apud te*" to the end.

To see Stravinsky at work after so many performers in the festival whose work was marked by casualness, vanity, phoniness, or outright incompetence, was itself inspiring. His movements are small, but they are forceful and precise. He is watchful, and I wish there were more conductors who do as well at holding the tempo. Except for a few details at the beginning of the first and second movements, the orchestra played well for Stravinsky, and the contrast with the shabby work from Robert Craft and especially Lukas Foss was striking.

The Philharmonic seems a totally demoralized orchestra: Professional musicians were scandalized by the adolescent delinquent behavior they observed at rehearsals, and at the rehearsal I attended of Stravinsky's *Flood* with Craft conducting, it was necessary for the personnel manager to stand on stage to maintain order and tell the players to keep quiet.

Interestingly, the most cogent, and purely musical, criticism of the orchestra's playing came from within the orchestra itself, that is, from the remarkable piano playing of Paul Jacobs. The piano is very prominent in all the works on the festival's final program, the Symphony in Three Movements, *The Flood*, and *Symphony of Psalms*. Jacobs's playing with its care for sound, for correct rhythm, for proper dynamics, for precision of release, provided an ever-present and devastating reminder of instrumental virtuosity, not to mention musical conscience, and it intensified one's revulsion at the coarse noises made most of the time by most of the orchestra.

Indifferently played though it was, *The Flood* seemed clearly to be one of the strongest and most fanciful of Stravinsky's late works. Two cuts were made by Craft, both damaging. One was the Mrs. Noah comedy episode; the other, more important, the return of the opening music and Satan's "The forbidden act." The two long set pieces for orchestra, "The Building of the Ark," and "The Flood," are most delicately balanced against the more episodic things of which most of the score is made, and omission of contrasting material throws the proportions off. The outstanding contribution to *The Flood* performance was made by John Hollander, who read the narration and the lines of Noah and the Animal Caller simply and becomingly and with fine art.

The penultimate festival program was called "Stravinsky and Recent Years," and the choice of music was falsely attributed to Stravinsky. That is, he had asked for Boulez's *Éclat* and for something by Varèse, but he also had asked for Carter's Double Concerto, which he has called a masterpiece, rather than the woodwind quartet Eight Etudes and a Fantasy, and even the necessary diplomacy toward the organizer of the festival had not moved him to suggest that the longest and most conspicuous work on the program be Foss's *Echoi.*

Stravinsky himself was represented by a tiny and very ingenious and amusing fanfare for two trumpets, and by the *Introitus, T. S. Eliot in Memoriam.* The *Introitus*, which uses part of the Requiem text, is brief, simple, and austere, scored for male chorus, most of whose music is in unison, with harp, piano, tam-tams, timpani, solo viola, and solo bass. Foss conducted this impressive work, and it was sung by members of the Camerata Singers who, prepared by Abraham Kaplan, did consistently good work whenever I heard them during the festival.

Boulez's *Éclat*, using mainly plucked and percussive sounds, is a slight piece with a seductive surface, elegant, coherent, and embodying a responsible total vision of a composition in a way that Foss's *Echoi* in its protracted voyage from one reminiscence and one gimmick to the next does not. Lukas Foss conducted *Éclat* and he was at the piano for *Echoi*, whose other excellent performers were Richard Dufallo, clarinet, Robert Martin, cello, and Jan Williams, percussion.

There were also two Webern pieces, a *Kinderstück* for piano (1924, a world premiere) and a Movement for String Trio (1925, listed as an American premiere, but believed by a number of musicians to be a work done at a Craft Town Hall concert some years ago). The program notes, incidentally, were generally inadequate and uninformative, when not actually mistaken, and the Stravinsky discography in the program was a staggering mess. Webern's published pieces contemporary to these newly discovered works (the songs Opus 17 and 18) are more interesting and intricate by far, and the piano piece and the Trio add little to one's knowledge of or feeling for Webern, though the *Kinderstück* is a useful addition to pedagogic literature. The Trio was adequately done by Charles Haupt, Jesse Levine, and Robert Martin.

The *Kinderstück* was done by a *Kind*, nine-year-old Caren Glasser, who played it with astonishing delicacy and control. Moreover, she gave an encore, a Diller-Quailish sort of arrangement of the *Petrushka* fanfare that had much of the audience in stitches and craning to see how the Stravinskys were faring.

The performance of Varèse's *Octandre*, sounding oddly like a reduction of *Le Sacre*, was horribly rigid under Richard Dufallo's conducting; that of Carter's Etudes and a Fantasy, badly cut, was by members of the Dorian Quintet and generally out-of-tune and inept.

Milton Babbitt's Ensembles for Synthesizer was offered as a kind of fashionable "intermezzo under the Lippolds."[8] Everyone stood out there and tried to listen, and the audience level was hardly worse than that of an opera audience. Still, Babbitt's lively and serious piece deserves better, and of all the composers of electronic music he is the one least inclined to the flashy and he belongs under the Lippolds as little as Brahms.

It was an imaginatively conceived festival with its idea to present a lot of Stravinsky's music in the context of its heritage and its legacy. It was inconsistently carried out, with some program building that was far-fetched as well as some that was illuminating. The level of musical performance was generally inadequate, and there was so insane a lapse of taste and sense as the Larry Rivers production of *Oedipus Rex*. It was mostly very well attended and it was, as intended, good advertising.

Major and Minor—Schoenberg for the Man Who Likes Webern

August 7, 1966

A reader has deplored my having made no comment on the Webern Five Pieces, Op. 5, and the Schoenberg String Quartet No. 2 when they were played here recently by the Guarneri String Quartet. He writes:

> Though they're always grouped together, there seems to me all the difference in the world between these two men. In the few Webern works I've had some chance to study . . . I think I hear an extremely fine and fastidious mind using what might be called a method of allusion to create, within the space of a few bars, a sense of enormous drama or grace or repose, and then somehow building these short sections into dramatic sequences that are not only moving and convincing but that seem to have great breadth and significance.
>
> What I hear in the Schoenberg Second Quartet, in the Fourth Quartet, in the dreadful *Verklärte Nacht*, and even in *Pierrot Lunaire* . . . is a coarse and rather pedestrian mind addicted to cheap melodrama and inclined to garrulity. . . . The Second Quartet still sounds to me mechanical and rhetorical, very much like the worst of Brahms's chamber music.

[8] Steinberg refers to Richard Lippold's "Orpheus and Apollo" sculpture, a monumental five-ton, 190-foot-long, 39-foot-high sculpture made up of polished metal strips that hung in the foyer of Philharmonic Hall at the time.

The most obvious reason for grouping the two men together is historical. As I am sure my correspondent knows, Webern, the younger man by nine years, was Schoenberg's pupil, an arrangement that began in 1904, and the two composers remained close as long as circumstances permitted, i.e., until about 1939.

Some of the grouping together of Schoenberg and Webern, and Berg also, is a careless convenience and meaningless. Schoenberg discovered and developed the new musical syntax he and Webern used, but what they both said and the manner in which they said it remained distinct. It is interesting to confirm this for one's self even in the works where they most approach each other: Schoenberg's Opus 27 and Webern's Opus 19 choruses, *Pierrot* and Webern's Opus 14 songs, and, in the most fascinating confrontation of all, Webern's Five Pieces for Orchestra, Op. 10, and the posthumously discovered two-and-a-fraction Pieces for Twelve Instruments Schoenberg wrote in 1910, included in Vol. II of the Columbia series of Schoenberg recordings.

The reader's characterization of Webern is perceptive and well put. Schoenberg would have been, indeed may have been, the first to agree. Recall his introduction to Webern's Bagatelles for String Quartet, Op. 9, where he wrote:

> Consider what moderation is required to express oneself as briefly. You can stretch every glance out into a poem, every sigh into a novel. But to express a novel in a single gesture, a joy, in a breath—such concentration can only be present in proportion to the absence of self-pity.

It may be, however, that a great sympathy for both composers is impossible. A large historical development has been founded on Webern, while passing Schoenberg by. Stravinsky does not underestimate Schoenberg, but Webern has been more important for his own recent development.

The lay public, once Webern's music came into circulation, first through the Craft records, then in an increasing number of performances, has found Webern, at least some of him, approachable and attractive, but it has tended to remain more suspicious of Schoenberg. Then again, among professionals who know Schoenberg's and Webern's music very well—I am thinking, for example, of composers as diverse in their esthetic outlook as Babbitt, Carter, and Sessions—one is more apt to find the view that Schoenberg is the giant and that Webern is a minor master.

The brevity of Webern's music is an important part of his appeal. That is true in the most trivial sense, but also more significantly because the brevity is part of the fastidiousness of a mind that knows its limitations. The imagination and the technical resourcefulness with which he used small forms and methods of allusion are astonishing.

Then, almost every one of us has had to learn to listen better because of Webern. The awareness he teaches us of the weight of the tiny phrase, the single note even, or the silence, is an exciting acquisition, as is learning to pay precise attention to the register of a note, its timbre, and its dynamic shape.

Webern is original, not concerned with merely polishing a pretty surface, and he writes a suggestive and atmospheric music. Though the difference between an essentially gestural music like Opus 10 and the Variations for Orchestra, Op. 30, is far greater than casual acquaintance suggests, Webern's expressive range is limited.

Nearly every one of Webern's works can delight one, and deeply, but as one gets to know them they do not, I think, add to one's knowledge and broad understanding of Webern and who he was. T. S. Eliot has discussed the point in his essay, "What Is Minor Poetry?" (in *On Poetry and Poets*), where he says: "The important difference is whether a knowledge of the whole, or at least of a very large part, of a poet's work, makes one enjoy more, because it makes one understand better, any one of his poems." Just before that, Eliot writes: " . . . the very greatest poets, who are few in number, have all had something to say which could only be said in a long poem."

One reason Schoenberg's art seems to me greater than Webern's is that it includes not only the occasional suggestive miniatures and the structures in small dimensions, but also the expansive and richly filled canvases like *Pelleas und Melisande*, *Erwartung*, the Quartet No. 3, the Variations for Orchestra, *Moses und Aron*, the Violin Concerto. I find the variety of all this exciting, and the man who wrote the *Genesis* Prelude (1945), the String Trio (1946), *A Survivor from Warsaw* (1947), the Violin Phantasy (1949), inhabited a large world indeed.

"Coarse . . . pedestrian . . . cheap melodrama . . . garrulity"—yes, Schoenberg's mind has its unattractive traits. His letters and essays contain disturbing confusions and inconsistencies, mostly as a result of getting carried away by something. There is also a certain amount of corn, the "O.K." essay in *Style and Idea*, for example, and the ugly and unfunny occasional canons. "Ach du lieber Augustin" in the Second Quartet is unconvincing, too, though the use of the oom-pah-pah to make a continuation after the disruptive quotation is masterful.

It seems clear, though, that the defense of Schoenberg has to be based on his music. A parallel with Wagner is in order: the text of the *Ring* is vulnerable as an intellectual achievement and certainly as a literary one, but most of the music, especially in the later dramas, seems to me unassailable.

The musical invention and the compelling and disciplined fitting of tone to word and situation make *Erwartung* an example of classical art in the sense that *Parsifal* was such an example for Tovey.

The survival of Romantic and post-Romantic modes of thought in Schoenberg is deceptive. They have deceived performers who in turn have deceived listeners—no more than Mahler can Schoenberg be played as though he were Strauss.

Schoenberg's textures are complex, and that makes his music very hard to perform. But the rare successful performance, Boulez's of the Five Pieces, Rosbaud's of the Variations, Silverstein's and Leinsdorf's of the Violin Concerto, reveals that he has written something remarkably clear, colorful (though not showy), and beautifully integrated with every other dimension of the discourse.

When his music sounds thick and like a parody of Brahms, that is a sign of a bad performance. Like Brahms, Schoenberg is hard to know. There is nothing seductive, and like Brahms, he is uneven.

I cannot like Schoenberg's Piano Concerto or the *Ode to Napoleon* and I do not really enjoy listening to the Fourth Quartet, but these things do not invalidate the Second Chamber Symphony, *Moses und Aron*, the Serenade, the wonderful Opus 22 Songs, or reduce the stature of their composer, any more than the Brahms B-flat Sextet or C minor Symphony alter the genius of the G major Quintet and the Symphony in E minor.

Composers Quartet Attains Distinction at Lenox

August 19, 1966

LENOX—With Tuesday's concert by the Composers Quartet, the Festival of Contemporary American Music at Tanglewood attained true distinction. Technically, this concert was not part of the festival, but the final event of the Tuesday chamber series here is always designed to fit into the festival's general scheme.

The Composers Quartet (Matthew Raimondi, Anahid Ajemian, Bernard Zaslav, Seymour Barab) played the String Quartets No. 2 by Roger Sessions, Milton Babbitt, and Henry Weinberg, and the only quartet (alas) by Ruth Crawford Seeger.

America has produced a few international virtuosi in a class with any. Our most special, and perhaps unique, contribution in the performance world has, however, been the training of players, many of them young and many of them specialized in contemporary music, whose virtuosic resourcefulness goes far beyond what is generally understood by virtuosity, and who are to an extraordinary degree possessed of musical intelligence and dedication.

This is a characteristically American phenomenon, and the Fromm program[9] at Tanglewood during the last decade has been very much responsible for bringing it about. The four players of the Composers Quartet are not Tanglewood-Fromm products, but they stunningly represent the new American virtuosity and intelligence.

The Sessions Second Quartet is a large and serious work. It seems to be directly descended from Beethoven's Opus 131, and that relationship and the rhetorical stance the work assumes make me a little uncomfortable. Yet the performance by the Composers Quartet for the first time let me hear the piece in all its compositional richness and variety. It was superbly paced and articulated, and the complex textures were wonderfully clarified to make it altogether one of the greatest string quartet performances in my experience.

Babbitt's Quartet No. 2 is all ginger and bite, with an excitingly tight relation of sonority and structure. Moreover, its sensuous appeal is a delight all on its own. Babbitt's ear for sonority is a fine one, and such a performance of so elegantly imagined a piece of writing made one regret what sometimes seems like his flight into electronic sounds, for all that one understands the necessity for the flight because there are not enough performers like the Composers Quartet.

The performance was remarkable as a whole, and nowhere more so in detail than in the octave passages near the end in which the octave doublings blossomed as tone colors in a way unprecedented in my experience of listening to string quartets.

For most persons, the Quartet by Ruth Crawford Seeger came as a special revelation. Ruth Crawford was born in 1901 and died in 1953. She studied with and married Charles Seeger (and became the mother of Pete), a musicologist and a remarkable musician who was the first to teach the new music in this country more than fifty years ago.

When Mrs. Seeger wrote her Quartet in 1931, neoclassicism and Nadia Boulanger staccatos dominated the thinking of American composers—the Open-Plains-of-Kansas school had not really materialized yet. Her Quartet was part of the expressionist world, whose manifestations in America we are only beginning to get an inkling of.

That Mrs. Seeger was doing something that in taste and technique was ahead of its time by a quarter-century is remarkable, but the more important thing about her Quartet is what an assured work it is and how individual and original regardless of its date and place of composition.

[9] The art-music patron Paul Fromm (1906–87) commissioned hundreds of composers for new works under the auspices of his eponymous foundation; launched the journal *Perspectives of New Music*; and for many years supported an annual week of contemporary music at Tanglewood. In 1972, he moved the foundation to Harvard, where it continues to commission new music and support related activities.

Each of its ideas is of striking and arresting character and their development is a natural extension of their nature. Not least, Mrs. Seeger was a punctual composer with a most precise sense of when a development or series of events has run its course. Her Quartet is a remarkable and beautiful creation, one that should become a part of standard repertory. It, too, was superbly played.

Henry Weinberg is a sensitive and serious musician and he writes the most complicated music I know. The dialectic of his Quartet No. 2, written from 1960 to 1964, rests on intricacies and subtleties, especially rhythmic, that I am not yet equipped to hear. I look forward to being able eventually to understand this music and to write about it; at present I cannot. I can, however, report the composer's own estimate of the performance as "wonderful."

Handel's Opera *Giulio Cesare* Suffers from Tampering

October 4, 1966

NEW YORK—Like the Boston Opera's *Hippolyte et Aricie*, the New York City Opera's new production of Handel's *Giulio Cesare* is better to look at than to listen to. Tito Capobianco's production, in sets by Ming Cho Lee and with costumes by Jose Varona, is generally convincing and often unusually handsome and tasteful. There are good singers in the cast of whom some actually sing well.

Ultimately, though, everything gives way under the leaden touch of the conductor, Julius Rudel, who produces a performance altogether weird, its general level of animation suggestive of Leinsdorf, its integrity that of a Lukas Foss, its tempi by the Handel and Haydn Society, and its vocal embellishments from heaven knows where between Mozart and Richard Bonynge.

Giulio Cesare, first produced by Handel in 1724, is very beautiful, with a great fertility of melodic and even structural invention and a marvelous ear for vocal and orchestral euphony. Its action is Caesar's defeat of Pompey, his conquest of Egypt, and his subsequent politico-erotic liaison with Cleopatra. It has two superbly drawn characters, the intelligent, sexy, pathetic Cleopatra, and the tragic Cornelia, Pompey's widow. Caesar himself has grand moments, and Sesto, Pompey's young son, is vivid, too.

Performance today presents one possibly insoluble problem: what to do about the title role, written for the castrato Senesino. It could be sung by a female alto, but could we accept a lady Caesar on the stage? It could be sung and acted by a countertenor, but their delicate voices have not the trumpet brilliance Handel expected in a leading role and which the great castrati provided. The solution adopted here was to drop the role into the register of an unfixed male and assign it to a bass-baritone.

Now one gets into difficulties with the orchestra and, of course, in vocal ensembles. Handel's ear was fastidious in matters of register. He always recast instrumental parts when he assigned a song to a new voice, and he would not have been pleased by some of the doublings or by the discrepancy between the octave of the voice and that of the obbligato horn in the aria, "Va tacito e nascosto." For all that, the baritone solution is probably the best for stage production.

In general, the sound, the texture of the performance was quite wrong. To be sure, pains had been taken to get most of the proper instruments for this astonishingly lush and colorful score. It scarcely mattered because the wind-string proportion was all wrong. There were far too many strings, and the string playing was atrocious.

That is, it was of a kind acceptable for the *Bohème* matinée, but the style of the modern orchestral player who will not on pain of death lift his bow from the strings or modify his heavy vibrato is death on Baroque music. No matter what Handel had written, everything sounded like the Vaughan Williams *Tallis Fantasy*.

And how curious an edition Rudel prepared, with its cuts, its borrowings, its shiftings about. Does his company's new production of *Traviata* introduce the Miserere from *Trovatore*? And in their new *Tosca* I am sure "O dolce mani" will be moved forward into Act I so the end won't drag so much. By far the best individual performance was that of Beverly Sills as Cleopatra. Some of her ornamentation seemed a little wayward—the Queen of the Night seemed always just in the wings—but from the beginning her voice was steady and lustrous, her taste in phrasing faultless, her technical execution brilliant, especially that of the spectacular trills. One thing, incidentally, Rudel was right about was to insist there be vocal ornaments so that one actually looked forward to the repeats in the arias instead of dreading them.

Maureen Forrester, who sang Cornelia, is a fine singer and a great artist in Brahms, Wolf, and Mahler. Handel, however, is apt to come out like a parody of *Elijah*, and she is musician enough to know better than to permit herself all that sentimental oozing in behind the beat.

Beverly Wolff, as Sesto, began with some misplaced oratorio singing of her own, but improved greatly. The metal of her voice is exciting, she has a good florid technique, and she gave a fiery and exceptionally well-acted performance.

Norman Treigle, looking astoundingly like Caesar, acted a bit like Don Giovanni, and sang well, though coloratura is not his natural element. Spiro Malas, also struggling with a transposed castrato part, Cleopatra's brother Tolomeo, was defeated by it; Domenic Cossa was passable as the Egyptian general Achilla.

To return for a moment to the visual production, Capobianco's grandly simplified motions for the singers were apt and effective; Lee's set is practical and also tasteful even if a little art-nouveau spindly; Varona's costumes are sumptuous.

With such visual sense and such gifted signers, what a pity *Giulio Cesare* does not have musical direction of greater flair or even of the kind willing to join the rest of us in believing that Handel really was quite a competent man who knew what he was doing.

Webern Festival—Fine Songs and Quartet in Posthumous Premieres

November 13, 1966

BUFFALO—This, on October 18–30, was the meeting place of the Third International Webern Festival, sponsored by the International Webern Society, the music department of the State University of New York at Buffalo, the Buffalo Fine Arts Academy, and the Buffalo Philharmonic. There were performances of Webern's music, there was talk about it by composers and scholars, and there was an exhibit of Weberniana in the auditorium of the Albright-Knox Art Gallery.

Anton Webern died in 1945, unknown outside the profession, hardly known within it, and even there regarded only by a very few as anything more than a hermetic, idiosyncratic follower of Schoenberg. Webern's public history began in 1957 when Columbia issued a four-record album containing his complete published works, despite its limitations an heroic and valuable project.

We have a long way to go still, but in 1957, to say nothing of 1945, not even the optimists foresaw the extent of interest in Webern today, the recognition of his importance and some of the exaggeration that has accompanied that recognition, and the fair number of performances of at least some of the works. It is in the area of performance that neglect and laziness are at their worst, with the conductors whose devotion stops with Opus 6, the quartets who enjoy their success with Opp. 5 and 9, but who will not touch Opp. 20 or 28.

The most interesting development of the last years has been the extension of our picture of Webern beyond the published works from Opus 1 to 31 and the Bach transcriptions.

Manuscripts of several unpublished compositions have come to light. Some precede Webern's studies with Schoenberg; others belong to his maturity. Some are of slight value; some are interesting in the light of published works for which they can perhaps be regarded as sketches or parerga; some are remarkably beautiful and presumably remained unpublished for reasons other than Webern's dissatisfaction with them.

A chamber concert in the Albright-Knox Gallery began with a String Quartet dated 1905, three years before Opus 1. The language is not as complex as that of the Quartet No. 1, Op. 7, which Schoenberg was working on at about the same time, but comes closer to that of *Pelleas und Melisande* or even *Verklärte Nacht.* While less abandoned than anything by Schoenberg, Webern's Quartet is of great expressive intensity. The opening, which is built on a figure similar to that at the beginning of Liszt's *Préludes*, as is the *Faust Symphony*, is wonderfully inventive in its handling of polyphony, line, and texture. The Quartet is attractive altogether, but in the opening pages there is already a real sense of the discovery of the poetry of form and of the eloquence of understanding so characteristic of Webern's later music.

A separate slow movement for quartet, also from 1905, has good themes, but its repetitions, both local and large-scale, are so literal that the work becomes very dull to listen to. There were also performances of the *Kinderstück* for piano and a slow movement for string trio (1924 and 1925, respectively) that were played at the Stravinsky Festival in New York during the summer. The *Kinderstück* will, I hope, become something piano teachers will find out about—these "new" Webern works are being brought out by [the music publisher] Carl Fischer—and the trio movement has a certain grace, though it is thin stuff not at all on a level with the published Trio of 1927.

There were also four apparently very early songs to texts by [Ferdinand] Avenarius and [Martin] Greif, and another four, from 1908–09 and very much finer, on poems by Stefan George. The singing of these songs was, however, so distractingly bad that I cannot be at all sure of my opinions. Other than the inadvertently comic lady, the performers were members of the University's Creative and Performing Arts Center or of the Philharmonic, and standards were generally high.

In honor of the festival, the regular subscription concert of the Buffalo Philharmonic was also built about Webern. Lukas Foss, who at his best has a remarkable imagination and sensibility in program-building, began with the middle three movements (the two *Nachtmusiken* and Scherzo) of the Mahler Seventh, continued with Webern's orchestrations of five Schubert Lieder, two newly discovered Webern songs from 1913 and 1914, Webern's Five Pieces, Op. 10, and the Four Songs, Op. 13, and the *Götterdämmerung* Funeral Music.

Actually the Schubert group was disappointing. The instrumentation is the same as that of the Schubert-Webern German Dances done in 1931. Hans Moldenhauer, who has been responsible for the recent Webern diggings, thinks that the songs, too, might be late works. Lukas Foss is inclined to believe that they might have been Webern's first assignment for Schoenberg. At any rate, the orchestrations are quite uncharacteristic and add nothing.

The two new Webern songs are treasures. Both are settings of poems by Webern himself, and Moldenhauer believes that the composer's diffidence about his verse may have made him withhold them. "O sanftes Glühen" belongs to a set of six pieces written in 1913, the year of Opus 10, and it is the only song among them. The pieces, which use a chamber ensemble like that of Opus 10, include two that are incomplete and not in performable condition. Three others were to have been played last month in Philadelphia by Ormandy, but their premiere has been delayed by the Philadelphia Orchestra's strike. Ormandy had planned to play the pieces with the Vienna Philharmonic. That, too, is off for the moment.

Moldenhauer, whose sense of justice in these matters has been formed and sharpened by his own experiences as a refugee from Nazi Germany, feels that Vienna does not deserve the honor of a Webern premiere.

Of the other songs, "Leise Düfte," also on a poem of Webern's own, is one of a pair written in 1914. The Buffalo Philharmonic program notes, by any standards among the worst in the country, gave no clue as to why "Leise Düfte" was not performed with its companion piece, "Die Einsame." Both "Leise Düfte" and "Sanftes Glühen" are lovely examples of Webern's art, though the wonderful songs of Opus 13, written in 1916, are richer, particularly in their rhythmic life. Marni Nixon, colorless in the Schubert, sang the Webern well, and Foss and the orchestra did good work in the songs and in the Opus 10 also.

That certain things in Mahler, especially the timbres of the Seventh's middle movements, look ahead to Webern is clear enough. It was curious, though, how even the beginning of the Wagner with its single kettledrum notes, its silence, its sinuous linear writing, seemed to become part of this world as well.

And finally there was the exhibit assembled by Moldenhauer. There were autograph manuscripts of some of the compositions heard during the weekend, and also of the Passacaglia, Op. 1. There was the last sketchbook containing drafts for a choral work to follow the Cantata No. 2. There are now, by the way, six notebooks that appear to contain all the sketches for the complete published oeuvre, and including things as interesting as a projected seventh movement for the Cantata No. 2 and rejected third movements for several published two-movement works.

But these are things to pore over, to study. Some of what was in the exhibit cases, of human interest even more than of musical, made its impact immediately. There was Webern's passport with the visa for the wartime trip to Switzerland for the premiere under Scherchen of the Variations, Op. 30, the last time he was to hear his own music. There were account books, notebooks, letters, all in the same almost painfully neat handwriting as the musical manuscripts. There was a bitter letter from the widow about Vienna's continuing neglect of Webern's music after his death—she called him Toni.

A pair of spectacles, a spectacle-case, a wallet, a cigar-case. The last time he walked out of his house it was to smoke a cigar.[10] A shattering photograph from August 1945. I must never before have seen one later than about 1938, and here he is almost unrecognizable, haunted eyes, emaciated, sagging skin. He suffered from dysentery the last year, and an identity card issued two days before his death tells the tale. Weight fifty kilos, 110 lbs.

The top right-hand corner of the identity card is shredded where a bullet passed through.

Moses and Aron—A Great Work Creditably Done

December 1, 1966

Moses and Aron has been done in America now. It was high time, for this is a very great work, not just for its philosophical content, but even more for its luminous, powerful music. It is a triumph for Sarah Caldwell and the company that *Moses and Aron* could be produced here in a non-theater[11] and with all the other limitations of resources to fight, and produced in a way that made a tremendous impact.

At the same time, one might lament that when such an important moment was at last here, *Moses and Aron* might not have been given the great performance it deserved. And then one's lament might well turn to outright complaint because the most severe handicap under which the performance labored was one that had nothing to do with budgetary or architectural problems, but that was a renewed example of a catastrophic policy of the company: its unwillingness to use an adequate conductor.

Moses and Aron is an opera about the birth of monotheism. At the beginning, Moses hears the voice of God in the burning bush. Aron interprets the Word to the people, but his translations of the concept of an invisible, inconceivable God into a string of concrete realities succeeds only in leading the people further away from the idea as understood by Moses. The golden calf is the ultimate degradation of the concept.

Moses and Aron is an opera of ideas. Some past productions have had the effect of leading the audience away from the essentials, in fact, from the idea to the golden calf orgy. Sarah Caldwell has given Schoenberg's work a production

[10] On September 15, 1945, while outside smoking in Mittersill, Austria, Webern was inadvertently shot and killed by a US soldier.

[11] The "non-theater" was the Back Bay Theatre, originally a movie theater. Caldwell never succeeded in building an opera house for her company, despite repeated attempts to acquire a permanent home.

that actually invites us to listen to the words and to the music. Her great success with it has been to make it perfectly clear to the audience what *Moses and Aron* is about, and any impact it makes it makes for relevant reasons.

Except for the golden calf, we are asked to imagine all the objects: rod, serpent, leprous hand, sacrificial animals, water, blood, drinking vessels. It fails to work just once, and that is in the absence of anything even to suggest the burning bush. But the diction is superbly clear and so is the pantomime devised by Claude Kipnis. It is a convincing solution to a difficult problem.

Playing space has been stretched by opening the stage to the brick wall at the back, by ramps that lead up to the boxes, by a platform that fully encircles the orchestra pit. Some of the groupings are brilliantly effective, but for people sitting at all close to the stage it is hard to tell what is happening because one can never bring the whole picture into view.

There are some inspired visual ideas: the most exciting is the revolving Janus figure made of Moses and Aron at their first appearance together. There are mistakes, too: the action of having the Israelites slowly pull down an obelisk before the music begins for the first great choral scene, for example, is sheer claptrap.

The orgy has been well staged, but it remains a problem. Other people's orgies perhaps are a bore anyway, and the music for the long scene is not Schoenberg's strongest. And what does one do about stage nudity: pink tights are miserably destructive of illusion. Again it should be said that the details of the action and pantomime are very good.

It has often been true of the productions by the Opera Company of Boston that the theatrical achievements, and for that matter the musical intentions, have been more impressive than the musical accomplishments. It was clear that Osbourne McConathy knew the score and that it had been rehearsed to a point at least of reasonable security. It was equally clear that he was not conducting *Moses and Aron*, but merely beating time for it. The tempi worked, but nothing was really phrased, balances were often bad, and the playing was often raucous and out of tune. The orchestra was made up of first-rate players, and we know their playing well enough to be sure that it was not necessary, for instance, for the violins to grope for the high B-flat on the last page had someone insisted they find it properly.

The chorus, which had been prepared by Roland Gagnon, James Billings, and McConathy, and which carries so much of the work, sang really impressively.

Richard Lewis sang and acted well as Aron. At the same time one could say that a solid and somewhat unimaginative workman had been given a part that calls for the dramatic power of a Julius Patzak.

Donald Gramm, a serious artist, worked hard to give a strong performance as Moses. He came close to success but missed, partly by confining the pitch range of his speech-song too much and partly by remaining too conventionally Biblical (with Hollywood overtones) rather than suggesting Schoenberg's unique conception of the part.

Among those who had smaller roles, there were outstanding performances from Eunice Alberts, as an Invalid Woman, and from Harry Theyard, a singer with an astonishingly brilliant and beautiful tenor voice, as a Young Man.

Diction was remarkable from almost everyone, chorus included. That served unfortunately to expose how unsatisfactory Allen Forte's translation really is. The unhappy truth is that *Moses and Aron* is, like Debussy's *Pelléas*, hopelessly untranslatable.

It will take time to figure out how to produce *Moses and Aron*, and future producers will benefit from Miss Caldwell's successes and from her mistakes. There were severe problems about this performance, and it must be emphasized that the evasion of the conductor problem is a major irresponsibility on the part of the company. Nonetheless, enough of the performance worked. What came across and so gripped the audience was unmistakably Schoenberg's *Moses and Aron*, specifically and uniquely.

Brendel's Luminous Enchantment Dazzles

December 12, 1966

Brendel is the best pianist I know. There are those whose playing is of an even more dazzling bravura, and there are those who command that special performer's witchcraft still more magnetically. But taking things all in all, for musical understanding, for intensity, for technical mastery, for commanding personality, all in combination, there is no living pianist I have heard who is Brendel's superior.

His most intense involvement has been with Beethoven, Schubert, and Liszt, and it was an extraordinary sort of Liszt-Beethoven program he put together for his Jordan Hall recital. The Liszt group was made up of immensely difficult pieces, none of which is flashy. The Third Hungarian Rhapsody is a dark piece, rather like half of one of the more familiar rhapsodies, consisting only of the slow Lassu without the gay, major key Friss to follow.[12]

"Pensées des morts," an almost completely unknown piece from the *Harmonies poétiques et religieuses*, is an extraordinary meditation on tolling

[12] In the 18th-century *verbunkos*, a Hungarian dance form, the *lassú* and *friss* are slow- and fast-moving sections, respectively, that alternate with each other.

knells, a black and dramatic piece Liszt envisioned accompanied by a speaking chorus reciting the "De profundis."

"Bénédiction de Dieu dans la solitude," from the same collection, is tranquility and luminosity. Of moving simplicity and magnificent sonority, it is one of the great monuments of Romanticism.

There are other Beethoven players, but as a Liszt player Brendel is unique now. The fantasy in the gypsy rhapsody, the grandeur and the nobility in the two religious meditations, were in quite different ways electrifying. It is easy to condescend to Liszt as camp. When Brendel plays Liszt, there is a sense of identification with and passionate commitment to a language and to a way of life and thought that language embodies. He attains the summit of what a performer can hope for: to make us understand why the music was written, and why it is as it is.

In Liszt, the musical idea and its physical-acoustic embodiment are inseparable. In that sense it is typical performer's music, though in the case of something like the "Bénédiction" at a near sublime level. Late Beethoven leads a life of its own, independent of any particular performance. The performer's goal here is almost to be forgotten. Nothing in Beethoven is more demanding than the *Diabelli* Variations, and at the end of the fifty-some minutes the performance took, I was aware only of having come through a confrontation with something that even by the standards of late Beethoven is a musical, intellectual, spiritual miracle. It was absorbing to the point of being exhausting, something I can only regard as a good thing.

Brendel's grasp of the piece, certainly the summit of Beethoven's achievement as a composer of music for piano, was sovereign. He gave special prominence to its wit, and in this connection I recall with particular gratitude his enchanting playing of the Minuet finale. Through the whole work, the sense of light and shade, the contrast between areas of clear daylight and of mystery already implicit in the theme, was communicated with marvelous clarity.

Altogether it was a beautiful program, beautifully played. Such brilliance in the service of such understanding gives us something we need badly in our concert life.

Let us have this man back.

Vienna's Alfred Brendel—Pianist With Sense of Humor

December 18, 1966

Alfred Brendel, the extraordinary Austrian pianist who was briefly in town for a Jordan Hall recital last Sunday,[13] is a very funny man with a keen sense for the

[13] See previous article.

absurd in all of its manifestations. And like all really humorous people he is intensely serious.

He likes talk of matters of consequence, but it is shot through with hilarious comments, illustrations, comic excursions of all kinds. His wallet bulges with examples of wild typographical errors in several languages, clipped from newspapers all over the world. He has, as the mad byproduct of the Schubert recitals he has given with the baritone Hermann Prey, a little album of photographs taken in booths in New York subway stations, in which the two, with only a scarf for a prop, "perform" the "Erl-King," with Prey as the demented and voracious peri, and Brendel as the obviously quite daft child.

At his recital here, Brendel had played a group of relatively unknown Liszt pieces, and I asked how he had come to be a Liszt specialist. Edwin Fischer, Brendel's teacher, did not play Liszt, though he admired certain pieces like the Sonata very much and taught them interestingly. "It had much to do with my recording career," Brendel said. "At the very beginning I recorded for a small company, SPA, who were looking for unusual repertory, and so I recorded Liszt's *Weihnachtsbaum*, and from there I came to other Liszt."

He finds Liszt dangerous to play because critics are in general hostile to it, and audiences are brought up to be snobbish about it. England, by exception, is "the most open country for Liszt now." The trouble begins, Brendel feels, with what is taught about Liszt in the conservatories, where he is generally represented as a writer only of flashy superficial virtuoso pieces.

The best Liszt, the composer of intensely original and noble music in which the virtuosity is organic and not superficially decorative, is hardly taught and little known even among pianists. "Yet one could make a selection of perhaps 40 or 50 of his piano pieces and find that they are very great music. I have not much hope, though, for the orchestral music."

What about the paraphrases and transcriptions of which he recorded a selection a number of years ago? "I learned them mainly for the recording and I do not play them now. The trouble is that it takes enormous work to keep up something like the paraphrase from *Norma*, and the opportunities to play it are not so very much. People often think you are a very foolish person to play such things."

At least one, though, Brendel mentioned as something he wanted to return to his repertory, and that is Liszt's transcription of the Love-Death from Wagner's *Tristan*, which he described as "absolutely marvelous."

Brendel's next Lisztian project is to learn the Hungarian Rhapsodies—"There are some very good pieces mixed in there"—and he plans to record them. He will play some at a Vienna recital along with Chopin polonaises, the first Chopin in his repertory in over 10 years.

"I always used to feel that to play Chopin one had to become a specialist. The great Chopin players were, and even if they played other things also, their center was Chopin. In Chopin you need a certain manneristic style for which you have no use elsewhere, and that makes Chopin very draining." And partly, Brendel speculated, it may have been awe of Chopin playing he heard in his youth, "particularly Cortot, who even as a very old man could sometimes do miraculous things. His record of the Chopin preludes is one of those I would take to a desert island."

Brendel plans in any event to take several months off from concerts for study and to learn repertory he knows in his head but has not had time to practice. Besides the Chopin, he wants to get to Schumann's *Kreisleriana* and to more Schubert, including the posthumous A major Sonata and the A minor Op. 143.

"It is pleasant," he added, "that so many musicians now admire the Schubert sonatas, neglected so long, but they are still mostly misunderstood in performance."

He mentioned a German pianist of the older generation, now dead, who enjoyed a reputation as a Schubert specialist. "He played so, like an old maid"—and there were little mincing gestures and poutings—"but always with little sentimental irrelevancies. You have not heard his records? Oh, but you should."

We discussed old instruments and the problem of playing Beethoven on a modern concert piano. The heavy untransparent bass on the modern instrument is a problem; the glassy top is a problem mainly peculiar to American pianos. But the hazards of the modern instruments are outweighed by the lack of *cantabile* sustaining power and dynamic differentiations on the treble of the pianos of Beethoven's day.

"Oh, yes," he said, "I have played on a Beethoven piano. Almost ruined it," he added thoughtfully. "Beethoven's piano music was always far ahead of the instrument even in the early sonatas. I am much more concerned with and guided by the range of dynamics and the use of accents in his string quartets and orchestral music."

In general he is a bit suspicious of fanaticism concerning old instruments, and with a mixture of pain and humor reported, with illustrations, on a performance he had recently heard of a Bach suite with baroque trumpets. He also finds the general Baroque craze a bit silly, a "higher sort of children's music." His happiest moment with Vivaldi was in Cocteau's film, *Les Enfants terribles*.

Did he play contemporary music? Only up to Schoenberg. And there he likes the early music best, Opus 11 and Opus 19. Among the still earlier works his favorite is *Pelleas und Melisande*. "For the really new music you must be a good sight-reader and have a photographic memory, and I offer neither." He is struck by how few players there are equally comfortable in the new and the old. He mentioned a young pianist whose playing of contemporary music he finds extraordinary, "but when he plays old music . . ." As a possible exception I mentioned Charles Rosen. Brendel brightened up. "I was waiting to hear that name. Yes, I have his record of Liszt's *Don Juan* Fantasy, and it is easily the most intelligent performance I have heard of it."

Even though he does not play it, Brendel keeps up with new music as a listener. He asked if I knew György Ligeti, whose *Aventures et aventures nouvelles* he had recently enjoyed in Vienna, and whose writings about music he admires. *Aventures*, Brendel reported, was a great success with everyone—"it is a good piece even so"—but, in spite of the audience's enthusiasm, it could not be repeated because it involved the sound of tearing paper—different kinds of paper, different thicknesses, and different speeds of tearing—and afterwards there was no more untorn paper in the house.

From Boston, Brendel went to Oberlin for master classes and a concert. Today he has a Beethoven recital in Philadelphia, and then home to Vienna. There he has a beautiful wife, Iris, who works in ceramics, and a 6-month-old daughter, Doris (which goes with Iris) Susanna (after Mozart). And the newest addition to the Brendel household is a merry-go-round horse, white, with outstretched legs and flaring nostrils, mounted on its original spring mechanism, "something I have always wanted."

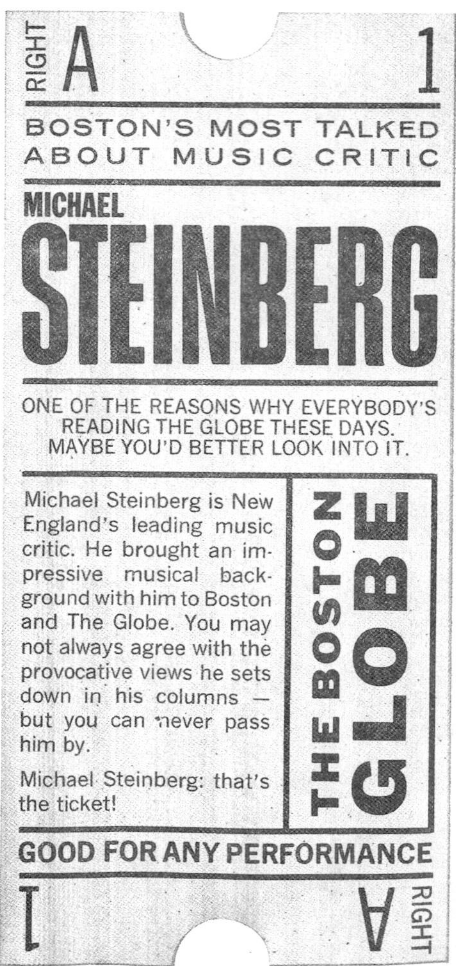

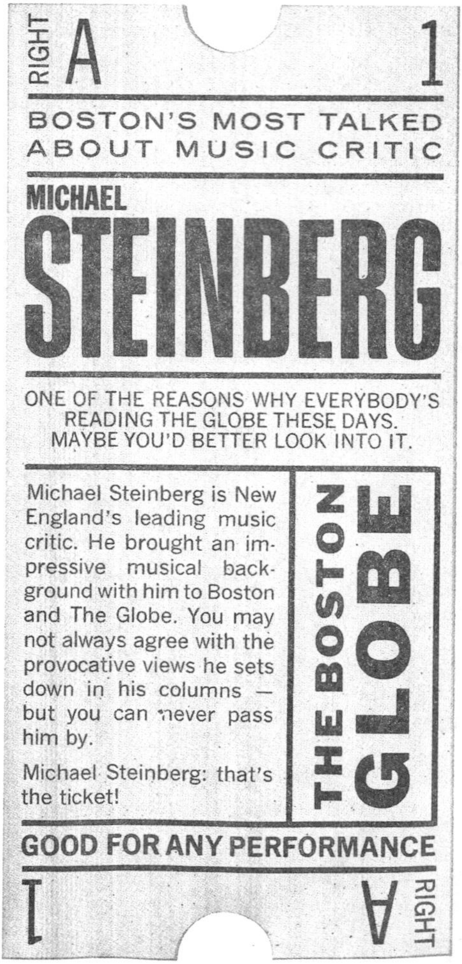

Boston Globe advertisement placed in the Boston Symphony's program book during the 1966–67 season. (Used with permission.)

1967

Carter's Concerto in Dramatic Debut

January 7, 1967

Elliott Carter's new Piano Concerto is the most original and powerful work by an American composer. I know of nothing of comparable quality and strength to have come out of Europe since the war.

Its strength is in its conservatism. Carter is conservative in that he believes in a work of art as a responsible statement, a unique articulation of a personal vision. He is not a toy manufacturer, and he is not a cynical player of games with listeners and performers.

He believes, too, that the validity of a work of art is in what it says. His musical ideas are as complex as any being imagined today, but their intricacies exist in the service of an emotional and intellectual activity that reach to the very roots of our lives, what we care about, and live by.

Carter's Concerto establishes the most dramatic confrontation of solo and orchestra since Beethoven. He has moved far from the Romantic concept of the soloist-hero cheered on by the crowd. Rather, the composer posits a conflict "between an individual of many changing moods and thoughts, and an orchestra treated more or less monolithically—massed effects pitted against Protean figures and expressions" (Carter's own words).

There are two movements. The first is fantastic in character. The dialogue moves rapidly, and ends at a climax when the orchestra block seems almost to have crushed the solo. But as in Carter's first String Quartet, the space between movements is not really a break at all. The second movement begins just where the first left off, but it moves into quite a different world of rhetoric.

The orchestral part becomes a complex fabric of regular, but mutually contrasted beats against which the rhythmic flexibility of the solo is set off. And there descends over the music a series of blankets of string tone, vastly thick chords—beyond sixty pitches each sometimes—quietly sustained in sinister contrast to the piano's increasingly urgent and impassioned utterance. Opposition breeds independence. The solo becomes more autonomous and free, and the Concerto concludes in the tranquility of a quiet and unopposed statement by the piano alone.

The originality of Carter's work is in its language, one fresh and individual in every dimension—not a hybrid of a traditional structure with a veneer or a graft of modernism. The harmonic vocabulary is uncommonly rich because Carter characterizes solo and orchestra by assigning to each its own repertory of triads.

Moreover, Carter's music is difficult to hear because his boldest inventions have been those concerned with treatment of speed and rhythm, the former an element ignored in most music as building material, the latter the very area where listeners and performers are most inexperienced and ill-trained.

The texture of Carter's Piano Concerto is fascinating. Carter has set a concertino of seven players (flute, English horn, bass clarinet, and one each of strings) to function as mediator between solo and orchestra. The concertino is a channel through which ideas are communicated from solo to orchestra. It shares the vocabulary of both, and in the series of cadenzas for the wind soloists in the second movement, which Carter has likened to the speeches of Job's comforters, it has a vital role in the human-musical drama. The actual piano writing, too, is extraordinary for the fantasy and ever-growing variety of the figurations.

This was the first Carter premiere since the Double Concerto of 1961.[1] To find for his original vision an equally original way of articulating it, and to get it all down to the actual finger details, as it were, is an immense labor. Not the least impressive achievement of Carter's is that as well as having written a beautiful and expressive work, he has written a new one.

Jacob Lateiner, who commissioned the Concerto through the Ford Foundation, was an admirable soloist. His feeling for polyphony is especially strong, and he had mastered the multi-textured layout of his part so that it sounded at times like the simultaneous performance of two players.

Erich Leinsdorf's work with the orchestra was alert and careful, and special praise goes to the members of the concertino, Doriot Anthony Dwyer, Laurence Thorstenberg, Felix Viscuglia, Joseph Silverstein, Burton Fine, Jules Eskin, and Henry Freeman.

Subsequent performances, some of them at least, will be more assured and will benefit from more transparency and more varied dynamics. But for a piece that is most assuredly an example of the sort of music not meant for the first performances, this premiere went well, and the second movement was very clearly in focus and came across with immense impact.

A local note, finally: this incredibly taxing performance was a most important thing for the Boston Symphony to undertake. It would be good to have this begin a renaissance of the tradition that Symphony Hall is where the important new orchestral works begin their performance histories.

[1] See November 18, 1965, review of the Double Concerto's Boston premiere.

Our special gratitude goes to Mr. Leinsdorf and to the Boston Symphony for their share in revealing a moving and exciting masterpiece.

St. John Passion—A Stunning Version

January 15, 1967

One of the most distinguished records to appear during 1966 was the Telefunken set of the Bach *St. John* Passion, and it is, furthermore, easily the best recorded performance available of that beautiful work (Telefunken SKH-19, three records). It is conducted by Hans Gillesberger, with the Vienna Choir Boys, the Chorus Viennensis (choir boy alumni), the Concentus Musicus of Vienna, the Leonhardt Consort of Amsterdam, with soloists Kurt Equiluz, Max van Egmond, Jacques Villisech, Bert van t'Hoff, Siegfried Schneeweiss, and an unnamed alto and soprano from the Choir Boys.

The performance is good because the tempi make sense, the phrasing has character, and the textures are lucid. It is unique in my experience to hear the opening chorus flow instead of pound at half speed in an interminable torment of 16th-notes, and unprecedented also to hear the sustained woodwind lines clearly through the busy string figurations. And almost everything from then on moves justly and clearly in a way that enables one to listen to Bach.

My only real reservation concerns the soprano aria with flutes, "Ich folge dir gleichfalls," which drags; and possibly the chorus about casting lots for Jesus' coat is a hair fast for its strongest rhythmic effect.

In general, though, the pacing is remarkably good, and the series of crowd choruses—up to the point when Jesus is delivered to be crucified—has superb sense of direction and impact. The atmosphere is less theatrical than in most performances now. The Evangelist's recitatives, which are done more rhythmically than usual (but not stiffly!), are sung without operatic or Lieder-like pathos, but with a master's feeling for words and music, and to superb effect.

Equiluz, the Evangelist, is one of the very strong elements in the performance; as is Van Egmond, who sings Jesus and also the arioso, "Betrachte," and the aria, "Mein teurer Heiland"; and as is the unnamed boy alto, who is marvelous in both his arias. All the solo singing is on a level of impressive excellence, and both choruses sing very beautifully indeed.

The instrumental playing is sensitively phrased and ravishing as sound, whether in the ensemble or in the solos of Alice Harnoncourt and Kurt Theiner (viola d'amore), Eugen Dombois (lute), Nikolaus Harnoncourt (cello and viola da gamba), and others. Gustav Leonhardt plays organ continuo for the recitatives and arias.

Old instruments or replicas of them are used, and the pitch is almost a half-tone lower than that to which we are accustomed. It makes no sense to make a fetish for its own sake of using old instruments and boy trebles and altos in the choruses and solos. There is no doubt, though, that the actual physical sound of this performance is a considerable part of what makes it so effective. A beautifully paced and phrased performance is still more effective the closer the actual sounds come to those the composer imagined, if there is no compromise in technical quality. That is just what has happened here: interpretation and sound are right, and the result is stunning.

One disappointment is that the sixth side is blank. It might have been nicely used for a first recording of the three arias Bach wrote for the unfamiliar second version of the *St. John* Passion, and room permitting, for its two special choruses as well, which are now part of the *St. Matthew* Passion and of Cantata No. 23. It would be useful and interesting to have a sort of *St. John* Passion kit.

Kubelik Conducts Great Mahler Ninth

January 21, 1967

Rafael Kubelik conducted a great performance of the Mahler Ninth on Friday afternoon. It was one, actually, that went counter to a couple of prejudices I generally cherish with respect to Mahler interpretation: that is, I believe Mahler needs to be extremely precise, and I like to hear him played with a sharp edge and, to borrow a phrase from Mr. Kubelik, "with fist."

Kubelik's temperament is the opposite of a drillmaster's, and he is sometimes fairly casual about technical fine points. The view he takes of Mahler's music is predominantly soft-edged and lyric, more like Walter's than like Mitropoulos's.

Kubelik's performance was intimate and vocal rather than dramatic. Its strength came from an unusual interpretive intelligence with remarkable powers of concentration, and from a deep, empathetic identification with the music.

The first movement is one of fantastical contrasts, partly implying, partly actually asking for a great range of speeds. Such a piece is especially difficult to conduct: its parts need to be highly characteristic, but the organic coherence of those parts must be established. Kubelik was especially masterful here. The performance was vivid, it had a strong sense of direction and a powerfully articulated shape. One could, from Kubelik's interpretation, unhesitatingly pinpoint the place in the score where Mahler writes "*Höchste Kraft*" ("maximum power").

Kubelik's feeling for pace is remarkable. It is rare to have Mahler's characteristic distinction between a flowing and an urgent kind of forward movement so sensitively felt, or to have the equally characteristic distinction between the abrupt and the gradual tempo changes so tellingly observed. I sensed a miscalculation just once: the end of the last waltz section of the second movement got going so fast that it was impossible to make the jump back to the original Ländler tempo without the preparatory ritard that Mahler wanted to avoid.

On the whole the second movement went superbly, being full of character even though the grotesqueness was gently illuminated. In the third movement, the Burleske, I felt some lack of fist and of furious speed. The lyric episode with the trumpet solo and the harp *glissandi* was beautifully done, with a remarkable and daring improvisatory quality. Throughout the whole Symphony, the conductor's feeling for quasi-improvisation, his willingness to leave things loose, contributed marvelously to the shapeliness and the eloquence of the performance.

The heart-piercing Adagio finale was what it must be, love, warmth, pain, cold, made audible. With all its poignant intensity, Kubelik never lost the sovereign inner calm that is so important here. And in no other performance have I experienced so completely the sense of suspended motion, the disintegration of substance on that incredible last page.

In a performance three years ago, Szell brought out in an extraordinary way the meaning of the infinite subtleties in Mahler's scoring.[2] Kubelik offered no such illuminating delineation of what Mahler achieves with textures and accents, and I felt a loss of that one dimension. Not that Kubelik is orchestrally unimaginative: the "soft" downbeats and the slow-blooming chords in the finale were masterfully conceived and tellingly executed.

But Mahler said that "the important part of music is not in the notes," and it was Kubelik's sure sense of what is behind the notes and his magnificent architectural grasp that made his performance so moving.

The Boston Symphony's warm, relaxed-sounding playing was a pleasure. There were also some beautifully done incidental solos, notably by Joseph Silverstein (violin), Doriot Anthony Dwyer (flute), Lois Schaefer (piccolo), Peter Hadcock (E-flat clarinet), Matthew Ruggiero (bassoon), James Stagliano (horn), and Armando Ghitalla (trumpet). There was distinguished percussion playing, and the Mahler Ninth is also a work that offers unusual opportunities to the superb second violin section.

The tiny symphony or overture by the 17-year-old Mozart[3] that opened the concert is a piece full of arresting rhythmic, harmonic, and textural details, and a touching melancholy hangs about its Andante section. It was elegantly done. Its brevity took the audience by surprise, though Kubelik was clearly right to keep the preliminaries short. It gave him a fresh and attentive audience for the

[2] See review of February 9, 1964.

[3] This was Mozart's Symphony No. 26 in E-flat, K.161a[184].

manifold wonders of the Mahler, and at the end of the concert there was an ovation of unusual warmth and length.

Irving Fine on Record, Thanks to Brandeis

January 22, 1967

RCA Victor has done a good thing in making available a record of music by Irving Fine, the American composer who died in 1962 when he was only 48. Fine was head of the music department at Brandeis, and without moral and financial assistance from Brandeis the record would not exist.

Fine was one of the American composers who for a while were strongly in the grip of Stravinskian neoclassicism, and his *Toccata Concertante* for orchestra of 1947 is closely dependent on Stravinsky's then new Symphony in Three Movements.

In the Symphony (1962), Stravinsky is still in evidence, but he no longer swamps Fine so, and the whole facture of the work is more serious, more elaborately inventive, more freely imaginative. The finale rises to a climax of impressive dramatic force.

The record also contains the intense, eloquent, and in character far more vocal *Serious Song: Lament for String Orchestra*, written on a Louisville commission in 1955.

The *Serious Song* and the *Toccata* are excellently performed by the Boston Symphony under Leinsdorf; the Symphony is given in the concert performance the Boston Symphony played under Fine's own direction at Tanglewood in August 1962, just eleven days before his sudden death (RCA Victor 2829).

Fine's teacher at Harvard was Walter Piston, one of whose most delightful early works, the Three Pieces for flute, clarinet, and bassoon, is recorded by members of the Soni Ventorum Quintet. The record includes the Quintet for winds by Joseph Goodman, a Piston pupil born in 1918, and, to judge from this well made and engaging work, a composer of high competence. Both this work and Ernst Krenek's crisp *Pentagram* are works with which wind quintets might well enrich their concert repertory. Performances are very good (Lyrichord 158-7158).

A strong work of Piston's from more recent years, the 1949 Quintet for piano and strings, is recorded by Earl Wild with the Walden Quartet, a Heliodor reissue of an MGM record—a good performance and rather boxy sound. *Khaldis*, a concerto for piano, trumpets, and percussion by Alan Hovhaness, played on the other side of the record by William Masselos with Izler Solomon, seems extraordinarily silly (Heliodor 25207).

If you have a taste for musical baby-talk, you probably already have a recording of Orff's *Carmina burana*. There is, however, a new and superb one conducted by Rafael Frühbeck de Burgos with the New Philharmonia Chorus and Orchestra, and soloists Lucia Popp, Gerhard Unger, Raymond Wolansky, and John Noble (Angel 36333).

And there is still more of Orff's strenuous strength-through-joy music in *Catulli carmina*. Here the contrast between the sophisticated erotic verse and the nursery school music occasionally leads to some amusing results, but in the end, Orff's studiously striving for emptiness and avoidance of doing anything interesting is self-defeating. The work is effectively done under Václav Smetáček with Czech singers and players (Crossroads 2216003-22160C04).

A Beautiful *Winterreise*

January 30, 1967

Hermann Prey and Ryan Edwards gave a beautiful performance [at Jordan Hall] of *Winterreise*. It was one that consistently drew attention to the work itself, to the pathos of Müller's verses and to the effectiveness that his images, with all their simple-mindedness, do have, and of course most of all to Schubert's miraculous transfiguration of those verses.

Prey is a singer of words as well as of music, but his interpretation found a singularly happy balance of the two elements. There are singers who seem excessively word-conscious, those about whom one almost feels they would rather be reciting than singing, those who itch to impose a musical shape of their own upon the verbal-poetic scenario.

Prey is always aware that somewhere Müller's verses became Schubert's songs and that it is the songs he must perform. One could put it that his way was a very sung performance of *Winterreise*. No verbal emphasis, no outburst of emotion shattered the musical sense of continuity of the songs.

It was tellingly projected as poetry, intensely expressive, and vocally beautiful. There is no self-pity in Prey's interpretation, nothing self-indulgent. The emotional life of the songs is pushed inward mainly, being allowed outward release on a large physical scale only in brief blazes of anger, bitterness, irony.

Prey's sense for words is keen, especially as it emerges in his awareness of their relationship to music. Words have denotative meanings, but they also have rhythm, color, density, weight. They are, in fact, a kind of music themselves. They tell one how the music goes, and at the same time the music controls and interprets the words.

The phrasing was unfailingly beautiful, subtly varied, but offering at each moment the most natural solution. Dynamics, often abrupt and deliberately unbeautiful, were a principal resource in expressing the drama of the songs, especially in view of the stern musical control exercised on words and phrasing.

Color, too, was masterfully handled. Prey has a ringing, virile baritone, one that retains its purity of timbre and pitch even at dynamic extremes. And again, without ever losing the larger musical continuity, he injected extraordinary variations of timbre, most haunting of them the incorporeal quality he brought to "Der Leiermann."

Handicapped though he was by an unfortunate piano, Ryan Edwards played superbly. From the start, his playing was sealed around the voice in a way that made it clear that he was engaged in chamber music, not an accompaniment. Whether urging, seconding, or pianistically declaiming or singing on his own, Edwards was an aware and sensitive partner. I would question his work only to the extent of suggesting it is worth paying more attention to the distinction between the songs that end in tempo and those with fermatas, preliminary ritards, or both.

Extraordinary Mahler

February 5, 1967

Two new recordings of Mahler's *Das Lied von der Erde* have come out. Each is extraordinary. Except for that, and the notes, they have nothing in common.

One is conducted by Leonard Bernstein, with tenor James King, baritone Dietrich Fischer-Dieskau, and the Vienna Philharmonic (London OM36005-OS26005); the other is conducted by Otto Klemperer, with tenor Fritz Wunderlich, mezzo-soprano Christa Ludwig, and the Philharmonia and New Philharmonia Orchestra (Angel B-SB3704, 2 records).

Bernstein's performance, though on one record, is the slower by two-and-a-quarter minutes, but the London engineers have done a good job of accommodating 66′10″ of music without loss of brilliance, volume, general impact. The Angel recording is more detailed, sometimes too much so, as in the excessive prominence of the mandolin in the last song. Klemperer's characteristically sensitive textural blends within the orchestra come out well. The singers, however, are placed very far forward: they seem too soloistic, and counterpoints between a voice and an instrument do not come out effectively.

Both tenors are excellent, with fresh, beautiful, strong voices. Good as King is, Wunderlich at every moment reveals himself as a finer singer and a more interesting musician. Nothing I have heard of his has made me mourn his tragic early death last summer as has his performance of these three Mahler songs.

Ludwig, in most beautiful voice throughout, is at her best in the fourth movement, "Von der Schönheit," which she does with just the right sort of sexuality and with lots of humor. In the other songs, she is weak in following Mahler's occasional direction to sing "without expression," for instance "*mit aufzutrocknen*" in No. 2, or in the narration, "*Er stieg vom Pferd*," that begins the second part of the last song.

And at the end, "*Die liebe Erde*," when Mahler says "*ppp!* without climax," followed by constant reminders of "*sempre pp*," she lets herself go in an orgy of vocal climax-building. It is some of the most gorgeous singing ever put on records, but it is not the piece Mahler wrote. In general, she is very good, but at a few crucial places, she disappoints badly.

Traditionally, the even-numbered songs have belonged to altos, though the score says "contralto (or baritone)." Bruno Walter, who conducted the posthumous premiere, once, out of piety, tried it with baritone but rejected the idea, finding the male voices monotonous. This seems silly, though one could make a stronger argument on behalf of the female voice by pointing out that Mahler's delicate vocal-instrumental relationships are designed essentially with the higher octave in mind. The downward transposition for baritone involves some musical loss, all exceedingly subtle.

The immediately relevant point, however, is that Fischer-Dieskau sings *Das Lied von der Erde* more compellingly than any alto I know of. He also sings it better now than when he previously recorded it for Angel in a performance poorly conducted by [Paul] Kletzki.

Mad music and the moods of the afflicted have always evoked a special response in Fischer-Dieskau. Here the powerful diction, the uniquely poignant voice, are used with imagination and discipline. He gives a performance both intensely expressive and in the most sovereign way musical, and it is his greatest achievement on records. One always reads in program notes about the heartbreaking sense of farewell in the last pages, and one sees it on the page. This is the first time I truly heard it.

But it is the conductors who impose the character on the two performances. Klemperer's, at its best, e.g., the A-flat minor in the first song, is a marvelous lesson in how to be expressive though in tempo. His performance is better planned than Bernstein's, with less extreme fluctuations of tempo, more continuity, a clearer sense of large form. Orchestral playing is excellent, with especially exciting and creative playing by the oboe soloist.

Bernstein goes more for the moods behind the music. The discontinuities in the first song are disturbing, but no other conductor has realized its savagery so well, or even got the sound of the last chord right before, for that matter. Falling in love with details, he is apt, for instance, to let the coda of No. 4 fall completely to pieces, though the details are done with breathtaking beauty. In the same way, for all its intensity, the interlude in the last song is less effective than in Klemperer's performance.

Bernstein's interpretation is the product of careful thinking and sensitive feeling, yet it is careless often; it is exaggerated and marvelous.

I must recommend both, though the best points of each make the other harder to listen to. The fourth side of the Angel album has Mahler songs with Ludwig and Klemperer, "Ich bin der Welt abhanden gekommen," "Um Mitternacht," "Ich atmet' einen linden Duft," from the Rückert series, and "Das irdische Leben" and "Wo die schönen Trompeten blasen" from *Des Knaben Wunderhorn*, done beautifully except for the last, of which Janet Baker's (Angel) is the only good performance.

Kubelik Chooses Exile to Privileges

February 5, 1967

Rafael Kubelik was the Boston Symphony's interesting and impressive guest conductor from January 13 to 31. He had last conducted in Boston in 1953: that was with the Chicago Symphony, which he then headed. Kubelik's present orchestra is the Bavarian Radio Symphony in Munich, though he and his wife, the Australian soprano Elsie Morison, live in Lucerne, Switzerland.

Kubelik holds a Swiss-issued stateless passport. He was born in Czecho-Slovakia in 1914, but left after the Communist takeover in 1948. As he puts it, "I lost my country in order not to lose my nation." He will not take the citizenship of another country, neither will he return home until there is another sort of government. "On that subject," he says, "I am adamant. I am anti, openly anti, I have been invited to conduct there often, but I could not go, being used by them as an item of propaganda, and accepting benefits and privileges that are denied the rest of my people."

Kubelik believes in principles and commitment. In Chicago, his insistence on his responsibility to contemporary music got him into trouble with his board. Later, at the Covent Garden Opera in London, it was his demand for copious rehearsal. No wonder that Mahler, whose Ninth Symphony he led here,[4] and who in the days of his dictatorship at the Vienna Opera was attacked by many as an unreasonable perfectionist, is a special sort of hero for Kubelik.

[4] See review of January 21, 1967.

"Strauss is a good composer, Mahler one of the great geniuses," said Kubelik, and went on to tell how he had outraged one of the first-desk men in the Vienna Philharmonic by saying so. He recalled also a Vienna Philharmonic rehearsal at a Salzburg Festival in the middle '50s when he was working on the Mahler Fifth. One of the string players remarked loudly that he thought Hitler had done a good thing in banning Mahler's music. Kubelik left the rehearsal to return only after the player's departure. The player apologized a year later.

Vienna was never, and is not now, a Mahler town, and Kubelik is convinced that Viennese political antisemitism is an important factor here. The Vienna Philharmonic's Mahler resistance is also personality-based in another way: "So many of the players have a father or grandfathers who played in the orchestra and who remember something disagreeable Herr Direktor Mahler said to them in 1907."

Amsterdam, thanks to Mengelberg, was the Mahler capital in the earliest part of the century, but Prague, according to Kubelik, was not far behind. Kubelik recalls annual visits from Bruno Walter, whose active Mahler repertory was limited, however, to only a few works. Locally, there were Václav Talich and Alexander von Zemlinsky, Schoenberg's teacher and brother-in-law by his first marriage.

When he speaks about Mahler's music, Kubelik emphasizes its human content and its reflection of Mahler's personal greatness. In the Ninth Symphony, for example, he talked of the distinction between the hatred expressed in the earlier movements and the redeeming, all-embracing love in the final Adagio. "But in that hatred Mahler included himself. He never felt superior, and he never stood to one side."

His love for Mahler does not go so far as to include the re-scorings of the Beethoven Ninth and of the Schumann symphonies. The former, with its heavy brass, he finds "horrible," the latter simply unnecessary. He is in general wary of much editing and retouching, and is convinced the Schumann symphonies can be made to sound as written. "One must be careful, of course."

Responsibility and self-scrutiny are frequent subjects of Kubelik's conversation. Conducting, he maintains, is difficult. "When I was younger, I often lay awake nights after concerts, mentally going through the whole thing again, analyzing my beat, wondering why something went wrong here, what I should have done better there." Now he works as hard and prepares as conscientiously as ever, "but I take perhaps a more fatalistic view of perfectibility."

If a good horn player makes a bubble, it is likely, according to Kubelik, to be the conductor's fault, perhaps some tenseness or hesitation in the beat that is translated into the player's physical response. "It is too easy to blame others without considering your own share. You must rule yourself before you can rule others."

Kubelik's musical personality and character were formed partly by his father, the celebrated violinist Jan Kubelík, and by a piano-playing uncle with whom he played duets, thus getting his basic education in classical symphonic repertory. He reveres his father as a great musician, and one whose career took an essentially tragic turn. "He was a kind of unfinished symphony," the son said. "He made his reputation at the beginning as a technical wizard, and one, I must say, of unparalleled facility and brilliance. You know, when he began in the 1890s, he was probably the first violinist in half a century to play the Paganini Caprices. Soon though, he became tired of that, but he had been typed in a certain way, and it was a terrible struggle for him to be accepted as something other than a player of showpieces."

"He did not have a large, sensuous sound like the Auer pupils," Kubelik continued. "I would say his tone was sweet, though with no sense of stickiness, except that he just hated the word '*dolce*.' '*Espressivo*' was something he understood very well, but '*dolce*' he hated. He was at his best in Bach and Beethoven, and these he played with a most marvelous purity."

I asked about the compositions of both father and son. Kubelik would like some day to conduct his father's A minor Symphony again, a work he remembers with affection, but whose only score was left behind in Prague and is now inaccessible. He also spoke of three violin concertos, romantic in sentiment but classical in layout, with much that is remarkably lively and original in the solo parts, though terribly difficult.

As for his own composing, there is the usual performer's problem of too little time. Recently Kubelik took a year off from conducting and spent much time composing, "but now I must remain silent again. By the way," he added, "my music is much more conservative than a lot that I conduct."

Kubelik recalled that his conducting debut in 1934 was at a concert at which his father played Rafael's Fantasia for violin and orchestra. The program also included the Beethoven Violin Concerto and the Tchaikovsky Fourth. It was deeply moving for the then 20-year-old musician, but he remembers that his father admonished him, "If you become more modern, I cannot go along with you."

Gertrude Schoenberg, 1898–1967—A Memoir

February 19, 1967

Late in 1951, some months after Arnold Schoenberg's death, a memorial concert was given at the YMHA in New York, at which all the piano works were played by Eduard Steuermann and the String Trio by a group with Rudolf Kolisch. Afterwards someone said to me, "You know, that was Mrs. Schoenberg you were sitting next to."

I hadn't known, and I cannot imagine what I would have done if I had. I recall very well, though, a slight, middle-aged woman with an interesting and rather severe face, and I think I recall that she sometimes glanced over at the printed music I held.

It was February 1965 when I actually met Mrs. Schoenberg. Even now I find it hard to believe that we met only once, and fairly briefly, so attached in a way did I become to her then and in what happened later.

She was in Boston for the American premiere of the opera *Intolleranza* by her son-in-law, Luigi Nono.[5] The composer later bitterly attacked the production of his work by Sarah Caldwell and the Boston Opera Company. To Mrs. Schoenberg, however, the production of *Intolleranza*, the mere fact of it and much about the actual accomplishment, was evidence that Sarah Caldwell was an opera producer of genius.

That summer, Mrs. Schoenberg and Miss Caldwell conferred in London, where Schoenberg's *Moses and Aron*, composed around 1930 but not heard until 1954, was being produced. In October it was announced that the Boston Opera would give the American premiere of *Moses and Aron*.

Moses and Aron was staged here on November 30, 1966,[6] but a couple of weeks before that it was already evident that Mrs. Schoenberg was already too ill to make the journey from Los Angeles. She died, aged 63, last Tuesday morning, February 14.

At the time of the *Moses and Aron* performances, she was in and out of the hospital, in pain, apprehensive, angry—"Medicine seems to be just as corrupt as the modern music world," she grumbled. She took great interest in the performance and stayed in touch by telephone with her friends here. It was most characteristic how she worked to interpret the reports she received, to discount on one hand what she called "the professional pessimism of the apostolic Schoenbergians," and on the other the accounts of friends whom she suspected of merely trying to make her feel better.

In a recently published reminiscence of her husband, Mrs. Schoenberg remarked that they shared the same sort of humor, and her observations had the typical Schoenbergian bite. She also shared Schoenberg's sense of mission, and her energies, both as a wife of twenty-seven years and a

[5] See review of February 22, 1965.
[6] See review of December 1, 1966.

widow of almost sixteen years, were wholly dedicated to Schoenberg and his music.

Gertrud Kolisch was a spirited young woman of 26 when she married the recently widowed 50-year-old composer. She was the younger sister of Schoenberg's pupil and friend, the distinguished quartet leader and great musician, Rudolf Kolisch. Under the pseudonym, Max Blonds, she wrote the libretto for Schoenberg's one-act comic opera, *Von Heute auf Morgen*.

In Austria, Germany, Spain, France, the United States, she shared a life involving much neglect and vilification within the profession, emigration, financial hardship, ill health. Into this life she brought an incalculable infusion of humor and courage.

There were three children: Nuria, now Mrs. Luigi Nono, born 1932; Ronald, born 1937, whose remarkable gifts as a tennis player gave his father particular pleasure; and Lawrence, born 1941. Mrs. Schoenberg is survived by these, by four grandchildren, by her brother and an elder sister, and by her 91-year-old mother, Mrs. Henriette Kolisch.

When the Schoenbergs came to America in 1933, the composer's first teaching appointment was at the now defunct Malkin Conservatory. The composer and his wife then lived at the Pelham Hall apartments, 1284 Beacon St., Brookline. Schoenberg, who was asthmatic, felt that the climate here would succeed in killing him rather rapidly, and so the Schoenbergs were not Bostonians for long. When Mrs. Schoenberg was here for *Intolleranza*, she noted that the climate had not improved.

An old friend remarked, "As Trude Kolisch she was the most delightful person, but as Mrs. Arnold Schoenberg she could be rather hard." She was tough, outspoken, exceedingly sharp about money.

She faced certain kinds of battles, at least, with relish. When she was here in 1965, she was cross about a well-known musician who, she felt, had made insufficient contribution to the effort to bring her politically controversial son-in-law into the country. I had to correct her impression and tell her that the musician had indeed been most helpful. "What a pity," she said, "I had so looked forward to dressing him down."

For her, Arnold Schoenberg was a cause, the battle for his music—a holy war. One is not always reasonable about such things. And so it came that when people spoke of Mrs. Schoenberg, they did it sometimes with both some fear and some irritation in the tone. And so it was, too, that I was surprised at first that the Mrs. Schoenberg I met here and stayed in touch with through correspondence and telephone, was a most gentle lady, a warrior not from choice, a humanly magnificent person, and one whose loss leaves the world much emptier.

His Dedication Was Selfless—A Century of Toscanini

March 19, 1967

The 100th anniversary of Arturo Toscanini's birth in Parma falls this Saturday, March 25, and it is just over ten years since his death in New York City. His career, which ended in 1954, had begun sixty-eight years earlier, on January 30, 1886, in Rio de Janeiro, when he was pushed from his place in the cello section to conduct a performance of *Aida* after the public had demonstrated against the scheduled conductor and one proferred substitute.

He was not in Boston often: he conducted a Metropolitan Opera performance of *Tristan und Isolde* in 1910, two concerts in 1921 on the America tour of the orchestra from La Scala, two in 1936 with the New York Philharmonic-Symphony, and one in 1939 with the NBC Symphony.

My generation knows Toscanini only incompletely, that is, from what he did in his 70s and 80s, with a few things from his 60s mainly from broadcasts and recordings whose acoustics were, often as not, mismanaged in a way that obliterated the effect of his concern for balance, dynamics, and fine sound. Apropos the last point, I remember well my amazed discovery that the NBC Symphony, when I first heard Toscanini conduct it in Carnegie Hall, made a beautiful sound that was nothing like the harsh, dry tone of the broadcasts.

While we heard his great performances of *Otello* and *Falstaff*, those of *Fidelio* and *Aida* were flawed by some poor singing, and there was no *Tristan*, *Meistersinger*, or *Parsifal*, no *Magic Flute*, no *Boris*, *Carmen*, or *Don Pasquale*, and, something I sense as a particular loss, no Gluck except Act II of *Orfeo*.

Toscanini's music-making was economical and direct. His performances were wonderful training in drawing the most information from the simplest possible statements, and I enjoyed acquiring, from listening to him, a taste for the unnecessary. I came later to appreciate complex performances as long as they were based on the accurate perception of real musical shapes, and in some pieces to enjoy such performances more than Toscanini's, but I learned to despise the underlining of points in a way that served to destroy them by asking nonsense of the context, and the vehemence, the sentimentalities, the cuteness, the vulgarity, that characterized the work of so many performers.

In that way, watching Toscanini was something like listening to him. His face was beautiful—not least for what it said—and it has been captured superbly in photographs, particularly in those by Robert Hupka in [Samuel] Antek's *This Was Toscanini*.

But his conducting was beautiful, too, partly just as visual design, as it were, but even more because of its honesty, because nothing was done other than for its effect on the orchestra. There was no ostentatious display of ecstasy, and he was incapable of any claptrap gesture.

Shapeliness, clarity, simplicity, and songfulness were the striking qualities of Toscanini's best performances. Take, for example, [early in] Act III of *Otello*, the scene that begins with Desdemona's greeting to Otello, "*Dio ti giocondi, o sposo*" ("God keep you happy, husband"), and that ends with Otello's unexpected, cruel, ironic recapitulation of the same melody, [at] "*Datemi ancor l'eburnea mano*" ("Give me again your ivory hand") [climaxing with, in the Shakespeare,] "I took you for that cunning whore of Venice/That married with Othello." No performance I have experienced equals Toscanini's in dramatic force because none has articulated the musical shape of the scene with such precision.

More than anything, it is his sense of pace that enables him to keep the basic tempo ("*Dio ti giocondi*") as a constant point of reference, even when there is a complete change of atmosphere ("*Esterrefatta fisso*" or "*Io prego il cielo*"), that establishes a correct relationship between Desdemona's "*Tu di me fai gioco*" and what goes before, and that produces, finally, that perfectly prepared and exactly gauged return to the opening melody and key.

You can hear the result of Toscanini's remarkable sense of pace and continuity in the working out of an interpretive problem so routine as to pass almost unnoticed. I listened again to his record of the Air from Bach's Suite No. 3, and I found myself very much moved by the beautiful naturalness of the breath between the end of the Air's second half and its repetition.

The performance of the Air was interesting from another point of view, too. Toscanini had no interest in musical scholarship as such, but his intense musicality, specifically his feeling for the vocal quality of the piece, led him to properly idiomatic, that is expressive, execution of the appoggiaturas and trills, something not achieved by most of his colleagues then or since.

More than anything else, I think of Toscanini as a sort of singer. There is a recording of him as he works with a chorus on the declamation on a repeated chord of "*Libera me, Domine*" at the beginning of the last movement of the Verdi Requiem, the pleadings, poundings, demonstrations, imprecations, that finally produce something that is free in its yielding to the speech rhythms, yet precise, and *pianissimo*, and, as Verdi asks, in tempo for the last two syllables. Or compare the rendering of the choral recitatives in the Berlioz *Roméo et Juliette* by Toscanini and Munch.

There is also quite a famous record of rehearsals for the 1946 *Traviata* broadcasts. These rehearsals are without singers, other than Toscanini, that is, and except for the voice and most of the actual pitches, he sings, among other things, "Sempre libera" with more verve, "De' miei bollenti spiriti" more elegantly and ardently, than I have heard them from the "real" singers. If you want an especially wonderful detail, try "*sorriso dell'amor*" in the tenor aria.

In that *Traviata* rehearsal, Toscanini at one point finds the orchestra inattentive about the figurations in the accompaniment. He reproaches the violins for sloppy articulation, and he adds, in Italian, "*Si puo suonare bene anche 'La Traviata*" ("It's possible to play *La Traviata* well, too"). The remark is made quickly, as though in passing, unpretentiously and without pathos, but I don't know of anything that illuminates more movingly what being a musician meant to Toscanini.

A musical performance was a moral commitment, something, in his own words, into which to put his blood. He hated the players and singers who would not put their blood because that represented the most terrible betrayal of the performer's ideal of service to the composer.

When he prepared Verdi's *Hymn of the Nations* for an OWI [Office of War Information] film, he changed the text so that Italy became "*patria mia tradita*" ("my betrayed fatherland"). By the firmness of his stand against the Fascists and the Nazis, and for actions like his work on behalf of the orchestra, later the Israel Philharmonic, which the great violinist Bronislaw Huberman had founded in Palestine, Toscanini became a political hero as well.

He was a great conductor, but surely not a uniquely great one. Nonetheless, he occupied a unique place, and in a world far larger than the world of music, for he was a great man who stood, burningly and beautifully, for integrity and selfless dedication.

Stravinsky's *Rake's Progress*—Sarah Remembers With Affection

March 26, 1967

It was in connection with Stravinsky's *Rake's Progress* that I first heard the name of Sarah Caldwell. The opera had its premiere in Venice in September 1951; it came to America the following season, but it seems to have been unsympathetically produced at the Metropolitan, certainly not effectively. It was really savagely treated by Olin Downes in the *New York Times*, and it failed.

Soon, though, one heard stories of a remarkable production in the provinces, specifically at the Boston University Opera Workshop, a performance conducted by the composer and directed by an extraordinarily talented young woman recently come from the Middle West, an assistant of Boris Goldovsky's named Sarah Caldwell. That was in May 1953, and now Sarah Caldwell, who still remembers the *Rake* chapter with special affection, is about to produce the work again with the Opera Company of Boston, March 29 and 31, and April 2.[7]

[7] See next article.

It is the first of three productions of *The Rake's Progress*, all likely to be remarkable, to be seen on this continent this year: the Royal Opera of Stockholm will bring its production, directed by Ingmar Bergman, to Montreal's Expo '67, and the Hamburg State Opera will bring its new production, directed by Gian Carlo Menotti, to New York City in June.

Stravinsky composed *The Rake's Progress* between 1948 and 1951. He asked W. H. Auden, who had been introduced to him by Aldous Huxley, to write the libretto—Auden's reaction: "I need hardly say that the chance of working with you is the greatest honor of my life"—and the poet later took in a collaborator, Chester Kallman. When Stravinsky approached Auden, he already had the *Rake's Progress* subject in mind. He had seen the engravings made from William Hogarth's set of eight paintings (1732–33) in Chicago in 1947, and he had been struck by them, and by *A Harlot's Progress*, "as by a series of operatic scenes."

Stravinsky was, in any event, anxious to write an opera in English. "By this I mean," he explained, "a music originated in the English prosody and worked out in my own way, as I did before with Russian (*The Nightingale*, *Mavra*, *The Wedding*), French (*Perséphone*), and Latin (*Oedipus Rex*, *Symphony of Psalms*) prosodies." Except for a couple of Bible verses in *Babel* (1944), Stravinsky's contribution to Nathaniel Shilkret's composite *Genesis* Suite, this was the composer's first setting of English, though, as it turned out, the first of many.

Stravinsky's treatment of English was as individual as his treatment of French and Latin had been in *Perséphone* and *Oedipus*, but one of the opera's most remarkable qualities is how clearly understandable the text is at all times, a matter of intense concern to Stravinsky.

Auden was delighted with the idea of a moral fable based on Hogarth. He wrote: "As (a) you have thought about the Rake's Progress for some time, and (b) it is the librettist's job to satisfy the composer, not the other way around, I should be most grateful if you could let me have any ideas you may have formed about characters, plot, etc."

Stravinsky, for his part, was determined that he was going to write an opera as opposed to a music drama. "I chose," he wrote in the notes for his 1964 recording of *The Rake's Progress*,

> to cast my work in the mould of an 18th-century "number" opera, one in which the dramatic progress depends upon the succession of separate pieces—arias, duets, trios, choruses, instrumental interludes, recitatives. The story is told, enacted, contained entirely in song—as distinguished from so-called speech-song, and Wagnerian "continuous melody" which consists, in effect, of orchestral commentary enveloping a continuous recitative. Having chosen a period-piece subject, I decided—naturally, as it seemed to me—to assume the conventions of the period as well. *The Rake's Progress* is a conventional

opera, therefore, but with the difference that these particular conventions were considered by respectable circles to be long since dead. My plan of revival did not include updating or modernizing, however—which would have been self-contradictory, in any case—and it follows that I have no ambitions as a "re-former," at least not in the line of a Gluck, a Wagner or a Berg.

In 1939, when Stravinsky gave the Charles Eliot Norton Lectures on *The Poetics of Music*, he had scandalized his Harvard audiences by declaring his admiration for composers like Bellini and Donizetti, though he was merely fifteen years ahead of fashion. *The Rake's Progress* is a kind of declaration of love to Italian "vocal" opera, though Italian here, to be sure, means *Così fan tutte* more than *Puritani*.

Except that it lacks trombones, the *Rake's Progress* orchestra is the same as the one Mozart uses in *Don Giovanni*: woodwinds, horns, and trumpets, all in pairs, timpani, and strings. Recitatives are accompanied by a harpsichord, and that instrument has almost the whole card-playing scene to itself. That is the scene in the churchyard when Tom Rakewell and Nick Shadow gamble for Tom's soul: a scene in which dramatic suspense mounts tremendously is accompanied by an instrument that refuses to change dynamic level, and to really chilling effect.

The vocal writing is predominantly lyric. Stravinsky also makes telling use of coloratura. In Anne's "I go, I go to him," which ends Act I, this is done for brilliance, ending on a high C. Here Stravinsky uses another convention because "I go" is the cabaletta, the fast concluding section, of a double aria, whose first, slow part is her "Quietly, night, Oh! Find him," and the double aria is a stock device of earlier opera, of, for example, Manrico's "Ah, sì, ben mio" and "Di quella pira" in *Trovatore*.

The coloratura style is parodied in Baba's rage aria, "Wretched me!" Then again it is used for its tender, expressive values in the Bedlam scene, in Tom's duet with Anne, "In a foolish dream," and for the "swanlike music" of Tom's dying soliloquy, "Where art thou, Venus?"

As in *Così fan tutte*, which Stravinsky studied intently while working on his opera, *Rake's Progress* uses a language of classical elegance to convey the pathos of Tom's "Love, too frequently betrayed," of "Quietly, night," of the death scene. And there is, of course, also the fun of the chorus of the Roaring Boys and Whores, the Auction Scene with its quasi-nonsense lines, of Baba's rage aria, which is interrupted and taken up exactly on the beat an hour later, and of the moralistic, before-the-curtain epilogue à la *Don Giovanni*.

But *Rake's Progress* is not pastiche, nor, except in a few details, is it parodistic. Most of Stravinsky's work has involved a kind of commentary on other styles and conventions, something that has been a stimulus for him to compose some of the most personal as well as the wittiest and most elegant music of our time.

Mod *Rake* Bold, Fantastic

March 31, 1967

With an excellent musical performance, this production [by the Opera Company of Boston at the Back Bay Theatre] gives a bold, even fantastic, dramatic and visual interpretation of a touching and subtle piece of theater.

The Auden-Kallman libretto, based loosely on Hogarth's "Rake's Progress" engravings, has Tom Rakewell [Alexander Young] leave his country sweetheart, Anne Trulove [Doris Yarick], when Nick Shadow [Raimund Herincx] brings him news of sudden wealth. The fleshpots of London pall, and Tom is persuaded by Nick, now his servant, first to marry Baba the Turk [John Ferrante], the bearded circus lady, then to invest his money in a fake machine for turning stones into bread.

He goes bankrupt and his possessions are auctioned. The year-and-a-day set by Shadow as the duration of his contract is over, and Shadow reveals himself as the devil, claiming Tom's soul. Shadow relents to the extent of agreeing to gamble for Tom's soul, but when Tom wins, Shadow, before sinking into the ground, condemns him to madness.

Tom, believing himself Adonis, ends in Bedlam where his Venus, Anne, bids him farewell. In an epilogue the actors step before the curtain to point the moral: "For idle hands and hearts and minds the devil finds a work to do."

On every page of the score, the melodies, the harmony and rhythm, the textures and timbres, proclaim Stravinsky's authorship. On every page, the score alludes to the conventions of Mozartian *opera buffa* in the clear demarcations of set pieces, in the harpsichord-accompanied recitatives with their tonic-and-dominant punctuation, in the reference to something specific like the *Don Giovanni* before-the-curtain epilogue, and in other matters of conception or detail. It is proudly artificial, and it is a conceit through which Stravinsky composed a score not only of delightful wit but of touching lyric beauty as well.

Its unique flavor resides in the balance of the 18th century with the 20th, and Sarah Caldwell, in a move whose daring is justified by the result, has shed a delicious and at times disturbing light on the matter by ignoring the direction, "the action takes place in 18th-century England," and setting *The Rake's Progress* in the England of 1967.

The sets by Senn and Pond[8] are black, white, and grey, their surface suggests line engraving. They are a pleasure to look at, more so than the opening scene

[8] Herbert Senn (1924–2003) and Helen Pond (1924–2017) were theatrical set designers based in Yarmouth Port, MA, active between 1950 and 2000, who frequently worked with the Opera Company of Boston as well as in New York City on and off Broadway.

with the drab semi-detached houses where the Truloves live. They also help to define the form of the work in the way they move from the nearly undifferentiated grey of the opening to ever more garishly pointed black-and-white contrasts, and from there back to the greyness of the burial ground, and finally to the all-white Bedlam.

Color appears only in projections and in the luminous disk, a light-and-color mobile, with which Tom decorates his London rooms. The aptly chosen clothes go from extremes of mod fashion, including plastic see-through dresses, in the discotheque—an inspired translation of Mother Goose's brothel—to plain conservative for the Truloves and sinister black for Shadow. Anne's skirts are knee-length, and so are those in the crowd of respectable citizens gloating at the auction.

The lighting is superb. Shadow appears first as a shadow on a housefront, and Tom's first conversation with him is a conversation with a voice and a patch of darkness. He takes Tom to London in a Rolls-Royce that is not quite a hearse, a vehicle that returns to extraordinary effect when its headlamps provide the only lighting for the graveyard scene.

There is the additional counterpoint of light provided by the visual effects of Cassen and Stern,[9] who make inventive use of the resources of kinetic and op art, sometimes with projections that comment on the perverse Stravinsky metrics, with the frenzied patterns for the discotheque, or for something as simple as the rainfall in the street scene in which Anne learns of Tom's marriage to Baba.

Only in the auction scene did the technology betray the play. It is run in front of the curtain and throughout the auditorium, which is delightful; however, the "unknown object," whose sale is to be the climax and which turns out to be Baba dumped by Tom, was shown in an enlarged projection on the curtain, but so murkily as to be unidentifiable to the people who didn't know the opera, and with the text blurred by the amplification of the offstage voice.

Baba is usually a mezzo-soprano, but Caldwell gave the role to a countertenor and, as it were, intensified the character from mere bearded lady to hermaphrodite. I must report that I was dead against this before I saw it, but persuaded by it when I saw it: the underlining of the queerness is unnecessary, but it worked, and even the pathos of Baba's scene with Anne came out within this conception.

Partly this was due, certainly, to the dignity and humor, to say nothing of astonishing vocal brilliance that John Ferrante brought to the role. Indeed, though there were some moments of nervousness, the entire cast was well suited to its musical and theatrical assignments, with especially vividly projecting

[9] Multimedia artists Jackie Cassen (c.1935–2010) and Rudi Stern (1936–2006) had recently provided luminous kinetic installations for Timothy Leary's psychedelic celebrations and also produced installations at the Electric Circus nightclub. Stern would become known for his work in neon.

performance coming from Raimund Herincx as Shadow and James Billings as the auctioneer.

Billings was also responsible for preparing the superb chorus, and credit for the overall musical excellence goes to Robert Craft, whose conducting provided coherence and continuity of pace, stylistic authority, and which also evoked beautiful playing from the orchestra.

Cliburn—Great, but Could Do Better

April 3, 1967

A performer establishes who he is by his choice of what to perform. A program—or better, a whole series from which, over a period, one can infer his concept of program making—is also a significant index to a performer's taste, intellect, industry, integrity, and sense of responsibility.

Van Cliburn's recital programs are most often timid and stale, and the one he played here on Sunday, whose nearest approach to freshness came in one Debussy Étude and in one of the less-played pieces of Liszt's *Années de pèlerinage*, was no exception. And not only does Cliburn concentrate on a repertory excessively battered by others, but he constantly repeats himself: Sunday's recital was the sixth he has given in Boston, and he has played Beethoven's *Appassionata* at three of them.

A special eccentricity of Cliburn's recitals is their beginning with "The Star-Spangled Banner." I don't know what Cliburn intends with this departure from concert convention, although the answer that suggests itself is that he wishes to make a forceful, if not aggressive, gesture of presenting himself as an American pianist. If that is his intention, I respectfully suggest that he could make the point more relevantly by playing perhaps one of the sonatas of Charles Ives, or something else from a considerable repertory of piano music by American composers. Cliburn's services to American music at his Boston concerts consist of two performances, in 1960 and 1963, of the Barber Sonata.

As a matter of fact, almost the oddest thing about Cliburn's "Star-Spangled Banner" performance is how uncharacteristic for his work in general is the taste represented by the soupy harmony and their affected phrasing.

The great strength of Cliburn's playing has been in its freedom from vulgarity and affectation. The public is excited by this powerhouse virtuoso, but he has always stood apart from the mere virtuosi because, most characteristically, he has used his skills to make direct, tasteful, coherent statements of the music he has chosen to play. Often, indeed, even the passages that one might legitimately consider as merely virtuosic, like the double-octave cascades in the first movement of Tchaikovsky's B-flat minor Concerto, have been remarkable for the grandeur and shapeliness of musical contour they have had when Cliburn has played them.

Sunday, Cliburn did his most impressive playing in the Chopin B-flat minor Scherzo, playing it with a pianistic resourcefulness, a formal and rhythmic coherence, and a nobility of style, that were exemplary in themselves, and typical of what makes him so remarkable a pianist. On a smaller scale, and not within the bravura manner, Cliburn did similar playing in the E major Nocturne as well.

The Debussy pieces went very well also, especially the light, darting middle section of the Étude, though a touch of the kind of fantasy that is not really part of Cliburn's equipment would have made them even more interesting to listen to. Liszt's most famous *Mephisto Waltz* was also an imposing musical statement rather than just an occasion for octaves and fast scales.

The *Petrarch Sonnet* No. 123 is an attractive piece, though not so strong, certainly not as impassioned, as the more familiar No. 104—fair enough, I suppose, when one compares the poems. Cliburn's playing of it, with its jangly punching out of the notes of the melody, was not good, though, and in the Brahms rhapsodies and in at least the first two movements of the *Appassionata* there was also much that was pianistically and musically wayward.

Van Cliburn, in spite of a certain reserve of intellect and fancy, is an enormously impressive pianist: hence one's impatient wish that, as he approaches the tenth year of his post-Moscow career, he address himself to more challenging tasks.

Gustav Holst India Opera Remarkably Original Piece

April 5, 1967

Gustav Holst was the most versatile of the English composers of his generation, and it is unfortunate that in America he is best-known either for pieces that are fairly unimportant like the *St. Paul's* Suite which all the bands play, or an annoyingly overblown piece like *The Planets*.

If I had to present a strong case for Holst, I should do it on the mystical *Hymn of Jesus*, of which there is a good recording conducted by Boult (London). A recent record has made me acquainted with another strong and remarkably original piece that I had not known before, the chamber opera, *Savitri*, which is given a superb performance under the direction of the composer's daughter, Imogen Holst, with Janet Baker as Savitri, Robert Tear as Satyavan, and Thomas Hemsley as Death (Argo ZNF 6).

Holst was much interested in Indian literature and music, and he took the story of *Savitri*, composed in 1907–08, from the legends of the *Mahabharata*. The story is simple: Savitri, the wife of the woodman Satyavan, waits for her husband to return home at day's end. She hears the voice of Death who has come to claim Satyavan as he enters the house. Savitri welcomes Death as "The Just One." Death, moved, promises to grant her anything except the life of Satyavan. Her request is for life at its fullest, but that, she tells Death after her wish is granted, can only mean life with her husband. Death, defeated, leaves. Satyavan wakes, and Savitri tells him they have been visited and blessed by one of the Holy Ones.

Holst uses a chamber ensemble of three woodwinds, double string quartet, and bass. Much of the singing is unaccompanied. A kind of stillness pervades *Savitri* at first and last, but the dialogues of Savitri and Death rise to a consuming, passionate intensity. Something remains here of Holst's early love for Wagner, but the music is as fresh and original as Debussy's *Pelléas* is with all its Wagnerian echoes.

A beautiful text is sensitively declaimed and delicately lit by the sparing instrumental music, and the result, for me, has been the discovery of something immensely moving. The record is filled out by four choral hymns from the *Rig Veda*, sung by the sopranos and altos of the Purcell Singers with the harpist Osian Ellis.

Holst, who died in 1934, taught at Harvard until 1932, and while he was here he wrote some pieces for male chorus and strings on English translations of medieval Latin lyrics. This is a superb set of marvelously alive pieces, and it has been recorded along with the slighter but still beguiling settings for female chorus with strings of seven poems by Robert Bridges. The excellent performances are by the Purcell Singers and the English Chamber Orchestra, Imogen Holst conducting (Argo 495/5495).

Holst also made an enduring contribution to the English folk song movement, and he is represented by four pieces on a record called *I Love My Love*, which also contains folk song settings by Vaughan Williams, Britten, Moeran, Grainger, Tippett, and others. It is a varied and pleasing collection, very well sung by the Elizabethan Singers, Louis Halsey conducting, with solos by Susan Longfield, Ian Partridge, and Owen Brannigan (Argo 496/5496).

The Symphony No. 6 in E minor by Vaughan Williams is uneven, but with remarkable things in it, especially the gripping trumpet-and-drum ostinato of the second movement, and the long hushed tragic epilogue. It is performed extremely well on a new recording by the Utah Symphony Orchestra, Maurice Abravanel conducting, and the record becomes even more valuable because it includes a good piece by Vaughan Williams not otherwise available, *Five Variants on "Dives and Lazarus"* for harp and string orchestra (Vanguard 1160/71160).

The Christmas Cantata, *Hodie*, which Vaughan Williams wrote in 1954, strikes me as exceedingly feeble and tedious, though it is very well conducted on a new record by David Willcocks, with soloists Janet Baker, Richard Lewis, and John Shirley-Quirk (Angel 36297).

RCA Victor has reissued Heifetz's slick and fussy performance of Elgar's Violin Concerto, with Sargent conducting (2910).

Handel and Haydn's New Boss—Thomas Dunn, the Purist

April 16, 1967

Thomas Dunn is music director of the Festival Orchestra Society, music director at Manhattan's Church of the Incarnation, and on the faculty of Union Theological Seminary. Next fall, according to an announcement four days ago, he also will assume musical directorship of Boston's 152-year-old Handel and Haydn Society, and his first concerts with the Society will be the annual performances of Handel's *Messiah* scheduled for December 8 and 10 in Symphony Hall.[10]

Dunn, brought up in Baltimore, went to New York from a post in Philadelphia in the late '50s. Word got around quickly that remarkable things were happening at the Church of the Incarnation. He was appointed conductor of the Cantata Singers, a group that under Arthur Mendel and Alfred Mann had specialized in Baroque music, and whose repertory Dunn extended to include major choral works from the 19th and 20th centuries.

In the first years, though, the performances of Baroque music, those of Handel's *Belshazzar* and of Rameau's opera, *Les Indes galantes*, outstanding among them, were what caused Dunn to get, first the attention, then the admiration, of his audiences.

He became known to a larger public through a Bach series he conducted in Carnegie Hall five seasons ago, especially the performance of the B minor Mass that began the cycle in October 1961. What helped to make him known then was not just the remarkable quality of the performance itself, but the outraged review of it in the *New York Times*, and the correspondence and further articles that were reactions both to the concert and the review.

Dunn had given the Mass with forces approximately equal to Bach's own, twenty-five singers and twenty-six players, and what outraged those who equate grandeur of conception with lots of bodies and lots of decibels was to many of us our first experience of really hearing the work. And there were similar experiences later with other works by Bach, and there was the revelation also of

[10] See review of December 11, 1967.

Dunn's series of *Messiah* performances in Carnegie and Philharmonic Halls at Christmastime 1963.

I asked Dunn about one of the consequences of all this, his reputation as a purist, apologizing for an expression which the loaded prose of certain critics has made a dirty word. "Not at all," said Dunn cheerfully, "I rather like the word."

He became a purist, he explained, during his second year at the Peabody Conservatory in Baltimore. He was an organist and he had studied, and happily, with Virgil Fox, a flamboyant virtuoso who is as far from purism as one can get. When Fox left Peabody, Dunn studied with an organist who was purer than pure, though, Dunn added, "I found out later that a lot of what he had passed on as factual, historical information was stuff he had made up himself."

Dunn, at any rate, was acutely unhappy with his new teacher and "seated one day at the organ," he played the overture to *Messiah* "with the *voix celeste*, opening and shutting the swell boxes, making the organ roar, really à la Stokowski." His teacher, whom Dunn thought to be at lunch, heard this exhibition and reported his pupil to the director.

As Dunn describes the subsequent drama as it implicated director, teacher, pupil, and fellow students, it must have been a Hollywood battle of inclination and duty, flaming youth and hoary tradition, and all the rest. The outcome, several crises later, was that Dunn decided to go along with the situation, do exactly what his teacher told him, planning, however, by the end of the year to have learned to do everything better than his teacher in order to thumb his nose at him.

The outcome of that was that Dunn suddenly realized what "purism" was all about. It meant that when one had to solve the problem of how to perform a piece, there was relevant information available, and that information was helpful. Whether the problem was, as in his years as an organ student the comparatively simple one of working out, say, a short piece by Couperin, or, as later, the exceedingly complex one of conducting the B minor Mass, there was always the principle that the composers, thoroughly practical musicians themselves, knew what they were doing, that such men were unlikely to have been bunglers and bores, and that knowledge of relevant tradition and history could only be helpful to the performer.

Later, as a graduate student at Harvard, Dunn came into contact with musicologists. He does not regard himself as one, though he has acquired considerable knowledge as the need for it has occurred. "I was too stupid," he says, "to realize that performers and musicologists were supposed to hate each other, and I just went around asking questions." He got answers, too, and remembers with particular gratitude the mail-order musicological services provided over the years by Arthur Mendel, America's most eminent Bach scholar and chairman of the Princeton music department.

As we discussed the performance of the Bach Passions and Handel's oratorios, Dunn emphasized a point of the greatest importance, and that is to take one's cues from the music. It is senseless to argue that an 18th-century composer felt the same emotions as the 20th-century listener, and then interpret the former to the latter via 19th-century expressive conventions.

When we perform Bach's or Handel's setting of a sacred text, Dunn explains, we must do it according to what we can infer Bach's or Handel's interpretation of that text to have been, not according to what we think of that text. "We mustn't go around interpreting theology ourselves." The issue is complicated by the tradition that equates slowness with reverence, and not just slowness, but tedium as well. He mentioned the recitatives of Christ in the Bach Passions as an example particularly apt to suffer: "Conductors and singers become paralyzed by the idea of dealing with the '*ipsissima verba*,' but the slow, solemn delivery that one gets is a sentimentalism that is completely at odds with the music and, for that matter, the words."

Dunn resigned as conductor of the Cantata Singers a year ago, severing, until the Boston appointment, his connections with the world of the large amateur chorus. He is committed to the idea that certain works, especially from the Baroque, must, because of their particular attributes of texture, balance, rhythm, articulation, tempo, be sung by small choruses. The 1967 *Messiah*s will be sung by the full membership of the Handel and Haydn Society, and to make this possible the Mozart orchestration (as opposed to Mozart-Prout which the Society has used recently) will be used. However exquisitely worked and interesting, Dunn regards this as a curiosity rather than as a real solution, and *Messiah*s after this year will be Handel's.

There is, however, Dunn points out, an enormous and exciting repertory of great choral music from the late 18th century on that is exactly suited to the large amateur chorus. From Haydn to Stravinsky there is much to be done and, Dunn adds emphatically, "when you don't handicap an amateur chorus by giving it music that is not suited to it, there is no need for compromise, for special standards for amateurs, or anything like that. The result should be first-rate."

Roland Hayes Verges on 80—Real Meaning of Great Man's Birthday

May 28, 1967

Roland Hayes will be 80 this Saturday, June 3.

Born in Curryville, GA, on a plantation where his mother had been a slave, Hayes was established as a successful singer by 1912, the year of his first Jordan

Hall recital, and ten years later he was world-famous, in demand everywhere as one of the most highly regarded concert singers of his generation.

Hayes had worked as a field laborer, as a mechanic in an iron foundry, as a waiter, as a behind-the-screen singer at movie theaters. He worked his way through Fisk University, and it was with the Fisk Jubilee Singers that he first came to Boston in 1911. He found work with the John Hancock Insurance Company, studied voice with Arthur J. Hubbard, and he has lived here ever since, for the last forty-two years in a house he bought in Brookline.

But Roland Hayes, struggling to make a career from 1912 on, was not just poor: he was a Negro, and as late as 1920, after many successful concerts, William Brennan, then manager of the Boston Symphony, told him that no Negro could be accepted as a serious musician in this country. Hayes's response was characteristic: he was not angry, but he knew he had not done enough. He went to Europe and gave a recital in London. Before three years had passed, he had given another fifteen there and had sung a command performance at Buckingham Palace.

In 1923, when Hayes had triumphed in Paris and Vienna as well, Pierre Monteux invited him to sing with the Boston Symphony, an aria from Berlioz's *L'Enfance du Christ.* The accounts in Hayes's memoirs (ghostwritten by Mme. Doris Monteux)[11] agree only on the basic points that there was opposition to Hayes's engagement, that Monteux insisted, and that the concert was a success. Moreover, Symphony Hall still stands. And in 1955, at Monteux's 80th birthday celebration, Hayes remembered the 1923 occasion as one that "purged tradition of a blot, the removal of which opened wide the door of opportunity to worthy artists of the Negro race."

It took the help of a man like Monteux, but even more, it needed the courage of a Roland Hayes. It took courage for Hayes to listen to Brennan's words, and to react as he did. It took courage again, and of a different sort, for Hayes in 1924 to face a Berlin audience that, stirred by propaganda about colored occupation troops in the Rhineland, booed, hissed, shouted, for ten solid minutes when he walked onto the platform.

Hayes's critical reception here and in Europe was overwhelmingly favorable. It was mostly rather patronizing though: not "he sings Schubert and Wolf, Fauré and Duparc beautifully," but more like "it's beautiful, and isn't it amazing to have it come from a Negro," or even "it isn't a bit like a minstrel show."

It is, I think, a significant advance that one hardly sees such writing any more. It is not just that we have learned to be more polite, but the thought behind it has pretty well disappeared, too.

[11] Steinberg must be referring here to Doris Monteux, *It's All in the Music: The Life and Work of Pierre Monteux* (New York: Farrar, Straus & Giroux, 1965), neither a memoir nor ghostwritten.

One still finds it in Europe sometimes—I remember it especially from the reviews Henry Lewis used to get in 1956 as conductor of the Seventh Army Symphony—but there it also is part of an attitude that regards any American cultural achievement with a certain polite astonishment.

Most of us, though, without giving it a second thought, judge Leontyne Price by the same standards as Tebaldi or Nilsson, George Shirley by the standards of Wunderlich and Gedda. They and their colleagues, in fact, are sufficiently equal even to get occasional bad reviews.

Since Hayes, and especially since Marian Anderson came on the scene in the mid-'30s, the list of American Negro singers has become long and distinguished. Opportunities in opera came more slowly. The Metropolitan engaged a Negro for the first time in 1955—it was Anderson, terribly past her prime, in *Ballo in maschera*—and by an impressive public relations snow-job, Rudolf Bing managed to have himself turned into a hero for doing so little so late.

It is still tough for musicians other than singers. Conductors like Dean Dixon and Everett Lee have made their careers outside America altogether, though in this connection one should point out that there is, even after Bernstein, a general disinclination to take young American conductors seriously here.[12] Among instrumentalists, only André Watts is making a big career, and certainly one sees almost no Negroes in the symphony orchestras.

A singer might not discover until he is well into his teens that he has the physical potential for a professional career, and if that potential is impressive enough, the chances are good that scholarships and other forms of patronage can be found to see him through his training. You don't, on the other hand, just discover a gift for playing the piano or cello in a boy or a girl of 16. It isn't something that is just there, like a voice, and anyway a good instrumentalist needs an early start of hard, concentrated work.

It means that if the successes of Negro singers can be interpreted as a victory, the fact that the singers are virtually alone among Negro musicians in their success points to an important failure. The conditions that go into making a singer allow a gifted Negro to overcome the fact that he cannot compete with his white contemporary on equal terms, economically, socially, and educationally. That is not true in the conditions that go into the making of an instrumentalist. The problem, then, goes beyond the confines of the musical world. It goes to the power of Gov. Wallace, of Mrs. Hicks, of Mr. Eisenstadt, of countless others, and of great economic forces and fears.[13]

[12] See also the article "Americans Ignored—Why Import Conductors?," June 22, 1969.

[13] Steinberg here refers to prominent political figures, national and local, in the Civil Rights movement: Alabama governor George C. Wallace (1919–98), at that time a staunch segregationist; Louise Day Hicks (1916–2003), a politician and lawyer fervently opposed to desegregation (especially court-ordered busing) in Boston's public schools; and Thomas S. Eisenstadt (b. 1936), a desegregationist who succeeded Hicks as chair of the Boston School Committee in 1966.

As we congratulate Roland Hayes this week, we shall be all too ready to congratulate ourselves as well, but before we become indecently eager to do so, thinking of all that has changed and that has been done since a young Negro tenor sang his first Jordan Hall recital fifty-five years ago, let us keep our minds firmly fixed on all that must still be done.

That is the real meaning of this great man's birthday. The job before us is even greater than the accomplishments behind us. I would suppose, though, that the birthday present Roland Hayes would most care to have from us all is our determination to carry on what he gallantly began alone. His exquisite artistry and his human greatness are occasions for our gratitude. They are also a challenge.

As we salute him, we can repeat Virgil Thomson's words to him on his 75th birthday: "You do the human race an honor to exist."

Roland Hayes Looks Back—"People Tell Me I Don't Realize What I Give"

June 1, 1967

A few days before his 80th birthday, which is this Saturday, Roland Hayes sat in the Brookline house where he has lived over forty years, reminisced, and talked about this and that.

On the birthday celebrations: "I was used to this sort of thing at one time, but I've been quiet for so many years now. It all seems very one-sided to me, people doing so much for me. . . . People tell me I don't realize what I give to them, and when I sing, I'm just off, gone, aware only that I've got a job to do, but not thinking about the effect. . . . It's overwhelming to me, people coming back still, year after year. . . . It's wonderful, too, to have all this recognition in my own country. You know, though, Washington hasn't said boo. That's all right, though."

On opera: "I studied five roles, including the Duke in *Rigoletto*, Rodolfo [in *La bohème*], Radamès [in *Aida*]. In Paris, Henry Russell, who had been the manager of the old Boston Opera, wanted to arrange for me to sing Des Grieux in *Manon* at the Opéra-Comique. But I told him, thinking this would be a way of putting it out of his head, that I wanted to make my debut in a part I created myself, and then I'd do Des Grieux, but there wasn't the composer for it then, and so it never happened."

On singing Lieder: "I know I did the right thing in going to Germany to learn more about the language and to understand more of the background from which the songs proceed. . . . In Germany I often sang whole evenings of Lieder, Mozart, Beethoven, Schubert, Schumann, Brahms, Wolf, just a few by Strauss. Schubert is like a corner of my heart, but Hugo Wolf to me was like the sum of them all. That word-sense!"

On *Boston Herald* critic Philip Hale: "A very serious man about music, and he gave me some fine, constructive criticism in the early days when I really wanted to know how I was coming along. Later, when I engaged a contingent of Boston Symphony men for a Mozart aria on one of my Symphony Hall recitals—that was before I'd been engaged by the Symphony for one of their concerts—he said, 'Be bold, be bold, Mr. Hayes, but not too bold.'

"Yes, I had one tour in Russia, and the arrangements about payment were complicated because you weren't supposed to take more money out than you'd brought in. I was invited to sing at the Kremlin once, and you know what they asked for? My religious folk songs. I sang there, but I didn't see anybody because the auditorium was in pitch darkness.... My companion all through that trip was Maxim Litvinov, you remember, he was ambassador in Washington later. I had asked to have a high official with me at all times, because evidently it was dangerous for Russians to speak to an *Auslander* without proper supervision. I made some pretty outspoken comments myself, and that was probably why I was never back there again.

"Even in 1924, when I first wanted to go to Germany after I had had successes in London, Paris, Vienna, and Prague, one of the things they warned about was Hitler. I was taken to see a sort of rite of someone being Nazified, being made to feel invincible. It was terrible, but it prepared me for the reception I got at my first Berlin concert, wave after wave of hisses, coming in relays, like a searing knife. But I just stood there like a soldier, and I, too, had learned something about invincibility.

"When I moved to Boston in 1912, I worked as a page in the executive department at John Hancock, and there I was taught something about business procedure because it was figured that as a Negro I wouldn't be able to get a regular concert manager. Later William Brennan, the Symphony's manager who at one time had told me that as a Negro I couldn't be accepted in this country as a serious artist, managed me. He was very good, and we had no disagreements ever. By myself I got the reputation of having a pretty rigid back about money. Over the years I said NO to many things that would have meant compromising my musical ideals. Yes, I was like a giant about that, and my conscience is clear, though if I'd acted otherwise with broadcasting and recording companies I might be better off financially now."

During all this there was a visit from Louis Speyer and A. Fred Prager,[14] who are arranging the celebration for Hayes at the Gardner Museum this Saturday evening. There was discussion about the musical part of the program, and at one

[14] Speyer was the English horn player of the BSO, Prager an area businessman and civic leader.

point Hayes said firmly, "No, no, no, you're thinking about the sentiment, but I want to think about the music." "And that," he added later, "is the battle I've been fighting all my life."

Discovered: Wealth of Talent—Rewarding Day With Russian Music

June 4, 1967

BRONXVILLE, NY—As recently as three years ago, contemporary, not to mention avant-garde, style in the Soviet Union was still an underground activity; so much so that when the International Society for Contemporary Music put a twelve-tone piano piece on the program for one of its New York concerts, the composer asked to remain anonymous for his protection at home.

When the young American composer Joel Spiegelman returned in January of last year from a five months' visit to Russia, the thaw in the musical world had continued to the point that he was able to bring back several new and unpublished scores.

For the first time, also, one could read in a *Globe* interview (February 6, 1966) the names of Andrei Volkonsky, Edison Denisov, Valentin Silvestrov, Leonid Grabovsky, and the others who represented a manner of musical thinking different from that of Shostakovich, Kabalevsky, Khachaturian, Khrennikov, etc.

Concerts devoted to the new music from Russia have been given at Buffalo, at Indiana University, and, on May 24, at Sarah Lawrence College, where Spiegelman is on the faculty. On May 18, 19, and 20, Leonard Bernstein had conducted Denisov's *Crescendo e diminuendo* at the New York Philharmonic with Spiegelman as harpsichord soloist. Bernstein also conducted *Mischievous Folk Ditties* by Rodion Shchedrin, done several times this season at the Boston Pops under the title *Naughty Limericks*. Shchedrin, however, is not part of the new current in Russia, his *Ditties* or *Limericks* being a bit of broad, rambunctious humor in the manner of Prokofiev or Shostakovich, very brilliantly scored.

The Sarah Lawrence concert consisted of two large pieces, *Lamentations of Shchaza* (1963) by Volkonsky, for soprano and five instruments, and *Sun of the Incas* (1964) by Denisov, for soprano with eleven instruments; and two small works, a Trio for flute, trumpet, and celeste, by Silvestrov (1962), and *Dimensions* (1965) for five instruments by Vladimir Zagortsev. Earlier in the day, Elliott Carter, Boris Schwarz, Lewis Kaplan, Spiegelman, and I, participated in a symposium on recent Russian music and its background.

Carter and Schwarz, who is the only American musicologist to have concerned himself extensively with contemporary musical life in Russia, spoke of Russian music in the early part of the century, especially in the '20s and early '30s. It was a period characterized by a lively sense of adventure, represented in the early years by composers as diverse as Stravinsky and Scriabin, a little later in things as remarkable as the Symphony No. 2 of Prokofiev, the Symphony No. 4 and particularly the opera, *The Nose*, by Shostakovich, and by the music of Nicolai Roslavetz (born 1881, assumed perished in Siberia some time after 1930) and that of Alexander Mossolov (born 1900).

What is being done today, then, by Volkonsky, Denisov, Silvestrov, and the others is far more relevant and true to the tradition of Russian artistic and intellectual life than one might at first assume. It is also worth remembering in this context that the only big-name international virtuoso who acknowledges the existence of advanced musical style is a citizen of the Soviet Union, the cellist Mstislav Rostropovich.

This new chapter in the history of Soviet music began only eleven years ago, in 1956, when Volkonsky, who had been a composition pupil of Nadia Boulanger and Dinu Lipatti, started to write serial music. One of the Moscow composers, the Rumanian Philipp Hershkovitz, had been one of Webern's last pupils, but in general it was often necessary to go outside of Russia to find out about the recent history of Western music. Hardly any new scores had entered the country for twenty years, and there were no performances to speak of. Spiegelman recalls hearing the Borodin Quartet play Webern's Opus 5 in 1965: it was the first performance in Moscow of anything by Webern. The Warsaw Festival became a significant educational institution for Russian musicians, and it was there that Americans, Carter and Spiegelman among them, first met their Russian colleagues.

It is not altogether surprising that some of the new Russian scores are a bit naive in their espousal and use of new techniques. Part of the significance of a concert like the one at Sarah Lawrence is historical, important because it conveys information about what composers in an interesting part of the world, and whose work we have not yet been able to know, are up to.

Of the four represented at this concert, Andrei Volkonsky, who is also a harpsichordist and the leader of an ensemble specializing in the performance of early music, is the most impressive. His *Lamentations of Shchaza* for soprano, with violin, viola, English horn, harpsichord, and percussion, a setting of a poem of his own, is a work of the most fastidious facture, rhythmically inventive, and strongly expressive with the sparest of means.

The Silvestrov Trio is a fairly slight work, with much charm, and effectively scored out for its flute-trumpet-celeste combination. Zagortsev is a pupil of Silvestrov's, and was only 21 when he wrote the quintet, *Dimensions*. This was the only piece on the program to make use of at least partially aleatory writing, for a coda made humorously effective in its sudden destruction of all the material and the assumptions associated with it.

One could tell from Denisov's somewhat Darmstadtian *Crescendo e diminuendo*, as well as from his more conventionally Russian *Sun of the Incas*, that he is a man of impressive and attractive musicality and of considerable vigor of invention, though both works were more remarkable for those qualities than for the ability to integrate manifold and often fascinating ideas into convincing compositions.

Stephanie Turash sang Volkonsky's *Lamentations* and the Denisov Cantata remarkably beautifully, and there was occasion also for fine playing from members of the Aeolian Players, in residence at Sarah Lawrence, other members of the college faculty, and various players from New York.

The day with recent Russian music was rewarding. The "new" composers represent a wealth of talent, and I look forward to knowing more of their work. It is good to know that the Soviet musicians who care can freely find out about the historical developments at one time closed to them and make the discoveries of a new musical world their own. It is also a pleasure, thanks to the ambassadorship of someone like Spiegelman, to be able to know what these musicians are doing and thus to be able to extend to them a welcome into our musical life.

Menuhin Uniquely Beautiful at Tanglewood

July 3, 1967

LENOX—At Friday evening's Boston Symphony concert at Tanglewood, the season's first, Yehudi Menuhin gave the most beautiful performance of Beethoven's Violin Concerto that I have ever heard. It was not the most perfect: intonation was often strange, and in the finale the rhythm was sometimes puzzling, too. At the same time, there were things about the violin playing as such that were really masterful: control of articulation, for example (and Menuhin makes severe demands on himself in that matter), and the lovely tone, which is delicate without being small or mincing, sweet and full without being heavy and blowzy, and concentrated even in the low register.

It was, though, the musical character of the playing that conveyed so well the breadth of form and the serenity of the work, and that made Menuhin's performance uniquely beautiful. For once the first-movement development, and especially the moving passage in G minor, remained part of the composition instead of becoming a self-indulgent, pathetic, and essentially irrelevant episode.

Menuhin played Kreisler's cadenza, itself a remarkable combination of virtuoso writing and compositional intelligence. Most violinists who play it—and I am thinking particularly of Isaac Stern's performance a couple of years ago—communicate only its virtuosity, and the famous passage when the two themes are played simultaneously becomes merely the climax of a series of outrageous technical difficulties.

When Menuhin played it with his greater maturity about relating local events to larger ones, it was clear that the heightened compositional density of this passage made it the cadenza's structural climax. Altogether, indeed, he showed how the cadenza continues, comments on, wraps up Beethoven's ideas, how, in other words, it is part of the concerto rather than an intrusion upon it.

Always when I have heard others play the Beethoven, the cadenza has become such an aggressive and detached display piece that audiences have taken its ending as the signal to relax and cough, thus spoiling Beethoven's beautiful strokes of bringing the lovely second theme back once more when the orchestra enters. With Menuhin, the cadenza was so obviously part of the piece, its ending open, and the orchestral entrance a continuation, rather than a break, that the hush remained, and for the first time in a public concert I could hear not only this magic moment but, as it were, the whole movement through to the end.

I am convinced that Rudolf Kolisch is right in insisting that Beethoven's markings for the second movement imply a faster tempo than the conventional one at which Menuhin, too, played it. Nevertheless, Menuhin's playing was the most engrossing I have experienced of this Larghetto because of the antisentimental, noble lyricism of the phrasing, the refinement of the sound itself, and the improvisatory fantasy with which the decorations to the theme were "spoken."

And for all this, Erich Leinsdorf provided a framework that started with a somewhat neutral playing of the first ritornello and became, with the soloist's entrance, stronger in character, sensitive, and finely integrated in detail as well as in large dimensions.

The concert began with Prokofiev's Symphony No. 5, played rather roughly, but with pleasing energy. Soggy weather kept the audience below 5,000.

A Natural Sounding *Tristan und Isolde*

July 9, 1967

Tristan und Isolde from the 1966 Bayreuth Festival is one of the very best of all Wagner recordings (Deutsche Grammophon 139221/5, 5 records). Karl Böhm conducts, and the cast includes Birgit Nilsson (Isolde), Wolfgang Windgassen (Tristan), Martti Talvela (Marke), Christa Ludwig (Brangäne), Eberhard Wächter (Kurwenal), Claude Heater (Melot), Erwin Wohlfahrt (Shepherd), and Peter Schreier (Sailor).

The performances of Böhm, Nilsson, and Windgassen are particularly strong; the sound is natural rather than souped up, and beautiful; and one senses the benefits of the work of Wieland Wagner, who originated the Bayreuth *Tristan* in 1962. Much of what Nilsson and Windgassen do so well is the product of a stage performance of uncommon penetration and intelligence. Windgassen's Act III, with its extraordinary projection of an existentialist despair, is the most powerful instance.

One should point out that Ludwig's Brangäne is a bit superficial, that Talvela's Marke is sometimes too pathetic, that Heater sounds dreadful in his brief but crucial moments, but even with these reservations the performance is exciting, convincing, true.

Furtwängler's way with music and orchestra remains uniquely marvelous (Angel), and his recording has Flagstad (less interesting than Nilsson), Suthaus (as good as Windgassen and more consistent), the very young Fischer-Dieskau, Greindl (better than Talvela, though less agreeable vocally), and a poor Brangäne. As a very different sort of performance, though, the new one should join the old in any collection, and I also recommend it to those who have no *Tristan* yet.

Furtwängler's *Walküre* recording, made in 1954 shortly before his death, has been reissued on Angel's low-price Seraphim label (6012, five records, monaural only). Martha Mödl is an exciting Brünnhilde, though often in technical difficulties; Suthaus is the best Siegmund on records; Frick a very good Hunding; Klose a very good Fricka; but Frantz only a routine Wotan, and Rysanek an often strident, uncontrolled Sieglinde. It is a performance of remarkable qualities and certainly the best conducted on records, the sound is good, and, especially at the price, I recommend it as something to put alongside one of the newer *Walküre* albums.

But which? London (A4509/OSA1509, five records) has completed its *Ring* with a *Walküre* conducted by Georg Solti, with Nilsson and Hans Hotter (Brünnhilde and Wotan), James King and Régine Crespin (Siegmund and Sieglinde), Frick (Hunding), and Ludwig (Fricka). Deutsche Grammophon (139229-33, 5 records) has begun a *Ring* with *Walküre*, von Karajan conducting, with Crespin and Thomas Stewart, Jon Vickers and Gundula Janowitz, Talvela, and Josephine Veasey.

Brünnhilde: Nilsson is great; Crespin, though very good, is not as impressive, and that she has not sung it on stage makes a difference.

Wotan: Hotter's is one of the great dramatic portrayals of our time, though in a few moments in Act III, his voice is not up to his demands on it; Stewart is the most impressive Wotan since Hotter.

Siegmund: Vickers, when he is good, as in the "Todesverkündigung," is much better than King, but he is less dependable and has bad moments.

Both Hundings and Frickas are good, and the London Valkyries are a bit better.

Solti achieves powerful climaxes, but he makes nervous tempo fluctuations, is incapable of calm, lets details dominate, and tends to vulgarize and trivialize this score, much as he has the rest of the *Ring*. Von Karajan's high points are not as brilliant as Solti's, but often the sense of line is grand. The performance is almost chamber-musical, and the delicacy of texture is fascinating and revealing. His recording is distant and sometimes disagreeably echo-y; London's is very present indeed and makes Wagner sound like Mantovani.

Tribute to Monteverdi

July 16, 1967

In celebration of the 400th anniversary of his birth, Claudio Monteverdi is unusually well represented in the new records this year. The most ambitious of these projects involves the opera, *L'incoronazione di Poppea*, which he wrote at 74, which is the greatest of his surviving works and the summit of achievement in opera composition before Mozart.

It shows us Nero sexually enslaved to Poppea, willing, for her, to exile his wife and empress, and to put his advisor, Seneca, to death. We see Poppea crowned Empress, and the work ends with herself and Nero in an ecstatic love duet, the whole a hard, immoral triumph of love over virtue. It is a subject that engaged all of Monteverdi's powers, his architectural sense, his penetration into human character, his tragic sense, his flair for comedy, his feeling for the rhythm and contours of language, his melodic invention, his staggeringly powerful harmonies, his imaginative ear for texture.

Cambridge has issued an excellent recording (CRM B 901-CRS B 1901, four records), made at the University of California, Berkeley, under the direction of Alan Curtis, with a cast that includes Carole Bogard (Poppea), Charles Bressler (Nero), Herbert Beattie (Seneca), Judy Nelson (Drusilla), Sharon Hayes (Octavia), and many others.

An earlier recording on Angel gave only about half the work, and that in an edition that made it sound a bit like Vaughan Williams, though there were some good characterizations from people like Richard Lewis, Oralia Dominguez, John Shirley-Quirk, and Hugues Cuénod. The Cambridge recording gives us Monteverdi's masterpiece with the right sound, the right notes, and most of the time with the right spirit.

A few individual performances are pallid, some of the Italian is bad, but generally the passion and humor of the work are well put across; Bogard and Bressler are notably good, as is James Fankhauser in a number of interesting small roles. There is a libretto in Italian and English, and full and excellent notes. This release is an admirable enterprise, most important, and something to give the deepest musical pleasure.

From the same source, and also highly recommended, comes a record of vocal chamber music and some keyboard pieces by Monteverdi and his great contemporary, Frescobaldi (Cambridge 708-1708). The selection is superb, and there is sensitive and often lovely sounding singing by, among others, Carole Bogard, James Fankhauser, and Judy Nelson, with Alan Curtis to establish the high musical and musicological standards, and to play the keyboard solos.

Monteverdi performance at a still higher level can be heard in the new (and first and only good) recording of that brilliant and varied masterpiece, the Vespers Service of 1610, that so excitingly combines the ecclesiastical tradition with the drama and virtuosity of the new operatic style (Telefunken SAWT 9501/2). Jürgen Jürgens leads this superbly eloquent and gloriously executed performance, with the Monteverdi Chorus of Hamburg, the Concentus Musicus of Vienna, harpsichordist Gustav Leonhardt, and a first-rate group of vocal soloists.

An Enoch Light recording (PR7001SD) offers parts of the charming, sometimes ("Eri già tutta mia" and "Io ch'armato sin hor") moving *Scherzi musicali* of 1607 and 1632. The tenors Hugues Cuénod and Charles Bressler sing beautifully, but both the violently "present" and exaggeratedly stereophonic recording and the often cute and tricky instrumentations and their performance by the New York Chamber Soloists, suggest ardent salesmanship more than musical dedication.

Some beautiful music by Monteverdi, his contemporaries Frescobaldi and Turini, and the earlier Della Casa, is well performed on a record called *Early Baroque Music of Italy*, with the New York Pro Musica under the late Noah Greenberg (Decca 9425-79425).

Also worth noting are a record of Monteverdi's intensely expressive *Lamento d'Adrianna*, together with works of earlier composers, Jannequin, Lassus, Marenzio, Gesualdo, and Josquin (his touching memorial to his teacher, Ockeghem), sung by the Deller Consort (Bach Guild 671); and a record of Monteverdi's two Mass settings and of two other sacred works, *Laudate pueri* and *Ut queant laxis*, sung by the Choir of St. John's College, Cambridge, George Guest conducting (Argo ZRG 5494).

Rosen's Debussy Bright

August 2, 1967

Charles Rosen has made a record of piano music by Debussy, including both books of *Images* (the first containing the popular "Reflets dans l'eau," the second consisting of three very fine pieces, "Cloches à travers les feuilles," "Et la lune descend sur le temple qui fut," and the remarkable "Poissons d'or"); *Estampes* (a set that includes the fine "Soirée dans Grenade"); and four single pieces, "La plus que lente," "Hommage à Haydn," "Berçeuse héroïque," and "L'Îsle joyeuse" (Epic 3945/1345).

Rosen is a pianist remarkable for his intelligence and his technical resourcefulness. Most pianists play Debussy mainly for atmosphere and as a slightly blurred wash of color. To compare even just the first couple of measures of "Reflets dan l'eau" in Rosen's performance with almost anyone else's is to realize that he reveals a line of activity in Debussy's music that is generally ignored: the marvelous and subtle polyphony achieved by the juxtaposition of [textures] and timbres.

This attention to texture and the role it plays in structure, and its rhythmic vitality, allows Rosen's playing to present a Debussy who is far stronger and more "musical," also correspondingly less trivially pictorial and less suggestive of cocktail-piano, than the one we mostly hear. Toscanini's and Boulez's performances of the orchestral music have comparable qualities. It adds up to an image of Debussy that is more relevant, more true, certainly more interesting, than the traditional one. I find Rosen's playing of "La plus que lente" and of the "Berçeuse" a bit mannered, but I very much recommend this important and impressive record.

Beethoven's Original *Fidelio* Tanglewood Delight

August 7, 1967

LENOX—An unforgettable evening: a great and vital work of Beethoven's given only a handful of times ever, and probably not at all in America; an exciting performance generally, whose special glory was the portrayal of Leonore by the most wonderful new singer heard in this country since the debut of Nilsson.

The *Fidelio* of 1805, as performed Saturday night at Tanglewood by the Boston Symphony Orchestra, is flawed, and the revisions of 1814 that produced the work we see in the theater and hear on records today were necessary to have a tenable proposition for the modern theater. Also, the 1814 score contains many strokes of genius that enrich the work in ways that go far beyond questions of practicability: the prisoners' music at the end of Act I, the amazing cross-rhythms in the second finale, the spoken interruption of the trumpet quartet, almost all the changes in the role of Pizarro, the hallucinatory second part of Florestan's aria, are examples.

Almost every improvement in the 1814 *Fidelio* carries some loss also: the recitative in pathetic style, "Ach brich noch nicht, du mattes Herz!," before Leonore's aria; the long version of the Leonore-Florestan duet with Beethoven's original and far better melody (the later one being meanly cropped back to eliminate high notes), and also the elaborate recitative before it; many points in the second finale, for instance the agitated duet, "O Gott, nun ist's um uns gescheh'n," but especially the prayer, "O Gott! o welch' ein Augenblick!," which in its magnificently broad original form is the most exalted page in all the *Fidelio* scores.

Scale was the crucial issue in the revisions. The period of the original *Fidelio* is that of Beethoven's most expansive music, of such things as the first movement of the Violin Concerto and of the Quartet Opus 59, No. 1. Such breadth, which dominates the 1805 opera score as well, is difficult, even dangerous, in the theater, and so Beethoven eliminated not merely whole pieces—among them a lovely, though dramatically badly placed, duet for Leonore and Marzelline—but also many short bits, a page here, six bars compressed to two there, a single measure gone somewhere else. The most fascinating thing about that is that the pieces whose length, whose insistence on being "musical" rather than theatrical, makes them most problematic in the familiar *Fidelio*, namely the two great trios, are stronger and more convincing in their bigger original forms.

The point altogether is that while the later score may replace the earlier one in the practical life of our theaters, it does not render the original one obsolete or invalid. The 1805 *Fidelio* is a work of surging vitality with a life all its own, full of strokes whose loss cannot represent Beethoven's uncompromised artistic conviction, one of which the traditional estimate, based on inexperience with performance, must be revised, and one that we must know even as we have come to recognize that among the overtures we must know *Leonore 2* as well as *Leonore 3*.

Hanne-Lore Kuhse, who sang Leonore, is an East German, probably in her middle 30s, who made her American debut in a *Tristan* performance in Philadelphia last season. A heavy woman, she could hardly make a convincing Fidelio on the stage. She has a dramatic gift: her performance was remarkable before she had sung a note, by virtue of her concentration and stillness as she stood waiting for her entrance in the quartet.

Her voice is a rich, warm, evenly textured soprano of great amplitude. For splendor and radiance I have heard nothing to equal the ten high B's and the two C's in the "O namen, namenlose Freude!" duet.

As an interpreter, she gives everything words and music demand, everything they imply, and nothing in excess. Her work is as free of mannerism and of externally imposed dramatics as her voice is free of forcing and pushing. That makes her a great artist, and the operation of her exceptional word sense, and of a remarkable, warm femininity, make her a great Leonore, by miles the greatest in my experience.

Her aria got Frau Kuhse an immense ovation, the duet an even bigger one, with Mr. Leinsdorf himself leading the applause. George Shirley contributed distinguished singing as Florestan, though his voice was still cold for his aria. Tom Krause was quite a good Pizarro, though he did not always have enough vocal impact. Ara Berberian, Nico Castel, Harold Enns, and William Brown did singing that was in various ways good and interesting, but Mary Ellen Pracht's Marzelline was, for lack of diction, not satisfactory.

Erich Leinsdorf, except for a few under-characterized numbers early in the first act, led a strong and intelligent performance, one in which he had access to a certain emotional energy which, when it is in action, can make him a most gripping conductor. The Boston Symphony played beautifully, though there were some bad horn moments at the start of Leonore's aria. The choral singing was very fine. The one really disturbing blot was in the narration put in place of the spoken dialogue of the original, the text itself being very well written by Andrew Raeburn, but ludicrously spoken by some ham from a theater in Stockbridge who was booed as he fully deserved.

Crisp Handel by Mann

September 17, 1967

Alfred Mann's notes for his recording of Handel's *Chandos Anthems* begin, "We know too little of Handel's work." This is often said but, sadly, it remains true that Handel's enormous popularity is based on a tiny number of works, most of them, at that, generally heard in forms in which Handel would hardly recognize them.

Records have occasionally helped this situation, and they do so now with this superb release by Bach Guild (227-8-9, 3 records, available boxed or separately) of performances previously available on the German Cantate label of the first six anthems Handel wrote in 1717–19 for the Duke of Chandos, Queen Anne's Paymaster General, and an affective and appreciative patron of music.

The *Chandos Anthems* are psalm settings in English, portions of Psalms 100, 11, 51, 96, 145, and 42 being used. They are all scored for three-part chorus with three-part string orchestra (no altos or violas) and oboes, used with endless resource to produce an entrancing variety of texture and surface. The six anthems also encompass a great variety of shape and character, and are altogether among Handel's most vigorous and beautiful inventions.

Alfred Mann conducts shapely and vivacious performances with the Rutgers University Collegium Musicum, various excellent instrumentalists for the obbligati, and with first-rate vocal soloists, Helen Boatwright, Charles Bressler, and Jerrold Held. I warmly recommend the whole set; if you prefer to take the records one at a time, I recommend starting either with No. 227 for the famous Anthem VI, "As pants the hart" (with IV, "O sing unto the Lord a new song!"), or with No. 228 for Anthem II, "In the Lord put I my trust" (with III, "Have mercy upon me, O God").

[*The remainder of this article addresses other topics.*]

Pears and Britten—A Vigorous Schubert

October 1, 1967

NEW YORK—Nineteen years absent, in two evenings of exalted artistry, Peter Pears and Benjamin Britten again performed in concert in this country. Norman Singer, director of the Hunter College concerts, induced them to come back to participate in a song cycle series offered as part of the 25th anniversary season of the Hunter concerts and to give another recital besides.

Friday, September 22, they gave Schubert's *Winterreise*; two days later they performed a group of five Purcell songs, two of Haydn's English canzonets, a group of five of Schubert's greatest songs ("Im Frühling," "Dass sie hier gewesen," "Auf dem Wasser zu singen," "Nacht und Träume," and "Auflösung"), Britten's own Pushkin cycle, *The Poet's Echo*, and some of his folk song arrangements.

There are song cycles whose poetic content is finer than that of *Winterreise* and many, certainly, in which it is more sophisticated. Schubert's music, with its unsentimental compassion and hard truthfulness, transfigures Müller's verses so that, after all, *Winterreise* is for most of us the richest and deepest of all song cycles. It is its musical qualities that make Pears's and Britten's performance so illuminating and so close to Schubert; not that Pears is inattentive to words, but rather that he and Britten seem to find the road to them through the music.

Their way with the music is at once simple and bold. There were no tricks in their performance and nothing in the least eccentric unless the slower-than-usual tempi for "Im Dorfe," by which I was not convinced, and "Die Nebensonnen," which, though unconventional, was not merely "*nicht zu langsam*" for Pears and Britten, but one of the great experiences in listening in my life.

Within the framework of simplicity and naturalness, they sculpt, define, articulate the songs with astonishing force and move about within them with an exhilarating sense of freedom, and, moreover suggesting that what one is hearing at the moment is just one of a limitless number of possibilities their strong and yielding concept allows.

With perhaps the single exception of Schnabel's playing of the B-flat Sonata, this *Winterreise* was the most adventurous meeting with Schubert's music I have ever experienced in performance. I believe, too, that the vigor of the musical interpretation made possible a corresponding understatement of the rhetorical side, and the combination of intensity without exaggerated pathos, thus avoiding the limitations both of a tightly reined Prey[15] and an overstating Fischer-Dieskau, as an essential part of what made this *Winterreise* so affecting.

One thinks of Pears first as a rhetorical and dramatic singer, the master of verbal and pictorial atmosphere, one of the great Evangelists in the Bach Passions, the magnificent actor in roles spanning the human and artistic range from Captain Vere in *Billy Budd* to the Madwoman in *Curlew River*, and this, too, is what Britten has emphasized in the music he has written for him. The deepest impression, perhaps because it involves a much rarer art, is, however, the one he makes with the exquisite line drawing of his lyric singing. He makes time seem to stop as, fulfilling everything but adding nothing, he traces the melody of Purcell's "I attempt from love's sickness to fly," Schubert's "Nacht und Träume," the Somerset folk song, "O Waly, Waly."

Singers are apt, in a peculiar sense, to be monolingual; that is, whatever languages they master, there is one in which they take fire. I still remember how, at the first Pears-Britten recital I ever heard, in 1948, after a performance of Schumann's *Dichterliebe* so impressive that my understanding of the cycle has always remained affected by it, the program continued with some songs by Frank Bridge, and suddenly it was like a new coming to life. Pears is most completely fulfilled when he sings in English, and the clarity and color of his diction is something extraordinary, whether in his own translation of Pushkin's "Lines written during a sleepless night" or the fun of "The Lincolnshire Poacher." Now 57, Pears always has relied on what he could do with his voice more than on the voice itself, and so he has based his art on an asset that would not leave him with age. I have loved the sound of his tenor ever since I first heard it on records twenty-one years ago—none of his records, by the way, does justice to the quality of his sound—though I can understand, too, how his intense, penetrating voice with its slow vibrato is not to everyone's taste. He is a singer of extraordinary dynamic

15 See review of January 30, 1967, for an account of Prey's *Winterreise*.

and coloristic fancy, his sense of pitch is so fine that his use of it is really creative, and I would say that at no time, in relation to his physical resources at the moment, has he sung as well, as easily as now.

Britten is one of the great pianists of our time. Mozart's piano concertos show it best of all, and then Schubert's songs. I do mean pianist as well as musician playing the piano: completely relaxed, he plays with an amazing facility, an unfailingly lovely and unpercussive tone, breathtaking mastery of dynamic and articulation ("Auf dem Flusse" in *Winterreise* was, among other things, one of the most marvelous accomplishments in sheer instrumental skill I have ever witnessed). He is the master, pianistically and musically, of those easy-sounding songs that destroy accompanists, things like "Im Frühling" and "Nacht und Träume."

Leading, yielding, listening, building a rock-solid frame as context for his partner's freedom of action, improvising, supporting, stimulating, restraining, commenting, varying, he creates a continuously exciting activity through his playing. The chamber music ideal is completely fulfilled through his and Pears's work together.

Because the level of inner musical vitality is so high, their performances never become mechanical and they are never hemmed up. It is incredible really that they could have done "The Sally Gardens" as they did, so alive, so melancholy, yet so understated and without the needless underlining of the chord change at "foolish," or to do "Oliver Cromwell," with which they must have ended literally many hundreds of recitals in the last twenty-five years, with such sparkle as though it were for the first time.

Nothing can make up to us for the nineteen years of their absence and the loss, during that time, of so fantastic a gift of musicianship, dedication, intelligence, nobility, virtuosity, passion, warmth, and humor. Let us hope, though, that Pears and Britten will come back, and often.

French Charm Pervades Bernac, Poulenc's Album

October 8, 1967

For several years in the late '40s and early '50s, there were opportunities in this country to hear occasional recitals by the French baritone Pierre Bernac with the composer Francis Poulenc at the piano.

These usually included some German Lieder—I remember a *Dichterliebe* of a kind of detached elegance that seemed closer to Heine's verses than to Schumann's settings of them—but the great moments came when Bernac and

Poulenc turned to French songs, Fauré, Duparc, Debussy, Ravel, Poulenc himself, repertory that I have never again heard touched with such grace, wit, and refinement of feeling.

Bernac's voice was light, reedy, and so personal that one could recognize it from the first note. In range and quality it came close to being a tenor: in fact, the first record of his I heard was one he made during the war with Munch of the spurious Bach Cantata 189,[16] a piece generally sung by tenors. He spun phrases with exquisite taste, and he was an incomparable master of French diction.

Poulenc was not a profound interpreter at the piano like Britten, and he could be careless. He played well though, sometimes very beautifully, he brought special insight to French songs, and he was an alert and stimulating chamber music player.

The records Bernac and Poulenc made for American Columbia in 1950 have been reissued as a two-record album on the low-price Odyssey label (32260009, monaural only), and it is something not to be missed. The repertory includes Poulenc's own cycles *Banalités, Chansons Villageoises, Quatre Poèmes de Guillaume Apollinaire, Callagrammes*, and two of his Éluard settings, "Tu vois le feu du soir" and "Main dominée par le coeur"; Ravel's *Histoires naturelles* and his Hebrew and Yiddish songs; Debussy's "Le Promenoir des deux amants" and two other songs; two by Chabrier; and three wonderfully funny songs of Satie. No texts or translations: only summaries.

Let us hope that Seraphim will come out with a Bernac-Poulenc record of the material they own, which includes Debussy's Villon settings and Ravel's *Don Quichotte à Dulcinée.*

Poulenc the accompanist is documented by earlier recordings, now reissued (Pathé COLC 317), on which he plays *Le Bestiaire* with the superbly cool and witty Claire Croiza; his *Airs chantés* with Suzanne Peignot, a singer with a light, bright soprano; and a number of Debussy songs including the *Ariettes oubliées* with Lucienne Tragin, who sounds like a tremulous little girl, and is even so a captivating performer. On the other side, Poulenc plays some of his pieces for solo piano including the popular "Mouvements perpétuels" (pianists should listen to this nice lesson in "throwing away"), and the "Improvisations," which are attractive enough to make one wonder why they are never heard.

[*The remainder of this article addresses other topics.*]

[16] After an early attribution to Georg Melchior Hoffmann (ca. 1679–1715), the cantata was generally attributed throughout the 19th century to Bach, then restored to Hoffmann in the second half of the 20th century.

Guarneri String Quartet—From Skillful to Marvelous

October 16, 1967

Since its beginnings in 1964, the Guarneri Quartet has played here more often than any other string quartet. Every piece on Sunday's program had at one time appeared on one of their Harvard Summer School series; their Jordan Hall concert, therefore, not only provided performances each of which was masterful as interpretation and as instrumental accomplishment, but also invited comparison with their previous work.

What has happened is marvelous. The Guarneri Quartet began its career with a collective instrumental skill that enabled it to play with the surest ensemble sense and the most beautiful sound of any group since the New Music Quartet in the early '50s, with the Composers Quartet the one possible exception. Their performances were intelligent and lively, they held the attention unfailingly, and were altogether on a level that from the very start clearly placed them among the top-ranking ensembles.

Their playing was not always very personal, though it could be mannered, sometimes by fussy phrasing (especially from the cellist), sometimes by frenzied dynamics à la Marlboro. Even as recently as two summers ago, their playing of the late Beethoven quartets showed slight, but telling, interpretive immaturities. They were terribly concerned with smoothness, and especially in classical repertory there was a nervous staying out of one another's way.

The beautiful sound is still there, though it is bolder now, and much more varied. The ensemble is both closer than ever and more flexible and responsive: they are still the only quartet I have heard make sense of the quick dialogues in the Beethoven scherzo [Quartet in C-sharp minor, Op. 131]. They no longer fuss nor resort to the old incessant *crescendos* and *diminuendos* for expressive emphasis.

But it is their interpretive growth that is most exciting. Their style has become more expansive, and they move confidently and imaginatively about in the music. Where on their early records you can hear formal repeats that sound as though a tape loop were being run over again, repeats—for example that in the first movement of the Haydn [Quartet in G major, Op. 76, No. 1]—are continuations now, essential and living.

Their rhythmic sense is magnificent, whether in handling a detail like the tricky off-beat beginning of the variations in the Beethoven, or in something large like the rhythmic structure of the Haydn first movement (which they had upside-down in 1964).

Now, when they move from one thing to another, in the Beethoven, for instance, from the fugue to the second movement, or from one variation to the next, you can listen to them and tell exactly what the organic compositional process was that took the composer from one idea to the next. They played the Berg [Opus 3] with sharp awareness of how the music is always and essentially changing from one beat to the next, giving, in fact, the sort of interpretation I have always wanted to hear of *Wozzeck*, and which no conductor has quite achieved.

In sum, the Guarneri Quartet has fulfilled its promise. Expressive, beautiful in sound, characterized by an unusual analytical intelligence, their performances are now most richly illuminating experiences.

BSO's Leinsdorf Explains—Why Others Have Orchestra Problems

November 19, 1967

"I can't blame any one of them who doesn't want it!" The speaker was Erich Leinsdorf, and the Boston Symphony's music director was talking about the young conductors who have been politely resisting attempts to make them music directors of the New York Philharmonic and the Chicago Symphony.

Both orchestras have a problem. Leonard Bernstein will leave the Philharmonic in the spring of 1969; Jean Martinon is in his last season in Chicago now.

Neither orchestra has named a successor; in fact, the New York Philharmonic has announced that for at least one season after Bernstein's departure it will use guest conductors with George Szell, who then will be in his twenty-fourth season as music director of the Cleveland Orchestra, appointed music advisor and senior guest conductor.

Many names have been mentioned in connection with both posts, among them those of Colin Davis (BBC Symphony), István Kertész (London Symphony, Cologne Opera), Lorin Maazel (Berlin Opera), Zubin Mehta (Los Angeles Philharmonic), and Seiji Ozawa (Toronto Symphony). The rumor mill is on the whole more productive at furnishing lists of people, including several of the above, who have turned the jobs down or who are likely to if offered them.

Leinsdorf agrees with most observers that the New York Philharmonic board has gone out of its way to make things difficult by giving Bernstein the life-long title of laureate conductor. Having to be in the shadow of the most glamorous and highly publicized figure in the field today does not make a job that is at best a back-breaking one more attractive to a young man professionally on the make. In addition, Bernstein will continue to be involved in recordings and television, cutting into his successor's ability to exploit these two important reputation-building devices.

Leinsdorf went on to point out that apart from such local problems, the post of music director of a major orchestra brings plenty of headaches anyhow. Among them are these:

As orchestras have demanded and won year-round employment, the conductor's burden in terms of increased repertory has become tremendous. One must remember, Leinsdorf said, that in assessing a conductor's workload, the actual number of concerts is not so relevant a measurement as the number of programs to be learned.

With pressure from all sides for more concerts, conductors face orchestras that are more tired as well as more prosperous. The problem of how to keep an orchestra mentally and physically fresh is one that nobody is even close to solving. Moreover, with the number of weekly services that can be asked from players limited by union regulations, there is a danger of selling rehearsal time short. Available rehearsal time is at a dangerous minimum now.

Part of the demand for more performances eventually will be met by television, Leinsdorf feels. There is, after all, no reason to assume that television sound always will be as poor as it is now, and when that technical problem is solved, television can become as important and serious a medium for the diffusion of music as the long-playing record.

Even with all the efforts to make an economically more attractive life for orchestra players, the personnel shortage becomes more drastic all the time. Leinsdorf is disturbed by a situation that forces major orchestras to hire young players for responsible positions for which they are likely to be superbly qualified as instrumentalists, but for which they are almost certainly insufficiently seasoned musically and humanly.

Most of all, Leinsdorf senses keenly the frustrations of being in a profession whose activities are determined by matters intrinsically irrelevant to what that profession is about.

In other words, musical considerations can never wholly determine what ought to be musical decisions, because other matters intervene, most of them to do with money. Music is a living, not a calling.

"I tell you frankly," said Leinsdorf at one point, speaking for himself and for his colleagues who are music directors of major orchestras in this country, "none of us needs it." None would suffer a loss of income from a guest conducting career, which is easier anyway since one can travel around with a few prepackaged memorized programs. And domestic considerations of having a year-round post in one place are not important for everyone either. "For myself," says Leinsdorf, "I'd rather live out of a suitcase than out of a house."

What, then, are the rewards? The possibility of repertory one cannot do as guest conductor.

Leinsdorf mentioned Schumann's *Scenes from Goethe's "Faust"* and last summer's Beethoven's *Leonore*[17] as examples. There are, too, the rich rewards of being able to participate in, and to help shape, the cultural life of the community the orchestra serves. Then there are the extensions of an orchestra's life into the field of education, something for which the Boston Symphony's Berkshire Music Center has been the prime exemplar.

Given the balances between rewards and frustrations in posts that offer some unique possibilities for service and that, on the other hand, are no longer altogether attractive or even "possible," how did Leinsdorf view his own future with respect to the music directorship of the Boston Symphony?

"When I have enough, I go," he replied quickly. "But," he added, thinking still of Schumann's *Faust* and of the possibilities of a symphony orchestra as educational institution, "so far I don't have enough. No, not at all."

Leinsdorf Has a Good Point, Says Steinberg

December 11, 1967

Erich Leinsdorf was not fired as music director of the Boston Symphony.

However, when a man is discontented with the conditions under which he is employed and murmurs about greener grass, his employers can do one of two things: they can make an effort to keep him by meeting his demands at least part way, or they can politely escort him to the door. The Symphony trustees took the latter course, and hence the announcement four days ago of Leinsdorf's resignation, effective at the end of summer 1969.

The announcement came as a surprise, or at least its timing did. Leinsdorf's side of the story was, however, clearly stated in an interview published in the *Boston Globe*, Sunday, November 19.[18]

Discussing the difficulty the New York Philharmonic and the Chicago Symphony were having in replacing their departing conductors (respectively Leonard Bernstein, leaving 1969, and Jean Martinon, leaving this spring), Leinsdorf said about the various reluctant candidates: "I can't blame any one of them who doesn't want it." And speaking for the music directors of this country's major orchestras, he added, "I tell you frankly, none of us needs it."

[17] The title *Leonore* here refers to the original version of *Fidelio*. See review of August 7, 1967. Steinberg's review of *Scenes from Goethe's "Faust"* appeared on February 26, 1966.

[18] See previous article.

Leinsdorf listed some of the reasons he considers such a post no longer attractive or even "possible." First came overwork, given also as the principal reason in the resignation announcement. As orchestras have demanded and won year-round employment, the conductor's burden in terms of the number of concerts and, even more significantly, of repertory to be learned, has grown tremendously.

Union regulations limit the number of services to be asked of a player, and with greater pressure to produce concerts and records, rehearsal time—already at, if not below, a dangerous minimum—is being sold short. Musical standards are sufficiently imperiled by the shortage of good string players, and Leinsdorf has said that he now hires unseasoned players he would not have taken five years ago.

In every direction, Leinsdorf senses the frustration of maintaining musical standards in a situation in which first considerations, whether on the part of trustees, recording executives, or players, are financial rather than artistic.

Asked how, in the light of his pessimism, he viewed his future here, Leinsdorf said, "When I have enough, I go." But, since that was not yet the occasion for making his announcement, he added, "But so far I don't have enough."

Mr. Leinsdorf's resignation was tendered and accepted with the customary civilities, but acrimony was perceptible enough. Henry B. Cabot, president of the orchestra's trustees, countered the overwork complaint with, "It is for him. But look at others—look at Ormandy. Now he even goes to Saratoga."

If you look at the schedule of Eugene Ormandy, music director of the Philadelphia Orchestra, you find that his concerts in Philadelphia involve fifteen out of twenty-eight Friday-Saturday subscription pairs, adding up, when you count the shorter series as well, to forty-five concerts.

Leinsdorf during an equivalent period has sixteen out of twenty-four Friday-Saturday pairs and a total in Boston of fifty-eight concerts. Leinsdorf-Boston have more out-of-town dates than Ormandy-Philadelphia; Leinsdorf's Tanglewood obligations are more arduous than Ormandy's at Saratoga, without even considering the additional responsibilities that fall to Leinsdorf as director of the Berkshire Music Center; and Philadelphia programs, winter and summer, show a higher percentage of repertory works repeated from season to season.

Cabot's "Look at Ormandy," therefore, only emphasizes the self-evident rightness of Leinsdorf's complaint. There is, in fact, no one else Cabot could have cited, for no other symphony conductor in this country has an even remotely comparable workload.

The trustees may have elected to ignore Leinsdorf's complaint (Cabot: "We didn't want to change our policy to meet his requirements") partly because of a lack of understanding of what is involved, for they are men, for the most part, out of touch with the musical world and its realities. It is probable, though, that they had other and more relevant reasons for scuttling Leinsdorf at this time.

The announcement of Mr. Leinsdorf's appointment here came as a surprise. He was known as a conductor experienced in opera and symphony, competent, generally unexciting, and with a penchant for getting into trouble, most famously as a very young man at the Metropolitan Opera and again at the New York City Opera in 1956.[19]

He was brought here to rehabilitate an orchestra that had been allowed to go to the dogs. His predecessor, Charles Munch, could be exciting and he had personal glamour and charm, but his faculty for continuous attention and his willingness to work hard were less developed. The sober, meticulous, verbally articulate Leinsdorf was a completely different type, and because of this, he was warmly welcomed at first by many—including, let us not forget, the orchestra.

But though the public relations industry continued to spread the story of the great love affair in Symphony Hall, it was over. Public, critics, and orchestra were bored much of the time. Though stuck with the consequences of some unwise appointments made by his predecessor, Leinsdorf raised orchestral standards again, but not enough to recapture the polish and virtuosity of the Koussevitzky days.

What would have impressed the trustees most is that Leinsdorf's records have sold poorly. A Boston Symphony player gets $2,000–3,000 a year from recording fees, and without this, which brings a beginner's salary to about $14,000, the Symphony could not compete for the best players.[20] RCA Victor, for which Boston has recorded since the '20s, has used the Chicago Symphony more and more in the last two years, and eleven days ago came the surprise announcement that the Philadelphia Orchestra had switched from Columbia to Victor. At worst, it could be that Victor means to phase Boston out of its plans altogether as contracts expire; at best, it means that a juicy bit of money is in jeopardy. The non-selling conducting had to go.

Leinsdorf is not an easy musician to assess, and the "head over heart" verdict is certainly too facile. He has given remarkable performances in Boston and at Tanglewood, and he has made some effort to freshen the repertory. A lot of his work, though, too much for most of us, has seemed inhibited, drab without relaxation or rhythmic energy.

[19] Following his Metropolitan Opera debut in 1938, Leinsdorf served as head of German repertoire there between 1939 and 1943, later appearing frequently between 1957 and 1983. His *New York Times* obituary, by Bernard Holland (September 12, 1993), states that "his contentious style—in particular an insistence on textual accuracy and more rehearsal—won him no friends among singers like Lauritz Melchior and Kirsten Flagstad."

[20] Adjusted for inflation, these dollar figures amount roughly to $19,200–28,800, and $134,300 in 2025.

What of the orchestra's future? The most likely candidate is 40-year-old Colin Davis, now in his first season with the BBC Symphony (London). Davis made a strong impression on orchestra, critics, and public when he was a guest conductor here last year (as did a man called Leinsdorf seven seasons ago). He has a wide range of musical interests, he is a dedicated and intelligent musician and a lively and personally attractive performer.

Other possibilities: István Kertész, 37, Hungarian, now with the London Symphony and the Cologne Opera, an intuitive musician rather than a profoundly intelligent one, and one whose world centers about 19th-century Romantic tradition.

Seiji Ozawa, 31, Japanese, now with the Toronto Symphony: he has had great success with the Boston Symphony at Tanglewood, and will make his Boston debut in January; brilliantly gifted, and at this point almost certainly unready for such a post.

Zubin Mehta, 31, Indian, now with the Los Angeles Philharmonic, brilliant, erratic, matinee idol looks, and a touch of show biz.

Lorin Maazel, 36, American, music director of the Berlin Opera, another erratic dazzler whose best is superb, with great capacity for survival, and believed a likely candidate for Philadelphia.

Less probably: Leonard Bernstein, not known to be looking for a job; Carlo Maria Giulini, good conductor, but small repertory and a slow study; Stanisław Skrowaczewski, good man, but like Leinsdorf thought of as a bit unsexy; Georges Prêtre, sexy all right, but inclined to vulgar music-making, an RCA Victor fair-haired boy.

Whoever it is, no matter how young and healthy, will discover for himself the truth of what old Pierre Monteux, music director here 1919–24, told Leinsdorf in 1961: "The job is for two orchestras and three conductors." He will probably discover too, that love affairs don't last the way they used to.

The trustees for their part in looking for a conductor who should, if possible, take an aggressively active part in the running of the Berkshire Music Center, one of the country's most valuable cultural assets, will probably find out that the job is not what it used to be, that they cannot treat a conductor with the hauteur they assumed thirty years ago when they thought it unreasonable of the orchestra to want to unionize, and that they will probably need to make the new conductor the concessions they have refused Leinsdorf.

The step after that will be the realization that Leinsdorf is right, and that the artistic and administrative structure of our orchestra is due for a more thorough shakeup than most of us can or do dare imagine at this time.

Exciting *Messiah* Via Mozart

December 11, 1967

Friday night in Symphony Hall was exciting. There was the first American performance, and presumably the first anywhere in 168 years, of one of the most fascinating scores ever written; it was also the Handel and Haydn Society's first concert under its superb new music director, Thomas Dunn.[21]

First, the score. *Messiah* is one of four Handel works that Mozart rescored at the request of Vienna's music patron and tastemaker, Baron van Swieten. The idea was to adapt Handel's oratorio to enlightened Viennese taste of 1789, which involved translating it into German (the performance here, however, restored the English text), making some cuts, redistributing material among the voices, and providing a rich orchestration.

George Gelles's program note suggested that Mozart's *Messiah* "offers us an invaluable lesson . . . in late 18th-century attitudes towards music of the High Baroque," and what we learn from that lesson is that they thought Handel, then dead thirty years, was a pretty naive cat who didn't have the faintest idea about how to write for orchestra.

This *Messiah* even contains one bit of original Mozart. Van Swieten thought Handel's aria, "If God be for us" too dry, and so we heard the words in a gorgeous recitative by Countess Almaviva (with one characteristic chord change borrowed from Donna Anna).[22]

To Handel's strings (with doubling oboes and bassoons) and sparingly used trumpets and drums, Mozart added flutes, clarinets, independent parts for oboes and bassoons, horns, and trombones. Sometimes he amplifies the already existing texture. More often he invents, adding echoes, imitations, new strands of counterpoint, for instance the chromatic run for woodwinds that is so startling at the beginning of "Thou shalt break them," or the lovely conversation with flute and bassoon in which he engages the soprano in "How beautiful are the feet."

Mozart's most amiable exuberance comes out in the chattering woodwinds and horns of "All we like sheep." By far his boldest stroke is in his realization, in the darkly glowing sonority of flute, two clarinets, and two bassoons, of what he takes to be the harmonic implications of Handel's stark unisons in "The people that walked in darkness," something that turns into the richest essay in chromatic harmony anywhere in Mozart.

21 See article of April 16, 1967.

22 Steinberg refers here to the Countess Almaviva from Mozart's *Le nozze di Figaro* and to Donna Anna from *Don Giovanni*.

The most vivid lesson here is that Handel is, after all, the best composer of his own music. Ebenezer Prout, whose version of *Messiah* the Handel and Haydn Society has used in recent years, was a dirt-dauber, and his score sounds like yesterday's coffee grounds. The issue with Mozart is quite different. As an arranger, Mozart is in a class by himself, and his *Messiah* is a marvel of fantasy, technical resourcefulness, and sensuous beauty.

It is also all wrong. Light years separate Handel's sonorous ideal from that of *Così fan tutte* and the E-flat Symphony. Mozart is round and lush where Handel is sharp-edged, busy rather than simple, decorative rather than direct, he paints where Handel suggests. *Messiah* is one of Mozart's most beautiful scores, but it is irrelevant to Handel. It offers no acceptable solution to the problem of how to perform Handel's *Messiah*; it is, however, an exciting part of our Mozart experience, one for which Friday's concert left me joyously grateful. I hope, too, that in a few years the Society will get around to it again, and that Mr. Dunn or some other good conductor will offer us a chance at another of Mozart's deliciously subjective Handel translations.

Thomas Dunn is a sensitive musician, he is a scholar, and he can conduct. He gave *Messiah* as it ought to be given, with tempi that made sense, with springy rhythm, with lively definition of the polyphony, and with plastic phrasing. I sensed some slackening of energy early in Part Two, but from "Lift up your heads" all went brilliantly to the end, and Mr. Dunn, greeted at his first appearance by a demonstrative round of goodwill applause, won a standing ovation at the end, the spontaneous kind in which the audience was on its feet within a few seconds of the last "Amen."

The Handel and Haydn Chorus has always had an agreeably warm sound, and Mr. Dunn has been able to add a new clarity of pitch and diction. The playing of the orchestra, actually Robert Brink's Cambridge Festival Orchestra, was especially good: the beautiful playing of Mozart's fanciful wind parts and the flexibility and solidity of the whole ensemble made it what one always wants to hear in such a work.

Tenor Jon Humphrey was outstanding for purity of voice and style and the elegance of his phrasing. Bass Andrew Poulimenos does not yet have the prophetic grandeur for "Behold, I tell you a mystery," but he sang the arias impressively and delivered as brilliant a "Why do the nations" as I have ever heard. Alto Eunice Alberts sang with her usual warmth and musicianship, though Mozart gave her a hard time by assigning several soprano recitatives to the alto voice, at the original pitch, and she had to tilt at some of the high notes rather. Soprano Barbara Wallace has a lovely voice and fine feeling for lyric phrase—"He shall feed his flock" was exceptionally good—but she has little word sense and she is handicapped, indeed panicked, by insufficient technique.

Boston Globe advertisement placed in the Boston Symphony's program book during the 1967–68 season. (Used with permission.)

1968

The Music Guild Quartet—A Reader Writes, a Critic Answers

January 28, 1968

A Weston reader, Eleanor G. Locke, has written a courteously angry letter, printed in the *Globe* of January 20, about my review of a Jordan Hall concert at which, in her words, "a highly skilled quartet of young Boston Symphony Orchestra players gave their first concert as the Music Guild Quartet." Miss Locke continued:

> With great dedication they spent precious hours of their rare spare time to bring the pleasure of fine, live chamber music to Boston concertgoers. This represents a renewal for them and us of the joy of playing. It was their effort to remedy the stultifying effect of hours of symphony playing. If the concert had weaknesses it was their strength, because it answered the question as to why such concerts.

Most orchestra players need the relief of chamber music, and badly. The announcement a few years ago of the founding of the Boston Symphony Chamber Players stated that the first aim was to make possible performances of chamber music in unusual instrumental combinations, but went on to admit that part of the purpose was therapeutic. Violinist George Zazofsky was not the only player to point out that the therapy was being directed where it was least needed, that is, to the section principals, who were in any case the only people with much chance of getting ego satisfaction from their work in the orchestra.

Fine, but most of the chamber music performances by Symphony players have not been good.[1] This may reflect a defect in the Boston Symphony's playing as an orchestra: the players are good when it comes to reacting to the baton, but they don't seem to listen and react to each other very much. The Boston Symphony is not a chamber-musical orchestra—the Berlin Philharmonic is, and so is

[1] See November 9, 1964, review of the inaugural Boston Symphony Chamber Players concert.

London's Philharmonia—and while the results can be disastrous in Webern's Variations, you can tell in *Scheherazade*, too.

With the Boston Symphony Chamber Players the problem has been the one G. B. Shaw called the scratch habit, characteristic of actors

> whose lot has been cast in theaters where a new play had to be presented every week or even every night. In such actors the scratch habit is an incurable disease. At the first rehearsal they astonish everyone, just as London orchestras always astonish foreign conductors and composers, by being almost letter-perfect and giving such a capable and promising reading of their parts that one feels that after a fortnight's work they will be magnificent, and leave all the others nowhere. And they never get a step further.

An orchestra works quickly and for safety. When something is rehearsed to the point at which a reasonable precision and clarity are assured, it is considered prepared, not perhaps in anyone's ideal view, but in the everyday, practical way of the orchestral world. Mahler's Ninth Symphony, eighty-five minutes of extremely difficult music, would get nine or ten hours' rehearsal, but a professional string quartet will give much more time than that to the preparation of a new Haydn quartet one-fourth the length and with far fewer complications.

Chamber Players concerts have often sounded as though prepared to the point where they were sure not to break down, but not much beyond that. There has been technical competence, though never the technical refinement that makes the orchestra's best playing so dazzling; hardly ever—in fact, the performance of the Brahms C minor Piano Quartet is the only exception I remember—have I heard a performance in which it seemed someone had had time to work out a musical idea of the piece. And of course there has been the uneven quality of the players, the contrast between intelligence and musicianship of Eskin, a Fine, a [Claude] Frank, at one extreme, and, at the other, the erratic taste of a Gomberg or the musical vacuity and bad pitch of a Cioffi.

But, to return to Miss Locke and to the Music Guild Quartet, the first thing to strike me at their concert was how carefully, from the instrumental point of view, everything had been prepared. Barring only a few insignificant technical blemishes, it was unanimous playing of a sort that testified to the many hours of dedicated rehearsal of which Miss Locke writes. No scratch habit here, certainly.

Yet the concert was bad. I didn't say so in my review, but I deplored the program: the Mozart A major, Bartók No. 3, and Beethoven's third *Rasumovsky*. Three masterpieces, to be sure, but a quartet that is exempt from the packaging and selling problems of a group that is full-time on the commercial circuit ought to have come up with something fresher both in content and in program arrangement. The Stockbridge Quartet, another Boston Symphony group that plays in Jordan Hall next month, is equally unimaginative in this respect.

At the Music Guild concert, the performances were musically poor for reasons I took as proceeding from insufficient linear feeling or analytical sense generally. Considerable demands are made on orchestra players' technical, human, and musical resources, but these demands do not include what it takes to organize a statement of something as complex as Beethoven's C major Quartet. Orchestras do include musicians of remarkable interpretive intelligence, but they are not your typical orchestra men. The ability to do what is required in most orchestral positions is not necessarily accompanied by the qualities needed in a first-rate quartet player.

Actually, Miss Locke's disagreement is not with my opinion of the concert, but with my expression of that opinion, which, she says, "serves to destroy the efforts of these gifted players to keep their muse alive." Miss Locke's interest in the work of the Music Guild Quartet is humane, it is in the usefulness of their work to themselves as anti-orchestral therapy. Why, in that case, must therapy take the form of a public concert to which admission is charged?

Once the commitment to a public concert is made by professional musicians, the critic cannot be distracted into irrelevant considerations. Playing quartets in public is, after all, not in itself an absolute good: the point is to play well. To say "if the concert had weaknesses it was their strength, because it answered the question as to why such concerts," is not sensible.

Someone's inability to play a concert well demonstrates the inappropriateness of his giving the concert. It may lead to various observations of the kind I make three paragraphs back, or to questions like "what [should] conservatories do to turn out more complete musicians?," but I see no way of parlaying such a "weakness" into a "strength," a relevant strength, that is, and without gross disregard of the interests of Mozart, Bartók, and Beethoven.

Public chamber music in Boston needs all the help it can get. But the quantitative fallacy, which says that anything is good just because it is happening, is a terrible trap. We need fresh programs, and in good performances. For that I'll cheer whenever it's offered.

A Kind of Executive Partner—Role of the Accompanist

February 25, 1968

At a party after a concert given in a posh suburb by a famous singer, accompanied at the piano by a man of equivalent eminence in his profession, a guest in search of her coat encountered the pianist as he sat with friends. After a moment she recognized him, paid him a compliment, then added in throatily well-bred tones:

"I was fascinated by the young man who turned the pages for you. Tell me, do you take turns? I mean, sometimes does he play and you turn?"

Dear lady, the man who makes the thundering hoof-beats for Schubert's "Erlkönig" and who evokes Gretchen's spinning wheel is not a faceless servant whose job, from the point of view of usefulness and of required skill, is on a par with the page-turner's, the parking-lot attendant's, and that of the man who turns the house lights down. And now a sociological footnote:

At the Country Evening Concerts in Weston, ushers get their names in the program in larger type than accompanists.

The accompanist's art is that of a chamber music player. In chamber music, roles shift: at one point you lead, at another you engage in dialogue, and sometimes you actually accompany in the sense of providing a figurational background. One difference between chamber music for voice with piano and that, say, for violin with piano, is that the voice never accompanies in this last sense.

A more important difference comes about because the voice makes a special claim on the listener's attention, for psychological reasons more than for acoustic. In most vocal literature, the voice is special by virtue of being a word-carrying instrument. As we listen to a Schumann song, we perceive it in double perspective. As musical discourse, voice and piano are on the same level, but as we sit in the concert hall, personal projection emanates only from the singer. If we are present at a performance by peers of a Brahms cello sonata, we will be equally aware of the persons of Fournier and Kempff, Du Pré and Barenboim, or whomever, but at such a performance of a Brahms song, we are aware of the person only of Crespin or Fischer-Dieskau, while Wustman and Moore become invisible, though keenly felt, musical presences.

The listener must learn to hear that which is not brought to his attention by strong personal projection. This is more likely to happen when the accompaniment is pictorial, as for example in Schubert's "Erlkönig" or "Gretchen am Spinnrade," and particularly when it is pianistically brilliant as well.

But listen to the first song in Schumann's cycle, *Dichterliebe*. It begins as a piano solo, not merely something the pianist plays by himself, but something written in the self-sufficient style of a solo piece. And suddenly there is a voice, singing Heine's words about love's awakening in the wondrously beautiful month of May, and doing it by joining with the piano in its melody. With "*da ist in meinem Herzen, die Liebe aufgegangen*," the line becomes more intense. The piano recedes to play broken chords, but the top notes of these chords sensitively touch the singer's melody on a few of its notes, "*in*," "*-nem*," "*-be*," "*-ge*." The second stanza is similarly divided, and after the singer's last word, the piano finishes the discourse which it had begun and whose tone and materials it had defined.

This eighty-second miniature contains the essence of what chamber music is about. The singer must mentally sing with the piano during the four preluding measures, to enter as though he had been singing all along, but had only just then become palpable.

What he has absolutely to avoid is an entrance that grandly proclaims, "here I am," as though his music were unrelated to the piano's, and degrading those four measures to vamp. In his turn, the pianist has to sing all of "*da ist in meinem Herzen . . .*" even though only four notes of it become actually audible.

The accompanist may, then, find himself duetting with his singer, sometimes the subtle way of Schumann's "Im wunderschönen Monat Mai," or maybe with the sonorous strands more separated as in Schubert's "Im Frühling." He may paint a representational picture, for instance the band that plays for the wedding in "Das ist ein Flöten und Geigen," or a suggestively atmospheric one, Cologne's Gothic cathedral in "Im Rhein, in heiligen Strome," both from Schumann's *Dichterliebe.*

In Wolf's "Mein Liebster ist so klein," the figure so drolly described by the singer materializes only when the pianist takes over in the postlude; the genre painting of "Schlechtes Wetter" is filled out only when we have heard Strauss's waltzing afterthoughts. There are even times when the piano in effect sings a whole song, two great examples being the voiceless return of the opening song at the end of Schumann's *Frauenliebe und -leben*, and the elaborated recapitulation of an earlier song at the end of *Dichterliebe.*

There are songs in which the piano is the leading voice. In a quiet way that is true of the first song in *Dichterliebe*, and it happens often in Wolf, for example in "Denk'es, O Seele" or "Anakreons Grab." In these, the pianist has to define the shape of the composition, and the singer has to be predominantly the listening partner, fitting his declamation into a context of more assertively formative power.

Even in a song like Schubert's "Nacht und Träume," where the accompaniment consists of a harmonic background articulated in the simplest possible pianistic terms, it is still the pianist who has the responsibility of establishing the rhythm and tempo for the listener, and, by what he does before the voice enters, after it finishes, between its phrases and in support of them, of building up a continuum of musical flow. In sum, no matter how unobtrusively the operation must be carried out at times, the accompanist's responsibility is not unlike a conductor's. In most instances the singer will be the one to have the most say about the general interpretive idea, but at the very least the pianist then becomes a kind of executive partner whose activity makes it possible for that idea to be realized.

A good singer probably will sing well even with a poor accompanist, though always better with a good one. A good performance of a song—which is a different matter—is possible only with a good accompanist, one who knows when and how to lead.

The text-carrying vocal part is the surface through which we make contact with a song. The accompaniment that surrounds it is the atmosphere in which the vocal line breathes, in which the words and the singing of them are perceived in perspective and attain life.

Bigger the Bang—The Art of Applauding

March 3, 1968

A Bach *Brandenburg* Concerto ends with the last note of its last melodic phrase. Beethoven's Fifth ends with more than forty measures' gunfire of tonic and dominant chords. It has to do with applause. At a court concert, there was none unless the Duke or whatever chose to lead it. The public concert hall audience to whom the Fifth is addressed functioned under no such constraint of protocol, therefore, it was fair game for Beethoven to do a bit of rabble-rousing, like an election orator bringing on Mother and The Flag. But you can't harangue just One Serene Highness in quite that way, and so applause-provoking gestures enter music only when the applause-tripping mechanism is not in an individual's response, but in that of a crowd. The law says: the bigger the bang, the louder the clap.

Applause is a function of response, though not necessarily of judgment. Ravel's *Boléro* always will be applauded more than the Mozart symphony at the beginning of the program, but that doesn't mean that most of the applauders think it the better piece, nor even that they enjoyed it more except in the specific sense of an immediate nerve stimulus.

Even with the Margraves and the Royal Highnesses pretty much gone, applause is still an activity affected by convention. These conventions vary in place and time, and perhaps because audiences are often uncertain both about their responses and about the convention, and because knowing when to applaud and when to refrain is often a matter of nice human judgment, applause can become the occasion for all sorts of awkwardness and folly.

At a recent *Tosca* here, the tenor's singing of his third-act aria was good, though not inflammatory. Puccini finishes the aria with a long postlude, which then moves without break into the music for the appearance of Tosca, Spoletta, and the others. Usually there is applause as soon as the tenor finishes. You may lose a few bars of postlude, or if the singer produces massive enthusiasm, the conductor may need to find a place to stop, Puccini having, I think, allowed for both possibilities.

Here, however, the audience missed its chance, but seemed to realize it only when the postlude was over, the music changed character, and new people came on stage. Then they decided they had committed a gaffe, whereupon they interrupted the beginning of Cavaradossi's conversation with Tosca with applause they hadn't genuinely been stimulated to give, and whose ill-timed arrival must have been as embarrassing to the singer as its absence earlier. It was a perfect example of convention winning out over response.

Then there is a classic series of trap pieces that make some sort of imposing bang before they are over, the Tchaikovsky Fifth, Chopin's F minor Ballade, being famous examples, with the *Academic Festival* Overture the most dangerous one of all and likely even to fool a "good" audience. One might point out that in such spots, knowing that it's not over depends not on one's memory of previous performances, but on one's attention and feeling for musical language: syntax, grammar, punctuation, tell you this silence does not signal the end.

The absence of applause can be destructive, too. In lots of opera, applause is composed into the music. German audiences are so well drilled that they won't stir as long as any music is going on, which is great when it comes to the last two bars of *Tristan*, but comical when everyone listens solemnly to the rum-tum at the end of "Di quella pira," obviously a racket to be clapped through rather than listened to.

We have become rather solemn about groups on song recitals. I heard a recital the other day that began with a group of charming Granados songs. Everything at the end of the first one, the piece itself and its performance, was an invitation to applause, but since the song was the first of a group, we were too stupidly well-bred to respond the way we really wanted to.

And I wonder, too, if the education about not applauding between movements of symphonies, and definitely concertos, has not been overdone. It does involve judgment, though, and sophistication. A silence at the end of the first movement of the Rachmaninoff C minor Concerto is out of place and probably painful. It is conceivably all right to applaud after the first movement of the *Spring* Sonata—I'm sure Beethoven's audience did—but then we must know that we must on no account clap between the movements of the Debussy Sonata, which is next on the program.

And apropos response, why not offer tokens of disapproval? I'm dead against any disturbances of a performance in progress, but I don't see that there's a case to be made against some healthy booing afterwards.

One of the functions of convention is to avoid the necessity of thinking through certain situations, and in many sorts of human contact that is obviously a great convenience and a splendid lubricant. But the avoidance of thought and response is what is most out of place when we are confronted with an art work. To applaud politely something that we dislike is really rather immoral. The more we can let response dominate convention, giving the artist a sense of engaging in dialogue rather than in an address to a bunch of laundry-bags, the happier and more lively I should think the whole situation would be.

Emperor Given a Fresh Airing

March 23, 1968

Russell Sherman's program note on Beethoven's E-flat Concerto rightly included the work among those "whose performances are offered in ritual by inertia." We see it listed on a program. "Ah, yes, the *Emperor*," we say, "we know how that goes." And that is then just how it does go, and we come away reminded but unenlightened, unstretched by the experience. The recent Boston Symphony performance with Johannesen and Leinsdorf was, on a respectable level, an example of the inert celebration of the *Emperor* ritual.

Russell Sherman's performance Thursday with Frederik Prausnitz and the New England Conservatory Orchestra was something else altogether. Its most obviously unusual features were the quick tempi for the first and second movements. What does Beethoven mean by "Allegro" (particularly in the light of the finale's "Allegro ma non tanto"), or by "Adagio un poco mosso" in cut time? A consideration of the way he uses these and other directions elsewhere in his music, as opposed to basing our ideas on the sum of our recollections of all the performances of the work we have heard, suggests the rightness of Sherman's approach. There was, however, still more valid evidence in the direct musical result, in the way melodies, figurations, whole paragraphs, took on a coherence in some respects unprecedented in my listening experience with this concerto.

Much of the work is, so to speak, about its figurations, a matter in which Beethoven's invention was prodigious. Sherman's playing of this material was remarkable in that his vivid articulation went so far to illuminate that inventiveness and the diversity it produced, and also in being analytically so intelligent as to show clearly, through the phasing, how the varied surface hangs together and is profoundly, and at every level, related to the root ideas of composition.

It was a performance that managed to ignore, and to make us ignore, all the information that has accumulated about the work in so many thoughtless performances, the obnoxious nickname included. If I had to cite just one example of where this freshness, this refusal to play the piece by ear again, was most evident, I should give you Sherman's playing of the finale's main theme: for a moment I really felt as though no pianist had ever before really looked at its phrasing, dynamics, articulation, and scoring.

The actual execution of all this was sometimes tense, especially in the first movement, but I found Sherman's super-articulated and individual playing arresting and impressive. It seemed sometimes as though Prausnitz had not quite persuaded the orchestra of the "new" tempo for the first movement, but otherwise, except for some out-of-tune winds (the second horn was strictly P. D. Q. Bach),[2] the orchestral collaboration was strong and apt.

The first half of the program had consistently the best playing I have heard from the Conservatory orchestra all season. The news here was the first Boston performance of the Ives *Robert Browning* Overture. It is, for sheer textural density, the most bewildering Ives score I know, and I was very impressed with the clarity and power of much of the performance, which was strikingly better than any of the three commercially recorded ones.

When it was over, a lady sitting nearby asked: "What does all that have to do with Robert Burns?" What indeed, or with Browning, for that matter, though the rough energy of it and a certain inconsiderateness of manner do seem apropos to the subject. It is unusual in its almost complete eschewal of quotations. It is of far greater than normal overture size, and I found it exciting and in the slow sections with their typically "American" hymnic sound moving as well.

Les Préludes is far from first-rate Liszt, but since through no merit of my own I hadn't heard it for about fifteen years, I took it as an enjoyable, full-of-beans novelty, that got a very good, well mapped out, and not unnecessarily aggressive performance from Prausnitz and the orchestra.

For the Opera Company an Unexciting Season

March 31, 1968

The 1967–68 season of the Opera Company of Boston wasn't much to cheer about. Some of it was not bad, but there was none of the kind of thing that has made the company an exciting one to watch in the past. Moreover, the bad things were bad in very disturbing ways.

We had first the three productions with which the American National Company toured in the fall. *Falstaff* was the best, Sarah Caldwell conducted it effectively and there was a strong cast, so that musically it went very well indeed.

[2] A fictitious and farcical member of the Bach family whose initials stand for "Pretty Damned Quick," P. D. Q. Bach was invented by composer and parodist Peter Schickele (1935–2024). Beginning in 1965, Schickele performed the "discovered" works for more than five decades.

Scenically, I would say it was a good realization of an idea that, in spite of some extraordinary touches, was a bit shallow. It seemed too much the conventional comedy about an old man's making a fool of himself, and *Falstaff* is more.

Berg's *Lulu* was musically clean—Osbourne McConathy conducted—and in that respect vastly superior to the [touring] Hamburg production seen last summer in Montreal and New York and which I overestimated, I suppose out of sheer excitement at seeing the work at all. The Boston *Lulu* had an extraordinary performance in Donald Gramm's Dr. Schön, easily the best single achievement of the season. Otherwise the cast, though nowhere incompetent, was not impressive, and Caldwell's staging was an inconsistent mixture of sense and fuss. And *Lulu* is anything other than the rather dull piece one would have taken it to be here.

Tosca, which the other critics in Boston loathed, was remarkably successful in conveying the political atmosphere of the drama. The staging represented Caldwell at her alert and inventive best, though its physical requirements were geared to a more slender and graceful soprano than the one who sang here. Rudolf Heinrich's ingenious idea of making the sets blown up photos of parts of the actual scenes worked strikingly for the church's interior, but less convincingly later on.

Then came *Carmen* produced here, but intended for touring. Praised in most of the Boston press, it had obviously hardly been staged at all, just thrown together. In a *Herald-Traveler* interview, conductor Henry Lewis subsequently made this clear in detail. For a Caldwell production to go on in rather unready condition is nothing new. The first *Rake's Progress* in 1967 looked like a lighting rehearsal.[3] In the past, we have accepted this sort of unprofessionalism because the performances suggested that at least they were on the way to something interesting whose intentions and general shape one could clearly read through the mess. *Carmen* not only looked unfinished, if not unbegun, but it was a bore as well, with no promise of ever turning into anything interesting.

No one can expect Sarah Caldwell always to operate at her most inspired level, to come up each time with something as remarkable as *Moses and Aron*,[4] *Rake's Progress*, the 1965 *Boris*, the 1966 *Don Giovanni.* It is reasonable, though, to expect her to have put on the stage a piece of responsible, professional looking work. I think she first failed to do this with the spring 1967 *Tosca*, which she allowed to be scrambled together by two of her assistants, who then had to take the rap for a mindless quasi-improvisation that would have been an embarrassment in

[3] See review of March 31, 1967.

[4] See review of December 1, 1966.

Bremerhaven, Pasadena, Terontola, or Nizhni Novgorod. *Carmen* was attributed to Caldwell, it was better than *Tosca*, but it was quite bad enough.

Both *Carmen* and the *Traviata* that followed reflected the company's tendency to woo its public with stars. It was Marilyn Horne in one, Joan Sutherland in the other. Guests of that sort have made impressive things possible, the *Puritani* with Sutherland,[5] for example, or *Semiramide* with Sutherland and Horne.

But these people have done a lot of damage, too. Nothing in Tebaldi's flat and rhythmless singing justified her engagement for *Otello*. The unity of the original *Boris Godunov* was broken because Caldwell gave in to George London's wish to sing a monologue from a later version. When *Boris* was repeated a year later, she gave in to Christoff's insistence on having the stage set just as he was accustomed, wrecking the effect of Heinrich's superb scenic design.

In 1966, Caldwell gave a superb *Don Giovanni*, conducting it herself, and using the original Prague edition, much the best version of the score. For 1967, she engaged Sutherland as Donna Anna. Sutherland brought her own conductor, Richard Bonynge, her husband, who did a less good job than Caldwell, and who restored the less satisfactory edition of the score that mixes the Prague and Vienna versions. I was sorry to see that Caldwell had higher regard for a big name like Sutherland than for her own conviction about the kind of opera *Don Giovanni* is. Ironically, almost everyone felt that Sutherland sang Donna Anna less impressively than Beverly Sills, whom she replaced.

Carmen and *Traviata* this year presented the depressing sight of stars put on display unintegrated into a proper artistic context. *Traviata* I would also call semi-staged. The sets were those Zeffirelli designed for the Dallas production with Sutherland some years back, and one of Caldwell's assistants was, late in the day, given the task of assembling the work on stage, presumably depending on a combination of Zeffirelli's prompt book and Sutherland's muscle memory. Traffic was regulated well enough, but the crowd scenes were ludicrously stiff, and there was no chance to project or develop the important small roles.

The Opera Company of Boston is disastrously on the wrong track, confused in its aims, and coming up with mediocre results for all the wrong reasons. It is not that Sarah Caldwell has been spoiled by success; rather, she seems harassed and distracted by being obliged always to operate on the edge of financial disaster. She badly needs a strong board and competent administrative organization that make it possible for her to do a proper job as artistic director and that keep her away from the non-artistic functions. It is a vicious circle, too, because she needs the massive public support she never could get from Boston at a time when her work was most exciting and promised the most, and which, in view of

[5] See review of February 13, 1964, where the editors have provided additional information on Caldwell's career and impact.

what looked like the sheer slovenliness and cynicism of the *Carmen* and *Traviata* productions, one can hardly blame people for withholding.

Romantic Piano Style Lost?

April 5, 1968

To say that we hear even fewer stylistically appropriate performances of Romantic music than of Baroque is to exaggerate; nonetheless, the period and manner represented in the piano music of Chopin, Schumann, and Liszt, is one for which, as far as performance practice is concerned, we seem to have lost the key.

Much of this music posits a nonliteral approach, particularly with respect to rhythmic flexibility. The structural frame of reference has to remain perceptible, whatever license is taken; the stretching and compression in the playing must correspond to, and thus emphasize, whatever is implicit in the music, and not contradict it; and the result must sound natural rather than contrived. Too often, one hears freedom unchecked by taste or sense; sometimes, especially from younger players, a revisionist approach of great strictness that, however commendably motivated, is not at all persuasive either.

Alfred Brendel, whose recording of two of the great Schumann piano works, the C major Fantasy and the Symphonic Etudes, has just been issued (Vanguard), is a pianist who sounds magisterial in this music, which will be no surprise to those who remember his Liszt in Jordan Hall[6] or the Chopin Polonaise-Fantasy at Castle Hill.

Their coherence on the largest scale is perhaps the most impressive feature of Brendel's playing here. The effect of his ability to balance the sharply, and personally, characterized detail against the hierarchic placement of that detail among a host of others, produces particularly exciting results in the Fantasy with its idiosyncratic—literally fantastic—organization of the material. In both pieces, though, there is a combination of intelligence, energy, imagination, and virtuosity, that makes this record something very remarkable indeed.

The Symphonic Etudes are definitely part of Schumann's "public" music, and the Fantasy almost is. The *Davidsbündlertänze*, though, are Schumann at his most intimate, eighteen short pieces full of character, all suggestion and sketch rather than bold statement, very lovely, and hardly ever effective in the concert hall. Wilhelm Kempff, though more neutral than Cortot (Pathé) or Rosen (Epic), catches much of the restrained sentiment of the *Davidsbündlertänze* effectively,

[6] See review of December 12, 1966.

though a few tempi are rather slow, and there is much pleasure to be had from his sensitive playing (Deutsche Grammophon). The record also includes a good performance of *Papillons*.

A reissue (London Stereo Treasury) of an earlier Chopin record of Kempff's has a lot of technical sloppiness about it, but is still worth hearing for some of his illuminating phrasing, especially with respect to the subtle ways in which phrases grow out of each other, in the A-flat Ballade, the F minor Fantasy, the Polonaise-Fantasy, and the *Andante spianato* with E-flat Polonaise.

Also of more than routine interest are three Liszt records: David Bar-Illan playing the *Dante* Sonata from the second book of *Années de pèlerinage*, and the Hungarian Rhapsody No. 15 (*Rákóczy* March), with Beethoven's *Eroica* Variations on the other side (RCA Victor); a reissue of Tamás Vásáry's performances of the Liszt Sonata, the *Don Juan* Fantasy, and the E major Polonaise (Heliodor); and, more for the repertory than for John Ogdon's blandly featureless playing of it, again the *Don Juan* Fantasy, the *Reminiscences de Boccanegra* (after Verdi, of course), and some of the mysterious, very late pieces, "Csárdás macabre," "En Rêve," "Trauervorspiel und Trauermarsch," and *Mephisto Waltz* No. 3 (Odeon).

Happy Maestro Steinberg Scoffs at "Interim" Talk

April 28, 1968

William Steinberg, who will take over the music directorship of the Boston Symphony for three years beginning with the 1969–70 season, describes himself as "exceedingly proud and happy, elated, and excited" at the prospect. He also intends to make his presence felt here.

The first thing that Erich Leinsdorf's 68-year-old successor told the *Globe* by phone from New York Saturday was, "I must tell you that I am not fond of interviews by telephone. I like to hold the eye of my partner."

The next thing was, "I want at once to make it clear that the word 'interim' was never mentioned by Mr. Cabot [Henry B. Cabot, president of the BSO trustees] in connection with my appointment." He added that nothing about "interim" is to be inferred from the fact that his contract is for three years, that being simply the usual length for an initial contract. Moreover, for however long he is here—and it may be more than three years—Steinberg intends fully to exercise the powers and responsibilities of a music director. That includes general determination of program policy, hiring and firing of players within the exceedingly tight limitations allowed by the union, and the engagement of soloists and guest conductors.

Will he be able to, though? It is clear that Leinsdorf's discontent that led to his resignation in December (effective end of summer 1969) stemmed from finding himself in a situation where, with the players, whose power is increasing on one side, and the trustees on the other, he was hemmed in so that he was unable to do the things he conceived as necessary to achieve the standards he had in mind for the orchestra, and which it was his responsibility as music director to attain. In other words, he had a job to do but not enough of the power that he needed to do it.[7]

Will it be different for Steinberg? In one respect, he is likely at least partially to abdicate authority, and that is in the matter of guest conductors.

Steinberg acknowledged that most of the guest conductors coming to the Boston Symphony during the next few years will be here as potential candidates to be the orchestra's music director, and because of this special situation, it is expected that the guests will be chosen by the trustees rather than by the music director. Steinberg plans to "go along" with their decisions, although he will advise and suggest also.

In long view, then, Steinberg's appointment is de facto "interim." Steinberg, however, foresees the possibility that there may be found among the guests a candidate who is attractive to the trustees, orchestra, and public but who, in experience, breadth of repertory, and so forth, may not be quite ready.

In such a case, the trustees might find it convenient to continue the arrangement with Steinberg for a while beyond the stipulated three years until it is appropriate for the younger man to take over. After all, Steinberg says, they would not have hired him if they didn't like him.

The search for a music director to take over the Boston Symphony after Steinberg will not be easy. The very fact of Steinberg's appointment is a clue in that it is well known, too, that the Chicago Symphony and the New York Philharmonic are having difficulty replacing their departing conductors.

Jean Martinon leaves Chicago at the end of this season. It is supposed he will be succeeded by Georg Solti, now with the Covent Garden Opera, London, but there are evidently difficulties in the way of fixing a contract, and Irwin Hoffman, the Chicago Symphony's assistant conductor, has been appointed acting music director.

Leonard Bernstein quits the New York Philharmonic next spring. The trustees there have appointed 70-year-old George Szell as a kind of interim senior advisor, and they will share his services with the Cleveland Orchestra, whose music director he has been since 1946.

Most younger conductors prefer careers of guest conducting or appointments that allow them a great deal of freedom. Given the speed and convenience of jet

[7] See articles of November 19 and December 11, 1967.

travel, the rewards in glamour and money seem greater than those that come with the arduous responsibilities, particularly in view of the amount of repertory to be mastered, that go with strong commitment to a single orchestra and a single city.

There are not enough first-rate conductors to go around and in today's orchestra-conductor situation, there clearly is a conductor's market. The days are over when an organization like the Boston Symphony could simply beckon and expect all the conductors to come running. Cabot recently said as much when he explained the nature of Steinberg's appointment to the players, saying the orchestra would have to make itself attractive to a desirable candidate.

Steinberg himself views today's accent on youth with some skepticism, even remembering his own appointment at 27 to the directorship of the German Opera in Prague and his becoming general music director of the Frankfurt Opera at 29. About Prague he says today: "I was too powerful too early, having in effect the life and death of 400 people in my hands."

He is worried, too, about the displacement of musical considerations by concern with publicity in the making of many decisions. "In my day the word 'publicity' was not used, not known, not necessary." The abuses of publicity today push too many young performers into careers and positions for which they are not ready. Steinberg says, "If my young colleagues would only learn their music, publicity would follow of itself."

Steinberg, born in Cologne in 1899, came up the usual training route for European conductors—in the opera houses, first as assistant to Otto Klemperer in Cologne, then in Prague and Frankfurt.

As a Jew, he was compelled to leave Germany in 1933. In 1936 he became first conductor of the Palestine Orchestra (now Israel Philharmonic) and first came to the United States in 1938 to conduct the NBC Symphony at Toscanini's invitation. From 1945–52 he was with the Buffalo Philharmonic, then moved to Pittsburgh.

His association with the Pittsburgh Symphony will continue for "an unlimited number of seasons to come." He is experienced with double responsibilities: from 1958–60 he was also musical director of the London Philharmonic, and next week he finishes a two-year appointment as the New York Philharmonic's senior guest conductor. In 1958, Steinberg did, however, turn down an offer to become general music director of the Städtische Oper in West Berlin.

During his first Boston season, Steinberg will have fifteen weeks with the Symphony (twelve here, three on tour), and sixteen with the Pittsburgh. Asked about the workload problem, he said only, "I am used to it."

Each of his two cities, he stressed, had its own repertory problems, affected principally by what had and had not been played there in recent years.

Certain pieces, both standard and unusual or new, would undoubtedly crop up in both places, but essentially the two programming operations would be independent.

Since, among other reasons, Steinberg has not yet looked over the Boston Symphony repertory of recent seasons, it was too soon for him to say anything about specific plans for what he will do here. "I believe in the mixed diet," he said; and yes, he would not fail to observe Beethoven's 200th birthday in 1970. "I am accustomed to observe the great *anniversaires*."

Two other questions Steinberg was not yet prepared to answer concerned the directorship of the Berkshire Music Center, which has in the past gone with the job of music director of the Boston Symphony, and recording plans.

The BMC question, he says, is "still open," but he added that the Pittsburgh Symphony has demanding summer plans of its own. He has a contract with Command Records, for whom he has made many recordings with Pittsburgh, but the contract is not exclusive, and there certainly exists the possibility of recording with Boston for RCA as well.

He added that he hopes it will be possible for the Boston Symphony to record with some of its guest conductors as well: "*Variatio delectat*" ("change delights"). Like many Germans of his generation, Steinberg liberally sprinkles his talk with Latin tags, for example, enumerating the points of an argument, "*pro prime, pro secundo . . .*"

Steinberg, certainly one of the world's most widely experienced conductors, is known in the profession as a solid orchestral technician and as an uneccentric, if rarely exciting, interpreter. In educated musical circles, the lavish cuts he makes, especially in Berlioz, Bruckner, Elgar, and Mahler, are noted and deplored.

One final point of clarification: the Boston Symphony's music director-elect and the *Globe*'s music critic are not related.

Harvard Student's Mozart Completion "Amazing"

May 20, 1968

Robert Levin, a music major at Harvard, wrote his senior thesis on the unfinished works of Mozart. As part of the project, Levin completed two fragments, a concerto movement for piano, violin, and orchestra, K.315f, and a movement of a quintet for clarinet and strings, K.516c.

Saturday, in an all-Mozart concert presented by Adams House, the two movements were performed for the first time, for an audience that filled Sanders Theatre and which gave Levin, conductor John Harbison, and the orchestra a standing ovation at the end of the evening.

Levin is a musician of extraordinary gifts, a composer (not only of Mozart, as it were, but of two kinds of Levin, one for Leon Kirchner's composition classes, one for Hasty Pudding shows), a scholar, and a pianist (he played the solo in the reconstructed concerto movement, all of another concerto, and a sonata).

Mozart began his Double Concerto in 1778 for the Mannheim violinist [Ignaz] Fränzl and himself as pianist, dropping it again when for non-musical reasons the opportunity for the performance evaporated. He had by then written about one-third of the first movement, a D major Allegro in martial style. That left Levin with part of the exposition to write, including one solo theme, and all of the development and recapitulation.

There have been completions of unfinished Mozart before, and some of them, like Süssmayr's of the Requiem or the Abbé Maximilian Stadler's of the C minor Piano Fantasy, K.385f, are often heard. They are "correct" enough, though almost paralyzed by caution, and their merit is in making it practical to get some marvelous music off the shelf and into performance.

Levin's work with the concerto movement goes beyond this. A piano-and-violin concerto is difficult to complete because there is no model to refer to; any concerto is difficult because in this form Mozart was most apt to be unpredictable in his recapitulation.

Levin chose to risk being in no way mechanical, predictable, merely safe, and he was right.

Armed with his unusual knowledge of and feeling for Mozart's music and with his own skill as a composer, he has expanded Mozart's beginning into a movement all of which delights one with its invention, shapeliness, and instrumental brilliance.

As for the B-flat Clarinet Quintet of 1787, we don't know if Mozart abandoned it or if part of the manuscript is lost. What survives is the exposition and the start of the development of an Allegro in the gently lyric manner characteristic of the works Mozart wrote for the clarinetist Anton Stadler (no kin to the Abbé).

Here, too, the completion was managed with superb professionalism and with perhaps a little more than that in the coda, though this piece, gracious as it is, does not make so strong an impression as the earlier, boldly original concerto movement.

The qualities that make Levin's work as a creative editor so impressive were to be heard in his playing as well. It is on a rather small scale, and purely as a matter of personal preference, I think of the C major Piano Concerto, K.503, as a big piece.

There is, however, so much vitality on every other plane, such awareness of and pleasure in the point-to-point progression of detail, such understanding of the vocal style and the complex anthropomorphic, operatic meaning in Mozart's instrumental writing as well as of what one might call the purely musical facts of rhythm and so forth, that makes Levin's playing a remarkable exercise of taste in the most positive and active sense.

This sense of life in performance was to a large degree matched by that wonderfully musical violinist, Rose Mary Harbison, Levin's partner in the B-flat Sonata, K.454, and even more in John Harbison's conducting.

Harbison has a super-relaxed manner that goes well with Levin's own, an outstanding musical intelligence, and an ensemble sense that was a sine qua non for a successful realization of the chamber-musical conception of the concertos, and an ability to get from his orchestra, non-professional except for a few music students, playing that was astonishing in its textural transparency, rhythmic definition, and stylishness.

Harbison also contributed a cadenza for the double concerto, a fascinating bit of composition and one not to be second-guessed.

It was, altogether, an amazing, a beautiful, an exciting concert.

Choice of Funeral Music Was Masterly

June 10, 1968

Even in grief a musician cannot stop hearing with a musician's ear. In the Kennedy funeral ceremonies in New York and Washington Saturday, music, chosen with imagination and tact, heightened the intensity of the experience.

It had been very different at the funeral of President John F. Kennedy in November 1963. Then the music—old-style Catholic liturgical music at its worst, and an embarrassing rendition of the sticky Bach-Gounod *Ave Maria*—had been something to make one ashamed.

It was the one failure in a tragic ceremonial otherwise imagined and carried out with exemplary dignity, and it was one more reason particularly to appreciate, as a kind of musical redress, Erich Leinsdorf's performance of Mozart's Requiem at the commemorative Mass celebrated at Boston's Cathedral of the Holy Cross in January 1964.

Every note of music I heard on telecasts of the services for Sen. Robert Kennedy was stirring, very deeply moving, and absolutely right. That it was possible was largely due to the liturgical liberalization following the second Vatican Council. It allowed the use of music whose associations are Protestant more than Catholic, the introduction of music with no liturgical associations at all, and it made possible the emphasis on the victory of life over death.

Kennedy the fighter was remembered in "The Battle Hymn of the Republic," one of the great marching hymns. It was sung by Andy Williams at St. Patrick's

Cathedral, and picked up by crowds at various points later, most moving at the Baltimore station just before the train passed through. It became the real theme music of the day.

One of the most beautiful moments was the brief halt of the funeral cortège at the Lincoln Memorial. There the Washington Choral Society sang Henry Purcell's anthem "Thou knowest, Lord, the secrets of our hearts," written for the funeral of Queen Mary II, wife of William III, on March 5, 1695, and used again at the 36-year-old Purcell's own Westminster Abbey burial nine months later.

As the procession moved on, the chorus sang the hymn that ends Bach's *St. John* Passion, "Lord Jesu, Thy dear angel send"—a wonderfully strong tune that was about thirty years old when Bach used it, having given it one of the most miraculous of all his harmonizations.

But I think the most shattering moment of all, and the most unexpected for such an occasion, was the playing in St. Patrick's of the Adagietto from Mahler's Symphony No. 5 by members of the New York Philharmonic under Leonard Bernstein. It was the one moment when music spoke of searing, nearly unbearable, personal pain. It said things that needed to be said at some point during the day, but beyond that, Bernstein's choice of Mahler was a humanly sensitive gesture symbolizing Kennedy's rapport with youth.

The Mahler boom of recent years has been associated especially with young listeners who hear in his utterances with their paradoxes, their sincerity and boldness, their strange mixture of angst and sweetness, something especially relevant and timely.

The Adagietto needs few instruments and it is short; that made it practical to play. It was perfectly judged as an expression of what was lost before the "Battle Hymn" and Handel's "Hallelujah!" again reminded us that death shall have no dominion.

You Can't Have It Both Ways—Accept Approval, Reject Disapproval?

June 23, 1968

At the funeral of President John F. Kennedy, the music—old style Catholic liturgical at its worst, and an embarrassing rendition of the sticky Bach-Gounod *Ave Maria*—was the one failure at a tragic ceremony otherwise characterized throughout by exemplary dignity.

There was occasion to comment to that effect while writing about the music heard from New York and Washington the day of Sen. Robert F. Kennedy's funeral, the inspired choices that were made of what to sing and play, and the moving effect. Some of the response to the article was dissent, and on three main points, each of which I can express by quoting from my mail:

1. "Gounod's *Ave Maria* is the most beautiful of all the Ave Marias."
2. "We who believe, will never consider the *Ave Maria*, no matter who the composer, neither (sic) embarrassing or sticky."
3. "You should refrain yourself from poking fun at Catholic liturgical music. . . . As a Catholic and respecter of other sects, I don't think one's sacred music should be criticized."

The author of the first quotation backs up her assertion confidently: "We know, we have a soul for music."

The second statement is not true. Many devout Catholics, both professional musicians and laymen, are embarrassed, even outraged, by some musical settings of liturgical texts, just as they are sickened by the equivalent manifestations in the visual arts. Gounod's *Ave Maria* is an example of what such persons find objectionable. I am sure, too, they would be quick to point out to a perhaps astounded non-churchgoer, that it is very far from the worst.

Sir Donald Tovey said of it, that in the ninth measure Gounod "addresses the Virgin with the musical equivalent of 'Darling.'" To many a Catholic, sensitive to musical values as well as to religious, Gounod's kitsch is sacrilegious.

In liturgical composition, the composer must live up to the text, which is the given part, and which articulates ideas that, for believers, are presumably the most important ones they know, and central to their existence. No one can assume that the composer's task here is easy, let alone automatic. You cannot assume, therefore, that all *Ave Maria* settings are valid, or that the text mystically confers worthiness on whatever music is associated with it.

The Catholic Church has, in fact, never assumed this. The history of its music is, among other things, the history of developments and reforms that were responses to the criticism that certain musics in use were inadequate to the texts they treated and the occasions they served.

What about criticism? The Boston College student who wrote the letter from which the third quotation is taken, says I "have no right to call Gounod's *Ave Maria* 'sticky.'" Why not? She does not say, though one can infer something of what is on her mind from a later remark about Catholic liturgical music, which, she says, "many consider . . . sacred as you would consider Bar Mitzvah ceremony music and other sacred Hebrew music." What if the byline had been Doyle or Smith? Or does it mean "no right" for anyone to differ about *Ave Marias*?

It gets complicated. Presumably it is proper to write criticism about Bach's Third *Brandenburg* Concerto. May I no longer comment on the same music when Bach uses it later as part of a Whitsuntide cantata, thus turning it into "sacred music"? For that matter, can I help that the remarks on the Concerto would automatically be at least partially applicable to the Cantata?

Then, some of the letter writers make a point of commending my favorable assessment of the music chosen for Robert Kennedy's Requiem and funeral. You cannot have it both ways, accepting approval, but on principle rejecting disapproval.

The most important point is that religion is not the private preoccupation of those who practice it. It perhaps should be, but it is not. Men have started wars and brought misery to thousands in order to show they loved God more intensely and more authoritatively than their neighbors. In its most peaceful manifestations, the church exercises enormous influence as a political, economic, and cultural force.

The ideas a church propagates, the buildings, the works of art, the musical compositions it calls into being, all become matters of public concern. The larger and more powerful the church, the truer this is. Offering themselves to public scrutiny, these things offer themselves to criticism.

The musician—and it doesn't matter whether he is a critic by profession, or a composer, performer, or scholar—cannot ignore the problem of religious art when he asks himself the inevitable questions about present conditions and about the future. The same, *mutatis mutandis*, is true of the painter, the sculptor, the architect, and the poet.

Most of the art that meets ear and eye in a church or synagogue is deplorable, and so—and this must be relevant—is the quality of most of the thought and sentiment pronounced from the pulpits. If this observation about the arts affects the Catholic Church most, it is only because the Catholic Church has assigned a larger role to the arts in its places and rites of worship.

A priest I know, talking about communion, said that men in authority at church had no scruple about serving at the Lord's table wine they would be ashamed to serve at their own. When it comes to music, the church cannot be counted on to offer the best there is either. Instead of being a force to elevate, music, like the polychrome statues that are its visual correlative, panders to the cheapest taste and the most facile sentiment.

From the plainsong that goes back to the first centuries of Christian history to the *Requiem Canticles* Stravinsky wrote two years ago, the Roman liturgy has inspired an incredibly rich repertory of profoundly beautiful music. Whether one's concern is religious, moral, artistic, or whatever combination of these, a preference for slops is something to lament.

"Tempo" and "Character"—Are Beethoven, Others Heard Properly?

July 14, 1968

When the pianist Russell Sherman played Beethoven's Concerto No. 5 with the New England Conservatory Orchestra under Frederik Prausnitz in Jordan Hall a few months ago,[8] the quick tempo in the first movement shocked me to begin with; in a few moments, though, the shock ceased to be one of astonishment or even alarm, and became the shock of revelation. I had the impression that I was hearing the piece properly for the first time. The effect of that, moreover, was cumulative: when the finale, taken at the "normal" tempo, arrived, I was made aware, as never before, of the difference in tempo and character between its Allegro with its broad 6/8 swing and that of the energetically thrusting first movement, and of the importance of maintaining that distinction. And between the two Allegros, the middle movement had been played with an awareness that Beethoven qualifies his Adagio with "*un poco mosso*" ("moving a bit"), and with an awareness also that the way the harmonies move implies the cut time, two beats to the bar rather than four, that is not specified.

I have linked the words "tempo" and "character" in deliberate reference to the title of Rudolf Kolisch's article, "Tempo and Character in Beethoven's Music," in the *Musical Quarterly* (1943). The article has failed to affect current performance practice, but it ought to be required reading for every performer.

Kolisch writes that Beethoven "was conscious of tempo as an essential part of his language, coordinated with that mysterious category which he himself termed 'character.' A wrong tempo would change the character, and for each character there is an appropriate tempo." For Beethoven, Kolisch points out, the issue of tempo was especially critical because he introduced so many new character types into music. The invention, during his lifetime, of the metronome was fortunate, and his enthusiasm for it was significant.

What is particularly illuminating for the musician concerned with the practical application of such a study is the way Kolisch shows how character is inferred by specific musical habits or configurations—"characteristics," in fact—the prevalence of certain rhythmic patterns, for instance, melodic shapes, or harmonic movement. Thus he groups the first movement of the Fifth Concerto with the parallel 4/4 Allegros in the Trio, Op. 1, No. 1, the Symphony No. 5 (finale), the E-flat Quartet, Op. 74, and the Violin Sonata, Op. 12, No. 3. These are all what he calls "normal" Allegros, as distinct, for example, from the *cantabile*

[8] See review of March 23, 1968.

Allegro or the "Allegro con brio," and the pause on the second beat and strongly accented quarters are characteristic for them.

In Bach's day, there was a common musical language, governed by convention, and universally understood by performers. That made it perfectly feasible most of the time to use only a very few basic tempo indications. Many pieces have none at all; others are marked "tempo ordinario," which is a way of saying to the player, "It's obvious how this one goes." And so it was, and for that matter most of the directions of Allegro, Presto, Andante, Adagio, will not have been necessary either: figurations, harmonic rhythm, the time signature, told the tale. And at the end of the century in the Haydn-Mozart years, the tempo code neither was, nor needed to be, much more elaborate.

The metronome, which came along in 1816 just at the right moment to be useful to Beethoven, is in disrepute among performers. It conjures up horrid memories of childhood music lessons. Then, except in contexts like "are you going to beat two or four?," "the second oboe is flat," and "$248 a week," musicians resist any attempt to connect numbers with their work.

More specifically, they will say that tempo cannot be fixed by arithmetic measurement, that at the very least it would have to vary a little according to the size and resonance of the room.

There is confusion here with the idea of playing "like a metronome," and obviously enough, a metronome's stiffgaitedness is, in all but special cases, an undesirable performance aim. If the composer puts down a metronome mark of 120—a metronome number indicates beats per minute—he does not mean that every beat in the piece moves at the same speed as every other one. On the contrary, there is reason to believe that very much music nowadays—and I would specifically include Beethoven's—is too rigidly played, with too little tempo flexibility both on local and large scale, in other words, too nearly metronomically. However, these variations should all happen with reference to the basic speed indicated by 120.

Again, if the composer puts down 120, he is not likely to find a performance at 116 unacceptable, nor one at 126. Any number of interpretive, analytic, technical, or acoustic considerations might bring about such a modification (or even greater ones) without distortion. Chances are, though, that he will scream if the tempo is 144 or 96, because you cannot make that kind of a change without altering the character of what he has written.

At worst, a wrong tempo can make a piece unintelligible on any terms. It can go so fast that it turns into unarticulated gabble, "like water from a public fountain," as Wagner said about one of Mendelssohn's Beethoven performances. It can be so slow that the listener's mind cannot establish the continuity. In how many performances of the "Song of Thanksgiving" in Beethoven's Quartet,

Op. 132, could you actually follow the chorale melody if you did not know it well already, or even tell that a melody was being played?

Real unintelligibility as the result of bad tempo is rare, though not as rare as one might suppose or hope. Distortion of character through a choice of tempo that inattentively or deliberately differs from the composer's indication is not at all rare. It is a serious matter, too, because as long as it is somehow intelligible, no matter how alien it is to the composer's intention, there is always the danger that the new character that has been established, or to put it more extremely, the new piece that has been made, will become sanctified by tradition.

Beethoven's E-flat Concerto is one of many works about which I am convinced that traditional performances have not allowed us to hear them properly, and next week I should like to write about some other examples.[9]

Is Beethoven's Tempo Too Fast?

July 21, 1968

The most famous problem tempo in the literature is, I suppose, that for the first movement of Beethoven's B-flat Piano Sonata, Op. 106, the so-called *Hammerklavier*. It even comes up in so unexpected a context as Fred Hoyle's science fiction novel, *The Black Cloud*, and Hoyle deals with the question more perceptively than many musicians.

Beethoven marked the movement "Allegro" and put down a metronome figure of 138 to the half-note. The only pianist I know who ever played it at 138 was Artur Schnabel. He was in many ways a pianist of extraordinary technical skill, but marksmanship was not his strength, and neither, under stress, were clear articulation and steady rhythm. On his 1935 recording—I never heard him play it in concert—most of the performance is chaotic.

This Allegro, with its stretches, leaps, and quick movement of full chords, is terribly difficult. I don't know whether it can be played at 138 or not. I am sure that it can be heard at that speed; in fact, like Professor Hoyle's cosmic cloud, I am convinced that in a clear performance it can be better heard and understood at that tempo than at a slower.

If we assume for the sake of argument that, given the present state of piano technique, 138 is an impossible tempo in practice, a pianist must still be aware that 138 is what Beethoven asked for (every pianist is), and he must use the metronome mark as part of the data from which to infer the character of the work (hardly any pianist does). In his *Musical Quarterly* (1943) article on "Tempo and

[9] See next article.

Character in Beethoven's Music," Rudolf Kolisch writes that Beethoven "was conscious of tempo as an essential part of his language, coordinated with that mysterious category which he himself termed 'character.' A wrong tempo would change the character, and for each character there is an appropriate tempo."

In other words, the pianist might say to himself: "I can't play the first movement of the *Hammerklavier* at 138, and I don't believe anybody can. But what would it be like that fast? What does the metronome mark tell about Beethoven's idea of the piece?"

It tells us, I would say, that the two opening barrages of massive chords are wild and impetuous rather than grandly declamatory, that the lyricism of the next phrase is markedly intense. Neither gesture is given to us in what you might call its most generalized form, nor, therefore, with its most generalized meeting: the expressive intent of the *Hammerklavier* opening is quite different from that of the first measures of Mozart's *Jupiter* Symphony, where you also find the forceful-lyric contrast, but in its "normal" form. The four-and-three-quarter-octave span of the *fortissimo* chords sees to it that Beethoven's adaptation of this sort of opening is "special" rather than "normal," so does the two-octave descent of the bass during the four-bar lyric phrase, so does the unmeasured pause that separates the two elements, and so, not least, does the tempo.

The rest of the movement follows from these first eight measures. It is a movement that abounds in abruptions of every sort, in powerful rhythmic expansions and contradictions, percussive accents, sudden changes of register, harmonic shifts, and so forth. These are the means with which Beethoven articulates the character of this movement, a character whose "special" quality is most consistently realized through tempo, the indication for which, in turn, is the first thing the pianist encounters in his confrontation with the music.

If 138 cannot be done, the c.126 at which Charles Rosen plays the movement on his now withdrawn recording is close enough to convey the unique quality of what Beethoven imagined.[10] Rosen's playing here, of course, has other virtues as well, but they are indissolubly linked with his tempo, that is, with his understanding of Beethoven's tempo. On the other hand, the c.108 of Vladimir Ashkenazy's recorded performance is too far away from Beethoven's 138, too far in terms of points on the metronome, and because of that too far away in character. And I would add that the other faults in Ashkenazy's performance of this movement—the underplaying of accents and the smoothing over of registral changes—are the result of his misapprehension most consistently expressed in the slow tempo.

The problem about the 138 for the first movement of the *Hammerklavier* is a famous one. It is curious, though, that no one ever seems to talk about the

[10] See also Steinberg's March 5, 1972, review of Rosen's later recording of the *Hammerklavier.*

tempo of the third movement, the Adagio. It is in 6/8, marked "Adagio sostenuto" ("slow and sustained"), which is supplemented by "Appassionato e con molto sentimento." Beethoven gives a metronome mark of 92 for the eighth-note, and on the four recordings I happen to have on hand I find that Egon Petri plays it at 84, Rosen at 74, Schnabel at 70, and Ashkenazy at 62. The figures represent basic tempi, flexibly treated in each case with excursions to either side.

Petri's tempo comes reasonably close to Beethoven's; in fact, its ratio of departure from the metronome mark is the same as Rosen's in the first movement. I don't think, however, that Petri's rather bland playing makes a completely convincing case for his tempo.

To try it myself at 92 was an unsettling experience, one that mind and muscles resisted for some time. It was a question of what I was used to hearing from Schnabel, Serkin, and others. More essentially I think it had to do with some valid convictions about the profundity of this movement, combined with a romantic prejudice that this profundity required an extremely slow tempo for its proper expression.

What I had to get through my head and into my fingers was the idea that "Adagio sostenuto" refers, not to the eighth-notes, but to the dotted quarters into which the eighths are collected in groups of three. In other words, there are two beats in a bar, not six, and each of the two moves at 30, which is very slow indeed. The solemn one-measure upbeat that Beethoven, in an afterthought, added to the beginning of the movement makes the in-two-ness of it as clear as can be.

Here, too, it turns out that Beethoven means what he says. Next week I should like to return to the tempo question once more,[11] to touch on some other problem spots in Beethoven as well as some in Mozart and Brahms, and to speculate on why it all happens.

Debussy—A Contemporary View

July 21, 1968

It has become a commonplace to treat Mahler not as, or perhaps better "not just as," one of the last manifestations of Romanticism, but as a Founding Father of 20th-century music, the precursor of the Schoenberg school, and as a source for more conservative composers like Shostakovich and Britten.

A parallel re-evaluation of Debussy is just beginning to reach public awareness. The process is slow because the Debussy relevant to later composers as diverse as Stravinsky, Bartók, and Boulez, is the Debussy of the late works, and

[11] See article of July 28, 1968.

those pieces, of which the most important are the ballet *Jeux*, the piano etudes, and the sonatas, are still stigmatized as dry, decadent style exercises in many of the most widely read writings on Debussy.

Jeux is included on a Debussy record by Pierre Boulez and the New Philharmonia, the other works being *La Mer* and *Afternoon of a Faun* (CBS). Boulez of course takes a contemporary view of Debussy. That is really necessary for *Jeux*, a score written in 1912 for a Nijinsky tennis-as-sex ballet. In this music, traditional ways about development of themes are abandoned, replaced by unceasing, irreversible forward-movement of ideas, sometimes juxtaposed, sometimes evolving one from another, but always concerned with moving on rather than with recapitulating. These varied events are unified by tempo and articulated by an approach to orchestration based on the assumption that texture and color are not the music's dressing but as much part of its essential substance as rhythm and harmony. Enough people to have filled the Théâtre de Champs-Élysées four times over now boast of having been present at the premiere of Stravinsky's *Rite of Spring*. *Jeux*, whose premiere took place just two weeks earlier in May 1913, is unlikely to attain the *réclame* to elicit similar claims; nonetheless, it is one of the key works of the 20th century, and one of his freshest and most beautiful. Its procedures are, however, so new, still so new in relation to most of the music we hear, that one must perhaps begin by learning not to listen to it as a decadent rehash of the compositional methods used in *La Mer*, to learn to follow its own characteristic "extremely tensile form of thought," as Boulez puts it.

The Boulez performance, its precision and vitality of rhythm, its luminous clarity of texture, its cohesive pacing, is a marvelous guide toward the understanding, and love, of *Jeux*. The only comparable performances of *Jeux* I have experienced have been Boulez's own with the BBC Symphony in New York three years ago, and one by another conductor whose mind was tuned to the 20th century, Hans Rosbaud, whom I heard do it with his own Südwestfunk Orchestra in Tübingen in 1956. On records, though Bernstein's performance (Columbia) is in many respects very good, there has been nothing to approach Boulez's achievement, and that alone is enough to make this disc an indispensable one.

The performance of *La Mer* is almost as remarkable. It is all in how the edges are treated, and those whose idea of Debussy is realized by the luminous blur of Karajan's or Ansermet's performances will be as disturbed by the Boulez *La Mer* as many listeners used to be and still are by the Toscanini interpretation. Boulez, with his fantastic textural precision, reveals in *La Mer* an amazing succession of exciting details. There are a few things, particularly those to do with tempo, that Toscanini (RCA) manages still better than Boulez; also, Toscanini's performance of the second movement gets much more of the rhythmic suppleness Debussy asks for. These are the two *La Mer* readings that outclass all other recorded ones.

The *Faun* has some puzzling failures. Boulez, for example, fails to make sure that the flutist holds the first note long enough to establish the correct rhythm, the end of the piece is anything other than the "*très lent*" Debussy wants, and on the way there are a number of ungraciously executed details. There are, however, important successes, too: the clarification of the whole form, the illuminating use of texture, of sound itself, as a structural element, the careful balance of solo and accompanying voices, the masterful transition into the D-flat major middle section. It is not a completely successful or beautiful performance, but it is one to know.

In this context I want to remind you of a record previously reviewed here, Charles Rosen's of Debussy piano music, including *Estampes* and both books of *Images* (Epic).[12] In a way that parallels Boulez's treatment of the orchestral pieces, Rosen rejects the notion of playing the piano music as soft-edged impressionistic, richly pedalled wash. I think it will hardly take more than the first few seconds of Rosen's playing of "Reflets dans l'eau" to show you how revelatory his performances of this music are.

Original Beethoven Hardly Recognizable

July 28, 1968

If Beethoven's Violin Concerto had been lost in 1810 and only recently rediscovered, its first 20th-century performance would, I am sure, be very different from almost any performance we are actually likely to find in concert or on records in 1968. The biggest difference probably would occur in the tempi of the first and second movements, both of which I should imagine to be played much faster than we are used to hearing them.

In this article, as well as the preceding two, which also dealt with the question of tempo,[13] I am indebted to Rudolf Kolisch, a great musician, and one of the very few ever to have thought systematically about the tempo problem. In his study of "Tempo and Character in Beethoven's Music," published in the *Musical Quarterly* in 1943, Kolisch suggests that the tempo for the first movement of the Violin Concerto ought to be about the same as that for the first movement of the A major Cello Sonata, Op. 69, and indeed the similarity of melodic, rhythmic, harmonic, and figurational detail that supports Kolisch's thesis is very striking. In fact, a standard tempo today for the sonata movement is somewhere between 60 and 70 to the half-note—Kolisch, invoking further similarities to other

[12] See review of August 2, 1967.
[13] See articles of July 14 and 21, 1968.

movements for which Beethoven gave metronome marks, thinks that something like 84 would be better—whereas a "normal," familiar for the concerto movement, is between 48 and 54.

Likewise, the evidence of similar things in Beethoven suggests that half-note= 30 is about right for the slow movement, Larghetto. Klemperer and Furtwängler (both with Menuhin) take it at 20 and 21, respectively, and with no suggestion that there are two beats in a bar rather than four; Leinsdorf (with Milstein) goes 22 and also, not only because of the tempo, does better on the two-vs.-four question. After his Harvard lecture last spring, Kolisch remarked that it was inconceivable that anyone who had any connection with the knowledge of music at all could take the score of that movement and infer from it the tempo that is usually taken.

Menuhin and Milstein, Furtwängler, Klemperer, and Leinsdorf are men whose relation to and knowledge of music is more than casual, and the same is true of the many violinists and conductors whose interpretations would, with respect to tempo, not be startlingly different from theirs. If these tempi do not come from a reading of Beethoven's score, which represents an experienced professional's best attempt to translate an idea onto paper for further translation into sound, where do they come from?

A violinist or conductor might tell you that the first movement of the Beethoven concerto is marked "Allegro ma non troppo" ("quick, but not too much so") and that it is a spaciously meditative composition whose character is best realized at 54 or so to the half-note. One might reply that "Allegro moderato" and "Allegro ma non troppo" are at the slow end of Beethoven's Allegro spectrum (with "Allegro molto" and "Allegro con brio" at the quick end, and plain "Allegro" in the middle), but that Beethoven's metronome marks tell us that even his "slow" Allegros are not meant to be all that slow.

Then we might raise the question of how we know that the character of the movement is spaciously contemplative or meditative. Since this idea of character seems to exist in defiance of what we can infer to be the composer's intentions about the tempo, the answer would seem to be that we "know" it because that is the way we always have heard it played.

It is a multi-faceted movement that survives being played slowly. We have heard it done beautifully that way; indeed, the performance I still remember as moving me more than any, one by Morini and Walter around 1950, may well have been the slowest I ever heard. But because of how the tempo affected the character, it was, no matter how beautiful, not the piece Beethoven intended. We have a nice circular argument here: we play the piece in a certain way in order to realize a character whose supposed existence we infer only from other performances.

Take a fresh look at the Violin Concerto's first movement and imagine it perhaps one-and-a-half times as fast as usual. Imagine it also without the further absurdity of the traditional extreme slowings-down for the G minor section at the end of the development (with the horn's invocation of the opening drum taps completely unintelligible at the no-tempo-at-all), and again in the passage immediately following the cadenza (where the coughing of audiences all over the world might have suggested to violinists that something was wrong). With that, and with an appropriate restoration of the Larghetto, we almost would have a different piece, no less beautiful, and more characteristic.

The problem of misrepresentation sanctified by tradition arises because fundamental confusions remain about the relation of performance to composition. That is why the ridiculous *Boris Godunov* controversy [regarding alternative editions] is still with us, based on the false assumption that a composer's score and someone else's "improvements" on it present equally valid alternatives. That is why a conductor who would be scandalized at the idea of himself rewriting a Haydn symphony does not, upon learning that the score he has been using is in fact full of changes by some other outsider, and upon having Haydn's own version made available to him, at once drop the spurious article for the genuine. Misprints in poetry are not continued in circulation once discovered and corrected, and no one in the visual arts has expressed a preference that the grime be restored to Rembrandt's *Night Watch*. Musicians are not generally trained to that kind of integrity and intelligence.

To find out what a composer meant, to eliminate what he could not have meant or would have wished to avoid, requires intelligent, imaginative, and knowing evaluation of complicated, often ambiguous evidence. Taste is necessary, but all by itself, unsupported by knowledge, it can become capricious preference and an unreliable guide to performance. Musicians' education should include equipping them to evaluate evidence, and to recognize the basic difference in value between what the composer tells us and what a performance tradition tells us.

It is no good to have pieces turned into other pieces, the various Beethoven works I have mentioned, the Mozart G minor Symphony, whose first movement has been turned from an impassioned "Molto allegro" to a pathetic Andante, the Brahms B-flat Piano Concerto, whose graceful Andante has become a sentimental Adagio. It is true that Toscanini's example restored something of the character of the second movement of Beethoven's Seventh after generations of conductors had dragged it. Perhaps it means there is hope, but it is a slender thread at best, and I can't help thinking that most of the men who took up the quicker tempo were imitating Toscanini rather than finding Beethoven.

Schumann "Premiere" by Frager, BSO First-Rate

August 6, 1968

LENOX—Last summer, the pianist Malcolm Frager participated in an informal reading with the Berkshire Music Center Orchestra of the first movement of the Schumann Concerto in its original version, which he had recently discovered in Germany. Last Saturday, a few hundred yards across the Tanglewood lawn and before an audience about fifty times the size of last year's, Frager was soloist with the Boston Symphony in the Schumann, playing the whole work, of course, but using the first version of the opening movement, giving its real American premiere. Erich Leinsdorf was the conductor on both occasions.

To recapitulate the background quickly, what is now the first movement existed to begin with as an independent Concert Fantasy, and the finale—using the terminology of Clara Schumann, who always thought of the Intermezzo and Allegro together as "the finale"—was added four years later. At some point between the first performance of the one-movement Fantasy and the publication of the whole Concerto, Schumann made changes in the first movement, producing the work familiar today.

Three changes are obvious. The work originally started without the bang from the orchestra on the first downbeat, but instead put a dramatic punctuation between the piano's first and second pairs of chords. Second, the last twelve measures of the cadenza as they stand now are the result of rewriting: the original led via more propulsive figuration to a startlingly unexpected orchestral entry on a diminished chord. Third, in the coda, the piano originally had a two-measure outburst on its own, theatrically delaying for a moment the final settling onto the tonic in bar 504.

The other changes affect scoring and figuration rather than structure and rhetoric. One attractive detail does stand out, though: the downward arpeggios that tailed each phrase of the C major clarinet melody that is first heard at measure 67, though Gino Cioffi's staccato clatter through them was remarkably ugly.

With Schumann, for reasons about which one can only speculate, the rule seems to be that his revisions make things less interesting than they were before because he tends to put safe moves in place of the audacious, original strokes he first thought of. Of course, the first movement of the Concerto is beautiful in the form in which we have always heard it, but almost without exception I regret the changes, now that I know what was there first.

Saturday's performance, however, made me see why some of the changes might have seemed desirable to Schumann or to his wife, who was the first soloist. That beginning, for instance, is hard to carry off. It seems that the only way the conductor can safely bring the orchestra in on its tricky entrance right after the piano's first da-DUM, is to give the downbeat Schumann so carefully left out. But that spoils it both for the pianist (he can't make his dramatic gesture at his own pleasure) and for the audience (we get a clear signal instead of the surprise of the solo entrance from nowhere). Also, the orchestral chord after the cadenza is hard to bring in. It sounded tentative rather than dramatic on Saturday, and Schumann, who was an exceedingly unconfident conductor, will have had much more trouble with it than Leinsdorf, and may, as well, have been disappointed by the lack of punch in the sonority itself.

These are technical problems that can be solved, though I expect Mr. Frager, and any other pianist who takes up this version, will often run into the typical conductor's prejudice against exhaustive rehearsal of a concerto, especially one "we all know" like the Schumann. I hope, at any rate, they will be solved. There is no reason why the 1841 version should replace the 1845 one altogether, nor is there any chance it will, but it has a boldness about it, a sense of adventure, that makes it an important and exciting find. It should stay in circulation.

Frager's warm, vocal, unpercussive playing became better and better, more free and with more expression of delicate fantasy, as it went on. It was marvelously nonmechanical, and throughout there was an exquisite rightness of taste in the way he moved about Schumann's *affettuoso* style. His tempi were close to the indicated ones, faster than usual in the first two movements, but broader in the third. I have never heard the finale done with such grace, and it really cannot be done properly at the conventional quick pace. Apart from the couple of reservations above, Leinsdorf and the orchestra provided first-rate collaboration, and even had there not been the special matters of interest, this performance would have been something singularly memorable and beautiful.

Baker-Barbirolli, a Fine Partnership

August 25, 1968

The young English mezzo-soprano Janet Baker is especially effective in French repertory. I hope before long she will record some Duparc and Fauré songs; meanwhile, we have her Phaedra, superb both dramatically and stylistically, in the Oiseau-Lyre recording of Rameau's *Hippolyte et Aricie*, and now a beautiful new record (Angel) on which she sings Berlioz's Gauthier cycle, *Les Nuits d'été*, and Ravel's *Shéhérazade*, both with Sir John Barbirolli conducting the New Philharmonia Orchestra.

In excellence of diction, intelligence, poetic sensibility and imagination, in musical taste, Baker's singing leaves nothing to be desired, and the sound is gorgeous through its whole range. The various atmospheres in the exquisite Berlioz songs are compellingly realized, most particularly perhaps the dream aura of "Le Spectre de la rose" and the gaiety of "Villanelle" and "L'Île inconnue."

Barbirolli sets some dangerously slow tempi, especially in "Le Spectre de la rose," which makes Baker's sustained phrasing even more miraculous, but he gets the New Philharmonia to realize the sonorities beautifully, and most of the time he works admirably with his singer.

About the performance of the Ravel I really have no reservation at all. Barbirolli is just right here, and it is an especial pleasure for one to hear these songs, with their mystery and irony, done without the heavily perfumed emphasis of, for example, the Tourel-Bernstein performance.

Another, slightly earlier Baker-Barbirolli collaboration, Mahler's *Wayfarer* Songs and *Kindertotenlieder*, both with the Hallé Orchestra, is a little disappointing (Angel). Baker, with her intelligence and sympathy, and her long phrases, the imagination that produces the chillingly numbed timbre and rhythm in the last of the *Kindertotenlieder*, has wonderful moments. But the sudden *pianissimo* on "*Nacht*" in the first of that cycle, and the same thing at the parallel passages on "*allgemein*" and "*Freudenlicht*," is cheap. I suspect, though, this is something she was talked into by Barbirolli, and in general what is wrong with the performances stems from the conductor's tendency to exaggerate, emphasize, and sentimentalize. In spite of this crudeness, and a persistent tendency to fuss about bar lines and cadences, Barbirolli also contributes good things, notably in matters of sonority (see especially the third and fourth *Wayfarers*). Baker's singing of "Ich bin der Welt abhanden gekommen," which fills the first side, is beautiful.

[*The remainder of this article addresses other topics.*]

Davis Conducts BSO Superbly

October 26, 1968

When Colin Davis first came to the Boston Symphony as guest conductor in February of last year, many among both players and public hoped some day to see the then 40-year-old Englishman take charge of the orchestra as music director. After the announcement last December of Erich Leinsdorf's resignation, Davis's name stood probably at the top of the rumor list. The subsequent appointment, effective next fall, of William Steinberg left Davis's supporters as much interested in him as ever, though the target date for their hopes was deferred until at least 1972, the expiration date of Steinberg's initial contract. At any rate, Davis's return to the Boston Symphony on Friday afternoon was anticipated with more than ordinary interest, and the audience, which, incidentally, included Dr. Steinberg, applauded him with unusual warmth.

Davis began with Haydn's Symphony No. 99 in E-flat (by coincidence last done here in 1960 by Steinberg at his first Boston Symphony concert). The first of the six symphonies Haydn wrote for his second London visit, it is one of those pieces of his late years in which the symphonic process takes place at an incredible level of luminous energy, and, of course, with the happiest blend of the popular with the exceedingly subtle, of humor and high spirits with the heart-piercing tenderness.

I could hardly imagine a more beautiful performance than the one Davis extracted from the Boston Symphony. Davis knows just who Haydn was and what his music is all about. There was energy, grace, lyricism, a delighted response to the winged play of Haydn's mind, a touch of something like swagger; moreover, the superlatively apt characterization of detail was marshaled into coherent and long-breathed progression, whose achievement was the result of uncommon perception and concentration.

The orchestra played beautifully for Davis, and in a way that was very different from the rather tense, anxious-to-please playing they did for him on his first visit. This time, there was none of the super-gloss that seems to Europeans so characteristic of American orchestras; there was, instead, a beautifully adjusted, relaxed, chamber-musical quality to the playing that reminded me of their work for Rafael Kubelik two season ago,[14] though the level of technical efficiency was higher. The solo woodwind writing in Haydn's Adagio was especially well taken by Mrs. Dwyer and Messrs. Gomberg, Holmes, and Walt.

Davis next conducted the Symphony No. 1 by the 32-year-old English composer, Richard Rodney Bennett. Written three years ago, it is a work of twenty minutes or so in the familiar quick-slow-quick pattern. Bennett's is not a particularly personal voice, but he manages a neo-Stravinskian language with considerable invention and with an awesome technical command. There is plenty of vitality to the first movement and considerable intensity to the Andante; the finale, though, seems to obviously be a rewriting of the "Danse sacrale" of Stravinsky's *Sacre*. The most unequivocal success Bennett achieves is with his dazzling scoring, and under Davis's leadership, the players responded to the virtuoso writing with zest and an infectious joy in their own skill.

The Brahms Third is frighteningly difficult. To be sure Brahms is easier than Haydn in the sense that the richer variegation on the surface of his music provides a more obvious guide to what is really happening at skeletal and bloodstream level, though it was precisely his ability to discern and project form through the relatively subtle differentiations in Haydn that made Davis's conducting of the

[14] See review of January 21, 1967.

Symphony No. 99 so remarkable. But nothing, absolutely nothing, in Brahms takes care of itself, and it wants unremitting vigilance on the part of a conductor to get the minimal intelligibility.

Davis's Brahms performance was never bad, but, except for the drive and force with which he gave the finale, and which, to some degree, he had anticipated in the first movement's recapitulation, it was unremarkable. He played the symphony for buoyancy and grace more than for mystery, sentiment, and drama, and that is by no means a bad idea. His conducting of it was coherent, intelligent, and tasteful, and that he made the relaxation of tempo into the epilogue occur where Brahms directs rather than with the viola triplets fifteen bars sooner (as most conductors do) is a tribute to all three qualities. Again, except for some less than first-rate horn playing, and the flat, but not quite as flat as usual, clarinet, the orchestra did beautifully for Davis. It was a careful, responsible job of house-cleaning, but the place didn't feel lived in.

Leonhardt Harpsichord Master

October 29, 1968

The Toccata by Frescobaldi with which Gustav Leonhardt began his harpsichord recital at Kresge Auditorium, MIT, Sunday afternoon, started with an ordinary broken chord. I would swear, though, that blindfolded, I would have known that it was Leonhardt playing. The timing of the chord's unfolding, the delicate stress on the dissonant notes in it, the grace of the gesture, the quiet authority in that little call to attention, all this represented a mastery that in today's harpsichord world is Leonhardt's alone.

Leonhardt's special glory is his playing of 17th-century music. He plays Bach, of course, and plays him beautifully, but other 18th-century music, Scarlatti, Rameau, Handel, hardly appears on his programs now. When he enters the still so mysterious world of earlier Baroque music, with its revealing demands on a player's fantasy and skill at reading between the lines—a world, incidentally, that most of his colleagues stay away from—he gives us access to a repertory to which hardly any other performer has anything like a workable key at all.

He began Sunday with four pieces by Frescobaldi, himself from all accounts a breathtaking performer who was organist at St. Peter's for thirty years, off and on, in the first half of the 17th century: two wide-ranging toccatas; a polyphonic ricercar that was spellbinding in its seriousness and chastity of idiom; a more extraverted, colorful canzona.

Leonhardt next played a passacaglia and a "Ballo della battaglia," a genre piece with military touches, by Bernardo Storace, an obscure composer probably of the generation after Frescobaldi and of whose life almost nothing is known. One quite large book of his compositions survives. The two pieces Leonhardt played suggest a stylistic bridge to the later, High Baroque, and their effect was, I would say, engaging rather than arresting. They nicely set off the Frescobaldi that came before and the two toccatas by Michelangelo Rossi, a pupil of Frescobaldi's, that came after. Rossi's music has a grandeur of gesture and a captivating unpredictability that suggests his teacher's work, and these two toccatas were not far from Frescobaldi in stature either.

After that, Leonhardt played a suite in F by Louis Couperin, a mid-17th-century master who was the uncle of François, the most famous of the Couperins. According to the program, this was to have been followed by "Tombeau de m. Blancrocher," Louis Couperin's memorial to a lutenist friend, and a very touching and lovely piece, but for some reason he either decided not to play it, or perhaps forgot to.

After intermission, there was Bach, or, more exactly, Bach-Leonhardt. There is a richly worked transcription for solo harpsichord, presumably by Bach himself, of the opening Adagio of the C major sonata for unaccompanied violin (the transcription has it in G). Leonhardt has often played this unattached Adagio—it was an encore at his last recital here—and he decided to make a complete harpsichord sonata by transcribing the other three movements as well, with the Adagio and with a similar transcription (perhaps not by Bach, but certainly contemporary) of the A minor Sonata available as models.

The idea of making a translation in which it is possible to state explicitly what the violinist can only struggle to suggest—I am thinking specifically of the immense fugue that Bach puts as a second movement—is, of course, very persuasive. It is also fascinating, and highly instructive, to discover in the event that it cannot quite be done, at least not without throwing up a whole set of new problems, so well are the instrumental "impossibilities" taken into account in the original composition and made inseparable from it.

It did, then, sound some of the time as though someone were playing violin music on a keyboard instrument. The third movement, an eloquent aria in Largo, came off beautifully and, to me, much more convincingly than the fugue and the final Allegro. There was, to be sure, an enormous and welcome gain in clarity in the fugue, but that had as much to do with Leonhardt's playing as with the fact of transcription to a medium less resistant to polyphony than an unaccompanied violin.

The news about Baroque style has hardly gotten through to string players yet. I can only think of about three violinists who understand such matters at a level of sophistication no longer so uncommon among keyboard players, and I have only heard one of them, Robert Koff, play unaccompanied Bach; one of the greatest values in Leonhardt's performance was in providing a virtually unique opportunity to hear one of those pieces made sense of. To that I should add that he played the slow movements with noble expression and the quick ones brilliantly. And I should add further how beautifully clear and mellow the sound of the Hubbard instrument was.

Copland at His Best

November 3, 1968

A recent record of chamber music by Aaron Copland (CBS) is automatically important because two of the three works on it are not otherwise available. It is a special pleasure to be able to report as well that the performances are superb. The works are the Sextet for Clarinet, Piano, and Strings, an arrangement actually of the *Short Symphony* of 1932–33, and the Quartet for Piano and Strings.

The Symphony-Sextet is in Copland's brightest, most vital, young American style. The Quartet, which marks the beginning of Copland's concern with serial writing, is in a much more contemplative mood, and its opening Adagio serio is one of the finest things in American music. Both pieces represent Copland at his best—that is considerable, too—and together they give an impressive demonstration of his range.

The record also includes Copland's early Jewish character study, *Vitebsk*, for piano, violin, and cello, and it, too, a strong, assertive work in the hard-edged manner Copland favored in the '20s. Copland himself plays the piano in all three works, and with a clarity of rhythm and sonority and a certain hardness that are thoroughly appropriate. His excellent collaborators are the members of the Juilliard Quartet and the clarinetist Harold Wright. An uncommonly valuable and worthwhile record.

The chamber music of Shostakovich is less familiar than it deserves. First encounters with it have often been an agreeable surprise to listeners who have been put off by his sometimes soap-boxy, over-extended symphonies. On its "Stereo Treasury" series, London has reissued the Borodin Quartet's superb performance of the Shostakovich Quartet No. 8, written in 1960, full like so much of his music, of autobiographical allusions, and a work whose restrained meditative rhetoric, distinctly touched by Mahler, makes it most impressive. On the other side you get Borodin's very lovely, lyric Quartet No. 2 in D, full of the tunes even *Kismet* could not ruin, and played to perfection.

[*The remainder of this article addresses other topics.*]

History Aids Bach

November 10, 1968

The Concentus Musicus Vienna, the remarkable old-instruments ensemble which will play a Bach program for the Cambridge Society for Early Music in Sanders Theatre this Wednesday evening, has been represented on a number of record releases in recent months. The most ambitious of them is a two-record album of the four Bach overtures or suites.

The Concentus exists because its director, Nikolaus Harnoncourt, believes that historically authentic timbres (and therefore historically authentic instruments) are essential in the proper realization of early music in performance, as essential in their way as right tempi, modes of articulation, and working out of ornaments. He insists also, and this is what gives the Concentus Musicus its special distinction as a performing group, that historical authenticity is no substitute for musical and instrumental competence, that we have a right to expect the same proficiency from a viol ensemble playing Purcell as from a string quartet playing Brahms.

By the most normal standards, the Concentus Musicus plays the Bach suites superbly. The most striking differences in the sound itself are in the woody softness of the flute in the B minor, and in the transparent, non-aggressive glow of the trumpets in the two D major suites (though I should add that the trumpet and kettledrum playing, fine as it is, is not as magical in sheer sensuous effect as that which the players of the Cappella Coloniensis produced at their Jordan Hall concert last season).

The dance movements in all four suites are a series of revelations as played here: I know of no other recorded performances so informed by a combination of musicianship and scholarship and able, therefore, to articulate, phrase, and pace these pieces with so much sense of character. The overtures themselves are a bit disappointing: the transitions from the quick middle sections to the slower codas jolt and don't quite come off convincingly, and I think, too, that to observe the second repeats in these movements, i.e., at the end to go all the way from the beginning of the Allegro to the end of a piece, is an act of merciless pedantry. In all, though, the level of vitality is high, and these are performances of quite special value and very much recommended (Telefunken).

The Concentus Musicus has also recorded Bach's violin concertos in E major and A minor, both with Alice Harnoncourt as soloist, and the Concerto in D minor for two violins, in which Mrs. Harnoncourt is joined by Walter Pfeiffer. The Double Concerto and the A minor are beautifully done, but the E major seems curiously lacking in fantasy and urgency, as with the rather cold account of the great Adagio, or the drily uninspired preparation for the first movement's *da capo* (Telefunken).

A record of double concertos by Bach's sons has the Concentus joining forces with the Leonhardt Consort of Amsterdam, Gustav Leonhardt conducting. The music includes a harpsichord and pianoforte concerto by Carl Philipp Emanuel (who, even without Elliott Carter to measure him against, is surprisingly unimaginative about exploiting the difference between the two keyboard instruments[15]); a delightful oboe and cello concerto by Johann Christian, getting its first modern performance here; and a very fine concerto for two harpsichords by Wilhelm Friedemann. The soloists include harpsichordists Anneke Uittenbosch and Alan Curtis, pianist Jean Antonietti, oboist Jürg Schaeftlein, and cellist Anner Bylsma. Very much worth having (Telefunken).

In the same vein, and very highly recommended as well, a concerto for two harpsichords in F by C. P. E. Bach, a superb piece, and a very agreeable B-flat major cello concerto by him, recorded by Gustav Leonhardt, Alan Curtis, and cellist Angelica May, with the Collegium Aureum (RCA Victrola); and J. S. Bach's great C major concerto for three harpsichords, his less interesting one in D minor for the same instruments, and a Leonhardt reconstruction of a fine D minor solo concerto, parts of which survive in the Cantata No. 35, with Leonhardt, Anneke Uittenbosch, and Alan Curtis as soloists with the Leonhardt Consort (Telefunken).

And to return, finally, to the Concentus Musicus, they have a fine new record of *Music at the Court of Louis XIV*, including one of the superb *Concerts royaux* of François Couperin, as well as some instrumental excerpts from Marin Marais' opera, *Alcyone*, a set of his pieces for viols, and the first book of Jacques Hotteterre's flute pieces (Vanguard Cardinal).

Two Good Performances—The Year of Schoenberg

November 17, 1968

There was a rare opportunity recently to hear good performances of both of Schoenberg's chamber symphonies within a twenty-four-hour period: Thursday evening, November 7, Frederik Prausnitz conducted No. 2 with the New England Conservatory Symphony Orchestra and the following afternoon Erich Leinsdorf conducted No. 1 at a Boston Symphony concert. This is Boston's year for those crucial, fascinating, and beautiful pieces: Prausnitz will conduct No. 1

[15] Steinberg here refers to Elliott Carter's Double Concerto for Harpsichord and Piano. Regarding this work, see concert review of November 18, 1965, and record review of December 22, 1968.

later in his season as part of a survey of Schoenberg's non-twelve-tone orchestral music, and the Philharmonia plans to include both symphonies in its series, Richard Burgin and Leon Kirchner conducting.

Schoenberg began two chamber symphonies in 1906. One, the E major, Op. 9, he finished the same year. The other, in E-flat minor, resisted him perhaps because Opus 9, as it developed, pointed toward so interesting and promising a future that it became impossible for Schoenberg to continue to work in what, when he had begun, was still the present. He continued to make sketches for No. 2 until 1911 and again in 1916. Then he abandoned it, but surprisingly picked it up and completed it in 1939.

By 1906 Schoenberg had written a number of songs both with piano and with orchestra, two string quartets, *Transfigured Night*, the symphonic poem *Pelleas und Melisande*, and, except for the instrumentation, *Gurre-Lieder*. Just ahead, in 1907–09, lie the works of his border-crossing out of the world of conventional tonality, the Quartet in F-sharp minor, the Stefan George songs, the piano pieces, Op. 11, Five Pieces for Orchestra, Op. 16, and *Erwartung*.

Here is Schoenberg's own comment on the critical moment at which the Chamber Symphony No. 1 appeared:

> When I had finished I told my friends, "Now I have established my style. I know now how I have to compose." But my next work showed a great deviation from this style: it was a first step toward my present style. My destiny had forced me in this direction—I was not destined to continue in the manner of *Transfigured Night* or *Gurre-Lieder* or even *Pelleas*. The Supreme Commander had ordered me on a harder road.

And No. 2? Between 1906 and 1939, Schoenberg composed, besides the works already mentioned, *Pierrot lunaire*, the operas *Die glückliche Hand*, *Von heute auf morgen*, and *Moses und Aron*, most of his piano music, the Serenade, Quintet, and Suite, the Quartets Nos. 3 and 4, the Songs, Op. 22, the Variations for Orchestra, and the Violin Concerto. Most of his creative life was bracketed inside that delicate arch of the E-flat minor Chamber Symphony.

How was it that Schoenberg, who was so much of a developing, experiencing personality, could return after so long a time and after such interventions? Nostalgia, of course—that nostalgia he mentioned when he was asked to explain why, in his 60s, he had begun writing occasional tonal pieces again; that nostalgia we can so easily hear in his music, that makes it so different from that of his nine-years-younger pupil, Webern, and that has brought him the contempt of some bright young people of all ages.

But nostalgia serves better as an explanation of why Schoenberg wanted to return than of how he, whose catalogue is full of incomplete works and projects not carried out, actually could return. When Schoenberg told his friends in 1906, "Now I have established my style. I now know how I have to compose," he was in the deepest sense right. A vast expansion of his vocabulary was to follow, and compositional innovations that were to change the face of music in the 20th century, but the essential Schoenberg, the man with something to say and with an unmistakable voice, was already all there.

Prausnitz spoke to this problem in the interesting program note he wrote for his concert, and he also quoted Schoenberg's biographer [H. H.] Stuckenschmidt on the subject of this music: "Stylistically, already by 1906 it presented such a definite unity that almost no important new characteristic was added to it later."

In the published score of No. 2, the first movement, an E-flat minor Adagio, bears the completion date, August 15, 1939. I do not know the details, but the assumption of Schoenberg experts seems to be that the Adagio was essentially complete in 1906, though obviously, because of the date in the score, that there must have been further work or revision later, and that Schoenberg's main task in 1939 was the making of a finale. He abandoned his original idea and arrived at his eventual plan, a quick movement in G major (the key relationship of the two movements is typical Haydn-Beethoven), followed by a return to the tempo, material, and key of the first movement.

The effect is not so much of finale with epilogue as of an arch. The central part effects the highest tension in the symphony, partly because it is harmonically more emancipated than either Adagio, and partly because of its peculiar fiery, and quite non-Romantic, intensity, which, from point of view of musical character, seems to me unique in Schoenberg's oeuvre. The retransition, in which the Adagio, when it returns, is subtly but deeply transformed by the experience of the "*con fuoco*" movement, to make what Prausnitz with perfect accuracy called "the shattering close of the work."

What of course has struck the E-flat minor Adagio music is not just the experience of the past few minutes, but that of three decades. The coincidence of technique and psychology, of form and expression, is complete. One could well apply to the end of the Chamber Symphony No. 2 what Schoenberg said about his 1940 Organ Variations (in D minor), that here is the filling of the gap between his early and his "dissonant" music. To that he added a significant further thought: "There are many still unused possibilities here."

The characters of the two quasi-simultaneous symphonies are marvelously different, and one's delight in their diversity is deepened by an understanding of the place each fills in Schoenberg's life: the exuberant No. 1, the springboard into an exciting and uncharted future, and the introspective No. 2, the arch over the life work, and, in a way that I am only now beginning to understand, the key to it.

I was glad of the chance that brought the two works together in consecutive concerts, and I should certainly not wish to end this note without again expressing gratitude to both conductors and to both orchestras for their meticulously prepared, understanding, and vital performances.

Beethoven in Puerto Rico—A Fellow Lecturer Sings Brendel's Praises

December 8, 1968

RIO PIEDRAS, PR—This evening, the Austrian pianist Alfred Brendel completes a seven-concert series devoted to Beethoven's thirty-two piano sonatas. He has played the complete cycle before, in London, Copenhagen, Vienna, and Graz. The series here was presented by the University of Puerto Rico, integrated into a course available to students in the music department, and supplemented by lectures, four by Brendel and two by this writer.

In London, Brendel played the sonatas in chronological order. But he rejects that plan now and makes mixed programs with contrasts of scale, character, and key, and on which the familiar appears together with the unfamiliar, the late with the middle and the early, and the perfect with the problematic. Being here for the third and fourth concerts, I heard first, Opus 7, Opus 27, No. 2 (*Moonlight*), Opus 78, Opus 10, No. 1, and Opus 101; then, Opus 79, Opus 14, No. 1, Opus 10, No. 4, Opus 2, No. 1, and Opus 53 (*Waldstein*).

It is immensely valuable now and again to survey the whole sonata cycle, and for reasons clear even to someone able to hear only a small part of it. The sonatas are one whole dimension of Beethoven's musical autobiography. To re-meet them all within a fairly short period is to be able to see them in clearer perspective. It sharpens apprehension of quality in the sense both of "excellence" and of "distinguishing characteristics." I do not know, for example, when Opus 101 last sounded so "late" to me, and therefore so fresh in a particular sense, as it did when heard in a context of other Beethoven sonatas composed from seven to nineteen years earlier.

Not least, performance of the complete cycle allows us to hear works that hardly ever appear on concert programs, some, ironically, because of their exceedingly great popularity, like the *Moonlight*, which is one of the finest, some because they are simply not fashionable at a given point, as the late sonatas were not a couple of generations ago, and as the early ones are not today.

The loss from working repertory of the early sonatas is bad. Beginning with Opus 2, No. 3, they are characteristic and masterful, more so, and bolder and more mature, than the corresponding first steps in quartet and symphony. At the two concerts I heard, Opus 7 (1797), Opus 14, No. 1 (1799), and particularly

Opus 10, No. 3 (1798), which Brendel regards as one of the five or six most perfect among the thirty-two, all made extraordinarily powerful impressions.

Brendel gave a superbly clarifying performance of the terribly difficult Opus 101, and one of the *Waldstein* that was poetic as well as brilliant. But it is his strong playing of the early sonatas that I remember with special gratitude. Each was so vividly characterized, so well caught in terms of its unique qualities, that for the duration of the performance he could always convince us that this music represented the farthest limit of Beethoven's inner experience and of the musical language through which to articulate the experience. We could hear the Largo of Opus 10, No. 3, for what it is, the greatest slow movement of its kind, a new kind, that had ever been written, utterly undistracted by the hindsight that might remind us of the slow movement to come twenty years later in the *Hammerklavier.*

Brendel's performance of Opus 10, No. 3—and I dwell on it because it was the greatest playing I heard Brendel do and because, indeed, it was one of the shattering moments in my experience of listening to music—was remarkable as well for its psychological unity. It is a rare performer who can hold an audience spellbound and breathlessly silent with that Largo, as Brendel did, but it is a still rarer one who can continue, or even knows that he ought to continue, the magic into the gentle minuet that follows, and from there into the quirkily humorous, but wistful and anything-other-than-casual, finale.

The human wisdom and nobility in Brendel's playing is one of its most remarkable qualities. It is comparatively easy to make this Largo "go" by enormous distention of the lamenting three-note figures in the right hand, but Brendel instead built the movement on the rhythmic and harmonic tensions of the basic substance of the movement rather than by a facile vulgarization of its ornamental surface.

Brendel's lectures showed him to be uncommonly aware and analytic about matters of compositional structure and textual accuracy. That was made amply clear by his playing as well, but what came across still more was an approach to performance that is at its root expressive, emotional, concerned with projecting the human statement the music makes, and in which the formidable intellectual equipment and knowledge are used as a checking mechanism.

Brendel likes to quote the German Romantic poet Novalis, who said: "In a work of art, the chaos should slightly shimmer through the fluorescence of organization." That serves beautifully to characterize the marvelously complete interpretations of this prodigiously developing artist. The mystery in Beethoven is always felt, but mystery is never an excuse to obscure the musical process through which it is expressed. The notes are not everything, but whatever is there is in the notes.

The Works of Elliott Carter—Where Drama and Music Intersect

December 22, 1968

Elliott Carter is 60. His birthday was December 11, and I imagine that he spent much of it working on the Concerto for Orchestra whose first performance will be given by Leonard Bernstein and the New York Philharmonic on May 1.[16]

That is a concert to which I excitedly look forward. Carter was 44 when his String Quartet No. 1 established his reputation as the most gifted and the most original American composer of his generation. The Quartet was followed by the charming and comparatively light-weight Sonata for Flute, Oboe, Cello, and Harpsichord. Then began the series of masterpieces on a large scale, Variations for Orchestra (1955), String Quartet No. 2 (1959), Double Concerto for Harpsichord and Piano with Two Chamber Orchestras (1961—see today's record column for this and the Variations),[17] and the Piano Concerto (1965).

Carter's reputation is based on a small body of works. He works slowly at his complex music. Once in New York I met Carter when he had just had a haircut. He was still exasperated at the barber's exhausting fussiness over detail. At the same time, Carter was somehow pleased, and, in a certain ironic way, amused to recognize a fellow craftsman. "After all," he commented wryly, "people might think I'm mad, too, for the way I worry about all these things in my music."

His music is difficult, difficult to compose, difficult to play, and difficult to listen to. Difficult though it is, it seems almost always strongly to affect an audience in a good performance. I first heard Carter's String Quartet No. 1 in the spring of 1954. I was rather inexperienced with contemporary music; at the end of that long, intense, emotionally draining work I did not know what had just happened to me, but I knew that I had just undergone something extraordinary. When the Piano Concerto was performed for the first time in Boston two years ago,[18] I thought I recognized in many of the audience the reaction, so poignantly familiar to me, of non-comprehension of everything except being in the presence of the prodigious.

Each of Carter's major works has had something new to say and each has a fully formed, wholly distinct personality of its own. At the same time, each is a further development, generally richer and more ambitious, of some line of thought pursued by its predecessor—and from the little that Carter has said about it, I should guess this to be true of the new Concerto for Orchestra as well.

[16] As it happened, the premiere of the Concerto for Orchestra did not take place until February 5, 1970. See review of February 15, 1970.

[17] See review of December 22, 1968.

[18] See review of January 7, 1967.

The continuity that underlies Carter's work is that of a bold conception of music expressed in something he said when he was finishing the Quartet No. 2: "I regard my scores as scenarios, auditory scenarios, for performers to act out with their instruments, dramatizing the players as individuals and as participants in the ensemble."

That Quartet was, up to then, the most vivid embodiment of Carter's special, anthropomorphic treatment of instrumental lines—the Double Concerto and the Piano Concerto were to explore the possibilities of this still more deeply and with farther-reaching expressive and compositional implications—but even earlier, in the dialogue of low and high instruments in the Adagio movement of the Quartet No. 1, I had been reminded of the Adagio in Schubert's Cello Quintet with its contrast of the calm melody in the middle instruments with the interjected comments of violin and cello.

A movement like Schubert's, or the Andante of Beethoven's G major Piano Concerto, which Liszt likened to the confrontation of Orpheus and the Furies, stands in spirit behind Carter's music. I recall, too, that once when Carter heard a Bach aria in which the voice, an instrumental obbligato, the bass line, and a superimposed chorale, all moved in coordinated independence, he said delightedly, "Why, it's just like my music." And of course Charles Ives, whom Carter knew well, is a vivid presence, upon whose audacious extension of the idea of polyphony his scenarios are based.

Its human content is of the greatest importance in Carter's music, and that, its powerful articulation of such basic feelings and situations, is what makes it so gripping, so immensely impressive even before, in another sense, we "understand." Mahler once wrote to the annotator of one of his works: "I should like to have it emphasized that the symphony begins where the love affair leaves off." Carter, too, warns us to remember that no matter how absorbing the literary or other background of one of his works may be—[the ancient Greek philosopher] Theophrastus for the Variations, Lucretius and [Alexander Pope's] *The Dunciad* for the Double Concerto, Carter's thoughts on the Hitler years for the Piano Concerto—"it all gets turned into music so fast."

The music, that concentrated, difficult, individual, beautiful music, is the challenge we face, and it is our road of access to its composer's profound, compassionate, rich, and humorous mind. In the best 20th-century music, each work, to a degree that I believe has never before been true in the history of music, is the unique embodiment of its own set of musical laws. Carter has remarked, not without pride, that he has had to break path to construct his musical language. As a parallel, players find that "normal" virtuosity, a routine craft for solving standard problems, is hardly applicable to Carter's music. The listener gets no help from habit either, except the habit of attention. A point to be made as well is that Carter's musical vision is most characteristically articulated through his manipulation of rhythm and speed, thus calling on us to exercise maximum sensitivity in the areas in which our training is apt to be the poorest and in which the past couple of centuries of musical history have most benumbed us.

Carter stands today with his powers at their height, at some marvelous crossroads where Bach meets Ives, where drama and music, innocence and sophistication, the American and European spirits intersect. His presence is a marvelous and much needed lesson on the existence together of passion and intelligence, feeling and intellect, heart and head. He of course has our warmest and most affectionate good wishes, though, unfairly, the gifts flow in the other direction as we sit here happily awaiting the Concerto for Orchestra, another string quartet perhaps, or whatever else he may choose to bring us.

An A-plus for Columbia

December 22, 1968

Columbia has just issued an extraordinarily valuable record that makes available excellent performances of Elliott Carter's Variations for Orchestra (1955) and of his Double Concerto for Harpsichord and Piano with Two Chamber Orchestras (1961). Both works have been recorded before, but not very well; in fact, the earlier versions, of which only the one from Louisville of the Variations is still available, illustrate a point once made by Stravinsky that an insufficient recording can greatly retard the circulation and appreciation of a new piece.

Carter's breakthrough, the point, as it were, at which he really became Elliott Carter, was the composition of the First String Quartet. The Variations were the next major work to follow, with the more divertimento-like Sonata for Flute, Oboe, Cello, and Harpsichord, coming between. The Variations, in an expressive language that owes something to Alban Berg, are the rich filling out of a sweeping and exciting design. Nine variations and a dramatic finale take the theme through a series of transformations that tend, toward the middle of the work, to neutralize and eliminate contrast of character, and, in the second half, again to increase sharpness of definition and conflict.

To this large-scale *decrescendo-crescendo* of tension, Carter adds two other lines of development in the form of two *ritornelli*, both heard in the Introduction, one as a rapid and rising declaration by the full orchestra, which becomes slower at each reappearance; the other, starting slow, and showing a corresponding series of speedings-up for each restatement. It is an uncommonly rich work, humanly as well as musically, and one of the special pleasures it offers is the virtuosic, and altogether original-sounding, orchestral writing.

Carter followed the Variations with his String Quartet No. 2, in which he extended his interest in musical character to the point where each of the four players became something like a personage in a drama, with characteristic rhythms and pitch intervals used to define each of the four personalities. The Double Concerto, completed two years later, carries this idea further.

It is surprising that the contrast of harpsichord and piano should have been so little explored by composers. Even the imaginative Carl Philipp Emanuel Bach muffed an opportunity one would suppose him to have relished, writing a bland sort of double concerto that could as well be for two harpsichords or two fortepianos. Frank Martin in his *Petite Symphonie concertante*, decorative as it is, does not approach coming to grips with this textural challenge.

Carter, with his double love of drama, that is, of an almost anthropomorphic characterization of instruments, and of virtuosity, made his Double Concerto a composition that draws the most fascinating conclusions from the incompatibility of the two keyboard instruments. Each is accompanied, and physically surrounded, by its own sextet (each includes a horn, but there is no other duplication), and there is a quartet of percussion players providing both punctuation and an acoustic backdrop, binding the worlds of the two chamber ensembles together.

The conductor for both performances is Frederik Prausnitz, well known here for his work at the New England Conservatory, where he has led both these works of Carter's. The orchestra for the Variations is the New Philharmonia (of London); the Double Concerto has Paul Jacobs as harpsichordist, Charles Rosen as pianist, and members of the English Chamber Orchestra. The Variations go very well, clearly and with considerable excitement and intensity; the performance of the Double Concerto is brilliantly effective, a really admirable product of intelligence and temperament.

Carter's is the sort of music that is especially well served by good recordings. The Variations and the Double Concerto are not easy to get to know, but unlike so many contemporary works that make a sensational impact at first hearing, they become more and [more rewarding the better one] knows them. Columbia's new record affords a wonderful opportunity, therefore, to listeners who still care about good music.

Superb! That's Sills

December 29, 1968

It is shocking to realize that the record called *Bellini and Donizetti Heroines* (Westminster) is the first solo recital recording by the soprano Beverly Sills, and to realize also how little, and how inadequately, her remarkable singing has been documented. Her repertory here includes a couple of well-known things, "Regnava nel silenzio" from *Lucia di Lammermoor* and "Come per me sereno" from *La sonnambula*, the lovely and less familiar "Oh! quante volte" from Bellini's *I Capuleti ed i Montecchi*, and three excursions into rarely explored Donizetti, "O luce di quest'anima," a fine aria from *Linda di Chamounix*, "Vivi, ingrato," a superb one from *Roberto Devereux*, and "Perche non ho del vento" from *Rosmonda d'Inghilterra*, which has a pleasant cabaletta, but which is otherwise less interesting.

Sills does it all beautifully. The voice itself is first-rate, warm, steady, and full of character throughout its range, all the way up to the high E-flat to which these arias carry her. She controls it superbly: the effortless approach to the high notes is marvelous, the coloratura is absolutely immaculate and brilliant in effect, and the long, slow *cantabile* phrases are grandly sustained. This equipment is at the service of a musician with exquisite taste in phrasing, and one who brings to the music commendable clarity of diction and captivating warmth of temperament.

It is interesting to compare Sills's singing of the *Roberto Devereux* aria with Caballé's (RCA), to discover the advantage of having the aria complete including its choral passages as Sills records it but Caballé does not, to be enchanted at first by the purity of Caballé's voice and by her tasteful phrasing, and to be very soon bored by the insipid sameness of her singing. To compare Sills with Callas in *Lucia* and *Sonnambula* is, on the other hand, to discover that Sills in most respects can sing circles around even the young Callas of the 1953 *Lucia*, but that Callas nonetheless is still a more extraordinary artist and with an uncanny ability to suggest character that Sills does not match.

Most coloratura buffs would probably hardly notice if their favorite ladies sang *a cappella*, except of course for the flute obbligatos; nevertheless, I want to take a moment to deplore the generally squalid accompaniments provided to Beverly Sills by Jussi Jalas and the Vienna Volksoper Orchestra. The solos, for example the horn in "Oh! quante volte" and the harp in *Lucia*, are spoiled, and the conducting is mostly mindless and the playing ugly. This is bad for Bellini and Donizetti, but I am concerned as well that it is bad for Sills, who can actually sing this music better than on the Westminster record. I have heard a private aircheck of a couple of these arias as Sills sang them at Radio Cologne, and one can hear from point to point how the greater vitality and intelligence of the conducting there, though it is not the last word in this repertory either, produces a correspondingly greater vitality and tension of line in the singing. I hope the next Sills record will be along soon, but I particularly hope that next time she will land up with a better conductor and orchestra.

Seraphim has reissued the 1953 Callas recording of *Lucia* I mentioned above. At that time, the strangely beautiful quality of Callas's lower voice had not yet fully emerged; the high voice, however, was still intact, and though the notes above high C were never Callas's most comfortable territory, she managed the coloratura well and with an expressive force that most of us had never experienced before in such music and which represented a real revolution in taste. Callas, in sum, does a breathtakingly beautiful Lucia. Giuseppe di Stefano is an insufficiently elegant Edgardo, but the rest of the cast, including Gobbi as Enrico, is good, and so, for the most part, is Serafin's conducting.

Boston Globe advertisement placed in the Boston Symphony's program book during the 1968–69 season. (Used with permission.)

1969

Sherman's Piano Concert Stimulating

January 13, 1969

The pianist Russell Sherman chose an uncommonly stimulating program for his Jordan Hall concert Friday evening; having begun with Schoenberg's Opus 33, which comprises his last two pieces for piano solo, he played a Suite by Edward Steuermann, *Form* by Stefan Wolpe, and Milton Babbitt's *Partitions*, each of the three being a branching off from Schoenberg, but in quite different directions. Next came the last Sonata, No. 10, by Schoenberg's contemporary, Scriabin, a work written in 1912–13, that astonishingly adventurous and door-opening moment in Western music. The second half was given over to the Twenty-four Preludes of Chopin, antecedent to Scriabin, and, in this context, assuming an unusual character as the clean and classical music of the evening.

Steuermann was best-known as a pianist (Sherman was a pupil of his at Juilliard), but the five-movement Suite that he wrote in 1953–54 shows that he was a composer not just with technical skill, but with individuality as well. The March with which it ends is perhaps rather pointedly Schoenbergian in its rhythms and figuration; elsewhere, though, there is no suggestion of its being a "school of . . . " piece. The fourth-movement Chorale, in which the melodies are encased in a grand encrustation of quasi-trills and tremolandos, is especially fine. The piano style itself reflects the virtuoso player's feeling for the instrument and is most imaginative.

Wolpe's music has most often been eruptive and violent, but in *Form* (1959), he has written a short piece whose gestures are characteristically vivid and arresting, but which is civil and possessed of a certain gentle humor. Someone at the concert aptly likened it to the work of Paul Klee. *Partitions*, which Babbitt wrote in 1957, is a highly compressed study in multilayered rhythmic and textural activity. With its independence of lines and its quick changes of register and dynamics, *Partitions* is like an extremely complex ensemble piece that has been somehow impacted into a single keyboard, and as a result it is also an etude in mid-20th-century pianism, and one of a most brilliant sort.

The Scriabin is a study in turning on, abounding in directions like "*avec une ardeur profonde et voilée*," "*avec ravissement et tendresse*," and "*avec une volupté douloureuse*." Pianistically, structurally, and often harmonically, it is music of provocative originality and interesting to hear; I regret, though, that I can't really make contact on that wavelength, and that I seem to catch only dazzlingly artful cocktail piano.

Sherman's playing of Schoenberg, Steuermann, Wolpe, and Babbitt was ideally sympathetic and perceptive, clarifying, and pianistically resourceful in the face of an exceedingly taxing and highly varied lot of demands. The delicate line-drawings of his Wolpe performance particularly gave exquisite pleasure. The details of the Scriabin Tenth Sonata were beautifully fashioned, but, for its architectural and communicative force to come fully clear, it needs more sweep than Sherman gave it. He is always a stimulating, informative player whose work represents the highest level of intelligence and responsibility, he is not often a very outgoing sort of pianist, and sometimes, given his reticence about projecting over the footlights, it is as though we ought to join him on stage to share in his music.

I enjoyed Sherman's performance of the Chopin Preludes, though my pleasure was increasingly disturbed by what came to be his maddening mannerism of sounding the right hand slightly ahead of the left. It was an understated, somehow guarded interpretation, apparently particularly concerned with, and certainly remarkably successful at, projecting the Preludes as a unified twenty-four-movement composition rather than as a sequence of vignettes. Here as well as in the Scriabin, I wished for more dynamic variety and more sheer physical impact, but certain Preludes—A major, E-flat major, F major, for example—were strikingly lovely, as moments in themselves and as links in a chain.

The New Fares Better Than Old

January 25, 1969

Friday afternoon's Boston Symphony concert brought a fairly new piece and a fairly new conductor. The piece was Olivier Messiaen's *Chronochromie*, written in 1960 and getting its first Boston performances this weekend; the conductor was the 44-year-old Frenchman, Georges Prêtre, making his Boston concert debut, though he did conduct a *Trovatore* here for the Metropolitan Opera in 1966.

Chronochromie can be translated as "the color of time," by which Messiaen means that he uses color-timbre primarily—though he also seems to include pitch in the concept—to underline and clarify the rhythm, the divisions of time.

The rhythm of *Chronochromie* is sometimes complicated in that many different subdivisions of the beat are superimposed on one another, though in such passages the beat itself is apt to be regular. Conversely, when the meter changes most often, the whole orchestra breathes and moves together. The colors are bright and vivid, thickly laid on, with the sounds of glockenspiel, xylophone, and marimba prominent, and a bit top-heavy.

An engaging feature of *Chronochromie*, and one it shares with several Messiaen scores of the last fifteen years, is that the melodic material draws heavily on bird-song. Almost forty species are composed into the score, the most remarkable *tour de force* of bird portraiture occurring in the section called "Epode" (which follows strophe and antistrophe just like in Greek dramatic verse), where twelve violins, four violas, and two cellos produce an almost unpunctuated dawn chorus. On the recording of *Chronochromie*, the sound of the Epode is too close and loud and shrill, but with the more diffuse acoustics of Symphony Hall, the effect was quite lovely.

Messiaen always threatens to be complicated. The apparatus awes, and the composer's grandiloquently humorless program notes are calculated to make the listener feel just a little bit unworthy. After all that, though, the music turns out rather simple. It is characteristically static and not always free from corn. *Chronochromie* is not without those faults, but it is less impaired by them than most of Messiaen's works.

Georges Prêtre is two conductors. *Chronochromie*, whose third public performance he conducted (Besançon, 1961) and which he introduced to this country (Cleveland, 1967), is so difficult that the public safety demands from the conductor the utmost in to-the-point efficiency and clarity, and no nonsense. This, together with his knowledge of the score and experience with the score, is just what Prêtre delivered, and the performance of *Chronochromie* was for the most part very good indeed.

In the more familiar music—Lalo's *Roi d'Ys* Overture, the Sibelius Fifth, and Ravel's *La Valse*—Prêtre was a shameless show-off. Rather than conducting for the orchestra, as he did in the Messiaen, he staged a *divertissement* for the audience, miming the affect of the music, but enduring bravely the ecstasies and pains that threatened to overwhelm him. It is well that *La Valse* is no longer than it is: another three minutes of soundtrack, and M. Prêtre might have found himself liable to arrest.

The performances of Lalo, Sibelius, and Ravel that accompanied these orgiastic celebrations moved from one exaggeration to the next, blown apart by extreme and musically unmotivated outbursts, and made incoherent by the irrational and violent dislocations of tempo. Lalo's little thesaurus of 19th-century dramatic and orchestral devices suffered least; Ravel's finely built poem came closest to being destroyed.

The orchestra played more loudly and more softly than in a long time, and generally gave evidence of being unusually wide awake. I, too, found myself in a state of alarmed attention during most of the concert. I would not want to commit myself to a case that being irritated to near-flipping is really better than being bored to the same point: it does make a change, though.

NY Philharmonic's 125th—The Pitfalls of a Complex Babbitt

January 26, 1969

Relata II by Milton Babbitt had its first performance anywhere on Thursday, January 16, at a concert of the New York Philharmonic, which had commissioned it for its 125th anniversary. But that was not the first moment of its public existence. It was in the news briefly last October when its scheduled premiere was postponed because at Leonard Bernstein's first rehearsal of it with the Philharmonic, it turned out that Babbitt's publishers had provided such a mistake-ridden set of parts for the orchestra to play from that it was impossible to proceed.

Then, on the Sunday preceding the rescheduled premiere, the *New York Times* printed an interview with Babbitt,[1] which was being much talked about at the Philharmonic concerts, and whose content evidently shocked a lot of readers. Among other things Babbitt pointed out that if each of the 600 measures—all difficult, and no two alike—were practiced for five minutes ("a minimal requirement for a Chopin piano piece"), fifty hours would be needed. "Instead, with luck, we'll manage to find six! So we bang, bang, we plow through it, we do it."

Bernstein did what he could to make time available for the Babbitt by planning a program that would otherwise require a minimum of the orchestra's time. Even so, what was finally available was too close to six hours and not close enough to fifty. That Thursday's performance proceeded without a total breakdown was remarkable under the circumstances.

Having heard two run-throughs at the dress rehearsal (one following the score) and the performances Thursday evening and Friday afternoon, I do not propose to "review" Babbitt's new composition because I have not heard it. There is no question of blaming the composer, the conductor, or the orchestra. I do think it important to consider the situation of each in their collision.

Babbitt, now 52, writes extremely complex music, and has for over twenty years. While he has been delighted to find in the electronic medium the possibility of realizing with the utmost accuracy the involved imaginings of his mind, he never has assumed that the human performer was now obsolete. But his music does ask for a new sort of virtuoso. Just as, say, Clementi's brilliant piano technique would have gotten him nowhere with one of Liszt's *Transcendental*

[1] Joan Peyser, "The Affair Proved Traumatic," *New York Times*, January 19, 1969.

Etudes, so is your prize-winning Rachmaninoff-and-octaves thunderer helpless in the two minutes of Babbitt's *Partitions*. Indeed, the situation is further complicated because this new virtuosity, as we find it even in classics like Schoenberg's Violin Concerto, is not just mechanical, but organic, inseparable from the compositional content.

Partitions, which is brilliantly recorded for RCA by Robert Helps, makes tremendous demands on the pianist, especially in constant changes, both extreme and minute, in dynamics and modes of articulation. If you imagine that *Relata II*, from point of view of performance difficulty, is *Partitions* multiplied in one dimension (length) by ten, in another (personnel) by 100, your picture is rather too pessimistic, if by no means quite off the mark. No orchestra player's part in *Relata II* is even remotely as difficult as the solo pianist's in *Partitions*; on the other hand, length, because of the toll it takes on the ability to concentrate and keep calm, and the question of ensemble, increase the dangers produced by the difficulties that are there.

The New York Philharmonic is a first-class orchestra of its kind, but that means it is a Cliburn or a Horowitz, not the Robert Helps, the Paul Jacobs, or the Robert Miller, needed here. It is inexperienced with music like Babbitt's, insofar as there is any such thing anyway, and its inexperience with contemporary orchestral techniques is so extreme that it is inclined to make heavy weather of the Webern Symphony as well. That is, of course, equally true of other major orchestras. As for the Babbitt, even an orchestra more fitted by experience for the task would have been defeated by the 36-seconds-per-measure ration of rehearsal time imposed by the system (before overtime it costs about $40 for each 36-second bit the Philharmonic rehearses[2]).

There is a new virtuosity to conducting, too, but Bernstein is of the old school. The "new" conductors include, among others, the late Hans Rosbaud (unique in his generation); Boulez, Maderna, Gustav Meier, Prausnitz, Schuller, in the middle generation; Boris Brott, Lawrence Foster, Michael Tilson Thomas, among the younger. Bernstein worked hard at a score that must have meant little to him in terms of understanding or sympathy, but I think it both fair and important to say that the Philharmonic's *Relata II* gained enormously in confidence and clarity when Boris Brott got up to conduct. Brott, a 24-year-old Canadian, greatly gifted and surprisingly experienced, is one of the four assistant conductors at the Philharmonic this season: he helped to prepare the work, and Bernstein generously gave him the opportunity of conducting the performances Friday afternoon and Monday evening.

The Philharmonic walked into a hornet's nest when it offered a commission to Milton Babbitt, and so did he in accepting. Yet both did the right thing. That

2 Adjusted for inflation, the dollar figure amounts roughly to $356 in 2025.

I think that Babbitt has written some of the most beautiful and interesting music of recent years is my subjective judgment and, as such, perhaps not relevant here; but he is by any standards one of the most important and influential composers now working, and for that reason it was proper for the New York Philharmonic to include his name, along with those of Berio, Carter, Gerhard, Sessions, and Stockhausen, among others, in the list of anniversary commissions.

Babbitt, for his part, had to assume that the difficulties of his music would not take the Philharmonic by surprise, and as a creative artist he had an obligation to take advantage of the possibility of exploiting "the most subtle resources of a most sophisticated orchestra." His brilliance as a composer is not an intellectual brilliance only: it includes his sonorous fantasy as well, and the evidence for that is in the exciting sound-surface of a purely instrumental work like *Partitions*, an electronic one like Ensembles for Synthesizer (recorded on Columbia), or one that draws on both worlds like *Philomel*.[3] As for *Relata II*, and remembering *Relata I* (performed in Cleveland in 1966), I have heard and seen enough to say with confidence that Babbitt commands a forceful and original orchestral style which I hope an adequate performance some day will reveal.

What most shocked people in Babbitt's *Times* interview was his remark that having his work played on a New York Philharmonic subscription concert was "as though a colleague of mine in the field of philosophy were to read his paper on the Johnny Carson show." I want next time to make this the point of departure for some further considerations of the *Relata II* premiere.[4]

Miss Sills Brilliant in Boston's *Lucia*

January 30, 1969

The new Boston Opera production of *Lucia di Lammermoor* shows Sarah Caldwell's work as director at its best. Donizetti's seems, besides being very lovely as lyricism, a surprisingly forceful and inventive piece of dramatic writing, dazzlingly skillful as stagecraft, and Miss Caldwell was determined evidently to make the most of that side of *Lucia*.

She has staged it as a dark opera, physically and spiritually. Its three principal characters positively seethe with suppressed violence—indeed, even the chaplain has a presence of almost manic intensity.

Lucia does not wait for her famous third act Mad Scene to be mad: her opening scene, "Regnava nel silenzio," finds her in a near lunatic condition of exaltation,

[3] See review of March 15, 1964.
[4] See article of February 2, 1969.

and the later scene in which she is forced to sign the marriage contract has her in a brooding state that is close to catatonic.

All this has been done attentively and consistently, and with a sensitive eye for stage pictures. The Senn and Pond sets are beautiful and interesting in the way they are set so freely and with so much visual variety within the rectangle of the stage.

The Mad Scene introduces a bridge that extends the stage around the front of the orchestra pit, and lighting is imaginatively used here, the crowd on stage gradually melting into darkness as Lucia drifts deeper into her mental isolation.

John Harvey's lighting is finely conceived, though its actual realization left a lot wanting technically. This is also the place to mention that Jan Skalicky's costumes are quite exceptionally handsome.

Miss Caldwell's one great miscalculation in direction was to precede the first two scenes with endless sequences of slides with text meant to clarify the story, though I also think that the audience hilarity that greeted this was exaggerated as well as forced.

Then, of course, the production is singularly fortunate in its Lucia, Beverly Sills. Her singing was stunningly brilliant, pure in tone, elegant, characteristically tasteful and intelligent. Her dramatic portrayal did not quite sustain the extraordinary force with which it began: that first scene with "Regnava nel silenzio" was so original, so richly detailed, with the embellishment so endowed with expressive quality, as to leave one shaken.

What followed never fell below a level that I daresay very few of Miss Sills's colleagues can even reach, but it was not so gripping, and its excellence was of a more conventional sort. Altogether, though, it was an affecting and communicative performance, and vocally something quite out of the ordinary.

With less opportunity to dazzle, Donald Gramm gave an equally distinguished performance as Raimondo, the chaplain. His acting was, as always, most accomplished, but it was his singing that was so remarkable, not just for its sonority and power, but for its clarity of diction and the marvelously enlivening plasticity of phrasing, especially in recitative.

The Edgardo was Jaroslav Kachel, a Czech tenor who works in East Berlin, and an interesting singer miscast. He is a competent actor and a sympathetic stage figure generally, but his singing though always intelligent, concerned, and tasteful, is really not very good: the voice is forceful, but the quiet singing is done in a husky, rather uncomfortable-sounding half-voice.

James Farrar, as Lucia's brother Enrico, was hearty and hammy. Eunice Alberts, wonderfully costumed and made up, did a beautiful job with the incredibly thankless role of Alisa; Salvador Novoa was effective in the almost equally submerged role of Lucia's unwanted suitor, Arturo; Lowell Harris was just on the margin of audibility as Normanno.

Sarah Caldwell conducted with a nice sense of style, but the performance was awfully shaky in detail, and the orchestral playing was mostly quite horrid.

Babbitt's Music Requires Special Audience

February 2, 1969

A composer with a commission and a performance by the New York Philharmonic is someone you probably picture as a proud and happy man. Recently, though, when the Philharmonic was about to play the premiere of one of its 125th Anniversary commissions, Milton Babbitt's *Relata II*, Babbitt said it was as though a philosopher were to read a learned paper on the Johnny Carson show. Leonard Bernstein's reaction to that evaluation of his shop is not recorded.

Babbitt, 52, a pioneer years ago on the twelve-tone scene in America, one of our first composers of electronic music, an outstanding theorist and influential teacher, made his remark in a *New York Times* interview that appeared on the Sunday before the January 16 premiere of his work. He talked about who would hear the piece which his publisher was not planning to publish, and of which there would be no broadcast, tape, or recording. His "interested musical colleagues, those for whom I really offer it," would have no access to the piece unless they could get to Philharmonic Hall for one of the four performances.

"On the other hand," Babbitt continued, "the regular Philharmonic audience does not want to hear this piece. And why should they have to? How can it be coherent for them? It is as though a colleague of mine in the field of philosophy were to read his paper on the Johnny Carson show. The milieu is inappropriate for the event."

Let us look. The program at the *Relata II* premiere went like this: Bach's *Brandenburg* Concerto No. 5 (violinist Isaac Stern, flutist Julius Baker, pianist Bernstein), Violin Concerto No. 1 by Prokofiev (Stern), the Babbitt, and Mozart's Violin Sonata in B-flat, K.378 (Stern, Bernstein). The inclusion of a sonata that does not involve the orchestra at all is of course extremely unusual, but it was done, obviously and commendably, to make a little more desperately needed rehearsal time available for the Babbitt. The Fifth *Brandenburg*, which also involved the orchestra minimally in personnel and time, was a contribution in that direction, too.

Even so, *Relata II* failed to get what it most wants, an adequate performance; moreover, given its difficulty and the realities of orchestral economics, we may be waiting for some time for that (see last Sunday's *Globe*).[5] What it next

[5] See article of January 26, 1969.

needs—and this is a question of tender, loving care more than of sheer survival—is sympathetic, intelligent placing on a program. The other works ought to be intellectually, expressively, and sensuously congruent to it, and the atmosphere has to convey some sense of congeniality. Starting, we must assume, from the best of reasons, Bernstein ended by constructing a program whose primary intent was to glorify two glamorous star performers. What it amounted to really was a Stern-Bernstein Festival, a family entertainment in which Babbitt's work, not helped by its completely unrepresentative performance, could only appear to most of the audience as a rude, incomprehensible, and unwanted intruder. That at the Thursday concert the playing of the *Brandenburg* was musically absurd and technically insufficient, that the Prokofiev performance was imprecise and flabby, that, in sum, the fabled performing establishment was on display in so indecent a condition of decrepitude, sharpened the irony of the occasion.

The Philharmonic's 7579th through 7582nd concerts, the group at which *Relata II* was played, are essentially representative of the values and the problems that militate against their being an appropriate milieu for "difficult" new music like Babbitt's. There are both professionals and amateurs for whom this is evidence that Babbitt is in some important sense wrong to compose his sort of music.

The symphony orchestra is a musical instrument whose vast and exciting possibilities are by no means exhausted. That is why Babbitt, as he says, "jumped at the chance to compose for the New York Philharmonic."

The nuisance of it is, though, that the symphony orchestra is an institution as well as an instrument. As an institution, it is burdened with economic problems so severe that the survival for long of the great instruments like the Philharmonic or the Boston Symphony is by no means to be taken for granted under present conditions. The pressing problem of financial security is one of the factors that have led orchestras to rely on the subscription system. That makes the orchestra a social institution as well. As anyone who goes to many public performances of different sorts can attest, a subscription audience is not a problematic beast. The importance of a subscription audience as a social cachet probably has been exaggerated by observers for all but a few series (Boston and Philadelphia on Friday afternoons, the Met on Mondays, for example), but even if there are relatively few people there for entirely non-musical reasons, the audience that has come out specifically for a particular event almost certainly will offer more in preparation, attention, and appreciation (not synonymous with a shouting and standing ovation), than that which has appeared because it is Tuesday or Saturday again.

Babbitt's music is for a special audience. That seems to me quite proper: it is true as well of *The Art of Fugue*, Thelonious Monk, the motets of the Ivrea Codex, *Falstaff* (as compared to *Rigoletto*), and the Beethoven Fifth. In an essay on Schoenberg's *Moses und Aron*, Babbitt has defined as "the most concrete principle of artistic conduct: The obligation of the responsible artist to do that which he is convinced must be done, and which others apparently are unable or unwilling to do." With respect to his own music, Babbitt always has been clear about his audience, "my interested musical colleagues, those for whom I really offer it."

The dilemma is that Babbitt will not find his "ideal other" (Stravinsky's phrase) embodied in the Philharmonic subscription audience. There is some validity to pointing that some other composers who have written abstruse music have not done so for orchestra, but have addressed themselves to highly specialized performers, small groups of listeners, or even smaller groups of professional colleagues. Think, for example, of Beethoven's late quartets and *Diabelli* Variations, of Bach's *Art of Fugue* and Canonic Variations, though some of this music, not all, did find a fairly large audience much later. Indeed, Babbitt himself suggested eleven years ago in his thoughtful, thought-provoking article, "Who Cares If You Listen?" (the snappy and misleading title was an editor's), "that the composer would do himself and his music an immediate and eventual service by total, resolute, and voluntary withdrawal from this public world to one of private performance and electronic media, with its very real possibility of complete elimination of the public and social aspects of musical composition."

He chose to ignore his own suggestion, as though making believe that that "complete elimination," that separation, had taken place, and I must say I think it attractive in him that the musician fascinated by the possibilities of the modern orchestra won out over the potential hermit. It may be that the atmosphere at orchestral concerts will change or that a second, more specialized orchestral life will grow up alongside the one we have, like comparable developments in chamber music. I would welcome both and am not truly optimistic about either. Perhaps Babbitt, with his rude candor, has added something to the slim hope for a system in which *Relata II* can be regarded as a piece of music rather than an irritant and source of frustration.

Schnabel and Cone—Good Talks and Advice about Music

February 23, 1969

Artur Schnabel's *Music and the Line of Most Resistance* is the title of three lectures given by that great musician at the University of Chicago in 1940. Originally published by the Princeton University Press in 1942, this wise and charming book has been out of print for something like twenty years. It is good to have it back at all, of course, but it is frustrating that instead of being available in paperback, because it is the kind of book one would want to have one's students read and that one would want to give to musical friends, it has returned in a wildly expensive ($8.50 for ninety-one pages![6]) hard-cover reprint, nicely made from the original plates by the Da Capo Press.

It is probable, therefore, and sad, that Schnabel's book will continue not to reach a large non-professional public. The lectures were Schnabel's first attempt at thinking and writing in English, something that makes their witty and precise language even more admirable. Their task was essentially to provide an introduction to the musical profession in its various aspects—composition, performance, teaching, editing, writing and talking about music—and Schnabel was particularly interested in the perpetual and inevitable tensions between the ideal and the practical. It all makes for stimulating contact with a lively mind.

The Schnabel lectures are good talk about the music world; Edward T. Cone's Oberlin College lectures of 1966, published by W. W. Norton as *Musical Form and Musical Performance*, are about music itself, specifically the problem of how to achieve valid and effective performance. For Schnabel, the performing artist is like a mountain guide who "must see to it that his charge, the guided climber, is more concerned with the mountain than with the guide." Cone teaches about mountains, and in doing so he teaches us, the guided climbers, how to evaluate guides.

Perhaps before I go further, I should admit special interest because I studied theory and analysis with Cone. That does not make him responsible for any specific opinions of mine; my general ideas about performance do, however, proceed from assumptions closely related to those that are so clearly thought through and lucidly stated in *Musical Form and Musical Performance*.

For most lay listeners, and for many performers as well, a successful performance is one first, that holds the attention, and second, in which the instrument makes sensuously beautiful sounds. No one would quarrel with the first point unless one is dealing with so obviously a special case as Satie's *Vexations* and some of its loonier progeny. The second point is already dangerous because it tends to assume that there is such a thing as, say, a uniformly applicable "beautiful violin sound," where the more mature musician would understand that "beautiful sound" means the appropriate sound for that particular work or phrase.

Cone takes "effectiveness" and "beauty" in these senses as given. He addresses himself to performance as being the task of clarifying the events of a piece of music, the events themselves, their succession, and their relation to each other. He is practical, he is resolutely non-mystical, and he deals only in audible categories. He is, as well, refreshingly undogmatic. He recognizes that the more interesting a piece is (and the more worth our attention, therefore), the more

6 Adjusted for inflation, the dollar figure amounts roughly to $76 in 2025.

multi-faceted it is, and the more irrelevant the notion of one definitive performance. The art of performance is an art of recognition and then an art of choice.

"It has been said that some of the most important scientific discoveries have resulted from taking seriously questions that are usually assumed to be trivial." That is Cone's opening sentence, and he goes on to cite, on the problem of performance, the King of Hearts instructing the White Rabbit that leads Cone to his first trivial question: "Where is the beginning of a piece of music?" From there he moves into his first large topic, the nature of musical form.

For Cone the performer's most important job is to perceive and clearly to project the rhythmic life of a piece. The question, therefore, is not only where does a piece begin and end, but how. Form, Cone says, is "basically rhythmic. It is not, as conventional analysis would have it, thematic, nor . . . harmonic. Both of these aspects are important, but rhythm is basic. That is why Ravel could have said, as the story goes, that he had finished his composition 'all but the themes.'"

Cone then goes on to illustrate this with specific performance problems and with an interesting exposition of how these problems take different forms in different musical styles. The lectures must have been copiously illustrated at the piano, and it is an inevitable disadvantage of a book that much of what would have been completely absorbing in a combination of talk, playing, and blackboard notations, makes a somewhat ungracious effect in mere print. The book is generous with musical examples, and the essential ones that Cone examines in some detail—among them, the theme of the variations in Mozart's A major Sonata, Chopin's A major and C minor Preludes, and a passage from Bach's D minor Harpsichord Concerto—fortunately require only a fairly modest skill at the keyboard.

Cone's is a remarkable book, quite the best thing I know on this aspect of responsible musical performance. It should be required reading for every performing musician—not as dogma to be swallowed but as stimulation and clarification—and it should prove an exciting ear-opener to the layman who is really interested in music as opposed to show biz.

Berlioz—Outstanding Release

March 9, 1969

Not much attention has been paid to the centenary yesterday of the death of Berlioz. There has been no observance at any concert in Boston, and the record companies have hardly been heard from. One exception is Philips, who have just released Colin Davis's recording of *Roméo et Juliette*, and whose plans include Davis recordings of *Les Troyens* and the Requiem.

Roméo et Juliette and *Les Troyens* have Berlioz's most beautiful music. *Les Troyens* is still almost entirely unknown in America, and the career of *Roméo* as part of the living repertory in this country began only with Toscanini's New York performances in 1942 and 1947. It is a strange and wonderful work, this "dramatic symphony," as Berlioz called it, one in which the action is entrusted to the orchestra and in which voices are used mainly for narration and atmosphere.

As a musical treatment of Shakespeare's play, it stands alone. The opera by Gounod, who found the Berlioz work "weird," is enchantingly pretty, but it has no trace of a specific "Romeo and Juliet" character. Tchaikovsky's popular Fantasy-Overture is a fine work, but if it and *Francesca da Rimini* had come down to us with their titles exchanged, we should hardly know the difference. It is Berlioz's setting that uniquely captures and articulates the youth of the lovers and that naiveté and helplessness in the face of the storm that carries them away—Berlioz's is, of course, a thoroughly Romantic interpretation, pre-Freud, pre-Kott.[7]

Shakespeare's tragedy engaged to the utmost Berlioz's dramatic imagination (the extraordinary scheme of the whole work, the choral recitatives, the orchestral-choral antiphony of Juliet's funeral music), his compassion (the great orchestral monologues for Romeo), the supreme delicacy of his sensibility (the sweet anguish of the love music, which Toscanini recklessly and understandably called the "most beautiful music in the world"), his fantasy (the orchestral "Queen Mab" is the incomparable example of Romantic fairy music). Berlioz fails only in the finale, which starts with characteristic and expressive writing, but in which Friar Laurence's moralistic haranguing of Montagues and Capulets becomes engulfed in soap-box conventionalities.

Roméo et Juliette is an exceedingly difficult work to interpret and to perform, and Colin Davis, for some years now the outstanding Berlioz conductor in the world, succeeds beautifully with it. Toscanini (RCA, a recording of the 1947 NBC broadcast) gets still more lightness and magic into "Queen Mab," sustains the love scene more completely, and infuses an even more intense despair into the episode of Romeo in the Capulets' tomb. Davis, however, is excellent even in these passages, and superb elsewhere. The London Symphony plays very well indeed (though the NBC Symphony in 1947 was an even more brilliant instrument), and the vocal soloists, mezzo-soprano Patricia Kern, tenor Robert Tear, and baritone John Shirley-Quirk, are first-rate. So is the chorus—the John Alldis

[7] Steinberg here refers to the Polish-born activist, critic, and theater theorist Jan Kott (1914–2001), known for his interpretation of theater classics. In *Shakespeare, Our Contemporary* (1964), he critiqued the plays in the context of 20th-century existentialism as well as his own life experiences. Kott's insights influenced many modern theater directors, notably Peter Brook, Giorgio Strehler, and Ariane Mnouchkine.

Choir and the London Symphony Chorus—and the choral recitatives in the prologue are much better done even than by Toscanini.

Monteux's recording (Westminster) is honest but stodgy. Munch's recording (RCA)[8] has been praised mainly by persons who learned *Roméo et Juliette* from Munch: it is, in fact, stiff (the choral recitatives are grotesque), heavy-handed (compare his "Queen Mab" with Toscanini's or Davis's), coarse in expression, and sometimes nonsensical in its tempos. Given the dry, sensuously unattractive sound of the Toscanini recording, even bearing in mind that the Philips sound is not as rich and luminous as one might wish, the Davis recording of *Roméo et Juliette* is something we have waited for and needed a long time. It is one of the most beautiful and important releases of the '60s.

Hub Treated to Early Beethoven

March 12, 1969

[*"The Hub" was a phrase coined in 1858 in the Atlantic Monthly by Oliver Wendell Holmes (possibly satirically) to describe the Boston State House: "Boston State-House is the hub of the solar system. You couldn't pry that out of a Boston man, if you had the tire of all creation straightened out for a crowbar." It was quickly adopted to describe Boston more generally.*]

Monday evening in Jordan Hall, Russell Sherman and Rudolf Kolisch played the first of three concerts devoted to Beethoven's ten sonatas for piano and violin. The programs go roughly in chronological order, the bill for Monday's concert therefore including the three sonatas of Opus 12 and the Sonata, Op. 23 (played for greater effectiveness in order 1, 4, 3, 2).

To play Beethoven's quartets, or piano sonatas, or orchestral works, in chronological sequence would be a mistake and a waste of opportunities for stimulating contrasts in content and style; it works well for the violin sonatas, though, of which the first nine fall within a five-year span (1799–1803), and with even the last of them, which is contemporary with the Seventh and Eighth symphonies, not representing Beethoven's late style at all.

Early Beethoven is persistently neglected. The quartets go for the pieces with opus numbers in three figures; so do the pianists now except when they play one of the big middle-period hit parade numbers like the *Appassionata* and the

[8] Munch recorded Berlioz's *Roméo et Juliette* twice with the BSO for RCA, in 1953 (monaural) and 1961 (stereo). Given his comments, Steinberg likely refers here to the 1961 recording.

Waldstein; violinists pick the *Spring*, the *Kreutzer*, the C minor from Opus 30, and the G major, Op. 96. In five years of reviewing concerts I have not once, before Monday, heard a public performance of any of the sonatas Kolisch and Sherman played this time.

Among other things, then, Monday's concert was an occasion to be reminded of how exciting a composer Beethoven was as he approached and became 30, which is not, after all, so terribly young for an artist. In Opp. 12 and 23 he is mature and masterful, prodigiously inventive, paying debts of various sorts to Haydn, Mozart, C. P. E. Bach, Clementi, but thoroughly his own man. The surface of these sonatas abounds in fresh detail, but, even more, it is the way these compositions behave at their core, the boldness of gesture, the concentration, the filling out of the time scale, that seems fairly to scream "new music."

Each of the four sonatas heard Monday contains music that is absolutely astonishing. Movements that struck me as extraordinary include in Opus 12, No. 2, the first with its sense of rhythmic fun, and the second with its touch of the exotic that looks forward to Schubert and to the Andante of the third *Rasumovsky* Quartet; in No. 3 (perhaps the finest of the Opus), the bold first movement, and the Adagio, which is one of Beethoven's first profound slow movements; the terse and urgent Presto and Allegro molto in Opus 23.

Kolisch and Sherman played beautifully. Intelligence and care are qualities to be expected when they perform, but this time one heard as well a vitality and a mutual responsiveness that were missing at their concert last year. Theirs is not a particularly free manner of playing and there is very little of a sense of improvisation, of taking advantage of the moment—a quality of performance the Zsigmondys suggest so well—and I do sometimes miss that.

Altogether, to hear the four sonatas played with such energy and concentration, and with so lively a sense of musical character, was an exciting experience, for me and evidently for all of the uncommonly attentive and enthusiastic audience.

I should add that I found Kolisch's playing remarkably rich and interesting from a violinistic point of view (without being in the least unaware of his limitations) because the intensity and depth of his response to the music elicits from him such a range in instrumental response. And apart from the way my Claude Frank–trained ears kept wishing for something more to be made of the bass line, I also thought Sherman's playing pianistically impressive and altogether the liveliest I have heard from him.

Whoom-pahs and Goosebumps—the Untraditional

March 16, 1969

About five minutes into Beethoven's Seventh Symphony there is a series of great gallumphing whoom-pahs, *fortissimo*, followed by a silence and then by another, shorter, lot of whoom-pahs. I can still, after five years or so, experience the most vivid sense of goosebumps when I recall a performance in which the silence was followed, not by what I "knew" came there, but by a quiet pip-pedip pip-pedip from flute and oboe. For the first time in my experience, the conductor—it was Erich Leinsdorf—had taken the repeat of the exposition in this movement.

Later I read a review in which the problem was dealt with as "musicological," with the reviewer implying that what for him was evidently an eccentric decision of Leinsdorf's was to be attributed to the conductor's well-known interest in scholarship and penchant for literal-mindedness. I never asked Leinsdorf about it; I should bet, though, that he made the repeat, not out of piety, but because he had imagined its dramatic effect. By that I mean not just the effect of the turn-back on listeners unaccustomed to it, but the greater effect made by the beginning of the development, which, like the repeat of the exposition, also starts with the pip-pedip figure, if you already have heard the immediately preceding music take off in a different and milder direction.

Musicology was invoked in that review as something that interferes. The point about musicology, certainly about that part of it that deals with problems of performance practice, is that it provides us with information whose proper interpretation will bring us closer to the music. In this particular situation, though, I don't believe that musicology was in it at all: a musical effect, rhetorical and structural, was involved, and my colleague simply never heard it happen. The question of whether or not to take a given repeat indicated by the conventional shorthand (colon and double-bar) is one to be resolved in each case on musical grounds; in fact, musicology is not even terribly helpful about it as it is, for example, about matters like Baroque ornaments.

The scherzo of Beethoven's Seventh begins with a section of twenty-four bars (it takes about ten seconds) whose repeat is always observed. Then comes a section of twenty-four bars which Beethoven also encloses within repeat marks.

There conductors almost invariably go on into the Trio; Leinsdorf, however, went back—also for the first time in my experience—and in doing so revealed one of Beethoven's most magnificent jokes. One should not explain musical jokes any more than verbal ones, but in violation of that rule let me say that the effect rests on a sort of pun. Beethoven lands on a long unison A, *fortissimo*, which he then uses as a catapult for the leaping three-note figure that is the movement's principal idea. When he arrives at the A for the second time, he makes a *diminuendo* and moves into the gentler, slightly slower Trio, still holding on to the A as a dominant pedal. To deprive this A of its double character—first rambunctious, then soothing—is to terribly impoverish the expressive richness of this movement.

A general rule can be inferred here. When the music just before the point of repetition has an important double meaning built in, the repeat is better taken. The dramatic beginning of a new section is often fully relished only when we already have heard its preparation lead to something else, usually something less dramatic, more "normal."

In the Seventh Symphony, Beethoven simply brings you up to the double bar, and you either go back or go on. Often, though, a composer will provide different paths to the two destinations. Omitting the repeat and going straight to the so-called second ending, you omit some music that probably occurs nowhere else in the piece. You are then dangerously near the area of thoroughly illegitimate cuts, passage over which the composer has taken particular pains.

My favorite example is the first movement of the Brahms Second Symphony. I still remember the excitement of the sudden invasion of quiet dramatic beauty the first time I heard the eight measures of the first ending. I had played them on the piano and I knew how they went, but hearing them was different and wonderful. The conductor that time was Pierre Monteux, and Frederik Prausnitz is the only conductor from whom I have also heard that repeat. One could argue that the movement as a whole doesn't urgently "need" the exposition to be heard twice, but I would urge doing it anyway for the sake of those incredible ten seconds.

Apropos needing the repeat, the most perplexing puzzle of this sort occurs in the first movement of Mendelssohn's *Italian* Symphony. The puzzle is not of Mendelssohn's making. The roads traveled by the exposition the first and second times diverge unusually early. The difference between the first and second endings is big, therefore, and the first ending even introduces a theme that does not figure in the second ending and that, in fact, comes back only in the coda. If the conductor goes directly to the second ending, he not only omits a large chunk of music, he produces the absurdity of making a recapitulation of a theme that we never heard in the first place. One would suppose the point to be one that any conservatory freshman could understand, and that no conductor could be so stupid and so insensitive as to skip this repeat—yet, listen to the recordings of Cantelli, Casals, Klemperer, Toscanini, among others.

A more general point about needing repeats comes up when the exposition is unusually terse or concentrated. The first movement of Beethoven's Fifth is a case in point, and so is the first movement of the Brahms Third. In both, having been sluiced through the exposition at such a rate, I just don't feel ready to go on yet. The Fifth has as well a special, perhaps unique, situation: exposition, development, recapitulation, and coda are so close to being the same length that Beethoven must have counted on the repeat to achieve a satisfactory balance of expository versus developmental sections.

Except for a few special examples, this is not a subject for dogmatism. I am no longer even as sure as I once was about the necessity of uniformly making all repeats in a variation set. It is something that asks for experiment and reevaluation. Some departures from custom will prove to be unrewarding. Some, even if they seemed unlikely at first, have worked beautifully: the repeat in the first movement of the *Eroica*, once unheard of but not so uncommon now, or the repeats even of the developments and recapitulations in Mozart finales for which Leinsdorf and Sir Adrian Boult have made convincing cases in performance.

It becomes part of the performer's obligation to be prepared to ignore that accretion of bad, and even some good, habits that we call tradition, and to confront each composition as though for the first time. A great performance, after all, is one that hits us like a world premiere.

Schubertiades Recalled

March 23, 1969

Many of Schubert's songs and piano pieces had their first performances—often, indeed, their only performances during the composer's lifetime—at the so-called Schubertiades. These were evenings devoted to Schubert's music in the homes of his friends, not professional musicians generally, gatherings that with suitable intervals for punch were apt to go on 'til three in the morning.

On its Victrola label, RCA has attempted to suggest the atmosphere of a Schubertiade with a record whose contents differ from those of the conventional recorded recital of Schubert songs in two ways: the sequence of songs is broken by a group of piano pieces, and the piano, being a Viennese one of 1835 (by Rausch), must be close in sound to those Schubert knew and played.

The remarkable thing about this record, which is called *A Program of Piano Music and Songs*, is, however, the singing itself. This is done by the Dutch soprano Elly Ameling, who has contributed lovely things to recordings of various repertory from Bach to Mahler, and who, as one might in fact have inferred from her "Bist du bei mir" and her Mahler Fourth, turns out to be an extraordinary Lieder singer. Here she does mostly quite well-known Schubert songs—"Der Hirt auf dem Felsen," "Seligkeit," "Gretchen am Spinnrade," "Du liebst mich nicht," "Im Frühling," and "Der Musensohn" among them—and I don't know that I have heard anything quite as lovely since Irmgard Seefried's concerts and records of about twenty years ago.

Ameling is a soprano with a bright and clear voice whose timbre leans toward the boy treble side. Erna Berger, the young Schwarzkopf, more recently Edith Mathis, have been or are somewhat similar singers. Sopranos of this kind are often rather instrumental in character and exaggeratedly sexless. Ameling is, however, thoroughly vocal, that is, human and verbal. Whatever she does is governed by impeccable taste and a remarkable sense of musical line, and her work is free of affectation and excess. It is vividly and interestingly inflected yet intimate and contained. It attains the balance of poetic and musical communication that is the essence of Lieder singing, and on the basis of her nine Schubert performances here, I would say that she is one of the few—not more than a dozen certainly—great Lieder singers of our time.

The pianist is Jörg Demus. He plays well in the Lieder, and gives pleasure even in "Im Frühling," one of those "simple" pieces of Schubert's that throw the toughest possible challenge at the pianist. In his solo group, a set of twelve Ländler, he gets entangled in an attempt to give a super-idiomatic performance and ends up with something uncomfortably close to caricature.

As for the piano itself, I am neither sold on it nor terribly disturbed by it, and it seems rather less attractive in tone, shallower, than the slightly later instrument used by Demus and Badura-Skoda in their recent Victrola record of Schubert duets. Hans Deinzer's clarinet playing in "Der Hirt auf dem Felsen" is excellent.

Argo has released a lovely and unusual record of Schubert part-songs, male or mixed voice quartets, some with obbligato solos, some accompanied by piano and some *a cappella*. Most of the pieces are late Schubert, and some are quite wonderful, the finest of them being the great "Nachthelle" of 1826, male chorus and tenor solo in a contemplation of heaven and the stars. A serenade to a Grillparzer poem, a piece called "Der Gondelfahrer," lovely rather in the manner of the famous solo song, "Auf dem Wasser zu singen," and a setting of Moses Mendelssohn's German translation of the Twenty-third Psalm, are also particularly worthwhile. These pieces are sung by the Elizabethan Singers under Louis Halsey, who, except for slightly English-sounding German, are first-rate. Robert Tear does the "Nachthelle" solo beautifully, there are fine solos by April Cantelo, Shirley Minty, Helen Watts, Ian Partridge, and Christopher Keye, and Viola Tunnard plays the accompaniments very well.

Henry Lewis's Credo—"For Music, Not Myself"

April 6, 1969

Saturday afternoon, eight days ago, Henry Lewis arrived for our appointment in a state of vivacious turmoil, articulately and energetically throwing off enthusiasm and annoyance in all directions.

The previous afternoon he had conducted a Boston Symphony concert for the first time, and he was pleased with how that had gone—"at least I found out I was ready for them." He was delighted by the excellence of the orchestra itself, and he was still excited by the musicianship of the soloist at the concert, the English pianist Clifford Curzon. The one thing, in fact, Lewis was cross about was a review in which Curzon's excellence had, to say it mildly, gone unrecognized.

Lewis was pleased that a radio interview he had just finished with Leo Snyder at WBUR had turned into "really interesting, really stimulating conversation."

He was very happy because he had just had a transatlantic telephone conversation with his wife, soprano Marilyn Horne, who is at La Scala, Milan, rehearsing Rossini's *Siege of Corinth*, whose overture, on its musical merits rather than for reasons of totemism, had figured on Lewis's Boston program. It was a new role for Jackie, as Miss Horne is called, he explained, and the first she had studied with him. "Why don't you come over?" she had said, and he thought he would for a few days. The Greek soprano Elena Suliotis had been visiting his wife when he had called and, said Lewis with a certain plaintive longing in his voice, "It sounded as though everybody was having such a good time."

Then—all this more or less at once, contrapuntally—he was worried about how to put together a suitable program for the concert he would conduct with the Boston Symphony at Tanglewood in August at which Marilyn Horne would be the soloist. It was a question of combining their desire to do Berlioz's intimate quasi-chamber-musical song cycle, *Nuits d'été* (Lewis, remembering a Horne performance with Charles Munch at the Edinburgh Festival: "Jackie sings it better than anybody else in the world") with the public's presumed desire to hear Marilyn Horne sing some of the bravura arias for which she had become famous. And it was a question as well, Erich Leinsdorf had reminded Lewis, of finding an orchestral piece to end with that would produce a big personal success for Lewis, too.

Lewis, California-born and 37, is music director of the New Jersey Symphony. The orchestra's offices are in Newark, and that is where the Lewises live also, but the orchestra is intended to serve the state, rather than Newark alone, and it gives concerts regularly in several cities and towns. It has been an orchestra of fairly modest pretensions, but, Lewis reported, it is now on its way to becoming a major orchestra, to which end the board has just approved an enormous increase in the budget.

The change of status means a corresponding and major change in the orchestra's musical makeup. A good many of the players in the past have been what Lewis calls "avocational musicians," and they, says Lewis, are against the stepping up of the orchestra's activities to a full-time basis because then they no longer will be able to participate. The process of conversion has led to conflicts as a result of which part of the current season has been lost in strike.

Lewis envisions an arrangement in which the orchestra can serve the entire state—"after all, everything is close enough so that we can always come home after a concert"—preparing programs that could be taken sometimes to as many as twenty-five places. While the newly made, fully professional orchestra is still in the process of being built, the repertory will be limited in sheer quantity. Later, as the orchestra acquires a certain collective virtuosity, more music will be absorbed more quickly. What Lewis would like to achieve is a considerable pool of available working repertory from which concert programs can be assembled with minimal necessity for clean-up rehearsal and maximal flexibility in suiting programs to the varying possibilities and needs of each community.

Newark itself offers both extraordinary problems and extraordinary possibilities. Lewis, himself Negro, has a deep personal concern for the problems, and during the unquiet summer of 1963, he conceived the idea of taking his New Jersey Symphony into Newark's center city (read "ghetto"), and giving concerts in an empty lot on three consecutive Sundays.

He was assured on all sides that the scheme would not work, even that it was dangerous. In the event, 1,500 people showed up for the first concert, and by the third, the audience had grown to 5,000. "They were hanging out of windows," Lewis reports, still aglow from the experience. "We played Bach, Tchaikovsky, nothing I wouldn't play at a regular symphony concert. The only difference was that I avoided big, extended pieces. William Warfield sang Copland's American folk song arrangements and Jackie came to sing at the last concert and did 'Summertime' from *Porgy and Bess*." And it all worked, Lewis is sure, because the whole operation was carried off in a style that made it, not a patronizing bringing of gifts to the slums, but a communication of his love and enthusiasm for the music and a persuasive sense of wanting to share it.

Lewis loves being in "an expanding situation" like that of the New Jersey Symphony. "The possibilities for building are really fantastic." He does not pretend indifference to success, but he is no careerist. That his success has been gradual rather than meteoric he can now regard as useful. "I'm more solid for having waited. And I'm in it for the music, not for myself."

Schoenberg Drama Awesomely Performed

April 19, 1969

Friday afternoon's Boston Symphony concert was the first half of Erich Leinsdorf's final Friday-Saturday pair as the orchestra's music director. Having come here in 1962, Leinsdorf will end his duties at the conclusion of the coming season at Tanglewood though he will return as guest conductor during the next five seasons.

Like many of his predecessors, including Sir George Henschel, the Boston Symphony's first conductor, Leinsdorf put Beethoven's Ninth Symphony on his farewell program. There was more applause than is usual at a Friday concert and there was a solid round of cheers when the conductor took a solo bow after the Beethoven; it was not an emotional occasion, though. During his seven years here, Leinsdorf had often engaged the audience's respect, but hardly their affection, and his farewell matched his tenure in tone.

Leinsdorf preceded Beethoven's Ninth with Schoenberg's *A Survivor from Warsaw*, a short, intensely concentrated music drama whose subject is an episode in the battle that began just twenty-six years ago, April 19, 1943, in the Warsaw ghetto. A survivor tells the story of a group of Jews who, at the moment of their deportation to the death camp, suddenly, in a last flaring of spirit and faith, burst into singing the prayer "Shemah Yisrael."

Schoenberg, who seems to have had the story from an actual Warsaw survivor, wrote the piece in 1947, and it was the last orchestral work he completed. He shaped the narrative so that the singing of the prayer is its culmination. This brief intervention for men's chorus in unison is the only singing we hear in *Survivor*, and it appears as the climax of a story told in speech-song (rhythms exactly prescribed, but pitch contours only loosely indicated) for the narrator's account in English, and in which the German sergeant's words are given special profile and character by their delivery in straight, percussive speech.

The compression of the music, its rhythmic life, the ferocious energy of impulse, the richness of cross reference of languages and corresponding and characteristic vocal techniques, the vividness of musical imagery, the unsurpassed orchestral virtuosity through which that imagery is articulated, all this produces a work that is terrifyingly adequate to its subject.

For once, too, Schoenberg received an adequate performance. To begin with, the playing was so clear and so clean that one could actually follow the acoustic events of the work, and that, as Schoenberg performances go, is in itself rare and noteworthy. That had been generally true as well of Leinsdorf's finely made performance of the Variations, Op. 31, some weeks ago. A certain caution had gone into the achieving of the effect then, but what made Friday's performance of *A Survivor from Warsaw* so marvelous was that all these sharply defined gestures were delivered with electrifying force, and that they were integrated into a tightly coherent progression of tremendous sweep.

Sherrill Milnes did the narration. It was done without a trace of cheap pathos, with an astonishing ability to project situation and character, with complete comprehension of the purpose and effect of Schoenbergian speech-song, with rhythmic vitality, with an extraordinary range of tone color, volume, intensity of attack (used with the utmost virtuosity, though quite unobtrusively), and, most significantly, with evident understanding and depth of feeling. It was one of the greatest vocal performances I have ever heard. The orchestral playing itself was superb, and the singing by the men of the New England Conservatory Chorus was good, if a little weak in sheer physical impact.

Leinsdorf immediately repeated the piece, a move that, to judge from the reception, worked well for most of the audience. The performance of *Survivor* will be remembered as one of the most valued, distinguished, and exciting achievements in Leinsdorf's seven years' directorship here.

The performance of the Beethoven Ninth was much like the one Leinsdorf gave at the opening of the 1965–66 season, generally effective in the first movement, in the scherzo, and in the bouncy parts of the finale, but too determinedly straight and unrhetorical for the scherzo's Trio, for the great slow movement, and for the mysterious passages in the finale. Nor was there much trace this time of the extremely beautiful playing of the 1965 performances.

The two choruses—Chorus Pro Musica and the New England Conservatory Chorus, prepared respectively by Alfred Nash Patterson and Lorna Cooke deVaron—sang very well. Sherrill Milnes, whose baritone voice has a sound of extraordinary brilliance, concentration, and power, again distinguished himself remarkably. Placido Domingo lacks the heroic force for the proto-Mahlerian march with the suns flying through heaven's splendid space, but in all other respects his work was stylish, musical, and very agreeable in sound. A mezzo friend once said that one should always wear the brightest possible dress when singing the alto solo in the Ninth, otherwise one won't be noticed at all; in sum, the alto has nothing conspicuous to do, and Josephine Veasey, a fine singer, made a solid contribution to the ensemble. Jane Marsh sang the soprano solo with a nice, easygoing athleticism in 1965, but this time she sounded strained and unhappy.

Peter Serkin at 21—Exceptionally Gifted Pianist

May 2, 1969

NEW YORK—Now 21, Peter Serkin is really a marvelously interesting pianist. He knows the music he plays, knows it thoroughly and deeply, has perceived it freshly, and has that powerful personal projection that makes him a real performer, even in sterile Philharmonic Hall.

He played there Wednesday in the "Great Performers at Philharmonic Hall" series. It is a subscription series meant to provide both glamour and musical quality. It is not much given to adventure, and Serkin worked out a brilliantly imagined and pleasingly defiant program for the occasion. In the first half, he played two pairs of matched but strikingly contrasted pieces, both parts of Schoenberg's Opus 33, and later, two Mozart rondos that offer a comparable difference of mood, the *galant* D major [K.485] and the melancholy A minor [K.511].

He followed each pair with something startlingly different in sound surface, but not unlike in other ways, moving back from Schoenberg to the warm and damp Sonata [Op. 1] by Alban Berg, and on from Mozart to the elegant, rather severely witty Variations by Webern. The Webern, incidentally, follows the Mozart A minor Rondo beautifully—it begins on the same E that functions as a kind of hinge note throughout the Mozart.

It may have looked crazy on paper, but it worked superbly. The second half, which I was unable to hear, was given over to four [Nos. 10, 11, 13, and 17] of the *Vingt Regards sur l'enfant-Jésus* by Messiaen.

Serkin played the Schoenberg with a lot of emphasis on contrast and sharp characterization of detail. It was clear and vivid, but a bit hard, too. His playing of the Berg Sonata had a lovely improvisatory quality and it was unusually varied and beautiful pianistically. In the Webern Variations, the piano sound was neutralized, made impersonal, the performance altogether being lucid and cool.

In Mozart's A minor Rondo, Serkin was audaciously personal. His is a "bigger" performance even than Brendel's recent recorded one. It was "Andante" in that it undoubtedly kept moving, and it was remarkably flexible in pace, too. But the basic tempo was spacious so as to allow for an unusually bold and large projection of melodic, rhythmic, harmonic, and phraseological detail.

It would be almost perverse to be able completely to avoid thinking of Rudolf Serkin's playing at a Peter Serkin concert, and the son has, in any event, long been out of the father's shadow; I was very much struck by the contrast between Rudolf Serkin's rather one-dimensional linear approach to Mozart and the classics generally, and Peter Serkin's astonishingly complex multi-faceted view of this A minor Rondo.

It was an extraordinary performance surely, informed both by love and intelligence. I also found it not quite in balance, just a little too explicit, too spelled out, perhaps a bit too aggressively tragic with those very slow turns and heavily emphasized dissonances.

It missed something of Mozart's characteristic elegance and finesse of diction and manner. It was nonetheless singularly gripping, neither harsh nor sentimental, and conveying a remarkable sense of exploring one's way through the piece as though for the first time. And it is clear that Peter Serkin is a musician of very special quality.

Newton Memorial Concert Takes Ancient Theme for Youthful Piece

June 2, 1969

Danny Mendelson was a student at Newton South High School, an outstanding football and baseball player and wrestler. He died at 17 in June of last year when complications developed after a gall bladder operation.

Louis Weingarden is a 25-year-old American composer, who has studied with Elliott Carter at the Juilliard School and at the American Academy in Rome, and who for three years has spent the month of May at Newton South High working on the school's Arts Festival. Last year Danny Mendelson appeared in a musical version of *Huckleberry Finn*, composed, conducted, and directed by Weingarden.

Garrick Ohlsson is a 21-year-old pianist, the winner of the Busoni Competition and the Montreal International Piano Competition. He is now working towards a Bachelor's at Juilliard. A friend of Louis Weingarden's, he was one of the pianists in the *Huckleberry Finn* production.

Friday night in the Newton South High auditorium, just a few days before Danny Mendelson should have graduated, there was something like a reunion of Danny and Louis Weingarden and Garrick Ohlsson. It was the Danny Mendelson Memorial Concert at which Ohlsson played Brahms and Chopin, but also the *Triptych* that Weingarden had just begun at the time of Danny's death and which became a memorial for him.

Weingarden's *Triptych* is about eighteen minutes of music. Each of its three sections evokes an episode from the Bible. The first is on *Genesis* 22, the temptation of Abraham, the terrible command: "Take now thy son, thine only son Isaac, whom thou lovest . . . " It is a fierce sort of music, harsh in sonority and harmony, declamatory, and with dramatic confrontations between what I take to be the musical symbols for the voices of God and of Abraham and the rugged, unyielding landscape.

Next, David minds his sheep and (in Weingarden's words) "for amusement takes up his harp and composes a spiritual etude: 'If the Lord be my shepherd, then I shall lack nothing.'" This is the *Triptych*'s lyric intermezzo, an improvisatory play between fanciful harp rhapsodies and the attempt to shape a simple song.

Last, the Marys at the tomb, and the angel who gently bars their way: "He is not here, but is risen." It is music full of the whirring of great wings, first awesomely dark, later luminous and bright, and pierced once by the radiant simplicity of a Gregorian chant.

Louis Weingarden has the gift you cannot buy: he has something to say. His three spiritual dramas are urgently conceived, and they are composed cohesively and with remarkably telling musical imagery. Some parts of his diction seem a bit impersonal, perhaps because they are rather eclectic: rhythmic details and the piano writing itself (which is, however, brilliantly effective of its kind) are less vital and original than other aspects of invention in the *Triptych*. My impression of the Twenty-third Psalm movement, too, was of something less surely sustained than the other sections, though on one hearing I cannot be sure whether the lapse was in the piece, in the performance, or, for that matter, in the listener.

The best of *Triptych* is compelling music. Eloquent, serious but not solemn, unsentimental though deeply felt, it is a beautiful memorial to a boy whose life and death evidently deeply entered those who knew him.

Garrick Ohlsson, who is one of the most impressive pianists I have heard, produced what seemed to me a powerfully effective statement of *Triptych*. He had begun with a strong, uncompromising performance of the Brahms F minor Sonata, and he played three of Chopin's greatest, subtlest, most difficult works—the E-flat Nocturne from Opus 55, the E major Scherzo, and the Barcarolle—not merely with pianistic virtuosity, but with imposing, altogether unusual, mastery of style and form.

Had Refused the Job—Boulez to Philharmonic

June 15, 1969

So the New York Philharmonic has landed Pierre Boulez as its new music director beginning with the 1971–72 season, and they must have promised him the moon to do it. It is a hard job, perhaps the hardest in the profession. Leonard Bernstein, whose eleven-year tenure came to an end a few weeks ago, survived it, but not his three predecessors. Dimitri Mitropoulos, Artur Rodzinski, and

John Barbirolli were all in some way defeated, even destroyed by it. Moreover, the Philharmonic board had not made the search for a new music director easier by retaining Bernstein as conductor laureate, which means that Bernstein will continue to give concerts, make records, and do television programs with the orchestra.

Boulez was guest conductor with the Philharmonic for the first time in March and April of this year. Inevitably he was asked if he had been offered The Job and if he was interested, and characteristically he explained in trenchant terms that the position was not one he wanted, that he had no desire to be a prisoner of fame as he felt the Philharmonic's music director must be.

In any event, Boulez already had a three-year commitment to the BBC Symphony Orchestra (London) also beginning in 1971. In a conversation earlier this year, Boulez explained that the BBC post attracted him because it provided the possibility of controlling, or at least being influential in the control of, a whole musical environment, not just one particular series of concerts. If, for example, he wanted to do a Schoenberg cycle with the BBC Symphony, its effect could be strengthened by having the BBC concurrently produce performances of some of the chamber music, operas, solo works, and so on. That difference, he explained, was the reason an "ordinary" orchestral post, like, for example, the New York Philharmonic, did not interest him.

There also had been speculation about Boulez's relations with the Cleveland Orchestra. That was an orchestra he had been particularly happy with, and George Szell, its music director since 1946, had taken a great shine to the thirty-years-younger Boulez. For three seasons, beginning next fall, Boulez will be Cleveland's principal guest conductor, with an increasing involvement each year, and some of us had wondered if he was being phased in as successor to the 72-year-old Szell. It is likely in any case that Szell, who last year was named music advisor and principal guest conductor by the New York Philharmonic to take care of the interim period following Bernstein's departure, was influential in leading the Philharmonic to the choice of Boulez, perhaps even in persuading the initially reluctant Boulez.

For three years at least, Boulez becomes one of the commuting conductors. In fact, during his first season as music director, Boulez will be available to New York for only eight weeks because of his commitments to London and Cleveland. For his second and third seasons, Boulez will be at the Philharmonic for a minimum of fourteen weeks each, which is two weeks more than Bernstein has given New York in recent years.

Next fall, Boston will become involved in a commuting arrangement since William Steinberg will retain the position he has had with the Pittsburgh Symphony since 1952. Bernard Haitink has the London Philharmonic as well as the Amsterdam Concertgebouw. Thomas Schippers will have the Cincinnati

Symphony together with a job with Radiotelevisione Italiana in Rome, and Herbert von Karajan notoriously is in Berlin and everywhere. But these *ménages à trois* are not always a success. Steinberg was not happy with a setup that some ten years ago had him take on the London Philharmonic as well as Pittsburgh. Zubin Mehta found he could not take care of Montreal as well as Los Angeles, and Houston just fired André Previn because they felt neglected by a conductor they shared with the London Symphony (Previn's Houston predecessor, Barbirolli, also had Manchester's Hallé Orchestra, but was evidently a more gifted juggler).

It is worth remembering, for that matter, that Erich Leinsdorf, a man of great mental and physical energy, found just the one enormous job of being the Boston Symphony's music director too much to take.[9] Quite a few of his colleagues would agree that conductors, or performers in general, tend to allow themselves too little time for recharging of batteries and for reflection, and that their work begins to suffer. It is very much a conductors' market just now: there simply are not enough first-rate people in the 35-to-60 generation to fill the available positions. The money and prestige that go with having not just one, but two, major orchestras, are tempting. Trying to imagine 1971–74, I wonder who the principal beneficiary will be: Boulez, the BBC, the Philharmonic and its public, or BOAC or Pan-Am?

For Boulez, it has been a quick four years in New York. When he first conducted there—it was with the BBC Symphony in May 1965[10]—his name was known to the general public, if at all, as that of a young avant-garde composer. The audience that attended his two extraordinarily impressive Carnegie Hall concerts then was a rather special one, including a high percentage of professionals, and with a particular interest in works like Debussy's *Jeux*, Schoenberg's Five Pieces, and the Webern Variations. Since then, Boulez has become a star conductor, one with a command of power in the musical establishment that makes him rank politically and financially only just below the superstars Bernstein and von Karajan. And Boulez the composer? Some of his works, I think, have survival power; even so, I should not be surprised if in 1990 Boulez is the most famous living conductor about whom it is dimly remembered that he was as a young man said to have been an interesting composer.

More remarkable still than Boulez's quick rise to fame as a conductor is that we have a very limited idea of what his conducting is like. He has specialized in the music of the first quarter of the 20th century, and even within that period he concentrated on a few works. His excursions into the music of the 19th and 18th centuries have been few and not often successful, and he has done almost no really contemporary music, hardly even his own.

[9] See article of November 19, 1967.
[10] See article of May 2, 1965.

His programs at the Cleveland Orchestra's Blossom Center this summer list works like the Beethoven Fifth and Bartók's Concerto for Orchestra, and they should give more of an idea of what he might be like as a day-in, day-out music director rather than as a guest conductor with his specialties.

Boulez's ear is phenomenal with respect both to pitch and texture. He has, as well, an uncommonly sharp rhythmic sense. He is devastatingly competent, hard-working, efficient and humorous, and orchestras like him. I would put Boulez with the virtuoso conductors whose particular strength is in getting orchestras to play brilliantly, rather than with the interpreters: as a musical personality, Boulez is closer to Szell, von Karajan, or Solti, than to Bernstein, Davis, Kubelik, or Klemperer. Boulez's interest in at least the classics of the 20th-century repertory, of course, makes him a virtuoso conductor with a difference. So far he has done best with the music that most benefits from his ability to produce clarity of texture and rhythmic detail, a clarity often unprecedented in our experience, and least well in music requiring control of a long line and involving imagination and personal warmth. I remember brilliant, breathtaking achievements of Boulez's with Debussy, Webern, Schoenberg, some Berlioz, some Stravinsky, but also failures, some of them smashing, with Purcell, Haydn, Bartók, Berg, some Berlioz, and some Stravinsky.

The New York Philharmonic is not just the local band. It is a national cultural resource. Who is in charge matters not just in New York. The Boulez appointment is interesting, not the least so because much about it is so thoroughly unpredictable. The Philharmonic has taken a risk, just as it did in choosing Bernstein in 1958, and it is to be congratulated, perhaps envied as well, for again having chosen to associate itself with one of the most fascinating and vital musicians of our time.

Americans Ignored—Why Import Conductors?

June 22, 1969

When the New York Philharmonic recently announced the appointment of Pierre Boulez as its new music director, one of the first things that came to mind was that once again an orchestra had turned to Europe when there was an important vacancy to be filled.

That struck me, first, because Boulez succeeds Leonard Bernstein, whose appointment in 1958 was the first occasion that an orchestra of the Philharmonic's stature had chosen an American-born and American-trained conductor, and second, because of Boulez's low regard for most American composers. Concerning the second point, I would guess that Boulez will do as much for

American music as many of his colleagues whose mouths are full of pious sayings on that subject, but who actually play very little, not to mention those who are convinced they have been sufficiently daring in putting [Barber's] *Medea's Meditation and Dance of Vengeance* or the Overture to *Candide* on a program.

But what is an American conductor anyway? To insist on American birth is too restrictive. Consider this list: Maurice Abravanel, Antal Doráti, Lukas Foss, Vladimir Golschmann, Erich Leinsdorf, Eugene Ormandy, André Previn, Hans Schwieger, Leopold Stokowski. Those are all conductors currently, recently, or soon to be, music directors of major American orchestras. All were born abroad, most are United States citizens now, some had their first musical training and professional experience in Europe, many of them began their real careers as conductors in this country, all of them have for many years and through most of their professional lives been associated with the American musical scene.

To be sure, there are some tricky borderline cases on the list. Still, I am sure that no matter how distinctively European a phenomenon Erich Leinsdorf is in many respects, no one would have thought in 1961, "the BSO has picked a European conductor" (as it had with Munch and all his predecessors). Nor would one think of William Steinberg's appointment that way, even though Steinberg, twenty years older upon taking over the Boston Symphony than Leinsdorf was, already had acquired a substantial reputation in Europe and Palestine before coming to America.

The Boulez-Philharmonic situation is essentially different because the New York trustees picked someone who was not already part of the American scene. There are twenty-eight major orchestras in the United States—a major orchestra, according to the American Symphony Orchestra League's official classification, is one whose annual budget is more than $500,000,[11] and eight of them have either present or future arrangements with conductors brought over specially by those orchestras. The eight are in Chicago (Georg Solti), Detroit (Sixten Ehrling), Los Angeles (Zubin Mehta), Minneapolis (Stanisław Skrowaczewski), New York (Boulez), Rochester (László Somogyi), St. Louis (Walter Susskind), and San Francisco (Seiji Ozawa). The National Symphony in Washington is another borderline situation: Doráti, the conductor-elect, is one of the conductors largely associated with American orchestras, though his last two posts have been with the BBC Symphony (London) and the Stockholm Philharmonic.

American orchestras long have been in the importing business. Boston, as I already have pointed out, got all its conductors that way until Leinsdorf. The New York Philharmonic did it until the appointment of Artur Rodzinski in 1943. Josef Krips, Foss's predecessor in Buffalo, was an import, and so were such comparatively recent figures as Rafael Kubelik (Chicago), Paul Paray (Detroit), John

[11] Adjusted for inflation, the dollar figure amounts roughly to $4,445,000 in 2025.

Barbirolli (Houston), Dimitri Mitropoulos (Minneapolis), Eduard van Beinum (Los Angeles), Golschmann, Edouard van Remoortel, and Eléazar de Carvalho (all St. Louis), and Enrique Jorda (San Francisco).

Some of these men made valuable contributions to our musical life: indeed, there is no performer to whom the community of American composers had more cause to be indebted than Mitropoulos. A few of these conductors did not stay in America long, in Kubelik's case to our great loss. Some of the list, though, looks like reverse serendipity at work. If not that, a death wish. Were we so badly off for conductors that it was necessary to bring a Jorda or a van Remoortel across the ocean on purpose?

At one time, of course, American orchestras used to import their players, too. The string shortage is so severe that we may need to continue to recruit violinists from Japan and Israel, but we no longer import wind players: I distinguish between employing recent arrivals and importing because many of the imports, players like Gillet, Laurent, Longy, Tabuteau, stayed to become superb teachers of young Americans.

We have arrived at an efficient system of equipping student instrumentalists to take their places in orchestras. We have not got a comparably efficient way of training conductors, because once they leave the conservatory—and mostly while they are at the conservatory for that matter—they have no access to an instrument to practice on. We have not got all those opera houses that have been such good training grounds, and eventually springboards, for young conductors in Europe. The Metropolitan and the New York City Operas use young Americans as coaches and to conduct the offstage band in *Carmen*, but unlike in Europe, there is almost no vertical mobility in those houses. Leinsdorf, who made it up through the ranks at the Met, is an almost solitary example. Assistants stay invisible: when a new conductor is wanted, he is brought in from outside. Even Julius Rudel, who has been good about American singers the way Rudolf Bing has not, has persisted in bringing one European mediocrity after another—and, rarely, someone good—while Americans of demonstrated competence were under-employed or ignored.

In sum, if there is a young American who has great gifts as a conductor, it is rather, and unfairly, hard for anyone to find out about him. It is also harder for such a gifted person to become a good conductor in America. Considering that America now produces the best equipped instrumentalists and singers in the world, both in enormous quantity, I cannot believe that our conservatory students do not also include a proportionate number of future and first-rate conductors. To discover them and to make use of them requires awareness and effort. The route—a Berkshire Music Center Fellowship and the Koussevitzky Prize—that has led 24-year-old Michael Tilson Thomas to the assistant conductorship of the Boston Symphony is example of what can be done, though, in context of the larger picture, perhaps no more than a drop on a hot stone. I hope that it will occur to more American orchestras, assuming they have energy to cope with problems other than those of their own immediate survival, to make themselves aware of the problem of the American conductor, and to address themselves to its solution. The summertime educational activities in which more and more orchestras are becoming involved may provide a basis for making a serious start.

Textbook from Bach

July 6, 1969

Bach's *Art of Fugue* has not yet been discovered as a popular work. That is partly in its nature: after all, its first purpose, unlike that of the *Goldberg* Variations, is instruction rather than entertainment. Also it has not been available on records in an appropriately seductive performance. I don't like the Glenn Gould record (Columbia) that propelled the *Goldbergs* into their coffee house popularity—too streamlined, it evades too many interpretive problems—but it is easy to understand the beguiling effect of its brilliant surface. *Art of Fugue* recordings, including Gould's incomplete one on organ, have been stiff, self-conscious, and unpersuasive.

The best yet is one recently issued by Odyssey played on the piano by Charles Rosen. The album is called *Johann Sebastian Bach: The Last Keyboard Works*, and it also includes the *Goldberg* Variations and the two ricercars from the *Musical Offering*. There is no reasonable doubt that the *Art of Fugue* is a keyboard work. There is no objection to other instrumental transcriptions of it, though there is plenty to object to in the claims of most transcribers that their labors are necessary because Bach allegedly left no clue about instrumentation.

As for playing Bach on the piano, you have to have a little sense about it. Some works lose a great deal in that translation, others go beautifully on the modern instrument. In general, the less rhetorical, the more structural a work is—if I may offer a distinction which I know is excessively simplistic—the more convincing it is as piano music. Specifically, Rosen makes a superb case for the *Art of Fugue* on the piano.

The work was meant as a compendium of everything Bach knew about writing keyboard fugues. It is a textbook written in notes rather than words, beginning from the simplest sort of four-voice fugue, progressing, using always the same theme, to a fugue unprecedented in richness and even sheer size, using four themes to be combined with one another. This final fugue was interrupted mid-way by Bach's blindness and death.

Art of Fugue is not something to listen to all at once: integral performances are a kind of perversion really. Start somewhere, perhaps with the beautiful, chromatic Fugue No. 3, then go on to the dazzling No. 7 or to the brilliant mirror fugues for two keyboards (recorded by over-dubbing), the grandly eloquent No. 5, the pensive and spacious No. 8, followed by No. 11, which uses the same three themes (plus one other) to make a still more wonderfully elaborate work. Discover, by whatever route, how expressive, vital, and moving, this last testament of Bach's is.

It is hard to disagree with Rosen's idea that the six-voice Ricercar from the *Musical Offering*, the piece Webern orchestrated so fascinatingly, is the greatest fugue ever written. Like the looser and brilliant three-voice Ricercar, it, too, is a keyboard fugue. I find Rosen's playing of the three-voice fugue a bit jolty; on the other hand, his performance of the six-voice fugue is almost beyond praise, a superb and beautiful achievement sensuously and intellectually.

Rosen plays the *Goldbergs* with all the repeats, which I think very worthwhile because of the way, as he puts it, "each part of each variation faces both ways, backwards and forwards, with a different grace and a different meaning each time." A few of the variations are so harpsichordal as to defeat even the most resourceful pianist. Then, Rosen's pianistic brilliance is aggressive rather than elegant, and the performance, though much of it is exceptionally beautiful, e.g., Vars. 4, 19, 21, 25, has given me a less complete pleasure than that of the *Art of Fugue*. I want to stress, though, that Rosen's *Goldbergs* performance is a profoundly considered and extraordinarily interesting and revealing one, and that the album altogether, including Rosen's own unusually full program notes, is one of the best Bach recordings around. Indeed, at the low Odyssey price, it is a fantastic buy really.

Tanglewood's *Otello* Saved by Cassilly

July 28, 1969

LENOX—For all his musical seriousness, Erich Leinsdorf is not the right conductor for Verdi's *Otello*, of which he led a concert performance at Tanglewood Saturday. His conducting has neither the fire for it, nor the humor either, and lacking those qualities, a musician is really at a loss with *Otello*.

Also, the tempi were not always convincing. I don't mean that they were perverse or silly: well-meant, they were not rightly, naturally, felt. Adjacent tempi, maybe off by no more than a nail's breadth, sat uncomfortably together, so that transitions were awkward and scenes like the Otello-Desdemona confrontation at the beginning of the third act, where the impact depends on beautifully fitted tempo relationships, tended to drift aimlessly.

Spongy at its core, the performance could not succeed as a whole. It was, even so, one uncommonly worth hearing because of an Otello and an Iago of stunning dramatic, musical, and vocal magnificence. Sherrill Milnes was the Iago, and his singing had an astonishing richness and variety of verbal, timbral, rhythmic, and articulatory nuance. Subtle and witty, Milnes's characterization, though of course his voice is heavier, had something of the lithe elegance that made Giuseppe Valdengo's performance for Toscanini so remarkable. The sound itself was splendid.

Richard Cassilly, the Otello, is not the familiar figure in America that the phenomenal and gifted Milnes has become in the last couple of years. At the New York City Opera he seemed to be quite an interesting tenor with a constricted sound. After he had dropped from sight for some time, he came to Montreal and New York with the Hamburg Opera in 1967 and gave performances in *Jenůfa* and *Mathis* that showed him to have become a singing actor of unusual force and artistry (having the year before done a good job in a Boston Beethoven Ninth).

I had heard enough to expect a good Otello, but I was not prepared for the overwhelming one Cassilly delivered Saturday. The voice is enormous and rather open and bright. It is perhaps not as sensuously beautiful in any conventional sense, but it has so much intensity and so much character that it is a marvelously exciting instrument.

Verdi wrote Otello for a voice one can hardly imagine existing, one that can freeze the marrow with "*Abbasso le spade!*" Some moments later, the tenderness and vocal elegance for the love duet, and still later in "*Dio! Mi potevi scagliar,*" have available a fantastic intensity in *pianissimo* and in that low register where most tenors just breathe hoarsely.

I have not heard another Otello send his opening "*Esultate!*" ringing out so fearlessly and brilliantly, and Cassilly's whole performance was astoundingly, and in my experience unprecedentedly, equal to the demands of the role.

As an interpreter of Otello, Cassilly belongs with the best, with McCracken and Vinay and Vickers. Something wild is in his voice from the beginning, his singing is that of a first-rate musician, he knows how to act with his voice. At the end of the second act I still had the impression that he was stronger, the more "musical," the less conversational the part was.

In the third act, though, it seemed to me that Cassilly found himself, and that he proved himself a master at using words. He was then a complete and a moving artist, perceptive and resourceful. Each tone and word and gesture contributed to the picture of a man who is destroyed as his two strangely ambiguous love-hate relationships with Desdemona and Iago disintegrate, the process in which he is both actor and victim.

Maralin Niska took the role of Desdemona. She has a vibrant but clear soprano about which there is something pleasingly fleshy. She sings musically and with a rare and enviable ease and elegance. She hasn't much temperament and she is mushy with words (and seems so especially in a performance in which Cassilly and Milnes are setting the standards), and I found her performance not completely interesting.

Rose Taylor did well with the visible, but not often audible, role of Emilia, and Joaquin Romaguera was an effective Cassio when high, though dull when sober. The other roles were competently sung by Richard Taylor (Montano), Luther Enstad (Roderigo), Ara Berberian (Lodovico), Ryan Edwards (Sailor), and Eugene Rabine (Herald).

The Tanglewood Festival Choir, Berkshire Chorus, Framingham Choral Society Chorale, and Berkshire Boy Choir, with Charles Wilson, John Oliver, and Allan Wicks all involved in the preparations, sang excellently though with distinctly American Italian. Charles Wilson conducted the Cypriots' offstage serenade to Desdemona, and provided the kind of animation of phrasing and rhythmic vitality that was so depressingly missing from most of the performance.

Laurence Thorstenberg's English horn solo in the Willow Song was beautifully played (the candy-eating chatterbox behind me loudly whispered "Gomberg!"[12] to her husband at that point), but much of the Boston Symphony's playing was roughly inattentive and out of tune.

Given the highly theatrical nature of *Otello*, Andrew Raeburn[13] was probably right to devise more action for the singers than is usual in concert performances of opera—and this did provide exciting opportunities for Cassilly and Milnes—but it also looked a bit like a rehearsal in formal evening dress, and that was rather peculiar.

Superb Chamber Music

July 29, 1969

No recording can give you the beginning of the Adagio in Mozart's G minor Viola Quintet the way it comes to you in the concert room—that first sound of strings with mutes, so hushed, mysterious, distant somehow, or quite simply, so different.

[12] This is a mistaken reference by the "candy-eating chatterbox" to Ralph Gomberg, the BSO's principal oboe.

[13] Andrew Raeburn joined the BSO in 1964 as musical assistant to Erich Leinsdorf and succeeded longtime annotator John N. Burk as the BSO's program editor in 1967, remaining with the BSO until 1973.

It was something to make one catch one's breath in the performance at the Harvard Summer School concert at Sanders Theatre Monday evening, and it was just one of many things to enjoy and to be amazed and moved by as that great work was played by violinists Alexander Schneider and Isidore Cohen, violists Walter Trampler and Michael Tree, and cellist Leslie Parnas.

It was part of a chamber music concert led and, as they would say in Detroit, "styled" by Schneider, the Mozart Quintet being preceded by Schumann's Piano Trio in F, Op. 80, and followed by the Dvořák Piano Quintet in A, Op. 81. At Schneider's concerts you can count on hearing good music and hearing it played with zip. The actual playing of instruments is often rough, and the concern for having everything lively sometimes leads to vehemence and exaggeration of every sort.

Monday's concert, to be sure, had lots of playing that was badly out of tune and some that was scratchy, partly accounted for by the paralyzing heat and damp, and there was, now and again, some overpointing. Most of the playing, though, was simply alive, straightforward, sensible, wonderfully musical, perhaps even too straight and tight in the Schumann Trio, and, after a somewhat uncertain first movement, remarkably perceptive and beautiful in the Mozart.

The pianist in the Schumann and Dvořák was the youngest and least familiar member of the ensemble, Murray Perahia. He has played here before with a group from Marlboro and as soloist with the Philharmonia, and his supple, tonally lovely, sensitive playing showed once again that he is one of the most richly gifted young performers coming along now. The first (and finest) movement of Dvořák's Quintet finished so brilliantly that the audience quite spontaneously wanted to applaud. That gave way at once to the educated knowledge that you are not supposed to clap between movements.

Then, after a considered silence of perhaps a second and a half, education in turn gave way to sense, and there was a quick round of warm applause. It was nice, and right.

Dartmouth Delight—Sessions Old and New a Heady Mix

August 3, 1969

HANOVER, NH, NORFOLK, CT—"*O wüsst' ich doch den Weg zurück*" ("Oh, would that I knew the way back"), the poet has sung.[14] Louis Spohr, in his memoirs, describes having occasion late in life to write companion pieces to

[14] A poem of that title by Klaus Groth (1819–99) was set to music by Brahms in his Opus 63 set of nine Lieder and songs.

some much earlier works of his own. He did it easily; if anything, it gave him special pleasure to seem to be carried back to his youth.

It is understandable, but curious, too, as we think about it, and not characteristic of a mature, developing artist. Can we imagine the Beethoven of 1825 writing a quartet to be added to Opus 18 or Verdi at 66, when he began *Otello*, composing an opera in the manner of *Nabucco*? Can we even imagine their wanting to do it?

Schoenberg wrote an essay which he called "*On revient toujours*" ("One always returns"), and his life was informed by nostalgia for the land that lay beyond the bridges he himself had burned. Still, when in 1939 he was moved to finish his Second Chamber Symphony, the newly composed music, a perfect completion and fulfilment of the beginning, was no mere return, but a profoundly contemplative synthesis of his thirty-three years' development since he had abandoned the work.[15]

The listener can perhaps afford what is denied the creative artist, the passing regret for what had to be sacrificed. Not that I deplore what became of Beethoven, but the intense pleasure I took in a recent performance of the A major Violin Sonata from Opus 30 made me, for a moment, sad that, to borrow a metaphor from Schoenberg, the Supreme Commander had ordered Beethoven on a harder road.

Three days later, last Sunday, I felt something similar at a concert of Dartmouth for the Arts, Mario di Bonaventura conducting the Dartmouth Festival Orchestra with Christine Asher, soprano soloist, when two works by Roger Sessions were strikingly juxtaposed. They were Psalm 140 (1963) and the Symphony No. 1 (1927), Sessions at 67 and 31. The terse, dramatic, powerfully felt psalm setting—"harsh and violent, inhospitable music" as the program note said—is a stunning work.

I am glad that Sessions's development brought him to a point of being able to compose the strong and moving music of Psalm 140, something he was not equipped for technically nor, I imagine, humanly, thirty-five years earlier; nevertheless, when that wonderfully vital, vibrant, so spontaneously "musical" E minor Symphony began, I was sad that its composer had had, so to speak, to move over.

The neglect of Sessions's later symphonies (No. 8, the most recent, is to be played at Dartmouth tonight) is a national cultural disgrace, though the music is dense, difficult for both performers and listeners, and perhaps in no obvious sense grateful. The neglect of the Symphony No. 1 is, on top of everything else, incomprehensible except as further evidence of conductors' laziness. It wants good players of course, and a conductor with strong rhythm and an ear for

[15] See article of November 17, 1968.

polyphony, but neither conceptually nor technically is it difficult as the later symphonies are, it speaks engagingly as well as lucidly, and, as the Dartmouth concert showed, it pleases.

In 1926–27, Sessions was most influenced by Stravinsky, whose most recent works then were the Piano Concerto, Sonata, Serenade, Octet, Symphonies of Wind Instruments, and with *Oedipus Rex* just to come. Stravinsky is surely audible in the steady, but irregularly accented, eighth-notes of Sessions's First Symphony, and the finale, with its start from a syncopated piccolo tune and its splashes of parallel triads later, even goes back to the Stravinsky of *Petrushka*.

Amusingly enough, it even calls to mind then unwritten Stravinsky, *Danses concertantes*, for example, and *Orpheus*. But even when he seems nearly to quote, as in those *Petrushka* bits of the third movement, the young Sessions is very much his own man, writing a stockier music than Stravinsky's. The music also has so strong a sense of a life of its own that it pays debts as well as contrasts them: it has nothing essential in common with the dry pseudo-Stravinskian crepitations that American neoclassicists were producing so plentifully in the '30s and '40s.

Sessions was to develop into a composer of grand utterance in an elevated style. The stance of the First Symphony, however, suggests the late 18th century rather than the 19th. It is neither dry nor unexpressive, but it says its say with grace.

The second movement, a Largo, runs deep. Its low *pianissimo* brass and bassoons and its much divided strings make a glorious, though somehow chaste, sound. Both its principal music and its more delicate episode in *concertante* style are gravely touching, and this Largo, surely one of the most beautiful pages in symphonic repertory, lends depth and perspective to the more divertimento-like quick movements. The whole symphony "sounds" wonderfully—one more source of pleasure in this joyful and lively work.

Yehudi Wyner's Cadenza for Clarinet and Harpsichord had its first performance on Friday, July 25, played by Keith Wilson and Ralph Kirkpatrick at a Yale Summer School of Music concert. It seems to be the first duet for the two instruments. By the time the clarinet began to lead a proper life of its own in the second half of the 18th century, the harpsichord was on its way out, and though, in the 20th century, the two have appeared together as parts of larger combinations, no other composer has thought to explore what turns out to be a delightful, charmingly matched combination.

Wyner's piece, originally more abstractly called Composition for Clarinet and Harpsichord, is in four fairly short movements, Cadenze (cadences, final and deceptive), Canzona, Dodecadenza, and Decadenza (trills, arpeggios, and broken figures). The ideas are drawn out of various meanings of "cadence" (English or French) and "cadenza."

The Canzona is a wide-ranged lyric movement of great expressive intensity, but most of the work, as its punning subtitles suggest, is inclined to be playful in a manner I do not recall meeting in Wyner's music before. The last movement in particular sets up a delightful storm of cascades and gushes of broken chords, twitches and trills, and other sorts of glittering musical dust.

I imagine players will take pleasure in Wyner's lively new piece, and I should enjoy hearing it again soon.

A Growing Symphonic Skill

August 3, 1969

Philips has issued recordings of all six Tchaikovsky symphonies, Igor Markevitch conducting the London Symphony Orchestra (six records, available separately). For most conductors, and for many listeners therefore, the Tchaikovsky symphonies begin with No. 4, much as Haydn symphonies used to begin with No. 88, and many people have a way of automatically dismissing the first three as "early" and thus presumably immature and insignificant.

It is interesting to stop and consider the chronology of Tchaikovsky's work. Final revisions of the First Symphony date to 1874, and they are the work of a man of 34. The Third Symphony was finished the following year. The final version of No. 2 belongs in 1879, which makes it a later work than the B-flat minor Piano Concerto, the Violin Concerto, *Swan Lake*, *Francesca da Rimini*, *Eugene Onegin*, and the Symphony No. 4. The Fifth Symphony and the *Pathétique* stand apart from the earlier four as genuine late works like *Pique Dame*, *Sleeping Beauty*, and *The Nutcracker*. Orchestral mastery is there from the beginning, though it becomes increasingly refined, culminating in the astonishing achievement of the first and third movements of the *Pathétique*. A fantastic melodic fertility is also characteristic of Tchaikovsky's work early and late. The earlier symphonies are more often balletic in style than the later.

It is fascinating and moving to observe Tchaikovsky's growing skill with symphonic writing. By the time he reaches his Fifth Symphony he is no longer content to churn up sequences and to produce emphasis by repetition: One of the most interesting features of that work, though one almost always blotted out in performance, is Tchaikovsky's way of using tempo relationships for structural purposes, especially in the last movement.

And in the *Pathétique*, while he can still introduce the balletic style in order to make a kind of intermezzo of the charming second movement, he produces elsewhere symphonic movements of remarkable power and originality, to say nothing of the freshness and the impact of the whole plan for this masterpiece.

In a way, the First seems the finest of the lesser-known symphonies, with its economical first movement, original and lovely Adagio, and fascinatingly fresh and delicate scherzo. No. 2, the *Little Russian*, the most familiar of the three, has an attractive march, a scherzo that shows the balletic Tchaikovsky at his best, and a nice, rambunctious finale. In No. 3, the *Polish*, the solemn beginning, the exquisite "*alla tedesca*," and the scherzo, stand out as exceptionally fine.

If for some reason, and I cannot really think of a good one, you want a set of Tchaikovsky symphonies all by one conductor, the choice is between Markevitch and Lorin Maazel (London), both finer than Svetlanov (Melodiya-Angel) and the lumpy Doráti (Mercury). Maazel's performances are more pleasingly recorded, and his Vienna Philharmonic does some playing that is more refined and some that is sloppier than Markevitch's London Symphony. The Markevitch performances are unexpansive, a shade dry, for the most part well-paced, scrupulous, and intelligent.

More specifically, on No. 1 I prefer and recommend Maazel, on No. 2 I enjoyed Abbado (Deutsche Grammophon) more than Markevitch or Maazel, though both are excellent; with No. 3 I thought Markevitch exceptionally good. With the other three symphonies the competition, of course, gets enormous, with the interesting records of all three by Klemperer (Angel), the fine ones of No. 4 by Monteux and Munch (both RCA), of No. 5 by Monteux (RCA) and Solti (London), and No. 6 by Toscanini (RCA). Even so I think Markevitch rates a special recommendation for No. 5 and perhaps also for No. 4.

On its Odyssey label, Columbia has reissued the recording of the *Pathétique* by Mitropoulos and the New York Philharmonic. The performance is characteristically tense, and it seems difficult for Mitropoulos to let anything happen naturally. Still the uniquely dramatic form of the first movement is superbly projected—Mitropoulos is better here at large units than with details—and altogether, for all its faults, the performance is consistently absorbing and at times uncommonly vital and exciting.

Aspen's Music Festival—An Accompaniment of Real Thunder

August 17, 1969

ASPEN, CO—This town has more dogs than Rome has cats. Three Belgian shepherds were playing in the park with a big stick. They were joined by a boy, and as they all loped over the grass, there was the troika from Balanchine's *Apollo*, a charming moment of nature imitating art. The corner drugstore sells Gauloises by the carton, and it is easier to get Lindt or Tobler than to find a Hershey bar.

Aspen seems to be all about leisure and money, which makes an atmosphere I do not find entirely attractive. Even some of the members of the small quasi-hippie community arrive in Porsches. One of the town's fancier restaurants has in its window an inhospitable sign, old-fashioned in terminology, saying "no beatniks allowed."

Aspen has been a silver boom town; since the '30s it has been a great and extraordinarily beautiful ski center, and the Goethe Bicentennial in 1949 made it the site of a music festival. A summer music school is worked in with the festival, the faculty, which in the most part is very distinguished, providing most of the concerts, with students giving some concerts of their own and joining in the symphony orchestra.

The festival is just a bit elderly. Some of the performers are young, but most of the music is old. The composers Darius Milhaud and Charles Jones are regularly on the Aspen faculty and their music is played. Someone is invited as composer-in-residence for a period each summer (Luigi Dallapiccola this year) but few other living composers are represented. Though conservative, the program policy is neither commercial nor banal, and the concerts seem addressed to Senior Citizens of refined and educated tastes.

I heard last Sunday afternoon an extraordinarily impressive orchestra concert conducted by James Levine, the very young assistant conductor of the Cleveland Orchestra. He is a fine pianist, a former student of Rosina Lhévinne's at Juilliard, and he began his program by playing Bach's D minor Concerto. He continued with the Berg Violin Concerto with Toshiya Eto as soloist, and finished with the Dvořák Symphony No. 8 in G.

By the time the Dvořák was due to begin, a fine Alpine thunderstorm had started up providing an accompaniment of applause on the roof of the festival tent. It offered, as well, stimulating competition to the orchestra's superb timpanist, Richard Holmes. Except for the heavenly interventions in the Dies irae in the Verdi Requiem at Tanglewood in 1964, I have never heard thunder so expertly timed, first by waiting for Dvořák, who could take it better than Bach or Berg, then by making some ingenious counterpoints for the terrestrial drum effects in the first movement, and by going in even for such musical refinements as a bolt of lightning for the beginning of a short dominant pedal and a thunderclap for the arrival on the tonic. Aside from all that, the performance was enormously exciting, perhaps a shade heavy (though under the circumstances that may be an unfair observation), and beautifully paced, especially in the series of lingering farewell variations near the end of the finale.

I have at various times heard performances of Berg's Concerto that have had remarkable qualities of perception and execution. This one recaptured for me an excitement the work had not communicated to me since I heard Szigeti and

Mitropoulos play it over twenty years ago. I want, in fact, to go farther and say that I felt Sunday that I was really hearing the piece for the first time.

I liked Eto's playing, which was possessed by passion and intensity, rhetorical fire, and intelligence. I do not know, though, what impression, with its rather tight sound and occasional technical inelegancies, it would have made in the framework of a more ordinary "accompaniment." Levine's work with the Aspen Festival Orchestra was in no sense ordinary, and it produced the special quality of the performance.

That was a matter both of technique and of imaginative understanding. The difficult texture was clear, with everything audible, and in proportion. One could say as much about most of the details of the orchestral context Erich Leinsdorf produced for Arthur Grumiaux with the Boston Symphony last season; however, where Levine's conducting went beyond that was in its realization of Berg's complex interplay of texture and forward motion. Except for Elliott Carter's Piano Concerto I do not know another concerto in which the marriage of solo and tutti is so involved and rugged, and one could say that on one level, Berg's concerto is "about" the emergence and submergence of themes, lines, colors, and rhythms, from and within one another. This, Levine realized unprecedentedly well, both in what he accomplished within the orchestra and with the orchestra in relation to the soloist.

Because the participants felt the work so strongly and because the letter was made so clear, the spirit became manifest as never before in my experience. I know what the quotations of folk song are about, and the descent in blessing of the Bach chorale and its apotheosis, but now, with the particular qualities of timing and lighting in this performance, I genuinely and spontaneously felt and believed it. And what a beautiful human and musical document it is, so angry, so loving, so accepting finally, so rich and great.

Levine's Bach performance was a wonderful pleasure, too. The first movement took a few pages to settle into its right tempo, having started a bit slow, but the pacing was remarkably convincing within a rather broad conception. There was rhythm, phrased basses (when did you last hear that in a Bach concert?), and a splendid sense of moving by large paragraphs. In the Adagio, Levine spun the long, embellished melody like Fonteyn defining the line of the Rose Adagio [in Tchaikovsky's *Sleeping Beauty*], lyrical and of amazing tensile strength, and a marvelous product of musical and instrumental skill.

In Levine's conducting of Mozart's *The Abduction from the Seraglio* the night before, similar vitality and understanding were at work; however, not even that—and it was the finest Mozart opera conducting I had heard in years—was enough to keep me there looking at a dramatic and visual production that was the most unmusical, flitty, kitschy, and vulgar I have ever seen or that I can foresee. The singers, who are at Aspen for the summer on a special Corbett Foundation grant, included Lois Crane, a good Constanze, and Richard McKee, a possible Osmin, and others whom I am not anxious to hear or see again soon, indeed, in the case of the Blonde, ever.

A Saturday-afternoon chamber concert including Strauss's engaging Violin Sonata, played by Eudice Shapiro and Brooks Smith; Dvořák's Piano Quintet, played by the Juilliard Quartet with Beveridge Webster; and, between the two, the very great pleasure of Benita Valente's singing, also with Brooks Smith, a superb ensemble pianist, of eight songs from Hugo Wolf's *Italian Songbook*. Valente, replacing Jennie Tourel at very short notice, turns out to be a real Lieder singer. She sings words, but she never fails to sing music as well, and especially in Wolf's occasional dangerously cute songs, it was lovely to hear someone completely free of the operetta and nightclub ickiness of the great madam Whatshername.[16]

Wishing Him the Best—Leinsdorf's Farewell

August 31, 1969

At a quarter past four last Sunday at Tanglewood Beethoven's Ninth came to an end in a din of Turkish music. A bit under nine minutes later, the applause had pattered away into silence, and Erich Leinsdorf's seven-year tenure as music director of the Boston Symphony—his stewardship, as he liked to call it—was over.

Such a stewardship centers about three things: playing interesting music, playing it well, and maintaining the orchestra in the best possible condition as an instrument. The first of these things Leinsdorf did well. It is true that his ideas of how to combine and place pieces within a program were not always happy. Also, while there was some useful catching up on the 20th-century classics, Symphony Hall was not a place in which to find out what was new on the orchestral scene. Aside from those two considerable reservations, Leinsdorf's programs were imaginative and, on balance, among the most varied and interesting presented by a major orchestra. Looking back I am particularly grateful for Leinsdorf's interest in exploring lesser known pieces by popular composers, his frequent programming of Haydn (twenty-two works, only three of them London symphonies), and his inclusion of vocal works.

With the second point, quality of performance, we come to controversy. Leinsdorf came to Boston with a reputation as a highly competent, widely experienced, versatile, meticulous, but rarely exciting conductor. That he was so

[16] Steinberg may be referring here to the soprano Eileen Farrell (1920–2002), whose career spanned both classical and popular music, for which reason she sometimes drew the disdain of critics. In 1960, she released what was said to be the first successful crossover album, *I've Got a Right to Sing the Blues*.

different from the erratic, lazy, reckless, still sometimes fiery Munch, put him, for the moment at least, in a position of advantage. But much of the audience felt disillusioned as it began to get the impression that the defiler had been replaced by an undertaker. Leinsdorf's performances tended more and more to belie the public relations snow job that tried to build up the sober, conscientious workman into the great conductor that he was not.

Leinsdorf seems to me above all things an inhibited conductor. In our occasional personal contacts, I always found him to be a man of extraordinary resources of warmth, sympathy, and kindness. As for the musician, I remember performances in which what he achieved with technical skill, thorough preparation, knowledge, and taste, was infused with that human openness and generosity. Sometimes it took the challenge of music with complex housekeeping problems to bring this about; often it happened in response to an emotionally laden text in German. What would come out then was a performance of marvelous intensity and completeness.

Some of these performances really made a difference to life, and I shall not cease to be grateful for them: *Fidelio*, the Requiem and other choral works by Brahms, the last Bruckner Seventh, Elgar's *Falstaff*, the Mahler Sixth in Philharmonic Hall, Schoenberg's *Survivor from Warsaw* and Chamber Symphony, Schumann's *Scenes from "Faust,"* the Strauss *Daphne* finale, both Verdi Requiem performances at Tanglewood, *Lohengrin* and the December '67 *Tristan* Prelude—these stand out for me. And the memory of Leinsdorf at work that I treasure most is of something I heard by eavesdropping rather than legitimately, his breathtakingly beautiful and moving playing at the piano of the last song of Mahler's *Lied von der Erde* at a singer's audition when I happened to be in Symphony Hall.

Leinsdorf, though, rarely had access to the qualities that made such performances possible. His conducting at its most characteristic, seemed somehow choked, flattened out, tensionless. When there was a silence, the music just stopped, and the silence was usually too short at that. In a curious state of anxiety and impatience, he would hurry the last beat so that measures of 4/4 seemed to contain only fifteen 16th-notes. In combination with a certain Apollonian sheen he cultivated, the result was a lax rhythmic slither, and that, I believe, was the principal cause of the boredom his conducting so often generated.

As to the third point, the condition of the Boston Symphony as an instrument, Leinsdorf leaves an orchestra that is in many ways bored and demoralized, that no longer plays well without special provocation. As one can hear from its occasional beautiful response—to Leinsdorf himself sometimes; to Davis, Ančerl, Zinman, Ozawa, Boulez, Kubelik, etc.—it can be a great orchestra. Leinsdorf has been responsible for some first-rate appointments—Silverstein (concertmaster),

Fine (viola), Eskin (cello), Thorstenberg (English horn), Schmitz (tuba)—and there is no doubt that he did an impressive job at helping the orchestra recover from the technical slump into which it had fallen toward the end of Munch's tenure. Intonation is probably Leinsdorf's biggest weakness technically, and it shows in the Symphony's playing; since good pitch is said to be practically an obsession with his successor, William Steinberg, we can presumably look forward to substantial improvement in that department.

The question of orchestral standards brings us to the reasons for Leinsdorf's resignation. That full story might not come out for some time. Leinsdorf has said that he might write a book.[17] I hope he does, and I hope that it will be candid, because he is in a position to give us something exceedingly valuable and informative about the system of checks and balances at work in the running of an orchestra, the tensions between the musical interests that he was engaged as music director to represent, and the apparently weightier financial and humanitarian interests the trustees (with some encouragement from the union and the orchestra committee) chose to represent.

The eagerness to part company, I speculated at the time of the announcement of Leinsdorf's resignation,[18] must have been mutual. The trustees, I guessed, were disappointed in a conductor who failed to produce the expected enthusiasm with public and press and whose recordings did not sell well (the last point must have hurt the more because the marriage was practically arranged by RCA). The conductor for his part, I imagine to have been disappointed in a board that engaged him to achieve certain musical results but deprived him of the power to do so. It may well be that one of his most notable accomplishments was his dramatization, by means of his resignation, of the impossibility, or at least the insanely taxing difficulty, of the human and artistic juggling act expected of the music director of a major orchestra.

In all, the seven years, 1962–69, are not likely to be remembered as the most glorious in the Boston Symphony's history; neither, I suppose, will Erich Leinsdorf think of them as the happiest of his career. I imagine his thinking of last Sunday afternoon as an escape. He is a restless man, though, and I should not be surprised if in a few years we hear that he has had it with living out of suitcases and that he has occupied a permanent headquarters again. His mission now is to rescue the musician in him, to let the musician function without the drain that goes with being a handcuffed administrator as well. In that, in everything else, and with gratitude for the beautiful and enlightening moments he gave us, we wish him the best.

[17] There were ultimately three books: *Cadenza: A Musical Career* (Houghton Mifflin, 1976), *The Composer's Advocate: A Radical Orthodoxy for Musicians* (Yale University Press, 1981), and the posthumously published *Erich Leinsdorf on Music* (Amadeus Press, 1997).

[18] See articles of November 19 and December 11, 1967.

Britten Knows His "Repeats"

September 7, 1969

For English Decca (London) to record Benjamin Britten's work with himself as conductor or pianist is surely useful. I have often wished, though, that more of Britten's performances of other people's music might be recorded.

The reluctance seems to be Britten's more than Decca's; at any rate, the recordings of songs with Peter Pears have been all too few, though they have included the two great Schubert cycles, and records by Britten of instrumental music have been rarer still. One issued here recently by London of Mozart's Symphony No. 40 in G minor and of the *Serenata notturna*, K.239, is the first record of Britten conducting something other than Britten to appear in America, and I recall nothing even from the English catalogue other than a couple of concert performances from the '50s of Haydn's Symphony No. 55 and Mozart's A major Concerto, K.414. I very much hope that someday we may get a Mahler Fourth, of which I vividly remember a marvelously revealing broadcast performance with the London Symphony about 1961.[19]

At any rate, Britten's record, with the English Chamber Orchestra, of the G minor Symphony is an exciting enrichment of the catalogue. The most obvious special feature of the performance is that Britten takes the usually omitted repeats of the developments and recapitulations in the first, second, and fourth movements. It is hardly enough to point out that this makes the symphony unusually long (it plays about thirty-eight minutes). The redistribution of the weight assigned to statement and development, to tension and release, has, in this interpretation of Britten's, an extraordinary effect.

Few performers really seem to know what a repeat is for and what to do about it. Some use the second traversal merely to do something fussy and essentially pointless; far more seem unaware altogether of the principle that a repeat must always be a continuation and never just a repeat, and they give us something like a tape loop, as nearly perfect a replica as possible of the first go-around.

The most striking characteristic of Britten's performance of the G minor altogether is its continuously developing nature. When he plays a recapitulation, he does not slacken because "we've been here before"; rather, he emphasizes the differences between this view of the material as opposed to the previous. The recapitulations are themselves interestingly "developed." And that interest is

[19] Britten led the London Symphony Orchestra, with soloist Joan Carlyle, in a performance broadcast from Oxford Church, Suffolk, on July 6, 1961—a performance released on a BBC Music CD in 1999.

raised to a still higher power by his knowing use of the optional, unconventional second repeat. On this record, the first-movement recapitulation is particularly striking, and in the Andante, even if there were nothing else, it would be worth having the second repeat just to hear how Britten begins it.

Generally, I was especially pleased by the good tempi (for a change, properly quick in the first movement), by the sense of character, by the beautifully gauged lead-backs, by the extremely texture-conscious conducting, and by the exemplary clarity of the polyphony in the minuet and in the magnificently built development section of the finale. I found, as well, a couple of details that are probably more convincing once in concert than repeatedly on record, especially the minuet's final ritard and the excessive Marlboro swells on the dotted half-notes in that movement. The performance of the charming serenade is very good in a rather emphatic style.

Not Enough New—What Symphony Lacks

September 28, 1969

There are some fresh things I am glad to see on the Boston Symphony's programs for the 1969–70 season: Haydn's symphonies 55 and 98 (the former new to the BSO, the latter not as rare as all that, but still too rare), Elgar's two symphonies and his Cello Concerto, *Three Places in New England* by Ives (not played at the BSO since 1948), at last Berg's *Altenberg* Songs and a piece of recent Stravinsky, the *Huxley* Variations, Tōru Takemitsu's *November Steps* No. 1, the Liszt *Faust-Symphony*, Webern's Five Pieces, Op. 10 (played last season, but rare enough for their quick reappearance to be very much justified), Franco Donatoni's *Puppenspiel* No. 2, the Second Symphony by Michael Tippett, the Reger *Mozart* Variations, *Paris* by Delius, Three Pieces by Seymour Shifrin, and something as yet unspecified by Gunther Schuller that I hope might turn out to be the interesting *Triplum*.

It is not really enough, though. Above all, I am bothered by the Boston Symphony's continued timidity about offering its audiences some notion of the contemporary, that is, with-the-times music. Yes, I am grateful for the *Huxley* Variations, for the Donatoni, and so forth, but all that is going to amount to at most is an hour's music for the whole season. On paper, the programs contain several names of 20th-century composers, but to play *Petrushka*, the concert excerpts from *Wozzeck*, Bartók's Music for Strings, Percussion, and Celesta or his Second Piano Concerto, and Webern's Six Pieces, Op. 6, is like playing the Schubert Ninth and *Till Eulenspiegel*. Those are acknowledged, established, and much played classics.

On another plane of compositional achievement, the appearance of works by composers like Robert Starer, Benjamin Lees, Nikolai Lopatnikoff, Ernst Toch, and Carl Orff is tokenism. Samuel Barber and William Walton are composers who have written interesting music of an exceedingly conservative stamp, but *Die Natali* and *Belshazzar's Feast* do not represent them at their best.

Meanwhile it would be a responsible and appropriate action for the Boston Symphony to let its audiences know about the orchestral music of, for example, Milton Babbitt, Luciano Berio, Pierre Boulez, Roberto Gerhard, Alexander Goehr, Andrew Imbrie, Ingvar Lidholm, György Ligeti, Donald Martino, Salvatore Martirano, Luigi Nono, Krzysztof Penderecki, Nikos Skalkottas, Karlheinz Stockhausen, Iannis Xenakis, to name just a few, all key figures in recent music or highly regarded in the profession, whose music never has been played by the orchestra.

I point out, too, that the Boston Symphony has not played Berg's Chamber Concerto nor even the Seven Early Songs; that it has played Britten's *Spring Symphony* only at Tanglewood, twenty years ago at that, and other fine works of his, including *Illuminations*, the Serenade, and the Nocturne, not at all; that Dallapiccola has been scandalously neglected, with *Canti di prigionia* and *Canti di liberazione* particularly due for a hearing (a more urgent priority, I should think, than yet another Boston performance of *Carmina burana*); that the Second, Fourth, and Fifth symphonies of Bohuslav Martinů have not been played; the Nielsen Fourth has not been done; that the only representative work of Petrassi's on a Boston Symphony program was the Concerto for Orchestra No. 5, fourteen years ago; that Carl Ruggles, one of the most individual figures in American music, has had only one performance of *Portals* in 1965, and one of *Sun-Treader* in 1966, but not in Boston; that there are important pieces by Schoenberg yet unplayed at these concerts, including *Erwartung*, the Songs, Op. 22, *Kol Nidre*, *Ode to Napoleon*, the *Genesis* Prelude, the Cello Concerto after Monn, and the Concerto Grosso after Handel, and, for that matter, that *Pelleas und Melisande* has not been played by the orchestra since 1934; that the Symphony has played no major work by Roger Sessions since 1957 (and, parenthetically that the performance of the Third Symphony then was butchery); that Stravinsky's *Flood*, Movements, *Sermon, Narrative, and Prayer*, and *Threni*, have not been heard; that until *Déserts* was done last season, not a note of Varèse had been played; that Webern's Five Pieces for Strings, Op. 5, his Symphony, his cantatas, and even his luminous transcription of Bach's six-voice Ricercare from *The Musical Offering*, have not yet appeared on Boston Symphony programs.

Now, I am aware that much of the Boston Symphony's subscription audience would be happy to continue not to know most of that music. Some of the music probably would not please; much of it, I am certain, would find an interested audience. I know that much of that music is difficult, therefore time-consuming, therefore expensive to prepare.

The fact is, though, that the Symphony has to all intents a monopoly in Boston on professional performance of music for large orchestra. With monopoly goes responsibility (as with the telephone company). There are things that the Boston Symphony ought to be doing and that it is not doing. My catalogue of complaints about repertory is specific, but it points to where the broader problems lie. But even with all of the economic miseries and with all of the frictional drag produced by the subscription audience as it is now constituted, these problems are not insoluble, though their solution will want a willingness to question some hitherto basic assumptions about symphony orchestras and how they are run. In the next Sunday column, I should like to explore the matter further.[20]

The Ladies Left Too Soon—Elgar Needs More Patience

October 4, 1969

In 1911, as Sir Edward Elgar left the platform of Queen's Hall in London where he had just conducted the premiere of his Second Symphony, he muttered to Henry J. Wood: "They don't like it, Henry, they don't like it."

The ladies[21] in Symphony Hall yesterday afternoon didn't like it much either, walking out in droves between movements, and, when it was over, staying for hardly more than a minimal show of politeness. Perhaps it is not a piece that speaks easily to an uninitiated and not altogether involved audience, but it is, I am certain, one deeply informed by human and musical greatness. It is also hard to imagine a performance of it more strongly conceived and more beautifully executed than that given yesterday by William Steinberg and the Boston Symphony.

Elgar's music is of disturbing emotional depth and complexity, and its subject often is pain. The most nearly comparable figure among his contemporaries is Mahler, but Elgar, lacking Mahler's relish for agony in public, masks his *Weltschmerz* and allows his music to be outspoken and explicit only in its moments of triumph and of nobility. Those seem to have become almost alien quantities to us today, and their representation in music so patently sincere, not completely purged of doubt, is no easy thing to face.

[20] See article of October 5, 1969.

[21] "Ladies" refers to the prominent, Boston-society women in the Friday-afternoon audience whose tickets were passed down to family members for generations from the time of the BSO's founding.

The mixture of optimism and melancholy is an altogether personal quality of Elgar's, and his music now moves me more deeply than any of its time. The grandly laid out Second Symphony travels a strange path, beginning exuberantly and in splendor, subsiding in hard-won serenity with the cascading opening music heard now as though distantly and in a luminous mist.

Yes, it comes from the Brahms Third, and Elgar is often rich with echoes of Brahms and Wagner, too. But his music, including the sunset close of the Second Symphony, is some of the most profoundly original ever composed, with glowing sonorities, rugged melodic shapes, and a harmonic gait all its own, immediately and uniquely recognizable as Elgar's.

The Larghetto extraordinarily combines public elegy and private: it mourns Edward VII, to whose memory the symphony is dedicated, but we know, too, that the genesis of its theme was Elgar's response years earlier to the death of a close friend. Again, we know other such dark processions, the *Eroica* and, for that matter, the first movement of Elgar's own First Symphony, but none speaking of quite the same thing so well shaped.

There is a scherzo, coruscating virtuoso music, but weird, even a touch nightmarish. After that, the finale, so unlike other finales even down to being in 3/4 time (Brahms's Fourth, Tchaikovsky's Sixth, but how few others!), yet so perfect a summation of and destination for the whole work.

The performance was very nearly beyond praise. Steinberg was superbly responsive to the flexibility of pace that is built into the symphony, to the variety and interaction of its mood, to its inherent nobility of style. With just the fewest reservations about some of the brass playing, the orchestra's work was both refined and splendid. It really sounded like the Boston Symphony.

Before the intermission, Steinberg conducted a Concerto for Violin, Cello, and Orchestra by the Vienna-born American composer Robert Starer, written in 1967 and first performed under Steinberg in Pittsburgh last October. The playing Friday, with Joseph Silverstein and Jules Eskin as soloists, was clear and at times pleasingly brilliant.

Reforming the BSO

October 5, 1969

Last week in this space I wrote that there was a lot of music that ought to be, but was not, in fact, appearing on the programs of the Boston Symphony.[22] The problem is by no means local only. With few exceptions, music directors, boards,

[22] See article of September 28, 1969.

and managers are unimaginative about programs. I mean something larger than specific questions about, for example, why it took the Boston Symphony until 1969 to get around to playing anything by Varèse, or why the last performance by the orchestra in Boston of Mozart's great C major Piano Concerto, K.503, took place in 1883.

Having a hundred or so instrumentalists under contract opens possibilities that have not been explored enough. To begin with, most of the music in what has come to be thought of as orchestral repertory from the early 18th century to the present does not need that many players. Tuba and second harp, for instance, have relatively little to do; half the music in a normal season does not need all four players the orchestra has available for each woodwind; a considerable part of the working repertory goes better with fewer than all sixty-some strings.

While Varèse's *Déserts* was rehearsed last season, more than eighty players had nothing to do. *Déserts* eats up all available percussion and a high proportion of brass; even so, and without even thinking of strings only, there is a large body of available repertory from the 18th, 19th, and 20th centuries that might have been rehearsed at the time.

Rehearsed by whom? By the assistant conductor, who in most orchestras is badly under-used. He is an understudy, an extra pair of ears at rehearsal, a good keyboard man perhaps, and useful in special tasks like the preparation of singers. He gets few opportunities for public performance, though, and some of these young men are very much worth hearing: Henry Lewis and Lawrence Foster, who used to be with the Los Angeles Philharmonic, James Levine in Cleveland, Leonard Slatkin in St. Louis, Michael Tilson Thomas here in Boston, and, of course, everybody knows the story of Artur Rodzinski's assistant at the New York Philharmonic twenty-six years ago, a chap called Bernstein.

The Boston Symphony's new assistant conductor is specifically, though not exclusively, experienced with and equipped to deal with difficult contemporary music. William Steinberg, the music director, is not thus equipped, and, going by the evidence of what he has put on his programs for Boston and what he has conducted in Pittsburgh and New York, his taste in 20th-century music is conservative. It is to be assumed that he would agree that there is music that should appear on programs, though he himself does not feel sympathy for it and is not willing, perhaps not able, to conduct it.

George Szell in Cleveland, for instance, has made a point of inviting guest conductors who are strong in music he feels to be outside his own territory. Pierre Boulez has indicated that he will do the same thing when he takes over the New York Philharmonic. Assistant and associate conductors sometimes have been able to do the same thing: Richard Burgin for years earned the gratitude of the Boston musical public through his performances of repertory that did not engage the interest of Koussevitzky and Munch.

This, I suggest, can be stepped up. The assistant conductor need not be limited to the one program of the year that is all his own (or two, or whatever the number may be), but he could on, say, half a dozen occasions during a season appear with a single piece, or a couple, on a concert most of which is conducted by someone else. The idea would be to pick pieces for less than full orchestra, so that two or more works could be rehearsed simultaneously. Yes, why not more than two, maybe a Haydn symphony, the Varèse *Octandre*, and the Third *Brandenburg* Concerto with the concertmaster in charge?

This leads to the idea of having more than one assistant conductor, and that makes sense, too. The combination of music director and principal conductor who is with his own orchestra during the largest part of a season is disappearing. The Boston Symphony board split with Erich Leinsdorf over that very issue, but it went on to engage a music director who is available to Boston for only twelve weeks out of the twenty-four of the main subscription series. That is a proportion that I would guess will be normal, if not generous, from here on.

Orchestras and audiences need the stimulation of guest conductors, and we neither shall nor should be without them. More, however, of a season's work could be in the hands of assistants and associates, and an orchestra like the Boston Symphony might well have two such people around.

Most of my specific references to repertory today and last week have been to contemporary music because that is the area in which reform of program policy is most urgently needed, but, *mutatis mutandis*, similar changes are in order in older repertory as well. An enormous amount of loosening up can be done. There could be more exploration in a chamber-musical direction. If a chorus has been engaged to sing the Bruckner Te Deum or the Stravinsky *Symphony of Psalms*, the program might aptly add some *a cappella* motets of Lassus or Brahms. A program that already introduces electronic sounds in a "legitimate" orchestral concert—Varèse's *Déserts* can serve as an example again—could be extended to include a purely electronic work like Babbitt's Ensembles for Synthesizer.

I hope these examples show that what I suggest is not a hodge-podge, but a broadening of the perspective in which we now view what we think of as orchestral music—more exactly, the music whose appearance on programs by orchestras we regard as normal—by the inclusion of works that will extend our pleasure and our experience as listeners, freshen our perceptions, and even—who knows?—shed new light on the Beethoven and Brahms symphonies and concertos that we are assuredly going to continue to love.

Thomas in Dazzling BSO Debut

October 11, 1969

Michael Tilson Thomas, now 24 and the Boston Symphony's assistant conductor, made his debut with the orchestra Friday afternoon.

Resisting the temptation to prophesy, let me say simply that right now he is one of the ablest and most interesting conductors in the profession. He knows how the pieces go, he appears to handle the orchestra with easy authority, and he is full of life. He has the ancillary advantages of interesting good looks and of just a touch of theatricality, but he plays on those stops only between numbers.

While conducting, he is all business, and he is, in fact, a pleasant conductor to watch, not only because his movements are in themselves arresting and even beautiful, but particularly because they are unfailingly relevant to the musical result. What came of all this Friday was one of the liveliest and finest concerts I have heard at the Boston Symphony, and it was so, to begin with, because of the music Thomas had chosen.

The program a performer puts together is the first statement he makes, and one of the most revealing he makes at any time about himself as a musician. Thomas made his statement with Haydn's Symphony No. 98 in B-flat, *Three Places in New England* by Ives, with the first performance here of Stravinsky's Variations (*Aldous Huxley in memoriam*), and Debussy's *La Mer*. The Debussy, though brilliant, is risky and anything other than sure-fire, and the program altogether was far from the customary debut bid for facile success.

Good Haydn conductors are rare, but Thomas is one. The Symphony No. 98 is, even among the marvelous, one of the most marvelous: dramatic, richly lyric in the farewell-to-Mozart Adagio, witty, and, in the finale, crazily funny with all those charmingly willful violin solos. I found the first Allegro just a little round, but otherwise the performance was incisive, both quick-witted and patient, varied and multi-faceted though always completely natural, and it was one with tremendous relish for the fun in the piece as well as feeling for its depths. The one really unsolved problem was the harpsichord, which was delightfully effective in the last movement, but not even audible (to say nothing of telling) elsewhere.

Three Places in New England is a beautiful achievement in musical poetry and, I would add, as a declaration of love to America and this corner of it. Ives's tragic interpretation of the solemn and commanding "'St. Gaudens' in Boston Common" is the grandest in scope, the most elaborately inventive, the most profoundly felt of the three movements, but "The Housatonic at Stockbridge" is a singularly touching landscape with figures and a piece of extraordinary sensuous beauty. Between the two, for the depiction of a Fourth of July picnic at "Putnam's

Camp," Ives made one of his breeziest, infectiously captivating "Pop Pourris" (to borrow a phrase from David Del Tredici). The performance was superb.[23]

Stravinsky's dozen Variations, written in 1964, are very different stuff. Everything is sharp-edged, precise, economical, multi-functional, lucidly audible. The music sometimes proceeds in the sparest imaginable textures, but three times, once with twelve violins, once with ten violas and two basses, and last with eleven woodwinds and a horn, it goes into time-suspending shocks of the densest polyphony anywhere in Stravinsky's music.

Not even Webern made five minutes of music so varied. Of the writing for orchestra, one might say what a London reviewer wrote about Haydn's Symphony 170 years ago, that "every instrument is respected by his Muse, for he gives to each his due proportion of efficacy." It is new and fresh music, totally characteristic of Stravinsky, an object of cold and fascinating beauty. The performance was first-rate on the conductor's part and on the players', and Thomas took advantage of the extreme brevity of the piece to repeat it at once to the benefit, I am sure, of all.

Meaning, I would guess, to build toward the last movement, Thomas held back rather drastically in the first of *La Mer*, and let it go slack in the process. In the second movement, a more characteristic plasticity and flexibility returned, and the finale went brilliantly, with an exciting pictorial suggestiveness. The orchestra's playing was near to ideal for the dazzling and fine score, and indeed it had been at an extraordinary high level all afternoon.

The concert pleased, and at its end there was vigorous cheering. "We're lucky," said one of the customers as she left the hall. I think so.

Public Concert Defended—More Than Meets Ear

October 26, 1969

> *"If God had wanted people to go to concerts, He would have given them tickets."*
>
> (Sign backstage at Symphony Hall)

A few weeks ago I was at a concert at which Beethoven's third *Leonore* Overture was played. As the cellos and basses climbed slowly in *pianissimo* from G to A to B, at last to release us from the slow music of the introduction into the Allegro,

[23] Ives's *Three Places in New England* was recorded by Michael Tilson Thomas with the BSO for Deutsche Grammophon on January 26, 1970—his first recording as conductor with the BSO, paired in its original LP release with Carl Ruggles's *Sun-treader*, which was recorded that March.

the woman in front of me turned to her neighbor and asked, "Didja getcha tickets for Isaac Stoin yet?"

She is, I suppose, an argument against the public concert as an institution. One hears many such arguments, some of them perhaps trivial, some only variously applicable, and some quite serious: the discomfort and overheating of concert halls, the inconveniences of getting to them, the expense (babysitters, parking lots, and so forth, beyond just the tickets), the noisiness and bad manners of audiences and the destructive atmosphere of indifference and boredom emanated by many of them, the dully repetitious programs.

Some record collectors might add that they feel confident of having a better performance already available at home than any they will get taking their chances at a concert (an advantage to be added to those of comfortable clothes, a glass of wine, and your own thermostat). A relatively recent addition to the catalogue of dissatisfactions is the feeling that a concert is a stuffy ritual more apt to erect walls than to build bridges, and partly in response to that feeling, attempts have been made to move live performance of music into new surroundings.

That is all more or less true, though variously important to different people. There is, on the other hand, much to be said for concerts, and some of it is so essential that the disappearance of the public concert would be tragic. Perhaps the most obvious point is that a good performer's presence and personal projection can sharpen the listener's attention, perception, and involvement. It matters most with singers, whose art is so linked to their physical personae, but it can be as true of instrumentalists, dramatic and outgoing ones like Rubinstein and Rostropovich, or those as severe in manner as Brendel and Leonhardt.

As a completely personal footnote let me add that, in spite of the silly things to be seen at times, and even though I sometimes prefer to read a score, in general I like to watch, to look as well as listen. Not quite unlike reading a score, it is a way of taking the information through an additional sense, which makes the experience somehow more absorbing, but there is also something joyful and exciting about sharing, by watching, a performer's concentration and exercise of skill.

Then, music has constant need to renew itself in performance. To deny the benefits of recordings would be foolish, but so would not recognizing their danger. That danger is in the identification of a work with a particular performance of it—aggravated by record critics and their throwing about of the word "definitive"—and no performance is so great that such an identification is anything other than a distortion (by narrowing) of one's understanding of the work and an impoverishment for whoever has come to believe in that identity. That the performance is beautiful makes no difference: the person who has come to think of Schnabel's recording as really being Schubert's B-flat Sonata and not just one man's realization of his idea of it on a particular day in 1939 has lost something terribly important about the Sonata.

To those points I would add one that is perhaps more subjective. Not all the music we hear at concerts was meant for that sort of public performance: some of it has done well transplanted into the concert hall, and some of it perhaps not. There is, however, also music that makes its proper impression, or at least a completely convincing one, only in public. Virtuoso music, for example, wants to be seen as well as heard, and the excitement in its successful performance wants to be shared. That is, I think, as true of the stuff with class (Bach, Chopin, Debussy, etc.) as of that which is just fun (Paganini, Sarasate, Scharwenka, and so forth).

There is a really important distinction between public and private rhetoric. Queen Victoria used to complain that Gladstone, four times her prime minister, used to address her as though she were at a public meeting, and sometimes when I listen to records I have to think about her. The last minutes of the Beethoven Fifth or the Mahler Second are hair-raising in concert, but I do not think that in my own living room. It is embarrassing and silly. The kind of statement that is made and the manner of making it demand plenty of physical space and a large audience, and there is a considerable body of music we shall fully experience only in concert. By the way, playing the Beethoven Fifth at home as a piano duet is quite another matter, and for reasons that I imagine are obvious.

To sum up, there are many ways in which public concerts can be made livelier. I have discussed some of these ways in recent articles here[24] and I intend soon to write about the others.

Music asks for silence in which to listen to it (with an exception perhaps to be made for some of that low-density dinner music—Vivaldi-by-the-yard, Mozart cassations, etc.—that has strayed into the concert hall by mistake), it wants good performance and a sympathetic, interested audience. These conditions are obtainable, in Symphony Hall as well as at the Fillmore East.

It seems to be too easy to put the blame in the wrong place. You sit in Symphony Hall on a Friday afternoon with a deadly performance of a Brahms symphony going on, and you ask yourself what this has to do with what you know music is all about, and you decide that The Concert Is Dead. Of course, it is more strenuous and more troubling to consider that we are hungry for something other than traveling in ruts or that the orchestra needs a more interesting conductor. I have been in places just bursting with communication and relevance and nowness, and I have been bored out of my mind in them; I also have sat in Symphony Hall where everybody sits in chairs that are set out in straight lines, and I have been so rapt that I did not know where I was.

[24] See, for example, the articles of September 28 and October 5, 1969.

Ormandy Does Mantovani Job

October 27, 1969

The Philadelphia Orchestra gave a concert in Symphony Hall Friday evening, its first since March 1962. It was conducted by Eugene Ormandy, accompanied by someone's hearing aid tuned to D *in altissimo*, and the program consisted of Piston's Toccata for Orchestra, Hindemith's *Mathis der Maler* Symphony, and Mahler's Symphony No. 1.

Ormandy does the Mahler with the "Blumine" movement that was dropped by the composer for his first performances in 1896, after which it was forgotten until its recent rediscovery and revival by Britten in England (1967) and by Frank Brieff at New Haven a year later.

"Blumine," marked "Andante Allegretto"—a peculiarity in itself in as much as the other directions about tempo and expression are in German—is a quiet, lyric piece that belongs between the first movement and the scherzo. Its title refers to a book by the German Romantic author Jean Paul Richter, the source as well of the symphony's name of "*Titan*" (also withdrawn by Mahler), and it is a word coined in the early 19th century and roughly translatable as "flora."

No one is sure of the specific reasons that prompted Mahler to drop "Blumine," but now that we have it back, the case for restoring it to the First Symphony is strong. It is, to begin with, a lovely movement, with a delicate sentimentality of the sort we find in the minuet of the Third Symphony (another flower piece) and in the posthorn interludes in the same work.

The Philadelphia Orchestra is an amazing ensemble machine, although I found most of the solo playing, excepting that on the trumpet, surprisingly flavorless. Ormandy, who has almost as few outright bad ideas about music as good ones, is an impressive master of orchestras: economically and efficiently, he can get an orchestra to do whatever he wants. It is too bad that he is not more varied in his desires and that he seems to think of orchestral playing as an activity independent from the interpretation of music.

His orchestra plays in tune, in rhythm, with splendid voicing, and with stunningly precise attacks and releases. You can hear the difference between *fortissimo* and *pianissimo*, but not often that between *piano* and *pianissimo*, and even when there is a considerable difference in decibel count, the distinction is fairly well blotted out because the intensity—mad—does not vary.

The concert was an imposing exhibition of professionalism of a sort, of one man's control of a hundred others. What Ormandy never got around to was using that skill to show how Piston's and Hindemith's and Mahler's pieces have characters and even sounds of their own. It was dazzling the way a Mantovani concert is, but it had awfully little to do with playing music, which is what I think orchestras are for.

Horowitz—Boring, Marvelous, and Exciting

October 28, 1969

When Horowitz finishes a piece they cheer; while he plays, they cough. The contrast is striking. How to interpret it? Quite a bit of his audience goes to see a legend and is perhaps not so interested in listening to Haydn sonatas and Chopin ballades. That is perhaps a partial explanation, but I would suggest another, which is that in much of the music he plays, Horowitz is, at the deepest level, boring.

The audience then is wowed by his extraordinary playing of the instrument and by the unobtrusive, well-mannered showmanship. It is moved to genuine affection of the kind few performers enjoy by the charm of the man; it is excited by the legend and by the sense of occasion; it withholds the greatest tribute within its gift—that of silence, of breathless, rapt attention.

When Horowitz has done with it, the music does not often make sense. His command of the instrument seems to be limitless, and I have not heard him play better than in the best parts of his Symphony Hall recital Sunday afternoon, with such power, swiftness, color, with such beauty and variety of sound. But he does seem to view pieces of music simply as occasions for him to do something amazing at the piano.

Some music, however, is not satisfied with that approach, and it will not survive having its own life ignored or subverted. Then a Horowitz performance is razzle-dazzle *in vacuo*, and it is not absorbing.

In the first half of his recital Sunday, he collided with Haydn (the late, two-movement C major Sonata) and Chopin (F minor Ballade, two mazurkas, B minor Scherzo), and with catastrophic results. It is true that in the C-sharp minor Mazurka from Opus 30, he used Chopin's notes to build up a sound structure which, even though crazily irrelevant to the one Chopin evidently had in mind, was entrancing on its own.

But in the other pieces he produced spectacular sonorities, deployed in phrasings that were in alternation distractingly fussy or flattened out into veritable tours de force of non-articulation, informed by his passion for speed and by his taste for the cute and his tendency to become prissy when he evidently meant to be refined, and adding up to a series of musical statements that often as not were simply incoherent.

When the music is right, the result is marvelous, perhaps uniquely exciting. That happened after intermission, when Horowitz played eight Scriabin Etudes, covering ground from the early, romantic lovely C-sharp minor Study, Op. 3, to a pair from the "atonal" set of 1912, Opus 65. These are fascinating pieces, compositionally, pianistically, and (like Debussy's Études) in the interaction of both aspects.

Horowitz selected and grouped them cunningly, and played them spectacularly well. They require what he, and perhaps he alone, can do—where else has one heard anything like the quasi-trills in the F-sharp major Study, Op. 42, No. 3, or sonorous voicing like that in the C-sharp minor of the same opus? And they are not disturbed by his occasional interpretive vagaries.

Liszt's Thirteenth Hungarian Rhapsody is a good Horowitz piece, too, if not quite as good as the Scriabin. His playing of it was a bit suave, and lacking in fantasy and bite in the declamatory slow section, but he delivered the bravura passages with a touch of black magic that Liszt's own playing must have had.

There was one fantastic run that made a man across the aisle from me laugh aloud in sheer joy at the thing: you find that reaction to dancers sometimes but among those who play musical instruments Horowitz is probably alone in being able to evoke it.

Pears, Britten—A Voyage of Discovery

October 29, 1969

Ripeness is all, Shakespeare tells us. Yes, and freshness, too. When you are face to face with the greatest art, you have come to where ripeness and freshness meet. The singing and playing that Peter Pears and Benjamin Britten did last night in Jordan Hall was an occasion for one of those confrontations.

A great performance is one that catches the excitement of hearing something for the first time. To that excitement, that newness, is added a sovereignty that comes from long, hard-won possession. Such a performance speaks with the urgency of utterance never before articulated in that form, but at the same time it partakes of an authority that tells us, "This is how it really goes."

Pears and Britten must have given Schumann's *Dichterliebe* dozens of times, and unless they had, no performers could explore it so deeply and in so many dimensions—verbal, linear, textural, as a series of marvelously characterized moments from the birth of a love affair to its end, as magically compelling poetic and musical continuity.

Yet the performance in Jordan Hall was a voyage of discovery, with an intensity, pathos, tenderness, and humor that you cannot will in advance, with a tensile strength of line that was maintained across the most extraordinary risks born of the boldly expansive style in which this interpretation was cast, with that uncanny rightness of timing that is the sine qua non of great performances.

One could cite detail after detail—the suspense built with just a few chords and silences in the introduction of Haydn's "She never told her love," the concentration with which the narrative of Britten's "The Choirmaster's Burial" or "At the Railway Station, Upway" was projected, the beautiful simplicity of line and the delicacy of "The Sally Gardens" and "Six Dukes Went a-Fishing."

There was rare natural and technical resource, perfection of ensemble (the living kind, not the sort that sounds rehearsed to death), an enormous imaginative range, musicianship and taste on the highest possible level, even showmanship of the most knowing sort.

Hearing *Dichterliebe* and Britten's own beautiful Hardy cycle, *Winter Words*, was an overwhelming experience of an order we shall not often again have in the concert room. And this audience knew.

Giulini and BSO With Brahms More Like Borge

November 8, 1969

If Danny Kaye or Victor Borge were to conduct a performance of the Brahms Fourth just like the one Carlo Maria Giulini conducted Friday afternoon in Symphony Hall, one so raging and overwrought, one with its upbeats so stretched, with such crazed dislocation of tempo and accompanied by a similar visual production with such prodigality in expressions of tragic suffering and deep knee-bends, the audience would have been in stitches.[25]

In the solemn context of a Friday-afternoon Boston Symphony concert, the audience instead took it seriously.

Perhaps Giulini's tempest-tossed performance can be read as proceeding from a man of original and humorous spirit, loathing Brahms and the institution of the symphony concert, and inspired to deliver a devastating put-on in the most elegant deadpan style. I fear, though, that what actually happened is less interesting. The performance, instead of being the first ever fully to explore the comic possibilities of the Brahms Fourth, proceeded from nothing more uncommon than opportunism and meretricious vulgarity.

[25] The repercussions of this notably infamous review are discussed in the introduction to this book. As to the Brahms performance itself, an audio CD generously provided by BSO Archives reveals that Giulini's approach at this concert to the Brahms Fourth, a "signature piece" of his, was consistent—if by no means as polished—with the interpretation preserved in his Chicago Symphony recording made for EMI just three weeks earlier, on October 15, 1969.

To warm up for wringing Brahms's withers, Giulini conducted Haydn's *Surprise* Symphony and a suite from Alfredo Casella's Pirandello ballet, *La Giara*. The Haydn performance was rather too harmless, very legato and under-articulated and all but a couple of bars kept between *mezzo piano* and *mezzo forte*; if he did not bring the symphony to life as Michael Tilson Thomas did with No. 98 weeks ago,[26] he did not suffocate it either (the way William Steinberg suffocated No. 55 in the second week of the season). Still, he reduced it to an amiable, pretty piece of no special character and no genius, and it really seemed rather wasted on him.

Casella, who died in 1947 at 63, was a revered father figure to many Italian musicians now themselves in their 60s. He was concerned with liberating Italian music from the confines of the opera house, one who spoke for the new in the face of the conservatism of men like Pizzetti (exhumed by Giulini last week) and Respighi (never given a decent burial), a conductor whose career included three seasons of running the Boston Pops just before Fiedler, a pianist, a Romantically extravagant and rather irresponsible editor of piano classics like Mozart and Beethoven sonatas.

He was, of course, a composer as well, one with discipline, craft, and experience, but with little spontaneous gift. His pieces sound stillborn, and the best to be said about *La Giara*, written in 1924, is that it at least offers a gaily and brightly surfaced music aesthetic. It goes rather like Tchaikovsky's *Capriccio italien*, but with wrong notes to make it sound modern. Giulini gave it a bouncy, thoroughly effective performance, and an offstage tenor solo—a good tune with an overdone *Firestone Hour* sort of accompaniment—was attractively sung by Robert Johnson.

The orchestral playing was pleasantly relaxed and warm in the first two movements of the Haydn, but relaxed to the point of sloppiness in the other two; snappy in the Casella; tending toward the wild in the Brahms and madly out of tune. In the *danse sacrale* of the Brahms, Mrs. Dwyer's flute solo was a welcome oasis of musical sanity and technical competence.

Philharmonic Dilemma—New Hall Still Wanting

November 9, 1969

NEW YORK—Along with a new Nixon, we seem to get a new Philharmonic Hall every season. The newest version, unveiled at the beginning of the present concert season, is not up to much either.

[26] See review of October 11, 1969.

Philharmonic Hall was a spectacular acoustical disaster when it was opened in 1962 as the first functioning part of Lincoln Center. It was, moreover, made to appear even worse than it was because Leo Beranek, the principal acoustician involved, had been imprudent enough to publish a book in advance that described how glorious the acoustics were going to be. The Cambridge-based firm of Bolt Beranek & Newman was fired from the job, and in 1965 Heinrich Keilholz, a German acoustician recommended by George Szell, and since built up in the press as a miracle worker, was brought in to salvage what he could.

Keilholz has made one substantial improvement. It used to be that one sat in the hall feeling terribly remote from whatever was going on. The music sounded small and the stage looked very far away. Both acoustically and visually the communication is better now. You feel that you are in the same room as the performance and that it makes a difference. The music has physical impact now, and in the new color scheme, which provides a light background, the musicians on stage even look bigger and closer.

While the sound is louder, it remains harsh, short on bass response, and generally unbeautiful. If the New York Philharmonic finds the courage and the money for still another renovation, perhaps the bass can be beefed up. It would be an effort worth making because that bit of difference could turn the hall at least into a good one, if not the great one that the *New York Times* has told its readers it is now, nor one that presents "the music of the Orchestra in its full beauty" that Amyas Ames, president of the New York Philharmonic, has assured its subscribers they have. Ames has said, "The new Philharmonic Hall is now finished," and it seems then that the Philharmonic would like to regard the 1969 edition of the hall as final.[27]

There is a new look as well, and it is undistinguished. The predominant tone is that of the natural finish of the acacia walls, set off by seat fabric in a hard and bright red. The acacia in so huge an expanse seems somehow falsely homey, and the recessed crystal bowls that now house the lighting fixtures in the new solid ceiling—there is no longer a trace of the BB&N "clouds" of course—are tacky in the worst way, on a par with the dimestore costume jewelry fixtures that disfigure the State Theater across the Plaza.

The New York Philharmonic is still collecting the commissions it gave for its 125th anniversary year (the present season being the orchestra's 128th). Elliott Carter's Concerto for Orchestra is due to have its first performance in February, and a piece by Karlheinz Stockhausen is not listed in the 1969–70 programs at all. The latest work actually to arrive was Leon Kirchner's Music for Orchestra, finished cliffhanger style October 7 in time for its first performance one day

[27] Needless to say, it was not.

later; Kirchner conducted, and the performance I heard was the fourth, given Monday, October 20.

Music for Orchestra is a work of good intentions that remains an intention. As I read the piece itself, as I read Kirchner's program note for it and other recent statements of his about music (for instance his comments on the sleeve of the Columbia record of his attractive Quartet No. 3), he wanted to write something direct, expressive, not calculated-sounding. The best of Kirchner's music has been compelling in just that way, but Music for Orchestra on one hearing seemed tired, unconvincing, its rhythmic life slack, its colors ordinary, its one aleatory excursion apparently so tightly controlled that it did not generate any excitement either.

It had success with the audience—more than most new pieces played at the Philharmonic, if by no means as much as Luciano Berio's *Sinfonia* in October of last year—and the story now is that the orchestra will include it in its tour repertory.

The first weeks of the current season, including the rest of the concert at which Kirchner conducted his Music for Orchestra, were done by Seiji Ozawa. I heard relatively little of his work, a surprisingly ponderous performance of Mozart's little Symphony No. 32 in G, and, at a concert later that week (October 23), György Ligeti's *Atmosphères* and Scriabin's *Prometheus*, the latter with Paul Jacobs as the fine piano soloist.

When Bernstein performed the Ligeti at the Philharmonic six years ago, people, psychologically cued by Bernstein's verbal introduction of it and presumably unaware that there was a 55-year-old piece by Schoenberg very much like it (the third of the Five Pieces for Orchestra, Op. 16), reacted as though it were something no end alarming and far out. Since then we have had *2001*, every schoolboy knows *Atmosphères*, and we can recognize it as a fastidiously composed, sonorously seductive, but by no means alarming piece. It was my first experience of hearing *Atmosphères* in the concert hall, and I was interested to discover that at the high-pitch climax about two-thirds through, the sound in the hall shatters just as it does on records—it is not just your inadequate speakers. Also, it is not a piece for blond acacia paneling at all.

Prometheus is meant to have lighting effects, and the next work in a tetralogy of symphonic poems, and which Scriabin did not live to compose, was to have added scent. Scriabin had planned the lighting scenario for *Prometheus*, and had devised a keyboard for the operation of the lights, its part written in conventional staff notation. At the premiere, which took place in Moscow in 1911, Koussevitzky conducting and with the composer at the piano, the "color organ" did not work, and the key to Scriabin's notation was subsequently lost.

Looking at the score of *Prometheus*, one can now infer little about what Scriabin wanted in light and colors beyond something about the rate of change, and a conductor who decides to try it with lights is pretty much on his own. The Philharmonic got Peter Wexler to fix up something. Wexler is a theater man, a kind of decorator with lights really, whereas what is wanted is someone who can compose with lights in a manner comparable to the way Scriabin composed with sounds. Much of what Wexler produced was pretty—I think the Bach toccata and the *Ave Maria* in Walt Disney's *Fantasia* are what I kept being reminded of—but it was also surprisingly crude technically, and in no clear or stimulating relationship with the music. I hope someone will try *Prometheus* with lights again, but this time the color play only made it difficult to attend to Scriabin's excited, brilliant, and probably most successful large-scale score.

Pablo Casals—"What a Musician"

November 9, 1969

SAN JUAN, PR—Elías López Sobá put an X and the words "Don Pablo" on a certain spot on our city map. López, a pianist and director of Cultural Activities at the University of Puerto Rico, was our host, and he also said that all was set for a visit in a few days to Pablo Casals, the legendary Spanish musician.

Atlantic View runs along the shore at the northeastern outskirts of San Juan. Its south side has modest one-family houses; on the north side, however, the Casals house, one story, white, with a very slightly raked red roof, set perhaps a hundred feet back from the sidewalk, giving directly on the beach in the back, is one of the few such houses left amid the enormous resort hotels and condominiums.

Life there begins each morning with Casals going into his small garden, sometimes onto the beach, "to mix with nature." He marvels at the plants, the clouds, the birds, the surf, at whatever it is nature offers that morning.

"Do you ever think," he asks, "that there are billions of leaves in the world, and all different? That of the billions of people in the world, no two are alike? We think each morning, 'I must do this or that' or 'I will receive such a visit,' but we never think what a marvelous thing we are. These are the things fathers should teach to their sons, but they do not. And their sons do not learn it in school. They learn two and two is four." The *crescendo* of the paragraph mounts to a disgusted snort.

It is the day of our visit. The visitors are Alfred Brendel, the Austrian pianist who is giving a cycle of seven Beethoven recitals and some lectures at the university; Mrs. Brendel and their two-and-a-half-year-old daughter, Doris; Elías López; my wife; and I. Brendel and López arrive first; the Steinbergs a little later; Iris and Doris Brendel still later, on foot from their rented house, which is nearby on the unfashionable side of the avenue.

Michael Steinberg, Alfred Brendel, and Pablo Casals (left to right) at Casals's home in San Juan, Puerto Rico, in November 1969. (Photo credit: L. Sierra, Universidad de Puerto Rico; Fleezanis personal collection; used by permission.)

The first impression is of Martita Casals, who comes to the gate to let us in. Martita was 19 when she married Casals, then 80, in August 1957. She was a cello student of his, and, I later learned from Brendel, a promising singer. She is Puerto Rican, but she has learned Catalan for her husband. It was in 1956 that Casals moved from Prades, in the southeast corner of France, to Puerto Rico, the home of his mother who emigrated to Spain at 18.

Martita is beautiful, in a way and to a degree for which no photograph has prepared me. The pictures coarsen her looks, and none more than vaguely suggests the vivaciousness, the naturalness, the charm, the warmth, that are the sources of her beauty even more than her physical loveliness. Fiercely protective of Casals, she has extraordinary resources of kindness and tact. She is the fence around a public monument and also the path to it, and she impresses me as humanely superb in an exceedingly difficult job.

We enter the house. As we move quickly through the hall, there is barely time to do more than receive a general impression that the house, at least in what you might call its public rooms, is as much museum as home. The walls are crowded with photographs, diplomas, and other memorabilia, and when we enter the living room I again have the impression that much of what I see is not so much as a function of the owners' choice and taste, as of their position in life. Casals is a perpetual receiver, of gifts, tributes, and visitors.

Casals is sitting on a pale-green satin coach, Brendel, who is something like fourteen inches taller, on his right, and López in one of several pale-green satin chairs on his left.

Grey slacks, a grey-green short-sleeved shirt with top and bottom buttons open, black shoes on improbably tiny feet, and, of course, a pipe in his mouth. "I have seen you before," he says. I was once introduced to Casals at Marlboro, though it seems unlikely that he would remember me from a five-minute post-concert meeting in 1964.

Anyway, this leads him to talk about Marlboro, which he calls "marvelous" and "unique," though, he adds, he once saw something like it, "though not so perfect," in Kiev. Unfortunately this interesting trail is lost at once, and an attempt later to steer him back to Kiev fails.

López tells Casals that this is the first time all the Beethoven sonatas have ever been played as a cycle in Puerto Rico. At that point Brendel has played four programs and has three to go, and in response to a question from Casals tells which are the principal works on the programs yet to come. At the mention of Opus 111, Casals says, "that was always my preference," and adds that he has somewhere reviews of a performance he played as a young man. "The critics said it was good too." With the cackle of someone who has finally triumphed over the critics, he adds, "Sometimes they are right."

He expresses his regret at missing the concerts, but he rarely goes out. "It's that damned air-conditioning everywhere," Martita explains.

Actually I don't think she said "damned"—she certainly would not be such a fool as to say "darned"—but the delivery is so spirited and the sense so unmistakable that the air-conditioning is damned, whether aloud or not.

With the violent changes of temperature between indoors and out, the danger of colds is severe for the old man. At the Casals Festival in June, only a slight cooling of the hall is allowed, and that begins only after the audience has begun to arrive, more to compensate for their added warmth than to produce a real change.

The climate in Puerto Rico is a problem. Musical instruments are in poor condition generally, and Casals tells us that his good cello is in New York. "Here I have only a bad one, but very strong," and able to survive the heat and the damp.

Casals goes through his scales and arpeggios every day, "though I am now 92 and know how to do them."

But the first music-making of the morning is at the piano. When he comes from his walk, his "mixing with nature," he plays two of Bach's Preludes and Fugues at the piano. "Every day of my life, every day. It gives the house the right atmosphere. I have never been able to begin a day with a sonata by Mozart or Beethoven"—which he accents on the second syllable—"it must be Bach Preludes and Fugues. A pair every morning. I advise everyone to do so."

On the way out, later on, I walk by the keyboard and the *Well-tempered Clavier* is on the music rack, F-sharp minor of the Second Book.

Still on climate, Brendel says that he finds he sleeps "an enormous amount" in Puerto Rico, often ten hours a night. Casals says that he had been brought up by his mother to think of time in bed as wasted time, that he has no use for people who spend more than eight hours in bed.

Martita is alerted to the impending social emergency, begins to speak rapidly in Catalan, and after some back and forth between them, he closes the subject, still firm, with "anyway, for me is not good, more than eight hours."

The talk shifts to Vienna, Brendel's home. Brendel, rather impatient with Vienna's establishmentarianism and smugness, says it is a provincial town with an orchestra that can sometimes play beautifully, and with opera and the theater capable of occasional good performances.

Casals either ignores or fails to hear this heresy, and says "Vienna will always be Vienna. Vienna will always be the city of music." When he was first there as a young man, he tells us, he always thought he might meet Beethoven or Schubert or Mozart or Haydn coming around some corner.

"When I played my first concert there, with the first note"—he makes the gesture of a downbow and, with it, a kind of percussive grunt that perfectly evokes the powerful Casals attack—"the bow flies from my hand, like so, so frightened was I."

He reminisces about conducting the Vienna Philharmonic in 1927, the Beethoven centenary. He sings the first measures of the Eighth Symphony to indicate which piece.

"In the minuet, the horn player makes like so," and Casals, with hilarious effect sings the solo in the Trio as done by a bored player with soggy rhythm, unfocused tone, and no sense of phrase. "I make him repeat."

Casals sings again. For a moment I have the idea it is his parody, as funny as the earlier performance, of the player who has now gone to the opposite extreme and who is overemphasizing phrasing absurdly. I realize, though, that the super-*espressivo*, with its tremendous *crescendo* on long notes and the exaggerated pauses between phrases, is typical late Casals style, that he is now acting out his attempt to convey his wishes to the hornist.

Casals continues: "He said to me, 'I have played this under the greatest conductors and they have been satisfied.' I say, 'I am here and they are wrong.' I make him repeat three times, is always the same. I molest the man, and he leaves. Later, players come to my hotel to apologize."

For a moment, Casals cannot remember why he got into this story, but with Martita's gentle prompting it comes back. He recalls a lunch given in his honor by the Vienna Philharmonic two years ago, and how he startled his hosts by suddenly pointing and yelling, "there he is," upon catching sight of the hornist's portrait. "You see, he was a very famous player." Casals sits bold upright, an imaginary French horn in his left arm, a perfect picture of a self-important man sitting for his portrait.

At such moments Casals comes extraordinarily alive. The arms, the stubby-fingered hands, are put into motion, the lower lip is thrust firmly forward, the blue eyes sparkle, the face can break into one of the most enchanting smiles one has ever experienced. Especially the moments that are a little theatrical, that engage the performer in him, are unforgettable. The personality is fantastically compelling, and contact with it, even the briefest, is something one would on no account wish to have missed.

At some point a diversion is created by the arrival of the Brendel ladies. Casals is enchanted by the little girl. And when he engages in that always compelling ritual of relighting his pipe—he smokes it, he says, "as much as possible"—he offers her the match to blow out, which, with some assistance from her father, she manages to do.

Are the curls natural, Casals asks, and when assured they are, he says, "I thought perhaps . . . " and makes gesture of using a curling iron. Doris, fresh from her nap, is gravely courteous—her normal attitude is one of ebullient friendliness—and the human bridge across ninety-and-one-half years is touching to watch.

The two most prevalent visual symbols about the house, other than Casals himself, are Don Quixote and the cello, both represented in many artistic manifestations.

To Casals's left, there is a hexagonal lampshade, each of whose sides bears the incipit of one of Bach's suites, and which was made for him by the widow of Paul Grümmer, the cellist of the Busch Quartet. But Casals's first musical love is not the cello as much as the orchestra. The work of which he seems proudest is the founding in Barcelona in 1919 with his own funds of the Orquestre Pau Casals ("Pau" is the Catalan form of the Spanish Pablo).

The shattering trauma of his life was the establishment in 1939 of Franco's Fascist dictatorship, an event which destroyed that orchestra, which made Casals an exile (except insofar as the settling in his mother's native land is a kind of homecoming for him), and which set him on the path that changed him from musician to oracle.

He was preparing Beethoven's Ninth when word came that occupation of Barcelona by Franco's Nationalist troops and the Italian and German mercenaries was imminent. The concert was cancelled. "But we have not yet played the finale, the Hymn to Joy," he said to the orchestra, "Shall we go through it?"

"And," he tells us, "everyone there shouted 'yes' "—the "Yes" erupts from the old man with shattering force—"and so we did it, all the players, all the singers. It was a good end, no?"

I believe completely that the joy of doing the Beethoven is strong enough to conquer the bitterness of his loss. Similarly, one of the most moving moments of our afternoon comes when Casals and Brendel agree that to be a musician is a very great privilege. Casals now turns to López and repeats the Beethoven Ninth story in Spanish. The orchestra's shout of "Sí" again has tremendous intensity, if less volume than before, and the smile when he gets to the end—"buenito, eh?"—is beatific, truly.

"The men in the orchestra were so afraid," he continues, "that for seven years I did not hear one word from one of them. But they adored me. They adored me. They were like my children to me. I was godfather to many of their children."

Casals still feels deeply the Western democracies' betrayal in maintaining Franco in power. "Thirty-two years, thirty-two years," he muses, thinking of the passage of time since the beginning of the Civil War. "You know, until three years ago, my name was not mentioned in Spain. Since 1939. Now they want me to come back. The newspapers write I should come back. But the newspapers that write it are Francoist newspapers. But they are wrong. They are wrong."

It is time to go. Brendel uncoils himself and says, "Maestro, I cannot leave without expressing my most profound admiration."

Casals nods, then says, "I am only a musician."

Brendel: "But what a musician!"

1970

Real Music Will Survive

January 4, 1970

There will still be music at the end of the '70s. For the happy few, it will be a life-and-death matter, something to tap all their reserves of love and fury, something, as Toscanini used to say, to put their blood into. For many more, it will be a gig, a commodity to be promoted and sold, grist for the academy, a decoration. And in that way, the end of the '70s will be just like the end of the '60s.

The public relations industry is likely to become more resourceful, more diligent, and more powerful. Much of what people now assume has to do with art is actually a function of public relations, and that condition is not going to diminish. Perhaps, though, by 1979, music will have found a Joe McGinniss[1] to study the selling of a Bernstein, an Ormandy, a George Szell. It will continue to be part of the sometimes difficult and unpopular task of criticism to make and to maintain distinctions between music and the fantasies of the public relations people.

A Chassidic Jew said in outrage to the skeptic: "How dare you mock a rabbi to whom God himself speaks every Friday night?" Said the skeptic: "How do you know he does?" "He told me so himself." "Maybe he was lying." Said the Chassid: "What do you mean? Would God speak with a liar?"

In composition, I imagine that there will be increasing interest in mixed media and in theater pieces of various sorts. I am certain that what we compendiously and confusingly lump together as "electronic music" will be still more important at the end of the coming decade. There will be lots of know-nothing doing-your-thingism by people with Moog Synthesizers, and that will fill the boredom quota of the '70s.

It makes little difference, in the end, to have The New Boredom replace the old; one might, however, say on behalf of the academic serial bores of the '50s and '60s that they were not so demagogic and not as Messianic as their successors and that their pieces were shorter.

[1] Joe McGinniss (1942–2014) was the best-selling author of *The Selling of the President 1968*, among other books.

Good pieces, as in the past, will be written by good composers. The good pieces will be few, as in the past, and they might include light shows, serialism, and the key of D minor, and they will be written by composers as different from one another as Berio, Babbitt, and Britten (all hating each other's music probably). The public will continue to be best informed about whichever pieces make the best journalistic copy.

I see two major problems for the music world of the '70s. One is the question of sound pollution. The medical dangers of city noise are far greater and more acute than most people have supposed, something far worse than a nuisance, as Dr. Lester W. Sontag[2] and colleagues of his made compellingly clear at the American Association for the Advancement of Science meetings here.

The musician needs to be concerned with the findings of Dr. Samuel Rosen[3] about a Sudanese tribe living "in an atmosphere of virtual silence," whose hearing at advanced ages is better than that of any modern Western population. It is also time, however, that we faced the problem of the blunting of musical sensibility that is brought about by the incessant rain of aural filth to which one is subjected in elevators, savings banks, shoe stores, airplanes awaiting takeoff, restaurants, and so forth. I see the right to silence on its way out.

Then, money is a drastic problem of quite a different sort. Unless some drastically new financial basis is established for it, we cannot take for granted that ten years from now, in January 1980, the Boston Symphony Orchestra will still exist. That goes as well, of course, for the other orchestras in this country and for the opera companies. An orchestra is an impossibly expensive luxury: two years ago, the Boston Symphony's business administrator estimated the cost per hour of keeping the orchestra playing at roughly $3,725 per hour![4] It is an institution based on a wage-slave economy, but we now believe that an orchestral player is entitled to a good living.

Is there a way of juggling the rising costs and the necessarily limited income? What are the possible sources of unearned income? Can increased government support help? If so, what is the chance of getting such support? Are the people for whom imagining the Boston Symphony's farewell concert is thinking the unthinkable writing to their representatives in Congress urging adequate funding for the National Endowment for the Arts?

[2] Dr. Lester W. Sontag (1901–91) was known for his work on a phenomenon he called "somatopsychics": the way that "basic physiological processes affect the personality structure, perception and performance of an individual." He found that war transformed fears of danger in the pregnant wives of soldiers, further heightening a child's biological susceptibility to emotional distress while still in the womb.

[3] Dr. Samuel Rosen (1897–1981) was a surgeon and pioneer of the "Rosen stapes" operation, a procedure for restoring hearing that followed from research on societies living in locations with virtually no noise pollution.

[4] Adjusted for inflation, the dollar figure amounts roughly to $31,200 in 2025.

How to pay the price—not just for the orchestras and the opera, but for the music schools and conservatories, for publishing music and recording it—that is going to be the critical question in the '70s. Whoever writes this column on the first Sunday of the '80s should know if there were answers and, if so, what they were, because by then we shall not have time to be asking any more.

New Memoirs Translation Revives Genius of Berlioz

January 11, 1970

Berlioz wrote his memoirs to correct the many errors and inaccuracies that had appeared in other published accounts of his "arduous and turbulent career." It used to be that Berlioz was popularly seen as a man and artist whose every gesture and pronouncement was hyperbole, and there was, along with that, a tendency to question the veracity of the Memoirs. It was undeniably a most entertaining book, but few accepted it as the corrective Berlioz said it was.

In the last twenty years, the view of Berlioz has changed. There had been enormous interest in his music in England, to the point where critics have already begun to worry if Berlioz has not been oversold, and America has had something of a Berlioz revival, too. The very popular works—the *Symphonie fantastique* and the concert excerpts from *The Damnation of Faust*—exist for us now in a perspective produced by familiarity as well with *Harold in Italy*, with the rest of *The Damnation*, with *L'Enfance du Christ*, *Roméo et Juliette*, *Nuits d'été*, and the Requiem.

CBS, trying to sell Boulez's recordings of the *Fantastique* and *Lélio*, presented Berlioz as the prophet of psychedelia, but it is now generally clear—as, indeed, it might have been clear years ago from the Sylph music in *The Damnation*, or the Waltz and the pastoral slow movement of the *Fantastique*—that Berlioz is not a composer whose only strength is in the weird and hyper-theatrical genres. As David Cairns, Berlioz's newest translator says, we accept Berlioz now: "His originality, without having lost its vividness, no longer seems eccentric. We can enjoy him, greatness and limitations, for what he is, a remarkable composer but one among many."

With the changed view of Berlioz, we can accept the Memoirs, too. The new translation by David Cairns (Knopf) is, in fact, an irresistible invitation to do so. The Memoirs in any event are so much more than a corrective. Like Berlioz's critical writing and so much of his correspondence, they are special because of what they reveal about the beauty—that sum of responsibility, integrity, passion, humor, generosity—of their author. He was a brilliant, even a virtuosic, prose writer, and when the estate of his music was low, it was clever to say that he was a better writer of French than of music; his extraordinary personal qualities, together with his powers of observation and judgment, the resourcefulness and immense range of his prose style, make the Memoirs not just one of the most entertaining of all books, but one of the most moving.

Of course, if you can, read them in French. For those, though, whose French is not up to it, the Cairns translation provides something that is not only exciting and delightful to read for itself, but writing that really makes possible access to Berlioz's mind. Katharine Boult's translation, which I had not known but looked up because of a reference to it in Cairn's preface, has something of that character, too, but it is incomplete and in any case decades out of print. American and English readers know the Memoirs through the 1884 translation by the Holmes sisters[5] (revised 1932 by Ernest Newman and recently reissued as a Dover paperback), and almost anyone who has made his way through that affair, which manages to be stilted and insipid at once, is likely to be astounded by the sizzling prose of the new version, and by the vitality of Berlioz's prose which Cairns transmits so effectively.

Berlioz was a man keenly aware of the worth of his work, enraged by its rejection in favor of glittering trash, by the absence in most of the professional world of an integrity matching his own, by the indifference to musical values among orchestra players and conductors. He was nobly and generously responsive to appreciation and to true professionalism wherever he found it.

That led him to things as diverse as the hilarious accounts of his collisions with Cherubini (whom Cairns has speak Chico Marx[6]), but also to the original ending of the Memoirs (he added a chapter in 1865): "I am in my 61st year; past hopes, past illusions, past high thoughts and lofty conceptions. . . . I am alone. My contempt for the folly and baseness of mankind, my hatred of its atrocious cruelty, have never been so intense. And I say hourly to Death: 'When you will.' Why does he delay?"

It produced also the beautifully poised portrait of his music that he wasted on a hack biographer:

> Generally speaking, my style is very bold, but there is no tendency in it whatsoever to destroy any of the fundamental elements of art. . . . The predominant features of my music are passionate expression, inward intensity, rhythmic impetus, and a quality of unexpectedness. When I say passionate expression,

[5] Rachel Scott Russell Holmes and Eleanor Holmes.

[6] In Chapter 18 of his *Memoirs*, Berlioz recounts a conversation in which he seeks permission from Cherubini to use a concert hall at the Conservatoire. Cairns translates Cherubini's part of the conversation with a sort of pidgin-Italianate, Chico Marx-like accent, e.g.: "So you wish to geeve a concert?" . . . "For that you will 'ave to 'ave the pairmission of the Secretary of Fine Arts" . . . "Also for the expenses you needa some money. I don't suppose you 'ave it?" . . . "And what will you play at this concert?" . . . "Thatta compeetition cantata? No, that I will not 'ave."

> I mean an expression bent on reproducing the inner meaning of its subject, even when that subject is the opposite of passion, and gentle, tender feelings are being expressed, or profound calm.

Or on its performance: writing about the works that use normal resources, he says:

> It is precisely their expressiveness, their inner fire and rhythmic originality that have done them the greatest harm, on account of the qualities they demand from the performer. To perform them well, everybody concerned, the conductor most of all, must feel, as I feel. They require a combination of irresistible verve and the utmost precision, a controlled vehemence, a dreamlike sensitivity, an almost morbid melancholy, without which the essential character of my phrases is falsified or even obliterated. For this reason I find it exceedingly painful to hear most of my works conducted by someone other than myself.

The reissue in a slightly revised edition and the occasion therefore to examine again, Jacques Barzun's *Berlioz and the Romantic Century*, does much to heighten one's appreciation of Berlioz's own Memoirs as the book through which to understand the man and the music he wrote. Barzun's two-volume production (Columbia University Press) is an orgy of name-dropping, ponderous and vacuous at once. B. H. Haggin, reviewing another book of Barzun's, *Pleasures of Music*, in 1952, wrote: "What he has done in this collection is to demonstrate again, as in his book on Berlioz, the enormous amount and range of his reading and his astounding lack of discrimination collecting bits of material into files, then an equally indiscriminate emptying of the files into a book."

To conclude, Tom Wotton's superb *Hector Berlioz*, the finest study of the music and long out of print, is available from Johnson Reprint Corp., 111 Fifth Avenue, New York 10003; and you will get pleasure from a miscellaneous series of Berlioz letters, chosen and well translated by Humphrey Searle (Harcourt, Brace & World).

André Previn in Hub Concert

January 12, 1970

Because the interpretations were unfailingly musical and alive, and because the standard of orchestral culture was extraordinarily high, the concert that André Previn conducted with the London Symphony on Sunday afternoon in Symphony Hall was a rare sort of event and remarkable.

The program: Beethoven's *Prometheus* Overture, Mendelssohn's *Italian* Symphony, and the Symphony No. 4 in F minor by Vaughan Williams.

The London Symphony is most characteristically a brilliant instrument rather than a mellow one, and the program showed them doing what they do best. In the finale of the Mendelssohn, Previn allowed himself to be tempted into a speed that not even the London Symphony could manage—and I should add that there was no other comparable miscalculation—but everywhere else the orchestra played with precision, elegance, and transparency of texture, that were delightful even more than they were dazzling.

There is no exact borderline between technical and musical virtues, but something that struck me particularly was being shown how musically organic this virtuoso playing was, something that manifested itself not only in the sonorous balances that I have already mentioned, but also in the attention paid to the finishing of notes, the chamber-musical interplay of parts, and in the care taken to make even short notes beautiful.

It is also a superb *pianissimo* orchestra, one that commands a phenomenal delicacy and that has available to it what seems an extraordinary range of dynamics all within *pianissimo.*

Previn is neither a profound nor a highly original interpreter of music. He is, however, a marvelously musical man, unpretentious, and unfussy, and the performances of the Beethoven and Mendelssohn pieces were, with the exception (in part) of the excessively quick finale to the *Italian*, shapely and rhythmic right up to the largest structural units, and miracles of lightness and grace. The one place where it was needed, in the slow introduction to *Prometheus*, there was a splendid spaciousness that, too, was traceable to Previn's rhythmic poise.

The Vaughan Williams Fourth is an impressive and absorbing piece by which I am not moved and that I find difficult to like. First heard in 1935, it startled the public with an expressive and harmonic aggressiveness that had not been associated with Vaughan Williams, then in his early 60s, that certainly had never before occurred in such concentration in any one work before, though it is actually not unprecedented in his music of the previous decade.

Like much of Vaughan Williams's music, the Fourth is a disconcerting mixture of successes and failures. The scoring is raucous and amateurish, but the piece is also full of stunning orchestral inspirations. The form is often stiff, but the harmonic layout of the first (and best) movement has been imagined by a master, and Vaughan Williams carries off the most unlikely feat of successfully imitating the darkness-to-daylight transition from scherzo to finale in the Beethoven Fifth.

It is a work that insists powerfully on being what it is, and perhaps it is that very exuberance of personality, a certain willfulness and a sense of "by God, this is written like that on purpose" that make it at least humanly so engaging.

The performance was exciting, and it gave honest and proper representation to the music. Previn did better by its many angry statements, whose range goes from fury to crossness, than by its calmer ones. Where Vaughan Williams writes "*tranquillo*," Previn was often cold, as far beyond tranquility as beyond passion.

Boult's recorded performances come to terms with more of the expressive territory covered by the music. No question, though, Previn gave not just a strong ending to the concert, but a real encounter with a real piece.

The Moscow Philharmonic Performs

February 2, 1970

To construct a program worse than the one Kiril Kondrashin and the Moscow Philharmonic played Sunday afternoon in Symphony Hall would take some ingenuity. They began with poor Rachmaninoff imitating Rachmaninoff writing a symphony (his Third), and followed that with the appalling—and much longer—exhibition of Shostakovich writing a symphony (his Eighth).

Rachmaninoff's non-piece was written in 1935–36. By then he seemed devoid of any creative impulse, the *Paganini* Rhapsody of 1934 being a lone brilliant moment in a couple of desert decades. The Third Symphony does offer some thin consolation in its scoring, done with the Philadelphia Orchestra in mind, and with marks of ingenuity and refinement of taste.

In his Eighth Symphony, written 1943, the greatly gifted but un-self-critical Shostakovich was acquiescing to a demand for musical war propaganda, and at the very period that he was working on pieces as inventive and as honestly composed as his E minor Trio and his Second String Quartet. The Eighth Symphony, with its interminable slow movements that are like acres of library paste, with its military and jocular routines and its brainless bucolics, is pompous, gross, and profoundly untrue.

The Moscow Philharmonic itself sounded well prepared, precise, and in tune, though, mainly because of the thin violin tone, it makes a somewhat strident, disagreeable sound. Kondrashin is efficient, energetic, and rather too deadpan when he is not actually tearing down walls. It seemed about right for the Shostakovich, but the Rachmaninoff Symphony would clearly have gained from a less one-dimensional treatment.

Mine is a minority report: most of the large audience liked the concert very much (as I did the one that Kondrashin and the Philharmonic gave here four years ago),[7] though I am sure that there are non-musical reasons to account

[7] See review of November 2, 1965.

for some of the Russian musical successes in this country. Symphony Hall was picketed by Student Struggle for Soviet Jewry, but the concert was not actually disturbed as earlier ones on the orchestra's tour had been, for example, those in Constitution Hall, Washington, and the Brooklyn Academy.

Carter Concerto Premiered

February 15, 1970

NEW YORK—The New York Philharmonic is in its 128th season now, but it is still taking delivery on works commissioned for its 125th anniversary. A contribution from Karlheinz Stockhausen is yet to come, but February 5–9 the Philharmonic gave the first performances of the last-but-one of its anniversary pieces, Elliott Carter's Concerto for Orchestra, completed last November 25.

Carter has written that the Concerto's

> general character . . . was suggested by the Nobel prize–winning poem "Vents" ("Winds") by the French poet who calls himself St. John Perse. The poem had attracted me by its expansive, almost Whitmanesque description of a United States constantly swept by forces like winds, forces that are always transforming, remolding, or obliterating the past and introducing the fresh and the new. . . . But Perse's poem served only as a point of departure, for as I worked on this Concerto, the music naturally began to take precedence over the poem and I began to find Perse's poetic tone, especially his, to me, rather contrived primitivism, did not correspond to the tone of the work that was taking shape, and so I took no further thought of the poem after a certain point and followed the musical conceptions the work seemed to impose on me.

The Concerto is an exciting piece, difficult for the listener and the performer because it is all event and no filler, and full of extraordinary ideas about compositional continuity, musical character, and the orchestra as an instrument. Carter's work of the last twenty years or so appears more and more to emerge as one huge, continuing, evolving opus; the Concerto continues Carter's thought and is, at the same time, a profoundly new piece.

With respect to sonority and in the way Carter enters the piece and leaves it again, the Concerto for Orchestra seems at first acquaintance most nearly to resemble the Double Concerto. With respect to musical expression, Carter has moved into lands he has not explored before. With all his characteristically intent playfulness, he has written an exceedingly serious work, but one whose discourse is not so overtly impassioned as before. It is magic, sinister, somehow distant. If this cooly intense masterpiece reminds me of anything, it would be Debussy (often a purely musical influence on Carter), of the strange world I sense behind his Sonata for Flute, Viola, and Harp (my view of that Sonata as something other than a gently limpid pastoral is one few will share) and of *Jeux*.

In his first String Quartet, Carter dealt with the problem of continuity and contrast wittily and paradoxically by going without break from one movement to the next, but making movement breaks within movements. The first movement of the much later Piano Concerto comes to a formal and full close, but the second movement begins from the very chord on which the first stops.[8] In the Concerto for Orchestra, Carter has carried his quest for balancing the claims of continuity and contrast still further.

The Concerto's twenty-three minutes of music contain four movements, more accurately described perhaps as four bodies of material, each with specific characteristics of rhythm, speed, interval, and above all, register and sonority. These four "movements" are unfolded one after another (one at moderate pace, a deceleration, a recitative, and an acceleration—to give summary descriptions), but no section is stated without being counterpointed by the three others. There is constant interpenetration, then, of all four parts, the interruptions or interferences being sometimes playful and sometimes threatening, and it means that what I refer to as a "movement" is merely the largest and most nearly continuous statement of that set of materials.

Each "movement" speaks in a particular voice: the first in low middle register (cellos, piano, harp, wood percussion), the second in high register (violins, flutes, metal percussion), the third in low register (basses, horns, tuba, timpani, bass drum, tubular bells), the fourth in high middle register (violas, oboes, clarinets, trumpets, vibraphone, snare and tenor drums). Carter has suggested a seating that spreads the four ensembles in a semicircle, in descending registral order from left to right and with some space between groups. Housekeeping arrangements at Philharmonic Hall apparently made it impractical for the performances; it was hoped, though, that the Columbia recording, which will have been made by the time this article appears, would either use or electronically simulate the special seating. It should not only clarify, but greatly dramatize, Carter's astonishing scenario.

The orchestral concept of Carter's Concerto is its most dazzling aspect. The writing for individual instruments (there is virtually no writing for sections in the conventional sense) is demanding, appropriate in a work meant to celebrate the anniversary of a great virtuoso orchestra, but it is considerate, "practical," and, when mastered, stunningly brilliant in its effect. There is, however, not a thing in it that would find a place in a future edition of [Gardner] Read's

8 See review of January 7, 1967.

Thesaurus of Orchestral Devices or any such work. Its freshness is not in "devices" (let alone gimmicks), but in the view of the orchestra as a whole; in that sense, Carter's Concerto is pathbreaking as Schoenberg's Five Pieces, Stravinsky's *Rite of Spring*, Debussy's *Jeux* were early in our century.

The sound is mantled in a virtually continuous envelope of percussion from which the music seems to emerge. Nothing is ordered in conventional sonorous combinations, but the real originality of the scoring stems directly from the compositional demands of the work, particularly the interpenetration of movements and materials and the way in which this brings about a constant flux as ideas and sonorities change their weights and functions, come forward through the texture, or recede again from foreground to background. If you can imagine a coordinate between Bach's richest and most complex "concerto-for-orchestra" writing (say the first movements of the First and Third *Brandenburgs*) and [Pavel] Tchelichew's [painting] "Hide-and-Seek," you can perhaps get some idea of Carter's luminous writing. He has made the orchestra into a new instrument, no less.

The first performance was carefully and effectively prepared, and the dramatic character of the Concerto was something for Leonard Bernstein to respond to as, for example, the patterns last year of Babbitt's *Relata II* were not.[9] The result was that the premiere was not one of these hanging-on-for-dear-life readings, but a real performance with almost as much clarity as the bass-starved acoustics of the hall would allow, and one with plenty of life and dramatic projection. The fourth performance, last Monday, which I also heard, started out even better, especially with respect to balance, but it became somehow unconcentrated and flat as it went along. It was interesting to observe the contrast between the polite reception Monday and the warm on the previous Thursday when Bernstein and the Philharmonic had really delivered the expressive point of the piece as well as its notes.

Schuller Leads BSO in His *Spectra*

March 28, 1970

Gunther Schuller was guest conductor with the Boston Symphony Orchestra yesterday afternoon and used the occasion to give the rather overdue Boston premiere of one of his strongest compositions, *Spectra*. Schuller wrote the work in 1958 on commission from the Board of Directors of the New York Philharmonic

[9] See review of January 26, 1969.

for presentation as a parting gift to Dimitri Mitropoulos whom they had just bumped out as music director.

Schuller was 32 then, and just beginning to be recognized as a serious composer, as one of the liveliest figures in this country's musical life generally. Actually, Schuller had been composing steadily since he was in his teens, and *Spectra*, as assured as it is imaginative, is anything other than a beginner's piece.

Schuller's striking orchestral fantasy and discipline is most vividly in evidence, and *Spectra* indeed is very much and very specifically a piece about the sonorities and the ensemble characteristics of the modern virtuoso orchestra. To emphasize that a composer in the 1950s combines instruments differently from one in the middle of the 19th century, Schuller asks for a special seating plan, as peculiarly efficient for his music as the conventional is for Brahms, which splits the orchestra into five groups from four to fourteen players, each containing some representation of strings, wood, and brass, placing the kitchen department at the back of the stage in the normal way, but otherwise mangling the five quasi-chamber groups within a surrounding semicircle of tutti strings.

Not surprisingly, then, the deployment of sounds in space—the difference in effect between, for example, the horn who sits where you would normally see the fifth cellist and the one who is mixed up among the second violins somewhere—plays an important role in the argument of *Spectra*.

It is a one-movement work, extended in scale, and perhaps less effective than *Triplum*, Schuller's more recent New York Philharmonic commission, only because it is not quite concise in saying its piece. It gets going a little slowly, but it finds its way eventually to some eloquent and appealing music, a spare and tense section in very slow tempo, then its one really quick outburst, and a glissando-laden coda that I hear as partaking both of the comic and the sinister. In all, I find much in *Spectra* that is absorbing, and more than a little that confirms my impression that Schuller at his best is one of the relatively few composers who not only have vocabulary and a technique but who have something to say, too.

Schuller produced a generally effective and at times impressively played performance of *Spectra*. He did well with Webern's Five Pieces, Op. 10, and the playing was good except for those clarinet solos which Mr. Cioffi blew into the room not in Webern's *pianissimo* and triple-*piano* but at a persistently hearty *mezzo forte*; however, these beautifully made examples of "*multum in parvo*" never really stood a chance against the noise-making resources of the restless audience.

The concert began with Haydn's Symphony No. 31 in D (*Hornsignal*), heard in a performance in which the lively playing of the first movement promised well, but which soon foundered in a number of stylistic solecisms, the impossibly slow tempi in the Adagio and the variation set being the most damaging, and with exceedingly undistinguished playing throughout. The program ended with a Good Friday observance in the form of orchestral excerpts from Act III of Wagner's *Parsifal.*

Britten's *Brandenburgs* Exceptional Recording

March 29, 1970

Even the best recordings of Bach's *Brandenburg* Concertos, those, for example, by Busch, the Collegium Aureum, [Szymon] Goldberg, the Concentus Musicus, or Menuhin, have included some performances crippled by interpretive or instrumental lapses. For that reason it has never been possible really to recommend any one version of the *Brandenburgs* as the one to have. Now, however, one has come along that at least very nearly changes all that, a two-record London album by Benjamin Britten and the English Chamber Orchestra. I have a couple of minor reservations about it, but the whole achievement is remarkable not just because there are no drastic departures from a marvelously high standard, but because the performances have positive virtues and reveal musical features and points of character at a level new to me in this repertory.

Their most special quality is the result of paradox: these performances are conducted, but they are the freest, the most chamber-musical I know. Imogen Holst is persuasive in her notes where she attributes this quality in part to Britten's long familiarity with and feeling for Purcell, and his readings are beautifully touched by the flexible 17th-century style. She adds, again convincingly, "And his years of experience as a continuo player have surely helped to bring about the satisfying orchestral balance in this performance, where the shape of each movement owes so much to the glowing support of the bass." The long unrollings of 16th-notes never become mechanical; rather, they unfold freely, wittily, adventurously, with incredible moment-to-moment variety. It is, in fact, the most dangerous movement in the *Brandenburgs* that gets the most reveal-ingly beautiful performance of all, the dark first Allegro of the Sixth Concerto.

At every level, from the vivid characterization of detail to the boldly powerful projection of large form, Britten's insight is astonishing and moving, but not more so than his way of stimulating the players into realizing his ideas. Every gesture bears the impress of his mind, but he has not over-conducted and worried the performance either. They are, by the way, quite richly ornamented, the players being generally left to their own devices of their own tastes, with results that are attractive, not always "correct," and by no means uncontroversial.

There is room to mention just a few particularly striking points: in No. 1, the fun with the ornery horn cross-rhythms, the lovely phrasing in the Adagio, and the uniquely understanding playing of that movement's curiously disintegrative, dissective ending; the freedom with which the soloists move about the slow movements in Nos. 2 and 5, the latter a truly convincing projection of what Bach means by "*affettuoso*"; in No. 4, the shaping of the cadence between Andante and finale, and the quick, sharply energetic, but non-vehement playing of the finale itself.

My reservations: the first movement of No. 4, which feels slow and, at least by Britten's standards, under-inflected; the first movement in No. 5, in which harpsichordist Philip Ledger is good, but not as transportingly exciting as Leonhardt (Collegium Aureum) or, in quite another manner, Van Wering (Goldberg). To that I might add that Ledger is an imaginative continuo player and clearly a very good musician, but that he plays a bit pianistically—you can hear an increase in jackrail[10] noise where he tries to make a *crescendo*—and that he is handicapped by one of those awful quasi-glockenspiel English harpsichords.

The English Chamber Orchestra plays brilliantly and with poised balance of passion and elegance in the framework of swiftness and lightness Britten imposes. The combined effect of conductor, players, and engineers, and the acoustic properties of The Maltings, Snape, makes for a glowing, warm, and transparent sound. The excellent soloists include Emanuel Hurwitz (violin), Peter Graeme (oboe), Richard Adeney (flute, which is used not only in No. 5, but also in place of recorder in Nos. 2 and 4), David Mason (trumpet), James and Anthony Randall (horns), but unfortunately the names of the fine violinists in No. 6 are not given.

Gifted Soprano Fills Gardner with Color

March 30, 1970

Jessye Norman is one of the many gifted young American singers now working in Germany, and a couple of excited reviews that I happened to have seen from there led me to her recital at the Gardner Museum on Sunday afternoon. With Carl Fürstner at the piano, she sang Wagner's *Wesendonck* Songs, Poulenc's *La Fraîcheur et le feu*, and *Confession Stone*, a cycle of spirituals by Robert Fleming.

Miss Norman, a large and handsome woman, was billed as a soprano, though had I only her singing to go on I should call her a mezzo with a strong high

[10] A wooden bar that sits above the register gap of a harpsichord, regulating the vertical movement of the jacks and plectra. Felt is usually placed underneath to limit mechanical noise.

register. The voice is remarkable: big—though I think I would have to hear it in a large hall to be sure just how big—rich, and pleasingly carnal. It is a somewhat slow-speaking instrument, accurate in pitch, well supported, and with interesting timbral and coloristic possibilities.

It is, moreover, at the service of a good musician and an engaging, at times even compelling, performer. Miss Norman does well with words; specifically, she sings German a bit better than French, and English most effectively of all (which is not necessarily true of American or English singers). In the Wagner cycle, passion was rather tempered by majesty, so that her singing of the songs was more nearly like Flagstad's than like that of Ludwig or Horne. She brought heavier vocal equipment to *La Fraîcheur et le feu* than one usually hears in that repertory, but made effective use of it in projecting what is surely one of Poulenc's most concentrated and generally fine sets of songs. The mixture of false verbal naiveté and genuine musical poverty makes *Confession Stone* a poor piece, but it provided the occasion for some intense and telling singing.

Carl Fürstner's playing was in many respects careful and correct. It was, at the same time, so percussive in sound and so drily perfunctory that it not only failed to generate any atmosphere of its own, but actually, and particularly in the postludes of songs, tended to operate destructively. None of the musical performances, therefore, was completely effective as a whole; Jessye Norman, however, did indeed turn out to be very much worth hearing.

Composers String Quartet Plays Elliott Carter Works

April 6, 1970

Over the past weekend, the New England Conservatory of Music was host to the sixth annual Symposium for Student Composers, at which composition students from ten music schools, colleges, and universities in Canada and the northeastern United States heard their own and each others' works. In the middle of all this interesting, fruitful, and impressive activity, the Conservatory presented its quartet-in-residence, the Composers String Quartet, in a program of the two quartets by Elliott Carter.

It was a good choice. Carter is one of the composers most admired by young musicians, and his music has given them much to think about. That he is a composer of altogether special powers has been clearly and widely evident since the first performances of his First Quartet in 1953; now, with the writing of the nearly 88-year-old Stravinsky sadly at an apparent standstill, it seems that of all living composers Carter is the one from whom we can most confidently expect the most compellingly communicative new music.

All-Carter programs have been given before—one, for example, at MIT in 1967—but none, so far as I know, with both quartets. Friday's concert just missed falling on the tenth anniversary of the premiere of the Second Quartet. Then, in 1960, I was most struck by the differences between it and the First, which had been finished in 1951. With today's longer perspective, with greater familiarity now with the pieces up to the Second Quartet, and of course with the additional information in the series of concertos since 1960,[11] it is clear that one of the most remarkable qualities of Carter's music is the unity of all of it. Both quartets share Carter's zest for a dramatic sort of music in which the instruments are conceived of as characters (though perhaps it took knowing the Second, in which this is explicit, to hear how much this was true even of the First). Adventurous manipulation of speed and rhythm (Friday it was almost as though I had never before heard a real *accelerando*), a tremendous sweep of musical form, and an astonishing way of harnessing a fantastic sophistication of means and a taste for complexity produce some of the most directly, disturbingly impassioned music there is.[12]

It happens differently in the two quartets. The First is huge and runs to more than forty minutes, while the Second says its say in less than twenty. The First still has traces of "ordinary" music, particularly in its Variations movement, while one of the things that makes the first experience of the Second so exciting is the sense of the completeness of its leap into the real Carter.

It is not merely that Carter in 1959 was a freer, more assured, and more economical composer than in 1951: the two quartets are very different people, as it were. The First is intensely serious, whose Adagio, a dialogue between remote, still violins and urgently declamatory lower strings, is its most impressive page and, for me, the most moving music in all of Carter. But the most characteristic achievements of the Second are the cadenzas (dramatic to parodistically theatrical) that link the movements, and it is altogether a wittier and more sensuous work.

Both because of what joins them and what characterizes each uniquely, the two quartets make a beautiful program. How often, after all, does one hear two pieces so richly expressive and absorbing at a concert? How often, too, does one hear performances as extraordinary as those by the Composers

[11] See reviews of November 18, 1965, January 7, 1967, and February 15, 1970, respectively, regarding Carter's Double Concerto for Harpsichord and Piano with Two Chamber Orchestras; Carter's Piano Concerto; and Carter's Concerto for Orchestra.

[12] On the later Quartet No. 3, see articles of February 11 and 19, 1973.

String Quartet (Matthew Raimondi, Anahid Ajemian, Jean Dupouy, Michael Rudiakov)?

Pianist André Watts Performs at Symphony Hall

April 7, 1970

André Watts gave a concert of piano music in Symphony Hall yesterday afternoon that was both charming and dazzling. He was in superb form—unlike last year at Sanders when, in addition, he was bothered by a program in which he seemed structurally out of his depth most of the time—and he had picked and tastefully assembled a group of pieces that suited him well: three Scarlatti sonatas, a Chopin group including the G minor Ballade and six etudes from both Opus 10 and Opus 25, and, after intermission, Liszt's *Grand Etudes after Paganini*, the whole set.

Except for the Ballade, it was a program all of keyboard studies—Scarlatti, after all, called his pieces "*essercizi*"—and that is just what Watts does best. I mean in no way for that to be patronizing: it has been my experience, however, that in pieces that require great sustaining power of thought, ones as different from one another as Liszt's Sonata or the Brahms B-flat Concerto, he tends to lose himself in details. That may have to do with his being only 23, but the "may" is writ large, for it would be easy to name pianists twice and three times his age whose playing suffers from similar problems, and worse.

It is certain, though, that I could name no pianist of any age who commands a more spectacular technique.

Watts played with incredible speed, sureness, clarity, a truly fine control of dynamics, and, as much as he could on a somewhat dully voiced Baldwin, with unfailing, beautiful, unpercussive sound. He did it, moreover, with grace and with that sense of ease in which the essence of bravura resides. While the Chopin Ballade got a handsome performance with grand and expansive musical gestures, the etudes—except the lyrically ecstatic C-sharp minor Etude from Opus 25, which was lovely and touching as played—were thrown away just a little because of some want of interpretive vividness in the way they were projected: there was too much sense of scale study, chord study, or whatever, and not enough of musical character. Liszt's Studies, however, and Scarlatti's as well, came over full of life, humor, and individuality, and playing so brilliant and so stylish as Watts gave us yesterday in "La Campanella" and in the Twenty-fourth Caprice (the one borrowed by Brahms and Rachmaninoff) is something that comes along rarely. Indeed, I bet even Watts does not often play them that well!

Thomas Conducts BSO in Mahler's Ninth Symphony

April 25, 1970

Last October, Michael Tilson Thomas described Mahler's Ninth Symphony to an interviewer as his current candidate for "the all-time great piece of music." Now, yesterday afternoon, at the end of the Boston Symphony season that brought the 25-year-old assistant conductor (just promoted to associate conductor, effective this summer) the unforeseen opportunities to lead the orchestra through over thirty concerts, Thomas put the Mahler Ninth on a program of his own.

Mercilessly demanding on performers and listeners, the Ninth is not what they call in the trade a guaranteed piece. Had Thomas been thinking primarily of a sure success for himself at season's close, he had a hundred easier routes open to him. How often has it happened that the last concert of an orchestral season anywhere has ended *pianissimo*?—a trivial question in a way, but one that does call attention to something important regarding the concept of success and its place in our concert life. And the most encompassing characteristic of Thomas's performance Friday was a kind of selflessness. The experience for me was one that hardly involved awareness of a performance, an interpretation, at all: there was only contact with the music itself, to which I should perhaps add that Thomas does not by much overestimate the Symphony's greatness.

There is no such thing, in the Mahler Ninth, as "letting the music play itself," and of course the playing yesterday was powerfully and purposefully shaped. The performance was, in fact, mature, intelligent, technically competent, and all those to a remarkable degree.

It was also a performance that moved me powerfully and disturbingly, though I thought at first that it was going to turn into a rather cool projection with a certain "objective" clarity as its principal goal. What I was hearing, though, was not lack of warmth, but the presence of more control than most Mahler conductors command. The first movement, for example, [had a shattering climax at measure 47, and just where Mahler placed it, after which the others followed convincingly in succession][13]; most performances, however, have already exhausted themselves in an orgy over the upbeat to measure 47, after which the movement is apt to fall apart into a shapeless series of climaxes in mutually frustrating competition.

[13] This passage presented the editors with a particularly egregious typesetting jumble (including a line duplicated, after six further lines, in its entirety, as well as an obvious omission of words). The original *Globe* review at this point read: "The first / movement, for example, / had a climax, a shattering / ure 47, after which the / others, and just where / Mahler placed it: most / performances, however, / have already exhausted / themselves in an orgy / over the upbeat to meas- / ure 47, after xhich [*sic*] the / movement is apt to fall / apart into a shapeless se- / ries of climaxes in mu- / tually frustrating competi- / tion."

The end of the Adagio, a farewell, a death still more agonizing than the one in *The Song of the Earth* because the accumulation of pain has been so much greater in the symphony, that, too, for once had the impact we all know it is supposed to have (we read about it in the program notes and we can recognize the musical gestures even when we cannot feel them), but which it hardly ever achieves in actual concert.

The performance was (or seemed) quick, which failed to convince me only in the second movement, where I thought the opening tempo too fast not only for the character right there, but also to accommodate the necessary later change to the faster "Tempo II." It was, more than any other I have heard, an "*in tempo*" performance, one in which Thomas made no large modifications of speed other than those specifically prescribed and in which he tended to observe even those to an almost minimal degree. That contributed to the cohesiveness of the experience, and it was all so much alive rhythmically that there was no suggestion whatever of rigidity. Dynamics and accent, too, were treated subtly rather than emphatically, and with remarkable effectiveness in clarifying the texture and giving life to the succession of events.

Not least, it was a performance in which Thomas made extraordinary and knowing use of the orchestra's capabilities. The orchestra, on its part, responded with beautiful playing, whether in the quiet closing pages for strings alone, the virtuoso writing for full band at the end of the Burlesque, or in beautifully played solos by, among others, Joseph Silverstein (violin), Burton Fine (viola), Jules Eskin (cello), Lois Schaefer (piccolo), Peter Hadcock (E-flat clarinet), James Stagliano (horn), Armando Ghitalla (trumpet). The audience's response to it all was an unusual, if not yet ideal, concentration, and a great ovation afterwards. And indeed, it really was something very special.

The performance of Bach's Cantata 140, *Wachet auf*, with which Thomas began the concert, was on the whole a disappointment. There was enough good in it to suggest that by affinity and education Thomas could do such a piece very well, but more went wrong than right. There was beautifully fluid and expressive singing by the soprano Bethany Beardslee, elegant violin playing by Silverstein, and lively, transparent singing by the Harvard Glee Club and Radcliffe Choral Society (but in bad German); on the other hand, there was an awfully "beat-y" quality to much of Thomas's conducting, the orchestra was much too small for the large chorus (assuming the latter as a necessary evil, why the former?), the grey-voiced bass soloist was wooden in his phrasing, both his and the tenor's recitatives were ungainly,[14] the oboe solo lurched, and the instrumentalists playing the bass line disgraced themselves with their mindless whoof-whoof-whoofing throughout their part.

[14] The bass was Vern Shinall, the tenor Robert Gartside.

New *Kreislerianas*

May 17, 1970

Kreisleriana, which Schumann considered the best of his works for solo piano and which was certainly the one he most loved, was long the property of a small number of connoisseurs. In the last few years it has been played more in concert and has found a larger audience. Its former estate is, nonetheless, understandable because it belongs among those pieces that seem meant not so much for public performance (like, say, *Carnaval*) as for private loving.

Big and intimate at the same time, this eight-movement suite is first of all a portrait of Kapellmeister Kreisler, a fictional creation of E. T. A. Hoffmann's. Kreisler can be read in part as a Hoffmann self-portrait. Schumann in his turn, used Kreisler as a Schumann image, and *Kreisleriana* therefore becomes a curious double portrait. Schumann's wife, Clara, appears to be in the picture as well, though, stolid rather than imaginative and generally a bit bourgeois in her taste, she was not much drawn to *Kreisleriana.*

Two new recordings of *Kreisleriana* have just come out, one by Artur Rubinstein (RCA), the other by Vladimir Horowitz (Columbia). Neither quite works, but the contrast is fascinating and so, in its idiosyncratic way, is the Horowitz performance. *Kreisleriana* takes a very special sort of pianist, because it is Schumann's most extreme piece, in dimensions, technical demands, and musical imagery. It wants, therefore, an infinitely resourceful instrumentalist, one who can be warm as well as hot, one, above all, who can respond to the Hoffmann-Schumann manic-depressed scene and the instant, unmodulated changes of temper it produces.

Rubinstein's playing of *Kreisleriana* is musically and pianistically lucid, restrained, tasteful, elegant, and it misses the point. He gives you thirty-three or so minutes of attractive music, but little sense of something fantastic.

Now you do get that from Horowitz, a bit too much, even. It is clear at once that this is no ordinary piece, but one that is in some way mad, and so in an essential way this interpretation is on the right track where Rubinstein's is not. Then, Horowitz's playing is so extraordinary as a way of dealing with the instrument that it makes more than any performance I have heard of the genius in Schumann's piano scoring. *Kreisleriana* is Schumann's most fanciful piece in that respect, and what Horowitz makes of the difference between the voicing or spacing of one chord and another, of changes of register, doublings, and so forth, is excitingly revealing.

Horowitz's temperament is not quite in tune with Schumann's either, and his playing is too consistently feverish. The third movement is marked "*sehr aufgeregt*" ("very excited"), and one would infer from Horowitz that that is the direction for the whole work (while Rubinstein, though vivacious, is never "*aufgeregt*"). Horowitz cannot leave anything alone really, and music that needs to be played simply—the second B-flat major slow movement, for example, in contrast to the first, more brooding and temperamentally complicated one—escapes him completely. It is wildly imaginative playing in which each event gets special treatment, and Horowitz's imagination sometimes takes over independently of Schumann's needs. It has its problems and peculiarities, this Horowitz record, but it is very much worth knowing.

The Rubinstein record is filled out with the Arabesque, Op. 18, and with "The Prophet Bird" from *Forest Scenes*, Op. 82; Horowitz includes the Variations on a Theme by Clara Wieck, which is also the slow movement of the F minor Piano Sonata.

The Arabesque also appears on a valuable record reissuing Horowitz performances from the early '30s (Seraphim), including Schumann's Toccata and the original finale of the G minor Sonata, and, as the main work, the Liszt Sonata. Highly recommended.

Problems of Big, Amateur Choruses

June 7, 1970

How does one listen to a concert by a large amateur chorus? That is a problem I had occasion to confront twice in the last couple of weeks, when the Framingham Choral Society, whose conductor is John Oliver, sang Bach's B minor Mass at Sanders Theatre, and when the Masterworks Chorale of Lexington, whose conductor is Allen Lannom, put on a Beethoven program in Carey Memorial Hall, Lexington, including the *Cantata on the Death of Emperor Joseph II* and the C major Mass. Moreover, it really is a problem, and the troubling issues raised by both concerts were in no way local or passing, but are apparently endemic to such events.

Both choruses are big, Framingham listing 116 members, Lexington 119. Both are really too big for most of the music they sing, a situation aggravated by factors I shall come to in a moment. Framingham is also too big in that it has too many people who are not good enough. As I watched the chorus I became fascinated by a woman in the soprano section who looked at the conductor only at final cadences, peered anxiously into her copy, sang perhaps two syllables out of three, and tended to begin those only after she had heard others come in and felt sure of where she was. Then, as I looked around, I found others of her kind, though none so extreme, and by the end of the Gloria I could have suggested two dozen singers for canning on obvious appearances alone. Reduced by a good third, the Framingham group could make a really good sound: bigger, brighter, and cleaner than the one it now makes.

The Lexington people, by contrast, function at a high level of efficiency, and, though there is less emphasis on sharp diction than there might be, I should call the Masterworks Chorale a first-rate ensemble of its kind. Lannom is an excellent trainer of choruses, but Oliver, as I have found by observing the results of his work at the New England Conservatory and Tanglewood, is very good, too. I am disinclined, therefore, to attribute the difference in effectiveness of the two choruses entirely to a difference of quality between their conductors. It was my impression that Oliver was making the best of available material, but that he was struggling with the results of insufficiently rigorous auditions, and that, I guess, is so because someone has decided that the pleasure of the participating singers is more important than the musical efficiency of the chorus in performance.

That problem is one the Handel and Haydn Society has faced courageously in the last few seasons, when it decided that, whatever it might offer in total membership of more than a hundred during the course of a season, the Christmas performances of *Messiah* must, in justice to Handel, be sung by no more than thirty-some singers.

Now, getting back to Lexington and Framingham, Beethoven does not need a chorus of 119 for the Cantata and the Mass in C, and as for the B minor Mass of Bach, it simply cannot be done coherently with 116.

You get into difficulties with the orchestra, whose contribution in most of the repertory that groups like Framingham and Lexington tackle, is very much more than a neutral "accompaniment" in the background. In the Beethoven pieces you could engage an orchestra large enough and good enough to make a reasonable balance with the massive choral sound. Lexington did not, in fact, do so, and that the hat was passed at intermission presumably tells why. But Bach, with his chamber-musical scoring and the subtle interaction of solo and tutti writing in his music, does not even allow the big orchestra option. You cannot make sense of the textures of the B minor Mass except with sonorities similar in weight to those Bach imagined—about forty each of singers and players is maximum—and you have to face that fact just as much as a lutenist has to face the fact that he is not the man to do a really convincing *1812* Overture.

The crux of the problem is in the choral conductors themselves. Most of them just cannot conduct. I am not even talking about questions of musical culture, in which many of them are really quite ready for the poverty program, but about the plain technical facts of conducting, one-two-three, one-two-three-four, cueing the oboes, that sort of thing. As the professional orchestra players or vocal soloists who are more or less regularly associated with these conductors will attest, they are, except for dealing with the specifically choral portions, apt to be unclear, forgetful, erratic, inconsistent between rehearsals and performance in matters of tempo and beat pattern. They might beat three when the music is in four, they sometimes fail to mark cuts, and occasionally the performances simply break down.

They are inexperienced with orchestras, often diffident or even terrified, while the players in turn find their Svengali routines or rug-weaving gestures unintelligible and regard the choral conductors variously with patronizing affection, indifference, apprehension, loathing, or derision. Not surprisingly the playing, even that of the very good people from the Symphony or the Philharmonia, is awful.

There are exceptions. Thomas Dunn of the Handel and Haydn Society is one and a thorough-going professional, and the Cantata Singers' John Harbison is another, but exceptions they remain.

Not long ago someone told me of having complimented a singer friend on her contribution to a duet in a Bach cantata. The other singer had been impossible, the instrumental obbligato and accompaniment indifferent, and the conducting inattentive. The soprano was aware of all that and she angrily rejected the compliment as irrelevant to the only thing that really mattered: how she happened to sing that afternoon made no difference, she explained, "either the duet sounds well or it doesn't."

That story of artistic probity came to mind as I thought about the Bach and Beethoven concerts. Good choral singing, yes, and some good soloists, Pamela Gore in the Bach, Elizabeth Phinney, Phyllis Elhady, Francis Hester in Beethoven. But that is not enough for those pieces, that is not what they are all about, and in the end there was no escaping that Bach and Beethoven had sounded lousy.

The education and professional system that makes of the choral conductor a separate species to whose members ordinary standards of technical and musical competence are not applicable is a disaster. The exceptions exist and I am thankful they do. Meanwhile the best experiences with choral music tend to come in those performances sponsored and arranged by symphony orchestras who engage choruses, while the choruses, when they act on their own, usually accomplish more by way of affording recreation to their members than as a means of providing good performances of choral repertory.

Monteverdi's *L'Orfeo* Impressively Produced

June 21, 1970

Two of Monteverdi's operas survive: *L'Orfeo*, first given at Mantua in 1607 when the composer would have been about 40, and *L'incoronazione di Poppea*, written thirty-five years later.[15] At the time of *L'Orfeo*, the first experiments in drama with continuous music were just a few years old. They are feeble and monotonous, but Monteverdi moved in as though he had worked for the stage all his life and, for that matter, as though there had been a fully developed operatic tradition for him to connect with.

L'Orfeo is a rich synthesis of past and present, with the pastoral and the madrigal of the Renaissance tied to the new declamatory recitative. It is a work of enormous variety, in rhythm (the shepherds' dances and the "free" recital of the messenger who brings the news of Euridice's death), in pacing (the quick succession of short numbers in the first two acts and the expansiveness of Orpheus's plea to Charon), in texture (the simply accompanied declamations and the moralizing madrigals at the ends of acts), and in scoring. Monteverdi's imaginative feeling for the coloristic, affective possibilities of instruments is wonderful, and again and again he pierces the heart with the thrust of his word-setting and the boldness of the harmonies (the Messenger or, even more, Euridice's "second death").

This deeply touching work speaks eloquently in a new recording (Telefunken: Das alte Werk) under the direction of Nikolaus Harnoncourt. I have one reservation: the performance is oriented more to musical values than to dramatic: the pauses between numbers are sometimes a hairsbreadth too long, and the effect is underlined by fairly dry acoustics. Otherwise, though, it is really lovely, expressive, spirited, completely absorbing.

Lajos Kozma sings Orpheus beautifully (his coloratura is not quite elegant enough, but he understands and conveys its expressive purpose). There are very good performances as well by Rotraud Hansmann as Euridice and particularly as the Spirit of Music, Kurt Equiluz (third shepherd, second spirit), Max van Egmond (Apollo, fourth shepherd, third spirit), Nikolaus Simkowsky (an alarming Charon), Eiko Katanosaka and Jacque Villisech (Proserpina and Pluto), and Cathy Berberian (the Messenger and Hope). There is good choral singing by the Munich Capella Antiqua. The real glory of the recording, however, is the extraordinary instrumental playing by the Vienna Concentus Musicus and such outstanding musicians as Herbert Tachezi, Gustav Leonhardt, and Johann Sonnleitner (keyboards), Alice Harnoncourt and Walter Pfeiffer (violins), Erna Gruber (harp), Eugen Dombois and [Michael] Schäffer (lutes and chitarroni), Don Smithers and Ulrich Brandhoff (cornetti). There is a trilingual libretto with amply documented and illustrated notes. An impressive and valuable achievement in every way.

[15] This is an oddity: Monteverdi composed three extant operas, the omission here being *Il ritorno d'Ulisse in patria*, which by the time of this review existed in several editions and had already been recorded in 1964.

Steinberg on Steinberg

August 23, 1970

LENOX—Between rehearsals for his second pair of Beethoven concerts at Tanglewood, William Steinberg discussed his work as music director of the Boston Symphony Orchestra. He was brought to Boston, as he sees it, to "stabilize" the situation after "musical values had become shaky."

"I am used to putting orchestras straight," he added. "This is by no means my first time. I have found it can be done with the Boston Symphony in an astonishingly short while. It is supposed that the educational—I hate that word—process takes a long time, but it is fast here, even when I have returned to find the orchestra—I choose my words carefully—in not so desirable a state. If I may quote Michael Steinberg after the Elgar symphony last season, 'The Boston Symphony sounded like the Boston Symphony again.'"

How a conductor puts an orchestra straight, Steinberg continued, is "his own mysterious private affair. Is it done with charm of personality . . . "—and here the Maestro had to break off in order to deal with his own amusement over THAT idea—" . . . no, some do it with grace, some with uncouth, some with terror." But, Steinberg, who likes to say that "modesty" is not a word that occurs in a conductor's vocabulary, went on: "What is sure is that it takes a lot of brains, and it takes a lot of knowledge of human psychology." In an orchestra like the Boston Symphony, "each player is a king in his own right. He wants to remain so, and he subjugates not easily."

Steinberg, just turned 71, looking tanned, rested, and a little thinner than before the series of illnesses that kept him off his podia in Boston and Pittsburgh most of last year, is getting ready for his two seasons that begin in Pittsburgh September 18 and in Boston a week later. His total volume of work is very slightly reduced and he is trying to use energy-conserving devices like sitting down during the long solo cadenzas in concertos. Nonetheless, 1970–71 will mean a fuller season's work for him than that taken on by almost any conductor in the country, and it will include a three-week European tour with the Boston Symphony in April.

Both his September openings include Beethoven's Seventh Symphony. For Pittsburgh, Steinberg will also conduct the Prelude to Act II of Hans Pfitzner's *Palestrina* and *Also sprach Zarathustra* by Richard Strauss. Asked about the prospects for all three *Palestrina* Preludes for a Boston program, Steinberg replied that if it came to talking him into that, it would not take much. *Palestrina* was one of the largest operas he conducted before leaving Frankfurt after the Nazi takeover in 1933, recalling that a revolving stage was installed especially to accommodate the complicated, "conversational" second act, which represents a session of the Council of Trent, and remembering that he angered Pfitzner by thinning out some of the orchestration—"here, just below the middle, where there is so easily too much"—but succeeding thereby in having all the words come through with brilliant clarity. As for *Palestrina* as a whole, "it is one of the greatest manifestations of—you will excuse the expression—the German spirit."

In Boston, the Beethoven Seventh will be preceded by Gustav Holst's *The Planets* and the first American performance of *Paths*, a symphonic elegy by the Hungarian-born Israeli composer, Oedoen Partos. After the death of his wife two-and-a-half years ago, Steinberg set up a foundation to commission, in memoriam, a series of compositions by Israeli composers, one year a work for full orchestra, next one for chamber orchestra, then a choral piece, and so through the cycle again. *Paths* represents the first fruits of the scheme; it and a concerto for violin, cello, and chamber orchestra by J. Tal, alias Gruenthal, have already had their premieres at the Ein Gev Festival at Passover-time in Israel.

Steinberg's link to Israeli's musical life goes back to 1936 when, together with the violinist Bronislaw Huberman, he organized and trained the Palestine Orchestra (now the Israel Philharmonic), whose first concert was conducted in December of that year by Toscanini. "For a time it was an orchestra of incomparable quality," said Steinberg. He still likes to call it "my orchestra," and has often returned to conduct it (including most of the concerts on its 1967 victory celebration tour through the United States).

Steinberg has stipulated that the works commissioned by him first be performed in Israel, but he reserves for himself the privilege of introducing them in the United States. Does he choose the composers who receive commissions? "Oh no, that would be the greatest possible mistake. No, for that I have appointed a most elegant committee," which is headed by Erich Toeplitz, whom Steinberg brought to Palestine in 1936 as the principal flutist of the new orchestra, and whom he regards as "a marvelous artist."

Finally, how did things stand regarding a possible Boston performance—premiere, it would be—of Mahler's Tenth Symphony? Though at the time of the announcement of his Boston appointment Steinberg had hoped to play it during his first Boston season, it had not been forthcoming then, and neither was it on the 1970–71 programs. Steinberg affirmed his belief in the work and mentioned, as well, his closeness to Mahler's widow, the late Alma Mahler Werfel, and to his daughter, Anna. He had learned, however, that Deryck Cooke, the English musician who had prepared a performing version from Mahler's unfinished manuscript, had withdrawn his score, declaring that he was dissatisfied and that he could do better. "And that is impressive," commented Steinberg.

Yes, he had meanwhile received Cooke's revised score and was disappointed only insofar as some extreme notational complexities, adding greatly to the difficulty of preparing and performing the work, had not been eliminated. That, in passing, reminded Steinberg of an encounter with Stravinsky in 1929, when he had suggested to the composer that changes in the notation of the first part of *Petrushka* would make things much easier for conductors and players. "Yes, I'd already thought of that," replied Stravinsky. "No, you hadn't Meister Stravinsky," countered young Steinberg, "because you looked startled when I mentioned it."

Getting back to the Mahler Tenth, Steinberg said that even with the New York Philharmonic, "which is after all quite a machine," he had to go into overtime rehearsing the work in 1968, "for which Mr. Carlos Moseley, the manager, had grudgingly to pay many, many dollars." As it is now set up, the Boston Symphony rehearsal schedule does not permit the adequate preparation of exceptionally difficult works, and so, for the moment, the Mahler Tenth was not on the schedule. No, that was certainly not a permanent condition. He had begun, Steinberg said, to discuss what could be done occasionally to alter the proportion of rehearsal and performance time in favor of the former so as to make possible the inclusion of works requiring more than ordinary preparation. "Quality counts. As for the Mahler Tenth, you will not be spared it."

Schwann's Wonderful Catalogue

September 13, 1970

Schwann, in musical households, is a household word. It's where you look up what recordings are available of what—classical, jazz, popular, country and western, poetry, basic Ga (which they speak in Ghana), heart auscultation, just about the whole gamut except stag party records—and lots of people find it handy for quickly checking a composer's first name and dates or the Köchel number of Mozart's M major Piano Concerto.

Schwann has been so much of an institution for so many years that I was, I think, too much in awe even to wonder about a putative Mr. Schwann at 137 Newbury St., the address given for his monthly record catalogue. But yes, behind W. Schwann Inc. there is William Schwann, 50-some, tall, quiet. For years a professional organist, he still plays the harpsichord for pleasure. He was a critic for a while, too, but the real moment of the intersection of life and destiny came when he opened a record store in 1939. That venture was interrupted by the war, but he was back with records when the long-playing microgroove disc appeared in 1948.

To dispel some of the confusion produced by that development, first for himself and his customers, then for his colleagues and theirs, Schwann typed a list of LP records available on all labels. That led to the appearance in October 1949 of Vol. I, No. 1, of the Long-Playing Record Catalog,[16] its modest twenty-four pages of listings still in Schwann's careful typescript, reproduced by photo offset, and with a page of Schubert's *Great* C major Symphony on the cover. The first Schwann had a few hundred listings on eleven labels (eight of them still exist); the August 1970 issue, which is Vol. 22, No. 8, gives somewhere between 35,000 and 40,000 records—"I don't vouch for any of my figures," warns Schwann—on 695 labels from A.A. to Zondervan.

Both those exotic entries, unlike, for example, Accent and Zapple, are marked with an asterisk, which means that their records are listed only in the Schwann Supplementary Catalog, which comes out twice a year and whose most recent issue, Spring 1970, has 156 pages of entries. The Supplement is a way of keeping the regular catalogue within bounds, that is, neither too fat nor too expensive (dealers get the monthly, about 100,000 copies per issue, at from 23 to 29 cents; slightly more than half are bought by customers at the list price at 60 cents, but almost as many get theirs free). Among other categories, the Supplement now includes imports, spoken, international pop and folk, a special Latin American section, non-current popular within bounds (through 1966, and it is a particularly entertaining section to read through), children's, and, as the most recent development, all non-stereo records.

But the Schwann group of catalogues includes still more members: the Artist Issue (of which more in a moment), a children's records supplement (last issued Christmas 1969), a Country and Western catalogue. Schwann also publishes a list of a suggested basic record library, recommending compositions rather than specific recordings. Schwann prepares that himself, saying that he is the sort who likes to make lists of what to take to that desert island. For that matter, you can also get a souvenir reprint of the original October 1949 Schwann, from which you can learn that, along with all the gains since that time, we are the poorer for [the loss of] some interesting, but also for some valuable, repertory that was available then and is not now (Bloch's Quartet No. 2, Pfitzner's *Palestrina* Preludes, Reger's Böcklin Suite and Serenade for Orchestra, and the Villa-Lobos Quartet No. 6).

Schwann, his editorial staff of eight, and for that matter Mrs. Schwann, a tall, blonde, and beautiful Finnish lady by name of Aire-Maija, who has been very much drawn into the catalogue scene, spent the late spring and early summer in a condition of intense preoccupation about getting out the 1970 Artists Issue, the first since 1966. It runs to 320 pages as against 308 for the last one, and it would be enormously larger had Schwann not decided drastically to streamline its contents. You can still find ensembles, trios to orchestras, from Aachen to Zürich,

[16] The use of "Catalog" reflects the spelling used by William Schwann for the actual title of the periodical.

conductors from Abbado to Zuraitis (who records Glière and Shchedrin), soloists from accordionist Yuri Kazakov to zither player Ruth Welcome, and singers from Abdoun to Zylis-Gara, but you can no longer look up individual members of ensembles. That means, for example, that an admirer of the pianist Claude Frank could learn from Schwann that he could buy a recording of Brahms's *Liebeslieder* Waltzes with Frank, but he would not learn that he could also get recorded performances with Frank of important trios and quartets by Mozart and Brahms because those are listed only under Boston Symphony Chamber Players.

Schwann realizes the nuisance of that and regrets it. That is true also of his listing full contents of anthologies and miscellaneous collections only upon their first appearance in the catalogue. That, too, he points out, is part of the price for the decision he has made to keep his catalogue as useful as possible to the largest number of collectors or potential buyers of records. His English counterpart, issued quarterly by the magazine, *The Gramophone*, can afford some more detailed listings, including which cadenzas are used in concerto recordings, because the number of records it lists is so much smaller. "We're also a lot more accurate," he adds.

Where Schwann himself lives musically is most of all the Baroque. One can get the impression that he sometimes would not mind if the history of music had stopped in 1791,[17] or even that in his struggle to keep the catalogue within bounds that he has been tempted to exclude some of the music of which he does not approve. Schwann can see thirteen churches from his office, and that pleases him. Another thing he will show you there is a pirated edition of Schwann in Japanese. The office is slightly more dashing in its appointments than many another in Boston. The reason is that Schwann once entered the furniture business, sure he could make a go of a store in which a friend had failed. He was wrong, but he did have the idea of making a specialty of interior decoration for offices. He furnished his own office to be a persuasive model—it was the one aspect of that venture that really went well—and its present handsome appearance is all that remains as a reminder of that brief excursion of Schwann's.

Obviously Schwann the institution is enormously useful. And, for the inveterate list-readers among us, who cannot pass a college bulletin board without going through the section assignments in History 303, who read every package of breakfast crumbs or can of chicken broth for the niacin and hydrolyzed vegetable proteins, and who like to read the names of all the altos in the Handel and Haydn Society, Schwann has also made the world a more amusing place through which to pass.

[17] 1791 was the year of Mozart's death.

The Boston Musica Viva

September 24, 1970

The Boston Musica Viva is an outfit founded last spring, when it began with a modest series of three concerts, no money, and not a whole lot of listeners. Still alive,[18] Musica Viva led off the 1970–71 season here with a concert at the Busch-Reisinger Museum at Harvard last night, still with no money, but this time with an overflow crowd. I hope they will find money, because what they have carved out for themselves to do is something worth doing, something Boston and Cambridge will be the richer for having.

Musica Viva's concern is 20th-century chamber music, its classics as well as new pieces. I gather that attention to Arnold Schoenberg is near the core of their repertory planning since each concert has included a major work of his. Richard Pittman is music director and conductor, and he has put together an ensemble of musicians who, for the most part, are sympathetic to recent music and skilled with it.

Last night's concert included the first and second performances of Joseph Schwantner's *Consortium* (it was done at the opening and repeated just before intermission); two song cycles by Webern, the Canons, Op. 16, and the Songs, Op. 14; *Interpolation* by Haubenstock-Ramati; *The Shape of Silence* by Joyce Mekeel; and the Schoenberg Serenade. Pittman conducted whatever required it, and the performers were soprano Joan Heller, baritone David Evitts, violinist Nancy Cirillo, violist Virginia Blakeman, flutist John Heiss, clarinetists William Wrzesien and Anthony Fulginiti, guitarist Robert Sullivan, and mandolinist Henry Wiktorowicz. Not enough money means not enough rehearsal, and the Schoenberg suffered a bit; most of the music, though, was projected clearly, vitally, and convincingly.

For most of the audience, Miss Mekeel's *The Shape of Silence* was the evening's hit, not altogether unsurprisingly, for it was the most theatrical piece on the program. It is for flutist alone, but along with fluting, which itself includes here many recent extensions of technique such as multiple stops, the player sings, hums, whispers, speaks, and finally walks off the stage playing a kind of recessional ostinato. It is in the fun-and-games department in a way, but it works because the transitions from one mode of producing sound to another seem to be at the heart of what *The Shape of Silence* is about, and those transitions are composed knowingly and surely. It made, as well, a pleasing and interesting complement and contrast to Haubenstock-Ramati's piece of 1959, in which the flutist gets to play

[18] Boston Musica Viva remained "alive" for another half-century, until founding director Richard Pittman stepped down in 2022.

with his own taped ghosts. John Heiss's playing of both works was outstandingly, indeed spectacularly, good.

Schwantner's *Consortium* (for violin, viola, cello, flute, and clarinet) is breezily virtuosic, with a delightful surface, what appear to be some quotations from Schoenberg, Berio, and perhaps others, and quite enough individuality and substance to make the second hearing as persuasive or engaging as the first.

Thomas Leads Symphony in Piston, Schuman Program

October 3, 1970

Something is muddled in the program notes for the Boston Symphony concert which Michael Tilson Thomas conducted in Symphony Hall yesterday afternoon. Walter Piston's Second Symphony and William Schuman's Violin Concerto were about to be recorded by the orchestra, that information being followed by this sentence: "In commemoration of their 30th anniversary, Broadcast Music Incorporated are sponsoring a project, in co-operation with Deutsche Grammophon, to record works which have won Pulitzer Prizes." Fine, except that neither work is a Pulitzer winner. The Piston got a New York Music Critics Circle award in 1945 and his later Third and Seventh symphonies won Pulitzers; Schuman, too, was a Pulitzer winner, in fact the first one ever [for music], but that was for his cantata, *A Free Song*, in 1943.

I don't quite see how to put the pieces of all that together, but I am grateful for whatever chain of ideas got Piston's Symphony No. 2, not heard here since Munch conducted it in 1955, onto a Boston Symphony program. The Second, completed in 1943, is a three-movement symphony, quick-slow-quick. Precise and contained, it comes from a point in his life when his music began to open up, to move more lyrically in longer, softer lines, to admit, quite simply, more personal warmth. The first two movements particularly are music of sensibility, and in the way that sensibility is articulated by way of a surface unfailingly cool and unruffled, in the elegant mastery of his writing, in his delightful inventiveness in matters of form (though always within the framework of very conservative assumptions), Piston comes across as something like a mid-20th-century Mendelssohn.

The first movement is enjoyable for those very qualities, and the interesting and suggestive transformations of material in the recapitulation and particularly in the pensive coda give great pleasure. The Adagio, with its gentle undulating melodies and delicate textures, has, as I hear it, some kinship of spirit with the Andante of Brahms's Third Symphony: it is gentle music, eloquent, and touching, astoundingly so. There is a bouncy finale which does not speak in a personal sort of way and for that difference loses something in interest: well carried off, it is fun and it certainly works on its own terms. The performance was beautiful, the playing in the Adagio of Harold Wright, the new solo clarinetist, particularly so, and the 76-year-old composer was greeted with a standing ovation by orchestra and audience when Michael Thomas brought him to the stage.

Schuman's twice-revised Violin Concerto—its three versions date from 1947, 1956, and 1959—is an accomplished piece of writing, and it is most interesting in things to do with solo-tutti contrasts in questions of both gesture and of texture. The form is well controlled, with lots of variety of pace packed into the two movements. The material itself has something ungainly and muscle-bound about it, and there is in Schuman's aggressive rhetoric something that reminds me of official architecture that is too big and too clean like Speer's Berlin Chancellery, the Foro Italico in Rome, or, for that matter, Lincoln Center where Mr. Schuman was boss for some years. There is slow and quiet music in the Concerto, too, just as even such buildings have johns and potted plants, but I must say that on Friday I found myself cringing from whatever it was the piece was trying to tell me, and more, I think, because of manner than content. The work got a coolly efficient performance with Paul Zukofsky as soloist, and Mr. Schuman was there to share in its friendly reception.

The concert began and ended with brilliant dance music in D, Bach's Fourth Suite, which is festive and the real thing, and Ravel's *La Valse*, which is dream and a strangely mixed message of horror and something between fascination and love. Thomas conducted both with great verve and the Bach, as well, with a knowing and acute feeling for style and language; the orchestra's playing was alert and often brilliant.

In Israel, Omit the Ratchet, Maestro

October 11, 1970

One of the pieces the Greater Boston Youth Symphony Orchestra (GBYSO) played at its concerts at the Israel Festival in August was Krzysztof Penderecki's Capriccio for Violin and Orchestra. The Capriccio makes growls, clusters, shrieks, slides, and noises generally that you don't get in the Mendelssohn Concerto—or at least you shouldn't—and almost any audience will include some people who aren't used to such things and find them funny or annoying. The audiences in Caesarea and Jerusalem that heard the violinist Roman Totenberg and the GBYSO play the Penderecki seemed quite normal in that way. There were a few who tittered and some who offered the Hebrew equivalent of "They call that music?" and there was more conversation generally than during a performance of Mendelssohn, but it was really OK up to a point about two-thirds through the piece when Penderecki brings in the ratchet for a few twirls. Then, at Caesarea and a few days later in Jerusalem with a very different sort of audience, the reaction—mainly incredulous laughter, it seemed to me—had something near-hysterical in its loudness and intensity. Moreover, it passed as soon as the ratchet itself did, and nothing before or after in the Capriccio produced anything like it.

When Israelis offer a fact and its explanation, they do not proceed from one to the other with a simple "because." Rather they tend to stop at the end of the fact, transfix you with a big rhetorical "WHY?," and then go on. So, about the ratchet or rattle, WHY?, I wondered, and I thought of two answers. One is the association for a Jewish audience of that sound with the festival of Purim when the kids make a diabolical racket with them at each mention of Haman, the villain of the Esther story. The other is that here is an audience that never gets to hear Strauss's *Till Eulenspiegel*, so that the ratchet has no concert hall association whatsoever.

What to do about Wagner and Richard Strauss is still hot in Israel. De facto, the situation quite simply is that they do not get played. For many Israelis these are tainted names and intolerable. That is far from a universally held opinion, but it enjoys great respect and attention because anything that suggests Nazi Germany carries so terrible an emotional freight. There is, as well, some unease about works like Bach's Passion settings and Handel's *Messiah*, and performances of them have sometimes, not always, been occasions for protest and demonstration.

In *Messiah* the problem line turned out to be "The sting of death is sin; and the strength of sin is the law" (I *Corinthians* XV), and it offended because of the affect embodied in the Hebrew word for law, "torah."

Yohanan Böhm, music critic of the *Jerusalem Post*, showed me the enormous clipping file he has accumulated on the Wagner-Strauss issue and, more peripherally, the Bach-Handel one. As I read the articles, editorials, statements for publication, readers' letters, and so forth, I saw how the arguments tended to shoot past one another, the same arguments year after year. You can treat it as a musical issue and say that a repertory without Wagner and Strauss makes no sense, you can say in effect, "I can't stand to look at what that music makes me think about," and there is no common ground at all and therefore no argument really.

Mendi Rodan, a relatively recent immigrant from Rumania, is the young conductor of the Kol Israel Radio Symphony Orchestra, and he also teaches at the Rubin Music Academy in Jerusalem. He told me that Wagner's music was studied in theory and analysis courses and that he had successfully made a case that playing Wagner's music and Strauss's was an indispensable experience in the training of an orchestral musician. Orchestral classes at the Academy regularly rehearse such music, and each new class of students is astonished and a bit guilty at the pleasure derived from getting fingers and embouchures around those taxing virtuoso pieces.

Like most musicians with whom I talked, Böhm thinks that the issue will be resolved in favor of musical interests, perhaps sooner than many people think, and certainly once the generation that had direct experience of the Nazis has passed from the scene. He pointed out that the controversy about the German language had been quietly settled, that not so many years ago works like the Beethoven Ninth or the Mahler song cycles and symphonies could be sung only in Hebrew translation or that a Lieder recital in German was out of the question. Those conditions simply do not exist anymore, and nobody objects to sung German.

During a very brief visit, I had no chance to hear performances by the two full symphony orchestras, neither the Israel Philharmonic nor the Kol Israel. Together with Gary Bertini and the Israel Chamber Orchestra, Rodan and the Kol Israel account for most of the performances of contemporary music. Rodan is well thought of for his conscientious work in that area, for his achievement in improving the technical quality of the orchestra, and for providing the hope that Kol Israel might provide something like a culturally left-wing gadfly in opposition to the Israel Philharmonic.

My question "How is the Philharmonic?" was usually answered by some variation of "a very good second-rate orchestra." I found no one optimistic enough to believe that it would soon regain the legendary brilliance it had at the time of its founding in the late 1930s, when it attracted for a while the cream of Germany's and Austria's displaced Jewish musicians. Zubin Mehta has the title of musical advisor. He is in effect music director, but I was told that his contract with the Los Angeles Philharmonic explicitly disallows his holding that title with any other orchestra. Mehta became something of a hero when he flew into Israel in order to be there during the Six-Day War in 1967 (his dashing gesture was set into higher relief by another American conductor who failed to show up for a rehearsal one morning and who, it turned out when inquiries were made at his hotel, had headed for the airport and left the country[19]), and the consensus about Mehta is that both musically and technically things at the Israel Philharmonic have been somewhat brighter since his association with it.

In a way the most astonishingly impressive thing about the Philharmonic is its loyal and huge audience. In Tel Aviv alone (population 400,000) it plays eight sold-out subscription series in a 3,000-seat auditorium, and it has regular series in Haifa and Jerusalem as well. Jerusalem has a reputation for being a hard town to play in, and actually the Philharmonic has trouble selling a second series there. Still, per capita attendance at symphony concerts is greater in Israel than

[19] This was Erich Leinsdorf.

in any country in the world, and where most American orchestras advertise that subscriptions are still available, the Israel Philharmonic inserts ads announcing the "registration of applicants for subscriptions," with a deposit of ten Israeli pounds required.

Except that German performers still, by and large, are not welcome, concert listings in Israel are much like those in any European country or America, and the Philharmonic's programs could be those of one of our own symphony orchestras, though very much at the conservative end of the spectrum. The Philharmonic programs for the 1970–71 season contain only a single Israeli work (by Mordechai Seter) and one American (Schuller's *Klee* Studies conducted by Solti). I was both entertained and surprised by Yohanan Böhm's article outlining the series in the Jerusalem *Post* and its candid editorializing: "Ančerl wisely sugars his program presenting the Schoenberg Violin Concerto" with Schubert and Franck; Solti "compensates his listeners" for the Schuller with Tchaikovsky's *Pathétique*; and, about Barenboim's intention to conduct Webern's Five Pieces, Op. 10, Böhm says, "no fear, you will also get the Schumann Cello Concerto and the Bruckner Seventh."

Böhm is kidding his readers, but at the same time, he really is no friend to contemporary music. And in all I found that dissatisfaction with the state of music criticism is widespread among Israeli musicians, so there is something else to link Israeli musical life with that here and elsewhere.

Harrison's Canticle No. 3 Fine, Sometimes Surprising

October 28, 1970

Lou Harrison, whose Canticle No. 3 Michael Tilson Thomas included on his Boston Symphony program last night, walks alone. Now 53, he has composed copiously and idiosyncratically for nearly forty years, his works defying classification and having relatively little stylistic uniformity among themselves. His teachers were Henry Cowell and Schoenberg, and I imagine that from the one he got his interest in non-Western musics, and from the other his precision of workmanship. He has remarkable gifts as a conductor, and in and out of music, his occupation and concerns have been astonishingly and engagingly diversified.

His Canticle No. 3 must have been startling in 1941 when it was first heard and when its gamelan-like sounds would have been totally unfamiliar to just about everyone in an American audience. By now we have heard dozens, hundreds of pieces with exotic instrumentations, especially ones that aggressively make a point of their delicacy, and there is little that is more tiresome. It really says something about the quality of Harrison's work that his Canticle No. 3 sounds so fresh today and makes so delightful an effect.

It is scored for ocarinas (played by Martin Hoherman, the Symphony's assistant principal cellist), guitar, and something like fifteen kinds of percussion instruments, including iron pipes (muted), brakedrums (five out of eight muted), dragons' mouths (temple blocks), Egyptian rattles, and elephant bells in three sizes. The ensemble makes fine and gentle and sometimes surprising sounds, and the music, which lasts a bit under a quarter-hour, moves with pleasing variety sometimes involved in ruminations round about tiny phrases, sometimes making percussive, irregular accompaniments to unheard melodies.

It is light in weight: I at least cannot hear what led Virgil Thomson, reviewing it in 1953, to call it "powerful in expression," though "subtle" it is, as he said, and "lovely to listen to." I found its rhythmic looseness refreshing, particularly in the symphony concert context where so much regular and beaty music is served up.

On stage, along with the fine players and their rather jumpy conductor, was an ambulatory television camera man. His softly irritating presence was the counterpart of that experience we have all had of being kept waiting in a store while the shopkeeper thought it more important to talk on the telephone than to deal with his real flesh-and-blood customers.

String Quartet Opens Series at MIT

November 9, 1970

The LaSalle String Quartet, which opened the MIT Humanities Series in Kresge Auditorium yesterday afternoon, is one in just a handful of really first-class quartets today. The concert, at which the quartet played Mozart's B-flat Quartet, K.458 (*Hunt*), the Beethoven F minor, Op. 95, and the first performance here of György Ligeti's Quartet No. 2, was in every way impressive.

Because of the use of some of it in *2001*, Ligeti's music is familiar to more people than his name. He seems limited in range, but he is a composer whose imagination is liberated particularly with respect to texture and pace; he is a precise, responsible workman, and he has humor. His Quartet No. 2, written 1968 for the LaSalle, is in five movements that fill twenty-three minutes or so very beguilingly. The third is the movement to make the most striking immediate impression: its marking is "like a precision mechanism," and it is a funny frozen scherzo, consisting much of the time of repeated notes in pizzicato, but with each instrument independent from the others in tempo. Ligeti once wrote a piece for 100 metronomes, a somewhat simple-minded joke, not displeasing, and only a little boring. The quartet movement is not so much a postscript to that piece as a realization finally of what the compositional possibilities of the metronome are.

The Quartet as a whole is mercurial and nervous, even in its *molto calmo* slow movement, with frequent and usually abrupt changes in every dimension, and emerging once in a while into a kind of daylight of clarifying unisons. Sometimes it is silent altogether, often it is barely audible, and it likes to speak in the register and as though in the voices of bats. The scoring is fanciful, but I thought the program note's claim that the piece "opens up unsuspected realms of . . . instrumental possibilities" exaggerated.

The Ligeti is a dazzling showpiece, and the LaSalle played it brilliantly. The quartet made its reputation mainly with its sympathetic and virtuosic performance of contemporary music, but it also plays Mozart and Beethoven superbly. Yesterday's performance, with its bold delineation of large structural units and its almost aggressively vivid sculpting of detail, was, above all, astoundingly clear. It was uncommonly arresting in its projection of musical gesture and character. The sound, which is predominantly delicate and cool, was transparent, not least because the playing was so well in tune.

The four musicians, Walter Levin, Henry Meyer, Peter Kamnitzer, and Jack Kirstein, have striking, quite personal ideas about what they play. Their work is, in fact, enormously opinionated—which delights me—and their performances are spirited, elegant statements of the case for their unfailingly intelligent, interesting, and lively musical perceptions.

BSO Plays Copland's *Short Symphony*

November 14, 1970

In his second week as guest conductor with the Boston Symphony Orchestra, Seiji Ozawa yesterday afternoon gave a concert that invited one's alert and pleased attention all the way through. The program: Copland's Short Symphony, *Atmosphères* by Ligeti, and the Berlioz *Symphonie fantastique*.

Today is Aaron Copland's 70th birthday, and playing the *Short Symphony* is an apt way to celebrate because it is rarely heard, very good, and a work for which the composer himself has a special fondness. It was finished in 1933, performed soon after by Carlos Chávez in Mexico, subsequently scheduled and cancelled by both Stokowski and Koussevitzky, ignored by other conductors, and introduced in the United States as late as 1944 when Stokowski evidently decided that he liked it after all. Meanwhile, in desperation as much as conviction, Copland had arranged the piece as a sextet for clarinet, piano, and strings, and it has become fairly well known in that form. Friday's was the first Boston Symphony performance of the original version.

The *Short Symphony* is in three movements—quick, slow, quick—and it is short indeed, about fifteen minutes. The beginning and end of the slow movement are, so far as I know, the earliest appearances of that wide-open-spaces American sound that was to be so characteristic a feature of Copland's later work, from Music for Radio through *The Tender Land*. The *Short Symphony* is not a landscape piece, though, and its quiet middle movement is an interlude in a work whose melodies are otherwise jagged, whose rhythms are nervously irregular, whose stance is ironic and detached, biting, often sharply humorous rather than poetic and reflective. These aspects of musical character grow out of the structure, which is highly concentrated at all levels and it is extended into the fascinating and individual sonority, lean (there is no heavy brass and no percussion) but carrying enormous punch.

Copland has guessed that the rhythmic complications in the *Short Symphony* were "an important factor" in its early non-performance history. Friday's performance was not bad, but it lacked that energy which is given by confidence, and it showed that the *Short Symphony* is still a very hard piece.

Ozawa had conducted György Ligeti's *Atmosphères* at Tanglewood last summer, but this was its first performance in Boston. It is a study in clusters in shifting registers and of varying density, terribly simple as a musical idea but complex in the details of the working-out. It is fantastic and suggestive, sounds gorgeous, and it got a most convincing performance.

So did the *Fantastique*, Ozawa being one of the few conductors who catch the delicacy of the work as well as its fire, its classicism along with its wildness. There needed to be more differentiation in dynamics at the *pianissimo* end of the scale, and I think the "March to the Scaffold" wants to go a little more slowly, or at least more doggedly, to be properly menacing; otherwise, Ozawa's interpretation was very sure indeed and exceptionally beautiful in the bold, far-sighted shaping of the pastoral Adagio. The orchestra played beautifully, with evident pleasure and enthusiasm. And Berlioz, I am certain, would have been touched by the delicacy of Wayne Rapier's offstage oboe solos in the slow movement, and delighted with the huge and hideous clangor of the bells in the finale (real, cast bells, and played by Charles Smith).

Steinberg Conducts BSO in Mahler's Seventh

December 19, 1970

Mahler's Seventh Symphony was introduced to Boston by Koussevitzky in 1948 (forty years after its premiere!), and William Steinberg's performance of it at yesterday's Boston Symphony concert was the first here since then.

This work, whose performances remain so rare even in this time of Mahler discovery, is a problematic one indeed. There are five movements, perceived as a triptych, with pieces on a large scale and of enormous weight on the outsides, and in the middle a set of three that are lighter in texture, individually shorter, though large enough when taken together to provide the triptych with a very spacious central panel. Lots of contrast is built into this scheme. The first movement, for example, is predominantly tragic; the finale, on the other hand, seems like a picture of Mahler stuck on a desert island without a score of *Meistersinger*, trying to remember how the overture goes and becoming enraged because he can't. The three movements in the middle are, respectively, pastoral (ruminant?), sinister (or somewhere in a triangle defined by sinister, spooky, and grotesque), and serenade-like.

It is one of Mahler's most adventurous pieces, in the originality of its overall form, in the harmony as it is worked out both in its largest dimensions as well as in many piquant details, and perhaps most so in the orchestral writing. The delicate, quasi-chamber-musical textures of the two "night musics" and the scherzo, with their cowbells, the "Bartók pizzicatos" that are so violent that the string snaps back against the fingerboard, the sounds of mandolin and guitar, are particularly fresh and special.

It seemed to me, though, that the Seventh is a work that a lot of the time engages mainly what one might call Mahler's gift as an arranger. As a show of how to do it, it is always fascinating, but real musical, compositional, expressive urgency was something I sensed only in the Adagio introduction (and its recurrences) of the first movement, that tenebrous scherzo, and the amorous and charmingly fanciful fourth movement.

Mahler is a composer who asks his listeners not only for attention, but for sympathy, commitment, identification. It may be that, though I think of myself as someone who is really into Mahler, yesterday just was not a day on which I could find the right wavelength and hear what Mahler was saying, and that this was the reason I was inclined to react with so many reservations. I also suspect, though, that the performance had something to do with it. There were surely good points to it: it had energy, though mostly of a burly sort rather than the fiery kind that was also needed; the big tempo relationships were coherently worked out, which is anything other than easy in so diffuse a work; and it was resolutely anti-hysterical.

But perhaps Steinberg's anti-hysteria went too far. Not that you want a performance in which the music is swamped under a layer of gratuitous conductorial hysteria (as in some of Bernstein's and Solti's Mahler performances), but you do want a sense of the madness in Mahler. Steinberg's reading, with its glossing over disruptive caesuras, its conversion of shrill, *fortissimo* woodwinds to passages played *forte* and with beautiful tone, its reduction of extremes altogether, normalized the music too much. It was as though Mahler had gone through a successful analysis and had talked all the conflicts and dissonances and bizarre fancies and juxtapositions out on Dr. Freud's couch rather than putting them into his symphonies.

The most damaging decision Steinberg made about performing the Mahler was to put the intermission between the first and second movements, the first having been preceded by Mozart's *Linz* Symphony. Mahler's first movement offers a possible, temporary ending, but the exchanges among solo winds in the second movement are not any possible kind of beginning. Then, given Mahler's special requirements from his audience, the disruption of atmosphere with an intermezzo all full of tobacco smoke and its counterpart in probably equally non-nutritive (not to say poisonous) conversation has a disastrous effect. Why not make a program of just the Mahler? It is, heaven knows, long enough and dense enough, and except for some beautifully finished playing, there was nothing in that terribly safe, ever so classical and respectful lumber through the *Linz* that made a strong plea for its inclusion.

1971

Thomas's Theater Sense Enlivens BSO

January 9, 1971

With Michael Tilson Thomas around, Boston Symphony concerts certainly are interesting. It begins with his programs. He explores fresh repertory, and that alone, particularly given his combination of sense, curiosity, and taste, would be occasion for thanks. Then—and I would suppose this to be part of his gift for theater—he has a remarkable feeling for what to put next to what, and his way of hanging a show, as it were, often with really startling juxtapositions of textures, scale, and style, is often marvelously illuminating. Friday afternoon's Symphony Hall program was a typical and fascinating Thomas show: *Sederunt principes* by Pérotin, Karlheinz Stockhausen's *Punkte*, and the Schumann *Rhenish* Symphony.

Pérotin was choirmaster at Notre Dame, Paris, around 1200, and *Sederunt* is thought to have been first sung in 1199 (conjectural but a pleasing date somehow), when the cathedral was still thirty years from being finished and was no doubt swarming with contractors, carpenters, masons, and glaziers.

Sederunt has special fame as one of only two surviving four-voice pieces of the period, but it is also a genuinely fine work, an elaboration on a large scale of a plainsong introit, of which some is sung in the normal way, but with more of it stretched into notes of enormous length serving as fundament for a fanciful and lively superstructure.

The sources for *Sederunt* give only the pitches exactly; any performance, therefore, involves an "arrangement," or the making at least of many decisions about rhythm and of all the decisions about tempo and scoring. Thomas used male voices—the Harvard Glee Club, which sang very well—and a small group of violas, woodwinds, organ, and bells. His perceptive and imaginative articulation of form through his choices of tempo made this performance of *Sederunt* by a considerable margin the best I have heard, the one most apt to persuade one of the real quality of the music.

Such music is harmonically static, but then, being written for an exceedingly resonant building it could afford to be. It was a good idea, therefore, to attempt to approximate cathedral acoustics by piping the sound of the singing to the Symphony Hall art gallery, re-recording it there, and sending it back into the organ loft. That produced a reverberation of something like eight seconds, and the experiment was short of being a complete success only because of a certain harshness in the sound of the electronic echo.

From 1199 (?), Thomas leaped to 1966. Stockhausen's *Punkte*, too, is a piece of rather special acoustic assumptions. First written in 1952, and twice revised, it seems to push orchestral writing to its outer limits, to that point at which the composer seems to be just about to discover, or perhaps invent, electronic music. The *Punkte* orchestra is fairly conventional in makeup, but it is a remarkable sequence of swirling, stuttering, gliding sounds that Stockhausen draws from it. At any given point the sonorous surface of *Punkte* is fascinating, and my first sense of the piece was of an experience mainly revolving about the kaleidoscopic play with texture and density.

As for other dimensions of *Punkte*, it is all stops and starts, thick jungles of sound, often with all twelve pitches at once, leading to a clearing, then to a silence, then into the next tangle again. As rhythm and motion, *Punkte* seems a bit primitive, or perhaps I would be fairer were I to say that so far I perceive the life of its details better than that of its wholeness. It is strange perhaps to seem not to follow the sense of a piece and to like it anyway, but for what it's worth, I did like hearing *Punkte* and it thoroughly compelled my attention, both more on the second hearing (Friday) than at the first (Thursday's dress rehearsal).

The *Rhenish* Symphony got a performance that was buoyant and well played in the first movement, but which then sank into an unhappy combination of caution and sloppiness.

Camerata Early Music Series Sells Out

January 24, 1971

The Camerata, Boston's early music group and the audible extension of the Old Instruments Collection at the Museum of Fine Arts, begins its season with a concert at the museum this Tuesday evening, the 26th. For the first time in the Camerata's fourteen-year history, the series is sold out in advance, and each concert will be repeated at Christ Church, Cambridge, the first on Tuesday, February 9. I asked Joel Cohen, now in his third year as the Camerata's director, how to account for this new success. His answer: "It's got to the point where you can listen to the concerts without feeling embarrassed." Cohen, 28, is a Harvard-trained composer who also studied in Europe with Nadia Boulanger. He has been a double bass player with the Rhode Island Philharmonic (he comes from Providence) and has played classical guitar ("I love the instrument, but there's no music for it"). He is a lutenist now and a conductor (left-handed), and he is also on the faculty at Brandeis, where he is mainly involved in performance. A duo consisting of himself as lutenist and the soprano, Jane Bryden, was co-winner last year of the Cambridge Early Music Society's Bodky Award, but Cohen ultimately refused his part of the prize because at the time of the concert of all the winners, he chose to accompany a group of his Brandeis students to Washington to protest the Kent State shootings.

He is ambitious for the Camerata, whose first recording—Monteverdi's *Scherzi musicali*, on the Turnabout label—has just been issued. He would like to be able to form and maintain "a real ensemble with a stipend for each singer and player, like the [historical] Chapelle Royale," but until a big foundation grant is dropped into his lap—"Yes, we're working on it"—he has to engage his performers on a per concert basis. Among other things, he sees his future ideal Camerata as a style school for the participants. He believes that in some respects the problems of adaptation to authentic Renaissance or medieval style are more readily dealt with by instrumentalists than by singers, because for the players some of the transitions are naturally tied to the switch to an instrument that is physically different from the one on which they play non-old music, while it is harder for a singer, using the same instrument for Josquin and Schumann, to get in the habit, for example, of using vibrato as an ornament rather than as a constant in tone production.

Cohen enjoys the way the performance of old music leaves lots of decisions up to performers, the works not being nearly as specifically written down as those from later periods. Questions like what is assigned to instrumentalists and what to voices, which voice parts should be doubled on instruments, have to be answered fresh for each piece, with the director having to rely on ear, taste, historical knowledge, and his available resources, rather than on specific instructions in the score: "We spend a lot of time in rehearsals trying to figure out what sounds best." His task as the Camerata's director also involves the editing of music and the grappling with all sorts of practical problems: "I like getting into all that blue-collar stuff." He thinks, at least hopes, that the barrier between performers and scholars is breaking down to some extent,[1] that the performer with no idea whatever of historical consideration or the musicologist who never got his hands dirty actually putting a performance together, are rarer beasts than they used to be.

"The concert is not the principal vehicle for the distribution of music any more," Cohen maintains. With the repertory the Camerata deals with, there is the additional problem that much of it is so intimate that it is not most effectively perceived in public performance. He has no intention of giving up concerts, though: "I'm trying to reform the system from within." He is pleased

[1] See also the article "Music and Scholars—Must There Be War?," May 24, 1964.

at the range of audience the Camerata concerts pull in, "from little ladies with ear trumpets to real freaks." The programs, he says, are designed to appeal to lots of sorts of people with very different relationships to this music, "some of it for the connoisseurs, some that everybody will enjoy." He wishes that practical problems did not make it virtually necessary to isolate early music on concerts by itself: "it's as bad as the segregation of contemporary music." Brahms, after all, is "old music" the way Ciconia, who died in 1412, is "old music," and perhaps, he suggests, "the Camerata has a better chance of survival than an 'old music' group like the Boston Symphony simply because it's cheaper to run."

Final rehearsals, plagued by flu, are now in progress for the opening concert, which is all of music by Flemish composers brought to Italy by the Renaissance courts and chapels: Ciconia ("a major composer, one of the really big finds"), Dufay, Josquin, Isaac, Cipriano de Rore ("one of the great composers nobody plays, like Schoenberg—he's too problematic. It's dense, with lots of close imitation, and it undoes all the good generalizations about Italian music about structure being subordinate to effect, beauty of sound being more important than complexity of thought"), and others.

Cohen speaks about the music with knowledge and enthusiasm, as a man as good as natively at home in it, and he stops for a moment to remember his teacher, Nadia Boulanger: "You never knew whether you'd find a Stravinsky score open on her piano or a Josquin Mass; that was wonderful, and she lived equally in both of them." He continues: "You use the past that you need. I need this past"—pointing at the stack of photostats of 15th-century music in his South Russell Street apartment—"and other people do, too."

Horenstein Rare Conductor Who Grasps Mahler's Intent

January 31, 1971

Mahler performances have got to be interesting and alive, and in that they are just like performances of anything else. But there are special Mahler problems, too, because his music has elements that tend to scatter it in performance. There is, to begin with, the expansiveness of his forms: most other composers simply don't pose the problems of how to hold a thirty-five-minute movement or an eighty-five-minute symphony together. There is an uncommon diversity, jarring heterogeneity even, of material. And far from least, the tremendous emotional intensity is a trap to the conductor in the slightest disposed to go to pieces and to give all too soon.

Mahler, of course, knew about those traps and problems, being not only a crazy composer but a highly intelligent one, and being as well an experienced, indeed a great, conductor. His music is most carefully unified, with the means of achieving coherence and integration plainly offered to the conductor, and chiefly by means of tempo. No matter how far afield a given movement goes, it will always have a principal tempo that functions as a frame of reference against which all the departures take place. Then, in his changes of tempo, he distinguishes carefully between those that are to take place gradually and those that must happen suddenly. Examples of the former pose the additional problem of long passages that are not in a tempo, but en route from one tempo to another. If you listen carefully to performances of Mahler's music, you soon discover that those words "gradual" and "sudden" seem not to be in the vocabulary of most conductors. When you have a conductor who can read those words and understand the expressive intent that moves Mahler to choose one rather than the other, when you have a conductor who can be impassioned even though disciplined, then you have a good Mahler conductor. It is rare.

A performance that has it all is that of the Symphony No. 1, with Jascha Horenstein conducting the London Symphony Orchestra (Nonesuch), and at its low price, it is an extraordinary buy. The low-price reissue (Odyssey) of Bruno Walter's recording with the Columbia Symphony has attractive points, particularly in the easy playing of the middle movements, but Walter's projection of the form is not as cohesive as Horenstein's (beginning with the omission of the first-movement repeat), and the splitting of the slow movement across two sides is decidedly a detriment.

Of the Symphony No. 2 (*Resurrection*), there are two recent recordings, one with Bernard Haitink conducting the Amsterdam Concertgebouw Orchestra, with alto Aafje Heynis, soprano Elly Ameling, and the Netherlands Radio Chorus (Philips), the other with Rafael Kubelik conducting the orchestra and chorus of the Bavarian Radio with alto Norma Procter and soprano Edith Mathis (Deutsche Grammophon).

Haitink has the considerable negative virtue of avoiding the vulgarity and coarseness common to so many Mahler conductors. He is serious and careful, his tempo changes come out reasonably well, and his orchestra, chorus, and soloists are very good indeed. He projects the gentle music of the second and fourth movements well, but as a whole the performance lacks something in intensity and drama.

With Kubelik, however, you at once find yourself dealing with another order of performance altogether. I do regret his underplaying of the first movement's disruptive caesuras, but otherwise it is a performance in which the realization of the spirit through the understanding of the letter (or is it the other way around?) is marvelous. As on other records in Kubelik's Mahler series, you are sometimes aware that his Munich orchestra is very good rather than superb—and we have become very much spoiled in the matter of the technical realization of these virtuoso works—and I would also say that Norma Procter is not quite as serene spiritually and technically as some other altos, though she is very good. But this is a noble and dramatic performance that builds extraordinarily, and it is the one of this work I would without hesitation recommend now.

Abbado . . . Davis . . . Kubelik . . . Ozawa?—Who'll Succeed Steinberg as BSO Conductor?

February 14, 1971

As of mid-1972, the Boston Symphony will again be without a music director. The three-year contract of William Steinberg, who turns 73 that summer, runs out then, and the Boston trustees had not yet invited him to stay when, last week, he announced his intention of again, for the 1972–73 season and beyond, giving his more or less full-time attention to the Pittsburgh Symphony, whose music director he has been since 1952. That would leave him a maximum of eight weeks to give Boston in 1972–73, and that, said Steinberg, was not enough for him to have the responsibilities and the title of music director. He suggested continuing to serve here as senior conductor or musical advisor, and that offer was to be discussed by the BSO trustees at a meeting scheduled after the writing of this article.

It is likely to be some time before the Boston Symphony announces who its new music director is to be; meanwhile, if the trustees have anything definite cooking, it is a well-kept secret. So now the guesswork can start again, much as it did in December 1967, when Erich Leinsdorf said he would leave at the end of summer 1969.[2] The game then was made interesting because the Chicago Symphony and the New York Philharmonic were also looking for conductors, whom they found in the persons respectively of Georg Solti, which was no surprise, and Pierre Boulez, which was. Now Cleveland needs a conductor after the death last spring of George Szell, and Philadelphia will have to deal with the problem before long, Eugene Ormandy now being 71.

Indulging in fantasies about the future of the Boston Symphony will be easier once next season's guest conductor list is published, but so far that is being sat on tight. Of course there are some conductors that one can probably eliminate as candidates: the ones who aren't good enough (. . . well? . . .), the ones who aren't famous enough, those who are too well employed elsewhere (Boulez and Solti, for example), those who are too old, probably the very young, even though enormously gifted (Daniel Barenboim, Lawrence Foster, James Levine, Michael

[2] See article of December 11, 1967.

Tilson Thomas, for instance), and surely Leinsdorf who is not apt to pass this way again except as a guest. Apart from all the obvious desiderata for a music director, it will also have to be someone who pleases Deutsche Grammophon Gesellschaft, with whom the BSO now has an exclusive recording contract.

To make a beginning, here is a short list of names to think about:

Claudio Abbado, 37, an Italian. A winner of the Koussevitzky Prize at Tanglewood and of the Mitropoulos Competition, he has made a big career quickly, being much involved with La Scala, Milan, and having just been named permanent conductor of the Vienna Philharmonic. He conducted here this season and last, and will not return next only because of scheduling difficulties. Except for an *Eroica* (all right, but not distinguished) and one Bellini opera (marvelous), I have heard him only in late 19th-century repertory and beyond, most of which he does with fine flair, particularly the really splashy things like Scriabin's *Poem of Ecstasy*. He is Deutsche Grammophon property, and he has made two recordings here (Debussy-Ravel and Scriabin-Tchaikovsky). Clearly one of the good guys, though not, I think, great, and in many ways an unknown quantity still.

Colin Davis, 43, English, now heading the Covent Garden Opera, and with a well-established reputation as one of the most serious, responsible, and versatile performers of his generation, outstanding in Mozart and Berlioz. Trouble is that already he has turned the BSO down twice, and though there were rumors that he had been very much interested in the New York Philharmonic, it seems unlikely that he would want to take any permanent post in the United States. A pity.

Rafael Kubelik, 56, a political exile from Czechoslovakia since the Communist takeover of 1948, now music director of the Bavarian Radio (Munich) and said recently to have turned down an offer from Cleveland. He comes here in March for his third guest engagement with the BSO. He, too, is with Deutsche Grammophon and will record Smetana's *My Fatherland* here next month. A profound musician, magnificently mature, strong in a wide portion of repertory, though in the 20th century his interests and effective range seem not to go beyond, say, Schoenberg and Bartók. As a young man he had a brutal experience with the Chicago Symphony (more exactly with Claudia Cassidy of the *Chicago Tribune*), and though he has been guest conductor of virtually every major American orchestra with success since then (including Chicago), he perhaps hesitates about a permanent affiliation with another orchestra in this country.

Seiji Ozawa, 33, music director of the San Francisco Symphony, and already ours in so far as he is artistic director of Tanglewood (jointly with Gunther Schuller). His *Così fan tutte* last summer was enjoyable, but he has not generally been impressive in the 18th century, and has been strongest in the Abbado repertory, and there often very strong indeed. Erratic, he has seemed sometimes to conduct pieces before really digesting them, but then he has also given Boston some of its most impressive concerts in recent years. It would be a lively time, though with exasperating days.

Michael Tilson Thomas at 26 probably belongs in my "too young" list. But his position here, assistant conductor last season, promoted to associate conductor for this year, coupled with the considerable impression he has been able to make since William Steinberg's illness last year provided him with extraordinary opportunities, means that he should be considered. If he is a future BSO music director, he is more likely—and surely more wisely—not the next, but the one after next. His musical qualifications are superb, but the continued terrific upward acceleration that such an appointment would mean, is about the last thing he needs just now for his development as a musician and, for that matter, for the shaping of his career. He can be more effective coming in later from somewhere else, and maybe he is our man for the 1980s and '90s.

Someone should organize a sweepstakes for the BSO's Pension Fund.

Haitink Even Better in the Flesh

March 3, 1971

The guest conductor for the Boston Symphony concerts at the end of last week and again last night was Bernard Haitink of the Amsterdam Concertgebouw and the London Philharmonic.

Haitink has made lots of records, and, to a certain point at least, he was a known quantity when he strode onto the Symphony Hall stage: a serious and careful musician, an able conductor, with nothing flashy to his work.

Now, seeing Haitink at work for the first time and hearing the results in concert was an enormously interesting experience, even more because he exuded a vitality of which his recordings only sporadically give some sense.

What I said about the absence of flashiness stays true, though. Haitink's "big piece" was Strauss's *Ein Heldenleben*, and the performance was a very different sort of affair from the all-stops-out attack by Zubin Mehta and the Los Angeles Philharmonic on the *Symphonia domestica* at the beginning of the season.

Perhaps it is true that *Heldenleben*, even by Straussian standards, rather overinforms the listener, but it is a masterfully controlled work that makes a sprawly effect only when it is conducted badly, which usually means too self-indulgently.

Haitink set it out so that it was as cohesive, as readily surveyed, as a Mozart Allegro. It was superlatively well paced, with a stable framework and an elastic surface, and beautifully proportioned. The performance was of the rare sort that is exciting through sheer lucidity, the clarity of view it afforded of an extraordinarily imaginative and still original composition.

Not least, *Ein Heldenleben* was the occasion for handsome and relaxed playing by the orchestra. Joseph Silverstein's work with the violin solos, not only the fond but malicious portrait of Mrs. Strauss, but also the lyric passage near the end of the work, was marvelous, as brilliant violinistically as you would expect, but also with a sense of character that I don't recall from the orchestra's last performances five years ago.

The first half was rather quieter, with a Mozart serenade for strings and kettledrums only (the *Serenata notturna* in D major, K.239), and Ravel's *Mother Goose*, where even the final climax is somehow muted, luminousness perceived through a scrim. Both are works that give great pleasure. The Mozart is charming, but it is also quietly amazing in its orchestral originality with the division of the players into a solo quartet of two violins, viola, and bass, playing into and out of a larger band of violins, violas, and cellos (no basses!), plus drums.

The Ravel is a wonder of economy and restraint, saying so much, and so much that is very touching in so few notes—and how extraordinary it seemed again that so much of the music that most rightly speaks of childhood, Tchaikovsky, Ravel, Britten, is the work of childless men.

In addition to the five most familiar movements of the *Mother Goose* suite, Haitink conducted the two pieces Ravel added later, a Prelude that is particularly lovely in its prefiguring of later ideas in the work, and an elegant "Dance of the Spinning-wheel." The performances were fine, too: good, that is to say natural and easy-flowing Mozart, and just the right sort of shy warmth for the Ravel, played by the orchestra so that it was a delight to hear.

Frank's Beethoven Sonata Series Best Buy

March 21, 1971

About Claude Frank's recording of all the Beethoven piano sonatas (RCA Victrola, twelve records), let me first declare a personal interest: the program notes are mine. To that I want to add that I accepted RCA's invitation because of my high regard for Frank's playing, though as a matter of fact I had never heard him do a Beethoven sonata. What I heard when the album came out gave me great pleasure. For the collector who can afford only one version of the sonatas, Frank's is the best buy; it also has characteristics that make it well worth adding to a collection where the works are already represented. I would suggest that a very good arrangement, and one that is financially reasonable, is to combine two low-price versions, Frank's and the vastly different one by his teacher, Artur

Schnabel (Seraphim—issued as a series of three-record albums, including also the major sets of variations, Bagatelles, and other miscellaneous pieces).

Frank's playing is simple, thoughtful, warm, and remarkably beautiful in sound. It has also been very well recorded. The first of the great sonatas, Opus 10, No. 3 in D major, has come out especially well, and so, among the earlier pieces, have the companion piece to the *Moonlight*, the E-flat major, Op. 27, No. 1, and the A-flat major, Op. 26. The playing in the last sonatas is very beautiful indeed. I was particularly moved by the *Hammerklavier*, Op. 106, and the more so because the conception is very different from mine and, I think, especially questionably with respect to tempi. Frank's are very slow both in the first movement and for the Adagio, but the playing is flexible and fluid, the chosen tempo so effectively used and therefore so well justified, that the result is marvelously persuasive.

Inevitably there are a few disappointments; the major one for me is the stiff and constrained playing of the lovely little F-sharp major Sonata, Op. 78. Those interested in textural matters will find certain of Frank's editorial decisions curious, and there is one at least that I find bothersome, which is the omission (following Schnabel's and some other older editions) of the repeat in the Trio of Opus 101. Altogether, though, this recording is an achievement on an exceptionally high level, and it is one of the finest to have come out of the Beethoven year.

I listened carefully to Daniel Barenboim's recording of the thirty-two sonatas (Angel, fourteen records), found the playing of Opp. 109 and 111 attentive and beautiful, but most of the rest either perverse, particularly when very slow, or casual, which is worse. Claudio Arrau's playing of the sonatas (Philips—four three-record albums) is wooden and says nothing to me at all. Admirers of Alfred Brendel will want to know that he has begun what is planned as a slow project of re-recording the Beethoven sonatas for Philips. The first records are due out in England quite soon, but the plans of American Philips for issue here are inscrutable.

Both Christoph Eschenbach's (Deutsche Grammophon) and John Ogdon's (RCA) recordings of the *Hammerklavier* Sonata seem to me interesting but unpersuasive. Eschenbach's is about the slowest I have ever heard (24′16″ for the Adagio!), and while he does a surprisingly good job of sustaining it, the emphasis is on the surprise, on the sense of the successful management of a tour de force. The performance abounds in beautiful detail. Ogdon's is highly intelligent about structure, pianistically clear, but as exaggerated in the direction of coolness as Barenboim's is in that of pathos.

Jacob Lateiner's record (RCA) of the *Waldstein* Sonata, of Opus 109, and of the *Andante favori*, which is the *Waldstein*'s original and rejected slow movement, is very much the product of a curious, incisive, and somehow unrelaxed mind. As on his earlier record of Opus 111 and the Opus 126 Bagatelles, the playing seems at times over-studied, but I again find it unusually arresting.

Also worth noting: Stephen Bishop's playing with Colin Davis and the London Symphony of the *Emperor* Concerto (Philips), the Rubinstein-Leinsdorf-BSO set of all five Beethoven concertos (RCA, four records), and, among reissues, Schnabel's of the Fourth and *Emperor* concertos with Frederick Stock and the Chicago Symphony (RCA Victrola, mono only), William Kapell's of the Concerto No. 2 with Vladmir Golschmann and the NBC Symphony (RCA Victrola, mono only, with an impressive Prokofiev Third Concerto with Antal Doráti and the Dallas Symphony), and the Beethoven Concerto No. 1 with Sviatoslav Richter and the Boston Symphony under Munch (RCA Victrola, with Richter's playing of the Sonata, Op. 54).

Cantata Singers Perform Bach and John Harbison

April 29, 1971

The Cantata Singers, John Harbison conducting, wound up their season with a Sanders Theatre concert last night. The program, as usual, centered about Bach, including this time the motet *Komm, Jesu, komm* and the cantatas No. 42, *Am Abend aber desselbigen Sabbats*, and No. 47, *Wer sich selbst erhöhet.* In the midst of all the Bach, however, there was a triptych in which an Orlando Gibbons madrigal, "Fair is the rose, yet fades," was preceded and followed by Harbison's Music for Mixed Chorus, which is a setting, composed in 1966, of Shelley's "Music when soft voices die vibrates in the memory."[3]

Harbison, one of the winners of the Brandeis University Creative Arts Awards this year, is an able, imaginative composer. In his Music for Mixed Chorus he has been concerned with "vibrates in the memory," and throughout this brief, texturally fascinating piece he writes what might be described as internal echoes, the reinforcing or repeating of vowels, begun so as to overlap with the original sounding, sometimes with the echo only left hanging as though from some distant point. As choral writing it is resourceful and quite demanding, and it makes for an affecting interpretation of the poem.

I was particularly grateful for a chance to hear the rare and subtle Cantata No. 42, whose subject is the appearance of Christ to the disciples as told in *St. John* XX:19. An elaborate instrumental overture, an immense and deeply probing alto aria ("Where two and three are gathered together"), and the astounding final chorale are its most remarkable movements, but really the whole cantata

[3] In Harbison's catalogue, this work is listed as "Music When Soft Voices Die."

presents one unforeseeable thing after another and is altogether informed by what Harbison in his program note aptly characterized as a "this-piece-only" quality.

Once again, Harbison's conducting of Bach proceeded from remarkable sensibility and intelligence, with moments of great energy and perhaps a couple of somewhat willful touches. The choral singing was fine, particularly in its lovely transparency in the extremely difficult *Komm, Jesu, komm*. Jane Bryden, D'Anna Fortunato, Karl Dan Sorensen, and Mark Baker were a good solo quartet, with Mrs. Bryden's singing in Cantata 47 being really outstanding. Oboists Raymond Toubman and Kenneth Roth did some superb playing, as did violinist Rose Mary Harbison; otherwise, however, the orchestral playing, though mostly exemplary in the phrasing of the upper parts, was less good than at past Cantata Singers concerts, being troubled by a somewhat lumpy and not quite unanimous bass department and by occasionally shaky tuning in the high strings.

A lovely end to a distinguished season by what is clearly now one of Boston's strongest and most valuable organizations.

What to Do With Your Eyes While the Orchestra Plays

July 11, 1971

At the end of my first half-season as the *Globe*'s music critic, I asked to change my seat at the Boston Symphony concerts from row O on the floor to the first balcony. The main reason was that I wanted to see more.

At a concert—opera, which gives you something you are really meant to look at, obviously is different—you can follow a score or with a vocal piece, the words (what is to be gotten from watching the score is an interesting question, but a separate one). You can look at the performers. You can also close your eyes, though that is useful only if it promotes concentration rather than daydreaming or sleep.

Beyond that there are, of course, several things to do with your eyes guaranteed to lead to not-listening. Reading is one. The fat program books at orchestral subscription concerts provide ample temptation, well-meant (program notes), financially necessary (advertisements), or neutral (lists and announcements). For that matter, you can bring your own, and I have had people next to me reading Shakespeare sonnets during a Mozart divertimento and Camus during the Schumann Fantasy. And there is the audience to look at, which I find fascinating and a greater temptation to distraction than things to read.

Score-reading is pretty special, and I am not interested in non-listeners. The average listening member of an audience is looking at the stage. What does he see?

You see people, from one to hundreds, concentrating on something enormously difficult requiring an extraordinary conjunction of mental and physical disciplines. Concentration does beautiful things to faces: look into a grade-school classroom where there is a good teacher and you see it at once. Watching a skilled craftsman or, for a more spectacular version, a good athlete, affords a higher order of the same experience. With a fine musician it can be still further heightened because to discipline and coordination is added the delicate equilibrium of passion and control, of leading and responding.

When the musical performance itself is beautiful and when what the eye sees is congruent with what the ear hears, in other words, when everything you see is in direct and economical relation to the musical effect produced, when the performer and his performing and the music are one, then the eye can help carry you right to the center of the music. Toscanini at his best was a performer of whom that was movingly true.

It is, in fact, always in some way interesting to have the eye confirm the ear's perception. And, though I perhaps move farther from the composition and closer to the fact of performance itself, to someone interested in the how of singing, playing, or conducting, the eye is extremely informative (singers particularly being liable to give themselves away totally and at once).

There are hazards, as well, to looking. Horn players have to empty moisture from their instruments, which is less poetic than most music; oboists adjust reeds, timpanists check tuning. That is all necessary and usually it is unobtrusive, but any of it, when you catch sight of it, will take you out of the musical discourse for a moment. Players will exchange an occasional remark: that, too, is likely to be only momentarily distracting though a long and evidently amusing conversation during the Adagio of the Mahler Ninth can be totally destructive. I remember, too, a former principal clarinetist in the Boston Symphony who could be counted on to disturb anything, with a quiet close and no clarinet part, because the moment he had played his last note he would begin his uninhibited operation of dismantling, cleaning, and packing his instrument.

There are players—I am thinking of soloists now—whom I dislike to watch, even though I admire and enjoy the performances they give, because they convey to a distracting degree a sense of their personal tension or their struggles with the instrument. Worse, though, are the exhibitors of public ecstasies, even when they are unaffected, because to be in on what they are going through seems like a really painful invasion of privacy. Most impossible of all are the ones who are so transparently doing a show for you.

It leads to a larger issue. Composers have always known they were writing for performers and most of them have been performers themselves. They have also always felt ambivalent about performers, enjoying and cherishing virtuosity on the one hand, but on the other, from Josquin through Bach and Rossini to

Stravinsky, hating those combinations of vanity, stupidity, and laziness that have led performers to obscure their music rather than to reveal it. But composers have liked stretching performers' skills and in turn being stimulated by those skills. And, of course, they have known that performers except organists sometimes, could be seen as well as heard and that man, being so overwhelmingly a visual animal, would use his eyes to supplement his aurally received information.

If the *Globe* had footnotes, I should have one here about phonograph and radio listening at home. I do, in fact, want to say something about electronic music where, at least with respect to the public concert, the social and psychological problems are perhaps more severe than the musical ones. Nobody has come up with a comfortable way of dealing with the embarrassment of a stage with just loudspeakers; note, however, the success with audiences, always, of those pieces like Davidovsky's *Synchronisms* or Babbitt's *Vision and Prayer* and *Philomel* that put live performers on stage with the speakers.

There are, then, lots of reasons for looking at performers and reasons for sometimes looking away. Actually, I find it hard to think of any composition so peculiarly inward and in which the fact of performance is not somehow a built-in part of the experience, that the performer is altogether an intrusion.

Bernstein—*Missa solemnis* at Tanglewood

July 26, 1971

LENOX—The *Missa solemnis* is Beethoven's greatest single achievement. A unique intersection of his grandest, most brilliant, public style and of that most private, uncompromisingly dense and complex style of his old age, it is surely the most searching interpretation to which any musician ever subjected the text of the Ordinary Mass, composed from out of a condition of spirit that afforded him limitless capacities for jubilation, terror, awe, and serenity. A further marvel, and a very moving one, is how his fantasy, after years of deafness, continued to be so in touch with the physical reality of sound.

Because of its stupefying difficulties for conductor, singers, and players, and because, being difficult for listeners as well it is by no means the guaranteed public success that the Ninth Symphony is, the *Missa solemnis* is also the most rarely performed of Beethoven's major works. A good performance, then, is instantly a festival, and the performance which Leonard Bernstein conducted in memory of Serge Koussevitzky at yesterday afternoon's Boston Symphony concert at Tanglewood was, in fact, a superb one.

The Tanglewood Festival Chorus and the Tanglewood Choir were prepared by John Oliver. The soloists were Phyllis Curtin, soprano; Maureen Forrester, alto; William Cochran, tenor, and Sherrill Milnes, bass, both women substituting at short notice for their indisposed colleagues Arleen Saunders and Florence Kopleff. Miss Curtin did not even have a chance to sing in the dress rehearsal Saturday morning.

Bernstein, in the right equilibrium of turned on and collected, is as able as any Beethoven conductor now working. He showed that when he conducted the Ninth in Boston in April of last year and again with the *Missa solemnis* yesterday, this time in a situation far more challenging conceptually and technically.

It was exciting, rhythmic, perceptive of musical character, and, with all that, powerfully disciplined. There was the fury and fire of discovery about the performance—the *Missa* sounded as it should like a new piece—and it was very clean, very straight. I had doubts only about two of the tempi, those for the "In gloria Dei patris" fugue and for "Pleni sunt coeli," which seemed fast, not so much for themselves as the still greater speed with which Beethoven follows each, and a question also about that final, quiet, echoes-of-war kettledrum action in the "Dona nobis pacem," which surely wants to be on B-flat and not B-natural.

The details of the performance were impressively filled in by all participants. The chorus was excellent, and the orchestra played with engagement, precision, and fine sound. The violin solo in the Benedictus was beautifully done by Joseph Silverstein, who has just the right sweetness and elegance for that extraordinary romance-become-sublime. The solo quartet, even with what I thought an excessive collective vibrato, was very good, and Miss Curtin's singing and especially Mr. Cochran's was very expressive and distinguished indeed.

The performance of the *Missa solemnis* wound up a whole weekend of Beethoven concerts, William Steinberg's programming including the Third, Fifth, and Seventh symphonies, and the Violin Concerto (Itzhak Perlman).

Beethoven, who was nearly sued by one publisher as a result of his attempt to cheat six of them over the rights to his Mass, might have been pleased to know that his three concerts brought Tanglewood an attendance approaching 40,000 and the biggest box office income for a single weekend in its history.

Thomas and Berkshire Excel With the *Rhenish*

August 7, 1971

LENOX—Granting that something like the Bernstein performance of *Missa solemnis* falls into a category by itself,[4] Michael Tilson Thomas's concert with the

[4] See previous article.

Berkshire Music Center Orchestra Thursday night was as lively and attractive as any I have heard at Tanglewood this summer.

When Thomas had Schumann's *Rhenish* Symphony on a Boston Symphony program last season, he preceded it with the 12th-century Parisian master, Pérotin, and with Stockhausen.[5] This time, the first half was *Fili mi Absalon* by Schütz, born just 100 years before Bach, and Messiaen's *Couleurs de la cité céleste*, written in 1963.

It was Messiaen's piece that first became the focal point of the concert. Huge applause followed its performance. Thomas then said that, considering the enormous labor involved in preparing a comparatively few minutes of music, "some of us on stage" would like to play it again. (More applause, also the departure of a couple dozen people.) After that, he spoke briefly about the work, having the players illustrate the points he made about the elements that make it up and then conducted it all once more, getting another ovation.

Illustrated explanation preceded and followed by complete performances is the best format for that sort of thing—even better, of course, when still more time can be taken for the middle of that sandwich, and Thomas is a good talker, informative, humorous, and not condescending.

Messiaen has complicated ways of arriving at a result that sounds extraordinarily naive. It would not sound nearly so naive, that is to say, so spontaneous and unplanned, so "natural," if it were less cannily and elaborately plotted. With its collisions of plainsong alleluias, presented sometimes in very complete textural and harmonic transformations, and of painstakingly transcribed and fantastically scored calls of exotic birds, *Couleurs de la cité céleste* is an extravaganza of syncretism.

Its surface is a series of explosions, of outbursts of song, of marvelous, suspended silences. Those silences, by the way, are an example of something that makes live performance indispensable: on record, they do not tell at all. The silences also dramatize Messiaen's most impressive achievement, his control of time as a dimension of his sonorous sculpture.

The colors of Messiaen's heavenly city are given by three clarinets, half a dozen brass, piano, and lots of bright percussion. The effect is raucous, gay, absolutely individual—and as loud as the Jefferson Airplane. The performance was a vivid statement of the work, though one of the percussion players said afterwards about his six-notes-per-second part that, while the rhythms were right, there must have been quite a few wrong pitches.

Thomas's performance of the *Rhenish*, which was still in many respects stiff and tentative last fall, and which had grown enormously in assurance by April and the Boston Symphony's European tour, is now superb, elastic, and with a

[5] See review of January 9, 1971.

wonderful sense of romantic enthusiasm. It was well-played, too, by this orchestra of gifted students, and the special bows and cheers for the horns and trombones were particularly deserved.

Schütz's *Lament for Absalon*, a compelling piece for low voice with a quartet of trombones and bass, had a partially strong performance, one, that is, whose instrumental portion was excellently shaped and played, but in which the singer, John Seabury, though splendidly sonorous, was wanting in cleanness of pitch and communicativeness.

Aventures Brilliantly Staged

August 10, 1971

LENOX—If avant-garde music theater has a comic masterpiece, it is surely György Ligeti's *Aventures* (1962) and its companion piece, *Nouvelles Aventures* (1965). The two were performed together by the Music Theater Project at Tanglewood Sunday evening (repeated August 11 and 12) as part of a triple bill also including the American premiere of *Down by the Greenwood Side* by Harrison Birtwistle and Satie's *Socrate*.

Ligeti's adventures, old and new, are short pieces, not quite fifteen minutes each, for three singers (the production here distributes the soprano part of the second between two singers) and seven instrumentalists. The phonetic, non-semantic text is the composer's own, and it includes almost every imaginable sound that can be produced by the human voice. The vocal parts stand in the foreground. But they are most imaginatively [interwoven] into the instrumental texture, often by means of delicate aural puns. The surface is fun and games, but Ligeti is always a composer, never a mere effects man, and the two sets of *Aventures* propound musical relationships that are rewarding and delightful to listen to, as many who own the excellent Heliodor recording will have discovered.

There is no scenario, but the texts in their musical setting are constantly suggestive of some effect or confrontation, and what Ian Strasfogel has done in his brilliant and very funny staging is to make visible what he has heard. In a receding box designed by Douglas Schmidt, four young singers, Syble Young, Joyce Castle, David Holloway, and Poppy Holden, do a super-virtuoso job of singing and a very good one of flinging themselves about, the whole thing being superbly paced by Gunther Schuller and excellently played by Berkshire Music Center students (playing includes tearing paper, rubbing piano strings with a hairbrush, and breaking a Coke bottle).

Satie's *Socrate*, a series of settings for voice and small orchestra of passages from Plato's *Symposium*, *Phaedrus*, and *Phaedo*, seems to me so chaste a masterpiece—Satie was not one of the 20th century's great composers but *Socrate* is one of its great works—as to resist the kind of reification that a staging (or even the division of its vocal line among several singers to indicate the different personages) brings with it. Strasfogel's staging was in fact as discreet as possible, except insofar as he both veiled and heightened the homosexual bias of the text by assigning the parts of Alcibiades and Phaedrus to a strikingly attractive young woman at whom Socrates in white pajamas smiled sweetly and without cease.

This, too, was beautifully conducted by Schuller, with particularly effective singing (plus rather too much mugging) by Barbara Hocher as Phaedo, and almost very good singing, spoiled by too punchy and Broadway-ish a delivery by Doris Peterson. With Debussy's *Pelléas*, *Socrate* must be one of the most untranslatable things in the world and the English version by Yale Marshall and Wesley Balk did an amazing job of dealing with the impossible.

Birtwistle's "dramatic pastoral," in which St. George is twice killed and resurrected, and through which there wanders a coloratura infanticide, seemed on the basis of one hearing to be (in contrast to *Aventures*) fun and games with not much music. Except for the bad mother, the parts are for speakers rather than singers, and the instruments neutrally punctuate rather than underline. Bruno Maderna conducted, and there were outstanding performances by Barbara Hocher as the shrill lady and by Stephen Klein as Father Christmas, who functions as master of ceremonies and Evangelist for this tale.

Ozawa's *Faust*

August 24, 1971

LENOX—The 1971 Berkshire Festival at Tanglewood finished Sunday afternoon with a performance conducted by Seiji Ozawa of Berlioz's dramatic legend, *The Damnation of Faust*. Berlioz first had a go at Goethe's *Faust* in 1828 when he was 24 and Goethe, still alive, 79. A few years later, though, he withdrew those Eight Scenes from *Faust*, his Opus 1, and returned to the material only in 1845, his experience as a musician enlarged particularly by his profound and original treatment of Shakespeare's *Romeo and Juliet*.

He was now equipped to deal not only with the lyric and coloristic elements that had dominated the Eight Scenes, but also with Mephistophelean irony, with the pain behind Faust's aspirations, and with the abyss of Faust's and Marguerite's love for each other.

The Damnation of Faust is still apt to disturb, rejected by most Germans on principle and unloved by many others who long for the mellifluous Gounod.

Less cohesive than *Romeo and Juliet*, *The Damnation of Faust* is nonetheless a masterpiece, and an extremely idiosyncratic one, to be sure. When Berlioz tackled *Faust* for the second time, he dealt with Goethe almost as possessively and ruthlessly as Goethe himself had dealt with the legend before him. Berlioz could not possibly accommodate all the dimensions of the play, and so he took what he most responded to, informing his view of Goethe with a musical fantasy that I find staggering and a nobility and compassion by which I am very much moved. His Goethe composition is as triumphantly self-justifying as his later, still more outrageously bold embrace of Virgil in *The Trojans*.

How the large audience Sunday really responded I cannot quite say. The applause was enthusiastic, but there seemed to be more restlessness than usual, which I incline to attribute to the inadequacy of a plot summary where a full libretto really is needed. I understand it was thought impossible to print so long a text in the program; just the same, might it not be possible on some future occasion to persuade some advertiser each with new acknowledgment to sponsor, as it were, a page or a half-page of text?

The performance I would describe as marvelous with some great flaws. What made it marvelous was Ozawa's fluid pacing, sensitive phrasing, general manner of delivery, and the extension of all that in the Boston Symphony's beautiful playing. This is all rare and remarkably defined in a performance in a major work of Berlioz. These qualities, particularly the ones to do with pacing and timing, were also wonderfully present Friday evening when Ozawa conducted the love scene from *Romeo and Juliet*, a breathtakingly insightful penetration into that music, marred only by a sound that was too open and, to say bluntly, often too loud.

But it was Ozawa too, who was responsible for the most disturbing flaw of the *Faust* performance, the series of cuts. One, that of the music as Faust walks about Marguerite's room, examining it "with passionate curiosity," dropping one of Berlioz's most telling touches of psychologically right detail, and those in the finale of Part III and in the pandemonium scene, badly distorted the form.

John Alexander sang Faust and did it admirably except for the careless French he shared with the Tanglewood Festival Chorus. Lois Marshall's unsteadiness of voice in the high register detracted slightly from her intelligent and intense performance as Marguerite. Ezio Flagello, the Mephistopheles, was good in a part that could do with a voice that is less sumptuous but which offers more of a cutting edge. Saverio Barbieri as Brander, who gets the sadistic Song of the Rat, did not come through sufficiently, but there was fine singing by David Cumberland as an Earthly Voice and D'Anna Fortunato as a heavenly one.

Other than linguistically, the Tanglewood Festival Chorus did its work very well, but the meagre dozen-and-a-half boys from the Hartford Cathedral and from St. James', West Hartford, were far too few not just for Berlioz's "some thirty" (to say nothing of his hopeful two or three hundred), but too few really, to add that last touch of angelic radiance to the apotheosis.

Bernstein's *Mass* at JFK Center

September 9, 1971

WASHINGTON, DC—The Kennedy Center for the Performing Arts, a monstrous building which seeks to make an aggressive and spectacular statement about how seriously we take art, was inaugurated last night with the performance in its red-on-red, New Orleans–bordello style opera house, of Leonard Bernstein's *Mass*, a work which makes an aggressive and spectacular statement of the composer's view, depressed, hopeful, and sentimental, of man's relation to God in the last third of the 20th century.

Mass is a musical on the subject of the Eucharist: the Jets and the Sharks meet Superstar. Its text is taken from the Roman liturgy, with additions by Stephen Schwartz, the composer and lyricist of *Godspell*, and by Bernstein himself. It is staged with a huge cast of singers and dancers, more than two dozen instrumentalists on stage as well as in the pit orchestra, and it goes without break, though quite sectionally, for just under two hours. The additional texts amplify, comment, question, sometimes just translate, often directly and with humor, but too often with diction of painful banality ("When my spirit falters / On decaying altars" is one couplet that sticks in my mind).

The music covers wide territory: Stravinsky's *Les Noces* right at the beginning and several times thereafter; blues; spirituals; rock; jazz; Broadway; Renaissance *a cappella*; Anglican; Mahler; Copland western. Bernstein has heard or read just about every kind of music there is, and he can imitate or suggest any of it with impressive skill; moreover, as an experienced performer, he has a keen sense for what works. More than that, as he has shown over a period of many years, ever since *On the Town*, he has an extraordinary theater sense, and *Mass*, just like *West Side Story*, really goes.

Mass asks whether man can cut his way through all the tangle and again face directly, without affectation, without using ritual as something to hide behind, the issue of a possible God, and of his own existence. It is a question worth asking, but Bernstein as theologian really has little to say about it except that we should find simplicity, stay more in touch with our feelings, and be nicer to one another. And I think we know that. Not that we don't all discover daily that the great truths are simple, but those truths have to be stated either so personally, with such fresh lighting, that they hit as though new, or else they must be said terribly simply and cleanly.

Bernstein has nothing new to say as a composer, and never has had, and only rarely does he have the discipline to stay clean and simple. A choral anthem, "Almighty Father," almost makes it and is spoiled by the tiniest touches of corny harmony; a one-part setting of the Lord's Prayer almost makes it and is spoiled by its melodramatic introduction; the good-humored, enormously energetic choruses come closest to being right.

It is dazzlingly slick and professional, all of it, beginning with the printing of the word *Mass*, whose initial is shaped so that its first peak becomes a steeple with a little cross on top. It is slickness masquerading as simplicity, and that makes me uncomfortable. It exploits street culture, but it addresses an affluent, middle-class audience. It is also, beyond question, sincere, and it is personal in the sense that all of it, its inconsistencies included, is so clearly the statement of one man whose presence is constantly felt, even though he is a man who can only select, not create. That presence and the urgency of the statement are compelling enough to confront one with the issues it wants to deal with.

With Bernstein's *Kaddish* in 1963 that was impossible: musically and verbally it was such junk that the question of what it was trying to say never arose seriously at all;[6] with *Mass*, even though I want to reject its constant and immediate recourse to the obvious, I also find myself wondering what a devout Catholic would feel about it.

In other words, the question of what *Mass* is all about, remains alive. It is so much of a show, though, and whenever I felt most drawn into the work, suddenly and unbidden there would be the awareness of its purposeful theatricality. For a moment the dramatization at the end of the kiss of peace is touching, but then there comes the spectre of the director who must at one point have told Larry to kiss Linda, "and then Cindy, you . . . " and it is all lost. It is a statement of the Mass for those who find *West Side Story* a satisfying statement of the *Romeo and Juliet* story.

Wednesday's audience certainly took it as a show, mostly declining to participate as a congregation when bidden to rise and pray (though Mrs. Rose Kennedy and the composer stood in the Presidential box), and at the end so concerned with the para-show of watching the box full of Kennedys as almost to forget to applaud the real show on stage.

[6] See review of February 1, 1964.

The performance under the musical direction of Maurice Peress seemed superbly assured and was certainly extremely lively. Oliver Smith had contrived a simple, versatile setting of steps and pews; Frank Thompson dressed everyone sexily; Alvin Ailey had provided a choreography that was the effective and banal counterpart to the music; and the performers included the Norman Scribner Choir, the Berkshire Boys Choir, the Alvin Ailey American Dance Theatre, and some excellent singers including Alan Titus as the Celebrant, and particularly David Cryer and Larry Marshall.

Fine Simplicity Marks Fleisher

September 26, 1971

It has been seven or eight years since Leon Fleisher, then still in his mid-30s, stopped playing the piano because of a disabled right hand. He has begun to conduct, and it was a pleasure to encounter his musical intelligence and taste in a new package when he led a Boston Symphony concert at Tanglewood in July, but I admit I had forgotten just how remarkable a pianist he was—and in part had, I think, never fully appreciated that while he was still active—until there was occasion to hear again his recordings with George Szell and the Cleveland Orchestra of the Schumann and Grieg piano concertos, just reissued by Columbia on its Odyssey label.

What touched me first was the simplicity of his playing of the Schumann. The piece, with its certain quality of inwardness and domesticity (as contrasted, say, with the idiosyncratic fantasy of *Kreisleriana*), likes that approach anyway, and beyond that it is an extra pleasure to be offered something so straight and clean in a work played as much as the Schumann is, one therefore particularly liable to attacks of originality in performance.

As you listen, you discover that the simplicity is also the frame for an extraordinary and subtle imagination, particularly with respect to rhythm. Everything is varied and elastic, though there is never a narcissistic statement of "watch me now," and the whole performance is a process of unfolding and developing, something that is the more remarkable given how mechanical Schumann's recapitulations are. The cadenza is the time for assertive personal statement, and what Fleisher unleashes there is torrential in its force because of the control and reserve exercised up to that point.

The Grieg is less of a piece than the Schumann, but the way to hear it, too, is certainly in playing as fresh as Fleisher's. Lipatti's beautiful playing of these two concertos (also Odyssey) has similar qualities, but Fleisher's, particularly in the

Schumann, is more fiery. The completeness of the success of these performances rests of course to an enormous extent on the closeness of Szell's collaboration and the fine playing he got the Cleveland Orchestra to do. To cite just one detail: Szell certainly brings the middle of the second movement with the big cello tune to white heat, but right to the top you can tell what the rhythm is.

It is interesting to compare Fleisher's playing with that of some of the famous pianists in the first half of the century whose playing of Romantic repertory is so often cited as exemplary, and some of whose recordings have recently been reissued. Hearing Josef Hofmann, for example, is for me the constantly repeated experience of being unable to find a connection between the interpretive marvels his admirers describe and what I can only read as the hatred for music most of his playing exudes. The 1935 studio recordings of Chopin, including the first movement of the B minor Sonata and the *Military* Polonaise, have none of the capriciousness of the live performances which are the sources of most available Hofmann recordings, but they go equally destructively in the direction of brittle rattling-off of notes: "very good Czerny playing," was the appropriate comment of a pianist for whom I played the record (Victrola, mono only).

Rachmaninoff's playing of Chopin could be arbitrary, his drastic rearrangement of the dynamics of the Funeral March in the B-flat minor Sonata being the most famous example of that, and compared with the economy and elegance of Fleisher, of Ashkenazy at his best, or of a younger pianist like Garrick Ohlsson, it is apt to sound wildly overstated; still, it is arresting, it has nothing in it of mere fooling around à la Hofmann, and even at its craziest, it allows you access to the music at some reasonable perceptual level (Victrola, mono only).

Hofmann and Rachmaninoff just get their names on the record jackets; Josef Lhevinne also gets the title of "Master of the Romantic Piano." Most of what you get in his playing of Chopin, of Schumann, and of the Schulz-Evler arrangement of *The Blue Danube*, is a lot of technical razzle-dazzle, but beyond that an unpleasing mixture of coldness and affectation. The playing with his wife, Rosina, of Ravel's two-piano version of Debussy's *Fêtes* is remarkably elegant, though (Victrola, mono only).

When Twelve Music Critics Meet All Is Not Perfect Harmony

December 19, 1971

ROCHESTER, NY—Among the ways the Eastman School of Music is celebrating its 50th anniversary is a series of symposia on music criticism, musicology, music education, and arts subsidy. The criticism meeting ran December 9–12, and was attended by William Bender (*Time*), Martin Bernheimer (*Los Angeles Times*), Alfred Frankenstein (*San Francisco Chronicle*), James Goodfriend (*Stereo Review*), Peter Heyworth (*The Observer*, London), Paul Hume (*Washington Post*), Miles Kastendieck (*Christian Science Monitor*), Irving Lowens (*Washington Evening Star*), William Mann (*The Times*, London), Henry Pleasants (*International Herald Tribune*), Alan Rich (*New York Magazine*), Harold Schonberg (*New York Times*), Michael Steinberg (*Boston Globe*), H. H. Stuckenschmidt (*Frankfurter Allgemeine Zeitung*, *Neue Zürcher Zeitung*), and Thomas Willis (*Chicago Tribune*). Most of us gave a formal paper; all participated in discussions—some based on the papers, others free—and met informally and at length with Eastman and University of Rochester students and faculty. The papers will be published as a book.[7]

On the first day, after a welcome from Walter Hendl, director of the Eastman School, Harold Schonberg, the tactful and charming chairman for the symposium, looked at us seated at a long table across the stage of Kilbourn Theater and told a story of how the *Times* some years ago had all its departments photographed for publicity purposes. The music department was particularly unhappy with how it came out, but a *Times* veteran said, "Why, Harold, how can you say that? That's the greatest group picture since *The Last Supper*." Schonberg looked us over again and said, "Well, I don't want to press the analogy too far. . . ." Henry Pleasants, I think, found the right one when he said that the meeting was like a convocation of tenors.

If you stuck around, you could hear almost every kind of opinion expressed by critics about their work: they should be subjective, objective, judges, commentators, reporters, musicians, amateurs; should or should not take scores to concerts, study new works ahead of time and attend rehearsals when possible; should write for those who attended the concert, those who did not, both, themselves only, or their mothers; be specialists in "classical" music or make a point of covering all music; should or should not discuss their colleagues' work, should or should not applaud. Even the question that really precedes all these—why criticism?—was touched on by some speakers.

Some of these questions are fairly trivial though amusing (applause), some are really non-questions (for whom do you write?). Others emerged as central preoccupations, and their discussion aroused considerable passion (including those members of the "emotion recollected in tranquility" school).

Frankenstein cited Irving Howe: "The effect of all good criticism is that of articulating for the inexperienced observer . . . feelings and insights he holds but

[7] The book seems never to have been published.

cannot structure, so that he says about the critic's work: Yes, that's just how I saw it, that's how I'd have said it if I could." Other colleagues were concerned about "right" and "wrong": who would be right and who the goat thirty years from now, Hume for thinking the Bernstein *Mass* marvelous or Schonberg for hating it. It was quickly pointed out that history offers a consolation prize to "wrong" critics in that more dead critics are remembered for their "mistakes" than for what they got "right," an issue far more complicated than it seems: were Hanslick and Shaw so simply all "wrong" in having reservations respectively about Wagner and Brahms? Certainly questions from the floor suggested that much of the public asks of a critic that he be "right," that he provide them with a dependable consumer's guide to correct opinions. In the middle of all that, Mann and Steinberg—and, if I read them properly, Heyworth and Hume—maintained that the critic should work without self-consciousness, without concern for his reputation in 2001, and hoping only to have the reader awakened and interested, thinking that the *Times*, the *Globe*, or whatever, has found someone alive, someone who can really see and hear, to tell him about music.

The closest we came to bloodshed was over the question first raised by Pleasants in his paper, "If I Were Managing Editor . . . " in which he portrayed critics as people who "identify themselves with, support, and even encourage the artist's arrogant, self-indulgent attitudes" (translated "Pleasants does not like contemporary music," and greeted, I should think, with a hollow laugh by most composers). Later someone asked what we regarded as appropriate music preparation for dealing with a new piece. After noises had been made about scores, rehearsals, and talking with composers, Pleasants (seconded by Kastendieck) said no to all those things, maintaining that a piece should be clear and straight enough not to require homework, that in any case the critic should not, by virtue of special preparation, assume a position of superiority vis-à-vis his reader.

The response to that was predictable. It revolved around the intrinsic difficulty of much new music, the likelihood of its being misrepresented in performance—"My music isn't modern," said Arnold Schoenberg, "it's just badly played"—and ultimately the question, "Why should I want to know what you think when you know just as little as I do, and particularly when you are the sort of person who chooses to put on blinders?"

We offered few answers (which I thought was fine), but from Thursday afternoon through a Sunday dormitory brunch, the collection we were of the quick and the dead, the grown-up and the infantile, the confident and the nervous, the subjective and the objective (good grief, is that thing about "objective criticism" still running around?), offered a range of attitudes that several listeners found surprising (though I thought we were too uniformly male, white, and middle-aged), and some good questions were asked. One Eastman student observed:

"I got the impression you were all saying 'if you want to be a good critic, you have to be just like me,'" adding somewhat hesitantly, "though I don't think you all support that position equally convincingly." I offered one student Pleasants's quip about the convocation of tenors. She grinned, "Yeah, and you want to be Franco Corelli!"

1972

The Inevitable Future of Michael Tilson Thomas—Where Is This Brilliant Young Musician Going?

January 2, 1972

What everybody wants to know about Michael Tilson Thomas now is, where is he going? Another question people ask is who is going to be music director of the Boston Symphony after the end of William Steinberg's three-year tenure this summer? Not surprisingly, the two questions want to live together. Michael Tilson Thomas is 27, associate conductor of the Boston Symphony, and music director of the Buffalo Philharmonic. And to dispose of it with two clichés, his rise has been meteoric and he is obviously destined for great things.

I first heard about Michael Tilson Thomas in the spring of 1967 when I gave a criticism seminar at the University of Southern California, Los Angeles. Thomas was then conductor of an orchestra sponsored by the Young Musicians Foundation. It gave no concerts during the few days I was out there, but the student critics in the seminar, who had by then spent seven or eight months in Los Angeles, were thoroughly turned on by Thomas, by his programs, by the high quality of the playing he got the young musicians in his orchestra to do, by the vitality and intelligence of his interpretive ideas. They also found him useful as a stick with which to beat Zubin Mehta, the flashy, gifted, not always thoughtful conductor of the not quite first-rate Los Angeles Philharmonic. About Thomas I was also told that he was an excellent pianist and that he seemed to "know everything."

A year later, at age 24, Thomas went to Tanglewood as a conducting student, made a strong impression in works as different as Schoenberg's Five Pieces for Orchestra and a sometimes amusing, sometimes sophomoric opera by Stanley Silverman called *Elephant Steps* in which the conductor needs to participate with some histrionic flair of his own. At the end of the summer, Thomas landed the Koussevitzky Prize, the Berkshire Music Center's highest award to a student conductor, one whose list of winners includes the names of Seiji Ozawa and Claudio Abbado. Meanwhile, in Symphony Hall, Erich Leinsdorf had announced his resignation as of summer 1969, and Charles Wilson, his assistant conductor, would leave at the same time. Thomas, by now, was a watched man, and a concert with the Boston Philharmonia convinced William Steinberg, Leinsdorf's successor, that the recommendation of concertmaster Joseph Silverstein and Symphony Hall staff made sense: Thomas was appointed the BSO's assistant conductor.

After that it was like in the movies. Thomas conducted the Boston Symphony for the first time in October and made a solid success, public and critical, in a hard program: Haydn's Symphony No. 98 and *Three Places in New England* by Charles Ives (both not played by the orchestra in ages), Stravinsky's enigmatic, jewel-like *Variations: Aldous Huxley in memoriam* (for the first time at a BSO concert), and Debussy's *La Mer*.[1] Not long after, when the orchestra played at Philharmonic Hall, New York, the 70-year-old Steinberg felt ill and at intermission told Thomas something like "put on your suit, you're going to conduct." No one who wrote up the story could do it without mentioning Leonard Bernstein who, as a 27-year-old assistant conductor, had stepped in more or less without notice to substitute for the suddenly indisposed Bruno Walter, thus one Sunday afternoon in 1943–44 becoming Leonard Bernstein. Thomas was delighted by a story Bernstein told him later about his own first time of having to cancel after his spectacular arrival: the concert was with the Pittsburgh Symphony, and the man brought in for the rescue was the conductor of the Buffalo Philharmonic and a future Pittsburgh Symphony music director, William Steinberg.

Steinberg's illness was serious and protracted, and he was out of action most of the remainder of that season. Thomas found himself not only famous, but with enormously more work than anticipated. He survived and was rewarded by promotion at the end of his first Boston season from assistant to associate conductor: more prestige, more money, more conducting (an assistant is usually given one program a season, but as associate conductor, Thomas has done almost as many concerts as the music director), and more freedom (an associate conductor is not expected to stick around as a rescue wagon in case of conductors' illnesses, transportation difficulties, and so on). The speed of Thomas's promotion was special, too: Richard Burgin had become associate conductor only after many years' service as concertmaster and assistant conductor; Wilson was never offered the rank.

Thomas is now in his first year at Buffalo, and he does not know or will not say how long he will stay in Boston. His contract here allows him the option of cancellation in case of the departure of the manager, Thomas D. Perry Jr., or the associate manager, Harry J. Kraut. Kraut, who also served as Thomas's personal manager, left the BSO at the end of last summer to join Leonard Bernstein's recording and videocassette enterprise, Amberson Productions, so that leaves Thomas free to quit Boston. The BSO has so far not said a word about who its music director, associate or assistant conductor, or guest conductors are to be for

[1] See review of October 11, 1969.

the 1972–73 season. Thomas admits to having dates with the orchestra that year and he has also said that he will not be in residence at Tanglewood this coming summer, though he will conduct there.

"Is Thomas really good?" one is often asked. It is not really the right question. There is no doubt about his being equipped with that parcel of qualities, the musical comprehension, physical coordination, and personal projection, that make him a real conductor. But again, where is he going? In his 80th-birthday tribute to Sigmund Freud, *Freud and the Future*, Thomas Mann discusses and plays at length with an idea formulated by a Viennese psychiatrist (whom, high-handedly and discourteously, he fails to name). Many men, that idea says, live out "a biographical type, the destiny of a class or rank or calling. The freedom in the shaping of a human being's life is obviously connected with that bond which we term 'lived vita.'" A little later, Mann describes the "lived life" in terms of "life as succession, as a moving in others' steps, as identification." Just now there is a lot of pressure to make Michael Tilson Thomas live the life of Leonard Bernstein. Not the least of that pressure comes from Bernstein himself, whose feelings for Thomas are strong, fond, and admiring—not without some narcissism either, because Bernstein has said that his sense of the likeness of the Thomas of 1971 and the Bernstein of 1943 is vivid and specific. Koussevitzky, when nudged into retirement in 1949, had hoped to see his protégé Bernstein succeed him in Boston, but the Symphony trustees would not buy the idea. It is easy to see how a kind of vindication, twenty-some years later and through an *alter ego*, would appeal to Bernstein. It is also possible to see how the trustees, whose rejection of Bernstein could be described as the first step that led them into a series of misjudgments in the matter of the appointments of music directors, misjudgments that have spelled trouble for the orchestra for years now, would face with some unease the prospect of their own variation on the theme of "life as succession, as a moving in other steps," if they now failed to engage the Bernstein of the '70s (as the PR machinery has inevitably labeled Thomas). And those are considerable pressures on a man of 27 whose career has entailed so rapid and violent a mobility upward as to hardly leave him time to think.

Thomas, on his part, feels very drawn to Bernstein, humanly as well as musically and regards him, along with others like Pierre Boulez and Gregor Piatigorsky, as one of the "polar personalities" who have shaped his musical life. Mentioning Boulez, he asked, "Did you know I used to conduct like this?" standing to demonstrate the facial deadpan and the symmetrical karate chops of Boulez's conducting. Thomas's conducting now certainly looks more nearly Bernstein than Boulezian: a generous beat, much pained play of his promising but sometimes still startlingly unfinished face, and, per concert, one guaranteed moment of jumping in the air with enough swirl to afford the audience a full-face view. His performances do not sound like Bernstein's though, being generally cooler and hardly ever in danger of over-statement, and his is a different sort of musical personality altogether. He does not have Bernstein's preternatural audience appeal either. The public likes Thomas, but that erotic magnetism which has brought Bernstein nothing but sold-out houses for twenty-eight years just is not there.

What Thomas most strikingly shares with Bernstein is doubt about really wanting to be a conductor. Bernstein wants to be thought of as a composer, and there is some identification with Mahler, not always or whole-heartedly accepted in his own day as a composer, though widely regarded and loved as possibly the greatest conductor of his time. If you throw the "what do you want to do when you grow up?" question at Thomas, the part of the answer that says "not a conductor" is quite clear, but the rest is not. Composer is not it: he has studied composition ("to see what it is like") and still works at it from time to time. He will even go so far as to say that if he writes something worth communicating to the world, he will certainly perform it, but he does not give the impression that inside the conductor there is a composer crying to get out.

Mainly, as I read him, he wants to be a musician in a world better set up to deal with specialists—composer, conductor, pianist, musicologist, and so on. He wants to conduct because among other things he wants to perform music that requires conducting, but he does not want to be frozen into the life of a career conductor. He wants to play the piano and is disturbed how much he has let that skill slide since his success as a conductor began to eat at his life. He wants to learn more music history and is now, in fact, considerably more informed in that field than almost any of his colleagues, both in questions that feed directly into a conductor's work—something like Baroque performance practice, for example—and in his awareness of several centuries worth of music written before the existence of the orchestra as an institution: Monteverdi, Josquin, Machaut, Pérotin, are just names to most conductors: Thomas, to some extent at least, really lives there.

The breadth of his view of professional responsibilities and possibilities he owes to the most compelling of the procession of "polar personalities," his teacher at the University of Southern California, the late Ingolf Dahl, a man more than merely skilled as a composer, conductor, pianist, scholar, critic, editor, linguist, but who left his mark by the totality he was as "musician," something that was more than the sum of the formidable parts. But Thomas's world goes beyond the bounds of Western art music (or whatever you want to call that stretch from Pérotin to Stockhausen within which his professional life has so far taken place): he is interested in Japanese and Indian music (particularly the former); he is very much into rock and soul, and I have heard him speak of James Brown as the musical personality that most engages, even moves, him; he grew up in a world of theater, his father being a Hollywood scriptwriter and director, his grandparents, Boris and Bessie Thomashefsky, having been involved in the founding of the Yiddish Theater in New York, and he would like some day to answer that call of blood, not limiting himself to opera or any form of musical theater; and, he adds, "I know a lot about television and about films, and those tempt and interest me enormously." There are even moments when he talks about going back into science and mathematics, having in high school won prizes in his work and having remained interested and informed.

Does all that mean that the offer of the musical directorship of the Boston Symphony would not really tempt or interest him? Of course it interests him. "Having an orchestra of your own," he says, "is to have a platform on which to get things done." Constantly, though, he makes it clear that he senses a conflict between music, which is what really interests him, and the whole machinery for packaging, distributing, and advertising performing musicians, to which he owes his success and, of course, the opportunity to make music on a grand scale. "In Mahler's *Lied von der Erde*, which at the moment is my absolutely favorite piece of music, there is a line, 'Ich wandle auf und nieder mit meiner Laute / Auf Wegen, die von weichem Grase schwellen'—('I wander up and down with my lute / on paths cushioned with soft grass'). There is my idea of the musical life, one man alone in the mountains with his lute, making music just for himself and for the music."

Coming back to the more probable realities of his professional life, Thomas makes it clear that an orchestra which engages him on a permanent or long-term basis has to understand that it is buying a rather special sort of package. He would like to see his orchestra be not just an ensemble specialized in what is commonly recognized as legitimate orchestral repertory of the 18th, 19th, and 20th centuries (with a few adventurous excursions into "early music" or avant-garde), but rather, he wants to see it as part of an organization set up to provide performances of orchestral music, but mixed up with choral music, chamber music, theater, and so forth. To illuminate other works on the program, for variety, and, of course, for their intrinsic value, he has put into his symphony concerts such things as the *a cappella* vocal *Déploration* which Josquin des Prez, arguably the greatest composer of his time, wrote about 1495 on the death of his master, Ockeghem; Steve Reich's Four Organs, in which Thomas played one of four electronic rock organs, which, plus a quartet of maracas, make up the whole instrumentation of the piece; and *Schön Hedwig*, a Schumann piece for spoken recitation with piano accompaniment, himself playing the piano. Thomas would like to go much, much further in such directions. The idea of a concert all of orchestral music has more to do with convention and economics (the orchestra is there and has to get paid, so let it play) than with musical considerations. Thomas wants concerts whose contents are determined by criteria of light and shade, density, pace, expressive contrast and compatibility, and he has an uncanny sense for program-building, which is probably one of the innate, unlearnable musical skills. The orchestra—and his would institutionally include a pool of singers—has resources offering a far greater range of possibilities than traditional program-making has allowed anyone to discover. There is even the practical consideration that the inclusion of non-orchestral repertory frees time badly needed and generally unavailable for rehearsal of unusual and particularly difficult works: right now, for instance, Thomas is putting time into the bank to make possible a Buffalo Philharmonic performance of the immense *Turangalîla* Symphony by Messiaen, whom Thomas regards as being, since Stravinsky's death, the strongest of living composers.

Is the Boston Symphony the kind of institution most suited for the realization of that Idea of an Orchestra? "I don't know. I wonder. Perhaps some of the smaller orchestras, the less prestigious ones, St. Louis, Atlanta, Buffalo, which are not so committed to a received idea of a particular sort of greatness, are by their nature more flexible."

To be sure, the playing membership of the Boston Symphony would regard Thomas's appointment with mixed feelings. Orchestras do not love him. When he was given the Koussevitzky Prize at Tanglewood, the Berkshire Music Center Orchestra, which was on stage for the ceremony, applauded him but also offered an ostentatious demonstration of preference for the man who won the institute's No. 2 conducting award. "He most decidedly did not make a hit with us," was the report of an exceptionally fine, widely experienced musician in the New York Philharmonic, where Thomas was guest conductor for the first time in November. His habit of repeating passages without saying why—something of which BSO players have also complained—was particularly resented. The younger players in Boston tend to respond enthusiastically. The older ones are more reserved, some are downright patronizing. That is a response in part to the trivial, like a certain flamboyance of dress, but also to things that go rather deeper, what they call "coming on," or what they see as the self-indulgence of the occasional tantrum (once when he threw his score into the air in fury, there was a responding storm of sheets of music from most stands in the orchestra). In part it is the response—shall I just say resentment?—to having before them in authority someone they remember as a kid, as a conducting student at Tanglewood. That is an uncomfortable fact about the orchestral world: for example, only in London does Colin Davis not command the very special esteem orchestral players grant him all over the world. "I suppose," as one of the London musicians once explained, "it's because we all remember him as a not particularly good clarinetist." The interesting, and for the moment the essential thing is that the Boston Symphony almost always plays very well for Thomas, and at a time when the orchestra has been much demoralized and is not in the least in the habit of playing "like the Boston Symphony" for all comers. "But," warns an older conductor, one very much concerned about Thomas, "they could kill him."

Conducting is always thought of as an old man's profession, perhaps because many conductors live a long time (attributable, George Zazofsky, a former BSO violinist, used to say, to all that ego satisfaction). We forget, though, that many of today's and yesterday's old men held positions of great responsibility when they were very young. Thomas's youth is often mentioned as a handicap, or anyway as something all right for Buffalo, but not for Boston. One would more accurately pinpoint the problem by looking at the hectic quality of his life in the last two years when he was pushed into a situation where he had to cope with more music than there was time to learn, even for someone of his astounding facility—really to learn, that is, not just to get through. Players have complained about his "learning on the job," but the striking thing is that he does learn: the progress from his first somewhat raw go at Schumann's *Rhenish* Symphony at a BSO concert last winter, to the Barcelona performance on the April tour, to the one in August with the Berkshire Music Center Orchestra, was really impressive.[2] Thomas admits he has been doing too much, and one of his first aims is to reduce his current ninety concerts per season (Buffalo, Boston, plus guest dates in this country, Europe, and Israel) to a more manageable fifty. "You know, that pressure wasn't all bad. You want to find the point where just the right amount of adrenalin gets going, and I'm really terrified by the thought of knowing a piece so well I'd be tempted to conduct it in my sleep. I really can't understand those conductors and pianists and singers who make their whole careers on a tiny repertory which they polish harder and harder."

Thomas at this point is overloaded with volunteered advice, advice to recognize that the tide which leads on to fortune is at the flood now and to be taken, advice that "Lennie, whose life consists only of big events," is the worst possible model and that what Thomas needs is to plug away quietly and steadily at the professional life for the first twenty years. He asks, "What do you think?," but the inexhaustible energy of his mind and fantasy does not always allow him to stop talking long enough to hear the answers to his questions.

He is not the only remarkable American conductor of his age group. Musically, James Levine (Metropolitan Opera) and Thomas's old Los Angeles friend, Lawrence Foster (Houston Symphony, Royal Philharmonic) are his peers. But Thomas is a glamorous, highly advertisable figure as the other two are not, which, along with the obvious advantages, makes him more of a potential victim as well. He is also special in that of the three he is the only one who would say, "the one thing I'm certain of, concerning twenty years from now, is that I won't

2 See reviews of January 9 (BSO) and August 7 (Berkshire Music Center Orchestra), 1971.

be a conductor, or at least not just a conductor." Or, as he said in October, "Can't we talk again in three months? Maybe I'll know more then."

Rubinstein Plays With BSO

January 6, 1972

Artur Rubinstein played with the Boston Symphony at the orchestra's Pension Fund Concert last night. Michael Tilson Thomas conducted, and the program consisted simply of two big piano concertos, the Brahms in B-flat and Rachmaninoff's in C minor. The printed program also listed Glinka's *Ruslan and Ludmila* Overture, but before the concert began BSO manager Thomas D. Perry Jr. announced that "at the suggestion of Mr. Rubinstein and with the agreement of all concerned" the overture had been dropped. One old-time Russian nationalist in the left balcony booed, and Mr. Perry began again: "At the suggestion of Mr. Rubinstein and with the agreement of ALL concerned . . . "

Rubinstein appeared a moment later. Everybody stood up and produced one of those rock-solid walls of applause, which only four or five performers command—but they always do—and then everybody settled into the Brahms. One of the loveliest features of the really extraordinary evening it turned out to be was the grace of the transitions from party to performance and back. Rubinstein on any concert stage instantly turns the occasion into festivity. But beyond that, this was a special party because it celebrated—albeit months late—the 50th anniversary of the 83-year-old pianist's first concert with the Boston Symphony.

Rubinstein played both concertos very beautifully. His playing has become somewhat reduced in physical scale, and he has turned that fact to extraordinary advantage. It works even in "big" pieces like the Brahms and Rachmaninoff—in fact, part of the special pleasure in last night's performances was that the pieces were big, but not big and fat.

What Rubinstein does now has a similarity of surface to what you can hear on the recordings he made in the '30s—the difference is that his work now is more serious, though not more solemn, and that his musical taste is informed by a refinement that is a very sure and very exciting statement of "I really know."

There was a marvelous sense of ownership in his approach to both concertos. Many of the gestures of old-fashioned rhetoric were ones which have virtually been frozen into the performance tradition: last night though, they sounded new. Rubinstein made those gestures not as though he had inherited them as part of a tradition, but with the special authority of one who had helped make that tradition.

The interpretations were cohesive, graceful, economical, truly elegant, and executed with unusual loveliness of sound, often with dazzling lightness, and always with marvelous dash. In whatever he did, Rubinstein was excellently backed by Thomas and the orchestra. The orchestral context was transparent and perfectly scaled to Rubinstein's playing, and in matters of both continuity and texture, this was—especially in the Brahms—some of the finest working together of a conductor and orchestra with a soloist that I have ever heard. And on its own terms, the playing of the Boston Symphony, much turned on by Rubinstein and by a sense of the occasion, was exceptionally fine.

BSO—An Impressive Concert

January 22, 1972

The Mahler Fifth was the principal work on the concert which Michael Tilson Thomas conducted with the Boston Symphony yesterday afternoon. It was an impressive performance, and one which showed the value of paying attention to Mahler's instructions about pace and intensity.

I don't understand most conductors. When they blur—as most of them do—Mahler's crucial distinctions between things that change suddenly and those that are transformed gradually, when they normalize his idiosyncratic dynamics, I don't know what combination is at work of failure of insight into musical character, of arrogance, laziness, or annoyance at having someone (and worse, another conductor!) so specifically lay down the law about matters whose determination they are used to regarding as their prerogative.

I hope that the Corinthians understood "The letter killeth, but the spirit giveth life" better than those musicians and theater directors who are so ready to offer St. Paul's admonition in justification of their own departures from the letter. The letter, in Mahler, is the key to the spirit, and when conductors wander from it in some of the ways I have described, they dull Mahler's music when they do not cheapen it.

This week produced two opportunities to hear the Mahler Fifth under conductors whose interpretive point of departure was to take the composer's most explicit directions very seriously, the other being Michael Gielen, who conducted the work with the National Orchestra of Belgium in Carnegie Hall, New York, on Tuesday. Gielen responded more vitally to Mahler's humor—at least I found the scherzo and finale just a bit straitlaced in Boston—but on the whole it was Thomas who showed a greater range of sympathy in dealing with diverse tempers. The most obvious difference between the performances was in the orchestral playing: the Belgian group, though attentive and disciplined, is exceedingly limited in technique and sound, while the Boston Symphony happily made yesterday's concerts one of those occasions for letting us know what a stunning virtuoso outfit it is.

To sum it up: Michael Thomas conducted a performance of a certain emotional restraint, though of great inner intensity and remarkably sustained, with that combination of intelligence, taste, and growing technical resourcefulness which makes him an outstandingly good conductor. The Boston Symphony responded with playing that was brilliant, but beautiful in many other ways as well. Solo bows, well earned, were taken by Charles Yancich (French horn) and Armando Ghitalla (trumpet).

To begin the concert, there was a C major oboe concerto from the 18th century but otherwise of uncertain origin—early in the 19th century somebody penciled "*Von Haydn?*" into the manuscript, which is not persuasive evidence of authorship. It is a charming work in an open, uncomplicated style—rather more interesting in fact than most of Haydn's solo works. Ralph Gomberg played it with no end of assurance and verve, and Thomas, working with a small orchestra of strings, oboes, horns, trumpets, and harpsichord, produced an elegant, beautifully in-scale framework.

Met's New *Pelléas* More Lucid Than Most

January 30, 1972

NEW YORK CITY—"Not for my money," said the pearl-rattling lady in the $17.50 seat next to mine[3] when the curtain came down at the end of the first act of the Metropolitan Opera's new production of Debussy's *Pelléas et Mélisande*. The late Pierre Monteux had a comment on her many years ago: "*Pelléas*," he said "is a work that was never meant to be a success."

Pelléas is for people who can follow its French: I once saw it in English, but the translation was poor, as was the direction, and so it was not a fair statement of the case for *Pelléas* in translation. I have my doubts, though. More essentially, it is a work for people who live happily in a world of allusions, suggestions, unfinished sentences, unanswered questions, of characters talking past one another, all that done in music much of which is quiet and little of which is fast, with the words projected against the subtly variegated orchestral background as a sort of conversational bas-relief. The only thing that sounds like a song is what Mélisande sings at the beginning of the scene in her tower window ("*Mes longs cheveux descendent*"), and that is both in quotation marks and unaccompanied.

[3] Adjusted for inflation, the dollar figure amounts roughly to $134 in 2025.

For many people, certainly including most who would label themselves "opera-lovers," *Pelléas* does not work at all. Others love it as they love no other opera—not more, but in a way that is altogether special, not least because it needs defending against the clods, but for its delicacy (in what other opera, after all, does the orchestra stop completely instead of screaming at the first "I love you"?), and for its haunting, scary story (it is the saddest of the star-crossed-lovers stories, because Pelléas and Mélisande come to the end of their journeys hardly knowing that they have been and where).

Pelléas et Mélisande consists of fourteen scenes, most of them fairly short, grouped in five acts (the Met mercifully and sensibly gave them as three), the scenes within each act being linked by orchestral interludes. Those interludes present several problems. Having intended to let the scenes move into one another swiftly (much as Berg was to do soon after in *Wozzeck*), Debussy added the interludes at the request of the directors of the Paris Opéra-Comique because the mechanics of scene-changing could not be managed quickly enough. The New England Conservatory *Pelléas* in 1969 showed that there is a strong case to be made for returning to Debussy's original idea about the pacing of his work; at the same time, the interludes are necessity-become-virtue, because they are an extraordinary series of scenic, psychological, and musical metamorphoses.

In most *Pelléas* performances, you cannot really tell because, with astonishing lack of perception and blindness to experience, directors drop the house curtain, something always taken by an audience as an invitation to talk, even when the music is catchier than that in the *Pelléas* interludes. I should guess that one of the first things conductor (Colin Davis), director (Paul-Émile Deiber), and designer (Desmond Heeley) of the Met's new *Pelléas* thought about was how to preserve continuity of illusion and attention, that one of their first decisions was "we shall not drop the house curtain during the interludes." What, in fact, happens is that the gold house curtain is already up when you enter the theater, that you see a great stippled scrim, and that the main curtain comes down only at the end of the evening, even then not beginning to budge until the last chord has stopped (so easy a solution to the problem of premature applause in operas that are really composed right up to the last note—*Don Giovanni*, *Tristan*—though I do not remember ever having seen it tried before).

To rationalize his open scene-changes, Deiber extends the action both backwards and forwards into the interludes. To add to *Pelléas* in any dimension is dangerous, and a couple of times Deiber wanders into perilous territory, once in too obvious a come-on from Mélisande, and again after the scene of Golaud's physical brutality to Mélisande, when Mélisande and Arkel leave together and she falls into his arms for comfort. Otherwise, though, Deiber has met even this particularly difficult part of his assignment sensitively and with intelligence.

In all respects, though, this is a *Pelléas* more open and lucid than most. The lighting (Rudolph Kuntner), which even when dim is definite rather than hazy, and the rich-textured, firmly outlined scenery contribute to that. The three principal characters develop clearly—Golaud into a degradation whose climactic point is the cold-blooded killing of his half-brother, Mélisande into growing boldness, Pelléas into the realization that Mélisande represents his only chance of salvation in the open tomb in which he lives—and the change when the news comes of the turn in the long illness of Pelléas's father is really felt. For the realization of so dynamic, non-misty a dramatic conception, Colin Davis is an ideal conductor: it was a musical performance all thrust and passion, sense of direction, with luminous clarity of texture and outline. The score, moreover, was beautifully played by the orchestra.

On stage, there were Barry McDaniel and Judith Blegen (Pelléas and Mélisande), Thomas Stewart (Golaud), Giorgio Tozzi (Arkel), Lili Chookasian (Geneviève), Adam Klein (Yniold), and Clifford Harvuot (physician), a strong cast on the whole. The outstandingly impressive person in it was Stewart, superb at conveying through voice and movement the terrible and desperate isolation of Golaud trapped as the only grown-up between children and those already well on the path, as Freud said, toward becoming inorganic. As Golaud's son, Yniold, usually done by the littlest soprano in the house, but here by a boy, Adam Klein offered a remarkable small-scale reflection of the Golaud characterization, all exasperation and impatience, and full of touches which no performer twenty years older and of the opposite sex could have caught so well, doing it, moreover, with superb confidence, audibly, in tune, and with excellent French.

Barry McDaniel, an American who has made a distinguished career in Europe and who has been known here only via a few Bach cantata recordings, was an effective Pelléas in sound and appearance. The production was originally planned around the Mélisande of Teresa Stratas, and what that fiery actress would have done is a tantalizing question-mark. She was, however, obliged to withdraw because of illness, and I thought Blegen a not completely convincing replacement. She is intelligent, sings clear French, has an attractive voice, and is very pretty (just a trifle too much in the direction of the girls behind car rental counters), but I found her lacking in overtones and in anything like erotic mystery. It was all rather hard-edged, though it became more convincing as the character grew more definite in resolution and action.

I am not sure Deiber ever finished making up his mind about Arkel, fool or wise man, senile, oracular, how blind and infirm? What Tozzi did at any given moment was compelling, but it did not add up into a coherent statement. To Geneviève, Chookasian brought the gorgeous voice the part does not need (though, of course, no one minds it), but failed to bring the clarity of diction it needed more than anything: it was all *wawawawawawawa.*

Harvuot did his brief but telling role very well. I want to say also that Heeley's costumes were admirably simple and conducive to the right sort of movement, and that I hope in future the management will be less stingy with the women servants who appear so mysterious at Mélisande's death (the mere two they have now make Golaud's "*toutes ces femmes*" either comic or needlessly petulant). In sum, the new *Pelléas* is a fresh, direct, daring, powerful statement of a moving and great work of musical theater.

Watts's Recital Brilliant in Part

February 8, 1972

While waiting for André Watts to come out and begin his piano recital in Symphony Hall Sunday afternoon, I read the program notes he had written about the pieces by Schubert (a set of waltzes, the A minor Sonata, Op. 143, and the *Wanderer Fantasy*) and Liszt (*The Fountains at the Villa d'Este* and the *Don Giovanni Fantasy*) he was going to play.

That Watts felt the urge to write his own notes was a good sign. The notes themselves were a mixture of plainly written good sense, excessive naïveté, and a nervous leaning on authority (manifest in all the quotations from Einstein, Busoni, Schumann, etc.). Watts's playing was also a mixture of knowing and not knowing, the thoroughly understood and the half-baked, the skillful and the clumsy.

He is an amazing instrumentalist, unsurpassed, so far as I know, in sheer facility. And with the facility there is a growing skill: what he did to realize the difficult textures of Schubert's piano scoring took ear and brain beyond the mere doing of what comes naturally.

As an interpreter of music, though, the 25-year-old pianist wandered disconcertingly from level to level. In Schubert's Opus 18 Waltzes, simply played, quiet pieces alternated with more vigorous where, in the name presumably of Viennese style, the rhythm was broken by violent hiccups. The Sonata is a piece so subtle and so intimate as almost to resist public performance altogether, yet Watts projected remarkably its dramatic changes of character and played it simply and interestingly. Then again, in the extroverted, virtuosic *Wanderer Fantasy*, he gave us not only a beautifully "heard" slow movement, but also much playing that was thoughtless, riddled with inconsistencies of rhythm and phrasing, and coarse in its rhetoric.

In the very short Liszt part of the program, Watts played the *Fountains* dazzlingly from the pianistic point of view, though without much atmosphere. In the operatic Fantasy, the instrumental sureness was breathtaking, but beyond that brilliance there was a seeing right into the center of *Don Giovanni* and into the mysteries of Mozart's orchestral sound, and that was extraordinary.

Beethoven's Triple Concerto—Two Versions

February 20, 1972

There is an interesting batch of recent recordings of unpopular Beethoven. Let me start with two of the Triple Concerto for piano, violin, and cello, one played by Sviatoslav Richter, David Oistrakh, and Mstislav Rostropovich, with Herbert von Karajan conducting the Berlin Philharmonic (Angel), the other played by Claudio Arrau, Henryk Szeryng, and Janos Starker, with Eliahu Inbal conducting the New Philharmonia (Philips).

To read about the work, you want to go to Tovey (*Essays in Musical Analysis*, Vol. 3). His combination of analysis and defense is brilliant, and I don't want to try to summarize it. No question, the Triple Concerto is a piece addressed to special tastes: Tovey nicely says that its "indiscretion . . . consists in combining a problem that makes for dryness of matter with a problem that makes for exceptional length." It has little of that aggressive emotional sweep that people love in middle Beethoven, and for the sake of greater malleability in development, Beethoven has given its themes a deliberately neutral cast. It is, on the other hand, energetic, brainy, elegant, a coolly stunning show of a composer's knowing his material and understanding how to make much from little.

Given its expansiveness and its way of making its point through architectural control rather than by rhetoric, the Triple Concerto, even by Beethovenian standards, depends exceptionally on its conductor for coherent performance. Von Karajan used to be an interesting, vigorous conductor. More and more, he has turned into one concerned only with getting his orchestra to make beautiful sounds, which for him means uncannily smooth sounds. As he has become better at this, particularly with an orchestra like the Berlin Philharmonic to which he is very close, he has tended to exercise less and less control over the articulation of the musical flow, seeming instead to sink into a trance of enchantment at the beautiful sounds coming at him.

In a work that so much requires, not Narcissus, but a conductor in the most active sense, Karajan is a disaster. A comparison of the first minute on the two recordings, of Karajan's seamless murmur against Inbal's purposefully articulated statement, is downright comic. Moreover, everything in the Karajan performance that tends toward non-definition is accentuated by Angel's mushy sound. Since the solo group on Philips is very good, it does not much matter that Rostropovich's playing is a notch ahead of Starker's in some points of taste.

The other Beethoven on my list is not so much unpopular—people actually sneer at the Triple Concerto as they do at the *Consecration of the House* Overture—as it is little known. Of the delightfully adventurous, full-of-beans String Quintet in C, Op. 29, there is a good new recording by members of the Vienna Octet (London). On the other side, they play a fairly bland, certainly very pleasant early work, the E-flat Sextet for strings and horns with the deceptively high opus number, 81b.

The Piano Sonata in E-flat, Op. 7, is early Beethoven at his strongest, with a fiery Allegro to begin with, a solemn and expressive slow movement full of marvelous silences, a minuet with a surprising and disturbing Trio, and a finale in that gentle mood which goes so badly with the standard Beethoven portrait that we forget how beautifully he wrote such movements. It has been recorded by Arturo Benedetti Michelangeli—one of his first recordings of anything in years—and his work here is fascinating and quite unsatisfying. The sheerly pianistic, coloristic imagination is extraordinary, as is the control that enables him to realize all he imagines. Michelangeli also plays with taste and intelligence. What I cannot deal with is the coldness and the absence of spontaneity, the playing of the first movement from which one could never infer that Beethoven has asked for "*allegro molto e con brio*," or the charmingly conceived rubato in the minuet, which then comes back twice more played exactly that way as though on a tape loop. I had, at the end, heard some of the most amazing piano playing of my life, but not Opus 7 (Deutsche Grammophon).

One of Beethoven's handy sources of income was the Scots publisher George Thomson, who repeatedly commissioned him to make settings suitable for the drawing room of folk songs, mainly from the British Isles. Beethoven's work was appropriately simple, but both in points of scoring and in the newly composed preludes and postludes, he had scope for an inventiveness that is delightful to encounter. The record on which the tenor, Frank Patterson, sings fifteen of the Irish songs with the Music Group of London—David Parkhouse, piano; Hugh Bean, violin; Eileen Croxford, cello—gives a most refreshing sort of pleasure (Philips).

A postscript on a piece of super-popular Beethoven, the *Emperor* Concerto: Tovey is persuasive in saying that Beethoven could not have achieved it without first having written the Triple Concerto. It, too, is a work of rather severely interpersonal themes and one where extraordinary care has been expended on the details of the virtuosic solo figurations. The performance by Vladimir Horowitz with the Chicago Symphony under Fritz Reiner which has just been reissued (RCA Victrola—fake stereo only, but not an impossible sound if played back via mono) illuminates that side of the *Emperor* most tellingly with its admirably quick tempo for the first movement and its emphasis generally on the virtuoso elements. With its extremely slow Adagio and its touches of brittle violence now and again (including some extra octave doublings in the bass), it is not an altogether likeable performance, but it is an extremely interesting one and, at least in the first movement, a good antidote to the more usual "heroic" approach. It is as though Horowitz and Reiner had never heard of the Anglo-American *Emperor* nickname, and that at least is a step in the right direction.

Rosen's Sonata Album a Distinguished Work

March 5, 1972

In the notes I took while listening to Charles Rosen's recording of Beethoven's last six piano sonatas (Columbia, three records), I find "you have to hear all of this performance to hear how good it is." That refers to Rosen's playing of Opus 109, which happened to be the one with which I chose to begin, but to some degree that could be said of all six performances. Rosen here is dealing with the music Schnabel said he liked to play because it was greater than any possible performance of it. Insofar as that might turn out to be frustrating on any single occasion of listening to one of these sonatas, Rosen's performances are no less frustrating than anyone else's. One quality, however, that makes them particularly impressive is that each adds up to an enormously compelling statement which is more than the sum of its parts.

These recordings, made in England a couple of years ago, are a distinguished musical and pianistic achievement. Given what Schnabel meant, that no one performance can come close to revealing all of one of these multi-faceted works, the Beethoven sonatas are most particularly the sorts of works of which you want more than one record. I would give Rosen's album high priority on a small list which includes the recordings by Schnabel (Seraphim), Frank (RCA Victrola, available only as a complete set),[4] Hess of Opus 109 (Seraphim), and Lateiner of Opus 111 (RCA). I have not heard any of Kempff's recordings (DGG) recently enough to make specific recommendations; as for Brendel, I suggest waiting until Philips releases in America the new recordings he has begun in England.

If I wanted to persuade someone of Rosen's stature as a pianist, I would make my case on the new recording of the *Hammerklavier*, Op. 106, which by the way is very different in effect from his earlier one (Epic, withdrawn), much better recorded, less violent, more humorous, altogether more interesting. The first movement is very "allegro" (that is, as opposed to most pianists' "allegro maestoso"), and by the way of a final chord held to what seems endless length, it is connected without break to the scherzo, which follows as a kind of sardonic satyr-play. The Adagio moves beautifully, is as impassioned and expressive as

[4] See review of March 21, 1971.

Beethoven directs, but in nobly restrained style in which the main line of activity and decorative detail are always clearly sorted out one from the other. It, too, moves without break into the finale. In the fugue, the clarity of the polyphony is exemplary, especially with respect to rhythm, and there is no sense of someone's wrestling (even successfully) with something nearly impossible; the wildest passage, the series of leaps with short, explosive trills immediately before the quiet D major episode, even sounds like the huge half-cadence it is, and not, as it usually does, like a battery of berserk ejaculations.

It is interesting how Rosen sets the *Hammerklavier* apart from the other five pieces by making it the only real *fortissimo* sonata in the group. His playing is notably restrained in dynamics—though, in articulation more varied and lively than most—and it can seem startlingly small-scale at times (which again provides many useful reminders of such things as the third variation in Opus 111 being *forte* with many accents, not a roaring *fortissimo*). And if you compare the new Opus 110 with the one previously coupled with the *Hammerklavier*, you hear how Rosen's playing now is less explicit, less aggressively didactic than before. A price has been paid for the changes—I miss some of the sharpness of accent and of *forte-piano* contrasts as well as the Schumannesque ecstasy of the ending—but the new Opus 110, with its more controlled pacing, the more imaginative declamation of the recitative and the two verses of the aria, the intricate play of light and shade in the first fugue, is amazingly beautiful.

In Opus 90, it is the slow, impassioned playing of the second movement that is striking, and in astounding contrast to Frank's graceful playing of it or to Schnabel's fantastic, almost capricious projection of it as a series of "big events." Rosen's playing is a little hard in sound, a little un-*pianissimo*, but here and elsewhere remarkably knowing and sensitive about Beethoven's bass lines. In Opus 101, the march is brilliantly clear, as is the finale; the slow movement starts out exceedingly reserved, and rubato is the more telling when it sets in (see the first sentence of this review). The performance of Opus 109, very held in at first, is a remarkable unfolding of a whole piece.

In the first movement of Opus 111, I would wish for more distinction between "*poco ritenente*" and Beethoven's more generously marked retardations, and the slow movement suggests at first that Rosen is temperamentally less congenial to its "*semplice*" than to the "*appassionato e con molto sentimento*" of the *Hammerklavier* Adagio (also, is his playing not more *parlando* than the *cantabile* for which Beethoven asks?). Here, too, is a performance that develops. There is profound mystery and immobility in the *pianissimo* double variation (IV), and from there to the end, the music—that is, Rosen's realization of Beethoven's idea—is rapt, unearthly, our normal clocks all stopped: "*In paradisum deducant angeli . . .*"

Even where I am not persuaded, I find Rosen's playing always compelling, constantly teaching me something about Beethoven. In fact I am persuaded more often than not, and can only say once more that these records preserve a rare combination of musical sensibility and imagination, intellectual force, and spectacular command of the instrument.

Dunn Leads Bach at Symphony Hall

March 11, 1972

Thomas Dunn first made his reputation as a conductor of Bach. Curiously, though, since he became music director of the Handel and Haydn Society four seasons ago, though he has done one of the short Masses and some instrumental pieces, he conducted no major work of Bach's here until last night, when the Society gave the *St. Matthew* Passion under his direction in Symphony Hall. I hope he will be around with Bach often and soon. It is what perhaps he does best, and certainly the performance yesterday was marvelous.

The *St. Matthew* Passion has the most richly complex structure of any work I know. It is not only the horizontal complexity that necessarily comes from its being seventy-eight sections which take just under three hours to sing and play, but there is also the series of vertical strata, the differentiation of narrative and commentary, of commentary in arias and in congregational hymns, of hymns presented simply and those embedded in elaborate structures, the arias with chorus which offer commentary, within commentary, and so forth.

The most impressive part of Dunn's performance was the control, the grasp at all times of the whole immense structure, the sense of having available in his font, at least a dozen punctuation marks of different strength. What was new, at least to me, in this reading was the clarity with which climaxes, points of arrival, heights and valleys, light and shade, action and contemplation, were projected. Much of that is sub-structure: the performance also presented a compelling surface, knowingly paced in detail as well as in the large, and with extraordinary character and life in the phrasing.

Dunn used the full Handel and Haydn Society chorus of eighty-five: this double-chorus Passion can stand a large group of singers better than most Bach, but even so the singing was remarkable for its transparency (and not less for its variety of color). Richard Shadley was the Evangelist, less journalistic than most, though wonderfully verbal as well as musical, and clearly ready to take his place among the great ones like Erb, Cuenod, Pears, and Haefliger. Francis Hester sang Jesus, always with dignity, and after a while with splendid sound and great intensity. Barbara Wallace, Eunice Alberts, Jon Humphrey, and Elwood Thornton (a bass new to me, light, even somewhat undistinguished in voice, but unusually sensitive) were a superb quartet for the arias. The Boston Philharmonia played beautifully, with Elinor Preble's flute solo in "Aus Liebe will mein Heiland sterben" the outstanding among many excellently played *obbligati*.

"Greatest Living Composer"?

March 26, 1972

WASHINGTON, DC—As long as Stravinsky was alive, it was clear that there was such a thing as the "greatest living composer." When Stravinsky died last April 6, though music was not about to stop, it was also clear that no one comparable was left, so much so that I stopped thinking about the "greatest living composer" category at all. And I remember how during the summer, Michael Tilson Thomas, then preparing a performance of *Colors of the Celestial City*,[5] surprised me by saying in conversation that Olivier Messiaen was now the most likely claimant to that quotation-mark-surrounded title. "Think about it," he said.

I have, off and on. There are composers whose music interests, also moves or excites me more than most of Messiaen's—Elliott Carter is at the top of that list—but now, some months after Thomas's challenge to think about who Messiaen is, I see him as a composer whose best music has tremendous force, a man of sharply defined artistic profile, an incalculably influential teacher (Boulez and Stockhausen being the most famous of his pupils), a man who is grandly, resolutely himself. He, more than anyone else living, is the figure without whom I cannot imagine the recent history of Western music.

On several occasions, Messiaen has given performances in this country of his two-piano music with his wife, Yvonne Loriod. As a performer, he is, however, most renowned as an organist, and last Tuesday he played his first organ concert in America, in the National Shrine of the Immaculate Conception, Washington. Whatever one's evaluation of the new piece Messiaen composed for that concert—*Meditations on the Mystery of the Holy Trinity*, whose eighty-six minutes made up the whole program—there was no mistaking the sense of occasion that marked the evening. The National Shrine is the largest Catholic church in this country and the seventh-largest church of any denomination anywhere in the world, and long before the concert began, it was filled by an audience of just under 3,000, representing at least thirty of the United States (there was, for example, a busload of fifty organ students from the University of Michigan). During the forty-minute intermission, you could at long distance watch the shirt-sleeved

[5] See review of August 7, 1971.

Messiaen setting up the pistons for the second half, with Mme. Loriod peering over the ledge of the organ loft from time to time to report on the progress of the audience as it made its way back into the pews.

There were nine meditations. The components of Messiaen's musical language have been fixed for some time: the rhythmic patterns he has learned from Indian music, the complex pitch and rhythmic shapes of birdcalls from all over the world, and Gregorian chant. To these he has added something new in the *Trinity Meditations*, something he calls "communicable language," which I understand as an attempt to find a musical analog for the language of angels as described by St. Thomas Aquinas in the *Summa Theologica*: "If the angel, through his will, directs his mental concept in order to communicate it to another, immediately the latter perceives it: in this way the angel speaks to another angel."

Messiaen has constructed a musical alphabet in which each letter from a to z has a pitch and duration assigned to it. He has devised special formulas to indicate grammatical cases, and two more for the verb "to be" (a descending figure "because all that exists comes from God, the Being par excellence, the One Who is") and "to have" (the transposed inversion of the latter, an ascending figure "because we can always have more by raising ourselves to God"). Through this "communicable language," Messiaen puts into three of his *Meditations* quotations in French from the *Summa Theologica*.

All that was contained in the composer's copiously illustrated 400-word program note, which also provided a theological analysis of each movement as well as a detailed point-to-point description of the musical procedures. Messiaen's associations of colors with music play their part, too, so that he speaks of "the white and gold light of the sixth chord of C major" or to the chosen registration (Swell reeds 16, 6, 4, plus cymbal) as giving "a brilliant golden yellow color, with some violet glint, silver grey, a little tint of brown, of red, and pale green."

It is complicated and naive, as indeed Messiaen's music is altogether a mixture—really and amazingly a mixture, not just a collision—of heterogeneous and even opposite elements and qualities. Among exceedingly expansive movements, he has put as the third section a meditation on "The true relation in God is really identical to the essence," which is over before we are ready for it to have properly begun (as in the Intermezzo in the *Quartet for the End of Time*). The harmony ranges from violently dislocated chord sequences to material that sounds like the organ music in the Saint-Sulpice scene of *Manon* by Massenet (a composer Messiaen admires).

His play with time, rhythm, and form is like that, too: there is the really marvelous freshness, the metric looseness of his birds and Indians and chanting monks, but he is capable as well of squarely mechanical symmetries and given to ponderous repetitions of huge sections ("lest you should think he never could recapture—The first fine careless rapture"). Where, when, how Messiaen's results will be interesting is not always foreseeable. The key to the *Meditations on the Mystery of the Holy Trinity* is Messiaen's subtext for his Eighth Meditation, "God is simple." In the whole work, which seems to me uneven mainly insofar as it is sometimes unconcentrated, the most boldly simple moments are the ones that speak most eloquently, the tender, exceedingly quiet meditation on the Alleluia for All Saints (Messiaen here was thinking about "My yoke is easy and my burden is light"), and many of his birds, the wild shriek of the black woodpecker, instantly contrasted with the muted *mm-mm-mm-mm-mm* of the owl of Tengmalm, and the call of the yellowhammer (seven times C-sharp and one longer D-sharp) which ends three of the movements and in fact the whole composition.

And there is in Messiaen the composer always Messiaen the virtuoso, the man capable of enormous delight in how instruments speak. As writing for organ, the *Trinity Meditations* are brilliant in the extended Liszt-Franck language he has evolved over the years. The National Shrine has a superb Möller organ of the Romantic cathedral type, and Messiaen had spent about ten days there preparing his performance, often beginning practice at 6:30 in the morning. He is an organist whose playing has astonishing rhythmic life, vividness and clarity of color, and dramatic presence—several of his recordings of earlier works of his own are available on imported Ducretet-Thomson records—and he gave a stunning performance here.

Steinberg Conducts *Romeo and Juliet*

March 27, 1972

Most people would not at once think of William Steinberg as a Berlioz conductor; yet he did *Faust's Damnation* in New York a couple of seasons ago. It is to him that I owe my first hearings of *Lélio* (long before the Boulez recording) and the *Symphonie funèbre et triomphale* (badly cut), and for the Boston Symphony concerts this past weekend he chose the complete *Romeo and Juliet.*

The work itself, still an exotic and generally misunderstood rarity at the time of Toscanini's 1947 broadcast and Munch's first Boston performance of it six years later, has become so well established and so universally recognized as one of the central masterpieces of Romanticism, that to praise it here is really not necessary. The finale, everything after Juliet's awakening and death, still seems an anticlimax in that nothing about Friar Laurence's pitch for reconciliation engaged Berlioz's love of Shakespeare and his musical imagination as did the feelings and the situation of Romeo and Juliet themselves. I did on Friday afternoon, however, make a special effort not to hear the finale as anticlimax, and while its general manner is terribly official, I was struck more than before by the quality of detail, particularly harmonic and orchestral, which makes something special of Berlioz's essay in that rather unpromising style.

The tautness of Steinberg's pacing and his determinedly non-pompous approach helped, as indeed his control of pace and of large-scale rhythm was impressive all afternoon. The performance was admirable for its coherence, and I was especially grateful for Steinberg's quite un-Munchian readiness to take the classically restrained side of Berlioz's language seriously. What was lacking in this honest performance was sheer brilliance and sometimes energy. The love scene went beautifully, also the vocal version of "Queen Mab," both with lovely *pianissimo*; but things that should have been exceedingly quiet were only half-quiet (the tambourines and the antique cymbals were notably disturbing in that way), and the blurred Queen Mab Scherzo and the frightful scrubbing in the opening fugue suggested that the orchestra had a hard time reading the conductor.

I was impressed by the New England Conservatory Chorus, prepared by Lorna Cooke deVaron. Their French sounded American, but at the same time it was so clear that one could understand every word. There was a nice transparent sound, too, and the choral recitatives in the Prologue were, for a change, really effective. Kenneth Riegel, the tenor soloist, delivered Mercutio's bravura dream with enchanting lightness, verbal clarity, and rhythmic snap. The women in the chorus were enormously turned on by Ara Berberian, the bass soloist, and shuffled and stamped their feet like anything when he appeared on stage and when he took his bow afterwards. He did the Friar Laurence scene musically and with dignity; otherwise I dissent in that I did not at all like his rough sound. Joanna Simon, done up very nightclub, sang the alto solo competently, if with no special distinction.

Brahms Concerto Well Done

March 29, 1972

At the Boston Symphony's Pension Fund Concert in January, Artur Rubinstein played the Brahms Piano Concerto No. 2 in B-flat major.[6] Last night, at a subscription concert, that work was on the program again, this time with Malcolm Frager as soloist, and, as before, with Michael Tilson Thomas conducting. It was a different piece.

Rubinstein played it as something elegant and slender, with delicate inflection of line and exquisite transparency. It was astonishing as an act of cleaning the

[6] See review of January 6, 1972.

crud off a monument too much taken for granted and no longer carefully looked at, as a kind of rejuvenation, and all that the more dramatic in coming from a pianist in his eighties.

Now came Frager to make first of all the statement that the Brahms B-flat is, except for the freaks like the Busoni and the Furtwängler, the most gigantic of all piano concertos. His playing was huge, with massive sound—he is one of those pianists who can make an immense *fortissimo* effortlessly and without banging—and with the inflections of line sculpted on the most generous scale. It was a performance in the grandly, even riskily rhetorical manner of which Arrau's recording with Haitink is the most extreme statement.

That is a debatable approach. Certainly it is playing what is in the piece, though one could make a case against emphasis of what is least attractive in Brahms, his Beethoven dreams of glory and his ambitions in the direction of world-shaking utterance. I was not sure at the beginning that I should not disqualify myself from reviewing at all. Having lived very intensely in a world of Schütz, Bach, and Stravinsky these last few days, I found it hard to face Brahms. It was like wanting a dozen oysters and clams, very fresh, with a glass of really good ale, and then having someone threaten you with a vast dish of steaming, very brown goulash.

Somewhere very soon, though, I found myself completely drawn into what Frager was doing and thoroughly enjoying what was happening. Not without some misgivings, mainly because the volume was so consistently up that the *pianissimo* end of the scale was gone altogether, and not without the wish to be shaken rather less hard by the lapels; still, the consistency, conviction, sheer energy, and structural intelligence of the interpretation were in the end enormously persuasive. Specifically I want gratefully to mention the good tempi, an opening that was actually part of the concerto instead of the usual maudlin fantasy outside it, and a third movement with a beautiful sense of flow.

Michael Tilson Thomas, having worked into and out of Rubinstein's playing with extraordinary delicacy, now adapted himself readily and enthusiastically to Frager's mega-performance. There were a couple of extreme lapses in orchestral execution—the wild difference of opinion about pitch between horn and piano at the very beginning, and then some rich disorder in the Trio of the second movement—but in general the playing was warm and very much alive.

. . . and Bing's Successor Plans His *Carmen*

April 23, 1972

NEW YORK—The general manager's office at the Metropolitan Opera House is a grand, dark brown place, filled now with mementos of Sir Rudolf Bing's

22 years of being a VIP in New York's cultural life. Goeran Gentele, until recently head of the Royal Opera in Stockholm, will move into that office on or about July 1. For now, Gentele, who has spent the last seven months in the house observing, "pretty much getting to know everybody and the house and how it all works," is quartered in a small, brightly sunlit room, its wall and those of the little corridor leading to it hung with posters announcing the week's repertory for the theaters and opera houses in West Berlin, Hamburg, Stockholm, Frankfurt, Vienna, and Stuttgart (and I must say that the dreariness of repertory and casts makes the Met look exciting and glamorous).

Gentele is busy. "Excuse me, but I must go to the rehearsal stage a minute and look at *Carmen*." *Carmen* will be Gentele's opening night. The Met has to plan far in advance, and 1972–73, the first Gentele season, was pretty much fixed by Bing and his staff before Gentele's appointment was decided on. The opening was to be *Tannhäuser*. Gentele found that prospect too dreary and, looking around for another work that could well use the principals who had been engaged, Marilyn Horne and James McCracken, thought of *Carmen*, engaged himself as director, Leonard Bernstein as conductor (with Michael Tilson Thomas to take over after the first six performances), and Josef Svoboda as designer (remembered in Boston as the designer for Sarah Caldwell's production of Nono's *Intolleranza* in 1965).

Carmen will be done with spoken dialogue rather than with the more usual posthumously added recitatives by Guiraud, which Gentele dislikes on principle as being "music which poor Bizet never heard," because they make statements never envisioned by librettist or composer (for example, Don Jose's to Zuniga that he loves Micaela), and because they are musically too "nice" for so fiery and un-nice a masterpiece. Gentele and Bernstein expect to restore a little, "a very little," of the music that was cut before the March 1875 premiere, some of which has been cropping up in recent recordings and revivals.

Carmen will be the only opera Gentele himself will direct in 1972–73, but what would he like to direct in future seasons? The answer came quickly: Berg's *Lulu* and *Wozzeck*, Busoni's *Doktor Faust*, "our Stockholm production of Verdi's *Ballo in Maschera*," "possibly" Blomdahl's space-ship opera, *Aniara*, "certainly some Janáček, either *Kátya Kabanová* or *From the House of the Dead* to begin with."

Mention of Janáček's Dostoyevsky opera brought Gentele to Rafael Kubelik, whom he recently heard conduct it in Hamburg. Gentele regards his appointment of Kubelik as the Met's music director, a post that has not previously existed at the house, as being as important a step as he has taken yet. "I am very experienced in opera, I can read a score, and so on, but after all I am not a professional musician, and in the running of an opera company there are many matters, particularly pertaining to the orchestra, that can be properly attended to only by a professional musician. I first heard Kubelik 11 years ago, have followed his career closely ever since, and I think it is going to be absolutely marvelous to have him here. He is a fantastic musician, with experience and maturity and also a man of the broadest general culture who knows and understands the whole world in which any opera he conducts exists, and I think that shows in his work. And we are both very happy with the thought of having James Levine as general conductor. I heard Jimmy's very first performance here, a *Tosca*, and I just thought 'yes.'" Apropos conductors, Gentele sees as one of his most important tasks "to bring down the number of not good conductors."

Gentele had seen everything that was in repertory in 1971–72. Had he seen anything that he liked or that represented the kind of musical theater he would want to show in a house he managed? Gentele smiled, thought a while, said "*Tristan*," thought some more, smiled again, and repeated "*Tristan*. Yes, *Tristan*. It was imaginative and understanding as a scenic interpretation, it was fresh and forward-looking, and it was musically good." Yes, he was in contact with the director, August Everding, in hopes of future collaborations. And speaking of hopes, Gentele would like to bring to the Met the production of Stravinsky's *Rake's Progress* which Ingmar Bergman did for him in Stockholm.

"Yes, of course we must do contemporary opera, but you know, you really can't count things like *Wozzeck* and *Lulu* and *Rake's Progress* as 'contemporary opera.' I know it will not draw as well as Verdi and Puccini and so on, and it is depressing to do such things in a one-third empty house, depressing for the public and depressing for the artists, but then why is it necessary to do them in this immense house? We must in any case have a small theater for chamber opera, experimental works, and so on, and I think the important thing is that the Metropolitan Opera Company produce *Lulu* but not necessarily to do it in this building, no? Lincoln Center is full of good theaters of different sizes, but of course I cannot yet speak of going to this or that one, to Juilliard or the Beaumont, with this or that work—it is very delicate and we are very early in our conversations. I think it is important that Lincoln Center works as a unit, that we take advantage of the possibilities."

As for his neighbor, the New York City Opera, "I don't think it's bad to have two operas next to each other. They do some interesting things, and I think they must have their *Traviata*s and *Carmen*s to bring in their public. The underdog thing? Oh, the whole world loves an underdog, David-Goliath, brave little City Opera and fat, rich, bad Met. It's the same everywhere. In Stockholm they knock you with Göteborg or Oslo."

Gentele is concerned with finding a new audience, and he aims to increase the number of student performances and to improve their quality.

"I think much of what has been done has been in the wrong direction. Those things with four singers and a piano, for example—there is no smell of theater to that. And our park concerts are lacking in the same way. Cable and closed-circuit television has immense possibilities for us, but television, too, has so far not been handled well. Have you seen any of those dreadful German productions? They will have made far more enemies for opera than friends. I think we must find ways of showing things that you cannot show in the theater, and those straight-on shots and these embarrassing close-ups in those German films are just not it. Also, television is a tiring medium, and I wonder if we want to show operas one act at a sitting, like *Forsyte Saga*. I think it is not necessary to eat the whole pound-cake at one time."

Gentele will not accompany the Met on the tour that begins in Boston tomorrow, "but I have visited all the cities and seen all the theaters. With everyone cleared out of here, I mean to use those weeks to catch up on many things, also to work on *Carmen*." He sees tours as continuing to have a place in the Met's future, though like his predecessor, he sees them as a financial and logistic nightmare and as a source of severe artistic frustration. In the negotiations with the unions now in progress, Gentele has proposed that the tour be broken into two segments, perhaps with two weeks before the season in New York and four in the spring. Besides reducing fatigue, that should improve things in that some of the best singers and conductors who cannot now be persuaded to participate in a six-week tour might be willing to go along for a shorter one, "particularly if we get them in September and tell them they can open the season in New York."

At that point, Gentele was summoned to return to the negotiations. "Please excuse me, I really cannot sit here any longer. I will see you at *Carmen*?" He smiled, stood, shook hands, picked up two huge ledgers, and disappeared into the negotiating room through whose door I could hear laughter.[7]

Fine Arts Quartet Plays Fine, Babbitt

May 16, 1972

String quartets have an incredible literature from which to draw for their concerts, but when it comes to learning repertory and building programs, there isn't a lazier, more unimaginative category of players. The prevailing attitude that the 20th century can be disposed of by one token Bartók per concert is

[7] Tragically, Gentele died in a car crash less than three months later, on July 18, 1972. See obituary of July 20, 1972.

particularly paralyzing: the excellent Fine Arts Quartet (Leonard Sorkin, Abram Loft, Bernard Zazlav, George Sopkin) is an exception. I don't think that a program all of more or less difficult contemporary pieces is a completely convincing alternative either, but that the Fine Arts could play such a program, as they did in Slosberg Recital Hall at Brandeis University Sunday night, and play it so ably, is itself remarkable.

A special occasion brought this about: the annual concert given in memory of Irving Fine, who was Professor of Music at Brandeis at the time of his early death ten years ago. Fine's own Quartet (1952), a lively, direct, engaging piece in a sort of twelve-tone C major, full of chugging ostinatos, was on the program, and it was preceded by Milton Babbitt's Quartet No. 3 (1969) and followed by Seymour Shifrin's Quartet No. 4 (1967).

The Babbitt, which is a single fifteen-minute movement that makes extraordinary demands on a listener's concentration, had me pretty much slain. When it was over, I wanted to go away somewhere quiet, think about it, then hear it again—none of that available. I have not seen the score and this was my first hearing (the Fine Arts did, however, play the piece at MIT in April of last year), and for me, Babbitt's music, except when there is a text to hang onto, requires a lot of acquaintance before I can begin to find my way in it.

I found it completely absorbing. I love the restraint, the economy of means, that produces so varied a surface only by the contrast of dynamics and of plucked versus bowed notes, all managed without resort to the "colorful," to say nothing of the merely colorful. I was fascinated by the way in which the restless surface where expressive but brief phrases seem always truncated by punctuations in pizzicato, lives with a stable, profoundly calm substructure. I was gripped by the gradual emergence of clarity out of ambiguity particularly with respect to rhythm—at least one thing that was happening in the music, not just my own growing confidence at getting my bearings in Babbitt's language. And that is about as much as I can say for the moment.

After Fine and the intermission, the audience had shrunk by about one-third. I don't know whether people were fleeing tone-row or the heat, but those who left missed an impressive piece. By ordinary standards, Shifrin's music was "difficult," too, but if what he writes is densely worked and dissonant, it offers the listener a familiar sort of musical rhetoric. In the first of three movements, for example, Shifrin takes deep breaths and lets out great expressive arabesques which, *mutatis mutandis*, are not so different from those in the slow movement of Mozart's C major Viola Quintet. There is a delightful, ticking scherzo, with frenzied Trio, and a concentrated finale, blocky and lean at the same time (marked "*maestevole*," a word not known to my quite fat Italian dictionary).

Gentele—Man of Many Parts

July 20, 1972

The death Tuesday night in an automobile-truck collision in Sardinia of Goeran Gentele, who had just taken over as general manager of the Metropolitan Opera, was news to hear with shock and incredulity. The shock is perhaps greatest for us in the United States who stood just before the beginning of what we hoped and thought would be a long period of friendship and Gentele-watching. The pain is the greater for the personal tragedy that took the lives also of his 21- and 15-year-old daughters, Anna and Beatrice, like their mother, the former actress Maria Bergson, and their older sister Janet, who survived in serious condition, young women of exceptional beauty and vitality.

The appointment of Gentele, who would have been 55 the day after his first opening night, September 16, was announced in December 1970, and the new general manager had spent the 1971–72 season, Sir Rudolf Bing's last, in a small office in the big building, watching, getting to know the house and the people in it, making long-range plans, appointing new staff, preparing the production of *Carmen* which he was going to direct for the opening of his first season, and experiencing the first frustrations in what is considered for good reason the toughest job in the artistic management world.[8]

The *Carmen* story is characteristic of Gentele's cool and his smarts. Since, because of the schedule of big-name singers and conductors, opera seasons have to be planned far in advance, the first season was in its outlines planned by Bing before he knew who his successor would be. The opening night was to be Wagner's *Tannhäuser*, edifying and worth reviving, but not the stuff on which great successes are built. Working in the most discreet *pianissimo*, Gentele found another opera that could use Marilyn Horne and James McCracken, the two stars signed up for *Tannhäuser*, namely *Carmen*, tried but failed to get Tom O'Horgan of *Hair* fame to direct, announced that he would do it himself, got Leonard Bernstein to conduct and Alvin Ailey to work out the dances. And that was going to be quite an opening.

Directing was Gentele's profession, and he had done much of it, in opera, film, and theater, before becoming director of the Royal Swedish Opera in 1963. The Stockholm company was the most distinguished of the European ones—the others included those from Vienna, Moscow, and Milan—that showed their wares in Montreal at Expo '67. They brought what for many was the operatic experience of a lifetime, Ingmar Bergman's production of Stravinsky's *Rake's Progress*, but also Gentele's own productions of Blomdahl's *Aniara* and Verdi's

[8] See article of April 23, 1972.

Masked Ball, both profoundly intelligent, imaginative, and musical through and through. The brief Stockholm engagement in Montreal said that there was a man who could do and a man who had standards.

Gentele was a man of many parts. He knew theater and opera, but he also knew people and understood plenty about money. Quietly, with tact and superb efficiency, and not only because he was enjoying the benefits of a honeymoon, he negotiated contracts with the nine unions the Met deals with, and, without precedent, got everything settled before the expiration of the old contract.

Gentele had made good appointments, outstandingly those of the conductors Rafael Kubelik and James Levine to head his musical staff. He had planned for a Piccolo Met, where new, experimental, or chamber operas could be staged. He was interested in exploring the possibilities of televised opera, and in full awareness of the deadliness of almost everything else that had so far been done in that field. He had planned to take student performances, ones that would really convey the authentic smell of theater, with utmost seriousness. While he had a good news sense that kept him from saying too much too far in advance, it was clear that his plans included such things as Berlioz's *Trojans*, Berg's two masterpieces *Wozzeck* and *Lulu* in versions staged by Gentele himself, some of the operas of Janáček, and a *Rake's Progress* and more from his compatriot and friend, Ingmar Bergman.

Everyone in the music world had seen Gentele's appointment as a promise of life and excitement. Where the Met will go is impossible even to guess at, either in long range or in immediate terms. Presumably, Gentele's second-in-command, Schuyler Chapin, will run the shop for the season that begins just fifty-eight days from today. For after that, we have to dig out those old lists again, the lists with the names of Bernstein, Harewood, Leinsdorf, Liebermann, the lists which nineteen months ago we thought we could put away for a long time.

The Stanislaw Method

July 23, 1972

LENOX—Stanislaw Skrowaczewski, music director of the Minnesota Orchestra, had his moment of greatest visibility at Tanglewood when, on the Saturday night of the season's first weekend, he conducted Bach, Beethoven, and Mozart with the Boston Symphony for an audience of over 8,000. In all, though, Skrowaczewski spent three weeks at the Berkshire Music Center, engaged most of the time in the less public but no less important tasks of training the Berkshire Music Center Orchestra, which means, to begin with, turning ninety-eight young players, most of whom have never before worked together, into an orchestra and of helping the seven holders of fellowships in conducting to learn their métier.

There is some overlap because the Conducting Fellows observe Skrowaczewski and the other professionals—this year they include Leonard Bernstein, Bruno Maderna, Seiji Ozawa, and Joseph Silverstein—as they work with the BMC Orchestra (they also attend as many Boston Symphony rehearsals as they can). Then, with one or more of the professionals watching them, the Fellows rehearse the BMC Orchestra and conduct it at public concerts. There are also seminars away from the orchestra at which questions from the most general ("What does 'knowing a score' really mean?") to the most particular ("If you make a gesture at hip-level, the violins can see it, but the horns probably can't") are discussed.

One Saturday morning, I watched Skrowaczewski work with the BMC Orchestra on the last movement of the Brahms First Symphony. I was impressed by his sense of harmony, by his concern, therefore, for the bass lines which define the harmony, and, in a more general way, by economy that led him to say what he had to say with sharp precision and also to know when to say nothing.

I also watched the student conductors watching Skrowaczewski, looking up from their scores as notorious trouble spots approached—the pizzicato passages in the introduction, the difficult syncopations in the middle of the movement, the acceleration into the coda—and then writing notes to themselves or sometimes just smiling as each hurdle was cleared.

I asked permission to attend one of the seminars, and a few days later found myself in Hawthorne Cottage on the Tanglewood grounds, in a rather stark room with straight chairs around the walls, a grand piano, and a blackboard, and of course with the lean, nervously energetic maestro and six of the Conducting Fellows. Eighteen notes were played on the piano, and the blackboard was used not at all. At least with respect to the piano, that session was atypical: normally, Skrowaczewski explained, there was analysis of scores—himself an able composer, he is highly organized about that sort of thing—as well as exercises when he sat at the keyboard and played according to the students' conducting. That evening, however, two students would be leading the BMC Orchestra in concert, they had just had their dress rehearsal, and a large part of the seminar would be given over to a post-mortem on the rehearsal.

Skrowaczewski began by praising Phillip Lehrman's well-chosen and well-maintained tempo for the Brahms *Tragic* Overture, but, he continued, the "*piano*" after the two slashing chords at the beginning was not Brahms's "*piano sotto voce*" but "*piano indifferente*." He made suggestions for how the piece could be made to get better that night even without benefit of further rehearsal: "Make *pianissimo* not with hips, elbows (he stood to demonstrate) but with hands and face . . . you look as though you're afraid the *pianissimo* will not be there . . . your face expresses doubt, so they cannot enjoy... always try to visualize your expression." The big viola tune, he assured him, "will come out warmer if you just ask for it. You have left hand, you can do." But elsewhere, "the beat not bigger, but more stinging."

More, though, Skrowaczewski commented on rehearsal technique, for future reference, as it were always with an eye to economy. "If you can show it by gesture, it is better not to speak about . . . don't overact, they'll do it themselves very well." Later: "At a *forte-piano*, say how long, say '*piano* after the first sixteenths,' 'first eighth,' or whatever... that replaces repeating, having to say 'not together'... but if at the beginning you say too many things without playing, you risk complete inattention." Then: "Don't say 'it's not rhythmic enough,' then they don't know what's wrong... say 'you're playing triplets instead of dotted quarters and eighths... use the word 'triplets' and then they will play it."

Then John Neschling and Mozart's *Prague* Symphony. Early on, this dialogue:

N: "They were rushing."
S: "No, sorry."
N: "I was rushing."
S: "Yes, sorry."

Always the motif, "They don't need your help, that goes automatically," and, about a series of eighth-notes too explicitly beaten for the violins, "Don't bother them . . . of course don't abandon them either." On providing a beat that would be sufficiently clear for the slow introduction, but not chop things up either: "No, don't beat eighths, subdivide four." Later: "Your downbeat is rough, like for *Elektra*," and, analogous to the viola tune in the Brahms, "You've never really asked them to play this beautifully (the second theme in the first movement) . . . do it tonight and they will" (he did, and they did). And: "Don't just indicate 'too loud,' show who is too loud... but if you indicate it with your left hand very far down, then the violins will see it and they will go away, but the horns and trumpets who actually are too loud will not see it, and the balance will be worse than before."

The discussion moved on to more general problems, for example, knowing a score enough to conduct it from memory, which, Skrowaczewski said, meant knowing it well enough to write it out and then some: "You must not be so busy remembering it that you cannot react as it goes by." On approaching a new score: pacing is the most essential part of articulating form, so from the beginning have the tempo clearly in mind. Almost the hardest part of conducting, Skrowaczewski said, is to have a tempo live in you so that at any time you can find it, at every rehearsal, performance, after each interruption of a recording session.

Recordings as a study tool have "very interesting possibilities. Yes, they are even OK, provided you don't conduct. Never conduct a record. You can only follow, and the essence of conducting is that you have to provoke it. Upbeats, the preparation, are so terribly important, and on records there are no upbeats." And he went on to describe a demonstration for a class at which George Szell had conducted a movement by indicating only the upbeats.

A student asked about opera, another about "difficult" soloists. It was upbeats again, the clear signal of what would happen next. The hazard in opera is not so much the prima donna ("the better they are the easier you can do things with them—really") as unmusical directors, not only those who interpret operas "against the music," but those with no feeling for moment-to-moment musical requirements, and he described trying to work out something as chamber-musical as "Komm', Hoffnung" in the Vienna production of *Fidelio* with a near-sighted Leonore whom the director had placed "at least 150 yards away and who could see me only on television, if at all." As for concerto soloists, even problematic ones can be stimulation—he cited an *Emperor* with Glenn Gould, "fourteen minutes slower than any I had ever conducted or heard, but with marvelous inner rhythm, though I wouldn't next time go to an orchestra and say, 'now, gentlemen, the tempo is . . . ' And if you have a soloist who really makes you crazy"—he mentioned a violinist for whom he had recently conducted the Paganini B minor in Stuttgart in a performance which became "an exercise in acrobatics and quick response"—"you can treat it always as a very interesting experience."

Bernstein at Tanglewood

July 24, 1972

LENOX—Rehearsing the slow movement of Brahms's Second Symphony at Tanglewood Wednesday afternoon, Leonard Bernstein pointed out to the Boston Symphony Orchestra that before the actual recapitulation, which Brahms "sneaks in very quietly," there are two false reprises, both in the wrong key and both promptly broken off. "But," he said, "you play each one as though it were the real reprise. Let's go back to letter D and we'll have the whole series," and he proceeded to work with the orchestra on getting the structural emphasis just right.

The passage was usefully managed at Saturday night's performance, but one of the things that made that concert, which began with the Fourth Symphony, so impressive was the way in which everything was so surely in proportion.

The evening was festive in that way Bernstein's concerts can be, especially with orchestras and audiences where an appearance of his is rare enough automatically to be an event, but it turned into a great occasion, surely unforgettable, because as well as the theater of his presence, Bernstein brought an uncommon blend of seriousness, control, and musical excitement.

He leaned fairly heavily into both symphonies and played them with a lively feeling for their rhetoric, but, though endless flexibility of detail was available, each movement was firmly magnetized to a central, controlling tempo. Even in the dangerous chaconne of the Fourth Symphony, where Bernstein's quickest and slowest speeds were some fair distance apart, the transitions were handled with so much of both sense and sensibility that each event proceeded organically from the one before.

About the direct, powerfully disciplined performances: I had a slight reservation only concerning the extreme and long slowing down that turned the end of the Second Symphony's third movement into an elegiac, though sweetly sentimental parting too much like the end of "Von der Schönheit" in Mahler's *Lied von der Erde.*

Bernstein's one other great tempo risk, the broad ritard just before the coda of the finale in the same work, was an effective stroke which, moreover, paid off in gold because it enabled Bernstein to give the impression of a finish of incredible speed and energy without actually having to go into the usual vulgar whipping of the tempo at that point. The orchestra played superbly and with evident pleasure.

The night before, Bruno Maderna conducted Brahms's First Symphony, about which he had discovered that passages of greater and of lesser intensity might be contrasted by playing the former very fast and the latter very slowly. He also sent up huge warning signals before transitions and breaks, most often by means of tremendous slowing down. An interpreter is meant to show what belongs together and what is distinct, and he must make clear where phrases, sentences, paragraphs, and chapters end. What Maderna produced Friday, though, was a telling of the story in which every character was grotesque and printed with the punctuation marks bigger than the words.

Whether the interpretation actually began somewhere around unnecessary-but-interesting and degenerated to the absurd, or whether it stayed pretty much at the same level and I became less and less able to deal with Maderna's bizarre sort of didacticism, I cannot say. In the performance, where everything was either flogged or stretched, the orchestra played with rough tone, difficulty, and some disbelief. For sure, not since Munch last flailed the finale of the Berlioz *Fantastique* have I heard the Boston Symphony in a tempo faster even than this virtuoso group could manage.

There were those who defended it on the grounds of Brahms's Lib—"let it all hang out," and "oh, I'm so sick of all that squareness." There is a place between square and silly, and in fact Bernstein the next evening, with his fine combination of passion and taste, delivered the most eloquent and economical possible criticism of Maderna's giddy show of originality at any price.

A Moving Mahler

July 28, 1972

LENOX—Among the things that Leonard Bernstein's conducting the Berkshire Music Center Orchestra Wednesday did was to solve one evening's worth of problems for just about every camp director in Berkshire County. What looked to be about 2,000 camera-flashing, gum-popping, chatty teenagers got unloaded into Tanglewood, and the concert had to be moved from the Theatre-Concert Hall to the Shed, which the audience easily filled as far back as the line of boxes and then some.

Bernstein conducted the third and fourth movements of Mahler's Ninth Symphony. With his other commitments here—a Boston Symphony concert making videocassette tapes of two Brahms symphonies, conducting and composition seminars—he had only three rehearsals with the BMC Orchestra, and he chose well to teach two exceedingly difficult movements (actually close to forty minutes together) very thoroughly. The specific choice of the Mahler Ninth came, I believe, from the desire to dedicate the Adagio to the memory of Goeran Gentele, general manager of the Metropolitan Opera, who was to have directed the new production of *Carmen* which Bernstein will conduct in September.[9]

It was an astounding performance, deeply moving as musical interpretation and as an act of teaching. By making the Burleske wildly fast and the Adagio hugely, immeasurably slow, Bernstein took risks before which most conductors would hesitate in front of the most virtuosic professional orchestras. He was right, absolutely on musical grounds, and right on technical and pedagogic terms, even though the student players, excited, at the beginning of the Burleske blurred a few details which they had managed in the comparative cool of the dress rehearsal.

I think I have never seen an orchestra and its conductor more closely in touch than in the last minutes of the Adagio, that most terrible dying and farewell in all music. I have hardly ever heard it played with such purity of intonation and

[9] See Gentele obituary of July 20, 1972.

string tone, never so *pianissimo*. It must be so sustained and held in all its quiet, and the silences and the moments when a single note is suspended across the void must seem endless. Most people in most audiences are not interested in such things—at the rehearsal Bernstein at the last bar asked the orchestra, "Do you feel it? Do you hear what he is saying?"—and they cough, shuffle, begin to reach for their coats. Then the conductor gets scared, he hurries, the repose is lost and instantly the *pianissimo* with it. This audience coughed and racketed most infernally, but Bernstein held the music where it needed to be, timeless and nearly inaudible, and that so moving act of patience, that sense of absolute and unswerving undistractibility, was so compelling that the ending spoke in spite of all.

Bernstein shared the concert with two BMC Conducting Fellows. The first was Charles Darden (Philadelphia), a flashy character whose entrances, bows, and exits are the wildest in my experience. His conducting looks fairly extravagant, too, but what it produced astonishingly enough was a 100 percent sober, careful, even somewhat slow and heavy performance of Mozart's *Haffner* Symphony. It was musical, simple and unmanipulated, and informed by a nice sense of the operatic element in Mozart. It was also beautifully played, though one single calming gesture in the direction of the kettledrummer would have done wonders for the clarity of the sound. I recognize, of course, that the unscheduled move to the very bass-friendly Shed, where the student conductors had presumably never rehearsed an orchestra, was also an unscheduled difficulty and challenge.

Then John Neschling conducted Strauss's *Don Juan*. He did it with lots of temperament, and the performance was full of effectively realized moments. It wanted, in the end, the control to make the last climax the clear high point (one could tell both from looking and from the preparatory breath that Neschling's intentions were right)—too much had been spent already. When his physical gestures were to the point, the orchestra played brilliantly for him; when he flailed, things got muddy.

Levine's Mahler Rich, Clear

August 1, 1972

LENOX—Having conducted Mozart in coat and tie Sunday afternoon at Tanglewood, James Levine reappeared after intermission in a blue polo shirt to cope with Mahler's seventy-five-minute Sixth Symphony. The statement of "there's work to be done" made, he thrust, like the good opera conductor he is, the start of Mahler's menacing march tread right into the noise of the still settling audience, and powerfully asserted his stupendous command over the music, the orchestra, and the audience.

I've often been troubled why most conductors make Mahler seem so hard, why, for example, they can't deal with his crucial distinction between sudden and gradual changes of speed, why an instruction not to hurry has to be translated into the ritard, the request for an unnoticeable enlivening of the tempo to become the sudden jolt forward, why, in sum, they have to make it all come out so awkward and confusing.

With Levine, no such problems arise at all. His performance was totally scrupulous, but better even than scrupulous, because the correctness was informed at all times by intelligence and insight. He gave a powerfully concentrated, totally clear, superbly organized performance, one rich in vivid detail. Moreover, with an extraordinary economy and clarity of gesture, he elicited absolutely superb playing from the Boston Symphony Orchestra.

The two reservations I would note are that, apparently through some accident, the first of Mahler's two always problematic hammer-blows in the finale misfired, coming out as some sort of perfunctory rap, and that in that aftermath of the performance of the Ninth Symphony which Bernstein conducted recently with the Berkshire Music Center Orchestra, I longed for *pianissimos* with more of a hushed and special quality to them. But, no doubt, Levine is one of the most impressive conductors, not only of his own young generation, but any, now before the American public.

The Mozart was the Violin Concerto in D major, K.218, with Joseph Silverstein as soloist. There was on Levine's part some overpointing of the second subject in the first movement, which I read as a lingering influence of George Szell, under whose guidance Levine began his career; otherwise his conducting of the Concerto was altogether natural and beautiful. Just, in fact, what Silverstein's exquisitely phrased, tasteful, delicately toned playing wanted.

Silverstein's own cadenzas, witty, violinistically brilliant extensions or reconsiderations of Joachim's, were added pleasure to a distinguished concert.

Soprano Almost Sensation

August 14, 1972

LENOX—If Jessye Norman were as famous as she is good, there would have been a mob at Tanglewood for the Friday-night Boston Symphony concert instead of the barely 5,000, in fact about as small an audience as the orchestra has drawn this summer.

Jessye Norman is a young Black soprano who in the last three years has made it big in Europe in operatic repertoire ranging from Purcell's *Dido* to *Aida*, and who is now in the process of being introduced to the public in her own country.

At Tanglewood she sang Wagner, *Wesendonck* Songs and the Love-Death from *Tristan*, and she brought to it a musical taste of a high order, intensity, and that kind of personal projection which instantly says "star," and beautiful, expressive German.

Yes, an extraordinary, ample voice, a bit heavily laden with vibrato at first and with just the slightest tendency sometimes to flirt with the underside of pitches, the latter impeccably in tune and steady, almost coldly steady, like a superb organ diapason.

She made an enormous impression, and I think with another conductor—or even with the same conductor, Colin Davis, on another day—she might have made a sensation. Davis, who has made his reputation as a great Mozart conductor and as a man who found the classicism and the cleanness in Berlioz, just may not be temperamentally a *Tristan* conductor (and the *Wesendonck* Songs are part of the *Tristan* world, too), or perhaps he was momentarily below form. I don't know which.

He provided attentive accompaniments for the songs, but the *Tristan* Prelude just lay there and never took fire. The voice buffs could and did get thoroughly turned on by the singer's marvelous sound. I, although aware of the beautiful things Miss Norman was doing, could not separate them from their unexciting context, and in the end, the experience was disappointing. It will be interesting to see how the same music goes when Miss Norman, Davis, and the orchestra do this again in Boston in March.[10]

Davis began the Wagner group with the *Flying Dutchman* Overture. It was energetic although rough, with accident-prone brass and wind tuning generally not up to snuff (true to some extent in the rest of the Wagner, too). The orchestra did so much fine playing earlier that it is startling in the last couple of weekends to be back in the roughness that so often prevailed in recent years.

After intermission, Davis conducted Verdi's Four Sacred Pieces, the *a cappella* Ave Maria and the setting of the thirty-third canto of Dante's *Paradiso*, and, with orchestra, a Stabat Mater and Te Deum: fantastic music, especially in the two big pieces. There was taste, although some lack of delicacy in the execution, a tendency to emphasize the line-by-line sectionality of the pieces more than their cohesiveness, and here, too, some failure of energy.

John Oliver's Tanglewood Festival Chorus and Tanglewood Choir sang with sound both handsome and transparent, with diction that was clear but seeming rather in the direction of "tay dayum."

[10] A review of this program (March 2–3, 1973) did not appear in the *Globe*.

Thomas Conducts BSO's 92nd Opening Concert

September 23, 1972

With Michael Tilson Thomas in charge—he shares with Colin Davis the title of principal guest conductor—the Boston Symphony Orchestra started its 92nd season yesterday afternoon. There was Prokofiev's *Scythian Suite* for a brilliant and loud beginning, and the Beethoven Seventh for a brilliant and pretty loud finish. Between them came the first performance of Walter Piston's Concerto for Flute and Orchestra, written for and played by Doriot Anthony Dwyer. That, by the way, is the only piece written within the last fifteen years which the orchestra will play on a regular (that is non-Spectrum)[11] subscription program.

Piston has written a chamber-musical work in three linked movements, going from a declamatory, recitative-like opening, through slower music in more sustained style, to what I should like to call paradoxically an interrupted *perpetuum mobile*. It is a grateful virtuoso piece in which, perhaps surprisingly, the slower music near the beginning provides a more effective show of the player's brilliance and taste than the fireworks later on. The virtuoso demands are of a conventional sort: no double-stops, key-clackings, and so on.

The orchestral writing is beautifully conceived and managed. The ensemble is fairly small, but its sounds are so delicate, so carefully chosen, and there is so nearly complete an avoidance of tutti style, that it sounds still smaller than it is. The sounds the orchestra makes are attractive and, in all their conservatism, wonderfully fresh. Sometimes an accompanist, the orchestra most of the time offers the soloist partners in dialogue. Or, to tell it another way, the soloist passes herself around to be conversed or played with in an almost balletic manner like, for example, the princess with her four cavaliers in the *Sleeping Beauty* Rose Adagio, or Siegfried moving among the six princesses in the ballroom scene of *Swan Lake*.

Piston warned an interviewer that the Flute Concerto was going to be "the same old Piston." For the finale, perhaps yes. For the beginning, no, with its arresting melodic shapes and its fine play of textures, he found his way to a place that is new for him. The end I thought perfunctory and therefore, disappointing; for the first two-thirds or so of his new concerto, he worked not only with the immaculate craftsmanship that has been the hallmark of his work for half a century

[11] Initiated and led by then-BSO Associate Conductor Michael Tilson Thomas, who also provided commentary from the stage, the BSO's reduced-price "Spectrum Concerts" offered three themed programs per season (available as single concerts or by subscription) aimed at attracting an audience younger than the BSO's typical subscription attendees. The Spectrum Concerts lasted for three seasons, from the fall of 1971 to the spring of 1974, when Thomas's BSO contract ended.

now, but also at an imposing level of intellectual concentration and vigor—inspiration, if you like. The performance was a brilliantly effective one.

For the Beethoven Seventh, Thomas re-seated the orchestra in the pre-Stokowski arrangement, with second violins on the right, opposite the firsts, with viola and cellos respectively left and right of center. (Kempe who will be here with the Royal Philharmonic October 29, and Boult are, so far as I know, the only conductors who do that regularly.) It delightfully clarified the scoring of the second movement, making much of the addition to low strings, first of second violins on one side, and only later of first violins on the other, or of the special sonorous character of the duet for first violins and violas. It also produced some telling moments in the other movements. I wonder to what extent the effectiveness was visual (could I tell the difference blindfolded?), but looking is after all a real part of concert experience for most people,[12] and for a performer to address his audience's eyes as well as its ears is legitimate, subject though it is to horrendous abuse.

There was in any case plenty for the ear in this intelligent, hugely energetic performance (though I am only half-persuaded that the finale wants to be quite so wild). For the most part it was beautifully played, with a bright, open, aerated sound—there is still, as a hangover from Leinsdorf's rhythmic slackness, some dissension about the trochees in the scherzo, a faction of winds led by Mrs. Dwyer making the long syllable rather too short, and with strings tending to overcompensate.

The *Scythian Suite*, which stands up as one of Prokofiev's strongest, most original pieces, sounded gorgeous in its controlled gaudiness.

Boston Symphony Taps Rich Era

October 23, 1972

In the history of Western music, is there another ten-year period as rich as the one immediately before the 1914 war? That was the decade in which what we still call "modern music" was invented, but beyond that, the sheer quality is staggering, as well as the variety of voices heard and the wonderful sense of doors and windows being thrown open.

For his first program this season with the Boston Symphony Orchestra, Friday afternoon in Symphony Hall, Colin Davis reached into that decade, and to two composers whose music is neither the most popular of the period (Strauss or Puccini) nor the most central and critical (Debussy, Stravinsky, Schoenberg,

[12] See "What to Do With Your Eyes While the Orchestra Plays," July 11, 1971.

Webern, Berg). He gave us the Third Symphony of Sibelius, written in 1907 and not played by the orchestra since 1939, and the Elgar Violin Concerto, finished in 1910 and done here just once before, in 1934, the year of the composer's death, and then on a Pension Fund Concert rather than in the regular series.

That I don't like the Sibelius Third is of no consequence, although I think very few other people like it either: with the Sixth, which Gunther Schuller revived at the New England Conservatory last year, it has always been the least played of Sibelius's symphonies, and by some margin. The Third has none of the sort of scratchily individual intellectual force of the Fourth and Seventh symphonies, nor is it a heartily vulgar "success piece" like the Second or the Fifth.

It is an essay in taste and classical writing, modest both in its dimension—three movements, none very long nor of great compositional or expressive density—and in its sonority—woodwinds by twos, no tuba, kettledrums as the only percussion. There is something uncompromising to that stance which is rather appealing, and the greyness of the textures is impressive and somehow compelling. The material, however, seems dry, except in the not-quite-slow middle movement, where it looms toward the sticky, and you really have to be Beethoven to make strong music out of such drastically neutral themes.

It is obsessive music with its insistent literal or rhyming repetitions of small fragments, and a bit boring. Even so, it is the statement that could have been made by that one man only—how fascinating its obstinate anti-romanticism must have seemed when this piece was new—and as we are threatened and surrounded today by musical facelessness worse and more distressing than the dumbest noodlings of the 18th-century concerto grosso factories, such assertion of individuality is a quality I come to appreciate more and more.

Elgar's was an unmistakable voice, too. He was also a great composer with much to say, but a professional through and through, with complete control on every structural level. In his ample, emotional violin concerto, there is much to admire. The surefootedness with which he marshals the progression from one event to the next, for example, or the miraculous orchestral style that is so lush and so transparent at the same time. There is also much to love in this concerto, from something as overriding as its mood, the sadness, and intense and consuming sadness, that lives so comfortably with energy and discipline, or the detail as touching as the pains he always takes to give the second violins something particularly beautiful to play. The most special feature of the concerto is the cadenza in the last movement, and surely this is the only concerto in which the cadenza is its most poetic and introspective point. The last movement, a very vivacious Allegro, with piquantly oblique harmonies, makes its way gradually toward the upward progression of two semitones with which the whole work began. With that the cadenza is opened, with what Elgar himself referred to as "a sad look back at the first movement."

It is an amazing invention, that cadenza, perhaps the most vivid composition of a dream in music, something that scarcely seems to happen in real time, as fragments from earlier in the work are recalled over miraculously shadowy sonorities in the orchestra. It is a stroke that is perfectly placed, compositionally, technically, and psychologically.

It was an afternoon of splendid performances. I have no reservations whatever about the performance of the Sibelius, which was cohesively conducted by Davis, and beautifully played by the orchestra. Joseph Silverstein, the orchestra's concertmaster, was the soloist in the concerto (by the way, his predecessor in the 1934 performance was Jascha Heifetz). I have almost nothing but praise for Silverstein's negotiation of this extraordinarily taxing work. Obviously, it is something that he loves and understands, and he has the musical and technical mastery with which to cope with it. The one reservation I do have pertains to his sound, which I found excessively laden with vibrato.

There is a lovely theme in the last movement which Elgar specifically requests to be played with vibrato and at that point Silverstein had nothing new to give it or with which to characterize it, and I found that the insistent intensity of his vibrating was both a little monotonous and a little fatiguing. Otherwise, let me say it again, both musically and from the technical and violinistic point of view, his performance seemed to me exemplary. And its excellence was of course made possible to the huge degree by the superb framework that Davis provided with the orchestra, a framework that was infallibly sturdy from the structural point of view, that assured a continuing progression of gorgeously beautiful sounds (and this is a concerto which is particularly physical, and in which the purely sensuous aspect is singularly important), and which was ideally attentive to the needs of the soloist. In sum, it is a concerto of exceptional distinction.

Heifetz—In a Class by Himself

October 25, 1972

LOS ANGELES—In the program, Franck was César Franck; Strauss was Richard Strauss; Bloch, Debussy, Rachmaninoff, de Falla, Kreisler, Ravel all had their first names; Bach had his initials, but the performer was simply Heifetz. In large, bold capitals, too, you had better believe.

Heifetz—Jascha—is nearly 72 and makes few public appearances nowadays. His violin recital Monday evening in the Dorothy Chandler Pavilion was the first in four years. It was given as a benefit for the University of Southern California music scholarship fund, and drew an audience whose musical know-nothingness and sense of entitlement were oppressive.

After the first two movements of the Franck Sonata, which began the program, there was a smattering of applause and a break during which a couple of hundred latecomers were admitted. Heifetz and Brooks Smith then played the third and fourth movement, after which there was a lot of applause and a rush for the lobby on the part of two-thirds of the audience, sure that it had now heard the Strauss Sonata as well.

"But it says intermission," said the young thing as she pushed past me.

But you want to know about Heifetz. He is just the same. True, he looks a little older—one might guess 63 or 64—and he was less unbending, permitting himself a wintery smile on three or four occasions during the evening. But really he is just the same, unique, unmistakable, and in no need of an identifying first name.

His playing of the instrument is dazzling and still in a class by itself; his playing of music, most of the time, is vulgar.

There were brief exceptions to both. In the first two movements of the Franck, he played straight, in fact, with almost exaggerated rigor. Bloch's *Nigun* was done beautifully and so was *Sea Murmurs* by Castelnuovo-Tedesco. Conversely, there was some technical unease in Heifetz's own transcription of Rachmaninoff's Étude-Tableau in E-flat, which was scratchy and off-pitch, and some of Ravel's *Tzigane*, like the scale with left-hand pizzicatos, got away from him. He made heavy weather also of the three movements he selected from Bach's E major Partita which were hectic and not quite in tune.

The Bach, with its nonarticulated perpetual motion style for the Prelude and Gigue, the elephantine, anti-balletic Louré, was singularly bad musically, but in ways that would apply to most violinists of Heifetz's generation.

More specialized Heifetz problems were in evidence most of the evening. The muting of his fine pianist so that neither the Franck nor the Strauss sonatas ever made sense naturally; the lack of temperament for a fiery, quasi-improvisatory piece like *Tzigane*; the passion for spiccato bowings, producing sequences of toneless, pitched clicks; the fussy, sometimes perverse phrasing, particularly the imposing of diminuendos where the music asks for the opposite (an example would be the way the second phrase of the theme of Franck's finale rose always to a mincing pianissimo on its highest note). It was the Strauss Sonata, where bad taste is built in, and de Falla's *Nana*, which wants utterly simple playing, that were the most tormented. Franck, by the way, was treated to some extra octaves in the violin part.

Heifetz's priorities are always violinistic rather than musical. One can understand, of course, his fascination with his own violin playing. Except for those few moments I mentioned, the left hand is sure, but it is the right arm that takes your breath away: the gleaming purity of tone (except when he chooses otherwise, as in those razzle-dazzle spiccatos), without a trace of anything gritty or blowsy; the power of that tone as well as the personal quality that makes it as uniquely his as the sound of his voice or his fingerprints; the enormous dynamic range and the fantastic, though often abused control of that aspect of playing. I don't know who else plays the violin like that, and coming from a man into his seventies, it is a miracle unparalleled so far as I am aware.

Part of me, the part at the center of me, wants to say: "I don't care about that while his playing remains so anti-musical." At the same time I found the completeness of his mastery of the instrument and the sheer professionalism of what Heifetz did fascinating, even very compelling.

Afterwards, in a short speech in which he excused himself from the post-concert party ("I am pooped"), he thanked the audience for having made him work very hard. Given how he plays the violin, I found that moving. It was a concert that lived in a strange place of uneasy equilibrium of the unbelievable and the unbelievably awful.

Berlioz's *Nuits d'été* Rare Treat

October 28, 1972

Good for Colin Davis! At yesterday afternoon's Boston Symphony concert, he turned around and actually told the audience something it ought long ago to have been told—from the stage—about its manners.

Berlioz's exquisite Gauthier cycle, *Nuits d'été*, was on the program, with Janet Baker to sing it. After the last couple of minutes of "Le Spectre de la rose" had been drowned in coughing and program rattling, Davis, after a quick consultation with Joseph Silverstein, the concertmaster, told the audience to "read the poetry when you get home and listen to the music while you are here." The non-stop rustling, he said, made it extremely difficult for the orchestra to play, and, he added, "you don't know when you will be able to hear these again."

The last time Boston Symphony subscribers had a chance at *Nuits d'été* was in April 1955 (which is when the beautiful record with Victoria de los Angeles and Charles Munch was made). That was also the first, which is even more astonishing than the nearly fifty-four-year interval since the last performance of Berlioz's *Francs-juges* Overture, which began yesterday's program.

It was marvelous to have both works back, and in such beautiful performances. *Nuits d'été* is more a sequence of six lovely songs than a unified cycle in the *Dichterliebe* sense, but they wonderfully represent what Berlioz could do at the delicate end of his expressive spectrum. The range of *Nuits d'été* is great, from "L'Île inconnue," all light and air, to the darkness and gravity of "Sur les Lagunes." That range, though, all happens within astonishingly narrow physical confines. There are no excursions into declamatory style, there is nothing loud, and even special orchestral effects like those eerie violin harmonics in "Au Cimetière" occur with extreme rarity.

But with what fantasy and virtuosity Berlioz handles his "plain" materials, and how individual his voice always is. So when the rose says to the dreaming girl, "I come from Paradise," Berlioz can turn you inside out just by adding the harp's simple A major cascade to his four woodwinds, two horns, and strings. A man who could find his way to the center even of giants like Shakespeare and Virgil, he responds fully to the images of Gauthier, and there is in *Nuits d'été* that conjunction of poetic sensibility and compositional power that makes great songs. *Nuits d'été* is one of the loveliest moments of the Romantic movement.

The overture to Berlioz's early, unperformed, then lost opera, *Les Francs-juges*, which deals with the creepy, underground Vehmic tribunals in medieval Germany, is engaging and surprising. A grand and powerful introduction leads to what starts out to be a harmless, then ravishingly pretty Allegro.

The Italian lightness is a surprise, within which is contained the further surprise of how well Berlioz could write a symmetrical tune (this one he lifted from a flute quintet he had written thirteen years earlier when he was all of 11). Then the next layer of surprise is revealed when from this material he takes you into directions as unexpected as the extremely slow-motion woodwind music over a highly jittery string accompaniment, or the scoring which seems to get almost demonstratively more colorful.

The Boston Symphony played *Francs-juges* with great brilliance for Davis, and their playing was transparent and beautifully shaded in the songs. Janet Baker is one of those people who make singing sound terribly easy, and who even make it seem quite natural to be intelligent, musical, and to pronounce French perfectly.

Davis completed the concert with a knowingly shaped, witty, vivacious performance of Beethoven's Symphony No. 2. But talk about surprises: how about that introduction and those "genie-out-of-the-bottle" codas to the first and last movements?

Oxford Issues Paperback of Tovey's Music Essays

November 22, 1972

So you think you're depressed? The American Guild of Organists can't stand it to the point where they have dated the current issue of *Music*, their monthly magazine, November 1971.

There is good news, though, from Oxford University Press, who have just made Sir Donald Francis Tovey's *Essays in Musical Analysis* available in paperback, and so probably accessible for the first time to thousands of new readers.

Tovey, 1875–1940, was an English composer (I should once like to hear his Cello Concerto, written for and greatly admired by Casals), pianist, conductor, historian, and critic. His reputation now rests on his writings about music. The core of that is in the six volumes of *Essays*, published in book form between 1935 and 1939, with a posthumous supplementary volume in 1944. Almost all the essays are program notes for concerts Tovey conducted with the Reid Orchestra in Edinburgh, at whose university he had become Professor of Music in 1914. Some of the material in the supplement, for instance the two big essays on Bach's *Goldberg* and Beethoven's *Diabelli* variations, goes back to piano recitals Tovey gave in London in 1900.

The books are organized by subject matter. Vol. 1 has symphonies by Beethoven, Haydn, Mozart, Brahms, Schubert; Vol. 2 has more symphonies and other orchestral works; Vol. 3 is on concertos, Vol. 4 on program music.

Vol. 5 is about vocal music, with particularly interesting pieces on the B minor Mass, Beethoven's *Missa solemnis*, the Haydn oratorios, and the Brahms and Verdi Requiems; Vol. 6 has miscellaneous essays, a section called "Retrospect and Corrigenda," a glossary, and the index (with some funny things planted in it). The supplementary volume has solo keyboard and chamber music.

The essays' musical density varies. Many have examples in notation, a few presuppose very close attention and a fair knowledge of music (the superb note on that disliked and misunderstood Beethoven masterpiece, *The Consecration of the House* Overture). Essentially, however, Tovey was writing for the cultivated amateur of music. His stuff is wise and idiosyncratic, best on the 16th, 18th, and 19th centuries (the 20th said little to him except in a few of its most conservative manifestations; the 17th he saw as the period of bizarre experiment between the Palestrinian Golden Age and the settled classicism of High Baroque—and that is one of his aberrations), but he was likely to be interesting, illuminating, and almost always amusing, on any matter he touched. Elegance and his musical ear made him an exceptional prose writer.

Tovey was put into my life when I was 14 by an English teacher, who did more for my musical education than any music teacher I ever had before I went to college, mostly by such simple expedients as, in the anti-musical atmosphere of an English boarding school, giving me clandestine access to his radio, persuading me that Mozart's K.467 was as well worth knowing as the Tchaikovsky B-flat minor, and occasionally giving me something like Tovey to read. Actually, Tovey was hard going in my state of ignorance and semi-literacy (musical and general), but I remembered, came back to him soon after, and by 17 was addicted. When I sang in the Princeton Chapel Choir, I always carried either some of Pepys's diary or a volume of Tovey under my robe to read during the sermon (except once a year when Reinhold Niebuhr preached), and I am sure that in all the time I have been professionally involved in music, not a fortnight has passed without an occasion for taking Tovey off the shelf to look something up, usually staying to browse for an unscheduled quarter-hour.

If Tovey's *Essays* are not yet in your life, now, at $2.95 a volume, seems the moment for them to be put there.[13] And for someone who loves reading about music as well as listening to it, you could hardly find a nicer Christmas present (or just one to counter the grey and wet of mid-November).

Bernstein Conducts Boston Symphony

December 9, 1972

The Boston Symphony concert Leonard Bernstein conducted yesterday afternoon was full of marvelous things, yet its impact was less than promised. The program was Beethoven's *Pastoral* Symphony and Stravinsky's opera-oratorio, *Oedipus Rex*, and the trouble began there. The two works have nothing to say to one another, and they make too long a program, at least for that audience, to which a punctual four o'clock departure is more important than any musical statement.

Pastoral-Oedipus is not a bill a conductor would normally think of conducting, but Bernstein concocted it anyway, being more concerned with assembling material to be videotaped for his Norton Lectures at Harvard than with sensible program building. At any rate, Stravinsky's grim drama really had little chance to assert itself through the stream of departing ladies.

"A great big lump of wonderful music, some of which never did come off right and still doesn't," is what Virgil Thomson once called *Oedipus Rex*. It is the work as a whole that doesn't come off rather than any of the music (or perhaps I misread Thomson's ambiguous "which"), and Stravinsky himself late in life was critical of the dramaturgy, particularly the spoken narration in the vernacular to link the tableaux whose text has been translated back into Latin for the sake of the concision and above all the incantatory possibilities of that language.

The distribution of dramatic stresses is strange (as odd, in fact, as some of Stravinsky's syllabic stresses), and you could not always immediately infer, from musical weight, which are dramatically the "important" scenes. That works when *Oedipus* is staged, and it works on records, when the listener is cued to use his imagination with extra sharpness. In concert, which is middle ground between the hotness of the one and the coolness of the other, it seems not so clear and not so convincing.

[13] Adjusting for inflation, the dollar figure amounts roughly to $22.66 in 2025.

Add to that one technical problem: when a work written for the theater, assuming the orchestra is in the pit, is given in concert, with singers and players on stage together, the singers are apt to be in trouble. Sometimes yesterday words disappeared in the orchestral tempest, which blurs the storytelling, but also irritates an audience, evaporating its concentration and sympathy.

Bernstein conducts *Oedipus Rex* superbly, with remarkable concentration, rhythmic bite, sense of dramatic timing and character. He lives in it with extraordinary intensity, and its monumental classicism makes it not something he can love to death. He has impressive collaborators through whom to realize his interpretation. The Boston Symphony played magnificently, and F. John Adams's Harvard Glee Club was admirable in the incisiveness of its singing, the clarity of text and pitch.

The eloquent choral music could hardly be better done, and the same imposing level was reached in the Jocasta of Tatiana Troyanos, who supplied exciting thrust of voice and articulation, finding also just the right combination of intensity and distance.

On the other hand, René Kollo as Oedipus left the whole performance somewhat hollow: his tenor is agreeable, his phrasing is musical, but he has no tragic stature. He is neither arrogant, nor angry, nor afraid, and, though he says "*Lux facta est!*," it is hard to believe he has seen anything. Singing, he remains too much the amiable, nice-looking young man who between arias sits there with his legs casually crossed.

Impressive competence in every way was provided by Tom Krause (Creon), David Evitts (Messenger), and Frank Hoffmeister (Shepherd), while Michael Wager was notably good, which means both simple and commanding, at dealing with the narration. The usually excellent Ezio Flagello (Tiresias) was disappointingly woolly in rhythm and diction.

The performance of the Beethoven *Pastoral* was serene, intelligent, imaginative, light, and transparently wonderfully played.

Saturday's *Oedipus Rex* an Event of Another Order

December 15, 1972

Sometimes, when there is music on the program I especially love and which is not often heard, I go back Saturday night for a Boston Symphony program I have already reviewed Friday afternoon. Last Saturday I went back mainly for Stravinsky's *Oedipus Rex*, and, I believe for the first time, I want to write a second review.

Friday, the impact was somehow scattered, and in a review I never managed to write to my satisfaction, I tried to tell why.[14] The central reason, I thought, was that René Kollo, taking the title role, was emotionally casual in a way that left the whole performance hollow at the center. Saturday's *Oedipus Rex* was an event of another order, one of the great musical experiences of my life, and I am sure that the critical difference was in Kollo.

Oedipus is a very, very difficult role. At the beginning, full of hubris, he sings in florid, sinuous lines—a strange union of Bach and Verdi, made by this century's greatest inventor of melodies. His fears and his discoveries he articulates in barely inflected *parlando*. You need a tenor of penetrating intelligence and exemplary diction, one who is forceful and elegant at the same time, with command of florid style, and able to invest the quietest music with the utmost intensity. He must convince you that the journey from the showy, proud sufficiency of his opening "*Liberi, vos liberabo*" ("Children, I will free you") to the starkness of "*Lux facta est!*" ("All now is made plain!") is a journey on which a soul is stripped.

That the 35-year-old Kollo is a tenor of unusual gifts is evident from his recordings of *Tannhäuser* (with Solti on London) and *Meistersinger* (with Karajan on Angel), and I was not prepared for the musical and personal blandness of what he offered Friday. Everything was tasteful and pleasant-sounding, but you just cannot tell that story about a hero who remains so untouched.

Saturday he was a changed man. That he stood through the whole performance except for Jocasta's address rather than sitting with an air of total non-involvement when not singing was the most obvious external token of change. The crucial impact of his changed attitude was on his singing. He projected the embellishments of his arias with arrogant élan, the voice itself now ringing, full of color and life. But the crises in *Oedipus Rex* are *pianissimo*, and this time Kollo put so much energy into the articulation of syllables and into the rhythm that, in all their quiet, their force was tremendous. The end of the journey, when Oedipus sees his triple shame of birth, marriage, and parricide—"*Lux facta est!*"—was overwhelming.

I don't know whether because of the difference in having so compelling a figure at the center of the story, or just coincidentally, but Saturday evening everyone seemed to have something special to give. Leonard Bernstein's conducting was highly charged and completely controlled, and the response of the Boston Symphony Orchestra and of the Harvard Glee Club, prepared by F. John Adams, was splendid. Tatiana Troyanos was an electrifying Jocasta; Tom Krause and Ezio Flagello filled the less stunningly grateful roles of Creon and Tiresias excellently. And it was a particular pleasure to observe how well the two young

[14] See review of December 9, 1972.

Bostonians in this distinguished international cast acquitted themselves, Frank Hoffmeister (Shepherd) and especially David Evitts (Messenger).

Some of the troublesome balances between voices and instruments which you always get when a work designed for pit orchestra is done in concert with everyone on stage together stayed sticky, though it was better than on Friday. Michael Wager's narration, still admirable, moved between Friday and Saturday very slightly in the direction of hamminess (gulp). I again felt that Beethoven's *Pastoral* is not the ideal preface to *Oedipus Rex*, and I was again very much moved by a performance both so simple and so discovering (and Saturday, by one dangerous percent, more self-indulgent in the last climax and coda).

The Posthumous Success of Wilhelm Furtwängler

December 17, 1972

My real knowing and loving of Wagner's *Der Ring des Nibelungen* began under extraordinary circumstances, in Rome, when Radio Italiana gave the whole thing in concert performance, one act at a time every Tuesday and Friday [October/November 1953]. It was exciting (part of the excitement was seeing whether I could scrounge tickets to the studio at the comically hideous Foro Mussolini with its statues of square-membered naked athletes, or whether I would have to listen on the radio); it was also, in a most Wagnerian, Romantic way, seductively paralyzing to be held in the grip of the unfolding drama for five weeks, unable really to think about anything else.

A lot of the excitement was in the performance. Wilhelm Furtwängler conducted, and there was no magician better equipped to hold the thread of continuity aloft across those three- and four-day intermissions. The cast was strong: it included Mödl as the most moving of Brünnhildes, Windgassen, Suthaus, Frantz, Klose, Neidlinger, Patzak (for Furtwängler he had the once-in-a-generation ideal Mime voice and style, but he was much too tall ever to have done the whiny dwarf on stage), and luxury casting like Grümmer as Freia or Jurinac as Woglinde and Gutrune. That is the performance which has recently been issued here (Seraphim—nineteen records, mono only), and, though that was not my first *Ring*, nor by any means the last, it was Furtwängler's performance more than any other that defined the work for me.

When some days ago I was asked would I like to meet Furtwängler's widow (he died November 1954), I jumped and for a moment it felt a bit as though I had been offered dinner with Anna Magdalena Bach or Clara Schumann. Mrs. Furtwängler, it turned out, was traveling through the United States, to say it bluntly, to promote the *Ring* recording. She was here as a guest of the National

Arts Foundation (a private foundation, not to be confused with the National Endowment), and she was quick to say how delighted she was to have no EMI-Angel-Seraphim money behind her trip, leaving her free to speak her mind about the record company. She had, in fact, quite pungent things to say about distribution and about the fact that several critics she had met had not received review copies.

It was her first visit here since 1934, which was nine years before she became Frau Elisabeth Furtwängler. It was a second marriage for both, and she was twenty-six years younger.

Her husband, for whom she had given up a career in painting and art history, was killed in the war, leaving her with four small children. Furtwängler had been separated from his wife for many years. Had Furtwängler children, I asked. "Not from his marriage—I am very good friends with all the mothers," replied Mrs. Furtwängler crisply. There was one child in the second marriage, Andreas, who looks amazingly like his father, but who followed his eminent grandfather, Adolf Furtwängler (known to his children as The Pope), into the profession of archaeology. Mrs. Furtwängler's daughter, an actress in Munich, is now called Furtwängler also, having married a nephew of her stepfather's.

Furtwängler himself conducted in America for the last time in 1927. His death occurred just a few months before his long planned-for return early in 1955, this time with his own orchestra, the Berlin Philharmonic (he was also supposed to tour with the Vienna Philharmonic the year after). The history of Furtwängler in America is complicated and sad. The New York Philharmonic, where he had been an idolized guest conductor in 1925–27, played him and Toscanini off against each other in a painful way, and Furtwängler left America feeling ill-used. Nevertheless, he was the first choice to succeed Toscanini at the Philharmonic in 1936, and again the first choice—to the point that there was a signed contract—to take over the Chicago Symphony in 1948.

Both times politics frustrated the appointment. Furtwängler was no Nazi; indeed, on several occasions he took somewhat risky stands against the regime on repertory, going to bat with considerable vigor on behalf of Hindemith and on the status of Jewish musicians in Germany. What he could not do was make up his mind to leave (Wagner's granddaughter, Friedelind, instructed him when they happened to meet in Paris: "It's very simple, just throw away your return ticket"). What he saw as a possibly useful "working within the system," as being in a position to bring his compatriots some taste of liberation through his performances of Beethoven, looked to many—remembering those who had been driven from their podiums, and those who had left voluntarily in protest—like an awfully comfortable way out (all the evidence says it was not). That he continued to conduct in Germany at all made him available to Goebbels as a cultural propaganda showpiece. Discourse was not always rational, and Furtwängler's insufficiently vigorous anti-Nazism, or non-Nazism, his attempt at being apolitical, were too easily translated into "Furtwängler, the Nazi sympathizer." He was desperately vulnerable, and his appointments in this country were out of the question.

Furtwängler's tour in 1955 would, then, have been no ordinary return, and Mrs. Furtwängler's journey just past has been informed with her need to redress some injustice to her husband's memory. To a group of San Francisco critics she said that she hoped they knew more about the *Nibelungenlied* than Wagner's version. She reminded them of the figure of Kriemhild, who after the murder of her husband, Siegfried, and after her remarriage to Etzel, king of the Huns, invited all the Burgundian nobles who had been responsible for Siegfried's death to a great feast, at which she had the lot of them slaughtered. "I am not Kriemhild," she said, "and I am not about to commit murders, but I must tell you that I have strong emotions to be travelling in the country where my husband was not allowed to conduct for so long, and to see now at least his posthumous success."

She was very much moved by the breadth and intensity of interest in Furtwängler's work, particularly among young people. It gave her particular pleasure that Carleton Smith, chairman of the National Arts Foundation, was able to announce in Boston that Leonard Bernstein had agreed to be president of the newly founded Furtwängler Society of America. Furtwängler, shortly before his death, heard Bernstein conduct, and noted in his diary that this was "the most talented conductor of his generation—I want to hear him again." The purpose of the Furtwängler Society is to promote interest in his recordings, to collect and make available recordings of radio broadcasts from places as far afield as Caracas, Cairo, and Moscow, also to stir up interest in performances of Furtwängler's own compositions. As for recordings, the first major project is to get out the last of his opera performances at Salzburg, including *Don Giovanni*, *Figaro*, *Magic Flute*, *Fidelio*, *Freischütz*, and *Otello*. Heading the Boston chapter of the Furtwängler Society is Zeph Stewart, master of Lowell House, Harvard University, and inquiries should be addressed to Professor Stewart.

Franz Brüggen Magnetizes Atmosphere at Jordan Hall

December 20, 1972

If you arrived a little early in Jordan Hall for Franz Brüggen's recorder recital last Sunday afternoon, you saw on the unlit stage two plain wooden chairs and a music stand. On one of the chairs, there were two cardboard boxes with recorders. Squatting near the chairs was a tall young man in grey slacks, black sweater, and black loafers, adjusting instruments, occasionally getting one of them to speak a soft "*doooooo*." After a bit he sat in the free chair, taking up a little recorder in C, and began to play quietly, more to himself than to us, not presentationally. He played "Est-ce Mars" and other songs from the hit parade of 350 years ago,[15] a prelude to while away the time for those already there, a gentle processional to welcome those still arriving (including a babe-in-arms who looked at the stage and cried "Papa"), and for himself a warmup. After maybe fifteen minutes of that, the Jordan Hall stage manager appeared, tapped Brüggen on the shoulder, Brüggen nodded and finished the piece, then the stage lights went on, there was applause, Brüggen stood, the ushers closed the doors, and the real concert began.

It was of music for recorder alone: Variations by the 17th-century Dutch composer, Jacob van Eyck, on *Doen Daphne d'overschoere Maeght*, two fantasias by Telemann, a Bach Partita in C minor (usually played on the transverse flute and in A minor); then two pieces recently written for Brüggen, Makoto Shinohara's *Fragmente* and Luciano Berio's *Gesti.*

I had doubts beforehand about an afternoon of unaccompanied recorder, but none whatever at the time. Brüggen is a fabulous player. His virtuosity is complete. Whatever he plays is alive, and he speaks the language of the 17th and 18th centuries with a native's confidence. As a performer he exercises special magnetism, being one of just a handful who command an audience's absolute silence. (The last time I sensed such silence at a concert was when Pears and Britten were in Jordan Hall in October 1969.[16])

Having said all that and adding specifically that the pleasure for me of Sunday's concert was enormous, I want to say also that at times Brüggen does things which make me squirm. He has, for example, devised a way of inflecting pitch for expressive purposes, blowing a long note till it goes quite sharp and then letting it down to its proper level again (analogous to the common effect of swelling and diminishing of volume on such a note). Brüggen does it with greater skill than on the recordings of five or so years ago on which one first heard it, but the discretion that dictates its use comes and goes irregularly. Sunday he was more restrained than at Harvard in October, but even now I found it fussy to the point of being somehow enervating.

That is the most controversial thing Brüggen does, and unfortunately he sometimes fails to resist a touch of cuteness. He played van Eyck's lovely *English Nightingale* Variations as his second encore, and when he came to the downward scale that ends it, he stopped just before the last note, made a tiny pause, and then sort of went "pop." It is as though someone asked you for your address, and you spoke it all straightforwardly, right into the zip code, "oh-two-one-six," but then

[15] Here Steinberg references performances by Jan Pieterszoon Sweelinck (1562–1621) in which the Dutch composer and organist would play variations on popular tunes.

[16] See review of October 29, 1969.

hesitating and tilting your head down, said "five" very softly into your cupped hand with a slight blush and the suggestion of a giggle.

Of the two contemporary pieces, Shinohara's is a slightly academic demonstration of what can be done on the recorder that van Eyck and Telemann never dreamed of—double-stops, flutter-tongue, extremely high notes, and so forth—a respectably done exam piece on avant-garde recorder technique. Berio's *Gesti* (*Gestures*), like the best of his *Sequenze*, is the occasion for an enchanting combination of virtuosity and theater. It begins with flying fingers but only an occasional sound, makes much altogether of the visual frenzy in certain kinds of music-making, and often has the performer duet with himself by singing into the recorder as well as playing it. Berio knows how to make all that funny and interesting, but he also knows where to stop.

Before his Telemann-Bach group, Brüggen spoke briefly about the propriety of playing works for transverse flute on the recorder (OK, he said, as long as the music is not too much in *le style galant*). Of Bach's notoriously impossible Partita (because it offers no breathing places) he said that he assumed it was already a transcription in its flute version, presumably from a work for a stringed instrument. He managed to make it sound only slightly troublesome rather than impossible, and, my reservations aside, I thought he played both it and the two fine Telemann Fantasias compellingly.

Furtwängler Revisited

December 24, 1972

Elisabeth Furtwängler, widow of the German conductor, Wilhelm Furtwängler, who died in 1954, recently passed through Boston as part of a kind of barnstorming through the United States, partly to draw attention to the release on commercial records of her husband's 1953 performance in Rome of Wagner's *Ring* cycle (Seraphim), partly to help arrange the founding of a Furtwängler Society of America.[17] The Society, whose main purpose is to promote interest in Furtwängler's recordings, including many performances yet unissued, was in fact founded here because Leonard Bernstein, just then guest conductor at the Boston Symphony, agreed to be President (Zeph Stewart, Professor of Classics at Harvard, and master of Lowell House, will head the local chapter).

Furtwängler was impressed by Bernstein the one time he heard him, and Mrs. Furtwängler admires him now. Another conductor of whom she has a high opinion is the Argentinian, Carlos Paita. This is not generally, she feels, a period

[17] See article of December 17, 1972.

of conductors of genius, and she is outspoken on the subject. Of the Austrian, Karl Böhm, who at 78 enjoys a grand-old-man status on the Central European scene, she said simply, "In the country of the blind, the one-eyed man is king."

Herbert von Karajan arouses particular irritation, not least because of the reverence he now claims to feel for Furtwängler and which she says was strikingly not in evidence when Furtwängler was still alive. Furtwängler, said his widow, was to Karajan's generation what Arthur Nikisch was to Furtwängler's—the great man among the older conductors. (Nikisch, Hungarian, 1855–1922, conductor of the Boston Symphony 1889–93, was probably the most universally and unqualifiedly admired conductor in the history of the profession.) The difference, Mrs. Furtwängler continued, was that Furtwängler never tried to work his way into Nikisch's posts, whereas Karajan did nothing else. As for Karajan's musical personality, "You have only to compare the two men's performances of Beethoven's *Pastoral* Symphony. No further comment is necessary."

Mrs. Furtwängler is a tall, slender lady, all energy, intensity, and soft-spoken humor, and looking considerably younger than her sixty years. Their marriage in 1943, to which she, as a young war widow brought four small children, was the second for each, and the age difference was twenty-six years. She described her second and decisive meeting with him in Vienna where she was visiting her sister ("This is a good time to come," she had written, "Furtwängler is conducting *Fidelio* and *Tristan*"), and how at the end of a fairly brief talk she felt as though the earth swayed under her feet. "My marriage had been a good marriage, really good and happy, but suddenly I saw that I had never really been in love before."

Their life together fulfilled what that moment promised. "It was incredible for me" and "a marvelous place to live" for the four children and for the fifth, Andreas, who was born to the new couple. "There is nothing more important or more beautiful that you can offer children than that kind of marriage, and we could. Every time Wilhelm came home, he would throw open the door and first thing let a great shout of 'ELISABETH!!!' through the house, and there was the whole story really."

At one point during the evening of this conversation a recording which included a couple of minutes of a Furtwängler rehearsal was put on, but en route there was the finale of Mozart's G minor Symphony to be traversed. "Ah, yes, those famous Furtwängler slow tempi," said Mrs. Furtwängler, as that movement went by with unsurpassed speed and energy. Furtwängler didn't think much of critics, she said, but never got over being annoyed by them either. "However, if one showed signs of being able to engage him in a real musical discussion of substance, he would always enter into that gladly. Then I might say to him, 'Don't you know that was so-and-so you were talking to, who just wrote such awful things about you? And he would say, 'You know, that's awfully feminine of you to insist on extending an enmity like that.'" She laughed, remembering.

Musical issues engaged him passionately. As a young man on a walk with the philosopher Ernst Cassirer, his closest friend in his last years ("his death wounded Furtwängler so much, it was the one thing that could never be spoken of in our house"), he declared at a fork in the road, "You will walk one way and I the other if you do not take back what you said about Brahms." And he was capable of picking up a conversation after years of not seeing an acquaintance with "Have you changed your mind about Bruckner yet?" Though Mrs. Furtwängler describes him as "essentially and deeply a tragic temperament," he could laugh hugely. "He had, however, no sense for irony. It is the reason, I believe, he was always uneasy with and about Stravinsky, though he conducted much of his music. Temperamentally and intellectually he felt closer to Schoenberg and Hindemith."

As for recordings, Furtwängler hated making them, partly because he disliked the fixing as "the Furtwängler performance" of what was for him just one among many, and all different. "He was always searching, and never believed he had completely found the interpretation. He was a man who lived more easily among questions than with answers. But he enjoyed making the *Tristan* recording in London in 1952. Those were people he found wonderful to work with, and I remember him listening to the end of Act I, and Tristan and Isolde in their confusion, Kurwenal and Brangäne trying to organize them for the landing, the offstage trumpets, and saying, 'Yes, such a thing has possibilities.'"

"And of course he hated the interruptions. One of the last recordings he made, the Schumann Fourth, with the Berlin Philharmonic, in 1953, he insisted on going straight through without a stop. They didn't want to try it, but he said he was going home if not—oh yes, though he was generally quiet, he could be *Jupiter tonans* when he wanted to—and it came out perhaps his most beautiful record.

"By the time you heard him in Italy in '53 and '54, he was already very much used up. The end began for him in '52. He had a bad bronchial infection, and one day he said 'You must speak louder, I can't hear you.' His hearing came back, but it was never quite all there again, particularly when he was nervous or very excited. So he decided to quit. 'Ich will kein Betrüger sein,' he said ('I don't want to be a fraud'). 'I'll do all the things for which I have signed contracts and then stop.' The Rome *Ring* was one, and I remember how he studied it every day as though it were a new work. His last concert was with the Berlin Philharmonic. He did his own Second Symphony, so he was extremely excited, and the hearing was very bad, and he was very down. Then there was the recording of *Walküre* in Vienna, and he had fun doing that.

"Soon after, he had another bronchial attack. He woke me in the night and said 'I'm going to die now. I am finished with my work, and it is time.' I got him back to sleep, and when I went in in the morning, he had his covers pulled all the way up to his chin and he was wearing a most serious expression on his face. Suddenly he threw off the covers, laughed, and leaped up—he was fully dressed.

He hated being sick in bed. But I called his doctor, who had a clinic in Baden-Baden, and drove him there."

Furtwängler continued quite sure of where he was going. "Nobody dies of such a bronchitis," he told his wife, "and this is a place where people come to recover, not to die, but you will see, I am going to die." Mrs. Furtwängler continued: "He became very quiet. I read to him a lot—Hemingway, and many things—and for the first time that I knew him, he no longer conducted himself all the time" (she imitated the gestures and the humming).

Furtwängler was to take the Berlin Philharmonic to America early in 1955 for his first concerts here since 1927. Gerhard von Westerman, the Philharmonic's manager, came to see Furtwängler, and the one time Furtwängler became angry during this illness was when he learned that his wife had rescheduled von Westermann's visit from one Sunday to the following one. "No, I will no longer be alive then." Von Westerman came on the earlier Sunday. Furtwängler thanked him for everything, asked him to carry his greetings to the orchestra to which he had been close since 1922. Von Westerman began to cry, whereupon Furtwängler changed his tone and said, "Now about those programs for America . . . "

When Mrs. Furtwängler returned from taking von Westerman to his car ("You certainly flunked that one," she told him), Furtwängler said delightedly, "Did you see how I got him to stop bawling?" Two days later, he died. "I used to think," Mrs. Furtwängler went on, "that the best death was the one that comes in sleep, or the sudden heart attack, the death you never know about. I learned instead that the most beautiful death is the one you experience in full awareness. I told that to a friend. 'Yes,' he said, 'but you have to know how.' "

1973

Sherman to Perform All Twelve Liszt Etudes

January 14, 1973

Not since José Iturbi in 1931 has any pianist here done what Russell Sherman will do in Jordan Hall this Friday evening, play all twelve of Franz Liszt's *Études d'exécution transcendante* at one concert. Iturbi, Sherman pointed out, worked harder: he warmed up on Beethoven's *Appassionata*. Sherman thinks the Liszt is enough—"the perfect proportions for a recital, 35–40 minutes for the first half, 35–40 minutes for the second half."

The *Transcendental Etudes* go back to a project Liszt conceived at 16, forty-eight studies, two in each major and minor key (à la *Well-tempered Clavier*), in a style one could describe as Czerny-plus. In fact, Liszt wrote only twelve pieces, but thirteen years later, he presented those twelve (having this time announced twenty-four) in enormously enlarged and elaborated form. They were now real compositions. Still later, in 1852—Liszt was now 41, and five years retired from the concert stage—the third and now standard edition appeared. Most of the studies now acquired titles—"Harmonies du soir," "Eroica," "Ricordanza," "Mazeppa," and so on—and they were somewhat cut as well as made less bizarrely difficult. Liszt dedicated both the second and third versions to his teacher, Czerny, and he retained the idea of a schematic arrangement of keys (the major-key studies go by descending fifths, C, F, B-flat, etc., and each is followed by a piece in the relative minor).

The repertory Sherman has played in Boston since he came five years ago to head the piano department at the New England Conservatory has ranged from Mozart to Milton Babbitt, but he has made few excursions into the dazzlingly virtuosic like his Liszt project (later this season, March 22 and 29, and April 5, he gives three recitals at the Conservatory devoted to Haydn, and May 29 at the Gardner Museum, he performs Schubert's *Die schöne Müllerin* with the soprano Jane Bryden).

He has acquired the reputation of being an "intellectual pianist," but apropos that, he told a story with which Katja Andy, a colleague on the Conservatory's piano faculty, had just delighted him. Artur Schnabel, often charged with the same thing, once said to her, "They say I am an intellectual, but my dear child, I'm much too lazy."

Having offered that demurrer, Sherman offered some of his thoughts about Liszt and the *Transcendental Etudes*. "Radical though this theory may be," he said, "I think they are damn good music." What makes music good, he went on to explain, is a dynamic sense of form, by which he means that ideas never recur in a mechanical or static manner. "Liszt gets his way of motivic development from Beethoven, and with his perpetual variation he looks forward to Schoenberg. The pieces are very thorough." The two he likes most are the untitled A minor and F minor, which embody these characteristics at the highest level of concentration; he likes *Mazeppa* least because its form is the most static. He quoted Debussy on Liszt: "to leave the hall with a disgusted expression is pure hypocrisy."

"I would like to play them drier than Jordan Hall makes possible," Sherman went on. "Music gets caught up in the ego of the modern grand piano, the temptation to overpedal, to turn everything into a grand harmonic orgy. But, damn it, it's 'Harmonies du soir,' not [the perfume] L'Heure bleue by Guerlain. It's not music that takes time for delicious extravagances and all sorts of wicked cadenzas. Each study is the portrayal of an ideal, and its performance must point all its elements toward a common goal, and not go passage by passage."

That is far from the normal received ideas about Liszt's music and how to perform it, and Sherman went on to talk about the difference between approaches, now reaching into sports for an analogy. "Take Mays and DiMaggio, the two greatest center-fielders of the last forty years. Mays was a radiant performer. Everything he did communicated exuberance and enjoyment. DiMaggio was graceful, lean, everything was control, efficiency, exquisite line."

In hockey, Sherman said, the Montreal Canadiens provided analogous examples, Maurice Richard, a Dionysiac player of the Mays type, and Jean Béliveau, the Apollonian counterpart to DiMaggio. "And Bobby Orr—by the way, I happen to be a Rangers fan—even though what he does is flagrantly conspicuous, extravagant, exceptional, it is always within the calculus of what is to the advantage of the team, always with an awareness of what's the score, which period it is, of what, in large terms, can be done. He is a classicist. Like Busoni. And that's my tradition and my allegiance, too."

Ferruccio Busoni, Italian-German composer, for many the greatest pianist of his generation (and briefly and unhappily in 1891–92 on the New England Conservatory's faculty), is an important part of Sherman's musical and pianistic pedigree. At 11, Sherman began to study with Eduard Steuermann, who, in the years just before the 1914 war, studied piano with Busoni at the same time that he worked on theory and composition with Schoenberg. Busoni was not a pupil of Liszt, but he was outstanding as a Liszt player, made an edition of his works, and continued much of his thought in his own compositions and arrangements.

Sherman is fascinated by mixed pedigrees: "Often the psychic spark comes from the fusion of contradictory sources." He cited Liszt, "there's the Magyar blood, but also the passionate involvement with Dante and Goethe. I always believed that in Stravinsky, much of the life came out of the tension between the Russian and French heritages. I myself have a mother who is Rumanian with gypsy blood, and that is not concealed in my playing. With that blood, I went at 11 to study with a pupil of Busoni and Schoenberg."

Sherman came back to the *Transcendental Etudes*, demonstrated in some detail what he calls the "strettofication," the foreshortening processes in the A minor, the perpetual variation to which the principal idea (three short notes and a long) is subjected, concluding, "Look, it's Schoenberg, Opus 33b." The Etude in E-flat, called "Eroica," he said is one he likes "better and better," admiring particularly the very Lisztian qualities of "*noblesse*" and refinement: "There's also a certain humor to it—Napoleon played by Peter Ustinov." He compared and contrasted the intensely private Beethoven with Liszt, whose "inquiries into the nature of love and redemption" are carried out more theatrically, more with an ever-present sense of performance.

Finally he returned to "the intellectual label. The common understanding is that intellect and feeling are mutually exclusive. It is supposed, for example, that Dr. Henry Kissinger is insensitive to the murder and carnage being committed because he thinks too much and feels too little, but it's really because he thinks too little."

Sherman the Best Yet

January 22, 1973

The season's most exciting concert so far? Last Friday night in Jordan Hall, when Russell Sherman played all twelve of Liszt's *Études d'exécution transcendante.*[1]

In his program notes, having acknowledged Liszt's ardor, caprice, tone-painting, pyrotechnics, and dramatic intensity, Sherman writes: "The power of Liszt derives from his skills as a composer. 'Fire' and 'abandon' would be useless conceits without the basis of a musical form rich and varied in internal relationships, and presided over by a valid concept of musical time."

Liszt took special pains over the *Transcendental Etudes*; in their finally revised form of 1851, they are thoroughly, and stunningly, composed. Moreover, fully to appreciate that, you want to hear them as a set (and in a performance as magisterial as Sherman's).

[1] See article of January 14, 1973.

It is an extraordinary book, a compendium to define Romantic bravura technique (unsurpassed really until Debussy's Etudes sixty-five years later "fixed" a whole new world of piano playing), and of great, knowingly planned variety. The C major Preludio is one extreme, a flourish, a call to attention, a trying out of the whole keyboard, an exercise for the loosening of nerves and muscles, and all over in forty seconds. The other extreme is the penultimate study, "Harmonies du soir," sixteen times the size of the Preludio, massive and lush. In a different sense, the "opposite" to Preludio is the untitled A minor study that immediately follows, the former improvisatory and cadenza-like, the latter ingeniously concentrated in its motivic facture (otherwise, speaking of opposites, only Brahms wrote such tightly made pieces in the space between Beethoven and Schoenberg).

The F minor, also untitled and occurring near the end, equally compressed and highly developed, is the counterpart at white heat of passion to the playful A minor. Followed by the grand "Harmonies du soir," it is preceded by a very different sort of big, slow movement, "Ricordanza," an elegant essay in the faded love-letters genre. Poetically, the most powerfully suggestive is the final study, "Casse-neige," which is from the world of those ghostly, threatening snows Stifter[2] evoked in *Rock Crystal*, the most beautiful of all Christmas stories.

Sherman's playing of the etudes—and, as encores, of two more works in which Liszt is at his most poetic and attentive, the *Petrarch Sonnet* 104 and "Jeux d'eau à la Villa d'Este"—was something wonderful. One knew he could play the piano brilliantly; otherwise, he could not have achieved the textural and rhythmic clarity that distinguished his Beethoven sonata recitals two seasons ago. But he had not undertaken so virtuosic a program before, and what he now let loose was astonishing, something not half a dozen pianists could equal.

It was more, though, than getting around the notes, and more than stamina (but note that no one here had tried in forty-two years to play the full dozen at one concert). The virtuosity in these etudes is organic, which makes them different from and harder than Liszt's brilliant, delightful, and better-known set after Paganini. The brain must be as sharp as the fingers are fleet and strong, and at Sherman's concert it was in fact the musical concentration that held us in its grip as much as the dazzling coruscations on the surface. The absolutely compelling power of projection was new in Sherman's performance: his playing was open, free, and exuberant in a way I had not heard it before.

He caught and communicated that curious fusion in Liszt of intellect, fancy, and passion. In doing so, he gave a complete performance of a masterpiece we know too little. Jordan Hall was packed. The connoisseurs probably knew from the beginning how remarkable an occasion it was; by the end of "Mazeppa," the

[2] Adalbert Stifter (1805–68), Austro-Bohemian author, poet, pedagogue, and artist.

fourth study, there was no mistaking it for anybody. The enthusiasm at intermission and at the end was as special as the playing that produced it.

BSO's Strauss Worth a Rainy Trip

February 3, 1973

It was a day for polar bears, ice-skaters, and seals, enough to keep a lot of people from going to hear the Boston Symphony yesterday afternoon. Those who did manage to wade or skid or swim to the hall were rewarded with a beautiful concert. The program was all by Richard Strauss—the suite from *Le Bourgeois Gentilhomme*, *Don Quixote*, and *Salome's Dance*—with William Steinberg to conduct and Jules Eskin as cello soloist.

Strauss advised conductors to handle *Salome* and *Elektra* as though dealing with Mendelssohnian fairy-music. He knew he wrote a terrible lot of notes (Mozart, after all, was his favorite composer, and he had standards), and he knew that his rhetoric was emphatic. He was also a great conductor, and he knew that there was a way of conducting Strauss "like Mendelssohn," delicately and with restraint. That still won't make it sound like *Midsummer Night's Dream*, not to mention Mozart, but it will produce a performance to show what a good composer Strauss was.

About William Steinberg it is a curious thing. His conducting has weight: the basses are really solid, the middle of the texture is richly filled out, metrical accents are firm. There is quite a range of music in which his work can be disagreeably heavy. The feel of it all is apt to be blunt rather than sharp, but somehow Strauss always brings out in him a delicious lightness. The music is transparent, the rhythm has spring. The jokes are funny, but they are quietly told—in fact, there is no shouting or lapel-grabbing ever. Less is more, and in that respect, Steinberg's conducting of Strauss is much and admirably like Strauss's own.

Le Bourgeois Gentilhomme can seem arch and precious, but Steinberg, playing it straight and with the lightest possible touch, found in it only the masterfulness of the writing. The playing was very fizzy, very gentle, very right.

With *Don Quixote*, the flavor of the event changed. It had been delightful, and now it was profoundly moving. It is a glorious work, funny, tender, imaginative (Xenakis, Penderecki, and the rest of the flutter-tongue boys come and go, but still those sheep in *Don Quixote* knock you on your ear every time), and nowhere did Strauss more successfully solve the problem of how to integrate pictorial or narrative detail into a large and musically coherent structure. The performance was a wonderfully understanding revelation of the piece, with just the right balance of trees and wood, of affection and irony.

Steinberg and the orchestra provided the ideal framework, and inside that, Eskin drew the Don's portrait with wonderful sense of character, also playing the instrument beautifully, with Burton Fine, Sancho Panza-as-viola, doing a superb job of support and comment.

Count on Strauss always to know how to end a piece. The epilogue in *Don Quixote* is so beautiful altogether, the last two chords with their soft cymbal wipes in particular, that I felt they had to be left untouched—so, with apologies to St. Mark, Oscar Wilde, Lord Alfred Douglas, Dr. Strauss, and all others concerned, I admit that I ran before Salome danced.

Abbado, Cleveland Orchestra

February 10, 1973

Monday, Claudio Abbado conducted the Mahler Sixth Symphony with the Cleveland Orchestra in New York. Harold Schonberg of the *New York Times*, seeing Abbado as representing "the younger generation . . . less eager to play up the kind of sentiment and tempo fluctuation that used to be part of the accepted Mahler style," heard a performance that was "unrelaxed and literal." Wednesday, Abbado conducted the same orchestra in Symphony Hall, and, to someone responding to the performance rather than to categories like "the younger generation," it was an interpretation in which the many tempo changes in the score were exactly observed and which, wherever flexibility was built in—most in the second and third movements—the approach was elastic to the point almost of risk.

Abbado understands the difference between those two crucial Mahlerian adjectives, "*plötzlich*" ("suddenly") and "*allmählich*" ("gradually"), which already puts him light-years ahead of most Mahler conductors. What, however, made his performance extraordinary was that he observed the tempo fluctuations which are so central a part of Mahler's repertory of expressive gestures not only exactly, but imaginatively. He knew "why" as well as "that," and his interpretation—at once fiery and lyrical, benevolent, anti-hysterical—wonderfully conveyed a sense of Mahler's enormous musical intelligence. I think I have never heard this work sound so composed.

I had not heard the orchestra since Szell's last-but-one concert in Cleveland in May 1970; Szell was already very ill, and the playing was ragged and without spirit. This, Wednesday, was vintage Cleveland: a sound with a cutting edge like a diamond, incredibly concentrated and compact, highly characterized, yet with perfection of blend—the voicing of those brass chords played as though by a single instrument—that speaks for uncommon care in assembling and training. Beyond those conventional, though remarkable, virtuosities, there was the orchestra's flexibility and capacity for instant response, the prerequisite for Abbado's rubato style. If finer Mahler is available today, it is from an orchestra and a conductor I have never heard of.

And not least, thanks to Abbado for letting the Mahler be the whole program.

Elliott Carter's String Quartet No. 3

February 11, 1973

This is more of a program note than a review. Its subject is Elliott Carter's String Quartet No. 3, which had its premiere just nineteen days ago in New York, and which will be played this Friday evening, February 16, at 8:30 in Sanders Theatre at a concert by the Juilliard Quartet.[3] The program also includes the Ives Quartet No. 2 and Bartók's No. 6, and the concert, which is presented by the Fromm Music Foundation at Harvard University, is open to the public free of charge.

The Quartet No. 3 was completed in December 1971, and it is Carter's first major work since the Concerto for Orchestra, which was first played in February 1970. It continues quite directly Carter's musical thought of these past twenty-some years. Go back to the Sonata for Cello and Piano, 1948 (Nonesuch J-71234), and listen to its simple and arresting beginning. The piano plays chords drily, metronomically; the cello unwinds an expressive melody whose notes occur in complete independence of the beat that is so painstakingly defined at the keyboard. The contrast is of sonority, rhythm, staccato and legato, but more than that, it is the contrast of two drastically dissociated musical characters.

Wilfrid Mellers prefaces the Carter chapter in *Music in a New Found Land* with these lines by Wallace Stevens[4]:

> Out of what one sees and hears and out
> Of what one feels, who could have thought to make
> So many selves, so many sensuous worlds,
> As if the air, the midday air, was swarming
> With the metaphysical changes that occur,
> Merely in living as and where we live.

[3] See review of February 19, 1973.
[4] From *Esthéthique du Mal*, XV (1944).

On this, Carter has commented:

> It is quite true that I have been concerned with contrasts of many kinds of musical characters—"many selves"; with forming these into poetically evocative combinations—"many sensuous worlds"; with filling musical time and space by a web of continually varying cross references—"the air . . . swarming with . . . changes." And to me, at least, my music grows "out of what one sees and hears and out / Of what one feels," out of what occurs "Merely in living as and where we live."

Let Carter speak twice more: (on the Quartet No. 2 of 1959) "I regard my scores as scenarios, auditory scenarios, for performers to act out with their instruments, dramatizing the players as individuals and as participants in the ensemble." (On the Concerto for Orchestra) "As with all my works, the primary intention is expressive, and the entire musical vocabulary, instrumentation and form have been chosen to further this."

In the Quartet No. 2 (Nonesuch H-71249), each player has his own particular vocabulary of expressive gestures with which he delineates and affirms his unique musical character (Carter suggested that the players sit far apart on stage, but most quartets have felt uncomfortable about that). In the Double Concerto (Columbia MS-7191), the dialogue is between harpsichord and piano, each with its own differently constituted chamber ensemble (with a band of percussion to link them), again each with its own vocabulary of intervals, rhythmic patterns, and characteristic gestures. In the 1965 Piano Concerto (RCA LSC-3001), a solo concertino of seven instruments mediates between piano and orchestra, carrying the news from one to the other, the piano being "an individual of many changing moods and thoughts" as opposed to the more or less monolithically treated orchestra. The Concerto for Orchestra (Columbia M30112) has four movements, each assigned to a different segment of the orchestra, but the four, instead of being played in sequence in the traditional way, are blended and intercut in film-like fashion and, as it were, "choreographed" so that each takes its place front and center on stage at a different point in the unfolding of the whole work."

This time, Carter has made a scenario by splitting the players into a pair of duos. Duo I is violin and cello (this violin part is taken by Earl Carlyss, the Juilliard's second violinist); Duo II is violin (Robert Mann, the first violinist) and viola.

Duo I has a repertory of four movements—Furioso; Leggerissimo (very lightly); Andante espressivo; Pizzicato, giocoso—and it plays *quasi rubato* throughout. Duo II has a repertory of six movements—Maestoso; Grazioso; Pizzicato giusto, meccanico; Scorrevole (running or fluent); Largo tranquillo; Appassionato—and it plays in quite strict rhythm throughout. As always in Carter's more recent music, certain intervals are especially prominent in each "character"—tritones and perfect fifths in the Maestoso, major sevenths in the Furioso, fourths and major seconds in the Leggerissimo, minor sevenths in the Grazioso, and so on.

Now as you can figure out for yourself, you can do thirty-four things: each of the ten "movements" or "characters" can be played alone, and twenty-four combinations are possible. Carter does all thirty-four, and the end of this article is a sort of road map. "The map is not the territory" (if it is still permissible to quote S. I. Hayakawa[5]). Don't confuse the description with the object. As Carter said recently, "If you made a schematic diagram of the plot of *Great Expectations* it would look much more complicated." In Carter's music, enormous complexity of procedure and richness of detail has always been used to make a statement whose impact—given a good performance—is powerful and direct. A note to score-kibitzers: Carter's music looks far more formidable than it sounds because, like the cello melody I mentioned earlier, its events characteristically happen just to one side or another of the beat, while our notation is geared to the convenience of on-the-beat composers.

The Quartet No. 3 attacks you with the Maestoso-Furioso combination (*fortissimo* in double- and triple-stops) at what is almost the point of maximum confusion. Very quickly, though, it thins out, and it attains such wildness again only at the very end, which, like *Finnegans Wake*, could go right back to the beginning, and where all ten ideas boil up together. En route, you pass through scherzo-like country where the two pizzicato movements coincide and the Scorrevole first comes in, then to a slow movement.

Beyond that, I want for the moment to report only such miscellaneous things as that it takes about nineteen minutes; that at the premiere, the Juilliard Quartet played it lucidly, with conviction and brilliance; that I found it a colder more Leverkühnish[6] sort of thing than Carter's other major works; that even with that quality, which disappointed me, I thought it confirmed Carter's position as the most interesting composer now writing; that I loved listening to it and can hardly wait to hear it again.

[5] Samuel Ichiye Hayakawa (1906–1992) was an academic and politician who had recently switched political affiliation from Democrat to Republican. The phrase itself originated with Polish-American philosopher Alfred Korzybski (1879–1950).

[6] Adrian Leverkühn is the composer-protagonist of Thomas Mann's final novel, *Doctor Faustus*. In a *New York Times* book review [March 18, 1984] of MacDonald Harris's Leverkühn-inspired novel, *Tenth*, Steinberg describes Leverkühn as "a composer primarily made up of biographical bits of Nietzsche and Schoenberg, along with some details Mann drew from Alban Berg and Hugo Wolf." The critic Alex Ross, a self-described *Faustus* obsessive, produced "An Adrian Leverkühn Companion" for his blog *The Rest Is Noise*, on March 6, 2016, in which he described Leverkühn as having evolved a non-tonal, at times idiosyncratically serialist language, although he also incorporated parodic imitations of past styles and anticipated certain developments of the postwar avant-garde." Leverkühn's fictional lifespan, 1885–1945, mirrored the rise and fall of the Third Reich and German intellectual culture during the same period.

Ohlsson Right All Way

February 12, 1973

Garrick Ohlsson is getting better, and he was enormously impressive when I first heard him not quite three years ago.[7] The 24-year-old pianist gave a recital for the BU Celebrity Series in Symphony Hall yesterday afternoon, choosing a tough program, then coolly demonstrating that he was right about his choices. He began with Beethoven's G major Rondo, Op. 51, No. 2, went on to Schumann's F-sharp minor Sonata and to a group of nine Scriabin Etudes (three each from Opp. 8 and 42, and all of Opus 65), and finished with Chopin (the A minor Mazurka from Opus 17 and the *Andante spianato* and *Grande Polonaise brillante*).

Ohlsson is intelligent, unaffected, relaxed, tasteful, good-humored, and he plays the instrument beautifully. He knows what is going on inside the pieces—even when, as in parts of Schumann's Sonata, that is a bit obscure—and, never one to score a tactical hit at the expense of a larger strategy, he has the patience and maturity to show his listeners what he knows. Another manifestation of his interpretive intelligence is that he makes vivid distinctions among styles and manners, the structural and the decorative, the cool and the hot, and so forth. He has, as well, highly developed feeling for piano scoring, not only in obviously coloristic music like the Scriabin studies, but also in Schumann's subtle and difficult manner of distributing the material, and even in things so seemingly simple as the Chopin Mazurka and the Beethoven Rondo.

Ohlsson plays simply. Everything—rubato, contrasts of color and dynamics, expression of sentiment—is offered with the greatest economy. He is never neutral and he does not underplay—there is nothing stingy about his temperament—but he seems to look always for the way of projecting the most life with the least fuss. In that he began now to remind me of Lipatti, a comparison which was suggested most forcefully by the aristocratic taste and elegance in his Chopin (one of his encores was the A-flat Waltz, Op. 34, No. 1).

His most imposing achievement was his performance of Schumann's crazily wonderful, wildly difficult Sonata. I wonder if the exceedingly problematic finale could not be dealt with other than by means of the cuts Ohlsson made; obviously, though, Ohlsson has thought about it more than I have, and he negotiated the jumps without leaving any sense of incoherence. He caught completely the humor, poetry, and fantasy of the piece, and made it sound gorgeous.

The Beethoven Rondo at the beginning was a bit overpointed in some of its details (though not without wit) and a trifle shallow in sound. Even remembering

[7] See article of June 2, 1969.

that, I would say the whole concert was a powerfully assertive statement of musical understanding, breadth, taste, and vitality.

Pianist Returns to Classroom

February 18, 1973

At Newton South High School Monday morning, there were signs in the corridors announcing "Garrick Ohlsson in the music room, 9 to 11:15," and a few that simply said "Welcome Garrick." The music room was easy to find: that was where there was a great bubble of people who seemed to have burst through the door into the hall. Through the people and the door I could hear the first movement of the *Appassionata*. Inside, in the middle, there was a Mason & Hamlin grand with the massive young pianist, informal in shirtsleeves, playing it; then, beginning not three feet from the instrument, people, close to 200 of them jammed into the room, a handful of teachers but mostly kids, on the floor near the center of the room, on desks, chairs, and tables as you got nearer the wall.

Ohlsson's visits to Newton South High began in 1967. They grow out of his friendship with Jonathan Slater, who teaches English there and who did his year of student teaching at the high school in White Plains, NY, where Ohlsson went to school.

Ohlsson tells the story: "Jon brought a crazy composer friend, Louis Weingarden,[8] around to write music for a school play. Weingarden asked what instrumentalists we had, and they told him, not much, but there's a terrific pianist. 'Yeah, so what else is new? Every school has a pianist,' thought Louis. But he heard me, and the next day he composed and brought me some unplayable music, and I played it."

The first time he visited Slater in Newton, a librarian at Newton South had just died, and Ohlsson went to the school to play Chopin's "Funeral March" Sonata. And, through high school, Juilliard, and now as a much-demanded concert artist, he has made his visits to Newton South and become something of an institution there, coming by two or three or four times a year, spending as much as possible of a day talking with students, but mostly just playing for them.

Last Sunday, Ohlsson played a Symphony Hall recital.[9] Monday at 9, he was at Newton South. First a choral group sang two Lassus madrigals to him. He responded with pieces by Pasquini, an obscure 17th-century Tuscan composer of whose music he is particularly fond, and the Jacobean, Thomas Tomkins.

8 See article of June 2, 1969.
9 See previous article.

Then he went on to the Bach-Busoni Chaconne, the *Appassionata*, Scriabin's Sixth Sonata and a group of Etudes, finally and by request, Chopin's F-sharp minor Polonaise. A short day because he had a TV tape to make—then back to New York and from there to Europe.

In two-and-a-half hours, Ohlsson can undo years of damage by music appreciation classes. He is a good teacher. When he talks about music, or occasionally about composers, he is funny in a low-keyed way, but he is never cute or showy; at the same time, without a trace of solemnity, he leaves no doubt that Beethoven is a serious matter. There is even, he suggests, joyfulness to being serious about some things. He treats his audience with respect: no one is made to feel that limited knowledge of music—or even limited interest in it—is a crime.

A lot of credit goes to the school for providing the right sort of unforced atmosphere for such an occasion. Kids are free to come and go, and under extremely difficult physical circumstances they manage their comings and goings with a courtesy of consideration that their elders in Symphony Hall or at the opera cannot summon. In the middle of the crowd, one girl sat on the floor reading, and I was impressed and grateful that no one offered to make her feel she shouldn't.

It is Ohlsson's candidness that gets to them, the courtesy and warmth to which they respond in kind, his directness about the pleasures of success (or when he says something like "this Etude is a great favorite with pianists, at least with those of us who can play it") and equally about doubts or failures (of Scriabin's Etude in ninths he said, "I'm sure it's never had an adequate performance since the day it was written"). He does the best thing a teacher can do: by standing there and being who he is, he makes a direct and compelling statement that the activity to which he is devoting his life is one worth giving a life to.

He has, at Newton South, a rapt audience that is really excited by Beethoven and Scriabin (and how many audiences would request the F-sharp minor Polonaise?). They are being shown something extraordinary about quality. And no doubt we shall continue to hear and read that it is impossible to interest young people in classical music.

Carter's Complexities Evoke Simple Ovation, Curiosity

February 19, 1973

Worth reading: Charles Rosen's essay on Elliott Carter in the February 22 issue of the *New York Review of Books*, and David Hamilton's review of Carter's new String Quartet No. 3 in the February 19 issue of *The Nation*. I shall borrow from both.

Rosen begins:

> Can a new work of music be played brilliantly by musicians who think that it is impossible to get through it technically with confidence, and also be wildly cheered to the galleries by a public most of whom would claim that it is too complex to understand? So it would seem from the first performance of Elliott Carter's Third Quartet by the Juilliard String Quartet in New York on January 23.[10]

It happened again in Sanders Theatre Friday night. This time, the more relaxed performance seemed more brilliant and sure, and the ovation for the composer and players was more solid. It was the second of four programs presented this year by the Harvard Music Department, with the Fromm Music Foundation, a wonderful occasion because there is something uniquely exciting about the early hearings of those few pieces which make a dent.

The intense, quick response to the music—Carter's quartet was preceded aptly by the Ives No. 2 and followed by Bartók No. 6—came from a predominantly young audience, which had Sanders jammed to bursting a half-hour before starting time. When applause for the Carter piece stopped, there was a rush to the stage to look at the music on the stands. Usually, it is a harpsichord that elicits such curiosity.

Characteristically, Carter has written a piece that is difficult, direct, and responsive to virtuosic performance. It is about nineteen minutes long and continuous, but its sequence of tempi and characters suggests the familiar succession of serious allegro, scherzo, slow movement, climactic finale.

Carter breaks the quartet into two duos—violin and cello, violin and viola. Each has its own repertory of "movements," four and six respectively. Each movement of Duo I is combined with that of Duo II, though only toward the end do the movements react and interact for a sense of climax. Each movement also is presented briefly alone, so starting from ten elements, Carter offers thirty-four musical experiences.

Hamilton likens it to "listening to two simultaneous conversations with the important difference that everything—details, interactions, and totality—has been imagined by a masterly ear and a masterly dramatic mind." The conversations are not casual, even in the enchanting double-pizzicato movement, and it is a new kind of listening Carter asks of us.

Carter has uncanny knowledge of human and musical character (and of the latter as metaphorical presentation of the former), of dramatic processes, of what "works" when you play with time. The result is paradox. His music is sometimes

[10] See article of February 11, 1973.

more "difficult" for the trained listener, who tries to "hear" everything, than for a more innocent kind of listener who is simply caught up in the powerfully compelling drama. Rosen's remark that "the simplicity and directness of Carter's achievement . . . are only beginning to be felt" is more applicable to players, for whom the immediate difficulties are enormous, than for general audiences.

The difference between this hearing and the first was huge, partly just because it was the second, partly because of the more relaxed playing, partly because of the softer acoustic ambience of Sanders as compared with the more aggressive tone of Tully Hall. My impression of greater transparency must stem from all three factors. I had no sense this time of a certain coldness that disturbed me at first, though I still hear the Quartet No. 3 as an expression of Carter as *homo ludens*—man at play, to be sure, at the highest level—or the *Goldbergs*, if you like, without a twenty-fifth variation. Still, in a passage like the Largo-Leggerissimo combination of stasis and agitation, we recognize Carter as a man who has seen far into the human condition.

Steinberg, Singers, Players Provide Treat at Symphony

March 17, 1973

Seeing a silent film of William Steinberg conducting the Dies irae of Verdi's Requiem as he conducted it in Symphony Hall yesterday afternoon, you might guess that the music being played was [Mendelssohn's] *Fingal's Cave*. To the ear it was the Day of Judgment, but what the eye saw was a stick moving in gentle curves and not more than two inches. It was a performance made with enormously reduced physical resources carefully and knowingly husbanded. Necessarily, it also became an understated performance of small theatrical flash, but the singers and players for the most part followed Steinberg with such attention, and Steinberg conducted with such intelligence and taste—and there was fire at the center—that this honorable, selfless statement had become, when all done, more moving than most performances offering a more exciting surface.

What made it go? First, Steinberg's seriousness, his disposition to take Verdi seriously, his refusal to cheapen the music by constant underlinings. Then, more specifically, the tempi. Not since Toscanini and Cantelli have I heard the Requiem so justly paced, and it is so easily done: just pay attention to Verdi's painstakingly clear directions. In the firmness, there was elasticity, a real Verdian *espansione*, and the understanding that, when the chorus declaims "*Libera me, Domine*" on a single chord and Verdi marks it "*senza misura*," you let the sound and the meaning of the words guide the music, don't punch it out in metronomic eighth-notes.

Steinberg's physically minimal conducting cannot always have been easy to follow, but he and Verdi together engaged sympathies and attention so that the performance had an easy precision—the busy, quick Sanctus even went with a delightfully off-hand virtuosity. The unexpected bonus of Steinberg's tip-of-the-baton conducting style was that it drew playing with a wonderfully relaxed sound from the Boston Symphony. It is a piece in which an orchestra can easily be roiled into racketiness, but I have never heard its internal balances more vividly, transparently worked out.

The orchestra made a superb contribution (though I wish Sherman Walt would learn to phrase the bassoon's accompanying figure to "*Quid sum miser*"—please, not with an accent on the fourth sixteenth in each group of six). The chorus—from the New England Conservatory, and prepared by Lorna Cooke deVaron—sang beautifully, with concentration, vivid diction, and solid, unforced sound.

The solo quartet was wonderful at the top, not so good below. At the top was Martina Arroyo, a woman who has moved right into the front rank of Verdian sopranos—indeed, if there is someone better in the Aida-Leonora-Requiem corner of the repertory now, I have not heard her. She sings with fire, intelligence, and taste, and she has a magnificent, intense, vibrantly alive voice with which to do it. Lili Chookasian is a good mezzo-soprano partner for Arroyo: the voices are compatible, and so are their temperatures and pulse-rates. On her own, Chookasian offers a grandly mature, gorgeous, relaxed voice, and no end of expressive power. The way she radiates love of Verdi's music—and not just the parts she sings—is something special, too. The tenor, Carlo Cossutta, is a puzzle: how does a man who can sing the Hostias so sensitively, who participates in ensembles with such care and courtesy, come to allow himself such coarse bellowing, such crude scooping, in the Kyrie and Ingemisco? The bass, Robert Hale, was disappointing, hollow-voiced, and incapable of even a moment's aware and expressive singing.

Eight Songs for a Mad King

March 22, 1973

Like pornography, *Eight Songs for a Mad King* is exciting but not interesting. The Peter Maxwell Davies composition—a dramatic *scena* on texts by Randolph Stow and including words by George III—was the principal work on the [contemporary music ensemble] Collage program Sunday evening at Walnut Hill School, Natick. It made a terrific impression, and I was as bug-eyed and breathless as anybody there while it was going on. But ten minutes later, there was nothing. They might as well have played Glazunov.

Stow's words are strong, evocative, and simple enough so that they like being completed by music. They are the King's wandering monologue as he listens to his trained bullfinches, and they issue from the reciter's mouth as speech, as song over a range from bass into highest falsetto, as howls, as incoherent, hardly intelligible groans and gutturals. An ensemble of six players—flute and piccolo, clarinet, violin, cello, piano and harpsichord, percussion and birdcall devices and a didgeridoo (a hollow tube played by Australian aborigines)—provides the King with accompaniment, partners in dialogue, and objects of rage.

Sunday's performance had the costumed King in a spacious cage and the players in their informal civies just outside the bars so that they were both occupying and not occupying the same space—an effective solution to a vexing theatrical problem. *Eight Songs* is theater and it is strong stuff, violent, and with painful glimpses of sanity [in contrast] to the King's perceptions.

Davies is clever. He is more than that, but I would base my claim for him as one of the strongest composers of his generation (he was born 1934) on something other than the *Eight Songs*, probably *Revelation and Fall* (I don't yet know his opera, *Taverner*). He has used parody and allusion powerfully in *Eight Songs*, his scoring is imaginative, he has a superb sense of pace and of how to place a climax, he has a highly developed flair for ghastly humor, but musical thread and substance seems thin. And no transformation has taken place. It is as though he stopped at providing an objective correlative to the King's madness, an imitation of it, but offering no comment or illumination.

It is also an occasion for virtuoso performance, almost always an element central to Davies's music, and the Collage players—Paul Fried, Felix Viscuglia, Ronald Knudsen, Ronald Feldman, Christopher Kies, Frank Epstein—did superbly by it. As reciter they brought in that remarkable musician, Philip Kelsey, whom on other occasions I have heard accompany a song recital, sing bass solos in Bach's *Christmas Oratorio*, and conduct Schoenberg's *Pierrot lunaire*. Kelsey is not by nature a spectacular, indeed freaky virtuoso like William Person, for whom I believe Davies wrote the part, but skill, fantasy, intelligence, and a potent dramatic presence produced a stunning performance.

Partly because of accidents—a bad piano, an air-blower louder than Webern's cello-and-piano pieces, the failure of the electronic equipment properly to reproduce the taped part of Davidovsky's *Synchronisms* No. 2—the first half of the concert did not work especially well. I was sorry primarily about Donald Lybbert's *Leopardi Canti* for soprano, flute, viola, and bass clarinet, which come out of that lovely world of Dallapiccola's sensitive, elegantly sinuous, somewhat fragile *Greek Lyrics*. While not tremendously strong or original, Lybbert's songs do respond intently to Leopardi's poems, and in a beautiful performance they could cast a spell. Sunday they succumbed to the onslaught of insipid singing (in bad Italian) and poundingly brutal flute playing.

Lorin Maazel Impressive Conducting Boston Symphony

March 24, 1973

At his Boston Symphony concert yesterday afternoon, Lorin Maazel dealt impressively with the music and with the orchestra. The music was Beethoven's *Egmont* Overture and the G major Piano Concerto with Vladimir Ashkenazy, then Schumann's Symphony No. 2 in C major.

Structural intelligence, fascination with detail, a sense of musical character, rhythmic energy, quite consistently certain coolness and reserve, some distrust of spontaneity—those traits were present in all of Maazel's interpretations. It does not sound like the proper recipe for Schumann, but it worked. A conductor who can control the form and keep the sound transparent has a lot to give to Schumann. The sharply defined rhythms gave an attractive, athletic buoyancy to the quick movements, and though Maazel looked rather dispassionately at the wonderful Adagio, he spread it out with so compelling a sense of harmony and got the orchestra to phrase it so beautifully that he produced a statement of it that was very lovely in a different, highly refined way (I am grateful as well that Maazel did not fake the warmth he did not feel).

Egmont was clear, controlled, calm, powerful. The slow introduction was particularly eloquent, most so in its grand silences: it was as though the event was the attack of the silence rather than the end of the preceding chord, and thus the silences became expressive and exciting events instead of mere spaces between events.

Maazel also built an extraordinary context—witty, subtly suspenseful, almost startling in what it revealed by way of "new" orchestral detail—for Ashkenazy's playing of the concerto. It was a fine ensemble performance altogether, both partners being superb listeners. Yet, for all their sympathy and ease with each other, Maazel and Ashkenazy seemed to be after very different things with respect to Beethoven. Ashkenazy gave a reading that was totally without drama. If you can accept that as a given—and I admit to finding it hard—you get from him a marvelously played performance, transparent and unfailingly elegant in sound, and phrased with exquisite taste. He created an appealing sonorous object, but I thought he never got near the center of what Beethoven is about.

Here, too, the Boston Symphony played beautifully. Maazel's conducting is specific, active, and a shade idiosyncratic with its prevalence of forward movements (as opposed to up, down, and across). It works, and at the end of the concert the applause on stage was as warm as that from the auditorium.

Isaac Stern and Friends "Rehearse"

April 5, 1973

On learning that I planned to go to the "Isaac Stern and friends" chamber music concert at Merrimack College last Tuesday evening, Stern, smiling, said: "Oh, well, you're going on your own time in that case. It's a rehearsal. We assume no responsibility." The rehearsal is for tomorrow when the program will be given in Carnegie Hall. Stern's friends are violinist Alexander Schneider, violists Jaime Laredo and Nabuko Imai, cellist Jules Eskin, and pianists Ruth Laredo and Alexander Zakin. The music: Mozart's G minor Quintet, the Prokofiev Sonata in F minor, and Dvořák's Piano Quintet.

All right, but the concert cost Merrimack College a pretty penny (with a hike in the fee when it turned out Stern was bringing six friends instead of just Zakin, his regular pianist, as everyone originally supposed), and the college charged admission. A little assumption of responsibility would have been in order. Actually I took Stern's disclaimer for amiable cocktail party bull. Dumb me. On the evidence of the Mozart Tuesday night, Stern was serious. Had he chosen to be serious about Mozart and about his audience instead, that would have been a better choice.

I don't think the playing of the Mozart wants describing in detail. Stern played beautifully the B-flat major theme in the Adagio that descends stepwise in groups of two, using long, quick, light bow-strokes, so adding to sweetness a wonderful swing. Twice, then, for fifteen seconds each, he offered this reminder that he is a master violinist. I thought, too, that Laredo, because less strident, sounded better on viola than he ever has on violin. But such pleasures came in a context of rough, unblended, out-of-tune, and musically brutal sawing. No one was listening to anybody else in this show of what seemed like the sight-reading of five experienced but lifeless instrumentalists.

Between movements, Stern looked angrily at the audience whose coughing and unrest never ceased. That audience was not going to be quieted by Stern's disapproval; it would have been quieted by playing which, by its involvement and care, suggested that here was something to be taken seriously. The applause was warm, and that was a funny thing often about audiences, their double response, the respect for reputation and the sense of "this is Isaac Stern, so it must be good," which is expressed in applause, and the boredom with dead playing, expressed through coughing, program-rattling, and all the other familiar signs of non-concentration.

The "and friends" should have been read as a warning. A serious performance of a Mozart quintet, one with respect for the music and the audience, is first of all thoroughly rehearsed, and it is played by five musicians whose names appear on the program in the same size print. "And friends" is an appeal to voyeurism: Isaac Stern in bathrobe and slippers reading chamber music with his friends (who happen to be people like Schneider and the Laredos). It is nice for Stern to indulge in a little carefree musical rough-housing at home with his friends. As a public spectacle it is unseemly, and it is not an exhibition one ought to charge anybody money to see.

After Hearing *Lily*—Leon Kirchner Should Compose More Often

April 25, 1973

It always makes composers mad when you tell them you wish they could do more performing, yet some of them—Boulez, Britten, Henze, Kirchner, Schuller, for some examples (and of course what makes them madder than anything are certain bracketings of names)—make extraordinary contributions as performers. Perhaps I can slightly placate Leon Kirchner, who Monday night in Sanders Theatre conducted a concert of music by himself, Messiaen, Schoenberg, and Webern, by saying also that I wish he would compose more.

The concert was one in the series presented this season by the Fromm Foundation and the Harvard Music Department, and so classy an event was it that the stage crew included the new music director of the Cantata Signers, Philip Kelsey. The Kirchner piece was *Lily*, heard for the first time last month in New York, and eventually to be incorporated into *Henderson*, a long-in-the-works theater piece based on Saul Bellow's *Henderson, the Rain King*. Music for Orchestra, which Kirchner conducted with the Boston Symphony last season, is part of the *Henderson* project as well, and the two make quite a teaser.

The music in *Lily* is of two different sorts. What is heard at the beginning and end is associated with the jungle princess, Mtalba, the words in an African-sounding language made up by Kirchner, and it is exotic (beginning with a sinuous flute solo), sensuous, atmospheric, full of small surprises, full also of charm and humor. The middle, reached via a soliloquy of Henderson's spoken on tape ("When I think of my condition!"), belongs to Henderson's wife, Lily. This is less convincing. The text, also the composer's own, does not work—"Meet me in my orgone box with a double bourbon on the rocks" is just a bad couplet, not a funny one—and the faintly nightclub-y, tipsy music just misses, too: Kirchner hasn't the parodic knack of someone like Stanley Silverman, and that is what it would take really to bring the scene off.

Lily is scored for soprano, taped and slightly manipulated soprano and male speaker, diverse electronic noises, wind quintet, string trio, keyboards, and percussion, and it makes a good sound: rich, colorful, and, like the other musical gestures in the piece, defiantly not neat. The performance, mostly with Boston Symphony players and with the composer conducting from the piano, was superbly effective. Its star, in a very old-fashioned way, was the soprano, Diana Hoagland: she has a light lyric voice of exceptional loveliness and warmth, a way of finding line and continuity even in the most jagged note sequences, fine pitch, humor, poise, and presence.

Her singing of Webern's Four Songs, Op. 13, was also something special (and would be still better if she would get the German quite right), and Kirchner with his BSO players produced a strong and delicate frame. Messiaen's high-spirited, slightly crazy *Oiseaux éxotiques* was also on the program—it screams and it really feels like birds—and got an exciting performance, sensitive and breathtakingly virtuosic, with Peter Serkin as piano soloist and with Robert Becker on the important xylophone part. But to achieve in Schoenberg's Chamber Symphony textural clarity commensurate with Kirchner's intelligence about rhythm and pace would have taken more rehearsal than was available.

Zander's "Fifth" Was a Mind Bender

May 10, 1973

Mahler or Schoenberg or one of those wise men to whom quotations are attributed said that new pieces should be made in performance to sound like classics, and classics like new pieces. Last Friday in Jordan Hall, Benjamin Zander offered a striking realization of the second half of that maxim in the performance he conducted with the Boston Civic Symphony of the Beethoven Fifth.

Yes, of all things the Beethoven Fifth, that super-classic, so hard to have new ideas about, but so desperately in need. But Zander, both influenced and encouraged by that eternal revolutionary, Rudolf Kolisch, thoroughly reconsidered the Fifth and gave a performance almost totally divorced from tradition, but profoundly in touch with what is clearly to be read in Beethoven's score.

In one respect he went beyond the printed score, restoring Beethoven's original plan of going around the scherzo-Trio-scherzo cycle twice (as for example in the Fourth and Seventh symphonies) so that the final, drastically compressed version of the scherzo comes only after the Trio has been heard twice. That, combined with the [exposition repeat of the] finale, which most conductors don't bother with, makes enormously more sense—structurally and psychologically, the two, of course, being completely linked—of the third and fourth movements, particularly of the sudden reappearance of the former within the latter.

Given that, plus Zander's from-the-ground-up reconsiderations of tempi and articulation, his feeling for cohesiveness and for musical character, the Fifth was suddenly a new piece—very exciting, because so unmistakably a new and thoroughly characteristic piece by Beethoven. The performance was of near-reckless vitality, and the Civic Symphony, which, to be sure, has a lot of conservatory students among its members, impressively realized most of Zander's demands. It was an event that left me with very much to think about, concerning specifically the Beethoven Fifth but also more generally about how to think about music.

Putting Reviews in Their Place

June 21, 1973

The other day, looking for an address in the *Musical America Directory of the Performing Arts*, I came across a full-page advertisement for the pianist Rita Bouboulidi, and was startled to find the certification, "a great pianist," attributed to Michael Steinberg, *Boston Globe*. I had forgotten. Bouboulidi played the Schoenberg Concerto with Leinsdorf and the Boston Symphony in the 1967–68 season, and in my review I identified her as "a Greek pianist." That was a good season for misprints, a funny one turned "Greek" into "great," and the innocently false quotation lives in the Bouboulidi dossier along with things like "*une virtuose de grande classe*" from *Le Figaro*.

It got me thinking, though, and it occurred to me that artists' agents must be among the few people who care about keeping the review as an institution alive. It helps them sell, or they think it does. Other than that, who needs it? I submit that nobody does, really.

To be sure, reviews have a certain appeal. If you see an accident or a fire, you like to read about it in the paper next day—that makes it "real"; similarly for some people the experience of a concert or the opening of a play is completed only with the reading of the review. They also have some allure as gossip. What amazing or outrageous thing has Steinberg said about Steinberg this time or Schonberg about Schoenberg? We want sometimes to see who loses and who wins, who's in or who's out. Surely though, these trivial appetites are stilled at an inordinate expense of spirit.

I am not proposing an end to criticism. A reader of criticism, I love good talk about books, plays, films, dances, paintings, and also about music and its performance. Such "talk," whether it comes literally as talk with a friend immediately after the experience, or whether you read it in the newspaper a couple of days later or in the magazine a few weeks later, or in a book dozens or hundreds of years later, informs, delights, clarifies, and stimulates. It makes you think, it leaves you hearing and seeing more clearly than before. It needs no defense.

The review—the account of a specific event or object can be the occasion for that kind of happy disturbance. But it does not always work out that way—not even often. Some events simply, in Stanley Kauffmann's phrase, do not aspire to criticism. If the event is not stimulating, the critic will not respond by telling its story interestingly. What you get then is the dull account of who, what, when, where, and faster, louder, slower, softer, and who needs it? I don't want to write such a review nor read them.

There will be events—the first performance of the original version of *Don Carlos*, a new Carter quartet, a first or rare appearance by a famous performer—to which the most natural and practical response is the "morning-after" description and evaluation, in a word, a review. But we must now question the assumption traditional to American musical journalism, the assumption that every concert—or as many as space in the paper and availability of writers permit—is followed by a review.

I shall not go to fewer concerts, and there will not be less writing about music in the *Globe*. I do, however, want to find a new texture for these pages, a more interesting relationship between event and reaction, between Boston's musical life and the kind of talk about music here.

Boston's musical life: that means composers and compositions; performers and performances; money and management; teaching and learning; records, radio, and television; new ways of packaging and presenting music, and music in unexpected places; the many musical publics and their critics. It is a scene of extraordinary richness. The traditional commitment to the review as the chief journalistic and critical form has not only locked us into writing about many things that were not worth writing about, but has also locked us out of the possibility of doing justice to that richness.

Rag Spells Cash

July 9, 1973

The composers riding high on *Billboard*'s classical best-seller chart are Scott Joplin, Bach, and Verdi. Gunther Schuller's record with the New England

Conservatory Ragtime Ensemble of the *Red Back Bock* (Angel) has moved to the No. 1 spot, which means not only prestige for the Conservatory but financial good news in as much as Schuller is turning over his share of royalties to the still still-pressed, if no longer desperate, school. No. 2 is the record that began it all, Joshua Rifkin—he is on the Brandeis faculty—playing piano rags (Nonesuch), with the sequel Nonesuch issued soon after in the No. 3 position.

That kind of concentration at the top on one figure may be without precedent. It is not hard to explain. There is the lively charm of the music itself, which will do as sonorous wallpaper but which also repays listening, and which has now been brought to a whole new audience. Trendiness has something to do with it as well: to lots of us kneejerk liberal whites, Joplin passes as an inexpensive and easy ride into the world of Black Culture. A question, though, that might well be asked is what Joplin is doing on the "classical" chart anyway? I leave it unanswered, except to point out that it says something about labels. Indeed, one might also question the *West Side Story* excerpts (to be sure, they are called "symphonic dances," but that only means over-scored), the Stephen Foster songs, and the *Sea Hawk*, *Now Voyager*, and *The Strauss Family* albums, occupying slots on the list from ten (Foster) to twenty-eight (Strauss).

For years, Van Cliburn, either with Tchaikovsky or Chopin, was the most nearly permanent fixture on the chart. But in the week ending June 23, Cliburn was nowhere to be seen—the classical pianists were Aldo Ciccolini, with his album of all the Saint-Saëns concertos (Seraphim), and Maurizio Pollini playing the Chopin Etudes (Deutsche Grammophon)—and the triumphant, long-term best-seller was still, since late 1968, *Switched-on Bach*, the Carlos-Folkman Moog-synthesized electronic transcriptions (Columbia).

I hate the damn thing, not for its gaudily cute coloration, but for its mechanical, unyielding rhythm. I am sure, though, that much of Bach's present popularity with the student generation was kicked off by the switch-on. Popular Bach is still primarily cheerful, energetic Bach, and the *Brandenburg* Concertos, which represent that side of him both richly and fetchingly, are on the chart three times, with the Harnoncourt-Concentus Musicus album as No. 7 (Telefunken), a Nonesuch recording which I don't remember and which, probably 20 miles from the nearest Schwann catalogue, I can't identify as No. 16, and the Collegium Aureum version as No. 33 (RCA Victrola). The complete flute sonatas with Rampal are No. 23 (Odyssey).

The Verdi group is interesting. *Rigoletto*, No. 13, is no surprise—a popular work served with big names, Sutherland, Milnes, Pavarotti (London). But the others are *Giovanna d'Arco*, No. 8 (Angel), *Attila*, No. 14, and *I Lombardi*, No. 40 (both Philips). *Giovanna d'Arco* is helped by Caballé, Domingo, Milnes, and Levine, but public response to works almost no one in this country has seen in the theater is based on curiosity—this is neither a highly promoted fad nor standard cultural *lares and penates*. Records both create and meet the desire to know.

Solti is the most represented conductor on the list, with Mahler's Eighth and *Lied von der Erde*. Beethoven's Ninth, and Wagner's *Parsifal*, respectively Nos. 4, 25, 15, and 9 (all London). There is a lesson in promotion, and I note that Billboard once abbreviates his orchestra as "CHIC SYMPHONY." The movies still matter, *Elvira Madigan* replaced by *Clockwork Orange*, but *2001* is still with us. Astrology does, too, with two recordings of Holst's *Planets* listed, Mehta's No. 31 (London), and Steinberg's with the BSO, No. 35 (Deutsche Grammophon), which, by the way, was the orchestral bestseller of 1972. And, thank God, there are always the surprises, the Saint-Saëns concertos, a reissued Delius record by Beecham, No. 17 (Seraphim), and *Music from the Court of Ferdinand and Isabella*, No. 39 (Angel). Just ten of the forty are on low-price labels.

Klemperer Fame Forged in Pain

July 11, 1973

The year has taken a terrible toll among conductors. We have lost, at ages from 44 to 88, István Kertész, Hans Schmidt-Isserstedt, Fritz Mahler, Jascha Horenstein, Paul Kletzki, Karel Ančerl, and now, last Friday, Otto Klemperer.

Ančerl, Horenstein, and Klemperer meant a lot to me. Ančerl, a Czech, had survived grueling experiences in German camps, but had, in spite of limited physical stamina, a distinguished career that led him at last to the music directorship of the Toronto Symphony. Through bad luck with schedules, I heard just one of his several concerts at Tanglewood—the Boston Symphony held him in high regard—but the eloquent nobility of Gluck's *Iphigenia* Overture and the fervor, in fact the sheer excitement of the Dvořák Eighth, set standards for me. His was the rare gift of a style that was elegant and full-blooded at the same time.

Horenstein, too, I heard just once. I recall it with some shame because I really let it go by me. It was in Rome twenty years ago. The orchestra was the Radio Italiana, and it was my first and bewildering encounter with the Mahler Third, and, as I learned some years later, incredibly enough the premiere of Alban Berg's *Altenberg* Songs, whose intended first performance in Vienna, 1913, had been aborted by the rioting audience and the arrival of the police. Anyway, I got next to nothing out of it all, and was unimpressed by Horenstein. Later, though, I was very impressed indeed, particularly by his recordings of Mahler, whose music he conducted more scrupulously, more intelligently, and with more sense of identification with the language, than anyone else in my experience. He had, at the end of his life, a smallish but devoted, discriminating following, and for those happy few, he was one of the genuine musical heroes of our time.

Klemperer was a giant, inside and out, and when he died, two years after his retirement as music director of the New Philharmonia in London, he had reached beyond question, and like Furtwängler and Toscanini, the status of legend.

I heard him conduct the Philadelphia Orchestra in what I believe was one of only two concerts he led in New York in the last thirty years of his career (appearances by him were constantly announced, including plans for a *Tristan* at the Met, but illness or accident always prevented him from coming except for his Philadelphia engagements).

It was 1962 and the most frightening day of Kennedy's Cuban missile mess. We were depressed as hell, and the evening turned into perhaps the great demonstration to me in my lifetime of music as a power that heals. A victim of strokes and accidents, he entered with pain and difficulty, sat, took off his glasses and closed his eyes, conducted mostly with one hand, and produced performances of the *Pastoral* and the *Eroica* I shall not forget. He got that orchestra to play as beautifully as only it and one or two others could play, but with no trace of "The Philadelphia Sound": this was all bone, full of good marrow. The performances were slow, but they didn't feel slow, and I learned more that evening about rhythm and texture than in any other two hours of my life.

Younger, he had been a firebrand (his Vox recordings of the late '40s and early '50s give some sense of the pre-Nestorian Klemperer), an aggressive champion of new music, at the Kroll Opera in Berlin, a proponent of innovative staging, and for those reasons as well as for his Jewishness, object of the Nazis' particular hatred. They almost destroyed his career. For years, in Los Angeles, and just drifting, nothing went really right with him. He was partially paralyzed by his stroke, and the almost too-good-to-be-true story is that he stood for the first time when at a performance of *Don Giovanni* somewhere in Europe he cued in the statue music.

In London in the '50s he began what was virtually a new career, and his perception and skills were then richly documented on Angel Records. They are their own most persuasive champions. Of that one sight of Klemperer plain, now almost eleven years ago, I remember, even more than the immediate musical statement, the sense of a man who had been through the crucible. I bid him farewell with a sentence of Nietzsche's which I have sometimes applied to Beethoven: "He who has built his own Heaven has found the strength for it only in his own Hell."

Cleveland, Tokyo Quartets Are the Real Thing

August 5, 1973

ASPEN, CO—PITTSFIELD—The Germans have a word for it—"*Nachwuchs*." It means literally "aftergrowth," and it is what you have to have to ensure continuity, young musicians to step forward as older ones reduce their activities, retire, die. It's fun and exciting to watch the *Nachwuchs*, to see some of it assert itself as unmistakably the real thing (and there is always the startling moment of waking up to realize that the Juilliard and the Italiano are no longer young quartets, that even the Guarneri has been around for nine years, that Brendel, Eschenbach, and Watts are no longer new pianists, and so on).

As for the new quartets, about a week and a half ago I heard the Cleveland (Donald Weilerstein, Peter Salaff, Martha Strongin Katz, Paul Katz) at the Aspen Music Festival, and last Saturday at South Mountain, Pittsfield, the Tokyo (Koichiro Harada, Yoshiko Nakura, Kazuhide Isomura, Sadao Harada). Both are the real thing—spectacularly so.

The Cleveland I heard this time only in a single Haydn quartet, the D minor, Op. 76, No. 2, which came at the end of a most implausible assortment of pieces, beginning with Schumann's Andante and Variations for two pianos, two cellos, and horn, then continuing with the Berg Piano Sonata, an Albinoni Concerto for trumpet with three oboes and figured bass, and a Persichetti Serenade for trombone, viola, and cello. Now I ask you, is that a program, or is that two hours of music?

Anyway, we got to the Haydn like the experienced battler of smorgasbords who knows that acres of beans and macaroni salad obstruct his path to shrimp and beef. That's not a line of imagery I intend to continue, but I do want to say how much I liked their aggressively confident relationship with Haydn. It was big playing, loving, but not struck dumb by reverence, energetic to the point of rambunctiousness, but including among its possibilities a remarkable delicacy in the slow variation movement. On another day and in another mood I might have been put off by such a tumult of high spirits (and even that afternoon I wished Weilerstein, a superb violinist, had the stylistic discretion not to begin the restatement of the first theme with a harmonic on the high A), but as it was, I was nothing but delighted to discover four more people who really dig Haydn.

As a matter of fact, the Tokyo had me on their side before they played a note, just by programming a rare and wonderful Haydn, the F-sharp minor, Op. 50, No. 4. Tokyo Haydn was, in the event, more conventional than Cleveland Haydn, that is, smaller in scale, more consciously 18th-century and classical, though the operation within those choices was a demonstration of impressive intelligence and sensibility as well as of impeccable quartet-playing.

They went on to Bartók No. 6 and to Smetana's *From my life*. Superb Bartók, the most carefully detailed, the wittiest I have ever heard, and refreshingly refined and economical: they had discovered the Haydn in Bartók. Smetana was big, unbuttoned, impassioned, stylistically absolutely sure: when they bounced through those Pilsner and Budweiser polkas, it was like all the stories whose punchline is "Funny, you don't look Jewish." The Tokyo play in Jordan Hall for the BU Celebrity Series on Mozart's birthday, January 27: mark it on your calendar.

Orchestra Gave All Ozawa Asked

September 29, 1973

Yesterday afternoon, Seiji Ozawa conducted his first concert as music director of the Boston Symphony. His welcome at the beginning of the afternoon was distinctly friendly, with many in the audience standing to applaud him, but next time he starts out on a new job he might be well advised to choose a program with a loud ending and something less long than Berlioz's *Damnation of Faust.* When it ended, most of the audience was concerned only with getting out, and, indeed, ladies had been determinedly shuffling or striding toward the exits for the last three quarters of an hour.

Ozawa conducted *Damnation of Faust* at Tanglewood in 1971,[11] but it seems we have not had it in Boston since Munch did it in 1954. High time then, because it is so beautiful. Berlioz was ruthless and possessive with Goethe—as ruthless and possessive as Goethe had been with the Faust legend—but by legitimate authority: he knew and understood the poet, completely and profoundly. The man was equipped to deal with the irony of Mephistopheles, to see the mixed pain and pride behind Faust's aspirations, to know the abyss of Faust's and Marguerite's love for each other. The composer had the range and command of musical language: no one has gone beyond what he said in Marguerite's "D'amour l'ardente flamme" to the theme of love betrayed, and the writing of that took heart and brain and ear, all three.

I see that with a few reservations, particularly about cuts, I found Ozawa's 1971 performance "marvelous," which I admit astonishes me. I don't know which of us has changed, but I thought his work yesterday often rather flat and on the surface. He strikes me as a Berlioz conductor by fiat (partly that of Deutsche Grammophon, who plan to record the major works with him) or by act of will more than by affinity. With *Faust,* he was respectful and energetic, but not imaginative or responsive. He tended to neutralize Berlioz's many modifications of speed and volume, and, for example, in the postlude to Faust's "Merci, doux crepuscule!" he gave us, with the straight-ahead, purely "musical" playing of the meandering violin line, no suggestion of the touching picture of Faust walking quietly about Marguerite's room for the first time, examining it "with passionate curiosity."

[11] See review of August 24, 1971.

The singing of Stuart Burrows as Faust was unflawed pleasure. His tenor voice is virile, pliant, lyric (and yesterday it was "there" from the first note; he uses it with intelligence, ardor, and taste). On the other hand, getting Edith Mathis to sing Marguerite is less a believable response to the question of who can do it best (or well) than the decision of a record company to push one of its important properties. Marguerite wants to be a mezzo with ease and lightness at the top, or, failing that, a soprano with unusual intensity and character in her low notes. Mathis is an admirable artist and singer, but as Pamina or Ännchen or Sophie; here, miscast, she was pallid. The Mephistopheles, Donald McIntyre, had wit, rhythm, presence, and projection, but not the sensuous warmth that is needed when you get to "Voici des roses" (in his operatic life in Europe, he specializes in growly and declamatory parts). Thomas Paul was incisive and quick as Brander, but a bit hollow and unsure in pitch when he returned in the Epilogue as an Earthly Voice, Judith Dickinson then being his satisfactory Celestial counterpart.

The orchestra gave Ozawa all he asked for, and had he asked for more like all the *pianissimos* Berlioz wanted, they would no doubt have given him that, too; they were in admirable condition and high spirits.

Casals and His Playing—"Unique Synthesis of Material and Spiritual Beauty"

October 28, 1973

The quintessential Casals note is the first one he plays on his recording with Szell and the Czech Philharmonic of Dvořák's Cello Concerto. It bites. A college classmate, Louis Berger, himself later a cellist in the Boston Symphony, first showed me that note as something special, and he liked to contrast it with Piatigorsky's soft ooze at the entrance (which Dvořák marks *forte* and *risoluto*).

As Charles Rosen says in *The Classical Style*, "The most important fact about concerto form is that the audience waits for the soloist to enter, and when he stops playing they wait for him to begin again." Casals's electrifying gesture is addressed to that fact. It is the most magnificent, dramatic assertion of self, of presence, and I can imagine the tension building in Casals as he both lived through the opening tutti with the orchestra and waited for it to be over—there is a wonderful photograph of him from that recording session, pipe in mouth—then at last allowed to make that wonderful . . . but how can I convey that noise to you in print?

The sound of Casals's playing was as personal, and as electrifying, as the musical gestures. Somebody says "cello," and my first thoughts are "warm," "lush," "mud baths," "hot chocolate." But Casals's tone was not a bit like that. He made an incredibly compact, intense sound, bright and firm, glowing, hardly "bass-ic" at all. Even in its lowest register, it was never grumbly or wooly, but wonderfully centered and transparent.

He could be vehement, but he was incapable of being sentimental or cheap. That is one reason I especially love the record called *The Art of Pablo Casals* (RCA IM-2699). It consists of encore pieces—"The Swan," Hillemacher's *Gavotte tendre*, "The Evening Star" from *Tannhäuser*, the Berceuse from *Jocelyn*, and such things—recorded 1926–28. The playing is full [of] fun and warmth, with moments of breathtaking off-hand bravura (the figurations in Chopin's E-flat Nocturne!), but there is no condescension. Casals plays Rubinstein's Melody in F with the probity, the cleanness, the intensity, the simple eloquence, with which he played the sonatas of Beethoven and Brahms.

As he grew older, and as Casals the Institution seemed sometimes to eat up Casals the Musician, he grew more vehement. I was no admirer of the Institution. The stories in Corredor's *Conversations with Casals* and in Casals's own *Joys and Sorrows* are delightful, touching, and revealing, but the opinions are apt to be banal claptrap. There are experiencing, expanding personalities, and there are those that become more intense, distilled versions of what they always were. Casals was one of the latter, and in his later performances—the Marlboro recordings of Bach's *Brandenburg* Concertos being the extreme example—he seemed sometimes to be fighting with ever-increasing bluster and anxiousness a long-won battle—won by him—in the cause of the once dangerous heresy that Bach might be lively as well as learned.

Perhaps the tendency toward the emphatically didactic was present in his conducting always. It has been many years since I heard the recordings he conducted in the '20s and '30s of Beethoven symphonies and overtures and of the Brahms *Haydn* Variations in London and with his own Orquestra Pau Casals in Barcelona, but I recall that it was difficult to reconcile the weight of some of those performances with his fiery cello playing.

Among the recordings he made late in his life and as a conductor, the album of the last six Mozart symphonies, though uneven, is very much worth knowing, and so are the performances, bursting with brio, of Beethoven's Eighth and the Mendelssohn *Italian* (all Columbia).

An indispensable item is Columbia's five-record album called simply *Pablo Casals* because it brings back his early recordings of Beethoven's A major Sonata with Otto Schulhof, the Brahms F major with Horszowski, the quasi-Boccherini Concerto in B-flat,[12] also the wonderful performance from about 1950 of Schubert's C major Quintet with Stern, Schneider, Katims, and Tortelier, a group

[12] Here Steinberg references an 1895 arrangement by Friedrich Grützmacher (1832–1903) of several Boccherini cello concertos into a single, Romantic-style concerto

of encore pieces, and, not quite so interestingly, the Schumann Concerto with Ormandy, the pleasant Marlboro version of the Brahms *Haydn* Variations, and a record of talk.

Otherwise, the situation with the earlier recordings (it always is a shock to remember that the great Dvořák record with Szell preserves the playing of a man past 60) is bleak. Perhaps some of this material will now reappear on Seraphim. For now, not even the classic, pathbreaking recordings of Bach's cello suites can be had, nor can Schumann's D minor Trio with Cortot and Thibaud. The only record by that combination available on a domestic label is the one of Mendelssohn's D minor Trio, which is in Seraphim's three-record album called *Six Chamber Music Masterpieces* (the Casals-Kreisler-Bauer Trio never recorded at all). Beyond what I have already mentioned, you have to go to imports, available, as they say, in better stores.

Spanish Odeon has a five-record album with Haydn's G major Trio, Schubert's B-flat Trio, and the Beethoven *Archduke*, all with Cortot and Thibaud; four Beethoven cello sonatas with Horszowski or Schulhof (for me the most magic moment on any Casals record is his playing of the *pianissimo* arpeggios that decorate the piano's playing of the melody in the slow movement of Beethoven's D major Sonata, Op. 102, No. 2—this one with Horszowski, not the later Columbia with Serkin), and one of Beethoven's *Magic Flute* variation sets with Cortot. The Haydn and Schubert trios alone are available on a Dacapo single.

A three-record album, also Spanish Odeon, has the "Boccherini" Concerto and the disappointing recording of Elgar's Concerto, but it provides the only access to two of Casals's greatest performances, the Dvořák with Szell, and the Brahms Double Concerto with Thibaud as violinist and Cortot conducting.

Finally, an Italian Odeon album brings together the Haydn, Schubert, and Beethoven trios, the *Magic Flute* variations, plus the *Kreutzer* Sonata played by Thibaud and Cortot. I have not heard these Spanish and Italian pressings and so cannot speak for their quality, but the playing is a miracle, refreshing and shocking every time in what Furtwängler called its "unique synthesis of material and spiritual beauty."

Bernstein Winds Up a Brilliant Norton Lecture Series

November 25, 1973

How many public speakers can you think of who can get applause by announcing that tonight's lecture would be exceptionally long and who could hold an audience of 1,650 from 7:30 until 11:20? Even after you discount a fifteen-minute delay in starting, a fifteen-minute intermission, and a fifty-minute film of a performance of Stravinsky's *Oedipus Rex*, it leaves you two-and-a-half hours of lecture. Who would even try? Leonard Bernstein did it Tuesday at the sixth and last of the lectures he gave during October and November as Charles Eliot Norton Professor of Poetry at Harvard. From the beginning of the series on October 9, Bernstein has had a success rarely equaled in the academic world in recent years—if you measure success in terms of attention, laughter, damp eyes, and adoration.

His subject was—well, what was it really? The title of the lectures was *The Unanswered Question*, in homage and reference to Charles Ives's brief and powerfully evocative masterpiece. The question, Bernstein suggested, was "Whither music?," and the attempt to answer it would have to be preceded by a look at "Whence music?" He proposed as well to explore the viability of musico-linguistics (on the modes of psycholinguistics, socio-linguistics, etc.)—linguistics, he said, is mankind's "newest key to self-awareness"—to apply the principles of Noam Chomsky's transformational grammar to musical analysis.

An interesting, difficult plan, carried out only in small part, entertainingly, sloppily, and tendentiously. After the first two lectures, Chomsky was pretty well forgotten, except for a brief appearance in the third talk and one still briefer in the last. Indeed, it seemed often that the presiding spirit at Bernstein's quest for musical universals was Dr. Sigmund Spaeth, the late "Tune Detective" (*Oedipus Rex* and *Aida* share a four-note figure, *do-re-si-do*, and a pattern of descending appoggiaturas, and both works are about pity and power).

Those who know Bernstein's musical philosophy either from his previous words about music or from certain of his compositions like *Kaddish* and *Mass*[13] had no surprises coming: tonality is the necessary condition for a truly poetic music, Schoenberg is the Bad Guy and Stravinsky the Good (that is, until he began writing serial music, which was like "a general defecting to the enemy camp," though his death freed composers "to rediscover their innate sense of tonality").

What did the linguists think of it all? Chomsky, who describes his relation to music as "purely passive," had been "too busy" to hear the lectures. "I look forward to reading them, though," he added, suggesting I call his MIT colleague, Morris Halle, and Ray Jackendoff at Brandeis. Halle had heard only one lecture. He disclaimed musical competence—"it's as though you were asking me to comment about baseball"—but said he had "enjoyed the lecture very much," praised Bernstein's use of illustrations at the piano and of slides, and said that it was the first time he felt he "understood how twelve-tone music worked." He too, suggested I call Jackendoff, adding that he would "practically sight unseen endorse anything Ray has to say."

[13] See reviews of February 1, 1964, and September 9, 1971, respectively.

Jackendoff is a linguist highly regarded by his colleagues and also a musician, a clarinetist who is a member of the Brandeis Contemporary Players. He began: "The musicians say 'so what's new?' and the linguists think it's crazy, he doesn't understand. I can see both." But he can see more: "Bernstein has very, very good intuitions . . . but he's not putting it across effectively because he's groping. He doesn't know linguistic theory and so he can't always come up with the right examples."

He sees Bernstein "in an inchoate way" pointing in a direction where interesting questions might be asked, questions that could lead to a "more formalized system of analysis to capture out intuitions about how a piece works. Will we find substantive universals indicating something about music as a whole? Are there innate properties of human perception or cognition that music shares with other forms of information processing? To what extent do formal principles of music parallel those in language and poetry?"

Like many musicians, he regrets that Bernstein has addressed himself only to classical Western music. On serial music Jackendoff said: "It is the first that was made up rather than just happened, and in that sense it is qualitatively different from other music. That's a charitable interpretation of Bernstein. He seems to be saying that the success of serial pieces depends on falling back on old principles, that for success you have to work against the system."

When Jackendoff says "not effective," he is talking about specifically the musico-linguistic content of the lectures. Some of what Bernstein said about music was effective: for example, his analysis of Mozart's G minor Symphony, his characterization of aspects of Stravinsky's style, his highly subjective interpretation of the extramusical meaning of the Mahler Ninth. Throughout, there was plenty of enlivening detail. But all that existed in a context of superficiality, of evasion, confusion, distortion. I would, for instance, like Professor Halle to know that what he was given to "understand" about twelve-tone music included much that was misleading (there, I believe, on purpose in order to make polemic points) and some things that were simply not true. Bernstein's gifts as a teacher were repeatedly praised by the various Harvard academics who introduced his lectures; to praise him as a persuader would have been more apt. A praiseworthy teacher is not only good at putting it over: he is responsible about the probity and integrity of what he puts over. It interested me that, while Bernstein's musical oddities went unchallenged, he was hissed when he said equivalently questionable things about modern poetry.

That it worked in the way it did is not surprising. Bernstein's gifts of personality, voice, enthusiasm, warmth, articulateness, fluency, and humor, his facility at the piano, his adeptness with the teleprompter and with various visual aids, are well known. Hardly any teaching about music on a popular level approaches his in vitality. No professor comes to his class with such a battery of technical resources nor with the power that comes from thirty years as a public institution. That it was a spectacular, generous entertainment is not in question. That it was the cultural or intellectual event that some heavy breathers around Cambridge have hyped it into is enormously in doubt.

1974

Splendid Bruckner Seventh by Steinberg and BSO

January 5, 1974

There is a story that Handel, describing what it was like to compose the "Hallelujah!" chorus in *Messiah*, said, "I thought I saw the Heavens open and the great God Himself." The other composer the story always brings to mind is Bruckner, who has moments, particularly in the last three symphonies, whose radiant openness of sound and feeling partake of that kind of untroubled faith and exaltation.

It is a wonderful adventure in simplicity, really, Bruckner's way of composing music, that unsophisticated but almost always very sure laying end to end of great blocks, the generous sense of euphony that is so unselfconscious but so original at the same time. The simplicity was clearly revealed in William Steinberg's beautiful performance of the Seventh Symphony at yesterday afternoon's Boston Symphony concert.

Steinberg's way with Bruckner is musical rather than mystical (Jochum most convincingly presents the opposite view). Neither the hush nor the blaze is extreme, and there is no possibility ever of confusion with Mahler or any other passionately to-be-leaned-into music, certainly not Wagner, to whom this is a kind of elegiac love letter. This was all out of Haydn and Schubert, inevitably some Beethoven as well, and Steinberg played it very directly, economically, and with a most sure sense of destination.

Walking on and off the stage, he looked frail, and he conducted the scherzo and the finale up to the beginning of the coda sitting down. But the gestures and signals this time were ample and vigorous, and the orchestra responded with defined, nobly sonorous playing. They also applauded the conductor warmly at the end, as did the audience.

The Bruckner was the only work on the program, and that was good. Not that the Seventh is extremely long, but even so the difference of coming to it completely fresh was remarkable. The most important point, though, is that the Beethoven Ninth and the great Bruckner and Mahler symphonies want to stand by themselves, for that makes their performances feel more like a celebration or even a rite and not as part of an entertainment. That is their spirit: like it or not, they do absolutely resist that clap-trap about making concerts casual and friendly, and the Bruckner Seventh, particularly in a performance of such selflessness, concentration, intelligence, and command, makes a musical declaration that justifies its hugely ambitious stance.

Palestrina Recorded, at Last

January 6, 1974

Hans Pfitzner's *Palestrina* and Stravinsky's *The Rake's Progress* are the two 20th-century operas I love most. Many others I admire, enjoy, am interested in, even excited by, but with those two I live in a special way. An odd coupling they are, too: I doubt that Stravinsky ever saw or read *Palestrina* or that he would have found much sympathy for it if he had, while the neoclassical mask-wearing, games-playing *Rake* is the neatest packaging of everything Pfitzner hated. As for *Palestrina*, I am in good company: Fritz Busch, Bruno Walter, and Thomas Mann (who discusses it at length in that most troubling book, *Reflections of an Apolitical Man*) were among those for whom it was the greatest achievement in music theater after Wagner.

Pfitzner was born in 1869 and died in 1949. First he was a composer, but he was also a conductor who left some interesting recordings of standard repertory, an opera director and manager (the young Charles Munch was his concertmaster at Strasbourg), a savage but superbly intelligent polemicist whose prime target was the 20th century, a recklessly passionate German nationalist, a professional conservative, and a man with a good streak of curmudgeon and martyr in him. As a composer he was overshadowed always by his slightly older, more brilliant facile contemporary, Richard Strauss. In their later years, both felt exiled and isolated in a swiftly forward-moving world, and neither was adroit at making his way safely through the political scene of the '30s and '40s. Pfitzner was a sensitive song composer, and that is the side of him, if any, that American listeners are likely to know (his beautiful Eichendorff cycle with orchestra, *Von deutscher Seele*, is recorded by Deutsche Grammophon). He wrote, however, in many vocal and instrumental genres. In his work, as far as I know it, there are, beside the finest songs, two things that are by the most rigorous standards great masterpieces: one is the C-sharp minor String Quartet, Op. 36 (1925), and the other is *Palestrina*.

Palestrina had its premiere in Munich in 1917, Walter conducting, and with the wonderful Karl Erb in the title role. It has kept a place in the repertory in German-speaking countries (and none anywhere else), though it has definitely become a special-occasion and festival opera. Now, thanks again to Deutsche

Grammophon, there is at last a recording, curiously enough with a conductor, Rafael Kubelik, and a Palestrina, Nicolai Gedda, neither of whom has performed the work in the theater.

Pfitzner wrote his own text, and one could make a strong case that *Palestrina* is the finest of all composer-written libretti. The hero of what Pfitzner calls his "musical legend" is the 16th-century Roman composer of church music, seen through powerfully Romantic lenses. The Palestrina biography of Giuseppe Baini, published 1828, did much to spread the story that the composer wrote his *Pope Marcellus* Mass in order to dissuade those forces at the Council of Trent that sought to abolish all service music except Gregorian chant, and that by virtue of his success he became "the savior of music." The composition of the Mass and its acceptance by Pius IV are the principal "events" of *Palestrina*. Never mind the shakiness of Pfitzner's musicology: the legend is the ideal point of departure for the story Pfitzner so movingly tells of what it is to be a composer.

We see Palestrina first silent and in despair, for since his wife's death he has not composed and now can only reject the challenge of his friend, Cardinal Borromeo, to write a work for Trent. He is identified also as the isolated conservative whose gifted pupil, Silla, finding the polyphonic style tiresome old-hat, is about to take up with the avant-gardists in Florence. But the spirits of nine masters of earlier times appear to Palestrina (Josquin and Isaac are identified by name) and tell him that his earthly task is not yet done. The spirit of his wife appears also, and then angels, from whose dictation in one feverish night he writes the Mass. That is the first act, and the great glory of bells in which it ends was, by the way, the inspiration years later for the first pages of Mann's *Holy Sinner*.

In a grand stroke of dramatic genius, Pfitzner then gives us a session of the Trent Council, where Palestrina's music is only a political tool of small importance to the big world, and almost lost in the large issues of the day. Witty, merciless, entertaining, brilliantly presentational, this, with its maneuvers, pressures, temptations, and lubrications, its carnival of the shrewd and the naive, operators and victims, idealists and Realpolitiker, ranks with Büchner's *Danton's Death* as a powerful and authentic picture of politics in action. And timely: change names and costumes, and, right to the brutal police intervention, it could be Chicago 1968.

After tumult, the third act is very brief and very quiet, its subjects the composer's justification and the saving of church music. Far away, with the mandolins and tarantella rhythms, the crowd celebrates Palestrina: he sits alone in his house, communing with his wife's portrait and, improvising at the organ, with music.

The parallel with *Meistersinger* is clear, though Wagner brings the celebration on stage (and of course wants to have it both ways, to be Walther, the young radical, and Sachs, the great and wise conciliator). *Palestrina,* steeped like Wagner and like Mann (most poignantly the Mann of *Buddenbrooks*) in Schopenhauer, is a work of loneliness, pessimism, and "sympathy with death," which last phrase of Pfitzner's struck a deeply responsive chord in Mann, who in 1917 had just put aside temporarily the project that was to become *The Magic Mountain.*

"One lives and weeps because one has been born," says Palestrina's son, Ighino. Palestrina himself says, "the world's innermost is loneliness." To that I would add one other key idea: the blessedness of continuity, of tradition, of the seamless web of life and of music. Palestrina's last words are, "Now forge me, the last and newest stone on one of your thousand rings, oh God, and I will be of good cheer and at peace." The mandolins and the shouts of "*Evviva Palestrina*" are barely audible, and the orchestra, in Mann's phrase, "speaks the final word that was in the beginning, and which is mystery."

In music and dramaturgy, Pfitzner is indebted to Wagner in countless points, large and small, but he used Wagner as a model, not a source, much as Wagner used Beethoven, and thus emerges personal and free. *Palestrina* is huge in concept, ambition, range, and scale, but its sound is lean (Bernstein's pairing, in one of the Norton Lectures, of Pfitzner and Reger as writers of thick music was ignorant). Pfitzner modulates rapidly, but he does not partake of sensuous turn-of-the-century chromaticism. He characterizes vividly, and this intensely, richly inspired score is full of beauties I find overwhelming: the theme (almost the first to detach itself in the Prelude) associated with "the seamless web," the tender music of Ighino, the scene with the Masters, the great corona of themes from the actual *Pope Marcellus* Mass, the humors of the Council scene, every page of Act III, to name just some.

The performance, recorded with marvelous presence and clarity, is good (discussion of flaws of detail can well wait until there is competition). Those involved besides Kubelik, who is at his great best especially in the first and third acts, and the excellent Gedda, include, among many others, Dietrich Fischer-Dieskau, Karl Ridderbusch, Hermann Prey, Gerd Nienstedt, Helen Donath, and Brigitte Fassbaender.

Oliver Knussen Readies Symphony for Premiere by BSO

January 13, 1974

The first big stir in this country about Oliver Knussen, whose Symphony No. 3 will have its first performances with Michael Tilson Thomas conducting the Boston Symphony January 24, 25, and 26, occurred in 1968. He was 16, and with great assurance he conducted his Symphony No. 1 at a Carnegie Hall concert by the London Symphony Orchestra. He had made an even more dramatic debut in London some months earlier: the late István Kertész, then the LSO's music director, became ill, and the 15-year-old composer took over the performance. "Luckily Dad had given me some conducting lessons." "Dad" is Stuart Knussen, then president of the self-run LSO as well as its principal double bass, now an orchestra manager in Canada. Daniel Barenboim was in the audience in London, and when he was asked to take over the LSO's four New York concerts in place of the still sick Kertész, he in turn asked Oliver to come along and repeat his symphony.

The 21-year-old Knussen, rehearing the premiere on WGBH-FM a couple of weeks ago, was inclined to be uncharitable. "What a bloody awful conductor I was then," he said, hanging still worse epithets on the Symphony itself. "Articles in *Time* and all that, and other composers looking me over and saying 'so you're the one'—it's all something you really want to pull away from. By 1969, when my Concerto for Orchestra was done in London, I'd managed to alienate just about all the critics there and I got universally panned, which was the end of that stage of my prodigious career." On the other hand, he points out, the value of being able physically to hear what you write is beyond measure: "If I hadn't then heard what my music actually sounded like, I couldn't do what I'm doing now."

Knussen began piano lessons at five and composing "just before or just after. By the time I was 9, I'd composed about 200 pieces, all for piano, and each from ten to fifty seconds long." At 11, he went to study with John Lambert, a Nadia Boulanger pupil. His fellow students included two boys whom he now esteems particularly among the composers of his own generation, Simon Bainbridge and Jonathan Lloyd (the three were together again last summer as Composition Fellows at Tanglewood). Not long after, he began attending a special school for musicians in London, a turning point in that it provided the first regular opportunities to hear his own music.

When he was 13, a television film was made about the London Symphony, and it focused on Oliver's father as "the individual with the corporate identity," with footage of home life *chez* Knussen, "including this brat who played the piano all the time" (home was a farm not far from London, and Oliver's family includes a sister and a brother, both younger, the latter a bass player like his father). The producer of the film got the idea that someone should write a symphony about television, and Oliver got the commission, "which either had to go to someone in TV or else to the youngest composer in the world. The fee was a tape recorder." The work, which turned out a set of variations, was scheduled for performance by the London Symphony. Meanwhile the TV company folded, but the orchestra's and Kertész's continuing interest led eventually to the composition and performance of the First Symphony.

Other commissions followed—from Gervase de Peyer, then principal clarinet in the LSO, for the famous Melos Ensemble; from Britten and for the Aldeburgh Festival; from the Florida International Festival at Daytona Beach, where the LSO was in residence for a few summers in the middle '60s. Most of that Knussen sees as probably necessary experimenting, "jumping around from style to style." After the Florida piece, the Concerto for Orchestra, he wrote for smaller ensembles, including the Symphony No. 2, performed March 1972 in Jordan Hall by the New England Conservatory Symphony, Tibor Pusztai conducting, with Christine Noel Whittlesey as soprano soloist (the work sets texts by Georg Trakl and Sylvia Plath). "First my music was brassy, then the opposite, and in the Third Symphony the two extremes are now coming together."

I met Knussen in 1969 at Daytona Beach. He was no velvet-knickers, corkscrew-curls prodigy (he hadn't been at 15 either), but a soberly professional, hardworking young man, physically huge in a rather endearingly soft way, an avid and curious reader and listener, awesomely well-informed, particularly (but not only) about the music of the last fifty years. He is now a much-matured version of the same serious and humorous creature, in a state, the other evening, of controlled frenzy as he worked to put the finishing touches on the Third Symphony. Copyists in New York and Atlanta were at work on the orchestral parts, and his wife, a horn player he met at Tanglewood three years ago, was copying brass parts in the next room of their Brighton apartment [and was] called in from time to time for historical verification ("Sue, how many times have I seen [Tippett's] *The Knot Garden*?").

Knussen describes his new symphony, which takes about twenty minutes, as "a dramatic piece within formal confines. It has a dramatic plot and a symphonic shape—you'd always have some sense of 'now we're in the slow movement, now we're in the scherzo,' and so on. Actually it's a big tone poem about the death of Ophelia, and the shape of the whole thing is that of a big *diminuendo* and *rallentando*. At the same time, the intensity rises as the speed slackens, because it moves from being highly diversified to unified and concentrated, and so it comes out overall as simultaneous *crescendo* and *decrescendo*."

Sketches were begun about a year ago, and the symphony is the coming together of what started out as several separate projects. "I'd thought of doing a theater piece with costumed players like street musicians playing against an indecisive Musak-like sound, maybe from an orchestra in a pit, but I scrapped it—it was so indecisive, I just couldn't get down to it. Then I started a Cortège, which in fact survived as the beginning of the last movement. In June I composed two dances for chamber group. They're called *Ophelia Dances*—'dances' is a noun or a verb, just as you please—and what I kept hearing as their last chord was also the chord that began the Cortège. And then I saw that I needed something like the street musicians to set those pieces off, and that turned into a first movement in which lots of little instrumental groups keep standing out with musical gestures of very definite character." It evolved into three sections, Introduction and Masque; Ophelia Dances (slow movement and scherzo); Cortège.

"Particularly since Mahler," Knussen went on, "the word 'symphony' invokes all sorts of connotations, emotional and archetypal. Writing a symphony has become a form of quote. Rather than trying to shed off the past, ignoring that it's there, I'm taking account of it. I'm by nature and inherently and everything else eclectic, and it should be fun to hear it with the work of three non-eclectics" (the other composers on the program are Pierre Boulez, Morton Feldman, and Steve Reich).[1]

Works-in-Progress at Spectrum

January 26, 1974

Funny how having the men in the orchestra wear jackets didn't seem at all to diminish the audience's huge enjoyment of Thursday evening's Boston Symphony Spectrum Concert. For that matter, a title less trendy and less ugly than "Where We're At" might have done all right, too. Again on the plus side (in addition to the music and the performances): the tightness and helpfulness of Michael Tilson Thomas's spoken commentary. He shouldn't, however, in the enthusiasm of salesmanship, permit himself nonsense like the claim that Stravinsky was the first composer able to write "a wholly characteristic music" within serialism, or the contention that "most composers have abandoned choosing, in favor of some system" (this apropos Morton Feldman, offered as an exception).

First, *Éclat*, the 1964 portion of *Éclat/Multiples*, a large work-in-progress by Pierre Boulez. Explosions and subsidences, stillness, fifteen players making polished and hard sounds: the ghost of *Jeux* and of Debussy's sonatas, it is at once pretty and sapless.

The Symphony No. 3 by the 21-year-old British composer, Oliver Knussen, is a work-in-progress, too. It was to have had its world premiere at this weekend's concerts,[2] but because it is just short of finished, the first movement only was played. It proposes a lot of ideas that are developed and completed later: by itself, it is frustrating. And it ends at a point of masterfully calculated suspense, just the place from which to go on, but impossible as a termination. So evaluation wants to wait. There is nothing here of Boulezian concinnity: this is robust, lavish with notes, richly scored, mega-*Brandenburg* in texture. Knussen, who

[1] See next article.
[2] See previous article.

has the priceless gift of writing absorbing, enormously vital music, was warmly applauded by audience and orchestra.

To make up for the ten minutes of Knussen we didn't get, Thomas put in Stravinsky's sacred ballad of Abraham and Isaac, a chastely expressive, touching masterpiece of the composer's last years. David Evitts was the baritone soloist, exemplary in clarity of pitch and Hebrew diction, expression, and beauty of voice. He had performed it with Thomas at a Boston Philharmonia concert in October, and I admire Thomas for his decision to repeat it so soon and for a wider audience.

Morton Feldman's pieces are *pianissimo* and slow. Some are keeningly melodic, and a few are quite long. *Cello and Orchestra* (Jules Eskin, soloist) is all four. I tuned in and out of that rather attenuated experience, but at the same time I found those soft elegies and that discreet gorgeousness very lovely. So, evidently, did the audience, which gave the composer and the performers an exceptionally friendly reception.

If you enjoy discovering after a while that the blinker on the car in front of you at the stoplight is almost but not quite in phase with yours, if you like listening to the way the frogs and the crickets get it together and then drift apart again, Steve Reich's music is for you. It is about phasing, the pleasures of almost-monotony and of tiny changes. It is for the patient and the playful. Music for Mallet Instruments, Voices, and Organ (Joan Heller, Pamela Fraley, Patricia A. Miller, voices), suggesting Bali, the Supremes, and the lush Debussy of "Sirènes" [from *Nocturnes*], is a wonderful sensuous indulgence, but delights the head too—mine anyway.

Cleveland Performs Bruckner Fifth

February 8, 1974

If the snow had come twenty-four hours sooner, we might be waiting another fifteen years for the Bruckner Fifth Symphony, which, in fact, the Cleveland Orchestra did play in Symphony Hall Wednesday evening. The work has a meager performance history here: Prausnitz and the New England Conservatory Orchestra in 1965, Burgin and the Boston Symphony in 1959, Gericke and the BSO in 1901, and that's it. Leinsdorf and Steinberg both announced it and cancelled again.

Among the later Bruckner symphonies, the ones in which his personality emerges fully matured and recognizable, Nos. 5 and 6 are the odd men out. Both have something exploratory about them; neither exactly delivers the innocent, thunderous uplift. No. 5 is a frightening piece, very long, driving, scratchy in its polyphony. It doesn't begin with the typical Bruckner buzz, nor does it end in the usual organ roar. It is a grand, idiosyncratic, magniloquent symphony, and it was good actually to taste its sounds in live performance.

Not, though, that I found this interpretation really convincing. Lorin Maazel, now in his second season as music director of the Cleveland Orchestra, is one of the most gifted and experienced conductors, and also one of the most erratic. How to reconcile, for example, the beautiful Tchaikovsky recordings, the fiery Schumann Second with the BSO last season,[3] the superbly, elegantly controlled *Elektra* in Carnegie Hall on Monday, with the hectic, raucous *Missa solemnis* I heard in Cleveland last April, the stilted records of Bach, and the icy, arbitrary Bruckner on Wednesday.

The ice was in the persistently, monotonously hard-edged sonorities, in the unyielding rhythm (relieved only occasionally by exceedingly calculated-sounding flexibilities), in the *pianissimi* that lacked a sense of distance and of mystery, in the absence of serenity.

Maazel knows how to get an orchestra to play—though in doing so he peacocks rather much for my taste—and the Cleveland Orchestra made handsome sounds of an extrovertedly brilliant sort. Only the rough pounding of the kettledrums was a sound that does not belong in a first-rate orchestra, which the Cleveland clearly still is. The concert began with a chilly, polished, eventless performance of Mozart's Symphony No. 29 in A major.

Tippett's Symphony No. 3—Excitement of a Decade

February 16, 1974

Do I begin with a reading of my personal barometer, noting that in ten years of going to Boston Symphony concerts nothing has been so exciting as the first American performance yesterday afternoon of the Symphony No. 3 by Sir Michael Tippett? Yes, because I want it understood how special the occasion was, and how special the work that has been added to our musical landscape.

It is a big work, almost an hour, and divided in two equal parts. First, an outburst of energy, energy compressed, energy released, blasts of brass and percussion, rushing strings, the two characters set side by side without transition, each pairing longer than the previous one. Suddenly, it turns the corner and becomes a nocturne, windless sky at first, with flecks of wide-spaced or isolated high sound and much silence, then a deep, densely orchestral music out of earth or sea, then

3 See review of March 24, 1973.

the sky-music again, more fragmented than before, with remembrances of earth and sea. That is the first part.

Then fun and games, bravura juggling with five crazily disparate objects, stopped by a violent gesture of dismissal, an archetypal gesture first made in music about a century-and-a-half ago. What it is all about, what it is all for, is then set out in a series of blues: a song that looks back to childhood; a song of physical love, of bodies; the song of bodies that have gone wrong, and a song also of compassion, of milk and kisses; finally, the commitment to love.

No, the Beethoven Ninth cannot be escaped. Literally. The Tippett Third is by no means Adrian Leverkühn's[4] "taking back" of the Ninth, but it is perhaps a response to Adorno's statement that "after Auschwitz, it is no longer possible to write a poem." An optimist's response, an affirmation, but made out of the awareness that after Auschwitz we need an affirmation in a different key—less straight out—from the Schiller-Beethoven one.

It is music of large ambition, technically and spiritually. The spirit speaks powerfully because the technique is so well in hand—and, of course, because Tippett's maverick fantasy, daring, and originality, are as large and generous as his ambition. Also, the urgency of his address is overwhelming.

He can bewilder (yesterday, thanks to rehearsals and to an advance copy of the Philips recording, was my seventh hearing in a week, and that helps). He covers a vast expressive range. He writes the gentlest music and the most abrasive, the most transparent and the most piled up, and he jumps as startlingly from one to the other as he moves from his Stravinsky-sparked language (which hardly ever sounds like Stravinsky) to Beethoven to raucous blues-with-flugelhorn. The orchestral conception is brilliant, the harmonic perspective rich (what an ear for right notes!), and the prodigality of detail in all dimensions is a wonder on and on. It is music I love to listen to.

It is difficult, but there, too, Tippett is an optimist with faith that the world will provide orchestras like the London Symphony (for which the work was written) and the BSO (which plays it still better), conductors like Colin Davis, and singers like Heather Harper (stunningly translated from exquisite *Messiah* soprano to impassioned blues-wailer). The performance was marvelous, and, given it was Friday and that some of the ladies must have been taken aback by some of Tippett's poetry as by his music, the reception of all concerned, composer included, was warm.

[4] See review of February 11, 1973, for more on Adrian Leverkühn, the composer-protagonist of Thomas Mann's novel *Doctor Faustus*.

Callas—A Career in Four Stages

February 24, 1974

Wednesday evening, Maria Callas, at 50, and probably to no one's disagreement fifteen years or so past her vocal prime, will make her belated Boston debut at a Symphony Hall recital with the tenor Giuseppe di Stefano, now 52, and with Robert Sutherland as accompanist.

It would have been about 1950 that I first heard Callas's name. She had made her professional debut singing *La Gioconda* in Verona in 1947, and her first commercial recording—"Qui la voce sua soave" from Bellini's *I puritani*, and wonderful—dates from 1949.

That was the first of her records heard—in '51 or '52—and it was a shock. In one of the novels of Thomas Love Peacock, there is a conversation about opera in which it is said that the florid excursions in Bellini and Donizetti are not just indulgence of a lust for bravura, but work as expressive devices; they indicate, not an absence of feeling, but an excess of it. I had never understood what Peacock meant. The standard Lucia (Donizetti, after Scott's *The Bride of Lammermoor*) of those days was Lily Pons, pert, fluent, often in tune, a mite colorless, and guaranteed not to be expressive. The *Lucia* Mad Scene was something spectacular—including a high F!—that a soprano did with a flute obbligato, something easily and often made fun of, though enjoyable when well done. Pathos, expression, and emotion, however, were nowhere in it.

There was the shock. Callas, singing "Qui la voce," in seven minutes made clear what Peacock meant by associating coloratura and feeling, and, which was more important, she made clear what that whole school of early 19th-century Italian opera was all about. Callas vocalized "Qui la voce" as elegantly, as brilliantly, as anyone we had ever heard, but, investing the aria with the graceful melancholy and sensibility of the sort we knew from the finest Chopin-playing of Rachmaninoff and Cortot, she also made us understand that it was about something.

With the quiet despair of "Qui la voce" itself and with everything she put into her singing of its quicker second part, "Vien, diletto"—the gentle seductiveness, the sense of on-the-edge-of-heartbreak, the sheer virtuosity of, for example, the sequences of descending scales—Callas changed the operatic taste of the second half of the 20th century.

Bellini, except for *Norma*, was dead, and so was Donizetti, except for *Lucia* and a few of his comic operas. Now they are with us again—no one, but no one, in 1949 can have expected to see *Anna Bolena* in his lifetime—and, Callas having led the way, there were others to follow her example. Some of the most popular singers of our day have made their careers in Callas's repertory: Joan

Sutherland (encouraged by Callas, and once Clotilde to her Norma), Beverly Sills, Montserrat Caballé, to name just three.

This is not the territory in which Callas first established herself. At first it was heavier stuff, *Gioconda*, and the biggest Wagner roles, Isolde, Brünnhilde, and Kundry (all in Italian). She sang the standard Verdi and Puccini, while her revivals included neglected Verdi as well as grandiosely dramatic works of rather classical orientation like Cherubini's *Medea* and Spontini's *Vestale*.

Perhaps a chronology is helpful here. Maria Kalogeropoulos was born in New York on December 3, 1923, and at age 13 she was taken to study at the Athens Conservatory, returning only in 1945, having done some operatic work in Greece. (There is a record of a certain Nina Foresti, age 12, singing "Un bel dì" from *Madama Butterfly* on the Major Bowes Amateur Hour, and there are those who claim it to be early Callas, but its authenticity is doubtful. I have not heard it, but Richard Dyer says it "sounds like a little girl singing 'Un bel dì.' ")

That much is pre-history. The first stage of Callas's real career as a performer is from 1947 to 1953–54, when she was a superb musician, vocally at ease to the point of hedonism, and fat. Stage Two, which lasted until about 1958, had her deciding to lose weight so as to make her appearance more appropriate to her stage roles, and there emerged an astonishingly beautiful woman and a superlatively effective, intelligent actress (I have seen photographs from this period of Callas in *Traviata*, and they say more than almost anyone else's singing of the role in my experience). The vocal hedonism disappeared, though not the vocal control: she resisted all temptation to subordinate musical and dramatic interest to vocal ones. This was the time when all elements of her art were in perfect equipoise.

Stage Three started when her voice began to go, 1958–59. The top became unreliable, pinched, and wobbly, a problem to which she tried to respond by turning vocal defects into expressive advantages and by modifying her repertory. This chapter ended with her retirement from the stage in 1966. The current series of concerts with di Stefano, which began in Hamburg in October, is a comeback and the beginning of Stage Four. (A Hollywood gossip columnist reports that she is now due to make a pop record—the remark of a longtime Callas buff that the end of her recording of "Printemps qui commence" from *Samson et Dalila* suggests that she would make an interesting blues singer is well taken.)

The extramusical side of Callas's life has been lavishly publicized—her decades-long quarrel with her mother, her differences with Sir Rudolf Bing (though, in fact, legitimate artistic issues were involved), the process servers at O'Hare airport, the men—and no doubt some of those who have bought $25 tickets[5] will be there out of curiosity about this larger-than-life public personality

[5] Adjusting for inflation, the dollar figure amounts roughly to $170.75 in 2025.

and because they want to see the woman who preceded Jackie Kennedy on Aristotle Onassis's yacht.

For that matter, much of the musical discussion has been pitched in keys that obscure understanding. There have always been those who could not make their way through her later vocal difficulties to the extraordinary musical and dramatic statements she was making. Or how foolish it was to stir up a great Callas-or-Tebaldi rivalry, as though the amiable Tebaldi (who loved her mother), the possessor, briefly, of one of the most gorgeous soprano voices of the century, were remotely in a league with that complete artist, that only-once figure that Callas at her greatest has been.

That greatness, it was in a voice of uniquely flavorful timbre, with something mysterious in it that was both tart and veiled, that carried almost always a touch of melancholy (though her Rosina and her Carmen leave no doubts about the fullness of her humor); a watchful sensibility about words; exceptional energy of phrasing and rhythm as well as tensile strength of line; the quality Alfred Brendel summed up when he said she was almost the only performer he could think of who had never made an error of musical taste. As intelligent as she is intense and expressive, she had, when she still performed on the stage, a way of seeing things whole, so that she was as exciting between the great set numbers as in them (which must also be the reason her studio recordings are less completely satisfying than her theater performances). As for how much of that can shine through on Wednesday, we shall see and we must hope.[6]

Shifrin, Schuller Quartets Have Boston Premieres

February 26, 1974

What a lot of interesting string quartets have been written in this country in the last twenty-five years or so—Babbitt, Berger, Boykan, Carter, Crumb, Elston, Huss, Johnston, Kirchner, Layton, Perle, Piston, Rochberg, Schuller, Sessions, Shapey, Shifrin, Wolpe—to name just some of their composers. Sunday evening in Sanders Theatre at a concert sponsored by the Fromm Foundation and the Harvard Music Department, the excellent Composers Quartet (Matthew Raimondi, Anahid Ajemian, Jesse Levine, Michael Rudiakov) played two of these works.

One is quite new—Seymour Shifrin's Quartet No. 5, completed 1972. It is in three tightly cohesive movements, the first a conversation in quiet, delicate tones, eschewing what the composer has called the "crisis rhetoric" of normal sonata

[6] See review of February 28, 1974.

discourse; a slow movement that contrasts aphorisms, fine-spun and tranquil melody, and something chorale-like that speaks almost as though in quotation marks; and, after a crackling introduction, a dance finale.

It is risky, so much quiet, and it is not the *pianissimo* of Bartók or Berg or Ligeti which itself becomes drama, but the intimate, reticent discourse of a soft-spoken man. Energy and intensity are turned inward, and that is a problem I think the Composers Quartet has yet to solve: too much of what they did sounded like music of no intensity rather than music of contained intensity. Also rhythm will have to be steadier for the wit of the finale to come across (all those feet tapping vigorously but not together—it's disconcerting).

But the music itself is fine, risks and all. The sense of repose, the clarity and cleanness, the quiet humor, the elegantly curved melody—all that gives me great pleasure.

Gunther Schuller's Quartet No. 1 goes back to 1957, though it, too, was having its Boston premiere. It puts a driving, biting quick movement between two slow, quiet ones, and of the two slow movements, the first leans more toward atmosphere, the second toward rhetoric. You sense Schuller's love for Berg's *Lyric Suite* and the Bartók quartets.

He doesn't quite speak with a voice of his own, but the concentration and skill with which he speaks are impressive. This is a beautifully made work, one which holds the attention and which, I should imagine, is rewarding to play.

I enjoyed György Ligeti's Quartet No. 2 when the LaSalle played it at MIT some years ago.[7] This time it seemed empty and mannered. It is fun as a demonstration of the sounds a virtuoso quartet can make—and the demonstration is dazzlingly arranged—but it refuses to say anything.

The fire sirens did their best to outperform the quartet. Schuller's first movement was repeated because so much of it was lost in noise, and I imagine only fatigue and discouragement kept the players from doing the same thing with Ligeti's finale.

Callas Struggles in Hub, but Adds to Operatic Legend

February 28, 1974

"What are they applauding?," asked a lady after the Maria Callas concert in Symphony Hall last night. But many of us, to the end of our memories, will be put into ecstatic reminiscence in finding this evening again.[8]

7 See review of November 9, 1970.
8 See also the article "Callas—A Career in Four Stages," February 24, 1974.

It was not as expected. Callas had set up this tour of European and American cities, this painful comeback after over seven years' retirement—and she was almost 50 when she started again in Hamburg in October—as a series of joint recitals with the tenor Giuseppe di Stefano, singing few arias, mostly duets, and the reports, wherever they came from, told how much she relied on her partner to help get her through.

Now here was Boston, and di Stefano was ill. Callas had already had to postpone the New York recital—you can imagine the talk—but this time she determined to go on. To fill in for di Stefano, the Hurok office produced the Greek pianist, Vasso Devetzi, a clattery player, greatly handicapped by a box that brought shame to the name of Steinway, and who obliged with a Handel Chaconne, Schumann's *Papillons*, and the Chopin *Andante spianato* and *Grande Polonaise*.

"This was very important for me," Callas told the audience at the end. Often, as well, it was a struggle. Early in the evening, she sang "Suicidio" from *Gioconda*, "Vissi d'arte" from *Tosca*, and "Voi lo sapete" from *Cavalleria*, blandly accompanied by Robert Sutherland. Suddenly there would be notes, phrases, colors, words, rhythms, that sounded like the singing of Maria Callas. But they came in a context of struggle, of apprehension about where the next B was coming from and the desperate lunge when it was due, of careful, even canny maneuvering around what she couldn't manage, but which couldn't conceal the failures in her struggle.

She was scared. She told us so, at the beginning, and a few times after that. Her frankness and warmth were, to me, unexpected. Her beauty, the grand carriage, the boldness of that big mouth and big nose, the blaze in the large and dark eyes, it was a shock in its way, but still, it was something one knew about Callas. The openness, the genuineness were something else, and they were much of what turned the key of the ovation from admiration to affection.

After intermission, she took great risks: "Sola, perduta, abbandonata" [from *Manon Lescaut*], which she had never before sung in public, and the immensely difficult "Tu che le vanità" from *Don Carlo*. "This is a great test for me," she said before "Tu che le vanità," and she sang both with the moral support of a spiral notebook in which the words were printed in letters one-and-three-quarter inches high.

I wish I could know what she felt about the great test. High notes gave trouble still, but she found the intensity, the color, the word sense, the rhythmic life, which together with her nobility of taste, made her Callas. Sutherland played with more life, too, and those qualities were there in her one encore, "O mio babbino caro," a piece she rather overwhelms. She had come home on this evening that will be part of operatic legend, and I knew just why they, why we, were applauding.

Brendel—Full of Tension, Never Tense

March 11, 1974

A characteristic way in which the pianist Alfred Brendel describes a performance he has given and which to some degree satisfies is to say that it was "full of tension." Brendel's best playing, or even his good playing, is hard to describe, so non-idiosyncratic is it, and so inclined to draw attention to the music rather than itself. He played in Jordan Hall yesterday afternoon—the second-best-known of Haydn's E-flat sonatas (the one [Hob. XVI/49] with the minuet finale), Beethoven's Opus 126 Bagatelles and Opus 101 Sonata, and the Schumann Fantasy—and his own, sparingly afforded praise, "full of tension," came often to mind.

Full of tension, but never tense. Brendel's sense of the whole of a piece is extraordinary, as is his ability to lead you through it, to clarify it for you, making decisions and distinctions that beautifully distribute centers of gravity, points of repose, light and shade. It is worked out so perceptively and then projected so compellingly that he can make you feel how in the first movement of Schumann's Fantasy there is, in fact, no point of true repose until the C major chord of the last measure, only to show you that even that is temporary and that the true moment of arrival and release comes only with the last sound of the last movement. From the bass G that fires the whole work into life to that final sinking into C major it has all been one curve, the drawing and discharge of a single breath, fantastic and varied though the traversed landscape has been. He is the one, acting of course for the composer, who decides when to let go; that is what "full of tension" means.

The details are filled out clearly and simply. Brendel's playing, though it wants nothing in inwardness, is big, bold, highly presentational. It is rare for him to play passionately, but, as he showed in Schumann's first movement, his resources in that respect are enormous. Perhaps none of the great pianists since Schnabel (a personality of totally different stamp) has played with so much humor. Brendel responds particularly to Beethoven's wildest comedy, and his playing of the B minor Bagatelle and of the Opus 101 finale was somehow ferocious and gentle together, funny, and very human.

I didn't find my way into Opus 101 right away. It is an elusive, enigmatic sonata, and Brendel sat down and began it almost into the applause for the Bagatelles. It took the audience a while to settle, and I know I was not yet prepared to deal with that first movement, at once so beatific and so concentrated. But the rest of the concert went beautifully, the straightness and poised grace of the Haydn, the mercurial and gloriously scored Bagatelles, the exuberant, melancholy and mysterious Schumann.

Brendel's playing is more unbuttoned than when he first played at the Gardner ten years ago,[9] and free of the forced-sounding, larger-than-life quality it sometimes had in the later '60s. It has been evident from the beginning and through all stages of his development that Brendel was a musician and pianist of the first order; now, with the elements of his art so finely in equipoise, I hear with new clarity that he is a great one.

Bruckner's Second—First Time in Boston

March 29, 1974

Amazing that Bruckner's Second Symphony, 102 years old, had never had a performance here until Carlo Maria Giulini conducted it at last night's Boston Symphony concert. Common knowledge of the Bruckner symphonies begins with No. 4—the Third is beginning to make its way, but Nos. 2, 1, and 0 (sorry, no time to tell that story now) remain in the waiting room.

No. 2, which Giulini played in the much-tightened revision of 1877, is the first to sound and behave like a Bruckner symphony: it has the vibrating, endlessly upbeating beginning, the sudden unisons in *pianissimo*, the theme with pizzicato accompaniment, the silences to mark formal articulations, the characteristic filigree around the returns of the slow movement's main melody, and so on. (Also, alas, a tendency to lose nerve and concentration in the finale, something that is aggravated rather than helped by the drastic cuts made for the 1877 version.)

But its tone is not yet the hortatory, visionary one of the later and grander symphonies: Schubert is still close, and surprisingly, Mendelssohn. It is lyric—comfortable, one almost wants to say—and lovely in that vein, with a touching warmth of melody. Its great moment is the Andante, beautifully built and sustained, with dissonances that are gentle yet firm, and whose reticently intense poignancy seems to look forward to Elgar.

Giulini loves the sound of Bruckner's effortlessly, radiantly opulent scoring, and he takes pains realizing it. He also revels in the passion of individual phrases and gets them played with impressive intensity and feeling for shape. In other ways, I don't always find him convincing as a Bruckner conductor: he fidgets

[9] See review of February 17, 1964.

with the tempi, hurries across silences, and perhaps has not the long-range rhythmic structure quite clearly set in his mind. And apart from questions of interpretation, there were problems of execution, odd wrong notes, tentative horn solos, momentary failures of ensemble. With its many eloquent moments, it was a performance that didn't quite come off.

That was a pity, a disappointment, and a surprise, because the first half of the concert had great distinction. Giulini began with Webern's Passacaglia, Op. 1, which he articulated and formed with exemplary clarity, and in which he found the hidden Debussy, the enchanting, sensuous loveliness that escapes most conductors.

Then came the *Mathis der Maler* Symphony, and from whom else has one heard Hindemith sound so softly sumptuous, flexible, elevated in style? It was the softness of attack that was so remarkable (and startling at first)—that it was thoroughly on purpose was made clear, even dramatized, by the finale's big punctuating chords which came down like the guillotine. And what wonderful coherence to that finale. The first and second movements are already whole pieces in the opera from which the symphony is drawn, the third, however, is a fantasy about which it isn't always clear that Hindemith succeeded in making it whole. With Giulini, though, finding the just tempi and carefully husbanding energy, all for once was lucid and strong.

The Mirror of Music

April 7, 1974

NEW YORK—When the applause began after Elliott Carter's sonata, cellist Fred Sherry and pianist Ursula Oppens stood and, before anything else, waved to the composer to rise. Then they bowed and left the stage of the Hunter College Playhouse. And each of the three times they were recalled, their first gesture was towards Carter. It seems a small thing, but it is not, and it tells the essential story of Speculum Musicae, the contemporary music ensemble of which Oppens and Sherry are founding members. The name, "the mirror of music," is taken from an encyclopedic treatise written in the 14th century by a certain Jacob of Liège, who takes a notably conservative view of the music of his own day.

A dozen or so young New York musicians started the group in 1971. They jobbed around the city for a living, everything from hair-rinse commercials to B minor Masses, and some of them played in contemporary groups, too. They were all superb instrumentalists who liked contemporary music, felt involved in it, and spoke its languages with native fluency. They wanted a group of their own that embodied only their convictions about quality in composition and performance. Out of their late-night conversations grew Speculum.

Their allegiance is to what is somewhat snootily but accurately called "the responsible avant-garde," no cellists draped in Saranwrap, no neo-Dada, nothing of the "do anything you like but be sure to put my name on the program" school. If they have a house composer, it is probably Charles Wuorinen, who runs his own superb Group for Contemporary Music at the Manhattan School of Music and who has just written Speculum a piece called *Speculum Speculi*. And Speculum plays the 20th-century classics, Schoenberg, Stravinsky, Bartók, Webern, and so forth.

About quality of performance they have strong convictions as well. Ursula Oppens spoke of "our particular brand of insanity, which is actually a kind of extreme sobriety," and which has to do with the willingness to spend mad amounts of time in the cause of getting every last 64th-note exactly in place and finding for every *pp* its just slot between *p* and *ppp*. Their obsessiveness is healthily under control. Speculum's Hunter concert ended with Bartók's Sonata for Two Pianos and Percussion, with Peter Serkin joining Oppens, Richard Fitz, and Joseph Passaro. Rehearsals always ended in great states of tension, said Oppens, "but at the concert I decided we'd have fun."

The refinement and clarity that had come out of the hard rehearsals made the perfect base for the spontaneity and sense of fun which were added as the last and necessary ingredient. (There was a lovely moment a few hours earlier. I stopped by to pick up my tickets, and the Bartók crew was having one last pre-concert run-through. Two Hunter students, one M, one F, walked by just in time to hear the great roar of cymbals on the first page. "Dynamite! Bartók!" yelled the girl, who clamped her hand on her friend's arm and pulled him inside.)

The prospect of Bartók with Oppens and Serkin was what had first seduced me into going to the concert, but the whole event was enormously exciting. Carter's Cello Sonata went with more passion, fantasy, and sensuous beauty than in any other performance I have heard (it is my impression that among this virtuosic, sensitive, intelligent group, Oppens and Sherry stand out as extraordinary even among the extraordinary). And I was happy to hear again the *Notturno* written last year for Speculum by Donald Martino, who teaches at the New England Conservatory. There was an at-best so-so performance at Tanglewood, but even then, Martino's nocturnal theater of the soul had excited me with its drama, imagination, magical sound, and sureness of step: now, with Daniel Shulman conducting, I could really hear it.

Above all, I had an unpaid debt to Peter Lieberson's Concerto for Four Groups of Instruments, also written in 1973 for Speculum. It had been, let's say, destroyed at Tanglewood last summer, the victim, not of lack of talent on the part of players and conductor, but of inept organization, an unrealistic sense on the part of the schedule makers of what kind of preparation such a piece requires, a failure to calculate how a bad performance may be worse than no performance, and a grand-seigneurial attitude on the part of the powers that it is a privilege for a young composer like Lieberson to get his music butchered under such high auspices. Anyhow, I wanted to hear the piece, and hearing it confirmed what I had only been able to guess at before of the liveliness of Lieberson's mind and the fineness of his ear.

And now we have just had the absurd episode of a French pianist who came to America with lots of money to spend on publicity (well invested in one of New York's most aggressive and effective agents) and a plan to play four concerts of contemporary music. Having attracted incredible attention, she gave a recital at which, according to a witness on whose reliability I would stake my professional life, she got totally, bizarrely, wildly lost in some of the Schoenberg on her program, for which she was rewarded by rave reviews of truly exceptional passion by two of New York's more bubble-headed but influential critics, and tons of bookings for next season.[10]

Clearly, if you do what Speculum does, you do it for a reward other than that kind of Success. There is a growing audience for contemporary music, growing in numbers, growing considerably in sympathy, growing somewhat in discernment, and as a matter of fact, Speculum has success and plays a lot of concerts around the country. But you really do it because it has to be done, and doing it right is its own reward. And of course you show the composer to the audience before you take your own bows. They work with composers whenever they can and they like the way that makes them part of a living tradition. They know what's wanted, they have taste and skill and love, and each of their rightly placed 64ths and justly gauged *pianissimi* is a victory and a reassurance.

1925 *Rosenkavalier* Movie Seen for First Time in US

April 7, 1974

NEW HAVEN—*Der Rosenkavalier*, the last undisputed operatic hit, was first performed in 1911, and Hugo von Hofmannsthal, its librettist and a man with a considerable literary career of his own, soon had ideas about drawing from it a scenario for a film, to be accompanied, of course, by some sort of adaptation of Strauss's music. He assumed that people who knew the opera would be curious

[10] The pianist was Marie-Françoise Bucquet, who made her New York debut in October 1973. This incident was later reported in great detail in a *New York Times* article of October 19, 1975, by Jack Hiemenz, "The Tale of the Forgetful Pianist and the Red-Faced Critics."

to see the film, and he hoped that those who had seen the film at their neighborhood movie house would be seduced into going to the opera.

The project was realized in 1925. Von Hofmannsthal chose Robert Wiene as director, but was, in the event, dissatisfied with his "clumsy and awkward" work. He found it nearly impossible to interest Strauss in the plan, but eventually, and largely with the help of Otto Singer (arranger of the best-known concert version of *Rosenkavalier* waltzes) and Karl Alwin (conductor, pianist, husband of Elisabeth Schumann, the most famous *Rosenkavalier* Sophie), a score was produced. Most of the music comes from the opera, with the vocal lines incorporated in the orchestral texture, but there are several borrowings (some of Strauss's earlier military marches, a movement from his recent Couperin orchestrations in the *Tanz-Suite*, etc.), plus a newly composed march. Strauss even conducted the premiere at the Dresden Opera in January 1926 and, because the timing of the score was careless, there being constantly too much music or too little, he had great difficulty staying with the pictures.

There were a few more showings that year; then the producing company went bankrupt, and only one copy of the film survived in the Czechoslovak Film Archive, Prague. Decaying badly, it is also missing twenty minutes, Ochs's visit to the Marschallin, and the denouement. The Library of Congress has a set of orchestral parts (though no full score) and on March 29 in Woolsey Hall, the labors of the Viennese film archivists who made a new print, and of John Mauceri, the enterprising and able conductor of the Yale Symphony, and Glenn Most, a Yale graduate student, who between them did the reconstructing, editing, and translation of titles necessary for a performing version, led to the first showing in nearly forty-eight years—and the first in America ever—of the silent *Rosenkavalier* film with Strauss's music. Mauceri, much applauded, conducted the Yale Symphony.

Von Hofmannsthal cherished a fantasy that he and Strauss were da Ponte and Mozart *redivivi* (when *Die Frau ohne Schatten* was a work in progress, he referred to it as "our *Magic Flute*, as *Rosenkavalier* had been 'our *Figaro*' "). And now, he proceeded to rewrite the end of *Rosenkavalier* to make it like the end of *Figaro*. There is no Inn Scene; rather, Ochs's assignation with Mariandl takes place at a masked ball in the Marschallin's garden, and, as in *Figaro* Act IV, there is much slipping in and out of a pavilion by people not wearing their own clothes, and mistaken sometimes about one another's identities. The Field-Marshal, summoned by a letter from Valzacchi, arrives home in the middle of all this, expecting to catch his wife and Octavian *in flagrante*, but the person wearing the Marschallin's mask and cloak turns out to be Sophie. Then a reconciliation scene, and, as Octavian and Sophie go off to have their life together, the Marschallin ends up, good grief, in the arms of the Field-Marshal.

In the opera, the Field-Marshal doesn't appear at all, and is no more than the subject of three minutes' conversation in Act I (and of a single line in Act III). In the film, we see a lot of him. He is not about anything so frivolous as hunting bear and lynx in Croatian forests, but is engaged in the earnest business of trouncing the Prussians (hence all that extra military music), and when Valzacchi's letter comes, he quickly wins a battle before galloping to Vienna. As played by the delicate-featured Paul Hartmann, he is a figure of a certain gentle and affecting pathos.

Other differences: we see the Marschallin's convent upbringing in a flashback (to the music of her monologue); we get an extended view of Ochs's dilapidated castle and scruffy household as he prepares to go to Vienna; Octavian and Sophie first meet and are pleased with each other at a sort of large picnic, but they are not introduced then, so that their official meeting on the occasion of the Presentation of the Rose is a delightful and painful shock to both.

The film, in dim sepia, has Huguette Duflos of the Comédie-Française as the Marschallin, and she is dreadful—a flinger, clutcher, staggerer, leaner, and sniffer without beauty or allure. However, the foppish Jaque Catelain as a gleam-eyed and lecherous Octavian is still worse. Sophie, played by Elly Felicie Berger, is interesting in that she is the realization of the character von Hofmannsthal meant her to be, a pretty girl but ordinary, of the sort you meet by the dozen (a plan undone in the opera by the vivacious, ecstatic music Strauss wrote for her).

Ochs is done by Michael Bohnen, one of the most famous interpreters of the part in the opera (and the only singer involved in the film). He is gross, tallowy, wry, dirty, superbly rhythmic in the timing of his movements, and absolutely splendid. There is a fine performance, too, by Karl Forest as von Faninal, his dumpy figure, flapping arms, and creased face eloquently conveying the mixture of unease and vanity in him. The sets and costumes are by Alfred Roller, who designed the Dresden *Rosenkavalier* of 1911—I realize, typing this, that I have never seen his name so nakedly presented, without prefatory Dr. or Prof.—but his work doesn't come across with much effect.

In all, *Der Rosenkavalier* is by no means a good film in itself, but it adds a little to our knowledge of von Hofmannsthal and is a fascinating footnote to the Hofmannsthal-Strauss correspondence with its philosophizing about opera, its chronicle of mutual sympathy and antipathy, and of a disputatious, wonderfully productive relationship.

The same weekend offered the New England Chamber Opera Group's concert performances at the Longy School, Cambridge, of the scenes for the Marschallin, Octavian, and Sophie. To get my complaints quickly out of the way: having only the pretty music and none of the rough stuff gets to be a bore; Arthur Komar played the piano (with some backup work by Philip Morehead) like a scholar, a pianist, and a gentleman, where something more reckless and suggestive—the kind of "conductor's piano-playing" Felix Wolfes used to do so wonderfully—would have satisfied more; and Alfred Kalisch's English translation, which puts the most colorful and precise operatic text into stilted libretto-ese, is abominable.

But I loved hearing *Rosenkavalier* in a small room and as chamber music. (The film score, by the way, also exists in a version for under twenty players, and perhaps when copyright expires, some brave and sensitive musician can use that as the basis for a complete *Rosenkavalier* chamber-opera score.) And to hear Bethany Beardslee sing the Marschallin was wonderful. We are used to hearing Sieglindes and even Brünnhildes in the role (not to mention mezzos), but [Frieda] Hempel, the first Marschallin in Berlin and New York, was a Queen of the Night, and a light soprano works beautifully. Not all the attar of Persia could say "rose" as evocatively as did the subtle modulation of volume and tone that Beardslee gave to the G that carries the word "rose" in the last phrase of the first act. Her singing, exquisitely vocalized, aware, and of the greatest musical distinction, was an unforgettable demonstration of acting with the voice.

Tourist's Report from Kresge Auditorium

April 9, 1974

Ustad Ali Akbar Khan gave a concert on the sarod with the tabla player, Zakir Hussain, in Kresge Auditorium, MIT, Sunday evening. It was stupendous, and this is a tourist's report.

Khansahib, jowly, sits, all but motionless, eyes closed, the right foot in the pale yellow cotton sock marking the beat occasionally. At long intervals, a wan and fleeting smile escapes, and rather more often, he cuts his eyes over to his partner to indicate that the tuning of the tabla wants touching up. Hussain, probably not half Khansahib's 52 years, is slight and animated, at least from the waist up: the bare feet are still, but the torso moves back and forth or slowly round and round, he murmurs words of encouragement and approbation, exchanges knowing and delighted smiles with Susan Rosenblum, the tamboura accompanist, who sits behind the two men as she patiently does her simple and indispensable work, and his face—eyes wide and lower lip tensely thrust forward—expresses the intensity of his concentration. Johnson's baby powder is unforgoable: some is in a dish in which Hussain dips his hand between beats, but sometimes, cheflike, he shakes it from the can onto his drumheads.

First, Khansahib plays an evening raga composed by his father, the great and already legendary Dr. Allaudin Khan. It expresses, he says, devotion and pathos, and this is where I feel like a tourist: often I think I can follow the musical unfolding, but I have no sense for the ethos or what an 18th-century Western theorist would have called the affect of a particular piece, nor any for the distinction between a morning and an evening raga. To the extent that I attend to my reactions, I notice that I hear better as the evening goes on, which means partly that I stop hearing in Western terms: the harmonic narrowness of the music, all of which is anchored to a C-G drone, becomes an anchor instead of a bother, and I am no longer reminded of familiar pieces (as, for example, the melodic shape that dominates the first raga tends to recall the "Sunday Morning" interlude from *Peter Grimes*).

The most exciting music is in the second piece, a Gat, a set of variations lasting just short of an hour. The very skeleton of the theme is so beautiful in contour that people in the audience clap and sigh—altogether, the knowingness, the quickness and freedom of response of this audience is something any musician might envy. Invention, bravura, concentration, control of the far-flung line are stunning. I love the feeling for dialogue, the mutual edging on, the risk-taking, that sense of "now surely he's going to lose him," an expectation undone by the limitless wit of both players. Wherever Khansahib goes, Hussain responds with something that already contains the seed of the next variation (or even a touch of parody)—and unimaginable, the variety of sound to be made with two each of hands and drums. And of course to have such a partner is infinitely stimulating to Khansahib's audacity and compositional powers.

After intermission, light classical ragas, this too growing to fifty minutes, more medley-like in character, the wit residing in the transitions and in the emergences from transitions to stable points, all of it done with the utmost exuberance. There is much to be learned, about rhythm, about standards of virtuosity, about a music that makes its listeners laugh aloud with sheer joy.

Record Industry Starts a Korngold Revival

April 21, 1974

Who would have thought we would ever hear about Erich Wolfgang Korngold again? But sure enough, the record industry is promoting a Korngold revival. RCA, having ridden the nostalgia wave to success with *The Sea Hawk*, a record with passages from a dozen of Korngold's film scores, followed it up with a similar disc called *Elizabeth and Essex*. And now we are getting his concert works, too, *The Classic Erich Wolfgang Korngold*, as Angel calls its record of the Violin Concerto, the *Much Ado About Nothing* Suite, and the orchestral Theme and

Variations. RCA has also put out the large and ambitious Symphony in F-sharp, completed in 1950.

If you are of a certain age and have ever been to the movies, you have heard Korngold: he composed scores for *Anthony Adverse*, *Adventures of Robin Hood*, *Juarez*, *The Private Lives of Elizabeth and Essex*, *The Constant Nymph*, *Of Human Bondage* (the 1945 version with Eleanor Parker and Paul Henreid), *Escape Me Never*, and then some.

Born in Brno, the capital of Moravia, in 1897, he was five when the family moved to Vienna. His father, Julius Korngold, was Hanslick's successor on the *Neue Freie Presse*, and a famously pompous, obtuse, corrupt, and powerful music critic. The boy was the most fussed-over prodigy since Mozart. At 8, he had composed two fairy-tale cantatas. At 10, he wowed Mahler, who suggested he study with Schoenberg's teacher and brother-in-law, Alexander von Zemlinsky. At 13, he had a publisher, and his pantomime, *The Snowman*, was performed at the Vienna Opera. At 20, he conducted two of his one-acters at the Vienna Opera, works which had already had huge success in Munich the year before. Just before his 23rd birthday, *Die tote Stadt* (*The Dead City*) had simultaneous premieres in Cologne and Hamburg, and was taken up by eighty-three theaters in Europe and America. (Countless sopranos have sung and recorded Marietta's aria, "Glück, das mir verblieb," and the whole work will be revived by the New York City Opera next season.)

In 1934, Max Reinhardt, with whom he had collaborated on the *Fledermaus* adaptation that was later famous in America as *Rosalind*, called him to Hollywood to make Mendelssohn arrangements for a *Midsummer Night's Dream* movie. He went and he stayed. In 1947, feeling that the studios had eaten him up, he retired from films, but never succeeded in re-establishing himself as a "serious" composer. He died in 1957 with a second symphony and his sixth opera in the works.

The *Much Ado About Nothing* music, composed for a Viennese production in 1918, does the romantic things pleasantly and the humorous ones a bit heavily, and, with Willy Mattes conducting the Stuttgart Radio Orchestra in a slightly touched-up version (augmented strings, electronic organ for harmonium, etc.), it slightly anticipates Hollywood.

Apropos that sound, Korngold's movie music was admired not only for its "seriousness," for its suggestion of concert hall and opera house, but also, and more justly, for a standard of craft then by no means common in the studios. However, I just read by chance that his score for *Captain Blood* was orchestrated by Hugo Friedhofer (Oscar for *The Best Years of Our Lives*), and was most surprised to learn that Korngold, too, was fixed up by arrangers.

Goodness knows, though, Korngold could do that Hollywood sound himself, which is in fact one of the troubles with his later concert music. The Violin

Concerto, written 1947 for Heifetz, with admirable, Bachian thrift recycles themes from *Another Dawn*, *Juarez*, *Anthony Adverse*, and *The Prince and the Pauper*. Korngold had an easy melodic gift, though the tunes are never as memorable as they seem for a moment to promise, and the knitting together of the material is neat. But that sound, those moonlit and horse-y commonplaces, that sugary and omnipresent and disgusting harp—oy! Ulf Hoelscher plays it well, but Heifetz, whose monaural RCA recording with Wallenstein is still available, plays it better: he is more sure in the tricky shifts of register, and his cool style and faintly sleazy mannerisms suit better than Hoelscher's heart-on-sleeve. Hoelscher, playing it fervently as though it really meant something, exposes that it doesn't: Heifetz doesn't disturb its status as a well-made and pretty facsimile of real music.

The fifty-minute Symphony in F-sharp, handsomely done by Rudolf Kempe and the Munich Philharmonic, has patches of real music. The beginning—angry chords on plucked low strings with piano—is forceful, and the quiet recollection of that beginning provides the first movement with an effective ending. The Tarantella second movement is crude, but the soft, economically scored, harmonically shifty Trio fascinates. The Adagio begins beautifully, but the climaxes, reached by uninvolved churning, are stale and artificial: it's playacting at writing a great symphony. The finale is doggerel.

The best moments suggest those last big symphonies, Shostakovich, Toch, the Copland Third, and so on. But the indiscretions appall, the overscoring, the inability to leave anything out, the absent-hearted manufacturing of effects, the reckless all-but-quotations from Stravinsky's Symphony in Three Movements, Copland's *Appalachian Spring*, the Shostakovich Fifth, and *Der Rosenkavalier*. Somewhere he lost his way. The *Elizabeth and Essex* record includes the Cello Concerto Claude Rains composed and Paul Henreid played in *Deception* (it's never played from beginning to end in the movie, but this is a concert version Korngold made later). It is very short, conventional in its gestures, but by no means without interest or quality. The opening, though, with its tam-tam crash and series of brass chords, is not possibly the opening of a Cello Concerto in the real world: unconnected with what follows, it is the opening of a classical piece as Hollywood thought its public liked to imagine such a thing.

He no longer knew the difference. The story of Erich Wolfgang Korngold—and was there ever such an instance of "*Nomen est omen?*"—was, like his father's story, a story of corruption. It mattered more, because it was the corruption of a creative gift. Extraordinarily endowed and totally uncritical, he was, or became, a bad composer: all his models were good composers, but he, if to compose ultimately means to make things whole, was a bad composer.

The Power of Critics

April 21, 1974

Ms. Jan Curtis[11]
Groton

Dear Jan:
Your letter was not addressed to me, but to Robert Taylor, our arts editor, and it was not about a review of mine, but one of Richard Dyer's; just the same, I hope you won't mind my responding at least to one particular question you bring up, one that puzzles and troubles me.

You write as a singer who took an important part in the Associate Artist Opera [AAO] double bill of Vaughan Williams's *Riders to the Sea* and Walton's *The Bear* (and who was praised), and, though you don't altogether come into the open about it, as the wife of the conductor (who got drubbed). You write angrily, and you at least play with the idea of blaming the reviewer for what I infer was thin attendance at the repeat performance ("It is impossible to know how many people read Mr. Dyer's review on Saturday morning and decided to watch TV that night instead of seeing the AAO double bill"). Actually the review included a specific statement that the bill, for all of the writer's reservations about it, was something that should be seen, but it's the broader question of the critic's influence—or, if you like, the critic's power—that interests me here.

I really don't know how it works, this power and influence thing, and the more narrowly we define it—power and influence meaning power and influence to sell tickets or to discourage people from buying them—the more unclear it becomes. It is obvious that the drama critic of the *New York Times* has such power. It doesn't even matter a lot who the critic is: the power goes with the job. But even that operates within limits. If the critic writes with utmost enthusiasm about a new play by Beckett, he will still sell fewer tickets than with an only moderately friendly review of a new Neil Simon comedy. The intrinsic salability of the object has a lot to do with it.

In music, it's a different situation. You're not dealing with runs. At the Met, where one production may get eight or ten or a dozen showings during a season, the first reviews could make some difference but you know quite well that no

[11] Jan Curtis was a soprano who, with her husband, conductor Newton Wayland, performed in the Associate Artist Opera's double bill in February 1974. Both Curtis and Wayland wrote letters to the editor objecting to Richard Dyer's review; his was printed, hers was not. On May 5, the *Globe* published Wayland's lengthy rejoinder, also about the power of the critic—accusing Steinberg of an "overreaction to criticism of [his] colleague," and suggesting that he was warning performers in Boston "that if they express themselves in contradiction to [him] or [his] colleague they risk public reprisal. Steinberg's brief response, which followed Wayland's letter, asserted that "there is, in fact, no performer whom I only praise or only damn."

amount of enthusiastic reviewing could sell *Wozzeck*, *Elektra*, *Peter Grimes*, or *Pelléas*, and for that matter, that they're breaking down the doors to see things which have not pleased the critics. And don't forget that box office response to favorable reviews depends in part on the fact that some of the performances are weeks away so that prospective customers can make their plans at some leisure.

Now take the AAO double bill. Never mind the question of intrinsic worth: a pair of one-acters by Vaughan Williams and Walton is caviar to the general (ditto, I imagine, a pair of one-acters by [John Millington] Synge and Chekhov). This is not a town with a curious, adventure-hungry audience for opera, as Sarah Caldwell has found out to her cost, and even the Met when it has come here with something so slightly off the A(*ida*)-B(*ohème*)-C(*armen*) circuit as Strauss's *Ariadne auf Naxos*. And thank God for the perseverance of Caldwell, of Ernest Triplett at AAO, and of the others who have insisted that the opera repertory consists of something other than the basic A-B-C. Their audience is growing, but that's a slow process.

It is possible that an out-and-out paroxysm of enthusiasm by the first-string critic in Saturday's paper might have greatly jogged ticket sales for that evening, but, much as I'd like to believe it, I doubt it. Hunger to see two unknown operas (unknown to most people, and bearing the stigma of "modern" at that) cannot be stimulated between breakfast and supper, bang, just like that. Besides, an awful lot of people already have their Saturday evening committed by the time the paper comes in the morning. And what if the occasion was one for something less than complete enthusiasm? I can't argue this case with you because I didn't see the double bill, but it is possible that the production had some dramatic or musical faults. If that was so, the critic can't, for the sake of supporting a good cause, pretend to an enthusiasm he doesn't feel. I wish it were otherwise. I wish I could convey and spread my enthusiasms around so as instantly to produce huge audiences for all the composers and performers whose work delights or excites me.

Of course critics hope and like to persuade. We write to persuade, but even more to stimulate, to interest, to point out, to make people think. It's a lot like teaching, really, including that it takes time. If I have helped get anyone in Boston interested in the music of Elliott Carter or the piano playing of Russell Sherman, to cite two things about which I've been rather stubborn, it has not happened overnight with a single article.

Conversely, there have been composers and performers who have had great public success in spite of the persistent non-admiration of "influential," "powerful" critics.

I had a bizarre experience not long ago. A woman I have known fondly for more than twenty years suddenly turned on a colleague and me, saying it was the fault of the critics that state and Federal arts councils and subsidies had to be created because we were keeping people away from concerts. (The setting for the attack was odd—a concert of contemporary music, and the place was full.) Not so, and I would give you a variant of what I said to her. Here in Boston, there is, by my carefully considered estimate, about 40 percent more public musical activity than when I first began to write in the *Globe* ten years ago. You can't tell me the story that I or my colleagues are killing musical life here. You might, however, consider that competition for the attention and attendance of music-lovers has grown correspondingly tougher.

I wouldn't go far to defend music criticism as practiced in most newspapers and magazines; however, you do yourself, your company, your cause a disservice by implying that the blame for poor box office is to be laid at the door of "irresponsible, vicious, erroneous and biased" critics.

Best wishes, always,
Michael

Monteverdi and Words of Love at the Aston Magna Festival

June 18, 1974

GREAT BARRINGTON—When Stravinsky got to Heaven, the first of his colleagues he asked to see was Claudio Monteverdi, who had preceded him there by 328 years. (A transcript of their conversations will be published in a bilingual edition with an introduction by Giuseppe Verdi.) Unlike Stravinsky, Monteverdi had most often written of matters of the heart, but much of the time, the two masters had stood on common ground in their ingrained feeling for precision of expression and for elegance, the delicacy of harmonic sense, the centrality of rhythm in their thought and their limitless invention in that realm, their wit, and also the idea of the sheer fun of composing which their music evokes.

Sunday afternoon's concert at the Aston Magna Festival at St. James Episcopal Church here offered the luxury of a program almost entirely devoted to Monteverdi's secular vocal music, sometimes fiercely impassioned, sometimes humorous, sometimes the two together, and at times dazzlingly virtuosic as well. We heard the "Lettera amorosa" from the Seventh Book of Madrigals (wonderful how its formality heightens that intensity for which no phone-spoiled modern lover could find more appropriate and urgent language): "Eccomi pront'ai baci," which is about the nuisance of after-love teeth-marks; the famous and brilliant "Zefiro torna"; four of the vocal "Scherzi"; and that joyous rhapsody to golden-haired women, "Chiome d'oro."

Wonderful to experience this music live and in a room as intimate as the St. James Parish House, to find an audience capable of gasping—literally—at Monteverdi's turns of harmony (as when his letter-writer prepares to separate pen from the paper which he imagines will soon rest in his lady's bosom), and—best of all—to be offered such extraordinary performances. The Love Letter was ardently sung by the young baritone, Ronald Corrado, who most dramatically revealed its lascivious potential. Most of the assignments, though, went to two tenors, Charles Bressler, who is one of our great singers, and Robert White, who has become one of our very good ones. Though quite different—Bressler being always intense and inclined to work across what seems a huge range of colors and dynamics, White both more blunt and more suave—they work superbly in duet. Beautifully paced and responsive accompaniments were provided by a relay of harpsichordists (Raymond Erickson, Albert Fuller, James Richman) and viola da gamba players (Fortunato Arico, John Hsu), plus one bass player (Andrée Brière).

Each half of the program began with an instrumental piece of the period, a playful Sonata for two violins by Francesco Turini and a more serious and operatic pair of movements for violin by Dario Castello. Stanley Ritchie played the latter with fine understanding and some momentary technical difficulties caused by sopping weather, and in the Turini he was joined by Jaap Schroeder, who looks like a high-school chemistry teacher, and whose playing, unsurpassed in Baroque music, partakes of the best of the worlds of both angels and devils. The two were also fantastic in Monteverdi's "Chiome d'oro."

Koussevitzky—The Legend Still Lives

July 21, 1974

The impressive thing about Serge Koussevitzky is how persistently, at the 100th anniversary of his birth, and twenty-three years after his death, he remains alive. To the Boston Symphony players who were here before 1949 when he was reluctantly nudged into retirement, his memory is vivid indeed. For the older subscribers—except those whose recall goes all the way back to Karl Muck—Koussevitzky still sets the standard to which they hold his successors. For Charles Munch, his immediate successor, this was inevitable, but I remember that Erich Leinsdorf and William Steinberg were most often measured by the public, not against their immediate predecessors, but against Koussevitzky (and found wanting), and I remember, too, that one of the first remarks I heard from one of the Friday-afternoon ladies about Seiji Ozawa's appointment was that perhaps things would again be as exciting as with Koussevitzky. (On another level: when, some years ago, one of the most eminent of living conductors walked onto the Symphony Hall stage for the first time, I heard a lady say, "I think we should send him to Dr. Koussevitzky's tailor.")

Of course there is nothing like longevity—not to mention death—to turn a conductor into a great conductor. Koussevitzky's place in musical hagiology is secure, but we forget that during his lifetime, and most especially in his early Boston years—it was 1924 that he came here—his musicianship and his technique were under continual attack.

Indeed, he was in all respects a controversial man. A fabled virtuoso on the double bass, he came to conducting fairly late and under circumstances, first in Russia and later in Paris, that made it possible for him to learn on the job at leisure. In short, he had money, which he had married. But his experience with, for example, the orchestra with which he made his tours up and down the Volga from 1910 to 1914, or with the often brilliant Concerts Koussevitzky in Paris after the 1914 war, did not prepare him for the demands—repertory to be learned, efficient technical routine for preparing it—made by the music directorship of a major American orchestra (demands which in 1924 were mild compared to those of a half-century later).

His inadequacies were noticed and pointed out. Reading Moses Smith's biography,[12] one is impressed by the strength of will that kept Koussevitzky here, determined to learn and to grow equal to his job when many easier ways out were open to him. Characteristically, he tried to have the book suppressed at its publication in 1947.

He disliked having the story of his unconventional and incomplete training told, and he was distressed to have anything of poverty and Jewishness as elements in his background, and angry to have the long shoved-under-the-rug story of his brief first marriage to a ballet dancer brought into the open for the first time.

No, he did not take kindly to *lèse-majesté*, and he took his person hardly less seriously than his art. My favorite Koussevitzky story—and I can't think of another conductor so garlanded with anecdote—is the one of his reply to the lady who came to the green room (he called it "the artistical room") and gushed, "Dr. Koussevitzky, to me you are God." "Madame," he replied, "I know my responsibilities."

But it is finally in the personality with its gigantic will and sense of mission that one must look for the key to Koussevitzky's greatness. It is not in his craft, though he learned very much about orchestras—in fact, given that he was 50 when he came to Boston, his capacity and energy for learning were astonishing. And at its

[12] Moses Smith, *Koussevitzky* (New York: Allen, Towne & Heath, 1947).

best, in repertory congenial as well as familiar to Koussevitzky, the playing of the Boston Symphony in these years was fabulous in brilliance and finish.

It is surely not for his musicianship, for his interpretive powers, that Koussevitzky is cherished and remembered. Passion and energy he had in plenty, and he could command unparalleled elegance (has he rivals in Mendelssohn's *Italian* or Prokofiev's *Classical* symphonies?). But he was not a searching, cultured, deeply intelligent musician, and his performances of classic and romantic repertoire suffered often from awkward discontinuities, clumsy transitions, detail emphasized at the expense of context and line.

He was never free from a central uncertainty about pace, a story told in its simplest form by the impossibly slow "Star-Spangled Banners" that began his wartime concerts. One goes to his commercial recordings—few are available now, and RCA, considering how much money he earned for them, has not treated him generously—and to tapes of his Boston Symphony broadcasts to enjoy the drive and excitement of some of the performances, the finesse of the playing, to find out or to be reminded what he was like, but rarely to discover how a composition goes (as we do indeed go back to the recordings of such colleagues as Toscanini, Furtwängler, Klemperer, Walter, Beecham, and perhaps even Mengelberg).

But Koussevitzky believed in the vitality, the immediacy, the power of constant renewal of the musical experience. For twenty-five years, the Boston Symphony concerts were an adventure, most so to those who attended regularly and for whom the lapses were absorbed in a setting of long-range excitement. Aside from Prokofiev, Copland, Piston, the young William Schuman, the catalogue of the new music Koussevitzky championed does not bear close scrutiny, but when he played modern works, most often he did communicate his sense of their importance (even when questionable), his commitment. Even when the interpretations suffered from the same liabilities as his readings of standard repertory, new pieces were almost always played as though they mattered. It was an act, not of duty, but of love, and that is something composers remember gratefully.

His real monument is 120 miles from here, at Tanglewood. It seems so obvious thirty-four years after he showed us the way, but still, Koussevitzky was the first to see that an orchestra was more than a collection of players who gave concerts regularly, that it could be the nucleus of a musical university, the embodiment—literally—of standards of excellence. He saw and he insisted. His vision, his fantasy, his sense that the world needs music and needs musicians, inform the life of every composer and every performer to have passed through that much-imitated and still unique institution, the Berkshire Music Center.

It is a happy monument. An orchestra, after all, is quickly changeable, perishable, and cannot make a lasting memorial. It is a happy thing, too, that

Koussevitzky's birthday falls in summer, on July 26, when the monument is alive all around him. Many of the Koussevitzky stories revolve about his English, whose obscurity was barely touched by twenty-seven years' residence in Jamaica Plain, Brookline, and Lenox. He was proud, though, of the citizenship he acquired, and few citizens have made so grand a gift to their country. Dedicated, vain, stubborn, full of paradox and enigma, aggressively alive, he gives us much to ponder and to celebrate this Friday.

A Memorable Tribute to Koussevitzky at Tanglewood

July 29, 1974

LENOX—Friday was Serge Koussevitzky Centennial Day in the Commonwealth.[13] Gov. Francis W. Sargent so proclaimed it from the Tanglewood stage at 9:42 p.m., Olga Koussevitzky, the conductor's widow, standing beside him. The governor's speech began, I swear, "For me, my wife Jessie, and I . . . " and the proclamation summarized Koussevitzky's career by saying that he rose to fame "first as a virtuoso on the double bass, then by joining the Boston Symphony Orchestra," which, even by Bostonian standards, is a parochial way of telling the story.

The ceremony came just before the Boston Symphony concert which wound up the marathon observation of the 100th birthday of the man who was the orchestra's music director from 1924 to 1949 and, in 1940, the founder of the Berkshire Music Center. Four orchestras and five conductors took part in a celebration arranged with nice feeling for sense and symbol.

Koussevitzky's concern for the training of the young was reflected in the participation of the Boston University Young Artists Orchestra, the World Youth Orchestra, and the Berkshire Music Center Orchestra. The conductors were Lawrence Smith, a Berkshire Music Center alumnus; Leonard Bernstein, the most famous of Koussevitzky's pupils, and the man he hoped would be chosen to succeed him at the Boston Symphony; Gunther Schuller, artistic co-director of Tanglewood; Aaron Copland, the finest and most eminent of the American composers in whom he believed and whom he championed; and Seiji Ozawa, a student and Koussevitzky Prize-winner at Tanglewood nine years after the doctor's death and his fourth successor as Boston Symphony director.

The repertory for the series of concerts, which ran from 2:30 until a little after 11 p.m., included among other things, Prokofiev's Fifth Symphony, introduced to America by Koussevitzky, and written on manuscript paper supplied to the

[13] See also previous article.

wartime-shortage-stricken composer on Koussevitzky's standing order to a Boston music store; the *American Festival* Overture by William Schuman, another of the young Americans whom Koussevitzky was the first to recognize; the *Elegy to My Friend Serge Koussevitzky* by Howard Hanson; Schoenberg's *Survivor from Warsaw*, a Koussevitzky Foundation commission (though the composer, it must be said, despised the conductor); Stravinsky's *Symphony of Psalms*, a Boston Symphony 50th anniversary commission; and Beethoven's Ninth Symphony, the work which meant more to Koussevitzky than any other.

The Koussevitzky presence continued beyond Friday. Saturday afternoon, Bernstein, Copland, and Richard Burgin, Koussevitzky's concertmaster and associate conductor, discussed "The Koussevitzky Heritage." Eugene Ormandy's program with the Boston Symphony that evening consisted of three Koussevitzky specialties, Roy Harris's Third Symphony, another of his American passions, Debussy's *La Mer*, of which his recording reigned supreme for years, and Bartók's Concerto for Orchestra, which he commissioned and was the first to conduct. Sunday's concert, before a change of conductors (from Bernard Haitink to Eugen Jochum) brought about a change of program, was to have culminated in one of the great Koussevitzky pieces, the Sibelius Second Symphony. Ironically, much of this, certainly including the Beethoven, Prokofiev, and Sibelius, is repertory no other conductor would have been allowed to touch in Boston or Tanglewood while Koussevitzky was alive.

It is possible to touch only on highlights. No question that the day's great turn-on was the playing of Schuman's Overture and of the Berlioz *Fantastique* by the World Youth Orchestra under Bernstein. This orchestra, whose members are between 16 and 23 and who come from more countries than anyone seemed able to count, is part of the international organization, Jeunesses Musicales. It is newly assembled each summer and spends a couple of months working with established conductors (this year, Ozawa and Michael Tilson Thomas as well as Bernstein).

The vitality, precision, and overall brilliance of the playing were something incredible, and that was as true in Schuman's quiet fugue and in Berlioz's delicate waltz as in the all-stops-out bits. In a fully matured orchestra, percussion and heavy brass are a touch more bridled, and woodwind solos usually unfold with more personality; otherwise, this was orchestral execution of world class. It raised the roof and so did the audience, and no wonder. Bernstein's way with the music was here and there overwrought, but his work with student players is always moving for its sense of commitment and superb competence.

The summit of musical distinction in that long day was attained by Gunther Schuller, the Berkshire Music Center Orchestra, and John Oliver's Tanglewood Festival Chorus in Stravinsky's *Symphony of Psalms*. This performance was ideally intelligent, concentrated, and pure in heart (translated: exact, loving, not self-regarding). Audiences, who so happily stand for Handel's "Hallelujah!," might well fall to their knees for the passage beginning "*Laudate eum in timpanis.*" Stravinsky said this music should sound as though it came from the sky: Friday it did.

The most touching moment: the ovation—clapping and cheering in the hall, thunder on the stage—which greeted Aaron Copland when he came on stage to conduct his lovely *Quiet City*.

And there were disappointments, too: Schoenberg's *Survivor*, in which Schuller and the BMC Orchestra did sharply, admirably detailed work, but in which the chorus was ludicrously and fatally too small, and whose narrator, Vera Zorina, being both refined and stagy, was in the wrong emotional key. Also, the Beethoven Ninth under Ozawa, an interpretation that refused to come awake until the finale, and which even then was not so much animated by intelligence as rudely galvanized. But then, Koussevitzky never understood much about the Ninth, either. In all, it added up to a lively and memorable party.

Schoenberg—A Passionate Intensity from the Heart

September 22, 1974

Schoenberg's music is difficult. Not because it is dissonant (when it is): Bartók out-seconds and out-sevenths and -ninths him. Nor because it has left tonality (when it has): Berg, and even much of Webern, have posed less severe problems. Schoenberg's music is difficult because, or rather when, it is exceedingly rich and dense, and when it avoids easy-to-grasp symmetry.

The difficulties of some new music dissolve with the years. It is hard to see now why Richard Strauss was a problem (except where, especially in the operas, he presents genuine incoherence). Brahms has become familiar—not just his idiom in general, but so many of the specific works themselves—but a rigorously attentive listener can go to such works as the C major and C minor trios with their condensations and ellipses, or to the C minor Piano Quartet, and discover why he was thought difficult. But Beethoven: each time I hear or play the fifth variation in the finale of the Piano Sonata, Op. 109, and get caught up in that harmonic whirlwind of its seventh and eighth measures, I find it difficult. I always shall, furthermore, and that goes as well for passages in the *Hammerklavier* Sonata, the *Diabelli* Variations, and some of the last quartets. As for Bach, does anyone find the first chorus of Cantata No. 101 easy?

Such music is permanently difficult because events suddenly hit us more rapidly than context has led us to expect (even on the second hearing or the 200th) or because the next event itself is not one you could anticipate. That is the kind of music Schoenberg liked to write.

Last Sunday I quoted the letter in which he said that he longed for nothing more intensely "than to be taken for a better sort of Tchaikovsky." He meant that he wanted to be judged and accepted as a musician and as an inventor of themes and melodies (not "as a modern dissonant twelve-note experimenter"), but in mentioning Tchaikovsky he was ironic. Tchaikovsky he despised—not for his sentiment, but for his perpetual two-plus-two. And Schoenberg, sure as he was of his own worth, had the deepest reverence for those he regarded as his masters, and so he was too modest to express a hope that comes much nearer the mark, stylistically and historically, and that is to be taken for another sort of Brahms.

Schoenberg's most stimulating essay in criticism and analysis is called "Brahms the Progressive" (in *Style and Idea*) and it shows how in rhythm and phrase structure, conservative Brahms was bolder than progressive Wagner. The unspoken point is that Brahms, the master of ellipsis, rhythmic surprise, and flexibility, was a crucial model for him—as Mozart and Beethoven were for the same reasons.

But Schoenberg also engaged in musical, as opposed to verbal, music criticism. Twice, that is, he recomposed 18th-century works according to his own idiosyncratic lights: his Cello Concerto is a free adaptation of a harpsichord concerto by G. M. Monn (1717–50), and he made a version for string quartet and orchestra of Handel's Concerto Grosso in B-flat, Op. 6, No. 7. Like Stravinsky, Schoenberg worshipped Bach and was impatient with Handel. But one needn't share that impatience in order to enjoy the energetic invention with which Schoenberg goes about "removing the defects of the Handelian style," getting rid of "handfuls of sequences . . . replacing them with real substance" and doing his best "to deal with the other main defect . . . which is that the theme is always best when it first appears and grows steadily more insignificant and trivial in the course of the piece." Even if you don't enjoy the results or can't accept Schoenberg's reworkings as valid statements about the music of Monn and Handel, the concertos are vivid, illuminating statements about Schoenberg's compositional way, about his abhorrence of wasted motion, redundancy, or anything predictable, and his passion for constant development and variation.

The concertos also show—as do his "straight" orchestral transcriptions of Bach organ works and certain of his original compositions—that stylistic nicety and taste were not his strongest suits. Indeed, the very word "taste," as he said, "excited" him: "Taste is sterile—it cannot produce. . . . Taste functions mainly as a restricting factor, as a negation of every problem, as a minus to every number."

Schoenberg's music is extremely hard to perform. Occasionally he makes tremendous demands in sheer dexterity—for example, on the soloist in the Violin Concerto, and on the string quartet in the Handel setting—but more often, the difficulties are musical rather than mechanical. And even in the most virtuosic pieces, the technical challenges are organically tied to the musical ones. His music, moreover, is singularly dependent on good performance. If you play Webern's Five Pieces for Orchestra, Op. 10, with not a note in place, it will still sound rather pretty.

For myself, I love that he is difficult, that he compels all the attention, involvement, and good listening I know how to give. That goes for me with loving Josquin, Bach, the music Haydn and Mozart wrote after they discovered Bach, with Beethoven, Brahms, Sessions, Carter, and it does not interfere with my love of Monteverdi, Handel, Verdi, and Stravinsky.

I find Schoenberg's melodies wonderful in their generous sweep, with their unexpected turns, extensions, and contractions, and I find them so in all his styles, in *Transfigured Night*, in Tove's "Nun sag ich dir" in *Gurre-Lieder*, Pierrot's "Der kranke Mond," the "Song without Words" in the Serenade, the last of the Four Pieces for Chorus, Op. 27, the Adagio of the Third String Quartet, the sighing sevenths in the Violin Concerto's slow movement, the opening of the Piano Concerto, the close of the String Trio.

No less is he a marvelous inventor of sonorities. *Transfigured Night* and *Gurre-Lieder* are the last word in the fat 19th-century sound, but if he never again wrote anything so massive or so upholstered, he never gave up his preference for tight, compact, high-density, intensely "efficient" sonorities. The variety is immense: the Five Pieces for Orchestra, Op. 16, open up a new world of orchestral fantasy, just as the Trio was to do for chamber music for strings thirty-seven years later. There is *Pierrot lunaire* with its textural combinations and liaisons (in twenty-one pieces no two alike), the spooky magic of *Erwartung*, the filigree hung around the voice in the Songs, Op. 22, the brilliance of the Opus 31 Variations, the ear-opening lesson in "conventional" string scoring in the Suite in G, and on and on.

I don't know that I shall ever be able to deal with the scratchy, angular Petrarch sonnet in the Serenade, nor with the distorted Viennese, folksy bits in that work and in the Suite, Op. 29, that sound like weird, dry chips off the Mahler Seventh. I foresee no coming to terms with his operatic comedy of manners, *Von heute auf morgen*, and I shall forever be puzzled why a man so full of humor could write funny music only in the grotesque and parodic genres.

In 1927, he wrote: "I usually answer the question why I no longer write as I did at the period of *Transfigured Night* by saying: 'I do, but I can't help it if people don't yet recognize the fact.'"

I was touched, long before I first read that sentence, by the oneness of Schoenberg's work, whether it was in D major or continuously dissonant, and the more I came to know the work, the more moved I was by the voice that spoke so consistently—or almost—with such passionate intensity, with a fantasy and originality that take me aback over and over, with such dazzling skill, across so wide a range of human and musical experience, and, to use a phrase he himself spoke with pride, so deeply from the heart.

Leipzig's Gewandhaus Orchestra Delights Symphony Audience

October 15, 1974

Boston is linked by three cousinships to the Leipzig Gewandhaus Orchestra, which gave a splendid Symphony Hall concert Sunday afternoon under the direction of Kurt Masur, its conductor since 1970. First, the old Gewandhaus—the textile merchants' Trade Fair Hall, destroyed in a 1943 air raid—was the primary model for Symphony Hall. Second, the greatest of the Boston Symphony's music directors, Arthur Nikisch, who served here 1889–93, was the Gewandhaus conductor for the last twenty-seven years of his life. Third, Charles Munch was the Leipzig orchestra's concertmaster under Furtwängler in the 1920s.

As record collectors know, the Gewandhaus is a superb orchestra. The strings are especially fine: there is flame in that high violin sound, the cellos and basses speak with a terrific "*whoom*," and everybody commands a wonderfully delicate, airy *pianissimo*. The sound of the brass is full and non-aggressive, though the splendor of the horn tone in proclamatory music is bought at some cost to agility. The woodwinds, too, are very fine—soft by American standards, and with a woody, reedy, atavistic oboe sound that I find a flavorful change after the more homogenized, striving-toward-clarinet-roundness ideal most American players go for. The oboist who played the solos in Beethoven's *Eroica* is also an exceptional, superlative artist.

Peripheral observations: hair is a bit shorter than in an American orchestra, sideburns are rare, the very few beards are on the middle-aged professional types and closely trimmed, and the players talk almost not at all between pieces. I was surprised to see only three women—the harpist and two violinists (one of whom, even though she sits on the outside, turns pages, a task usually performed by the inside player of each stand)—and that is one area where I would have expected more equality from the German Democratic Republic.

Kurt Masur, successor to the podium of Mendelssohn, Nikisch, Furtwängler, and Walter, is in his late forties, a large, burly, very German type—a harmless Emil Jannings perhaps—who conducts with an energetic beat, fluid in the Schumann Fourth and rather paunchy in the *Eroica*, and with no baton.

He has a really good ear: I have hardly ever heard the Schumann, so notoriously tricky in matters of balance, sound with so beautiful a blend. His interpretations will in no way shake up your *Weltanschauung*, but I must say that I could wish that more conductors, including some of the exciting individualists, could lay out central-repertory symphonies with his sense of proportion, vigor, and feeling for euphony.

Siegfried Lorenz, a baritone still in his twenties, who sang Mahler's *Wayfarer* Songs, has a voice flowing with milk and honey. I can't think of a better place for it to be than attached to so sensitive a musician, one with so fine a feeling for the musical phrase and with so engagingly direct a way of telling a story in word and song. Masur and the orchestra gave him an accompaniment worked with utmost care and finesse.

"Pied Piper" Peter Pears

November 17, 1974

NEW YORK—It was sunny and for November the morning was mild, but there will not have been many rooms in the city whose occupant was sitting in shirt-sleeves by an open window. Especially not if he was a singer. Yet, that—lavender shirt, Black Watch tartan slacks, red slippers, gold-rimmed bifocals—is how I find Peter Pears the other day: a touch of England on Central Park West.

Pears is not your ordinary singer anyhow. His tenor, once heard, is unforgettable, a sound you would any time identify in a second. There are those who dislike it, who have found it whiny and quavery—it is also one of those voices to which records do not do justice—and there are those of us for whom it is one of the most expressive and beautiful of all musical sounds. His musicianship has always been acknowledged as exceptional, and he has an extraordinary way with words, particularly in German (which he does not speak: "my pronunciation is supposed to be quite good actually, but my vocabulary is small and my grammar dreadful"), but most so in English. He is a singularly gripping performer: not more than two or three times have I sensed an audience so held in breathless silence as the one in Jordan Hall when Pears and Benjamin gave a Britten recital in October 1969.[14]

New York just had an opportunity to find out that Pears is also a remarkable actor, for he was midway through a series of performances at the Metropolitan Opera as Gustav von Aschenbach in Britten's 1973 Thomas Mann opera, *Death in Venice*. For that matter, it is not your ordinary singer who makes his Metropolitan debut at 64. So for now, New York was headquarters while Pears gave his nine performances of *Death in Venice* and sang a few recitals, some with

[14] See review of October 29, 1969.

an old and admired friend, the English lutenist and guitarist Julian Bream, and some with a new and admired friend, the American pianist Murray Perahia. Pears and Perahia will be in Jordan Hall Saturday, November 23, doing a Schubert group, Schumann's Eichendorff *Liederkreis*, Britten's Pushkin cycle, *The Poet's Echo*, and some of Britten's folk song arrangements.[15]

For thirty years, Britten was Pears's keyboard partner at recitals. That is over. Last year, just before the premiere of *Death in Venice* at the Aldeburgh Festival which the two men founded in 1948, Britten was struck down by a heart attack. Open heart surgery was performed, "but it was not a success. They put in the new valve all right, but there was brain damage and, barring some sort of a miracle, his right side won't function properly again." Pears reports, though, that Britten is improving steadily, slowly, that he is more cheerful and mobile, but with times of bad depression. "He was a hard worker always, and it's not easy for him to get used to the life of a semi-invalid." And yes, he is composing again, "something very lightweight to begin with, an orchestral suite of British folk songs.

"Of course, performing in some ways had become harder and harder for him. He was dreadfully nervous about recitals, his circulation would nearly stop, his hands would be like ice, and nothing but brandy, brandy just before the performance, would do to get it going again. But you know, at Aldeburgh, where he felt at home and among musicians he loved, he really rather enjoyed conducting."

How did Murray Perahia come to inherit this mantle? "Murray won the Leeds Competition two years ago, and we have an arrangement that the Leeds winner gives a recital at Aldeburgh, and that's how we came to know him. Actually it was he who suggested some concerts together, and I was surprised, and pleased of course, that a young virtuoso so much in demand—really, he's dashing all over the world all the time—should be interested in accompanying a singer. But I had thought him a marvelously sensitive musician, and we did one concert in England and now we're doing this series over here. He has worked on some of this music with Ben, who, by the way, admires and likes him enormously. No, it's an arrangement with which I'm most happy."

Could Pears explain how he came to be doing the best singing of his life in his 60s? "Well, to begin with, I'm awfully glad you think so. I suppose I do, too, really. In spite of the *New York Times*,"[16] he added in *pianissimo* aside. Pears, by the way, is exceedingly self-critical and proceeded to discuss his Aschenbachs in some detail, having found the first two "quite satisfactory, the first perhaps marginally better," the third "dry and not very good"—"not" was almost "nought," and there was a quizzical crinkling of the brows and a silence before the "very"

[15] See review of November 25, 1974.

[16] This refers to Harold Schonberg's October 19, 1974, *New York Times* review of *Death in Venice*'s Metropolitan Opera premiere the previous evening.

with its precisely trilled "r"—and he admitted to some nervousness about the fourth, due to happen the next day: "but I'm arranging to leave more glasses of water about in the proper places for when I go off stage. Yes, of course the Met is a terrifying space. But how wonderful Tully Hall is where one can do songs to that sweet, adorable sound of the lute just as finely as in a drawing room." Jordan Hall, too, he remembered with pleasure, and spoke with warmth of "your extraordinary Symphony Hall."

Returning to the question of vocal longevity, he attributed it partly to a strong constitution and Lucie Manén. Ten years ago he had a bad season and was physically low altogether, thinking seriously of retiring. It was then he began flying to Austria for occasional lessons with Manén, a lyric-coloratura soprano then in her 60s and, incidentally, the wife of the West German political defector, Otto John. Pears sees her less often than he would like, though she now teaches at Aldeburgh every year, but in his mind it is certainly Manén, with a method that involves an unusual awareness in detail of what the body is doing—"she knows more about singing, about all the physiological and psychological aspects of it, than anyone I've ever known"—who got and kept him going again.

"Yes, I suppose I can almost do everything I want to now in order to make music. Of course, I've never had a big voice and I don't suppose I could materially enlarge my voice now without going all the way to the beginning. But the last year-and-a-half has been terribly hard, particularly singing the opera Ben nearly killed himself trying to finish for me. Emotional disturbance gets you by the throat. Literally, I've long known that, singing at friends' funerals, something simple like 'Bist du bei mir,' and . . . " The hand at the throat and the pained face told the story. "And now, ringing up and never quite knowing what the news is going to be . . . "

Pears spoke about *The Poet's Echo*, one of the few Britten cycles not written for himself (it was written for Galina Vishnevskaya and Mstislav Rostropovich, who performed it in Symphony Hall in 1965),[17] and the *Liederkreis*, which he has not sung in America—"somehow one seems always to have been occupied with *Winterreise* and *Dichterliebe*"—and which he sees as "terribly elusive and mysterious" and including "surely, three or four of Schumann's very greatest songs." ("Zwielicht" is the one that stirs him most.)

"I wonder how you'll like our tempo for the first song: we take that '*nicht schnell*' ('not quick') very seriously." As I waited for the elevator, the unmistakable voice began its morning warmup.

[17] See review of December 21, 1965.

Serkin's Perilous Risk Illuminates Beethoven

November 18, 1974

Pianists usually approach Beethoven's *Diabelli* Variations with caution, thinking twice and more before playing that attention-taxing work in public (and what a strange mixture it presents of the mandarin and the bumptious), and, when they do, being most circumspect about how to lead up to it. But last February, Charles Rosen prefaced it with nothing less than the *Hammerklavier* Sonata, demonstrating that such a pairing was inspired as well as daredevil, and yesterday, in a most wonderful Symphony Hall recital, Rudolf Serkin took the perhaps less spectacular but even more perilous risk of playing Beethoven's first and last sonatas, Opus 2, No. 1 in F minor and Opus 111 in C minor, before getting to the *Diabelli*.

The specific peril is that Opus 111 and the *Diabelli* offer two long sets of variations in the same key, C major, in succession, each concerned with the same pattern of intervals (C-G-D-G), each making its one considerable harmonic excursion to the same region of E-flat, and each dissolving finally in sheer figuration.

A great performance, though, is among other things one that reveals the unique characteristics of a composition, and Serkin vividly projected the differences between the two works—the few broadly laid out variations in the Sonata against the *Diabelli* set, which are many and which, until just before the end, move so mercurially that it takes the quickest listening you can do to catch them; the difference in harmonic detail, so simple in the Sonata and so exotic—and ultimately downright crazy—in the *Diabelli*; the closed style of the one against the encyclopedic gathering of moods, dialects, and keyboard techniques in the other; and above that, one is sublime and the other sublimely playful.

So, if putting Opus 111 and *Diabelli* together seemed like a wild idea, it worked perfectly in the event. Everything did. From the first stalking broken chord in Opus 2, No. 1, Serkin, who so often is painfully nervous, sounded relaxed and confident, quite as though he were near the end of a program rather than at its beginning. There were occasional and glaring wrong notes and they seemed to be totally efficient lightning conductors for all his tensions. He played with concentration and drive, with angelic serenity in the last pages of Opus 111, and, in this recital which kept getting miraculously better and better, adding finally hugely rambunctious humor as well as uncommon beauty of tone and range of color. Never in thirty years of hearing him have I known Serkin's honesty and loving musicality to be so completely and so uninterruptedly revealed.

Pears-Perahia Concert Unforgettable

November 25, 1974

Peter Pears and Murray Perahia gave a concert in Jordan Hall on Saturday, and not since Pears sang there five years ago with Benjamin Britten has there been anything comparable by way of song recitals in this town.[18] The program: a Schubert group ("Liebesbotschaft," "Der Neugierige," the seldom-sung and strange "Atys," "An die Entfernte," "Nacht und Traüme"), Schumann's Eichendorff *Liederkreis*, Britten's Pushkin cycle, *The Poet's Echo*, and some of Britten's folk song arrangements.

Since his heart operation last year, Britten, with whom Pears has sung nearly all his recitals of the last three decades, can no longer play the piano,[19] and so, one began by being curious about the partnership of the English tenor with an American pianist of considerably less than his own 64 years. It was wonderful, and quite different.

Not that Perahia is an unknown quantity: he has made interesting records of Schumann and Chopin and he has often played here in chamber music and concertos. He is, we know from all that—and it was confirmed over and over the other night—a player of exquisite musical and poetic sensibility, of soft and yielding temperament, and with a lovely touch, a master of *sfumatura*. In texture and color, volume, flexibility, in every respect, he was for Pears the most quick and responsive companion.

Britten, however, used to lead. He was a great pianist, completely natural, bold and sometimes idiosyncratic, plainer than his colleagues, the career-pianists, yet at the same time more imaginative and resourceful than almost any of them. But the musician dominated the pianist: Britten didn't play songs and sonatas and concertos for you, he showed you what it was like to compose them. Except in his own folk song settings, the act of performance disappeared: afterwards one might think about Pears's phrasing or Britten's pedaling, but at the concert, performance and music became an indivisible entity. And if Saturday we heard a great singer accompanied by an extraordinary pianist, Pears and Britten together made a transcendent oneness: that was music-making whose like I dare not hope to experience again in my lifetime.

No, Pears led, with the fantasy, word sense, musicality, the poignant beauty of his strange tenor—so slight, but so focused and intense, so far-ranging in its colors—and with more boldness and sheer vocal bravura than ever before. And what bravura, in those long-spun phrases of "The Sally Gardens" or the

[18] See review of October 29, 1969.

[19] See article of November 17, 1974.

octave-and-a-half leaps into *pianissimo* in "Sally in our Alley." It was more outgoing, more audacious in phrasing and expression, more "performed" than anything I had heard from him.

Tension is the root of art. Pears shows us all the conflicts and ambiguities in the music—seeing into the bottomless depths of Schumann's *Liederkreis* or telling with incredible simplicity and freshness the story of the bachelor and "The Foggy, Foggy Dew"—and he forgets his singing in the tension between the forces that push and cry out, and those others, bidding control and reserve, that hold back. An unforgettable evening of vocal, pianistic, musical, and poetic art.

Tennstedt's BSO Debut Breathes Life into Brahms

December 13, 1974

Last night's Boston Symphony concert brought a new face (and back) to the audience, and to most of us, I imagine, even a new name. The name is Klaus Tennstedt, and it belongs to a 48-year-old conductor, not long escaped from East Germany, and now *Generalmusikdirektor* of the opera in Kiel, with steady commitments in Hamburg and Munich. He has conducted in South America and in Toronto, but yesterday's concert was his United States debut.

The music, on the other hand, was familiar. It was all Brahms: the *Academic Festival* Overture, the Violin Concerto with Miriam Fried as soloist, and the Fourth Symphony (whose American premiere, right here in Boston, was led by a conductor who began by assuming that the opening bars indicated the composer's collapse into senility and who ended by confessing his incomprehension and cancelling the Saturday-night repeat performance, and took place within the lifetime, if not the memory, of a few BSO subscribers).[20]

In these decades, though, Brahms has become so familiar that he is awfully liable to automatic performance and automatic listening. One of the great merits, among many, of Tennstedt's concert was his ability to make so much of the music come across as something just astoundingly fresh. Tennstedt is, in fact, an impressive conductor, smart, and vibrantly alive, though looking at last night's concert as a whole, I would have to say that it was uneven as realization and presentation of strong ideas.

[20] Nearly ninety years earlier, the official American premiere of the Brahms Fourth was in fact given by the New York Philharmonic, Walter Damrosch conducting, on December 11, 1886. The Boston Symphony Orchestra would have owned that distinction if BSO conductor Wilhelm Gericke, after conducting what was technically a public rehearsal on Friday afternoon, November 26, 1886, had not postponed the Saturday-night performance to the following month.

To be sure, it began brilliantly. I have not heard the *Academic Festival* Overture done with so much air (rests are allowed in Brahms, too, we were reminded), with such wit, with so fine a sense of orchestral detail, with so cracklingly joyous a "Gaudeamus igitur" at the finish.

The Fourth Symphony, too, started beautifully. Tennstedt's upbeats lead with unobtrusive and irresistible energy to more upbeats, building paragraphs of immense breadth unfolded so as to give a view of wonderful clarity and spaciousness, projecting the movement in all its mobility and scratchiness. The scherzo was a rousing, roistering celebration, and the slow movement was full of fine detail (the combination of eloquence and reticence in the violin figures that accompany the big cello tune, or the force of the horn calls that shatter the tranquility of the closing pages).

But the great passacaglia finale seemed to get away from Tennstedt. Up to that point he had played according to the maxim of "less is more," achieving particularly exceptional definition of rhythm and texture, and sharp distinction of musical character with minimal modifications of speed. But now things began to bend and sway, not always convincingly, and I, at least, lost my sense of destination. Tension, understandable in such circumstances, may well have been the problem and the orchestra, which clearly liked the conductor and did some superb playing for him, fell now and again into surprising nervous mistakes.

Miriam Fried is a strong violinist with a tone, in her best moments, of diamond brilliance and boldness. She is remote of temperament and hardly inclined to search, and one would never infer from her playing that Brahms, discreetly but urgently, asks that the discourse sometimes be modified in the direction of "*espressivo*," "*dolce*," and "*teneramente*." Tennstedt supported this chilling, unvaried show with intelligence and vitality. Here, though, unlike in symphony and overture, he was not making a statement, but only being a first-rate workman.

Chicago Symphony, Solti Impressive

December 17, 1974

Forty-some years ago, when Arnold Schoenberg's Variations for Orchestra were brand-new, the composer gave an illustrated radio talk about them, and when he came to the seventh variation with its snaky bassoon and clarinet solos with flutter-tongued flutes and little pops on the piccolo and glockenspiel, he said with plaintive and sweet pathos: "I hope that perhaps one day these sounds will be found beautiful."

He may well have thought to himself, "I hope that perhaps one day these sounds will be played beautifully," and he did indeed once remark that his music was not modern, just badly performed. Last night in Symphony Hall, Sir Georg Solti led his brilliant Chicago Symphony Orchestra through Schoenberg's brilliant Variations—such pieces and such orchestras are made for one another—and the sounds, all of them, were beautifully played, and, to judge from the applause and cheering after the final bang, the audience found them beautiful.

Some of Solti's choices of tempo were a touch willful, and the more scrupulous Hans Rosbaud and Gunther Schuller have projected the long line of the Variations more effectively. Solti's performance was a bit sectional, but each section was a jewel. The piece is, among other things, "about" extraordinary orchestral sonorities—ones that still come across as stunningly original and imaginative—and it was wonderful to have that aspect of the music offered with unprecedented confidence and conviction.

The evening's other big piece was the Tchaikovsky Fifth. I was thinking after the Schoenberg that Solti had in fact always been better on texture than on continuity, and then the Tchaikovsky showed how cohesive and concentrated he could be (except for two huge and unproductive ritards in the finale). Solti hasn't got a sentimental fiber in him, and that helps: play Tchaikovsky straight, with intensity and respect, with sharply defined rhythm and with care for the exquisite scoring, and he will emerge expressive enough to turn you inside out.

That is what happened in Solti's performance. It was high tension all the way—even in much of the waltz, which is perhaps not such a good idea—but also elastic in a coiled-spring sort of way. Solti played the piece for its drama, and I would say that in that spirit he took it quite as seriously as Tchaikovsky did; at any rate, the huge grapplings of maledictions and benedictions in the first two movements were of stupendous impact. The orchestra—loud, fierce, given to formidable chomping, and with brass attacks that feel like what you get when you stick your finger into an electric socket—seconded Solti wonderfully. The famous and lovely horn solo was most beautifully played by Dale Clevenger in a manner rather less yieldingly sensuous than the usual.

Along with this marvelous double center—Schoenberg and Tchaikovsky—Solti offered a bad beginning and end, comparatively bad, that is. The beginning was Bach's *Brandenburg* Concerto No. 2, its middle movement nicely played by the orchestra's great solo oboist, Ray Still, and by recorder player Ralph Zeitlin, and a bit soupily by concertmaster Samuel Magad, but with the Allegros woodenly stomped through. Adolph Herseth's high trumpet solo was remarkable for its delicacy and near-accuracy. And the end was an encore, Verdi's *Forza del destino* Overture, for which the orchestra was simply and understandably too tired.

Bruckner, Tennstedt, BSO—Once-in-a-Lifetime Music

December 20, 1974

There is a story that Handel, describing what it was like to compose the "Hallelujah!" Chorus, said, "I thought I saw the Heavens open, and the great Lord Himself." I haven't any idea whether the story is true, but if it is, I wish Handel had waited for Anton Bruckner to say it, for it is his music that it describes perfectly.

Last night, the Boston Symphony gave us one of those great Brucknerian epiphanies—the Eighth Symphony under Klaus Tennstedt, conducted and played as one hears few things conducted and played in a lifetime.

The Eighth, composed in Bruckner's 60th year, though drastically revised and vastly clarified some years later, is the most audacious, the most superbly controlled, the most exalted of the series. It is, like his other symphonies, unimaginable without Beethoven and Wagner as models both for what to do and how to do it. But nowhere else does Bruckner draw such extreme, such far-reaching conclusions from the loving study of his forefathers. The leap from the Seventh to the Eighth is immense.

He gives you a theme—a dark and troubling one—and he gives you a key, but he will not put the two together. The whole vast structure—eighty minutes more or less, and four movements of highly differentiated character—is held in tension and suspense until just moments before the end when the theme, now neither troubled nor dark, is set for the first time in its right harmonic home. The sense of one arch, one voyage, is overwhelming.

The one voyage, it seems to go "through much tribulation into the Kingdom of God." But Bruckner writes after the tribulation: his is not music about struggle, but about the recollection that once there was struggle. He writes not only about Heaven, but as though from Heaven. The Adagio, about which out of custom and piety one often says that it is the greatest since Beethoven (but where among Beethoven's Adagios is its equal?), this Adagio—with its wonderful paradox of setting its exalted melodies to the throbbing accompaniment of Tristan's and Isolde's love-night—is itself the grandest and the deepest of Bruckner's visionary utterances.

Tennstedt moved the piece powerfully and intelligently, but with an extraordinary and confident sense of space. Many conductors project Bruckner as monumental stasis, and some—William Steinberg, for example[21]—do it magnificently. Tennstedt treated it more like "ordinary" music, like Beethoven and Wagner, who need to keep going and in whom the sense of destination is all. It works: the

[21] See review of January 5, 1974.

grandeur is not lost, but the drama of the voyage, the hugeness and vigor of the breath, is wonderfully marvelous. Tennstedt also sees a more complete Bruckner than most interpreters—one whose world includes, with rusticity and faith, humor, thunderous physical energy, a taste for the quirky and the bizarre, and limitless pleasure in the sensuous side of music. The orchestra played beautifully, with a glorious nobility in the brass, but above all, with a luminous and deep string tone that probably has not been heard here in decades. At the end, there was a yelling, foot-stomping ovation—the players, too, applauded warmly—and it is clear that Tennstedt's appearance is one of the best things to have happened to the Boston Symphony in a long time. He will surely be back.

1975–76*

Observing Ozawa: The Many Sides of the Maestro of the Boston Symphony Orchestra

January 5, 1975

Not knowing quite where to begin, I begin with my first meeting with Seiji Ozawa. It was a few summers ago when he was not yet the Boston Symphony's music director, though already artistic co-director (with Gunther Schuller) of the Berkshire Festival. The Fromm Foundation's annual Festival of Contemporary Music was in progress, and, suffering from the condition I always think of as Fromm Fatigue, I suddenly and drastically needed to escape from an especially rebarbative piece of musical calculation. I wandered about the Tanglewood lawns, and out of the near-pitch darkness someone softly called my name. It was Ozawa, also bent on escape, and I was surprised because we had never met and I had no reason to suppose he knew me by sight, but we stopped and talked for maybe ten minutes, for a while about the music we had both run away from, and for a while about Tchaikovsky, whose *Pathétique* he had just done with the Boston Symphony.

Reserved and open at the same time, more aware than he sometimes appears, not attracted to music whose appeal is overridingly intellectual rather than sensuous or emotional—reading backwards some time later when I knew a little more about him, I saw how characteristic that incident had been.

At 39, Seiji Ozawa is at the top of a pole he never found particularly greasy—music director of two major symphony orchestras, one of them in the world's top half-dozen on anybody's list, director of the biggest summer music festival in this country, in possession of a good recording contract with a ranking firm of international distribution, hugely in demand as a guest conductor (almost all of the offers being turned down in deference to his commitments to the Boston and San Francisco symphony orchestras). Naturally, no one is about to publish Ozawa's income, but those who like to measure success in those terms will be comforted

* In 1975–76, for a period of about a year, Steinberg took a leave of absence from the *Globe* to write a book on Elliott Carter, a project that unfortunately never reached completion. Owing to the limited number of articles from these two years, they have been consolidated into a single chapter.

to know that it must be in the neighborhood of a quarter-million. In public recognition, he comes just after the Bernstein-Karajan-Solti superstar trinity.

Ozawa was born in Hoten, Manchuria. His father was a dentist by profession, a Buddhist by faith, and "strong father, strong man, normal man, very normal man. He drank much. I drink much." Ozawa thinks a lot about being a father, too, to his real children, Seira, born December 29, 1971, and Yuki Yoshi, born June 6, 1974, and also to the players in his orchestras. His mother is a Presbyterian, and that is how the four Ozawa boys were brought up, though his eldest brother, a sculptor by vocation but an innkeeper for bread, returned to Buddhism. The other two brothers are a professor of German literature and an actor in the Japanese counterpart of Broadway musicals. As boys, the four sang together as the Golden Gate Quartet—Seiji as first bass—borrowing the repertory, learned off recordings, as well as the name of the famous Black close-harmony gospel group.

He began piano at seven and enrolled in the then new Toho School in Tokyo. He broke both index fingers at rugby—"I wanted to be a really good rugby player, at highest level"—and that ended his prospects as a pianist. He turned to composition, something he no longer pursues, though for a while he was quite successful with film scores. The first experience of hearing an orchestra—"like this!" (fist brought sharply to the side of the head)—showed him the direction in which he wanted to go. The successively still more exciting shocks of hearing the Symphony of the Air (the former NBC Symphony) and the Boston Symphony under Munch—"so full of fire"—made him surer still. His teacher, Hideo Saito, most eminent musician and pedagogue, had advised him from the beginning to go to Europe. Music—Western music, that is—is like bread there, was the gist of his message, a necessity. "In Japan," says Ozawa, "they don't want to miss anything, they enjoy, but is not like bread." So, at 24 he went to Europe, by freighter to Messina with a scooter and a guitar. He was to promote the brand of scooter, which was to be his source of income; and the guitar, which he didn't know how to play, came along because he thought he ought to have some sort of musical instrument.

From there, things moved quickly. A friend—in fact his future first wife—saw an announcement of the Besançon Conductors Competition on the bulletin board of the Paris Conservatoire where he was studying piano. Ozawa entered and won. Charles Munch was one of the judges and brought him to Tanglewood in 1960, where he won the Koussevitzky Prize. Then came an assistant conductorship under Bernstein at the New York Philharmonic, and the first professional engagements, guest dates in San Francisco in 1962 and Boston in 1964, the music directorship at the Ravinia Festival (the Chicago Symphony's summer activity), of the Toronto Symphony, the San Francisco Symphony, and the Boston. In Japan, he maintained ties until last year with the Japan Philharmonic.

Now what everybody wants to know about Ozawa is: how long will he stay with his dual San Francisco–Boston life? His San Francisco contract runs for one season beyond this, until summer 1976; his Boston one is, like that of most of his predecessors here, open. In February 1972, when his Boston appointment was announced, the official line was that he would keep San Francisco. *Newsweek* leaked the story of his coming to Boston a few days ahead of the announcement and got part of the story wrong, saying he was quitting San Francisco: Ozawa's sense of honor was so wounded that not only did he fly to San Francisco between Philadelphia Orchestra concerts only for the purpose of telling his players face to face that he was not breaking his contract, but hesitated for several days before signing the agreement with Boston. His own fondness for San Francisco and, more, that of his wife, Vera, was much dwelled upon.

But no one in San Francisco has ever been as sure, not for distrust of Ozawa, but because in the long run, the splitting of a music director across two orchestras simply seems not to work, and because there is no argument that if your choice is between music directorships in Boston and San Francisco, you are going to choose Boston. Boston has an orchestra of world class, and even in February 1972, Ozawa was saying that Boston was the "most musical city in America, where music is most like bread." Increasingly, San Francisco views its relationship with Ozawa with the melancholy of a lover who knows that the end of the affair is inevitable.

Moreover, within the last year, something has happened to make Ozawa's early parting from San Francisco a virtual certainty. The San Francisco Symphony's contract includes a clause that puts decisions on promotion and tenure into the hands of a committee of players. Last spring, two principal players brought in by Ozawa, bassoonist Ryohei Nakagawa and timpanist Elayne Jones,[1] were refused tenure by the committee. Ozawa is personally popular with the orchestra, but still, it was widely assumed and nowhere contradicted that the committee's move was its response to the conductor's expressed desire to demote four players and ultimately others. His artistic ambitions for that orchestra were exceedingly serious. The Jones-Nakagawa affair was public and ugly, and Ozawa was profoundly distressed by it. Voting is on a scale from zero to 100. By Ozawa's estimate, the players were deserving of maybe seventy-five for one, eighty for the other. He could understand, he said, disagreement that might cause someone to vote as low as fifty, but for the total votes of the seven-man committee to come out as they did, some members would have had to assign grades like zero and five. That was plainly political, and the misuse for political purposes of a privilege designed to help preserve artistic standards was

[1] Elayne Jones was the first Black principal of a major symphony orchestra, appointed to the San Francisco Symphony in 1972 after winning a blind audition.

something he had not anticipated and which hurt him. He speaks about it sadly, though without rancor. "California is like two islands, you know. In the East and in the Middle West, if you lose a job or want to move, next city, next orchestra is not so far. In California, I think people are more anxious." But he admits that the system has eroded his power as music director and that a shadow has fallen over the contentment he had felt in San Francisco. Would he stay anyway? "I don't think so. I don't know. I don't think so."

There is no telling what Ozawa will do from 1976 on. Will he give more time to Boston than the half-season plus Tanglewood (where he conducts relatively little) we get now, or will the time that giving up San Francisco makes available be turned over for lucrative guest conducting? And indeed, another line of speculation—uncommented on by Ozawa—is beginning to be heard, namely, that his eventual destination, if not his goal, is Philadelphia. He has been a frequent and well-liked guest there and at the orchestra's summer season in Saratoga, and Eugene Ormandy is 75 and known to think well of Ozawa.

By temperament, Ozawa seems more suited to the stay-at-home life of a music director than to the jetting about of the eternal or even part-time guest conductor. It is curious—Erich Leinsdorf, so European and so conservative in so many respects, seems to be having a much better time as the world's No. 1 guest conductor than he ever did as music director; Ozawa, who seems so swinging, is much more of a domestic type. Consider the surface: longish hair, discreetly exotic shirts (he no longer owns a necktie—at evening concerts he wears a white turtleneck and beads with his tails), the boyish run from stage door to podium. But the substance is one of commitment to established ways. In contrast to many young and younger conductors, he speaks with respect of older colleagues. He regards adventure as something to be taken in homeopathic doses. He is neither intellectual, explorer, nor martyr. He has no appetite for publicity, and he would love it if the Boston Symphony's press department could learn to see their job *his* way, that is, to shield him from press, radio, and television altogether.

He works hard, and he guards his health and privacy. Health has given him some trouble, too. In 1971, he did himself painful disc and nerve damage in the region of his neck during four days' rehearsing and three performances of the Mahler Eighth at La Scala, Milan, where the soloists and the hundreds of choristers were on high platforms. That has continued to trouble him, and he missed several weeks near the end of his 1973–74 season in San Francisco. And an injury to his hand sustained in toting the family baggage had him in an Ace bandage for many months and still mostly shaking hands with his left over a year later.

Life in his houses, those he owns in the Twin Peaks section of San Francisco and in Brookline, and in the one he rents in Lenox, is quiet and private. He plays leisurely tennis—"Ronald Wilford, my manager, is my enemy in summer—we take sometimes many days to finish one set"—goes to an occasional movie, sees a few friends. Most of his life, though, seems to revolve around Vera, Seira, and Yuki Yoshi.

Above all, he works hard. His standard regimen involves getting up at 4:30 to study scores, and the days of conducting programs not fully prepared—and there was some of that during the period five or six years ago when his career took off like a rocket and his repertory studies could not keep up with the demands on his time—those days are over.

Given that his professional life is now so rooted on this continent, does he intend to become a US citizen? He is unsure. He has taken out first papers, but hesitates about the next step. The East-West question still seems to a certain extent unresolved for him. Western music he describes as "fresh" for him rather than "foreign," but he points out that he has lived with it much more intimately than with Japanese music, with which he has been forced into a close contact mostly through the work of Japanese composers like [Maki] Ishii and Takemitsu who have sought to blend the two traditions in their own music. Becoming a father has made him think about the question a lot. Not long after Seira's birth he said, "My daughter will look Japanese, and I want her to know what that's all about."

For sure, Japanese is still the one language in which he is thoroughly at ease. His English, next to nonexistent when he was a student at Tanglewood in 1960, is quite fluent now, though accented, not always quite correct, and inclined to be missing definite articles. Sometimes his wife, who was born in Yokohama to a Japanese mother and a White Russian émigré father, is summoned for linguistic help: her English is easier than his, and almost free of accent. Names, especially names of German composers and compositions, still confound him, and, coming from a language with open syllables and in which consonants occur one at a time, he is uneasy about thick consonantal clusters. Communication with orchestras is uninhibited. Rehearsing Tchaikovsky's *Eugene Onegin* at Tanglewood, there was a momentary ensemble difficulty at the point where Lensky challenges Onegin to a duel. "I hereby sever all bonds of friendship," he declaims in the grandest style. Ozawa explained to the orchestra that the punctuating chords could not come to tempo: "He needs a little more time, he is saying . . . er, something." He was not reluctant to join in the general laughter. I have the feeling, though, that just as he only makes complete contact with those authors he can read in Japanese translation, so it would be impossible ever to know this man unless one could speak with him in his own language.

He is a stunningly gifted and by now extraordinarily accomplished conductor. No other conductor is such a "natural" for it physically. It is active conducting, but economic and elegant, completely un-self-conscious. And you can't, in the end, escape saying that it is beautiful. One member of a Tanglewood audience said last summer, "I've seen things offered as dance that were less beautiful and expressive." And it is wonderfully efficient. At Tanglewood, there is never enough rehearsal time, with three different programs having to be prepared each week. To watch Ozawa teach things as big and complex (and new to the orchestra) as *Eugene Onegin* or particularly Schoenberg's *Gurre-Lieder* with which he set an audience of over 10,000 into virtually unparalleled uproar last August, that is extraordinary. Calm, control, the total absence of tension and frenzy, the impeccable ear, the combination of good humor and seriousness that is not to be questioned, the common sense about knowing what wants to be corrected and what will take care of itself—all that is a staggering, even moving, show of skill and intelligence, human as well as professional. I find the musician hard to generalize about.

Probably one should never generalize anyway, and I am grateful to Ozawa for making it difficult. Mozart's *Così fan tutte*, the first two symphonies of Brahms, *Onegin* and the *Pathétique*, several Schoenberg pieces, Ravel's magic opera, *L'Enfant et les sortilèges*, *Firebird* (and more) have been superb. On the other hand, much of his Berlioz has been flat and characterless, the Beethoven Ninth at Tanglewood was a staid bore, the Verdi Requiem was conceptually confused and terribly moment-to-moment, his Mahler has not gone much below the surface. Things occasionally sound a little soft, not so fiery as they look—another Ozawa paradox.

If you bring up the question of contemporary music, he looks troubled. "Yes, I should do more" (he does virtually none here)—so he said in summer 1974, as he has in 1973 and in 1972. He has a conscience, and the question pricks it. And then speaks the man who is professional and craftsman before he is the intellectually curious explorer (let alone the boat-rocker): "But I think first I must establish myself here with orchestra and with audience."

He makes a wry face into his Campari, sitting with his left leg over the arm of his chair. He speaks with warmth of George Crumb's *Echoes of Time and the River* (though to begin with he can't remember the name of either composer or composition) and of Elliott Carter's Concerto for Orchestra, both of which are on his San Francisco programs this season. He says again, "Yes, I must do more."

He hears the conflict implicit in what he is saying as accurately as he hears a lopsided balance in a chord of brasses, and he is so open about the difficulties of being a grownup and a professional that it makes him suddenly a very touching figure on the patio of his house in the rapidly cooling Berkshire evening. I am almost as relieved as he when Seira, pretty and demanding, comes in. In the role of father, he looks happy.

BSO Bassist Wolfe Impressive as a Soloist

January 11, 1975

Lawrence Wolfe is number nine in the Boston Symphony's nine-man double bass section, a burly young man of friendly appearance who is just beginning to look a little older than a high school student, and last night in Jordan Hall he did something few bass players ever dare, which is to give a solo recital. His fellow bassists no doubt have the best of reasons for their reticence; he himself quite convinced us that for him, playing recitals is absolutely the right thing. He is extraordinary.

The bass hasn't much literature of its own, though more than Wolfe's program might lead one to infer. He played two recent pieces for bass unaccompanied, *Hommage à J. S. Bach* by Julien-François Zbinden, a graceful fantasy on the B–A–C–H (B-flat–A–C–B) note sequence, evoking the manner of one of Bach's preludes for solo cello, and a Fantasy, a bit on the dry side, by Robert Paul Block. With Jerome Patterson, a BSO colleague, he played a duet for cello plus piano accompaniment, by François Servais, a Belgian composer from the first half of the 19th century, the piece itself being amusing operatic high-jinks, Norma and Adalgisa wordlessly buzzing about, crooning in thirds, and all that.

For the rest, Wolfe borrowed from the cellists—some of François Couperin's *Pièces en concert*, Schubert's *Arpeggione* Sonata (which the cellists themselves borrowed for want of arpeggione virtuosi since the original one for whom that lovely piece was written), and Bruch's *Kol Nidrei*—and for his derring-do finale he took on one of the most alarming highwire acts in the violin literature, Paganini's Fantasy on the Prayer from Rossini's *Moses.* His keyboard collaborator was Jonathan Feldman, not especially impressive on the harpsichord, but an exceptional ensemble pianist, sensitive both as a musician and an instrumentalist.

Wolfe has a good left hand: the fingers come down in the right places and so the pitch is near to impeccable. (There are famous cellists whose playing is not that reliably in tune.) It is, however, the right hand, or rather the right arm, that is so astonishing. Wolfe's bow technique is deft and resourceful, sometimes almost beyond belief, and the tone emerges so pure, so transparent, so varied, so far from even the slightest suggestion of growl or grumble, that most of the time one forgets totally that everything is happening in the sub-basement.

Indeed, the best and most important thing I can say about Wolfe's mastery of the instrument is that it allows you, without obstacle, to attend to how beautifully he plays music. In fact, he plays music so beautifully, with simplicity and concentration, that the performance disappears and only the piece remains; it was at the end of Schubert's *Arpeggione* that I realized that for twenty minutes my mind had been wholly on the piece, not on the playing of it.

Most musicians about to embark on a solo recital concentrate on practicing and pamper themselves as much as possible. When you consider that Wolfe had within twenty-four hours played two strenuous concerts with the Symphony, having spent the week rehearsing for them, not to mention another BSO concert and several recording sessions, his achievement becomes the more amazing. A very, very impressive show it was, and a thoroughly enjoyable one as well.

Richard Tucker Was All Tenor

January 19, 1975

[*Tenor Richard Tucker died on January 8, 1975, aged 61.*]

The last time I saw Richard Tucker he didn't sing, but he gave as tenorial a performance as I have ever witnessed. It was at the International Verdi Symposium last September. There was a critic's panel, and from the stage we spotted two opera singers in the audience: one was Anna Moffo, sitting in the second or third row between two Verdi scholars (I don't know why she happened to be in town), and the other was Tucker, in Chicago to sing the High Holiday services at the Park Synagogue.

Irving Kolodin, moderator of the panel, soon made occasion for Moffo to come to the stage, where she added brief comment to a couple of topics that had been discussed and sat down again to polite applause. Some minutes later, Kolodin invited Tucker to come up and speak about his experience singing in *Aida* under Toscanini in 1949.

When Kolodin had finished his introduction, Tucker's hands were the first to be raised in applause, and to continuing clapping from the audience, the tenor walked slowly to the stage from his seat in the auditorium's back row. The issue was "Celeste Aida," for which Verdi wrote a *pianissimo* ending, but which tenors generally finish with the final high B-flat taken good and loud. Toscanini offered Tucker a compromise: take the ringing high B-flat, then repeat the last three words *pianissimo* an octave lower, which Tucker was willing to accept providing historical authentication could be found ("'Maestro,' I said, 'if you can produce a letter . . .'")

The story was told, plus its sequel: "hundreds of telegrams" of protest or dismay, a single attempt to introduce the *pianissimo* ending at the Metropolitan Opera, more upset, and the resolution to return to the traditional way. Kolodin thanked Tucker, the audience applauded warmly, Tucker bowed, then made his way along the table of critics with a handshake and a greeting for all eleven of us—"goodbye Bob . . . thank you, Martin . . . niceta seeya, Speight . . . take care, Michael . . . "—during all of which time, and through the leisurely walk to the back row, the applause perforce continued. It was magnificent. Later, someone remembered that we had not been told whether Toscanini had actually been able to produce convincing documentation. The question was put. "Yes," called out Tucker, waving a bundle of papers.

Yes, he was all tenor, reveling in high B-flats, in the pleasure they gave, and in the applause they produced. ("Didn't you hear a voice?" "Only, my own. Isn't it beautiful?"—an exchange from *Fledermaus*, in which he most charmingly sang Alfred, who makes that response.)

He knew there was more of an audience for B-flats than for music (or vocal subtleties), and he was happy to be the tenor for that audience. "They don't come to see you bunt, they want to watch you hit home runs," he said. What made him lovable, in his elevator shoes, and what made him earn and hold such a measure of respect all through the profession was, among other things, his honesty. There was not a touch of pretense to him. Never claiming to be anything other than what he was—a man with an exceptional voice—he talked exactly the game he played.

Margaret Webster tells of directing him in Verdi's *Don Carlo* at the Met in 1950. Where, in a certain duet, did he take the soprano's hand, he asked. "'When you say you do.' He said, 'Where's that?' I said, pointing to the score, '*Io prendo la tua mano*.' He said, 'Oh. Is that what that means?'" Webster exaggerates in saying that Tucker subsequently "transformed himself into a very good actor." In later years, though, he seemed to know what was going on, never just standing around like a dropped lump (as Bjoerling, a greater musical and vocal artist, did), but, looking always and irrepressibly like Richard Tucker, threw himself into the stage business with vigor and enthusiasm.

This year, his thirtieth at the Met (the anniversary would have fallen this Saturday), he added his thirtieth leading role in the house, Arrigo in *Vespri siciliani*. (To his grief, the Met never granted him what he most longed for, a revival of Halévy's *La Juive* in which he would sing Eléazar, though he had a few opportunities to sing it elsewhere.) His repertory was large and it included a few surprising excursions outside his normal Italian and French territories: Lensky in Tchaikovsky's *Eugene Onegin*, for example, and two Mozart roles, Tamino in *Magic Flute* and Ferrando in *Così fan tutte*, all of which he sang beautifully. I remember how much he relished the comedy in *Così*, particularly the first appearance in the absurd "Albanian" disguise in Act I: tenors don't often get a chance to make people laugh.

He recorded eleven complete operas (four of them twice), a Verdi Requiem, and a number of recital discs. For a singer of his eminence and popularity that is not much. He was under contract to Columbia, which had a brief alliance with the Met, but at a time when most of the best singers were with RCA Victor. Most of Tucker's early recordings, therefore, have him in company that runs from mediocre to wretched, Eleanor Steber in *Butterfly* and *Così* being the glorious exception. Twice he recorded for EMI-Angel with Callas—they had made their Italian debuts in the same *Gioconda* in Verona in 1947—*Aida* and *La forza del destino* (the opera he was to have sung here with the Met this April). However, they wanted him to record *Trovatore* and *Lucia* with von Karajan conducting, and Tucker chose to give up the contract rather than associate with that ex-Nazi. The only recordings, then, that give large-scale documentation of Tucker's later achievement come from the four occasions when RCA borrowed him for *Butterfly*, *Bohème*, *Forza*, and *Trovatore*, the last, which has him in strong company, being by far the best of the lot.

What you first notice is the voice, ringing and free, produced with energy, even in youth suggesting metal more than velvet, never harsh, and with the metal lightly and mysteriously cloaked and darkened in a most individual, instantly identifiable timbre. And that voice held. In the last years he avoided high Cs and Bs but when I last heard him—it was a *Boccanegra* in December 1973 when he was 59—he was in splendid form, pitching into a rather ungrateful part with unstinting intensity. His career was a virtuoso performance of vocal husbandry. He never allowed himself to be seduced into roles heavier than he felt ready for and, while other tenors, many of them his juniors, came and went, he stayed and sang. He could have continued with distinction far into his sixties.

What he missed was variety and vitality of characterization: Egyptian general, Spanish corporal, German philosopher, Parisian journalist, Sicilian country boy, all sounded pretty much alike. He could be crude in expression, more uniformly loud than the composer had bargained for, sometimes singing Verdi with Mascagni manners, indulging in sobs and chokes, shouting on odd words (none of which he did as grossly and indiscriminately as most of his Italian colleagues). He sounds always most personal in the music he grew up with—in cantorial chants or in something as captivating as the little Goldfaden song, "Roshinkes mit Mandelin," which he sings as an encore on the otherwise pretty dreadful, circus-y Carnegie Hall recital album with Robert Merrill. He was a good musician, though. His phrasing is always simple, musical, unfussed, and his pitch was impeccable. He was admirably scrupulous and clear in Italian and English diction, though his French was as outrageous as that of any real Italian tenor.

He had seen his friend Leonard Warren collapse and die on the Met stage. Death came to Tucker less glamorously—in a Kalamazoo motel room—but with equal and merciful swiftness. He was so in life, so glad of it, capable of such pleasure in his work, that the news of his passing came as an exceptional and saddening shock. We always assumed he would be with us forever, and we shall miss his human cleanness and liveliness.

It is hard not to tie his death to that, five days earlier, of his friend, Milton Cross. Tucker's comment that day—he said that they always greeted each other with an *abbraccio*, an embrace, because "there are fewer and fewer of us left"—spoke more than most others of real distress and grief. And who, after all, completely understands the links of the physical heart or the metaphorical?

Cross, too, with his passion for the glitter of opera—do you remember the combined awe and grandeur whenever he said "the Great Gold Curtain"—was someone about whom it was easy to be snooty. But he was impressively professional in work he managed so smoothly that we never stopped to think about how tricky it was. It is odd to think that we shall never again hear that joyous bounce with which he intoned "the Texaco Company,"[2] and even if it is fairly trivial, something genuine and full of personality and life has been taken from us.

Schuller Helps Students Succeed With Mahler

January 23, 1975

Last night's Jordan Hall concert by the New England Conservatory Symphony Orchestra was supposed to begin with Schoenberg's Violin Concerto, but an attack of flu on Rudolf Kolisch forced a postponement. It was disappointing not to find out what two musicians who know Schoenberg as intimately and as profoundly as Kolisch and Gunther Schuller had to say about that brilliant and difficult Concerto. From every other point of view, though, its omission was a mercy, given that the rest of the program consisted merely of Mahler's Third Symphony, those few 102 minutes of it (plus intermission). On the way out a young man was saying to the young woman on his arm: "You gotta realize this is one of his shorter symphonies—there's one that's twice as long." Well, not quite . . .

The Mahler Third is quite something for any orchestra to take on, and for a student group to bring it off as the players did is amazing. Of course, to have Gunther Schuller in charge in itself amounts to a huge bunch of steps in the right direction. He knows how instruments work; he is clear, unruffled, rhythmic, and he teaches good habits on the order of paying attention to composers' directions (and thinking about why), listening to what others are up to and not blaring or banging.

His strength as an interpreter is his grasp of the long line of a piece, his surefooted sense of direction. A useful quality to bring to a Mahler symphony, that, and it is rare to hear one of those works laid out in so orderly and clarifying a way. He will sometimes undercharacterize detail, and, while the countless shifts of pace and modifications of loudness were duly attended to, they were often done at a minimally perceptible level.

[2] Texaco sponsored the Metropolitan Opera's live Saturday radio broadcasts from 1940 to 2004.

The performance started out being interesting, because the piece itself is interesting and because of the lucidity of the presentation, also because of the prevailing energy. It was, at that point, also rather cool—what I have always thought of as the catastrophe that interrupts the series of marches in the first movement was no catastrophe but simply some scales and a precisely articulated loud noise. But with the offstage posthorn music in the third movement came the first intimation of magic. From the fourth movement, the Nietzsche song, on to the end, the performance became more involving and intense with each bar. The final Adagio was shepherded and built—very, very slowly, which few conductors dare, and which is absolutely necessary—with wonderful patience and control, and sung out with a most moving nobility.

Mahler taxes the most virtuosic and experienced orchestra, and the collective and individual achievements on the Jordan Hall stage were impressive, and in a way from which a few moments of fatigue or nerves did not detract. I loved the *pianissimo* string playing, and there were fine solos by Bruce Hopkins on the posthorn (wonderfully delicate, but perhaps not quite sentimental), by the principal trombonist (strong and splendid in sound, a bit stiff in declamation), the horn (melting tone and a lovely sense of the Mahler phrase), the superb trumpet, and some of the woodwind, particularly the first clarinet. (The Conservatory would rather be democratic than informative, and unfortunately I cannot identify most of the players from their alphabetical listing in the program.) The percussion playing was, all of it, wonderfully stylish.

Janice Meyerson, who sang Nietzsche's midnight poem, has one of those rich altos that just pours out effortlessly, and she sings words and music beautifully. A lovely job. And the choral parts were attractively done by members of the Conservatory Chorus, the Opera Department, and the Preparatory School.

The Conservatory does, however, owe its public two courtesies. One is to supply texts and translations (it was a nice touch to turn up the house lights for the two vocal movements so that we could read the words we didn't have). The other is not to set a photographer roaming at large and going click-click in people's ears for two hours.

A Lovely Party for Mozart

January 28, 1975

January 27 is the birthday—the 219th this year—of Joannes Chrysostomus Wolfgangus Theophilus Mozart. Last year the musical household of Emmanuel

Church, Newbury Street, decided to celebrate with a free concert and drew an overflow crowd. Yesterday they did it again—a celebration in sound and as large an audience as the church can hold.

Craig Smith, under whose musical ministry Emmanuel has become one of Boston's liveliest musical beehives, conducted about half the program and was the gentle, sensitive soloist in the C minor Piano Concerto. Edward Simon conducted the remainder. The other soloists were three members of the Emmanuel Choir—soprano Susan Larson, mezzo-soprano D'Anna Fortunato, tenor Bruce Fithian—and one alumna, soprano Jane Bryden. The orchestra was a slightly expanded version of the one that plays Bach cantatas at the Sunday services there.

They began with one of those sets of dance music Mozart wrote to pay the rent, the twelve *Deutsche*, K.586. There will have been some surprised dancers on that floor, though, because those pieces astonish, delight, and amuse over and over with their quirks of rhythm and harmony, and of course with their fabulous scoring.

Then came the vocal music, beginning with a concert aria, "Alma grande e nobil core," K.578, formal, taut, and like a brilliant Allegro in a concerto. D'Anna Fortunato sang it virtuosically and with grand style. Her maturity and her musical and vocal command grow ever more impressive, and she led the great quartet from *Idomeneo* with a nobility that was deeply moving. Susan Larson contributed to that rich and, in its last moments, so painful ensemble with a wonderful intensity and musicality. She had had, however, not quite so much luck with the lovely aria, "Zeffiretti lusinghieri," where her attempt to sing it with great delicacy was undone by a rather muddy accompaniment. Smith is a superlatively musical conductor, but not always an altogether skillful one.

When they come to me, and say I can hear just one more Mozart aria before I die, I expect I shall choose "Ruhe sanft" from *Zaide*. It is touching in its lullaby simplicity, but I also love all the things about it that are so unexpected, like, that in its openness of shape, its perfume of muted strings, its very innocence, it hardly sounds like Mozart at all, but more like—I don't know—Weber perhaps? It is, for sure, a glorious opportunity for the perfectly poised lyric soprano, and Jane Bryden, singing in her coolest choirboy tones, brought the house down.

A lovely party, touching and joyous, friendly and serious. Coffee was served afterwards, and some of the audience brought cake. But with the Window Shop gone, is there, I wonder, any place to get Mozartkugeln?

Turangalîla Tiresomely Gorgeous

February 28, 1975

A good shout went up in Symphony Hall last night when Olivier Messiaen appeared on stage after the performance of his *Turangalîla* Symphony, followed by another hearty roar when Seiji Ozawa had the players of the Boston Symphony Orchestra stand. Right enough: the playing had sounded magnificent and, no question, there was a real sense of occasion to the evening.

It is just a few weeks past twenty-five years since Leonard Bernstein led the premiere of *Turangalîla* in the same hall. Except to a few adventurous organists, Messiaen was hardly known in this country, and it was not until the '60s that his name became widely known and his evocative *Quartet for the End of Time* took off to become one of the few genuinely popular pieces of contemporary music.

Messiaen's has been a striking, original voice, one that has given us much to consider—and reconsider—about how and why music is made. But *Turangalîla* I find hard to get along with. The multiple meanings of the Sanskrit title, Messiaen tells us, include "a love song, a hymn to joy, time, movement, rhythm, life and death." Along with the song cycle, *Harawi*, and the *Cinq Rechants* for twelve voices, it forms part of a *Tristan* trilogy.

Its ten movements, scored for very large orchestra, plus solos for piano and the electronic keyboard instrument called an ondes Martenot, take about eighty minutes. Remarkable things happen during that time, like the many Liszt-to-the-nth-power piano cadenzas and the fascinatingly fragmented penultimate movement. Surprising things, too, like the bouncy "Joy of the Stars' Blood," with which, in a shortened version, you could bring the house down at the Pops. And much of it is a more complicated version—unmistakable nonetheless—of period-Hollywood.

But the imprecision and vagueness of Messiaen's thought and his self-indulgent repetitiousness bother me. It is odd to find him, in his self-congratulatory program note, describe a section as "a complex scaffolding of ten superimposed musical entities" when the giddy tumult suggests that he is not much concerned with what exactly it sounds like, and odder still to read his pronouncements on development—this apropos the movement called "Development of Love" ("What does one think of immediately? Of lovers who can never be separated, like Tristan and Isolde"—How's that again?)—when he develops nothing, but only repeats more loudly and more insistently.

Because the composition is crude in facture and taste, the expressive content is diffuse. The results are hardly in tune with the lofty aim: *Turangalîla*, gorgeous, and in the end tiresomely gorgeous noise, is *Tristan* as kitsch, *Tristan* for flower-children (if you remember those).

Yvonne Loriod, married to Messiaen since 1961, played the piano solo with incisive brilliance, though much of what she has to do gets lost in the reckless abandon of her husband's scoring. Jeanne Loriod, her younger sister, presided at the ondes Martenot, whose eerie out-in-space wail suggests now banshee and now soap opera. Ozawa and the Loriods worked from memory, but the composer followed the miniature score as eagerly as any student.

Luigi Dallapiccola, 1904–75

March 2, 1975

At the sight or mention of Luigi Dallapiccola's name, I always and at once hear two things. One is the sound of Suzanne Danco's vernal soprano in the first phrase of the *Machado Songs*—"*La primavera ha venido*"—a colorfully spaced scale, seven notes up to "*ni*" and five down again to finish the word. The other, in the acoustic of an empty street at night, is Dallapiccola's own sonorous voice saying, in English, "I beg to be of another opinion."

The street was in Stuttgart, and Dallapiccola was there for a production of his Saint-Exupéry opera, *Night Flight—Colo di notte* to him and *Nachtflug* in that vernacular. He was telling a story about his 1952 visit to California and how, at a dinner, he had become enraged by his host who was slandering FDR in a most virulent 1930s manner, how he, Dallapiccola, could finally bear it no longer, allowing convictions to overcome good manners, and so on. Except for the self-quotation, the story was told in Italian, with an intoxicating sense of theater, superb timing, and, for emphasis, with many stops on our walk. I remember how a group of teenage boys was halted in its tracks by the sight and sound of the tiny, hugely energized, gesticulating foreigner. And ever since seeing his picture on the *Times* obituary page—he died in Florence on February 19—I haven't known what to do with the idea that this dynamic voice is stilled.

He was born in 1904 in Istria, then part of the Austro-Hungarian Empire. In the 1914 war, the family was interned in Graz, and there he first made acquaintance with the central symphonic and operatic repertoire. He studied in Trieste and later in Florence, where he became "supernumerary" professor of piano ("adjunct," we would say) at the Cherubini Conservatory.

He was a splendid pianist and gave concerts for years with the violinist Sandro Materassi. He became an extremely able conductor, though there he stuck to occasional performances of his own music, viewing with some scorn those of his composer-colleagues who could not resist the temptation to don white tie and tails and to let themselves be applauded. Here, too, I cannot forget the sound of his ringing voice in the phrase "*per farsi applaudire*" nor the sardonic gesture that accompanied his words—he had just been much "*applaudito*" after conducting the premiere of his *Parole di San Paolo* at the Library of Congress—the deep inhalation, the rising and pulling back of the shoulders, the uplifted, slightly tilted head, and, at last, the deep, slow, delicately parodic bow.

The 1933 premiere in Florence of his orchestral Partita attracted wide attention to him as a composer. The next decade in Fascist Italy, though, was one, for him, of torment, anxiety about his Jewish wife, and quasi-seclusion. (He told the story of that time with characteristic vividness and absence of self-pity in the July 1953 *Musical Quarterly*.) The daughter who was born at the end of those dark years he named Annalibera.

After the war, he, who had always been international in musical outlook and who had been the first Italian composer to use the path-breaking discoveries of Arnold Schoenberg, worked hard to bring his country into contact with the European musical community again. His love for Schoenberg's music was old. He liked to tell the story of the 1924 performance at the Pitti Palace in Florence of *Pierrot lunaire* under the composer's direction. Two people in the audience had brought a pocket score; one was the shy 20-year-old student, the other the 65-year-old and dying Puccini. He watched with awe as the two masters conversed in a corner. He could not bring himself to speak to Schoenberg, and it was over twenty years before he dared write to him.

In the '40s, Dallapiccola began to establish a reputation for the second time. In 1951 and 1952 he taught at Tanglewood, and from then on, young Americans—among them Pulitzer Prize–winning Donald Martino of the New England Conservatory faculty—went in droves to Florence on their Fulbrights to study with him. The Cherubini Conservatory then still carried him on his books as a piano teacher.

How to describe his music? It is precise, economical, in that sense classical. It is radiated by a wonderful lyricism. The melodies wind and stretch with strength and grace, with true Italian "*vocalistà*." "When he composes he sings," one of his singers once said. The melodies are set in the most delicately wrought textures. All this one hears especially in the compositions of *Greek Lyrics*, the *Machado Songs*, in the Laude that he incorporated into the *Concerto for the Night of Christmas 1956*, and in *An Mathilde*, a miraculous setting of Heine's most touching poems to his wife.

Then there is the series of works in which he dealt with his anguish at the state of the world, the choral *Canti di prigionia* (*Songs of Imprisonment*—settings of Mary Queen of Scots, Boethius, and Savonarola), written 1938–41, and after the war, its powerful rich sequel, *Canti di liberazione*, the grim one-act opera, *Il prigioniero* (*The Prisoner*), and the staged oratorio on *Job*, grander, harder, less sensuous, but, like his lyric outpourings of love for words and the human voice, inventive and strong in rhythm. His masterpiece—completed 1968, it represents decades of planning—is his opera *Ulysse*, Homer read by a man who knew and loved Joyce.

The instrumental works, which are relatively few, tend toward the ascetic. The *divertissement*-like reworkings of Tartini and Paganini are the least convincing, but the notebook of short piano pieces for his daughter, the *Quaderno musicale di Annalibera*, is lovely, especially in its transcribed form as *Variazioni per orchestra*.

All of it reflects the man, the profoundly religious humanist who lived so intimately with the work of Joyce, Proust, and Mann, but who liked to say that his teachers were the medieval mystics; who seemed to know not only every note of Western music, but the Greek and Roman classics, Dante, Shakespeare, and Goethe; who loved Blake, Donne, the cross-shaped poems of George Herbert, and what he once called "the adamantine words" of the first letter [of Paul] to the Corinthians; the man fluent in classical tongues and in French and German (and getting there in English), all spoken with resounding Florentine accent; the man who loved Webern for his purity, but found relatively little to take from his music; the analytic intellectual who adores the physical sensation of voices and instruments (when most of a New England Conservatory Orchestra program was devoted to his music in 1967, himself conducting some of the *Greek Lyrics*, he asked that Ravel's *Boléro* conclude the concert); who was pained by corruption and slovenliness in language, or wherever he found it; who viewed the world tragically and humankind with compassion; who was endlessly curious and limitlessly erudite.

When our first son was born, Dallapiccola sent him a postcard as a welcome into the world and included these lines:

> *The Laestrygones and the Cyclops*
> *And angry Poseidon you shall not meet*
> *If you carry them not in your soul,*
> *If your soul sets them not up before you.*[3]

That is followed by a stern: "*Memento!*" He had seen those cannibal giants who ate up all of the crew of Odysseus and he carried them not in his soul.

The meeting in Stuttgart I described happened not long after the death of Thomas Mann. Dallapiccola said that he had written to Mann's daughter, Monika, a former piano pupil of his, to express his hope that Mann, "The inventor of so many deaths," had been granted the "modest death" of Mont-kaw,

[3] From C. P. Cavafy's *Ithaka* (1911).

Potiphar's steward in *Joseph in Egypt*. I hope Dallapiccola's crossing the *Magic Mountain* world was easy.

One of the figures he revered was Ferruccio Busoni. At Busoni's death in 1924, one of his disciples said, "We have lost, not a man, but a standard." In that spirit, then, "*Addio, Maestro, e grazie*."

Once, in Concord, I Heard John Kirkpatrick Play the *Concord* Sonata

March 9, 1975

CONCORD, MA—I have heard the *Italian* Symphony in Italy and I don't care if I never hear the *Scotch* Symphony in Scotland, but Charles Ives's *Concord* Sonata in Concord—particularly if played by John Kirkpatrick, who gave its first public performances thirty-five years ago—that was irresistible. And just that, thanks to the Middlesex School, the Concord Academy, the Thoreau Lyceum, and a number of individuals in the area, was offered at the Performing Arts Center of Concord Academy last Tuesday evening.

It is hard now, and particularly after the centenary last year, to imagine a time when Ives was less than a hugely fascinating figure on the musical landscape. I am sure, though, that when I was in college and graduate school I never once heard the name of Ives pronounced in a class or seminar, and worse, I am sure that it was not until quite late, probably 1961, that I made a reasonable lot of room for him in a 20th-century course I was then teaching regularly.

Various events have been cited as crucial to the recognition of Ives in the profession (how tough that was!) and by the public, notably his 1947 Pulitzer Prize for the Third Symphony, forty-three years old but unperformed until April 1946. But the single moment when the tide turned was surely John Kirkpatrick's Town Hall recital of January 20, 1939, when Lawrence Gilman responded in the *Herald-Tribune* by calling it "the greatest music composed by an American, and the most deeply and essentially American in impulse and implication." Kirkpatrick played the Sonata in Concord later that year, and now, having him back again, the cause won, made something altogether special of the concert. It was, however, far more than a sentimental occasion: the Sonata magnificently projects the range of Ives's poetic fantasy and untrammeled energy of invention, and Kirkpatrick, whom Gilman called "an unobtrusive minister of genius," still plays it incomparably.

"Though a great poet and prophet, he is greater, possibly as an invader of the unknown—America's deepest explorer of the spiritual immensities—a seer painting his discoveries in masses and with any color that may lie at hand—cosmic, religious, human, even sensuous . . . not afraid to ride Arion's Dolphin, and to go wherever he is carried—to Parnassus or the 'Musketaquid.'"[4] That is Ives on Emerson, but is it not a striking characterization of Ives himself?

Not surprisingly the long "Emerson" movement with its ambition to compose philosophy, as it were, is the least controlled and remains the most problematic, even perplexing part of the Sonata, while the domestic "Alcotts" yields its simplest, most immediately accessible music. "Hawthorne" is a fantastic scherzo, and flute-playing "Thoreau" is the finale, the most "musical" of the movements, pastoral in genre, tending towards impressionism in language. All of it grows from the double kernel of Charles Zeuner's Missionary Hymn and the first four notes of Beethoven's Fifth Symphony.

With its shifting meters, its leaps and stretches, its recklessly piled masses of notes, the *Concord* Sonata is exceedingly difficult by any ordinary pianistic standards, and Kirkpatrick gets around in it with marvelous confidence and seeming ease. Introducing one of his encores, Ives's "The Seen and Unseen?," he said: "You may have noticed that Ives is not averse to writing several kinds of music within one piece." To "rationalize" that, to make those crazy juxtapositions of original and quoted material, of scratchiest dissonance and homely, harmonious consonants plausible to a listener is a greater difficulty still, and that is where Kirkpatrick is peerless. His sense for the style of the quoted hymns and marches, for the allusions to church bells and distant flutes, his feeling for the degree to which these "found objects" need to be at one and the same time italicized and integrated is uncanny. He quotes like a man who knows the whole context of what he is quoting, and no one else I have heard play the *Concord*—not even Easley Blackwood, who does it impressively and excitingly—plays it so "completely" and lets you hear so much of its letter and its spirit.

He is a leading Ives scholar and he maintains a special freshness of outlook on the *Concord* by departing from the printed text of the second edition, revised by Ives himself between 1940 and 1947, moving into all kinds of variants drawn from the first edition of 1920, from the heaps of sketches, from his recollection of Ives's own playing, even including what appear to be some arbitrary touches of his own. And that is very much in the spirit of Ives, who liked to think of this piece as continuously evolving rather than as a fixed object. (The question of the place of improvisation in the *Concord* Sonata is interestingly argued by Sondra Rae Clark in the April 1974 *Musical Quarterly.*) What Kirkpatrick played the other night was much like you can hear on his 1970 Columbia recording, with new departures in detail both toward and away from the printed edition.

[4] "Musketaquid"—meaning "place where the waters flow through the grasses," or "grassy plain"—was the Algonquin name for Concord.

His unique way with the piece is in part a triumph of empathy and intellect, but it is as much attestation of remarkable pianistic resources. Kirkpatrick is no ordinary pianist. He began the concert with—what does one call it? a Mozart group? a Mozart sonata?—the last D major Sonata, K.576, which, however, he precedes with the D minor Fantasy and into which he inserts the D major Minuet, K.355 (the amazing chromatic one which Tchaikovsky included in his *Mozartiana*), and there, his performance seemed hardly as much that of a professional pianist as one by a highly cultivated amateur who plays quite a lot of piano.

Moreover, what came afterwards—the *Evocations* of Carl Ruggles (what a contrast between these two wild musical hermits, the precise and reluctant Ruggles and the ebulliently prolific, all-over-the-place Ives) and four pieces by Louis Moreau Gottschalk—confirmed the impression of "amateur." I mean nothing bad by that. This pianistic and musical character is also wonderfully consonant with Kirkpatrick's stage personality, the impeccable manners which are those of a gentleman rather than a performer's. The narrow skull, refined features, silver hair of a 1930s prep-school headmaster, the combination of incisive vocabulary and muted delivery that goes with that appearance.

It is, all that, a perfect embodiment of the world Ives wrote about, of Concord. Then, whatever Kirkpatrick does is illuminated by wonderful intelligence and musicality. He played the Ruggles so well, especially when he repeated the second Evocation, the one dedicated to him, as another encore; and in the amusing but rather stretched Gottschalk pieces, if he could do no more than suggest their virtuosic component, he caught perfectly their humor and, with a certain detachment, their raffishness. If he is not, in the Mozartian sense, always a fleet, elegantly precise pianist, in Ives those qualities are hardly at issue anyway.

So it was a stimulating concert, full of character, and completely unlike any I have ever heard. If I live to be ancient, long after I have forgotten how to spell Arrau or Barenboim or Ciccolini, I shall be telling my great-grandchildren that once, in Concord, I heard John Kirkpatrick play the *Concord* Sonata.

Sessions Cantata to Have East Coast Premiere Here Tomorrow

March 23, 1975

Tomorrow at 8:30 p.m. at Sanders Theatre, Cambridge, Roger Sessions's Walt Whitman cantata, *When Lilacs Last in the Dooryard Bloom'd*, will have its first East Coast performance.[5] Michael Senturia conducts the Harvard University

[5] See next article.

Choir, the soloists are Diana Hoagland, D'Anna Fortunato, and Alan Baker, and the concert, which is presented by the Harvard Music Department and the Fromm Foundation, is open to the public free of charge.

Andrew Imbrie writes of Sessions: "Those of us who have studied with him will remember with affection his tone of voice in speaking of 'the large gesture,' 'the long line.'" Sessions's music at its most characteristic is big—densely packed with events, rich in internal associations and connections, large in expressive ambition.

The Whitman cantata, written 1968–70 for the 100th anniversary of the University of California at Berkeley, where Sessions taught 1945–52, is, except for his two operas, his biggest work. Whitman wrote the poem in response to the death of Lincoln. An earlier and famous setting by Hindemith commemorates the death of President Franklin D. Roosevelt. The Sessions score is in memory of Martin Luther King, Jr., and Robert F. Kennedy, and tomorrow's performance of it will be dedicated to Sessions's friend, Luigi Dallapiccola, who died in Florence February 19.[6] The cantata continues a series of elegies begun with the Adagio of the Second Symphony, during whose writing the death of President Roosevelt occurred, and including the Piano Sonata No. 3, which commemorates President Kennedy.

Whitman always wanted to write a book in which he might gather his Civil War experience together. It would be part mosaic, part history, he thought, but it never came about. (*Walt Whitman's Civil War* edited by Walter Lowenfels—Knopf, 1960—is something like a realization of the plan, based on letters, lectures, journalistic reports, poems, etc.) The war, in which Whitman served as a sort of nurse's aide and "consolant" in military hospitals, was a critical emotional experience in his life.

Sessions is in the anomalous position of being a great eminence on the musical scene—not least as a teacher whose students have included composers as distinguished and as diverse as Milton Babbitt, John Harbison, Andrew Imbrie, Earl Kim, Leon Kirchner, and Fred Lerdahl—whose own music remains relatively little-known. That music is immensely difficult to perform. There is so much going on in it, with no idling, no coasting, and with accompaniments apt to assume so "specific" a character as to become independent lines. *Lilacs* at forty-some minutes is hardly less concentrated than the intense and witty Symphony No. 8 at fifteen. But the music immensely rewards superb performance, not only careful performance, which is of course essential, but performance with flair, with a sense for "The large gesture," for the rhetorical and—let us not shirk it—the ethical assumptions of the Beethoven-Brahms-Schoenberg tradition which Sessions uniquely represents today.

[6] See Dallapiccola obituary of March 2, 1975.

The Cantata, projecting the poetry now in simple chordal declamation, now in the long, high-arched melodies of which Sessions is such a master, is especially good at giving the sense of Whitman's recklessly large-breathed, quasi-Biblical rhythms. (Hindemith strait-laces them rather, while Delius in the lovely *Sea Drift*, which is beautifully responsive to the poet's emotional world, tends to let everything run awfully liquid.) Sessions also has an extraordinary sense of rhythm in the largest sense. How clearly one is made to feel the thrush's carol of death (solo for contralto) as the point toward which all things lead and from which everything recedes:

Come lovely and soothing death,
Undulate round the world, serenely arriving, arriving,
In the day, in the night, to all, to each,
Sooner or later, delicate death.
. . . I glorify thee above all,
I bring thee a song that when thou must indeed come, come unfalteringly.

When you listen, attend to the poem: it is the way into the music, as the music is the way—a way—into it. Some details I love especially: the plaintive conversation of flute and clarinet with which the work opens; the whippoorwill phrases of offstage flute and piccolo (sometimes with xylophone); the undulating, swaying violins for the "sea-winds blown from east and west"; the vaulted melody with which the violins follow the phrase, "Night and day journeys a coffin"; the wonderful mixture, part doublings, part variants, near the end, at "yet each to keep and all, retrievements out of the night"; the last phrase for bass clarinet, alto flute, trombone, clarinet, which does not stop so much as move across the last double-bar out of earshot . . .

Walt Whitman's Poem-Turned-Into-a-Cantata

March 25, 1975

Music that brings tears is still being written. Roger Sessions's cantata on Walt Whitman's *When Lilacs Last in the Dooryard Bloom'd*, heard twice last night in Sanders Theatre, is an example of it.[7] The poem was for Lincoln's death. The composition, finished in December 1970, was in memory of Martin Luther King, Jr. and Robert F. Kennedy. These performances were dedicated to Luigi

[7] See previous article.

Dallapiccola. Hearing it took, I am sure, almost all of us straight to whatever and whomever we have mourned.

Sessions meets Whitman's extravagance with a shaping, articulating discipline that heightens the intensity of feelings, that risky splendor of words in the elegy. What identification, what passion, what a sense of the gentleness in Whitman, what musical imagination and mastery in this cantata with its powerful, elastic rhythms, its dark and clean harmonies, its evocative orchestra, its marvelously fluid way of moving the text in and out among the voices of the chorus and the three soloists.

The performance, exhaustively prepared—and thanks for that to the Fromm Foundation—was conducted by Michael Senturia, who also had been in charge of the premiere four years ago at Berkeley. His was a superb achievement, precise and fiery. The orchestra of Boston freelancers was very good. Prepared by John Ferris, the Harvard University Choir did some of the most transparent, musical singing in my experience.

The crucial solo part is that of contralto, who sings the Carol of Death. D'Anna Fortunato hasn't the Marian Anderson low notes Sessions had in mind, but I'd pay that price gladly for the radiance of her high G on the repeated "joy" at the carol's end and for all the rest of the human, musical, and vocal beauty in her singing. Baritone and soprano intervene more as though in passing: Alan Baker and Diana Hoagland contributed unforgettably. From the capacity audience there was concentrated attention during the music and, after the second time through the forty-minute cantata, a long ovation for the performers and the 78-year-old master.

Sills Smash at Met Debut

April 8, 1975

NEW YORK—It was 11:30 when the curtain came down. Eighteen minutes and twenty seconds and twenty-six curtain calls later, the show was really over. The show was the long-awaited Metropolitan Opera debut of lyric-coloratura soprano Beverly Sills, the sort of woman who actually catches the bouquets that are thrown at her across orchestra pits and footlights.

The demand for tickets for the five performances of Rossini's *Siege of Corinth* with Beverly Sills in these two weeks was the most frantic any Met staff member could recall, and the concluding ovation was one of the longest. Yesterday's performance, a benefit for the Metropolitan Opera Production Fund, was sold out virtually as soon as it was announced in spite of prices like $60 for an orchestra seat, $500 for a parterre box seating eight, or $9 in the family circle. Standing room was at its usual $2 and $3.[8] A couple of dozen hopefuls stood outside 'til almost the end hoping to inherit the stubs of early leavers.

I had no expert celebrity-spotter with me. On my own, however, I spotted among others Danny Kaye, letting out ear-piercing whistles and calling for a speech, and from the musical world such luminaries as Maria Jeritza, Jessye Norman, Licia Albanese, Bidu Sayão, Risë Stevens, Robert Merrill, and André Kostelanetz.

Thirty yards separate the New York State Theater, the home of the New York City Opera for whom Beverly Sills has sung for more than twenty years, from the Metropolitan Opera House. Especially given the mediocrities who have appeared on the Met stage in that time and who have disappeared from it again (most of them anyway), the question of why wasn't Sills singing there has been asked for some time. Since she became a superstar seven or eight years ago, her non-appearance there had become a *cause célèbre* in the operatic world.

It had been a year of delayed debuts here. In October the tenor, Peter Pears, came to the house at 63 to sing nine sold-out performances of Benjamin Britten's *Death in Venice*.[9] Last Thursday, the legendary and controversial Magda Olivero, also at 63 (or possibly a bit more), made a clamorous debut as Tosca. Sills, a month from her 46th birthday, is by comparison a babe in arms, but her appearance last night was for her fans an event not much short of the second coming.

This is not the Pears-Olivero kind of debut at all, nor was it comparable to those of Callas and Nilsson (who, by the way, due to some irreconcilable differences with the Internal Revenue Service, made her unannounced farewell to this country last Wednesday). Sills, after all, has sung opera all over the country for years and has made hundreds of appearances with the company those few yards across Lincoln Center Plaza.

She herself had tried to play down her delayed coming to the Met. She does not consider it a "pinnacle in her career," she has said, adding on another occasion that she was doing it because she could no longer afford the time for twenty-minute explanations of why she was not singing at the Met. Her fans, however, did not take the event in that spirit. They interrupted the music with fifty-three seconds of applause at her first appearance and gave her second-act aria, which is her first real solo in *The Siege of Corinth*, an ovation of four minutes and forty seconds. The Met has after all a unique glamour for most opera buffs, and to most of that audience this was the union at last of the greatest and the greatest, given an additional fillip by the sense that an absurd and long overdue injustice was being righted.

[8] Adjusted for inflation, the dollar figures amount roughly to $365; $3,000; $54.75; $12; and $18 in 2025.

[9] See article of November 17, 1974.

The debut vehicle, Rossini's *The Siege of Corinth*, had served her for the same purpose at La Scala, Milan, in May 1969, and indeed the Met production, conducted by Thomas Schippers, directed by Sandro Sequi, and sumptuously designed by Nicola Benois, is largely the same.

The role of the Corinthian governor's daughter, Pamira, who is supposed to marry the young military hero, Neocle (Shirley Verrett in a trouser role), but who loves the enemy, the Turkish leader Maometto (Justino Diaz), offers Sills plenty of chances at the pathos in which she can be so touching and the coloratura she negotiates so brilliantly. (You can hear her readily on the new Angel recording, on the broadcast of April 19, and of course when the Met comes to town on April 21).

Though the audience was a partisan one that had come primarily to hear Beverly Sills, it was by no means impervious to good singing by others. Shirley Verrett, mustachioed and looking just a bit like Sugar Ray Robinson, earned three-and-a-half minutes of shouting with her great third-act aria.

Steve Reich's *Drumming* Should Also Be Filed Under Magic

April 20, 1975

BROOKLYN, NY—My pleasure in the music of Steve Reich is a division between me and most musical friends and associates, the exceptions being the composer, Oliver Knussen, and Michael Tilson Thomas, who introduced me to Reich's work in the first place. Boston has had opportunities to hear what Reich is up to. His own group, Steve Reich and Musicians, has appeared at the Museum of Fine Arts, and Thomas put *Four Organs* on his first BSO Spectrum Concert in 1971[10] and included *Music for Mallet Instruments, Voices, and Organ* on one of the last. And there have been some recordings: *Violin Phase* and *It's Gonna Rain* on Columbia MS-7265 and *Come Out* on Odyssey 32160160 (these all cleverly hidden under "electronic music" in Mr. Schwann's catalogue[11]), then *Four Organs* on Angel, and now from Deutsche Grammophon, a three-record album including *Six Pianos*, *Music for Mallet Instruments* etc., and Reich's biggest work to date, the eighty-five-minute *Drumming*.

Reich is a 38-year-old New Yorker touched a bit by California, trained in philosophy and music, and for the last nine years set on his own path with his own performing group. He spent several months of 1970 in Africa studying drumming.

[10] For background on the BSO's "Spectrum Concerts," see footnote to the earlier Spectrum Concert reference in the review of September 23, 1972.
[11] See article of September 13, 1970.

In 1967 he conceived but for technological reasons did not execute a piece called *Slow Motion Sound*. Characteristically, his music is about slow and slight change, and that gets to the people who are bored or maddened or both by what he does in the slowness of those changes. *Four Organs*, for example, consists of a single chord. Its pitches never change, but their distribution among the four rock organs does, and the durations become longer. The process continues for just under twenty-five minutes. A characteristic way of spinning out Reich's music is the process he has called "phasing," the gradual shifting away from an established pattern by having one part imitate another but at a slightly different speed so that the two lines become more and more separated. *It's Gonna Rain*, whose raw material consists of those three words taken from a sermon and whirled along on tape loops, plays delightfully with that idea. That dates from 1965, and *Drumming*, 1970–71, completes Reich's explorations of its possibilities.

Music for Mallet Instruments, Voices, and Organ and *Six Pianos* (a practical reduction of the charming notion of writing a piece for all the pianos in a piano store), both from 1973, deal more with percussive buildups rather than with gradual shifts of phase. The effect, however, is the characteristic Reichian one. If you don't pay much attention, it all sounds the same. If you do, you keep discovering that it is changing, or more often, that it has changed. Reich has likened it to watching the minute hand of a watch: you can learn to see it move.

Four Organs was the first Reich piece I heard, and I still remember how enchanted I was by those tiny shifts of duration and density in that one juicy and stubborn chord and by the fastidiousness of the mind that imagined those shifts. It is in that fastidiousness and precision and purposefulness that Reich's music differs profoundly from the potty empty-headedness of Terry Riley's, with which it is sometimes grouped by the rougher pigeonholers.

I have never ceased to be delighted by Reich's mind and the noises it dreams up. It is almost the only recent music I know that makes me smile: that sense of something being the same yet different, and then really different, those imperceptible emergings of a new beat or of a new sound in the texture, it gets to me every time. It reminds me a little of the metric modulations in Elliott Carter's music, with the difference that in Carter everything happens quickly and at high intensity while Reich proceeds with a sense of leisure so extreme that you really have to reset your mental metabolism. (Except in my head there is no connection between those worlds: Carter finds Reich unspeakably boring, and Reich disavows contamination by any of his Western contemporaries.)

Laura Dean is a 28-year-old New York choreographer whose fancies move along much the same paths as Reich's. She has described how she spent months alone in a San Francisco studio just sitting. Then came walking, first in straight lines, then in circles. That led to spinning, something she learned to do for three hours at a time, finding in it "a direct physical connection to the whirling motion of the mind . . . experienced while sitting."

In 1972 she began to imagine a choreography for *Drumming*, and on 3–6 April in the tall and handsome hexahedron known as the Lepercq Space at the Brooklyn Academy of Music, Laura Dean and Dance Company with Steve Reich and Musicians presented their combined work.

There were eight dancers in all. Dressed in white silk trousers and white embroidered shirts, they moved in patterns as simple in themselves and as intricately related as Reich's music. Jogging in place, hopping, rapid twirling of the forearms about each other, occasional games for two. Everyone does the same, and on every one it looks different, no attempt is made to homogenize the styles of the eight women whose individuality Dean clearly enjoys, and much of the pleasure in *Drumming* comes from this unplanned process of continuous variation. Dean has passed on what she knows about spinning and twice, in the second and third sections of *Drumming*, she sets up solar systems, herself spinning slowly in the center and other dancers moving about her in orbits of varying speeds and tightness. I noticed, and was happy to notice, that like me, the dancers tended to smile when they had moved into a change, when a new momentum had taken over, when they were being danced, as it were, by a new measure.

Endings do puzzle me in Reich. How do you stop such a process? Reich just quits, as though the tape had been snipped. Dance softens the process. The dancers have no idea when the music will cease, details of duration and transition being subject to on-the-spot improvisation (the night I saw *Drumming* it ran short and tight, a mere sixty-five minutes, which is rather too terse and businesslike for its unearthly length—I never have any feeling in Reich for how much or how little time has passed): they stop when they hear the silence, but their bodies and their clothes need a few moments to come to rest.

Perhaps *Drumming* should be filed under "magic" as well as under "music." Somebody, at any rate, should get it to Boston with Laura Dean's engagingly concentrated, humorous, devout dancers. Meanwhile, to have DG's generous, well-annotated album is a wonderful pleasure.

Von Karajan Remarkable, a Conductor of Immense Resources

May 2, 1976

SALZBURG, AUSTRIA—Mozartkugeln are chocolate balls about an inch-and-a-quarter in diameter, filled with a seductive series of revelations of cream, nougat, and marzipan, and wrapped in gold foil bearing one of the spurious portraits of the master. Without doubt their manufacturer nets more in a single day than Mozart earned from his compositions in his whole life.

People here like to say that in twenty or thirty years, they will be selling Karajankugeln. Nothing so far is named after Salzburg's second most famous musical son, but only because he's still living. Even if you are not interested in music, it is hard to escape awareness of Herbert von Karajan here.

The public relations staff of Deutsche Grammophon and EMI earned their keep during von Karajan's own Tenth Easter Festival, which ran April 10–19. There seemed to be no shop or cafe window, no kiosk, without its photo of Karajan, Karajan up, down, walking, sitting, conducting eyes open, eyes closed, driving, flying, skiing, smiling, frowning, alone, with others (including the tenor who left the Festspiele in a huff midway and the bass who swore he would never sing with Karajan again after this year's last *Lohengrin*).[12]

The newspapers are full of stories about von Karajan, including some that complain about how he hogs the media, and when his grey Rolls-Royce with Swiss license-plates—GR-14779 from the Canton of Graubünden—glides through the streets all heads whip about in hopes of a glimpse. If all else fails, you can go to the mobile post office set up in front of the Festspielhaus and get your letters and cards canceled with a special Karajan stamp with swan and grail. He begins to compete with Snoopy.

It is as well that these vicarious experiences are available. They are about as much as most Salzburgers can get: the prices—up to $82.50 for an orchestra seat to the opera[13]—enforce a certain exclusiveness. An hour before performance time, people line the Hoftstallgasse and watch the well-to-do, over-dressed (black tie at 4:30 p.m.) expensive-smelling visitors from Vienna, Switzerland, and Germany enter into the house.

Yes, one gets irritated and can be quite tempted to forget that the man is an extraordinary conductor and sometimes a remarkable interpretive musician. There are, to be sure, occasions that allow you to keep forgetting that, and it may be that this year, with Karajan still incompletely recovered from a back operation, offered more than its share. The festival schedule would be hard on a younger man (Karajan is 68) in perfect health: this year, in ten days three performances of *Lohengrin*, two of the Verdi Requiem, and two each of two orchestral concerts. There was some grumpiness, too, about last-minute changes of program, explained by the illness and its effects on recording and rehearsal schedules. Some of us at least were disappointed at the cancellation of the Mahler Sixth and of the Opus 6's of Berg and Webern.

[12] As specified below, these singers were tenor René Kollo and bass Karl Ridderbusch.
[13] Adjusted for inflation, this dollar figure amounts roughly to $470 in 2025.

The orchestral concert I did hear—Mozart No. 39 in E-flat and Strauss's *Also sprach Zarathustra*—was a misery. Mozart, heavy in sound with its doubled woodwinds, and beyond that unaware, tensionless, with no transitions—just suddenly, for no reason, there you were in the next theme or in a new key—and with an unmotivated, vulgar outburst of noise for the last fifteen seconds. Strauss messily, brutally played, out of tune and without rhythmic unanimity. The Berlin Philharmonic has fantastic strings and, for all I know, the best brass anywhere, but the woodwinds are a mixed lot that includes several toneless wobblers, and most of the percussion playing is violent.

That evening, Karajan walked and looked like an old man with a sore back, and his conducting was muzzy. The following evening, according to the reports I got, he must have been very much all there for the Verdi Requiem, and certainly he was for *Lohengrin* the day after that. Immense resources of energy, extraordinary feeling for orchestral sound—who would have thought so many colorations could be given to the fanfares that run all through that magical opera?—a cool and incorruptible sense of direction: it was all as canny as could be, and immensely exciting.

There is, alas, no robbing von Karajan of his delusion that he is a great stage director. It is hard to imagine his putting up in another, whether director, singer, or orchestral player, with the amateurishness he allows himself. The *Lohengrin* production imitated the Manesse Manuscript, a famous medieval collection of minnesinger music. In Günther Schneider-Siemssen's design, this provided a wonderfully pretty curtain, but as soon as the closed book was opened, there was trouble. The chorus, more crucial in *Lohengrin* than in any opera before *Moses und Aron*, was exiled behind scrims at both sides because the book illusion required a shallow stage. Because of this constriction, the Minster looked like a modest parish church and nothing one could see matched the splendor of what one heard. Singers stood as still as they could, often with their backs to those who were addressing them (Elsa's rudeness to the King was as striking as it was out of character), and Lohengrin addressed his thanks to the invisible swan to the rear wall of the stage. As they were no longer needed, persons were slowly smuggled backwards off the stage. As for delineation of character or situation through gesture and demeanor, no hope.

But there certainly was a lot to listen to. All gossip-loving Salzburg was in suspense as to whether Anna Tomowa-Sintow and René Kollo would be well enough to appear at the premiere (Karajan upset several hundred ticket holders by closing the dress rehearsal at the last moment). By the second performance, the one I saw, Tomowa-Sintow was recovered and Kollo, after a running series of disagreements with the Maestro, had cancelled at 11 that morning and left town.

His substitute was an almost unknown young tenor from Nuremberg, Karl-Walter Böhm, who fortunately had been present at rehearsals since Kollo's voice began troubling him before the premiere. Böhm is just a little raw of voice in the top register, but he produced a steady sound that was impeccably in tune, he was clear and intelligent with words, less phlegmatic than Kollo is apt to be, and he managed a difficult situation with admirable aplomb. He is a useful Wagner tenor, and there are not too many of those about.

Tomowa-Sintow, a young Bulgarian, is a large woman with a not very large voice, musical, verging toward the wordless, not wildly interesting. For wicked, pagan Ortrud, Karajan offered a bit of surprise casting, Ursula Schröder-Feinen, a dramatic soprano in a mezzo role. Moreover, I was surprised by what she did with it. I had heard her sing Elektra, her most famous part, in a concert performance with the Cleveland Orchestra and recalled tirelessly efficient, cold belting out of note after note. This, on the other hand, was all fire and involvement, vocal and verbal variety, rather mannered (I think she has been listening to Astrid Varnay and her effective, studied ugliness rather too much), and, while one does miss the mezzo timbre, for itself as well as for contrast to Elsa, this was exciting stuff.

Siegmund Nimsgern was an immensely forceful, slightly crazed Telramund. He is a baritone with a weight of voice that explains why he is not terribly convincing on all those Harnoncourt Bach cantata recordings. Karl Ridderbusch, the man who says he will not appear with Karajan again, sang a splendid King Henry, and Robert Kerns was a brightly sonorous Herald. All this, though with Kollo, you will be able to hear on an Angel recording before the year is out.

Violin-Harpsichord Concert

May 5, 1976

Francesco Geminiani was a contemporary of Bach's, a fine fiddler if not much of a composer, the author of a famous violin treatise, a musician with an international reputation established largely in Paris, London, and Dublin, where he died. The Duo Geminiani—Stanley Ritchie, an Australian violinist long resident in this country, and Elisabeth Wright, an American harpsichordist—gave a fascinating, provocative, elegant concert at the Longy School in Cambridge last night.

Ritchie is by no means exclusively specialized in Baroque music; he has been concertmaster with the Metropolitan Opera and he now leads the Philadelphia String Quartet (which, as you might not at once infer from its name, works out of the University of Washington in Seattle). He has, however, mastered the language of that musical world with its passions and artifices so that he can speak in it commandingly and virtually without a noticeable accent.

He is a sure instrumentalist, with a quick, accurate left hand and a bow arm at once powerful and delicate.

Unaccompanied, he played a long Passacaglia by the 17th-century composer, von Biber. It is a grave piece, but its purpose is quietly to dazzle the connoisseurs, or rather, to allow the virtuoso violinist to do so. And what Ritchie did here—by way of sorting out voices, producing myriad differentiations of color and intensity, knowing always when what effect was musically in place—was fair breathtaking.

Elizabeth Wright is a fluent, alert ensemble partner with a fine sense for long and grand melodies. Sometimes, though, the little extra articulations and distensions that are witty and charmingly capricious in Ritchie's playing come out a touch bumpy and overstated in hers. Interestingly, she played a harpsichord by Keith Hill, a builder from Michigan whose work is not much known hereabouts. It certainly is different from the Hubbard- and Dowd-descended instruments we mostly hear, less lean and colorful, with a certain thickness, almost viscosity in the center of the tone, and a powerful singing voice.

The Geminianis gave a beautifully imagined program. It began and ended with Bach, the sonatas with harpsichord obbligato in G major and E major.

On either side of the intermission, there was something French, a fanciful and courtly sonata by Jean Baptiste Senaille (we ask you to imagine an acute accent on the final e) before, and an unmeasured, improvisatory harpsichord prelude by d'Anglebert after.

And in the middle of each half, they turned to the greatly inventive and exploring 17th-century Germans, Schmelzer and his presumed pupil, von Biber. To hear that fantastical and passionate Sonata in C minor by Schmelzer played with such sympathy is an experience of a sort not often granted,

The audience was small and distinguished, about four-fifths of it consisting of scholars, performers, and instrument builders of eminence. That was nice. As for the other part, I hope by the time the Duo Geminiani returns, word will have gotten around. What they do has class.

The Fortepiano Revolution

June 22, 1976

By the year 2006, half the performances of the piano music of Haydn, Mozart, and the early Beethoven will be played on replicas of the 18th-century instruments. Then I'd give it another twenty or thirty years for the invasion of period instruments to have taken over late Beethoven, Schubert, Chopin, and Schumann as well. If that prediction seems far out to you, consider how improbable it seemed in 1965 that by the mid-'70s Bach on the harpsichord would have developed from exoticism to norm.

Last week and this, the fortepiano revolution is being quietly and effectively nurtured at a workshop at Wellesley College. There are nine students, several auditors, six instruments, and one remarkable teacher, the pianist Malcolm Bilson, who is on the faculty of Cornell University. The students and auditors, all women, are performers, teachers, scholars (most often more than one of these at a time). Most are in their 20s and their 30s, some are considerably older, and one is a high-school freshman. They come from as near as the Wellesley campus and as far as Berkeley, CA. Two own fortepianos, one is building her own from a kit.

The piano was invented about 1700 by a Florentine builder named Cristofori (stress on the second syllable). The complaint about the otherwise perfect harpsichord was that you cannot play soft or loud by touch, its strings are activated by a plucking mechanism that is pre-set for a certain pressure. Cristofori wanted to fix that and he called his new instrument the "*gravicembalo col piano e forte*," harpsichord with soft and loud. This was soon abbreviated to pianoforte, later just to piano. In the 18th century, the Germans and French for some reason reversed the word to fortepiano, and we now use that word when talking about the old instruments because it's handier than saying "18th-century piano."

Bilson, 40, originally from Los Angeles, educated at Bard College under Paul Nordoff and later in Vienna and Paris, has been playing the fortepiano for six years. He is a tall, powerfully built man with large hands and describes himself as "absolutely unsuited to this thing." He refers to the fact that virtually everything the modern pianist knows about arm-weight and playing with the energy of the entire body has to be unlearned. Attack a fortepiano as you would your Steinway and you will be rewarded only by bleak, shattered tone.

"Everything I have to teach falls under two headings," says Bilson: "articulation and lightness." He points out that on the modern piano the key goes down nine millimeters in response to a pressure of fifty-five grams; on his fortepiano, a replica by Philip Belt of a Louis Dulcken instrument in the Smithsonian Institution, the figures are three millimeters and fourteen grams. For their fresher tone and greater mechanical reliability, Bilson favors replicas over originals, a point in which he differs from his most famous European colleagues, Jörg Demus and Paul Badura-Skoda.

At the workshop, Bilson discusses history, gives individual lessons, teaches master classes, offers instruction in tuning and regulating, passes on some of his own mechanical know-how (he carries a black doctor-bag full of tools). One of the pleasures of being a fortepianist or harpsichordist is that of being so immediately in touch with your hardware; taking the thing apart and getting at the works isn't the big deal it has become on the modern grand. Though he has reservations about many of them, he also plays recordings (his favorite is a BASF disc on which Demus accompanies Elly Ameling in Schumann songs, using an 1833 piano by Conrad Graf).

Two factors, he believes, are immensely influential in the fortepiano revival: one is the growing number of builders, some of whom make their instruments available in kit form, and the other is the prevalence of recordings, which radically and profoundly affect public taste. Bilson will soon be adding to those: late summer, Advent will issue his performances on two different fortepianos of sonatas by Haydn and Beethoven plus shorter pieces by Mozart.

He teaches with humor and energy, with attention to what he calls the psychology of a Haydn sonata ("in this music you have to make yourself a manic-depressive" and later, "if you play this piece and nobody laughs you're a failure") and to the question of whether the B-flat wants to be played with the second finger or the third. "Leave it to how you feel," he advises a student uncertain about what to do with ornaments, "but educate the way you feel."

"The world is divided into two kinds of pianists, those who believe you can make a *crescendo* on one note and those who believe you can't. I believe you can. I know you can't but I believe you can." Constantly he emphasizes the importance of "what goes on between the notes." The students feel clumsy at the unfamiliar, exquisitely responsive instrument, and Bilson stresses that he is still learning, too. He shows how he practices and adds, "I'm learning the hard way that only this terrible patience ever pays off with anything." And, in humorous encouragement as they engage in this quiet revolution, he tells them: "You'll find that when you give a concert on a fortepiano, nobody comes backstage to see you. They all go to look at the instrument."

Harvard Summer Series Opens

July 7, 1976

"The piano is an imperialistic instrument." That's what a violinist buddy of mine used to say, and had he heard the performance of Bach's F minor Sonata at Sanders he would have said, "See?" Because there was Leon Kirchner at the piano, making a blanketing though colorless sound, and there was [violinist] Robert Portney being held down to a veiled and also colorless *pianissimo*. Back to back they faced each other, as the verse goes, each in a separate trance, each seeming to have given up on Bach as well as on his alleged partner, Kirchner spinning romantic fantasies off Bach's notes, Portney at a loss how to give a performance that would in some way be effective though inaudible.

Considering that these concerts come out of a program that mixes seasoned players and young in a school for chamber music, this was a most peculiar beginning. Downright perverse, in fact.

The counter-demonstration of what chamber music sounds like—even what it looks like—came after intermission. It is getting to be clear that when Richard Kogan, Lynn Chang, and Yo-Yo Ma play together, the only thing to do is to drop everything and go hear them.

Monday they took on Schubert's Trio in E-flat, a hard piece because it is expansive and shifts constantly between leisure and compression. It can sound long-winded and crazy, but this time it simply sounded right. The three young players—Chang was graduated from Harvard last year, Ma last month, and Kogan will be in '77—played according to the ideal that less is more. Tempos were steady, inflections subtle. Characterization and contrasts were vivid but understated. They charmed, they touched, they amazed—or rather, they let Schubert do all those things—but nothing was italicized.

There is a case to be made, though, for a quicker tempo in the second movement, not just because Schubert does modify "Andante" with "con moto," but because when its melancholy proto-Mahlerian tune returns so unexpectedly and miraculously in the finale, it wants to do so at its original speed. This time it came back rather faster (and the tempo for the finale was perfectly set) and the link across the two movements was to that degree less sure.

Between Bach and Schubert came Walter Piston's 1946 Divertimento for Nine Instruments, a natty and amusing work of (very generally speaking) Stravinskian accent. The performance conducted by Leon Kirchner was a bit rough around the edges, particularly with respect to textures not quite sorted out, but it was engaging and lively.

Happy Birthday, Rudolf Kolisch

July 18, 1976

Day after tomorrow, Rudolf Kolisch will be 80. The reference books identify him as a violinist, which is true but so inadequate as to seem silly: he is a musician of transcendent insight, fantasy, and responsibility whose instrument is the violin.

Since 1967 he has lived around Boston, associated with the New England Conservatory, and his patriarchal beard is an addition of those years. More than half his life he has been a quartet leader, and in the '20s and '30s, the Kolisch Quartet was one of the four or five great ones. It differed from others in two obvious respects: it championed new music and it always played from memory.

The 22-year-old Kolisch was one of the brilliant young musicians whom Arnold Schoenberg involved in the Society for Private Performances he founded in Vienna in 1918, the Society being an attempt, quickly doomed by the collapse of the Austrian currency, to provide a model setting for the hearing of new music. In a letter to his wife, the composer Alban Berg describes a distracted Kolisch, without violin, drifting onto the stage at one of these concerts, suddenly saying in surprise, "Oh, am I on now?"

The quartet, first called the New Vienna Quartet, grew out of the Society's activities. Renowned for its Mozart, Beethoven, Schubert, it was still more famous as the group that played the premieres—and many performances thereafter—of Schoenberg's Third and Fourth quartets and of the Concerto after Handel for Quartet and Orchestra, of Berg's *Lyric Suite*, of the Trio and Quartet of Webern (the latter first heard at Elizabeth Sprague Coolidge's South Mountain concerts in Pittsfield), and of the Third, Fifth, and Sixth quartets of Bartók. The close, lifelong tie to Schoenberg was personal as well as musical, for in 1924 the composer married Kolisch's sister Gertrud.

As for playing from memory, unheard of then for a quartet, that was no gimmick. Once, describing what was involved in coaching chamber music, Kolisch said, "All the time they have to be taught to listen and not to play so loud." Listening is for him the heart of musicianship, and if real ensemble, real listening are to be achieved, the eye must not be fixed on the printed page. Moreover, while studying their repertory, the quartet did not play in the customary way from individual parts but each from a complete score, dismembered and pasted onto large sheets of cardboard: that way the player would think of himself as playing a string quartet rather than a violin, viola, or cello part.

With Kolisch, everything has always been different, right from the start. Klamm, where he was born, turns out not even to be a real town but a mountaintop pilgrimage church near Salzburg where his mother had gone on a forbidden hike. And Kolisch, who no longer performs in public but still practices daily, plays left-handed. As a child, he lost the first joint of the middle finger of his left hand in an accident with a railway carriage door. He had been playing for about a year then and he relearned the instrument, bowing left and fingering right. "Never, thank Heaven," has he played in an orchestra: the accident saved him.

Boston Symphony violist Eugene Lehner joined the Kolisch Quartet as a 20-year-old conservatory student and he says that the six-hour train ride from Budapest to Vienna carried him a longer distance than a voyage from the South Pole to the North. "The quartet would begin to rehearse at ten in the morning and we would still be together at midnight, and for Anton Webern to spend one hour explaining a single rest was nothing. Kolisch lived then, as he still does, in the private heaven of pure idea, entirely without compromise. The strength of his conviction of his creed was such as to render the very idea of compromise absurd."

The pianist Russell Sherman, who first played for Kolisch at 13 and who has been particularly close to him since they both came to the New England Conservatory nine years ago, would modify the picture of Kolisch the absolutist. He tells a story of a rehearsal with the cellist Stefan Auber of Beethoven's *Archduke* Trio. Dissatisfied with the pallid playing of a particularly passionate sequence, Kolisch, in his slow, gently growling, Austrian-accented tones said, "It must be here the principle of the shivering goosepimple." To Sherman, the essential Kolisch touch here is the blend of the categorical and the idiomatic. He recalls, too, how after long and detailed rehearsal of a Beethoven sonata, Kolisch asked, "But does it sound free?" Sherman, his partner at the piano, thought not. "Then," said Kolisch, "let us play it very free," and out of the window went bundles of decisions made in the last few days.

The Kolisch Quartet was often praised for its way of making its performances sound spontaneous, almost improvised, though Kolisch would never allow the indulgence of freedom except on a foundation of the most painstaking, searching study. Jean Dane, who worked with Kolisch at the New England Conservatory and who is now violist of the Composers String Quartet, especially recalls learning "that there are certain things you have to give up. Maybe there's a very good note to be played, one that comes on a good finger or one your instrument likes, but if it conflicts with what the music wants there . . . "

The pianist Rudolf Serkin was 15 when he met Kolisch and played chamber music with him at the Society for Private Performances. "Unconditional admiration" is how he describes his feeling for the older man ("of course then the seven years made a lot of difference"). "I got criticism from him I have never forgotten and learned values that have remained with me always. He represented openness in that Viennese world of small circles. It was liberation for me."

And where to find room for the master of German words; the friend of the philosopher, sociologist, and musician, Theodor Wiesengrund Adorno; the moviegoer; the animal lover; the man who has played tennis with Charlie Chaplin (another left-handed fiddler) and who still stays up until 3 a.m. to watch matches on TV; the chess maniac; the only member of the Conservatory faculty to have a photo of Bobby Orr in his office; the man who confessed to wishing he were Derek Sanderson ("then I would know how to hit"); the author of a revolutionary, still controversial, profound yet simple essay, on performing Beethoven, published thirty-four years ago in the *Musical Quarterly* and now being expanded into a book?[14]

[14] For Kolisch on Beethoven, see articles of July 14 and July 21, 1968.

Once I introduced Kolisch on a public occasion, and afterwards he pounced on me angrily to say, "I am not a piece of history, I am a working musician." Still, our friend, the violinist Rose Mary Harbison, who has known Kolisch since she studied with him at the University of Wisconsin, is absolutely convincing when she calls him "a personality so powerful he makes me believe that the threads of history do exist, that they change us all, and that we become the future." Kolisch, she adds with emphasis, is an advocate of that future, and thinking of that and of Tuesday's gentle birthday child, I was reminded of what Busoni says somewhere, that he whose eye is on the future wears a happy look.

The Maestro Finally Comes to Tanglewood

July 25, 1976

LENOX—When I saw Visconti's *Death in Venice*, I hardly could wait to learn who had conducted the Adagietto of the Mahler Fifth used all through the film. The intensity of passion, the sure sense of direction as those long melodies unfolded, were far out of the ordinary, and that was the more amazing because the tempo was slower than any that most conductors would dare.

When, finally, the screen credits revealed the name of Franco Ferrara, my mind leaped back to Rome 1953. At the intermission of a concert, a friend had pointed out a strikingly handsome man who had been hailed at his debut just before the war as the most exciting Italian conductor of his generation, but whose career had almost at once been tragically interrupted when he turned out regularly to be afflicted by blackouts and seizures whenever he was on the podium before an audience. Now, my friend continued, Franco Ferrara conducted only for films and the radio. She believed as well that he was beginning to make quite a name as a teacher of conducting.

All that was true. What had changed by the beginning of this month when Ferrara arrived at Tanglewood to take charge for two weeks of a conducting seminar at the Berkshire Music Center was that his reputation as a teacher had become legendary. Now 65—he was born on the 4th of July, 1911, in Palermo, Sicily—Ferrara travels all over to teach, and his summer course at the Chigi Academy in Siena is truly a pilgrimage for young conductors.

Because of that annual obligation, it was not easy for Tanglewood to get him. It was four years since Gunther Schuller had led a delegation of three to Philadelphia where Ferrara was teaching a course on Mozart's *Don Giovanni*. Planning was complicated because Ferrara would not fly, something about which he changed his mind a couple of months ago in order to accept an invitation from Mrs. Imelda Marcos, wife of the president of the Philippines, to teach in Manila.

But here at last he was. Not the least remarkable thing about the first of several rehearsals and classes I visited was the attentive presence of some pretty good conductors, among them Seiji Ozawa (in a Boston Symphony T-shirt, usually sitting in the middle of the Berkshire Music Center student orchestra, helping out as a string coach); Gunther Schuller; Theodore Antoniou, a specialist in contemporary music and a member of the faculty at Tanglewood; Nikolaus Wyss, who has been Ozawa's assistant at the San Francisco Symphony; and the pianist Christoph Eschenbach, who had been soloist with the Boston Symphony the previous evening and who also conducts.

Ferrara's approach to teaching is practical. Unlike some colleagues, he engages in no theoretical discussion, nor does he seem interested in the analysis of scores. He likes to have an orchestra right there and seemed less sure of how to use the time at sessions when only two pianos are available. He is actually an adroit pianist and on such occasions would play such things as Hindemith's *Mathis der Maler*, Respighi's *Fountains of Rome*, and Rossini's *Silken Ladder* Overture with a good deal of dash and color.

At rehearsals with orchestra, a row of chairs was lined up at the front of the stage for the student conductors, Ferrara, and his interpreter, William Routch (Ferrara speaks next to no English). Ferrara's equipment included a baton and a music stand. The stand held no scores—he has those in his head—but it came in useful for tapping (and sometimes banging) on. Routch was needed mostly for things Ferrara wanted to say to the orchestra directly or for translation into Italian. Most of the conductors understood enough Italian to cope with what Ferrara said to them. He addressed them in the intimate "*tu*" form and by their first names, which he Italianized into Eduardo, Alfredo, and so forth. At no point did I hear anyone other than Mrs. Ferrara address him as anything other than "Maestro."

Speech issued forth at spitfire rate, the words few but vivid. "*Deciso*" ("decisive") was a frequent exhortation, and once, when a conductor waffled about a crucial entrance, the command was "*imperativo!*" A student's tempo would wander, producing an instant "*non rallentare*" and the rhythmic click of the stick on the metal stand.

In Beethoven's *Leonore* Overture No. 3, a brass entrance blotted out the rest of the orchestra. "*Forte, si, ma dentro*" ("loud, yes, but inside") was Ferrara's advice, and I thought of it a week later when Leonard Bernstein, rehearsing the Tchaikovsky Fourth, was trying to get the strings to play extra loud so that they could be heard over the roof-raising trumpets and trombones.

On the first page of the last movement of Debussy's *La Mer*, called "Dialogue of Wind and Sea," the six-note *pianissimo* figures in cellos and basses were too defined, too "musical." Ferrara strode over to the players, puffed out his cheeks hugely, said "*non strumenti, vento*" ("not instruments, wind"), and returned to his chair. Suddenly it sounded right, and composer Betsy Jolas down in the auditorium turned up her collar and said, "I think there's going to be some bad weather." "*Atmosfera*" was a frequent issue.

Ferrara, who was thrilled with the quality and responsiveness of the Berkshire Music Center Orchestra, finds that student conductors everywhere have the same difficulties. They talk too much: "*E inutile parlare, GUARDA!*" ("it's useless to talk, LOOK!"), he had let fly at one rehearsal, and students beginning lengthy explanations were constantly told to "show, show" and to use the arm, the hand, the baton. They don't know what to do with their left hands: a symmetrical movement of both arms guaranteed an outburst, "*non con due mani*" ("not with two hands"), how are you going to indicate the *pianissimo*? With your nose?

They learn by doing, and Ferrara disagrees radically with colleagues like Igor Markevitch and the late Hans Swarowsky, who always address the orchestra themselves instead of letting the student do so. When at Tanglewood rehearsals something went wrong and the student would first turn to the Maestro for help, the first response was apt to be "*ma prova, prova*" ("well, rehearse, rehearse").

Until they have efficient technique, students are not free to make personal statements about the music. "*Pensa alla musica*" ("think of the music") is the central clause of the Ferrara creed. Nikolaus Wyss, "Nicola" to Ferrara, remembered those words from his studies with him in Hilversum, Holland, fifteen years ago. Now he told about talking with one of the Tanglewood students who was puzzled by "*pensa alla musica*" when he wanted to be told "faster, slower, louder, softer." "He was still stuck on down, up, one, two," Wyss continued, "and I think maybe that's the moment when I first really understood the Maestro's '*pensa alla musica*.'"

Ferrara talked about ways of not thinking about music and told the story of a young conductor—"*non dire il nome*" ("don't say the name"), interposed the Signora anxiously—who had recently given a concert in Rome. His program was to begin with Strauss's *Don Juan*, whose beginning, a propulsive off-the-beat upward rush of strings, is notoriously difficult. He rehearsed it to his satisfaction, then told the orchestra he wanted to stride as rapidly as possible to the podium, barely bow to the audience, and dive right into the music, and he would now rehearse it that way. "Whereupon, if you can believe it," said Ferrara, "he actually left the platform and rehearsed his own dramatic entrance six times, *Madonna mia!*"

A Poignant Roar at Tanglewood

August 9, 1976

LENOX—Nikos Kazantzakis has written: "We come from a dark abyss, we end in a dark abyss, and we call the luminous interval life." Beethoven's great Solemn Mass proceeds from his knowledge of both the darkness and the luminosity. It stands alone in the poignance of the cry for mercy with which it begins, mercy that we may somehow deal with the luminous interval, and in the poignance also of the hope and thanks in the prayer for peace with which it ends.

Between beginning and end, Beethoven being Beethoven, everything is extreme—glorification, belief, empathy for suffering, awe, surrender, terror, and again, hope. Even the Kyrie eleison and Dona nobis pacem are given in a poignant roar.

Many—musicians and laymen—are disturbed by the *Missa solemnis*: by its rhetoric, its quirky spirituality, its notes. Colin Davis, who conducted it on Saturday, is not. At the center of what makes his interpretation so moving is his unconditional faith in the rightness of the piece. Neither drawing attention to its oddities (and from the first D major chord, it hasn't a conventional gesture nor an ordinary sound), nor smoothing them over, he gives it straight, clean, large.

That is his way into the piece. For the way out again, for the translation of interpretation into performance, he has ear, technique, experience, temperament, a mature sense of husbandry and continuity, and enough of all to make the music sound as wonderfully huge, blazing, and mysterious as the pages of the score promise.

The Boston Symphony, a couple moments of rough brass voicing aside, played with ideal commitment and attention, and John Oliver's choruses once again covered themselves with glory. The solo quartet was strong, though the listener who remarked that Anna Reynolds might as well have been ironing was not altogether wrong. Susan Davenny Wyner's singing was radiant and what Marius Rintzler communicated with his ample, pleasing grainy voice was especially gripping. The most miraculous solo performance of all, though, was Joseph Silverstein's pure playing—pure in spirit and in tone—of the violin solo that is threaded through the Benedictus: the holy ghost can do it no better.

Sunday afternoon, Klaus Tennstedt returned with an *Egmont* Overture that makes one long to hear him in opera, and a Fifth Symphony of exemplary intelligence, vitality, and uncomplicated freshness. There is a special pleasure in the sort of at-oneness that marked Malcolm Frager's and Tennstedt's work together in the C minor Piano Concerto, of which they gave a leaning energetic, quietly humorous, gentle poetic reading. It and the symphony were much commented on by a starling who probably feels about Beethoven the way Tanglewood's neighbors feel about James Taylor, but who, as nuisance, couldn't begin to compete with the cigar smokers and bracelet janglers.

Friday was not so happy. At the Weekend Prelude, Frager played Beethoven sonatas with a degree of calm that came close to placidity, not the quality you must want in the *Appassionata*. Davis began the symphony concert with a *Coriolan* Overture that was powerful even though perversely slow. At its end, though, someone felt compelled to show off his acquaintance with the work by applauding directly after its last note, demonstrating at the same time his unawareness that the silence after the last note is also part of the music (not to mention some want of sensibility). The contretemps left the conductor visibly angry and upset, and it was a while before things were on the rails again. The Symphony No. 1 was full of energy and charming detail, but to No. 7, Davis contributed little beyond a generalized vigorous getting-on-with-it. The playing in the latter was deplorable: I thought at the end they might have a plebiscite to determine whose version of the rhythms in the first and third movements we liked best, the strings' or the winds'.

Harvard Series Ends Memorably

August 11, 1976

Delayed twenty-four hours by [Hurricane] Belle, preceded by the appearance on stage of a charming and dirty black-and-white dog, and made festive by the presentation of a silver cup to Thomas Crooks, director of the Harvard Summer School, this year's series of "Monday Concerts" came to its end last night. For financial reasons, the concerts and the chamber music workshop from which they proceed are endangered, though a Summer School representative last night spoke with guarded optimism about their "hopeful" continuance.

Perhaps the silver cup will help. It came as a token of appreciation from this year's chamber players, but all kidding aside, I hope Crooks is aware how much those concerts have meant to that part of the music-hungry community that stays in Boston for the summer. Having performed five of his American composer colleagues at the season's earlier concerts, Leon Kirchner this time performed his own music. His Concerto for Violin, Cello, Ten Winds, and Percussion sounds newer now than at its premiere fifteen years ago. It shared the evening then—a memorable one it was—with the premieres of Milton Babbitt's Dylan Thomas setting for soprano and electronic accompaniment, *Vision and Prayer*, and with Elliott Carter's Double Concerto for Harpsichord, Piano, and Two Orchestras. Both Babbitt's work and Carter's were so startlingly pathbreaking that Kirchner's familiar rhetoric, which is warmly impassioned, and his "easier" harmonies and straighter rhythms sounded by comparison old-fashioned.

I remember, though, enormously liking the piece at one of the first concerts I heard here in 1964 (Joseph Silverstein and Madeline Foley were the soloists)[15] and I did so again yesterday. Violin and cello sing not only with urgency but also with engaging variety, especially in the matter of how deep the breaths they draw are, and the argument between them and the accompaniment—the five woodwinds most song-like, the brass more given to percussive punctuation, the real percussion most peremptory of all—is consistently engaging. If anything the Concerto is oversupplied with ideas, a work of more convincing beginnings than conclusions, but this lavishness is an amiable fault.

It sounded handsome last night. Robert Portney's ample violin tone, Romantic inclinations, and easy technique, were all superbly employed here, and Laurence Lesser once again turned in a musically and cellistically impeccable virtuoso performance. The composer had things snappy and in order, and the texture was wonderfully illuminated by the phrases of flutist Paula Robison, oboist Jan Eberle, and clarinetist Frank Cohen.

The evening began with the Sinfonia to Bach's Cantata No. 209. It sounds like the first movement of a flute concerto and was neatly done with Paula Robison as soloist. The performance of Schubert's Symphony No. 9 in C major disappointed, being generally rough in execution—again, with beautiful moments from Eberle and Cohen—and vague in conception. Much of it was so discontinuous as to sound like tape-splices from different performances, and the feeble *diminuendo* on the last note—a famous misprint, the misreading of one of Schubert's unusually emphatic accent-signs—was the crowning absurdity.

La Scala Scores Triumph in *La Cenerentola*

September 11, 1976

WASHINGTON, DC—If Wednesday's *Bohème* [at the Kennedy Center] has shown that La Scala could, among opera houses, be as shabby as any, *La Cenerentola* (*Cinderella*) took us right back to our belief in the theater as a place where magic is made.

We laughed—and how we laughed—at the speed with which words popped from the actors' lips, at the rhythmic articulation of their scales and divisions, at the rolling of their eyes and the wrinkling of their noses, at the way they carried

[15] See review of February 11, 1964.

real chairs and sat in imaginary ones, at their seduction by Prosciutto and their surrender to Gelati.

All of it was scripted to perfection by Rossini and his gifted librettist, Jacopo Ferretti, paced, shaped, textured, and colored to perfection by Claudio Abbado and Jean-Pierre Ponnelle, and executed brilliantly by all hands from prima donna to piccolo. The most outrageous corn was put over with Swiss watch precision. You could totally abandon yourself to the illusion that it was all being done for the first time, so fresh was it. And it was a challenge to the quickness of body and spirit of everyone involved.

Abbado, who usually wears his handsome face straight almost to the point of austerity, smiled as the singers, one by one, drum rolled their r's in the "Questo è un gruppo rintrecciato" sextet. And no use for him, when he took his curtain calls, to motion to the orchestra to rise: they were already on their feet to applaud him and the rest.

Ponnelle is the wittiest designer since Eugene Berman, if without his great classic gift of restraint. His *Cenerentola* sets off riots of comic invention in black and white. Cinderella and Don Ramiro, her Prince Charming, depart from their colors as far as bottled green and silver. The others moved further: the ineffectually ambitious sisters ventured into reds and oranges, and Dandini, Don Ramiro's resourceful servant, sports a metallic honey-bee cloak and magenta topper.

Ponnelle is a superb director, superb because so musical. Things start off quietly enough, but suddenly you see that in all its exactness the patterning, the stage has gone mad. That intoxicating sneakiness is what you find in the music, too, and Ponnelle has heard it. I have never before experienced the Rossini delirium so completely. It is in the combined lightness and crackle of Abbado's conducting, in the elegant perfection and authority of that uncannily good orchestra, in the command of Romano Gandolfi's virtuosic chorus, and in what the soloists do.

Lucia Valentini Terrani rouladed her way into fame when she took over this role one evening two years ago for the indisposed Teresa Berganza. Here is a large, magnificently smoldering voice, and to hear it put through its paces like that is thrilling. In rags, she has a certain simple allure; finery she wears less successfully, seeming somehow dressed beyond her looks, and needing in any event more help from the make-up department. When she finally smiled—very late, in the famous "Non più mesta"—she lit up the theater.

Luigi Alva's perfection of style and rhythm is such that you hardly care that he is sometimes beyond singing the actual pitches. Flawed though it was, his performance delighted. Enzo Dara, right in that wonderful Italian proletariat tradition, does his stuff brilliantly: he is an extraordinary comic actor and there are dozens of parts in which I want at once to see and hear him. Paolo Montarsolo, too, represents splendid expertness, and the others, as well, did their parts effectively. Not least, it was fascinating how Margherita Guglielmi, so destructive as Musetta in *Bohème* because in that messy context she could only explode in ways that were diffuse and aimless but destructive just the same, could now use her cunning gifts to such good effects as soon as they were precisely channeled.

Israel Philharmonic an Event

September 14, 1976

"At least one-third of the audience will be Christian," said Kitty Dukakis at yesterday's press conference for Zubin Mehta and representatives of the Israel Philharmonic. And of course a concert by this orchestra outside of Israel always becomes a political, social, ideological event. This has its moving corollary when the audience sings "Hatikvah" with as much fervor as "The Star-Spangled Banner." Then again, you get the impression that a large part of the audience has never attended a concert before, and all records for talking, rustling, program rattling are on the way to being broken. The concertmaster loses none of six occasions to look outraged when there is applause between movements; Mehta, as always, looks unruffled and disdainful.

At the same press conference, Mehta remarked that for Americans outside New York, classical music is "borrowed culture." As an Indian trained in Vienna, and with orchestras in Los Angeles and Tel Aviv, Mr. Mehta should know something about acculturation. At his best, he is in fact more in touch with the central European tradition than most of his colleagues of any age and origin.

If you can accept at all the premise of his kind of soft, almost sentimental Mozart, you can hear that he does the G minor Symphony really beautifully. The sounds have grace and glow and an easy, athletic sort of energy. It is interesting, given his taste for mild sonorities and cushioned cadences, that he chooses the original, rather tart version without clarinets. And I am impressed that he is one of the very few conductors to avoid the vulgar solecism of slurring the first two notes of the Andante.

The Brahms Fourth, too, is impressive for three movements, being at once generous and contained. But there is also a bad central European tradition that, by ignoring Brahms's careful and specific directions in the matter of tempo, tears the finale into a scattering of barely related episodes. The dangerous corner is the fourth variation, and sure enough, at that point Mehta turned to the violins, took an immense breath, and cut the tempo down by a third. After that, as Richard Strauss once said about a Nikisch performance of *Death and Transfiguration*, "he really conducted only the orchestration."

Strauss added ruefully that the audience loved it. So did this one. Mehta made it work hard for an encore, but the reward, when it came, was a splendidly vigorous performance of Verdi's *Forza del destino* Overture.

After the two national anthems, Mehta had begun the concert with *Paths*, a symphonic elegy by the Hungarian-born Israeli composer Oedoen Partos. William Steinberg opened the 1970–71 Boston Symphony season with it—it was the first in a series of commissions in memory of his wife—and I must admit that I had no recollection of the piece, nor of my reaction to it six years ago. It makes colorful sounds, invokes Near Eastern melody, and somewhat unhappily embeds both in a neutral, dissonant modernism. I suspect that a performance of textural delicacy—Mehta is not in general a refined workman—might have made for a more convincing statement of *Paths*.

The orchestra itself has excellent strings (and I don't doubt they could deliver more finesse than Mehta asks) and some very good woodwinds. Brass and percussion are more ordinary. The energy level is infectiously, often excitingly high.

Michael Steinberg's Twelve Years of Music in Boston

September 19, 1976

Michael Steinberg has resigned from the Globe *to join the Boston Symphony Orchestra as editor of their program book and newsletter, effective October 1. He will be succeeded by Richard Dyer.*

On January 31, 1964, the first time I sat at this typewriter (rather past its best years even then) to write a review for the *Globe*, Erich Leinsdorf was the Boston Symphony's new white hope; no one was whistling "The Entertainer"; Sarah Caldwell was a local phenomenon, not fully accepted even here; plans had just been made to give a recent Tanglewood alumnus called Seiji Ozawa his first shot at guest-conducting the BSO during the summer; the 81-year-old Igor Stravinsky was composing vigorously and wonderfully; the first Beatles records had just been played on American radio stations; the name of Colin Davis was just beginning to be known to record collectors; there was no National Endowment for the Arts, nor a Council on the Arts and Humanities in this Commonwealth; the doings of Ravi Shankar and Ali Akbar Khan were altogether esoteric; Philharmonic Hall was the only completed part of Lincoln Center in New York, and the opening of the Kennedy Center in Washington was more than six years away; Beverly Sills (Mrs. Peter Greenough of Milton) was not a household name, nor did any imagine that a respected Russian cellist with a hard-to-spell name of Mstislav Rostropovich and a Hungarian-born opera conductor in London named Georg Solti would soon be superstars of the greatest magnitude; Michael Tilson Thomas and James Levine were in school; and Richard Dyer was a Harvard graduate student who sent passionately argued, impeccably informed, elegantly phrased letters of disagreement whenever I wrote about opera.

Stravinsky is gone. So are Karel Ančerl, Sir John Barbirolli, John N. Burk, Robert Casadesus, Pau Casals, Luigi Dallapiccola, Mabel Daniels, Thurston Dart, Goeran Gentele, Roberto Gerhard, Noah Greenberg, Jascha Horenstein, Frank Hubbard, Sol Hurok, Otto Klemperer, Hans Knappertsbusch, Josef Krips, Lotte Lehmann.

As are also Frida Leider, Bruno Maderna, Lauritz Melchior, Pierre Monteux (his was the first obituary I wrote for the *Globe*), Charles Munch, David Munrow, David Oistrakh, Gregor Piatigorsky, Elisabeth Rethberg, Carl Ruggles, Sir Malcolm Sargent, Dmitri Shostakovich, Eduard Steuermann, George Szell, Joseph Szigeti, Dame Maggie Teyte, Jennie Tourel, Richard Tucker, Wolfgang Windgassen, Felix Wolfes, Stefan Wolpe. They had made our world grander, more colorful, tune-ier.

Music itself is unquenchably alive. We have had in these dozen years Babbitt's *Philomel* and *Correspondences*; the Piano Concerto, Concerto for Orchestra, and Quartet No. 3 of Carter; from Sessions, four symphonies and the Whitman cantata, *When Lilacs Last in the Dooryard Bloom'd*; Stravinsky's *Requiem Canticles*; Tippett's Symphony No. 3 and another opera, *The Knot Garden*; George Crumb's *Ancient Voices of Children* and *Vox Balaenae*; the last Shostakovich quartets and sonatas; Earl Kim's *Exercises en route*; Donald Martino's *Notturno* and the *Paradiso* choruses; Maderna's *Giardino Religioso*; strong new pieces by Peter Maxwell Davies, John Harbison, Jacob Druckman, Luciano Berio, Betsy Jolas, Peter Lieberson, David Del Tredici, Gunther Schuller, Pierre Boulez, Yehudi Wyner, Charles Wuorinen, Oliver Knussen, Joyce Mekeel, Karlheinz Stockhausen, Daniel Lentz.

Aaron Copland has all but fallen silent, one hears little from György Ligeti, and Krzysztof Penderecki seems bogged down in self-imitation. Not all the promise of the young has been realized: what, for instance, became of Fredric Myrow, whose Music for Orchestra made such a brilliant impression at Tanglewood ten years ago?

Altogether, music has become more centrist and more varied. Total serialization of all elements and total abdication of control (in reaction to the former) are less fascinating to composers. Many new pieces bear out Schoenberg's contention that there was still plenty of good music to be written in C major. Collage and quotation have become prominent. That comes from Ives, whose presence has grown more vivid, and so does the questioning of the validity of the barrier separating "popular" from "serious."

There is little now by way of neo-Dada fun and games, but a lot of theater has come into music. Singers and conductors play instruments, instrumentalists sing and speak. And if ten years ago one felt lucky to find something interesting at a festival of contemporary music, today you can go in reasonable expectation of hearing something that touches, amuses, or moves you. The scene is looser, happier, more alive.

Boston, these twelve-and-a-half years, has been exciting. The Symphony has shaken off its torpor, though it has continued irresponsible about new music. Sarah Caldwell has become more settled (and no less adventurous), and we may yet live to see her in an opera house on the UMass campus. Gunther Schuller has most amazingly stirred up the New England Conservatory. To judge from the sound of the Boston University Concert Orchestra on the eve of their departure for an international competition in Berlin, they are clearly doing something right at 855 Commonwealth Ave., where the composer Norman Dello Joio has been dean since 1972.

The Cantata Singers, Musica Viva, Collage, and Associated Artists Opera did not exist in 1964. The Handel and Haydn Society, the Boston Civic Symphony, the Cecilia Society, respectively directed now by Thomas Dunn, Benjamin Zander, and Donald Teeters, have risen from the edges of their graves to new vitality. The churches, led by Emmanuel in Boston, which offers a Bach cantata at each Sunday service, by King's Chapel and First Congregational in Cambridge, have become important centers of musical activity.

Under Joel Cohen, the Camerata has become one of the country's outstanding early-music groups, and Barbara Lambert, in charge of the instruments collection at the Museum of Fine Arts, has put new musical life into that institution. Some ventures have not made it: the Philharmonia is the one most regretted. In all, though, public musical life in Boston is today close to double what it was in 1964, and of impressive quality.

Other new faces in town have included musician-at-large Rudolf Kolisch, pianist Russell Sherman, composers Earl Kim, Donald Martino, Seymour Shifrin, musicologist Christoph Wolff. Some remarkable young performers have settled or done part of their growing here: David Arnold, Jane Bryden, Jan Curtis, David Evitts, D'Anna Fortunato, John Gibbons, Pamela Gore, Diana Hoagland, Frank Hoffmeister, Laura Jeppesen, Stephanie Jutt, Beth Levin, Beverly Morgan, are some of them.

In all, we hear more kinds of music now than in 1964, at least we hear it more easily. Baroque music no longer means only Bach, Handel, and Vivaldi (and there is, thank God, less obsession with the dregs of that period): the 17th century has become a more familiar landscape and its masters, Monteverdi, Schütz, Louis Couperin, find a larger audience. Performers like Gustav Leonhardt and

Nikolaus Harnoncourt's Concentus Musicus have considerable followings. Performance practices in matters of articulation, embellishment, and rhythm, that a dozen years ago were the secret of a few, have become common knowledge. The sound of old instruments and their replicas has become familiar, and we are almost at the stage where Bach on the piano is coming back as an exotic revival. There are early-music groups all over the country now, many of them excellent, and in the last decade, the builders of recorders, harpsichords, and lutes must have quadrupled.

Non-Western music, with a considerable assist from the Beatles and their much-publicized interest in Ravi Shankar, has become a natural part of our sound-world. The record industry is fascinated by and anxious to court "cross-over," the phenomenon that has some of the "classical" audience listening to rock and rediscovering jazz, that has a composer like Gunther Schuller recording Sousa marches and country fiddlers' dance music, a Renaissance-music expert like Joshua Rifkin playing the rags of Scott Joplin, and the pop audience buying *Switched-on Bach*, an electronic version of *Pictures at an Exhibition*, and a straight one of an obscure 17th-century canon by Pachelbel.

In the world of performers, there have been many new names. In 1964, we were just beginning to know Joan Sutherland (she made her Boston debut in Caldwell's production of Bellini's *Puritani* in February of that year) but hadn't yet heard of Montserrat Caballé. Shirley Verrett, then Verrett-Carter, was just beginning to make a reputation, but Janet Baker and Luciano Pavarotti were not yet on our maps. Garrick Ohlsson was in high school in White Plains, NY. The Budapest Quartet was playing its last season of concerts, but there was no Guarneri or Cleveland Quartet. When Pierre Boulez came over with the BBC Symphony in 1965, few knew his name at all: those who did were aware of him as an avant-garde composer but mostly had no idea he also conducted.

Artur Rubinstein, Maria Callas, and Elisabeth Schwarzkopf have gone into retirement, and Jascha Heifetz seems to have. Vladimir Horowitz and Nathan Milstein, after some silent years, are playing again.

The Big Five orchestras have changed hands, New York from Bernstein to Boulez to Mehta, Boston from Leinsdorf to Steinberg to Ozawa, Chicago from Martinon to Solti, Cleveland from Szell to Maazel. In Philadelphia, though, Ormandy goes on forever.

Quadraphonic recording has come, making less of a splash than the industry hoped, but tape cassettes have made an enormous impact. The Romantic Revival so often announced by the *New York Times* has failed to materialize. Satie was a flash in the pan. Who remembers Rosemary Brown, taking dictation from the spirits of Beethoven, Liszt, and Chopin? Charles Rosen's book on *The Classical Style* has turned out to be a landmark in criticism and scholarship. Andrew

Porter's presence at *The New Yorker* has been A Good Thing, but by and large, journalistic criticism continues an irritant and a depressant.

The years since January 1964 have been full of change and full of life. I have loved listening, watching, commenting, hoping, badgering, and evidently I have survived the disappointments. To this "*addio*" I add my thanks to all who have read, asked, complained, and sent bouquets.

Coda

The Appetitosissimi Cookbook of Ada Boni—A Fond Tribute to the Author of *Il Talismano della Felicità*

September 2, 1973

When Ada Boni died in Rome on May 2 at the age of 92, she got not quite three inches on the obituary page of the *New York Times* and none at all in the *Globe*. In this family, though, Ada Boni is a household name, and I am sure that we talked about her death more than about Stravinsky's or Picasso's.

Her *Talismano della Felicità* was our first cookbook and, stained, annotated, and rebound, it remains the favored and best. The household came to be one in Rome thanks to the Fulbright fellowship program, and when I sought advice on cookbooks from Letizia Ciotti, who was the secretary in the Fulbright office and knew or found the answers to everything, she said that *Il Talismano* was the *only* one. How long it had been in such eminence I do not know: our copy, bought October 1952, is of the twenty-second edition, and it quotes from the foreword of a 1934 edition whose wording makes it clear that it was a classic then.

It is a good, solid book—three pounds and 919 pages. And it works. From the beginning, I loved its language, characterized by Enrico Boni, the author's admiring husband, as being of "seigniorial simplicity and elegance." With the wonderful resonance of Signora Boni's Italian prose goes a splendid expansiveness of style, one perfectly consonant with simplicity and elegance. I doubt the practical usefulness of the English-language edition of *The Talisman of Happiness* not at all, but the resonance and the expansiveness are gone, and with them the sensuous pleasure of reading. Frost will have understood.

Of course an author in a language with the grand subjunctives of Italian has a lot going for her. Boni begins her discourse on potatoes—thirty-three recipes plus a note on the extraction of fecula—by borrowing from Voltaire: "If potatoes did not already exist, one would need to invent them." But how much finer it is in Italian: "*Se le patate non esistessero già, bisognerebbe inventarle.*" Then, instantly and characteristically, she is down to earth and talking about amides, phosphorous, and vitamin B.

Now and again, for a sense of other assumptions and another world, also for the presence of Donna Ada herself, I read the recipe for meat jelly, "*elegante e indispensabile accompagamento*" to cold dishes.

It is, she says, one of those preparations which rather frighten or daunt the ladies ("*spaventano*" is her word, one any opera buff will recognize): in fact, nothing is easier or less wearing. Whereupon she has you assemble carrots, chopped onion and parsley, cloves, bay, black pepper, ham, bacon rind, veal or beef, fowl, a finger of water and salt, all that to be cooked gently until barely blond. Many stages, plenty of water, six hours of slow and regular boiling, much skimming, a few veal feet and heads, and one straining later, comes the great challenge: clarification. (Animadversion en route: "Limpidness is one of the criteria of good jelly.")

Add two egg whites and a glass of marsala for each liter of broth and beat it with a whip of iron. Then, she says, you will see the egg white tear apart into a net in whose interstices the broth will emerge "*limpidissimo*." She makes of it an epiphany almost like Virgil's description in *Georgics* IV of the bees generated in the skin of the slain lion. But there is more. You keep the limpid fluid on the fire at just the temperature where it boils, yet does not boil ("*bolla e non bolla*").

Meanwhile you put a chair upside down on the kitchen table, tie a wet, wrung-out napkin to its four feet, place a pan under the chair, climb up and pass the mixture through twice, check for salt, and, when cooled—it, not you—pour it into a mold. Five hundred words of grandly unfolding epic, and then, by the way, she tells you how to use commercial gelatin powder instead of heads and feet.

If *Il Talismano* is her *Well-tempered Clavier*, her *Goldberg* Variations, her *Art of Fugue*, she also has her *Little Notebook for Wilhelm Friedemann*, which is called *Prime esperienze di una piccola cuoca* ("First experiences of a little cook"—five ounces and fifty-three pages).

The future housewife—"*padrona di casa*" is grander—is first instructed in the merits of attention, order, and cleanliness. After that comes an inventory of necessary equipment, a manual of basic procedures (I love where she writes, "thus far we have spoken of only one egg," and proceeds to explain what to do if you are frying two), then the first Great Station: "This morning your parents will find a surprise: their little girl has already prepared breakfast for them, and in the best of fashion!" And on, through pasta and soup, with a long sojourn in "the kingdom of sweets," and a postlude on table-setting. You can then go to Mamma and claim a kiss as reward, but Mamma will in fact give you not one, but a hundred, a thousand, a rain of kisses, "and that is the sweetest, the most beneficent rain which the Lord God Almighty grants to mortals . . . "

But to get back to *Il Talismano*—the recipe I most wanted to try was Caponata alla siciliana. I knew caponata as a pleasant eggplant hors d'oeuvre or garnish (Boni calls that "*caponatina*," a little caponata), but this was obviously an experience of quite another order. We talked about it for perhaps ten years, finally found just the occasion and the company, and I am sure that ten years later some of the survivors are still talking about it.

Sicilian gourmets, writes Boni, are justly proud of this classic preparation, which requires eggplant, celery hearts (delicately she suggests that blood has been shed between those who believe in flouring before frying and those who do not, herself coming out fearlessly and firmly for no flour), onion, tomato paste, sugar, vinegar, capers, olives, smoked tuna roe, parsley, octopus, lobster, and swordfish. Refined Sicilian chefs, she advises, add asparagus and artichoke. Over all that you pour Salsa San Bernardo, which I am sorry to say must be translated as St. Bernard Sauce, then decorating according to your ability and fancy with egg slices, shrimp, what have you.

St. Bernard's Sauce is made of toasted almonds and oven-toasted bread, anchovy fillets, and orange juice, to which you add a little vinegar, sugar, water, *and* a good spoonful of grated bitter chocolate. Because we are dealing here with "refined cuisine," you want to pass it through a silk cloth twice.

Some of us reacted with disbelief—actually I found it in a perverse way rather fascinating—but I still remember the look of absolute panic, that sense of "where's the exit?" on the face of one of our guests, a young pianist, who quickly decided she could more easily deal with the crisis of conscience brought on by accepting some slices of ham than with her eggplant-and-seafood sundae before her.

Though a disaster, it was one in grand style, and such theater that I can say that *Il Talismano* has never produced a disappointment. Let me, in justice to Mrs. Boni and for your pleasure, give you one of her simplest, most unusual, and best recipes—spaghetti all'ostrica. "*Ostrica*" means oyster, which does not occur in the recipe, and perhaps this wants to be translated as "mock-oyster spaghetti."

You slice mushrooms fine, put them in a pan with oil and cook them rapidly over very high heat until they are dark brown and look almost like dried mushrooms. Season them with salt, pepper, chopped parsley, and, once off the fire, a few drops of lemon juice. Over your drained spaghetti you pour plenty of olive oil and abundant freshly ground black pepper, then the mushrooms. An extra drop of lemon juice at the last second does no harm. She offers it as a "*bizzarria*" for those who eat pasta often and are bored with the standard sauces, but, she assures her readers, they will find these spaghetti "*appetitossissimi*." And that's right.

Acknowledgments

The long gestation of this book means there are many people to thank, including some who undoubtedly will have been inadvertently omitted here. As noted in the introduction, Jorja Fleezanis conceived the idea to compile Michael Steinberg's writings for the *Boston Globe* shortly after his death in 2009; she established the Michael Steinberg & Jorja Fleezanis Fund (SFF) in part to help realize her vision by underwriting editorial expenses. Our thanks go to the entire SFF Board, particularly current president Mari Carlson, treasurer John Nuechterlein, and secretary Robert P. Guter (who was also one of Jorja's early readers of the manuscript, and who read an early version of our introduction).

Although Jorja undertook the initial selection of articles on her own, she was aided in accessing and culling the *Globe* files by researchers and editorial assistants Lynn Walterick, Charlene Kluegel, *Globe* librarian Lisa Tuite, and, most especially, her former student Jacob Jahiel (subsequently a co-editor of the present volume). Jorja's closest friend Patricia Lewy was her constant sounding board and supporter, and provided invaluable assistance to us in the aftermath of Jorja's death.

Once we took over the editing of the book, we enlisted people with knowledge of place and period to help shape the introduction. In particular, we are grateful to the late Richard Dyer, Michael's successor at the *Boston Globe*, for his many detailed insights; as well as to John Harbison, David Moran, Thomas W. Morris, and Lloyd Schwartz, for their clarifications on a variety of Boston-related details. Richard, David, and Lloyd also pointed us toward a number of Michael's *Globe* reviews without which this compilation would be less complete and compelling, and generously read and commented upon the introduction, as did Helen M. Greenwald of the New England Conservatory. Bridget Carr and Sarah Funke Donovan of the Boston Symphony Archives provided gracious and efficient assistance in responding to inquiries and making contemporary documentation available. Robert Kirzinger and Jim Connolly of the Boston Symphony Publications Office also offered assistance in answering a variety of questions and providing materials. Jim also proved to be an enthusiastic and first-rate indexer.

Jane Steinberg and Adam Steinberg graciously filled in some biographical blanks. For music-related minutiae, Allan Kozinn and John Rockwell responded quickly and knowingly to our queries, as did Mike Ouzounian and Harvey Sachs to questions of Jorja's. Jeremy Eichler, in his capacity at the time as the *Globe*'s classical music critic, helpfully put us in touch with his *Globe* colleague Katie Lazares, who proved immensely and speedily efficient in facilitating our permissions inquiries. Other forms of generous, knowledgeable assistance came from Charles Baxter (who also read the draft of the introduction), Trey Devey (and the Interlochen Arts Academy, which he leads), Jonathan Fleezanis, Dr. Nickolas Fleezanis, Michael Gross, Silke Hilger, James M. Kendrick, Harry Liebersohn, Warren Mack, Garrick Ohlsson, and another reader of the introduction, Larry Rothe (who collaborated with Michael for many years at the San Francisco Symphony).

It was Jorja who initially approached Oxford University Press about adding this book to its prior publications of Michael's collected writings. First Suzanne Ryan, then Norman Hirschy and Michelle Chen, expressed their enthusiasm for the project. We very much appreciated Michelle's commitment and patience, and also extend appreciation to her OUP colleagues, Anna-Lise Santella and Rachel Ruisard, who took over the project after her departure. During the production process we appreciated our long-distance collaboration with Leo Mosquline, project manager, and Timothy DeWerff, our meticulous copy editor. We give special thanks to our spouses, Tony Butler, Gracie Carney, and Todd Gordon, for moral, intellectual, and technical support, as well as for tolerating our countless hours-long Zoom calls.

And, finally, our enduring gratitude to Jorja and Michael for their abundance of love, friendship, and guidance.

About the Editors

Jorja Fleezanis

Concertmaster of the Minnesota Orchestra from 1989 to 2009, Jorja Fleezanis was the orchestra's longest-tenured concertmaster and only the second woman to hold that title at a major American orchestra. Prior to that she was associate concertmaster of the San Francisco Symphony and a violinist with the Chicago Symphony. A devoted teacher, she held chairs in violin and orchestral studies at Indiana University (2009–20) and taught at the University of Minnesota, Round Top International Festival Institute, Aldeburgh Britten Pears School, San Francisco Conservatory, Music@Menlo Festival, New World Symphony, Music Academy of the West, and Interlochen Academy, among other places. Fleezanis studied at the Cincinnati Conservatory of Music and the Cleveland Institute of Music. John Adams's Violin Concerto and John Tavener's *Ikon of Eros* were composed for her. She met Michael Steinberg at the San Francisco Symphony and they married in 1983. After his death in 2009, she established the Michael Steinberg & Jorja Fleezanis Fund to commission and perform text-based compositions by emerging composers. She died in 2022 at age 70.

Susan Feder

Susan Feder's multifaceted career in the arts culminated in a fifteen-year tenure as program officer in the Arts and Culture program at the Mellon Foundation, the largest private funder of the arts and humanities in the United States. There, she designed and supported programs resulting in a significant expansion of contemporary arts repertoire across the performing arts. She also developed a series of collaborative, systems-building initiatives and funder partnerships in both the public and private sectors on behalf of artists and organizations long under-resourced by philanthropy. Earlier, as vice president of the music publisher G. Schirmer, she nurtured the careers of composers in the United States, Europe, and former Soviet Union. She was also editorial coordinator of *The New Grove Dictionary of American Music* (1986) and program editor at the San Francisco Symphony, where she was hired by Michael Steinberg in 1979. Feder currently serves on the boards of a number of arts nonprofits and foundations. She holds music degrees from Princeton University and the University of California, Berkeley.

Jacob Jahiel

Jacob Jahiel is a PhD student in Historical Musicology at the University of Pennsylvania. He holds an MA in Musicology from Indiana University, Bloomington's Jacobs School of Music, where he studied modern violin with Jorja Fleezanis, Baroque violin with Stanley Ritchie, and viola da gamba with Joanna Blendulf. He writes frequently for *EMAg: The Magazine of Early Music America* and contributes program notes to the Baltimore Symphony Orchestra and Boston Artists Ensemble. As a historical bowed string specialist, he has performed at the Academy for Early Music (MI) and the University of Chicago's Howard Mayer Brown International Early Music Series, among others.

Marc Mandel

Hired to the staff of the Boston Symphony Orchestra by Michael Steinberg in 1978, Marc Mandel managed and edited the BSO program book from 1979 to 2020, also serving for many years as the orchestra's principal pre-concert speaker. While at the BSO, he initiated the adult education series "BSO 101," in which members of the orchestra joined him for discussions of music programmed by the orchestra. His program notes have appeared in the program books of the Boston Symphony Orchestra, San Francisco Symphony, Carnegie Hall, and New York Philharmonic, among others; he has written liner notes and essays for labels including BSO Classics, Deutsche Grammophon, Nonesuch, Philips, and Telarc; and he reviewed CDs for *Fanfare Magazine* for twenty years. Following his undergraduate work at Brandeis University, where he majored in biology while also studying music, he earned graduate degrees in music history and musicology from Yale University and Princeton University, respectively.

Index

For the benefit of digital users, indexed terms that span two pages (e.g., 52–53) may, on occasion, appear on only one of those pages.

Figures are indicated by an italic *f* following the page number.

Abbado, Claudio, 379, 460–61, 578
accompanists, role of, 217–20
Adams, F. John, 445, 446–47
Aeolian Players, 192
Alberts, Eunice, 10, 152, 212, 271, 416–17
Alexander, John, 391
Alva, Luigi, 578–79
Amara, Lucine, 79
amateur performers, 185, 353–55
Ameling, Elly, 282–83
American Symphony Orchestra, 67–69
Ames, Amyas, 326
Ančerl, Karel, 367, 478
Anderson, Marian, 34–35, 187
antisemitism, 169, 479
  See also Israel, concert culture in; Nazism and Nazi Germany
Arrau, Claudio, 382
Arroyo, Martina, 469
Ashkenazy, Vladimir, 239–40, 471
Aspen Music Festival, 304–7
Associate Artist Opera, 514–16
Aston Magna Music Festival, 516–17
Auden, W. H., 46, 124, 176, 178
audience behavior, 28–30, 120, 220–22, 258, 300, 318–20, 322, 384–86, 439–40, 472–73, 511, 576

Babbitt, Milton, xix–xx, 268–70, 272–74
  Ensembles for Synthesizer, 140
  Partitions, 265–66, 269
  Philomel, 20–22, 386
  and the public, 270, 272–74
  Relata II, 268–70, 272–74
  String Quartet No. 2, 144
  String Quartet No. 3, 425
  Vision and Prayer, 21, 386, 576–77
Bach, Carl Philipp Emanuel, 261
  recordings, 253
Bach, Johann Christian, 8–9, 261
  recordings, 253
Bach, Johann Sebastian, 95–96, 185, 237, 483
  Air on the G String, 69–70, 174
  Art of Fugue, 296–97
  Brandenburg Concertos, 272–73, 345–46, 533
  cantatas, 351, 383–84, 577
  Chaconne (Busoni transcription), 110
  Goldberg Variations, 121–23, 297
  Keyboard Concerto in D minor, 305, 306
  Mass in B minor, 183–84, 354
  motets, 383–84
  Musical Offering, 297
  orchestral suites, 174, 252, 364
  partitas, 440, 450, 451
  recordings, 161–62, 252–53, 296–97, 345–46, 477
  St. John Passion, 161–62, 233
  St. Matthew Passion, 416–17
  violin sonatas, 250–51, 568–69
  Well-tempered Clavier, 17, 330–31
Bach, P. D. Q., 223
Bachauer, Gina, 15–17
Back Bay Theatre (Boston), 150–52
Baker, Alan, 558
Baker, Janet, 121, 168, 181, 246–47, 441, 442
balance
  choral/vocal with orchestra, 166, 185, 353–54, 447
  in Lieder, 59
  orchestral, 2, 19–20, 92–93, 96, 108–9, 146, 151, 173, 242, 339, 343, 345, 429, 460–61, 469, 472, 525–26, 541
  pianistic, 16–17, 47
  See also doubling
Balk, Wesley, 390
Bar-Illan, David, 23
Barbieri, Saverio, 391
Barbirolli, John, 7, 48–50, 121, 246–47, 290–91
Barenboim, Daniel, 367, 382, 491–92
Bartók, Béla, 522
  Sonata for Two Pianos and Percussion, 506
  String Quartet No. 5, 127
  String Quartet No. 6, 480–81

Barzun, Jacques
Berlioz and the Romantic Century, 338
"Battle Hymn of the Republic," 232–33
Bavarian Radio Symphony Orchestra, 168, 377–78
BBC Symphony Orchestra, 71, 241, 291
Beardslee, Bethany, 20–22, 351, 510
Beatles, The, 70, 73, 80–81, 583
Beethoven, Ludwig van
Bagatelles, Op. 126, 503–4
Cantata on the Death of Emperor Joseph II, 353, 354
Consecration of the House Overture, xxxiin.21, 105, 413, 443
Coriolan Overture, 576
Creatures of Prometheus Overture, 339
Diabelli Variations, Op. 120, 106, 153, 529
Egmont Overture, 471, 575–76
Fidelio/Leonore, 197–99, 318–19, 430, 452, 573
folk settings, 413
Mass in C, 353, 354
Missa solemnis, 386–87, 575–76
Piano Concerto No. 1, 76–77
Piano Concerto No. 5, *Emperor*, 222–23, 236–37, 413–14, 430
piano sonatas, 256–57, 381–83, 414–16
Piano Sonata No. 4 in E-flat, Op. 7, 413
Piano Sonata No. 23 in F minor, Op. 57, *Appassionata*, 180–81, 465–66
Piano Sonata No. 27 in E minor, Op. 90, 415
Piano Sonata No. 28 in A, Op. 101, 16–17, 503–4
Piano Sonata No. 29 in B-flat, Op. 106, *Hammerklavier*, 13–14, 37, 47, 238–40, 415
Piano Sonata No. 30 in E, Op. 109, 3, 63
Piano Sonata No. 31 in A-flat, Op. 110, 8
Piano Sonata No. 32 in C minor, Op. 111, 94–95, 105–8, 110–11, 330, 415, 529
recordings, 381–83, 412–16
Rondos, Op. 51, 464–65
String Quartet No. 12 in E-flat, Op. 127, 130–31
String Quartet No. 14 in C-sharp minor, Op. 131, 204–5
String Quintet in C, Op. 29, 413
Symphony No. 2, 442
Symphony No. 3, *Eroica*, 108–9, 282, 379, 525
Symphony No. 5, 106, 220, 282, 474–75, 575–76
Symphony No. 6, *Pastoral*, 45–46, 445, 447, 452
Symphony No. 7, 26, 244, 280–81, 436–37
Symphony No. 8, 62–63, 331–32
Symphony No. 9, 80, 169, 286–87, 332–33, 497, 520–21, 522
Triple Concerto, 412–13
Violin Concerto, 41, 192–93, 242–44
violin sonatas, 278
See also tempo: in Beethoven
Bellini, Vincenzo
I puritani, 11–13, 498
recordings, 261–63, 498–99
Bennett, Richard Rodney
Symphony No. 1, 248
Berberian, Ara, 199, 299, 420
Berg, Alban, 522, 570
Altenberg Songs, 478
Lulu, 224
Piano Sonata, 288
String Quartet, 204–5
Violin Concerto, 64, 305–6
Wozzeck, 128–29
Berger, Elly Felicie, 509
Berger, Louis, 482
Berio, Luciano
Gesti, 451
Berkshire Festival. *See* Tanglewood
Berkshire Music Center at Tanglewood, 35–37, 207, 208, 210, 230, 295–96, 389–90, 399–400, 572–74
Koussevitzky and, 519–20
orchestra of, 129–30, 132, 134, 245, 387–89, 404–5, 427–30, 432–33, 521–22
Berlioz, Hector
Damnation of Faust, 390–92, 481–82
Francs-juges Overture, 441–42
memoirs of, 336–38
Les Nuits d'été, 246–47, 441–42
recordings, 276–78
Roméo et Juliette, 276–78, 419–20
Symphonie fantastique, 4–5, 370, 521
Les Troyens, 277
Bernac, Pierre, 202–3
Bernstein, Felicia Montealegre, 2
Bernstein, Leonard
and BSO, xxviii, 210, 386–87, 430–32, 444–45, 446–47
and Wilhelm Furtwängler, 449, 451–52
Mass, 392–94
and Metropolitan Opera, 422, 426
and New York Philharmonic, 99–103, 190, 205–6, 207, 228, 233, 268–70, 272–73, 290–91, 293–94, 327, 343
Norton Lectures, 444, 484–87, 491

recordings by, 166–68, 241
on segregation, 23
and student orchestras, 432–33, 520, 521, 573
Symphony No. 3, *Kaddish*, 1–2, 393
and Michael Tilson Thomas, 400–2
Bertolini, Ercole, 61–62
Biber, Heinrich von
Passacaglia, 566
Biggs, E. Power, 86
Billboard classical chart, 476–78
Billings, James, 151, 179–80
Bilson, Malcolm, 566–68
Bing, Rudolf, 119–20, 187, 295
Birtwistle, Harrison
Down by the Greenwood Side, 390
Bizet, Georges
Carmen, 41–43, 224–26, 295, 422, 426
recording, 41–43
Symphony in C, 2
Bjoerling, Jussi, 28, 544
Blegen, Judith, 410
Blitzstein, Marc, 124
Bloch, Ernest
Nigun, 440
Bloom, Myron, 7
Böhm, Karl (conductor), 128–29, 193–94, 451–52
Böhm, Karl-Walter (tenor), 564–65
Böhm, Yohanan, 365–67
Bohnen, Michael, 509
Bonacker, Jane. *See* Steinberg, Jane
Boni, Ada, 585–87
Bonynge, Richard, 13, 225
Boretz, Benjamin, 7
Borg, Kim, 121
Boston Camerata, xxv–xxvi, 14–15, 374–76, 582
Boston Civic Symphony, 474–75, 582
Boston Globe
Michael Steinberg's career at, xx–xxiii, xxi*f*, xxv–xxx, xxxi–xxxiii, xxxviii*f*, 158*f*, 214*f*, 264*f*, 580–84
See also letters to the editor
Boston Herald, xxx, 189, 224
Boston Musica Viva, 362–63
Boston Opera Group. *See* Opera Company of Boston
Boston Philharmonia, 399–400, 416–17, 495
Boston Pops, 69–70, 190, 325
Boston Symphony Chamber Players, 50–51, 215–16
Boston Symphony Orchestra (BSO), 186
controversy with Michael Steinberg, xxix–xxx, 54–56, 324–25
music directorship of, 38–39, 205–10, 227–30, 247–48, 307–9, 378–80
programming, 5, 67, 307, 311–13, 314–16, 372, 488–89
Spectrum Concerts, 436n.11, 494–95, 560
Michael Steinberg's career at, xxx–xxxi, 580
Boston Symphony Orchestra, reviews of performances
1964: Feb. 1, 1–2; Feb. 8, 4–5; Mar. 7, 17–18; Sep. 26, 45–46; Nov. 7, 48–50
1965: Mar. 27, 66–67; Jul. 3, 75–76; Jul. 5, 76–78; Aug. 23, 78–79; Sep. 19, 81–83; Oct. 23, 86–88
1966: Jan. 22, 108–9; Feb. 26, 114–16
1967: Jan. 7, 159–61; Jan. 21, 162–64; Jul. 3, 192–93; Aug. 7, 197–99
1968: Aug. 6, 245–46; Oct. 26, 247–49
1969: Jan. 25, 266–68; Apr. 19, 286–87; Jul. 28, 297–99; Aug. 31, 307–9; Oct. 4, 313–14; Oct. 11, 317–18; Nov. 8, 324–25
1970: Feb. 15, 341–43; Mar. 28, 343–45; Apr. 25, 350–51; Oct. 3, 363–64; Oct. 28, 367–68; Nov. 14, 369–70; Dec. 19, 371–72
1971: Jan. 9, 373–74; Mar. 3, 380–81; Jul. 26, 386–87; Aug. 24, 390–92
1972: Jan. 6, 406–7; Jan. 22, 407–8; Mar. 27, 419–20; Mar. 29, 420–21; Jul. 24, 430–32; Aug. 1, 433–34; Aug. 14, 434–35; Sep. 23, 436–37; Oct. 23, 437–39; Oct. 28, 441–42; Dec. 9, 444–45; Dec. 15, 445–47
1973: Feb. 3, 459–60; Mar. 17, 468–69; Mar. 24, 471–72; Sep. 29, 481–82
1974: Jan. 5, 488–89; Jan. 26, 494–95; Feb. 16, 496–97; Mar. 29, 504–5; Jul. 29, 520–22; Dec. 13, 531–32; Dec. 20, 534–35
1975: Feb. 28, 549–50
1976: Aug. 9, 575–76
Boston University
Concert Orchestra, 582
Opera Workshop, 175
Young Artists Orchestra, 520
Boulanger, Nadia, 376
Boulez, Pierre
and BBC Symphony Orchestra, 71–72, 291, 583
and Cleveland Orchestra, 291, 293
Éclat, 139, 494
and New York Philharmonic, 290–94, 315–16, 378
recordings by, 111–12, 241–42
Boult, Adrian, 49–50, 129–30, 132–34, 282, 340, 437
Boyden, John, 101

Boykan, Martin, 117
Brahms, Johannes, 36, 133, 522–23
  Academic Festival Overture, 45–46, 221, 532
  Clarinet Quintet in B minor, Op. 115, 134
  Piano Concerto No. 1, 25–26
  Piano Concerto No. 2, 244, 406–7, 420–21
  piano sonatas, 290
  Rhapsodies, Op. 79, 181
  Symphony No. 1, 428, 431
  Symphony No. 2, 281, 430–31
  Symphony No. 3, 48, 248–49, 282, 314, 363–64
  Symphony No. 4, xxiiin.8, xxix–xxx, 324–25, 430–31, 531–32, 579
  Tragic Overture, 428–29
  Violin Concerto, 65, 532
  See also tempo: in Brahms
Brecht, Bertolt, 123–26
Brendel, Alfred, 4, 13–14, 152–56, 256–57, 328–33, 382, 503–4
  on Callas, 500
  on Liszt, 154
  recordings by, 226
  on Michael Steinberg, xix
Brennan, William, 186, 189
Bressler, Charles, 196, 517
Britten, Benjamin
  cello suites, 90
  as conductor, 120, 310–11, 321, 345–46
  Death in Venice, 526–28, 559
  The Poet's Echo, 90, 103, 528
  as recitalist, 200–2, 323–24, 527, 530
  and Rostropovich, 88–91
  Symphony for Cello and Orchestra, xxxiin.21, 86–87, 88, 90–91
Broadway, 124–25
Brott, Boris, 269
Bruckner, Anton
  Symphony No. 2, 504–5
  Symphony No. 3, 19
  Symphony No. 5, 495–96
  Symphony No. 7, 488–89
  Symphony No. 8, 534–35
Brüggen, Frans, 123, 449–51
Bryden, Jane, 374–75, 384, 548
Bucquet, Marie-Françoise, 507
Buffalo Philharmonic, 148–49, 399, 400–1, 403–4, 405
Burgin, Richard, 315–16, 400, 521
Burrows, Stuart, 482
Busoni, Ferruccio, 456, 553, 572
  piano works, 95–96, 110
Caballé, Montserrat, 262
Cabot, Henry B., xxix, 208–9, 227, 229
  open letter to, 54–56
Cairns, David
  Berlioz memoirs translation, 336–38
  on Michael Steinberg, xxii–xxiii, xxix
Caldwell, Sarah, 11, 56n.2, 60, 62, 150–51, 152, 171, 175, 178–79, 223–26, 270–72, 515, 582
Callas, Maria, 262–63, 501–3
  career and influence of, 498–500
Cambridge Festival Orchestra, 212
Camerata. *See* Boston Camerata
Camerata Singers, 136, 139
Cantata Singers, 183, 185, 383–84
Cantelo, April, 283
Capobianco, Tito, 145, 146–47
Carter, Elliott, xxx–xxxi, 190–91, 258–60, 417, 536n.*, 561
  Cello Sonata, 461, 505–6
  Concerto for Orchestra, 341–43, 541
  Double Concerto, 93–94, 139, 260–61
  Eight Etudes and a Fantasy, 139
  Piano Concerto, 159–61
  recordings, 260–61
  Sonata for Flute, Oboe, Cello, and Harpsichord, 258
  string quartets, 347–49
  String Quartet No. 1, 258–59
  String Quartet No. 2, 75, 259
  String Quartet No. 3, 461–63, 466–68
  Variations for Orchestra, xxxiin.21, 22–23, 260–61
  See also tempo: in Carter
Casals, Pablo, 328–33
  recordings by, 482–84
Casella, Alfredo
  La Giara, 325
Cassen, Jackie, 179
Cassilly, Richard, 298–99
Castello, Dario, 517
Castelnuovo-Tedesco, Mario
  Sea Murmurs, 440
Catelain, Jacques, 509
chamber vs. orchestral musicianship, 39–40, 50–51, 215–17
Chang, Lynn, 569
Chicago Symphony Orchestra, 47–48, 168, 205–7, 532–33
  music directorship of, 48, 205, 207, 228, 378, 448
Chomsky, Noam, 485
Chookasian, Lili, 410, 469

Chopin, Frédéric, 30–31, 290, 322, 464
  Ballades, 349
  Brendel on, 154–55
  Études, 349
  Piano Sonata No. 3 in B minor, 16, 17
  Preludes, 265, 266
  recordings, 227, 395
  Scherzo No. 2 in B-flat minor, 110, 111, 181
choruses
  amateur, 353–55
  Ambrosian Singers, 121
  Chorus Pro Musica, 79, 287
  of Cleveland Orchestra, 96
  Columbus Boychoir, 2
  Elizabethan Singers, 283
  Hallé Choir, 121
  of Handel and Haydn Society, 52, 185, 212, 354, 416–17
  of Harvard University, 116, 351, 373, 445, 446–47, 555–56, 558
  John Alldis Choir, 277–78
  of London Symphony Orchestra, 277–78
  Munich Capella Antiqua, 356
  of New England Conservatory, 2, 116, 287, 420, 469
  St. Gabriel's Boychoir, 116
  Sheffield Philharmonic Choir, 121
  of Tanglewood, 299, 386–87, 391–92, 435, 521–22
  Vienna Choir Boys, 161
Ciconia, Johannes, 376
Cioffi, Gino, 17, 50, 87–88, 216, 245, 344
Cleva, Fausto, 28
Cleveland Orchestra, 6–7, 71, 96–99, 205, 228, 291, 293, 460–61, 495–96
  music directorship of, 378, 379, 460–61, 496
  recordings by, 120, 394–95
Cleveland Quartet, 479–80
Clevenger, Dale, 533
Cliburn, Van, 35, 180–81, 477
Club 47, 116–17
Cochran, William, 386–87
Cohen, Frank, 577
Cohen, Joel, xxv–xxvi, xxxii, 374–76
collaborative piano. *See* accompanists, role of
Collage New Music, 469–71
composer-performers, 9–10, 32–34, 48, 137–38
composers and musicologists, xix–xx
Composers String Quartet, 143–45, 347–49, 500–1
Concentus Musicus Vienna, 161–62, 196, 252–53, 356
concerto (genre), 482
Concerto Amsterdam, 123
conducting
  as career, 205–10, 228–29
  technique, 18–20, 169–70, 401–2, 427–30
conductors
  American, overlooked, 293–96
  assistant/associate, role of, 315–16
  choral, 354–55
  music directorships, 205–10, 227–30
    (*see also under* BSO; Chicago Symphony Orchestra; Cleveland Orchestra; Leinsdorf, Erich; Munch, Charles; New York Philharmonic; Ozawa, Seiji; Steinberg, William)
Cone, Edward T., xix–xx
  Musical Form and Musical Performance, 275–76
cookbooks, 585–87
Cooke, Deryck, 358–59
Coolidge, Elizabeth Sprague, xxn.5
Copland, Aaron, 520–21, 522, 581
  folk song arrangements, 285
  Quiet City, 522
  recordings, 251
  Short Symphony, 369–70
Corelli, Franco, 42, 119, 397–98
Corrado, Ronald, 517
Cortot, Alfred, 154–55, 484
Cossa, Domenic, 146
Cossutta, Carlo, 469
Couperin, François
  Les Nations, 123
Couperin, Louis, 250
Cowell, Henry, 68, 367
Craft, Robert, 138, 180
Craig, Charles, 12
Crespin, Régine, 118, 194
criticism, xxv–xxx, xxxi–xxxiii, 48, 54–56, 215–17, 233–35, 514–16
  reviews reconsidered, 475–76
  Rostropovich on, 91
  symposium on, 395–98
  See also under race
Cross, Milton, 545–46
Cross, Richard, 12
Crumb, George
  Echoes of Time and the River, 541
Cryer, David, 394
Cumberland, David, 391
Curtin, Phyllis, 386–87
Curtis, Alan, 195–96
Curtis, Jan, 514–16
Curzon, Clifford, 284

cuts, 56–58, 78, 82–83, 97, 138, 139, 146, 211, 230, 281, 391, 464, 481, 504
Cvejić, Biserka, 118
Czechoslovakia, 168, 379

Dahl, Ingolf, 402–3
Dallapiccola, Luigi, 305, 312, 556, 557–58
  obituary, 550–53
Dalley, John, 126–27
  See also Guarneri String Quartet
Dane, Jean, 571
Dara, Enzo, 578–79
Darden, Charles, 433
Davidovsky, Mario
  Synchronisms, 386, 470–71
Davies, Peter Maxwell
  Eight Songs for a Mad King, 469–70
Davis, Colin, 210, 247–49, 276–78, 379, 404–5, 409–10, 435, 437–39, 441–42, 575–76
Dean, Laura, and dance company, 561–62
Debussy, Claude, 240–42, 341–42, 456
  Études, 180–81, 458
  Images for orchestra, 71
  Images for piano, 110–11
  Jeux, 241
  La Mer, 23, 241, 317–18, 521, 574
  Pelléas et Mélisande, 408–11
  Prelude to The Afternoon of a Faun, 242
  recordings, 178–80, 203, 241–42
Deiber, Paul-Émile, 409–10
Demus, Jörg, 283, 567–68
Denisov, Edison, 190–92
Deutsche Grammophon, 363, 378–79, 481, 563
deVaron, Lorna Cooke, 2, 116, 287, 420, 469
Devetzi, Vasso, 502
di Stefano, Giuseppe, 262–63, 498, 502
Dimmock, Ellalou, 15
Donizetti, Gaetano
  Lucia di Lammermoor, 270–72, 498
  recordings, 261–63
Dooley, William, 79
Dorian Wind Quintet, 139
doubling, 25, 26, 108–9, 211
Downes, Olin, 131, 175
Dufallo, Richard, 139
Duflos, Huguette, 509
Dunn, Thomas, xxv–xxvi, xxxii, 183–85, 211–12, 355, 416–17
Duo Geminiani, 565–66
Dvořák, Antonín
  Cello Concerto, 87–88, 482–83
  Piano Quintet No. 2 in A, Op. 81, 127, 300
  String Quartet No. 14 in A-flat, Op. 105, 127
  Symphony No. 3, 56
  Symphony No. 8, 305
Dwyer, Doriot Anthony, 50, 160, 163, 248, 325, 436, 437
Dyer, Richard, 11n.4, 499, 514, 580–81
  on Michael Steinberg, xxviii–xxix, xxxii

Eberle, Jan, 577
education and teaching, xx
Edwards, Ryan, 165–66
Egmond, Max van, 161
Elgar, Edward
  Dream of Gerontius, 120–21
  Enigma Variations, 33
  Symphony No. 2, 49–50, 313–14
  Violin Concerto, 183, 438–39
Ellis, Anita, 124
Emmanuel Music, xxv–xxvi, 547–48
English Chamber Orchestra, 310–11, 345–46
Epstein, Frank, 470
Equiluz, Kurt, 161, 356
Eschenbach, Christoph, 382
Eskin, Jules, 50, 51, 77, 160, 314, 351, 460, 495
Eto, Toshiya, 306
Evitts, David, 445, 446–47, 495

Falla, Manuel de
  Nana, 440
Farrar, James, 271
fascism, 175, 332–33, 551
Feldman, Jonathan, 542
Feldman, Morton
  Cello and Orchestra, 495
Feldman, Ronald, 470
Ferrante, John, 179–80
Ferrara, Franco, 572–74
Ferris, John, 558
Fiedler, Arthur, 23, 69–70
finale, formal problem of, 49, 105–6
finances of ensembles, 273, 294, 335–36, 362
Fine Arts Quartet, 424–25
Fine, Burton, 50, 77, 160, 351, 460
Fine, Irving
  recordings, 164–65
  String Quartet, 425
Firkušný, Rudolf, 6
Fischer-Dieskau, Dietrich, 128–29, 167, 194, 491
Fischer, Edwin, 36–37, 154
Flagello, Ezio, 101, 391, 445, 446–47
Fleezanis, Jorja, vii*f*, xxii
Fleisher, Leon, 394–95
Fleming, Robert
  Confession Stone, 346–47

Foley, Madeline, 9–10
Forest, Karl, 509
Forrester, Maureen, 146, 386–87
fortepiano, 566–68
Fortunato, D'Anna, 384, 391, 548, 555–56, 558
Foss, Lukas, 135–37, 148–49
  Echoi, 139
Frager, Malcolm, 75–77, 245–46, 420–21, 576
Franck, César
  Violin Sonata, 440
Frank, Claude, 76–77, 381–82
Frankenstein, Alfred, 395–97
Freeman, Henry, 160
Freni, Mirella, 42
Frescobaldi, Girolamo, 249–50
Fried, Miriam, 531–32
Fried, Paul, 470
Fromm, Paul, 144n.9
Fulbright scholarship, xx, 551, 585
Fürstner, Carl, 346–47
Furtwängler, Elisabeth, 447–49, 451–54
Furtwängler, Wilhelm, 24, 83, 194, 243, 447–49, 451–54, 484

Gabrieli, Giovanni
  Canzon Quarti Toni, 17–18
Gagnon, Roland, 151
Gandolfi, Romano, 578
Gedda, Nicolai, 118, 491
Gelles, George, xxx, 211
Geminiani, Francesco, 565
Genovese, June, 51–52
Gentele, Goeran, 421–24, 432
  obituary, 426–27
Gielen, Michael, 407–8
Gilday, Edward, 51–53, 55
Gillesberger, Hans, 161
Gilman, Lawrence, 553
Giulini, Carlo Maria, xxiiin.8, xxix–xxx, 210, 324–25, 504–5
Glasser, Caren, 139
Godfrey, Batyah, 116
Goethe, Johann Wolfgang von, 44, 113–14, 132n.5, 457
  See also Berlioz, Hector: *Damnation of Faust*; Gounod, Charles: *Faust*; Schumann, Robert: *Faust-Scenes*
Gomberg, Ralph, 17, 50–51, 77, 87–88, 248, 299, 408
Goodman, Joseph
  Quintet for Wind Instruments, 164
Gorr, Rita, 78–79
Gottschalk, Louis Moreau, 555
Gould, Glenn, 3–4, 8–9, 296, 430
Gounod, Charles
  Ave Maria, 232, 233–34
  Faust, 118, 390–91
  Roméo et Juliette, 277
Graffman, Gary, 23
Gramm, Donald, 151–52, 224, 271
Greater Boston Youth Symphony Orchestra, 364–65
Grieg, Edvard
  recordings, 394–95
Guarneri String Quartet, 126–28, 130–31, 134–35, 204–5
Guglielmi, Margherita, 578–79

Hadley, Henry, 78
Haefliger, Ernst, 58–60, 137
Haggin, B. H., xxv, 126, 338
Haitink, Bernard, 291–92, 377, 380–81
Hale, Philip, 189
Hale, Robert, 469
Halle, Morris, 485, 486
Hallé Orchestra, 121, 247
Hamilton, David
  on Carter, 466–67
Handel, George Frideric
  Chandos Anthems, 199–200
  Concerti Grossi, Op. 6, 2, 523–24
  Giulio Cesare, 145–47
  Messiah, 51–53, 54–56, 96–99, 211–12, 233, 354, 365, 488
Handel and Haydn Society, xxv–xxvi, xxxii, 51–53, 54–56, 183, 185, 211–12, 354, 416–17
Harbison, Helen, 117
Harbison, John, 117, 230, 232, 355, 383–84
  "Music When Soft Voices Die," 383
Harbison, Rose Mary, 117, 232, 384
  on Rudolf Kolisch, 572
Harnoncourt, Nikolaus, 252
  See also Concentus Musicus Vienna
Harrell, Mack, 129
Harris, Lowell, 271
Harrison, Lou
  Canticle No. 3, 367–68
Harsanyi, Janice, 97
Hartmann, Paul, 509
Harvard-Radcliffe Orchestra, 28
Harvey, John, 271
Harvuot, Clifford, 410
Hatch, Francis W., 69–70
Haubenstock-Ramati, Roman
  Interpolation, 362–63
Haupt, Charles, 139

Haydn, Franz Joseph, 3, 303, 307, 568
  Cello Concerto in C, 86, 87–88, 89
  Piano Sonata in E-flat, Hob. XVI/49, 503–4
  Seasons, 57–58
  Sinfonia concertante in B-flat, 77
  string quartets, 204, 480
  Symphony No. 31, *Hornsignal*, 344–45
  Symphony No. 92, *Oxford*, 48–49
  Symphony No. 94, *Surprise*, 325
  Symphony No. 98, 317
  Symphony No. 99, 248
Hayes, Roland, 34, 185–90
Haywood, Lorna, 97
Heater, Claude, 193–94
Heeley, Desmond, 409–11
Heifetz, Jascha, 439–41, 512–13
Heiller, Anton, 84, 86
Heinrich, Rudolf, 224–25
Heiss, John, 362–63
Henriot-Schweitzer, Nicole, 5
Herincx, Raimund, 178, 179–80
Herseth, Adolph, 533
Heyworth, Peter, 395–97
Hill, Keith, harpsichord by, 566
Hindemith, Paul
  Konzertmusik, 108
  Mathis der Maler Symphony, 321, 505
  When Lilacs Last in the Dooryard Bloom'd, 556–57
Hindustani classical music, 510–11
Hines, Jerome, 28, 78, 79
historically informed performance, 162, 183–85, 249–51, 252–53, 375–76, 565–68, 582–83
Hoagland, Diana, 474, 555–56, 558
Hocher, Barbara, 390
Hoekman, Guus, 60n.3, 61–62
Hoelscher, Ulf, 512–13
Hoffmeister, Frank, 445, 446–47
Hofmann, Josef, 395
Hofmannsthal, Hugo von, 507–9
Hollander, John, 20–21, 138
Holst, Gustav
  choral/vocal works, 182
  recordings, 181–83
  Savitri, xxxiin.21, 181–82
Holst, Imogen, 181, 182, 345
Hopkins, Bruce, 547
Horenstein, Jascha, 377, 478
Horne, Marilyn, 225, 284
Horowitz, Vladimir, 23, 322–23, 352–53, 413–14
Hovhaness, Alan
  Khaldis, 164
  Prelude and Quadruple Fugue, 18
Hume, Paul, 395–97
Humphrey, Jon, 212, 416–17
Hunter College, 200
Hurley, Laurel, 28
Hussain, Zakir, 510–11

Imbrie, Andrew, 556
Inbal, Eliahu, 412
Isaac, Heinrich, 116–17
Israel, concert culture in, 364–67
Israel Philharmonic, 366–67, 579–80
Istomin, Eugene, 23
Ives, Charles, 75, 259, 581
  Three Places in New England, 317–18, 400
  Piano Sonata No. 2, *Concord*, 553–55
  Robert Browning Overture, 223
  Symphony No. 4, 67–69, 74
  violin sonatas, 72–73

Jackendoff, Ray, 486
Jacobs, Paul, 93–94, 138, 261, 327
Jacobs School of Music, Indiana University, xxiii–xxiv
Jagel, Frederick, 129
Jalas, Jussi, 262
Johnson, Robert (tenor), 325
Jones, Elayne, 538–39
Joplin, Scott, 476–77
Josquin des Prez, 15
Juilliard String Quartet, 251, 307, 461, 462, 463, 466–68

Kachel, Jaroslav, 271
Kalisch, Alfred, 509–10
Kalish, Gilbert, 72–73
Kallman, Chester, 176, 178
Kaplan, Abraham, 136, 139
Karajan, Herbert von, 24, 42–43, 194–95, 412, 452, 544–45, 562–65
Kastendieck, Miles, 395–96, 397
Kelsey, Philip, 470, 473
Kempe, Rudolph, 437, 513
Kennedy Center for the Performing Arts, 392
Kennedy, John F., 232
Kennedy, Robert F., 232–33, 235
Kerns, Robert, 565
Kertész, István, 210, 491–92
Keye, Christopher, 283
Khan, Ali Akbar, 510–11
Kies, Christopher, 470
King, James, 166–67, 194–95
Kipnis, Claude, 151
Kirchner, Leon, 9–10, 568, 569

Concerto for Violin, Cello, Ten Winds, and Percussion, 9–10, 576–77
Lily, 473–74
Music for Orchestra, 326–27
Kirkpatrick, John, 553–55
Klein, Adam, 410
Klemperer, Otto, 166–68, 229, 243
obituary, 478–79
Knudsen, Ronald, 470
Knussen, Oliver, 491–94
Symphony No. 3, 493–95
Knussen, Stuart, 491–92
Kogan, Richard, 569
Kohn, Karl Christian, 128
Kol Israel Radio Symphony Orchestra, 365–66
Kolisch, Gertrud. *See* Schoenberg, Gertrude
Kolisch Quartet, 39, 40, 569–71
Kolisch, Rudolf, 39–41, 172, 242–43, 278, 546, 569–72
"Tempo and Character in Beethoven's Music," 193, 236–37, 238–39, 242–43
Kollo, René, 445, 446–47, 563n.12, 564–65
Kolodin, Irving, 543–44
Komar, Arthur, 509–10
Kondrashin, Kiril, 91–93, 340–41
Kónya, Sándor, 78–79, 82, 120
Kopleff, Florence, 97–98, 116
Korngold, Erich Wolfgang, 511–13
Koussevitzky, Serge, 35n.12, 55, 88, 108, 327, 371, 401, 517–20
centennial tribute at Tanglewood, 520–22
Koussevitzky Prize, 295–96, 379, 399–400, 404–5, 520, 537
Kozma, Lajos, 356
Krasner, Louis, 64–65
Krause, Tom, 199, 445, 446–47
Kreisler, Fritz
cadenzas for Beethoven Violin Concerto, 193
Krenek, Ernst
Circle, Chain, and Mirror, 62–63
Pentagram, 164
Kubelík, Jan, 170
Kubelik, Rafael, 162–64, 168–70, 294–95, 377–78, 379, 422–23, 427, 491
Kuhse, Hanne-Lore, 198–99

Lablache, Luigi, 12
Lalo, Édouard
Roi d'Ys Overture, 267–68
Landowska, Wanda, 122
Lane, William, 129–30
Lannom, Allen, 353–54
Laredo, Jaime, 472–73
Larson, Susan, 548
LaSalle String Quartet, 368–69
Lateiner, Jacob, 160, 382–83
Layton, Bentley, 117
Lear, Evelyn, 128
Ledger, Philip, 346
Lee, Ming Cho, 145, 146–47
Lehner, Eugene, 40, 570–71
Leinsdorf, Erich, 47, 54, 243, 366n.19, 539
BSO music directorship, 30, 35–37, 205–10, 227–28, 286–87, 292, 294, 307–9, 437, 517–18
BSO performances, xxix, 25–26, 45–46, 56–58, 66–67, 75–76, 77–79, 81–83, 116, 160–61, 164, 193, 199, 222, 232, 245–46, 280–82, 286–87, 297–99, 307–9
cuts and other edits, 25–26, 56–58
on segregation, 23–25
Leipzig Gewandhaus Orchestra, 25, 525–26
Lenya, Lotte, 123–26
Leonhardt, Gustav, 121–23, 161, 196, 249–51, 253
Lesser, Laurence, 577
letters to the editor, xxiiin.8, xxv–xxvi, xxix–xxx, 2n.1, 54–56, 140–43, 215–17, 233–35, 514–16, 580–81
Leverkühn, Adrian, 463, 497
Levin, Robert, 230–32
Levine, James, 305–7, 315, 405–6, 422–23, 427, 433–34
Levine, Jesse, 139
Lewis, Henry, xx, 187, 224, 284–85, 315
Lewis, Richard, 121, 151, 195–96
Lewy, Patricia, xxiv
Lhevinne, Josef, 395
Lhevinne, Rosina, 395
Lieberson, Peter
Concerto for Four Groups of Instruments, 506–7
Ligeti, György, 531
Atmosphères, 327, 369–70
Aventures and *Nouvelles Aventures*, 156, 389
String Quartet No. 2, 368–69, 501
linguistics, 485–86
Liszt, Franz, 13–14, 153, 456
Années de pèlerinage, 180
Brendel on, 154
Dante Sonata, 13–14
Don Juan Fantasy, 155–56, 411–12
Etudes, 349
Fountains at the Villa d'Este, 411–12
Grand Etudes after Paganini, 349, 458
Harmonies poétiques et religieuses, 152–53

Liszt, Franz (*cont.*)
Hungarian Rhapsodies, 152, 154, 323
Mephisto Waltzes, 181
paraphrases and transcriptions, 154
Petrarch Sonnets, 181, 458
Les Préludes, 223
recordings, 227
Transcendental Etudes, 455–59
Lloyd, David, 129
Locke, Eleanor G., 215–17
London Symphony Orchestra, 303–4, 338–40, 574
Lorenz, Siegfried, 526
Loriod, Yvonne, 417–18, 550
Ludwig, Christa, 166–67, 168, 193–94
Lybbert, Donald
Leopardi Canti, 470–71

Ma, Yo-Yo, 569
Maazel, Lorin, 210, 304, 471–72, 496
Maderna, Bruno, 60–62, 269, 390, 431–32
Magad, Samuel, 533
Mahler, Gustav, 7, 163, 168–69, 240, 259, 494
"Blumine," 321
demands of performing, 102–3, 376–77, 546–47
Das Lied von der Erde, 166–68, 308, 403
Kindertotenlieder, 247
recordings, 120, 166–68, 247, 377–78
Songs of a Wayfarer, 247, 526
Symphony No. 1, 321–22
Symphony No. 3, 478, 546–47
Symphony No. 4, 120, 282–83, 310
Symphony No. 5, 62, 233, 407–8, 572
Symphony No. 6, 433–34, 460–61
Symphony No. 7, 101, 148, 149, 371–72
Symphony No. 8, 101–3, 114, 115
Symphony No. 9, 6–7, 92–93, 100, 162–64, 169, 216, 350–51, 432–33
Symphony No. 10, 358–59
See also tempo: in Mahler
Malas, Spiro, 12, 146
Manén, Lucie, 528
Mann, Alfred, 97, 183, 199–200
Mann, Thomas, 44, 107, 401, 463n.6, 489, 490–91, 526–27, 552–53
Mann, William, 395–97
Markevitch, Igor, 303–4
Marlboro Music (VT), 39–40, 126–27, 204, 311, 330, 483–84
Marsh, Calvin, 28, 79
Marshall, Larry, 394
Marshall, Lois, 391
Marshall, Yale, 390
Martin, Frank, 261
Martin, Robert, 139
Martino, Donald, 551
Notturno, 506
Martinon, Jean, 47–48, 108–9, 205, 207, 228, 583
Overture for a Greek Tragedy, 108
Martinů, Bohuslav, xixn.2
Masur, Kurt, 525–26
Mathis, Edith, 283, 482
Mattfeld, Victor, 14–15
Mauceri, John, 508
McConathy, Osbourne, 151, 224
McCoy, Seth, 97
McDaniel, Barry, 410
McIntyre, Donald, 482
Mehta, Zubin, 120, 210, 291–92, 366, 399, 579–80, 583
Mekeel, Joyce
The Shape of Silence, 362–63
Mendel, Arthur, 183, 184
Mendelson, Danny, 289
Mendelssohn, Felix
Piano Concerto No. 1, 70
String Quartet No. 2 in A minor, Op. 13, 127
Symphony No. 4, *Italian*, 281, 339
Menuhin, Yehudi, 192–93, 243
Merrill, Robert, 42, 119–20, 545
Messiaen, Olivier
Chronochromie, 266–67
Couleurs de la cité céleste, 388, 417
Meditations on the Mystery of the Holy Trinity, 417–19
Oiseaux éxotiques, 474
Turangalîla-symphonie, 549–50
Metropolitan Opera, 28, 118–20, 187, 209, 295, 408–11, 421–24, 426–27, 514–15, 526–28, 543–46, 558–60, 565
Meyerson, Janice, 547
Michelangeli, Arturo Benedetti, 109–11, 413
Milnes, Sherrill, 287, 298, 299, 477
Minnesota Orchestra, xxii
Minty, Shirley, 283
Mitropoulos, Dimitri, 7, 82, 99, 100, 128–29, 290–91, 295, 304, 305–6, 343–44
Moffo, Anna, 118, 543
Moldenhauer, Hans, 148–49
Moleux, Georges, 50
Montarsolo, Paolo, 578–79
Montealegre, Felicia. *See* Bernstein, Felicia Montealegre

Monteux, Pierre, 32, 186
obituary, 37–39
Monteverdi, Claudio
L'incoronazione di Poppea, 195–96
L'Orfeo, 355–56
recordings, 195–97, 355–56
secular vocal music, 516–17
Mordino, Joseph, 129
Morris, Thomas W., xxxi
Moscow Philharmonic, 91–93, 340–41
Mozart, Wolfgang Amadè, 547–48
12 German Dances, K.586, 548
Abduction from the Seraglio, 56, 306–7
completions (Levin), 230–32
Così fan tutte, 177, 544–45
Divertimento in B-flat, K.287, 77–78
Marriage of Figaro, 6, 508
Messiah re-orchestration, 51–53
Piano Concerto No. 12, 76–77
Piano Concerto No. 13, 75–76
Piano Concerto No. 15, 6
recordings, 310–11
rondos, 288
Serenata notturna in D, K.239, 381
Sinfonia concertante for four winds, 17–18
Sinfonia concertante for violin and viola, 77
String Quintet No. 4 in G minor, K.516, 472–73
Symphony No. 26, 163–64
Symphony No. 33, 76
Symphony No. 35, *Haffner*, 433
Symphony No. 36, *Linz*, 372
Symphony No. 38, *Prague*, 76
Symphony No. 39, 77–78, 564
Symphony No. 40, 310–11, 579
Symphony No. 41, 19
Violin Concerto No. 4, 434
Zaide, 548
Mozartkugeln, 548, 562–63
Munch, Charles, 2, 4–5, 55–56, 278, 419–20, 431, 489, 517–18, 525, 537
BSO music directorship, 88n.16, 209, 307–9
Munich Philharmonic, 513
music criticism. *See* criticism
Music Critics Circle of New York, 74
Music Guild Quartet, 215–17
musicologists, xix, 68, 144, 190–91
and performers, 30–31, 35–37, 184, 280, 375
Mussorgsky, Modest
Boris Godunov, 224–25, 244
Pictures at an Exhibition, 15–16
songs, 103–4
National Orchestra of Belgium, 407–8
Nazism and Nazi Germany, 149, 175, 189, 357–58, 365, 366, 448–49, 479, 544–45
See also antisemitism
Neschling, John, 429, 433
New England Chamber Opera Group, 509–10
New England Conservatory, 34
ragtime ensemble, 476–77
symphony orchestra, 23, 62–63, 93–94, 222–23, 253–54, 495, 546–47
See also under choruses
New Grove Dictionary of Music and Musicians, xxii
New Jersey Symphony, 284–85
New Philharmonia Orchestra, 165, 166–68, 240–42, 246–47, 261, 412
New York City Opera, 82, 145–47, 209, 295, 423, 559
New York Philharmonic, 32, 82, 128–29, 135–40, 207, 228, 229, 233, 268–70, 272–74, 304, 325–28, 341–44, 359, 404–5, 537
music directorship of, 205–6, 228, 290–95, 315–16, 448
New York Times, xx, 81, 118, 136, 175, 183, 268, 272, 326, 460, 527–28, 583–84
New Yorker (magazine), xxiiin.8, 74, 583–84
Nicolai, Otto
Merry Wives of Windsor Overture, 69
Nikisch, Arthur, 132–33, 452, 525, 579
Nilsson, Birgit, 118, 193–95, 559
Nimsgern, Siegmund, 565
Niska, Maralin, 299
Nixon, Marni, 149
noise pollution, 335
Nono, Luigi
Intolleranza 1960, 60–62, 171
Norman, Jessye, 346–47, 434–35
Norton Lectures, 177, 444, 484–87, 491
notation, interpretation of, 30–31, 33, 327–28
Novoa, Salvador, 271

Ogdon, John, 227, 382
Ohlsson, Garrick, 289–90, 464–66
Oliver, John, 299, 353–54, 386–87, 435, 521–22, 575
Olivero, Magda, 559
Opera Company of Boston, 11–13, 11n.4, 56–57, 60–62, 82, 150–52, 171, 175–76, 178–80, 223–26, 270–72
opera, concert performance of, 78–79, 444–45, 447
Oppens, Ursula, 505–6
Orff, Carl, 165

organ performance, 84–86, 184, 417–19
Ormandy, Eugene, xxx, 149, 208, 321–22, 539, 583
Ozawa, Seiji, xxx, 327, 536–41
  BSO music directorship, 210, 379–80, 481, 517–18, 520, 536–41
  BSO performances, 369–70, 390–92, 481–82, 522, 549–50

Paganini, Niccolò, 170, 430
Page, Tim
  on Michael Steinberg, xxii–xxiii
Partos, Oedoen
  Paths, 358, 580
Partridge, Ian, 283
Paul, Thomas, 97, 116, 482
Pears, Peter, 103, 200–2, 310, 323–24, 450, 526–28, 530–31, 559
Penderecki, Krzysztof, 581
  Capriccio for Violin and Orchestra, 364–65
Perahia, Murray, 300, 526–27, 530–31
Peress, Maurice, 394
performers, training of, 65, 244
  American, 187
Pérotin
  Sederunt principes, 373–74
Perry, Thomas D., Jr., 400–1, 406
Peterson, Doris, 390
Petri, Egon, 239–40
Pfitzner, Hans
  Palestrina, 357–58, 489–91
Philadelphia Orchestra, xxx, 149, 208, 321–22, 378, 583
Philharmonia Orchestra, 166–68, 300, 582
Philharmonic Hall (New York), 100–1, 288, 325–28, 342, 580–81
piano playing, Romantic style of, 226, 395, 406, 458
Piston, Walter
  Divertimento for Nine Instruments, 569
  Flute Concerto, 436–37
  recordings, 164
  Symphony No. 2, 363–64
  Toccata for Orchestra, 321–22
Pittman, Richard, 362
Pleasants, Henry, 395–98
Ponchielli, Amilcare
  La Gioconda, 118, 498, 499, 502, 544–45
Pond, Helen, 178–79, 271
Ponnelle, Jean-Pierre, 578
Portney, Robert, 568, 577
Poulenc, Francis, 202–3
  La Fraîcheur et le feu, 346–47
Poulimenos, Andrew, 212
Pracht, Mary Ellen, 199
Prager, A. Fred, 189–90
Prausnitz, Frederik, 22–23, 62–63, 93–94, 222–23, 236, 253–54, 255, 261
Preble, Elinor, 72–73, 416–17
Prêtre, Georges, 210, 266–68
Previn, André, 291–92, 338–40
Prey, Hermann, 116, 154, 165–66
Price, Leontyne, 41–43, 66, 67, 118, 119
Princeton University, xix–xx, 443–44
prizes for music, 73–75
  See also Koussevitzky Prize
Procter, Norma, 377–78
programming, xxxiin.21, 50–51, 66–67, 180, 216–17, 256, 272–73, 278, 284–85, 307, 311–13, 314–16, 373, 403–4, 424–25, 444, 447, 480
  See also BSO: programming
Prokofiev, Sergei
  Scythian Suite, 436, 437
  Symphony No. 5, 88, 89, 193, 520–21
  Violin Concerto in D, Op. 19, 272–73
Puccini, Giacomo
  La bohème, 27–28, 578–79
  Manon Lescaut, 118, 502
  Tosca, 220–21, 224–25, 422–23, 502, 559
Pulitzer prizes, 73–75, 363
Purcell, Henry
  dramatic music of, 48
  "Thou knowest, Lord...," 233

Quadro Amsterdam, 123

race
  and criticism, 186–87, 397–98
  and performing/training opportunities, 186, 187, 189
  See also antisemitism; Nazism and Nazi Germany; segregation
Rachmaninoff, Sergei, 395
  Études-Tableaux, 440
  Piano Concerto No. 2, 406–7
  Symphony No. 3, 340
Raeburn, Andrew, 199, 299
ragtime, 476–77
Rameau, Jean-Philippe
  Hippolyte et Aricie, 246
Rapier, Wayne, 370
Raskin, Judith, 118, 120
Ravel, Maurice
  Boléro, 69
  Mother Goose Suite, 381
  Piano Concerto in G, 5
  Shéhérazade (song cycle), 247
  Tzigane, 440

La Valse, 267
Rehfuss, Heinz, 136–37
Reich, Steve
Drumming, 560–62
Music for Mallet Instruments, Voices, and Organ, 495
Renaissance music, 14–15, 116–17, 376
See also historically informed performance
repeats, 53, 204, 252, 297, 377, 382, 474–75
essays on, 280–82, 310–11
Reynolds, Anna, 575
Richter, Hans, 132–33
Richter-Haaser, Hans, 23–24
Ridderbusch, Karl, 563, 565
Riegel, Kenneth, 420
Rifkin, Joshua, 476–77
Riley, Terry, 561
Rintzler, Marius, 575
Ritchie, Stanley, 517, 565–66
Rivers, Larry, 135–37, 140
Robards, Jason, 135–37
Roberto, Francesca, 51–52
Robison, Paula, 577
Rodan, Mendi, 365–66
Rodzinski, Artur, 290–91, 294–95
Roggero, Margaret, 60n.3, 61–62
Romaguera, Joaquin, 299
Rore, Cipriano de, 376
Rorem, Ned, 73
Eagles, 18
Rosen, Charles, xix–xx, 93–94, 155–56, 197, 239–40, 242, 261, 296–97, 414–16
on Carter, 466–68
The Classical Style, 482, 583–84
Rosenblum, Susan, 510
Rosenstock, Joseph, 118
Rossi, Michelangelo, 249–50
Rossini, Gioachino
La Cenerentola, 577–79
Siege of Corinth, 284, 558–60
Rostropovich, Mstislav, 86–91, 103–4, 191, 412, 580–81
Roth, Kenneth, 384
Roussel, Albert
Symphony No. 3, 5
Rubin Music Academy, 365–66
Rubinstein, Anton
Melody in F, 483
Rubinstein, Artur, 23, 36–37, 352–53, 406–7, 420–21
Rudel, Julius, 145–46, 295
Ruggles, Carl, 312
Evocations, 555
Russia
music of, 190–92
Roland Hayes in, 189
Rutgers University Collegium Musicum, 200

Salzburg Easter Festival, 563
San Francisco Symphony, xxii, 538–39
Sanders Theatre (Cambridge, MA), acoustics of, 9–10, 130–31, 501
Sargeant, Winthrop, xxiin.8, 74
Sargent, Francis W., 520
Satie, Erik, 203
Socrate, 389–90
Vexations, 275
Sawallisch, Wolfgang, 18–20
Scala, La, 577–79
Scarlatti, Domenico
sonatas, 349
Schaefer, Lois, 163, 351
Schickele, Peter, 223n.2
Schmelzer, Johann Heinrich, 566
Schnabel, Artur, 14, 32, 47, 94–95, 105, 238–40, 381–82, 414–15, 455–56
Music and the Line of Most Resistance, 274–75
Schneider, Alexander, 127, 299–300, 472–73, 483–84
Schneider-Siemssen, Günther, 564
Schoenberg, Arnold, 43–44, 253–56, 522–25
Two Piano Pieces, Op. 33, 265–66, 288
"Brahms the Progressive," 523
chamber symphonies, 39–40, 253–56, 301, 474
as conductor, 40
Gurre-Lieder, 540–41
Moses and Aron, 150–52, 171, 202–3, 273–74
on performance and reception of his music, 44, 397, 524, 532–33
Pierrot lunaire, 551
re-compositions and transcriptions by, 523
and Gertrude Schoenberg, 171–72
and Rudolf Kolisch, 39–41
Serenade, 362
String Quartet No. 2, 140
String Trio, 43
stylistic development of, 254–55
A Survivor from Warsaw, 286–87, 520–21, 522
Variations for Orchestra, 532–33
Violin Concerto, xxxiin.21, 64–67
Von Heute auf Morgen, 172
and Webern, 140–43, 148
Schoenberg, Gertrude, 170–72
scholars. *See* musicologists
Schonberg, Harold, xxvii, 83, 118, 126, 395–97, 460, 527–28

Schröder-Feinen, Ursula, 565
Schröder, Jaap, 123, 517
Schubert, Franz, 219
  Arpeggione Sonata, D.821, 90, 542
  Fantasy in F minor, D.940, 9–10
  Impromptus, D.899, 36–37
  Lieder, 59, 148, 188–89, 201, 202, 218–19, 282–83, 530
  piano sonatas, 155
  Piano Sonata No. 14 in A minor, D.784, 411
  Piano Sonata No. 21 in C minor, D.958, 13
  Piano Trio No. 2 in E-flat, D.929, 569
  recordings, 282–83, 483–84
  Schubertiades, 282
  Symphony No. 3, 94
  Symphony No. 9, *The Great*, 577
  Variations in A-flat, D.813, 9–10
  Waltzes, D.145, 411
  Wanderer Fantasy, D.760, 411
  Winterreise, 165–66, 200–2
Schuller, Gunther, 269, 343–45, 389–90, 476–77, 521–22, 533, 546–47, 572–73, 582, 583
  Klee Studies, 30
  Spectra, 343–44
  String Quartet No. 1, 501
Schuman, William, 74–75, 363
  American Festival Overture, 520–21
  Violin Concerto, 363–64
Schumann, Robert
  Carnaval, 95–96
  Davidsbündlertänze, 226–27
  Dichterliebe, 59, 218–19, 323–24
  Fantasy in C, Op. 17, 226–27, 503–4
  Faust-Scenes, xxxiin.21, 112–16, 207
  Kreisleriana, 352–53
  Liederkreis, Op. 39, 528, 531
  Piano Quintet in E-flat, Op. 44, 130–31
  Piano Concerto, 245–46, 394–95
  Piano Sonata No. 1 in F-sharp minor, Op. 11, 464
  Piano Sonata No. 3 in F minor, Op. 14, 8–9
  Piano Trio No. 1 in D minor, Op. 63, 300
  recordings, 226–27, 352–53, 394–95, 483–84
  Symphonic Etudes, Op.13, 226–27
  symphonies (Mahler re-scorings), 169
  Symphony No. 2, 471
  Symphony No. 3, *Rhenish*, 374, 388–89, 405
  Symphony No. 4, 453, 525–26
Schütz, Heinrich
  Fili mi Absalon, 388–89
Schwann, William, catalogue of, 359–61
Schwantner, Joseph
  Consortium, 362–63
Schwarz, Boris, 190–91
Scriabin, Alexander
  Etudes, 323, 464, 465–66
  Piano Sonata No. 10, 265–66
  Prometheus, Poem of Fire, 327–28
Seabury, John, 389
Seeger, Charles, 144
Seeger, Ruth Crawford
  String Quartet, 143–45
segregation, 23–25, 34–35
Senn, Herbert, 178–79, 271
Senturia, Michael, 558
Serkin, Peter, 288–89, 474, 506, 529
Serkin, Rudolf, 14, 94–96, 105, 288, 529, 571
Servais, François, 542
Sessions, Roger
  Stravinsky's influence on, 302
  Psalm 140, 301
  String Quartet No. 2, 143–44
  Symphony No. 1, 301–2
  When Lilacs Last in the Dooryard Bloom'd, xxxiin.21, 555–58
Seventh Army Orchestra (US), xx, 187
Shadley, Richard, 136–37, 416–17
Shaw, Robert, 96–99, 137–38
Shchedrin, Rodion
  Mischievous Folk Ditties, 190
Sherman, Russell, 222–23, 236, 265–66, 278, 455–59, 571
Sherry, Fred, 505–6
Shifrin, Seymour
  String Quartet No. 4, 425
  String Quartet No. 5, 500–1
Shinohara, Makoto
  Fragmente, 450–51
Shirley, George, 199
Shostakovich, Dmitri, 89, 90, 91
  String Quartet No. 8, 251
  Symphony No. 1, 45
  Symphony No. 8, 340
Shulman, Daniel, 506
Shure, Leonard, 8–9, 130–31
Sibelius, Jean
  Symphony No. 2, 521
  Symphony No. 3, 437–39
  Symphony No. 5, 267
Sills, Beverly, 10, 61–62, 116, 146, 261–63, 271, 558–60
Silverman, Stanley
  Elephant Steps, 399–400
Silverstein, Joseph, 9–10, 50, 64–67, 77, 143, 160, 314, 351, 381, 387, 434, 439, 575

Silvestrov, Valentin, 190–92
  Trio for flute, trumpet, and celeste, 191–92
Skalicky, Jan, 271
Skrowaczewski, Stanisław, 210, 427–30
Slater, Jonathan, 465
Smetana, Bedřich
  String Quartet No. 1, *From My Life*, 126, 480–81
Smith, Craig, xxv–xxvi, xxxii, 548
Smith, Moses
  Koussevitzky biography, 518
smorgasbord battler, 480
Solti, Georg, 194–95, 228, 378, 478, 532–33
Sommerfest, Minnesota Orchestra, xxii
sonata form, crisis of, 3–4, 8–9
Sopher, Joseph, 51–52
Soyer, David, xxiiin.8, 126–27
  See also Guarneri String Quartet
Spectrum Concerts. *See under* Boston Symphony Orchestra
Speculum Musicae, 505–7
Speyer, Louis, 5, 189–90
Spiegelman, Joel, 190–92
Stagliano, James, 7, 17, 50–51, 163, 351
"Star-Spangled Banner, The," 180, 519
Starer, Robert
  Concerto for Violin, Cello, and Orchestra, 314
Starker, Janos, 412
Starr, Susan, 70
Steinbach, Fritz, 133
Steinberg, Jane, xx
Steinberg, Michael, vii*f*, 592
  career at *Boston Globe*, xx–xxiii, xxi*f*, xxv–xxx, xxxi–xxxiii, xxxviii*f*, 158*f*, 214*f*, 264*f*, 580–84
  career at BSO, xxx–xxxi, 580
  controversies surrounding, xxiiin.8, xxix–xxx, 325n.26
  early life, xix–xx
  friendships with review subjects, xxvii
  See also criticism
Steinberg, William, 101, 580
  BSO music directorship, 227–30, 247–48, 291–92, 294, 308–9, 315, 357–59, 378, 400, 517–18
  BSO performances, 313–14, 371–72, 419–20, 459–60, 468–69, 488–89
  conducting technique, 468–69, 488
  and Israel Philharmonic, 358
Steinhardt, Arnold, 126–27, 131
  See also Guarneri String Quartet
Stern, Isaac, 193, 272–73, 472–73, 483–84
Stern, Rudi, 179
Steuermann, Edward
  Suite, 265–66
Stewart, Thomas, 194–95, 410
Stockhausen, Karlheinz
  Groups, 62–63
  Punkte, 374
Stokowski, Leopold, 17–18, 67–69
Storace, Bernardo, 249–50
Strasfogel, Ian, 389–90
Strauss, Johann II
  Blue Danube, 19–20
Strauss, Richard, 24, 459, 489
  Ägyptische Helena, 67
  Also sprach Zarathustra, 564
  Le Bourgeois Gentilhomme, 459
  Death and Transfiguration, 579–80
  Don Juan, 433, 574
  Don Quixote, 459–60
  Ein Heldenleben, 380–81
  Horn Concerto No. 2, 129–30
  and Israel, 365–66
  Rosenkavalier, 118
  Rosenkavalier (film adaptation), 507–10
  Salome, 67
  Violin Sonata, 307, 440
Stravinsky, Igor, 417, 494, 516
  Abraham and Isaac, 495
  Concertino, 134–35
  Concerto in D for strings, 94
  as conductor, 32, 137–38
  festival, 135–40
  The Flood, 138
  Introitus, T.S. Eliot in Memoriam, 139
  Les Noces, 9–10
  Oedipus Rex, 135–37, 444–47
  Petrushka, 18, 358–59
  Rake's Progress, 175–77, 178–80, 423, 426–27, 489
  recordings, 32, 111–12
  Rite of Spring, 38, 111–12
  Symphony of Psalms, 137–38, 520–22
  Symphony in Three Movements, 32
  Variations (*Aldous Huxley in memoriam*), 317–18
Stravinsky, Vera, 135–36
strings, seating of, 133, 436–37
Strunk, Oliver, xix–xx
Stuckenschmidt, H. H., 220
Sutherland, Joan, 11–13, 21–22, 225
Sutherland, Robert, 498, 502–3
Svoboda, Josef, 422
symphony (genre), connotations of, 494

Symphony Hall (Boston), 70, 88, 373–74, 525, 527–28
Szell, George, 6–7, 92, 96, 163, 205, 228, 291, 315–16, 378, 430, 434, 460–61
  recordings, 120, 394–95, 482–84

Talvela, Martti, 193–94
Tanglewood, 75–79, 379–80, 387, 520–22
  administration, 506–7
  audiences, 83, 432
  Festival of Contemporary Music, 144, 536
  Koussevitzky and, 519–20
  Music Theater Project, 389–90
  See also Berkshire Music Center at Tanglewood; Choruses: of Tanglewood
Taylor, Rose, 299
Tchaikovsky, Boris
  Cello Concerto, 91
Tchaikovsky, Pyotr Ilyich
  Eugene Onegin, 91–93, 540
  recordings, 303–4
  Romeo and Juliet Fantasy-Overture, 277
  Sleeping Beauty, 306
  songs, 103
  symphonies, xxxiin.21, 303–4
  Symphony No. 4, 573
  Symphony No. 5, 221, 533
Tear, Robert, 181, 277–78, 283
Tebaldi, Renata, 27, 118–19, 225, 500
Telemann, Georg Philipp
  fantasias, 451
television themes, 70
tempo
  in Beethoven, 193, 222–23, 236–40, 242–44, 387, 475
  in Brahms, 244, 421, 431–32, 579
  in Carter, 22, 93, 160, 259–60, 342, 347–49
  in Mahler, 376–77, 460
  in Tchaikovsky, 303
  in Verdi, 297–98, 468
Tennstedt, Klaus, 531–32, 534–35, 575–76
Terrani, Lucia Valentini, 578
Theyard, Harry, 152
Thomas, Michael Tilson, 269, 295–96, 315, 320n.24, 380, 387–89, 399–406, 417, 422, 560
  BSO performances, 317–18, 325, 350–51, 363–64, 367–68, 373–74, 406–8, 420–21, 436–37, 494–95
Thomson, Virgil, 188, 368, 444
Thorstenberg, Laurence, 160, 299, 308–9
Tippett, Michael
  Symphony No. 3, 496–97
Titus, Alan, 394
Tokyo String Quartet, 479–81
Tommasini, Anthony
  on Michael Steinberg, xxii–xxiii
Tomowa-Sintow, Anna, 564–65
Toscanini, Arturo, 19, 38, 241, 277–78, 358, 385, 543–44
  centennial essay on, 173–75
  recordings by, 33, 241, 244, 277–78, 304
Toubman, Raymond, 384
Tourel, Jennie, 2, 101
Tovey, Donald Francis
  Essays in Musical Analysis, xxv, 412, 413–14, 442–44
Tozzi, Giorgio, 119, 410
translations of sung text, 103, 124, 152, 201–2, 390, 408, 509–10
Tree, Michael, 126–27, 300
  See also Guarneri String Quartet
Treigle, Norman, 146
Troyanos, Tatiana, 116, 445, 446–47
Tucci, Gabriella, 118
Tucker, Richard, 28, 119
  obituary, 543–46
Tunnard, Viola, 283
Turash, Stephanie, 192
Turini, Francesco, 196, 517–18
Tyler, Veronica, 116

Ulanowsky, Paul, 58–60
unions, 206, 208, 227, 309, 424, 427
Utah Symphony Orchestra, 182

van Eyck, Jacob
  English Nightingale Variations, 450–51
Varèse, Edgard
  Déserts, 315, 316
  Octandre, 139, 316
variation form, 106–7
Varona, Jose, 145, 146–47
Vaughan Williams, Ralph, 133–34, 182–83
  A London Symphony, 129–30
  Greensleeves Fantasy, 70
  Riders to the Sea, 514–15
  Symphony No. 4, 338–40
  Symphony No. 6, 182
Verdi, Giuseppe
  Aida, 543
  Don Carlo, 502, 544
  Falstaff, 223–24
  Forza del destino, 533, 580
  Otello, 174, 297–99
  Requiem, 174, 468–69, 541, 564
  Toscanini and, 174–75
  Trovatore, 118, 146, 544–45
  See also tempo: in Verdi
Verrett, Shirley, 136–37, 560

Vickers, Jon, 118–20, 194–95
Vienna Philharmonic, 166–68, 169, 304, 331–32, 379
Vienna Symphony, 18–20
Vienna Volksoper Orchestra, 262
virtuosity
  and contemporary music, 143–44, 268–69
  on the nature of, 46–48
Viscuglia, Felix, 470
Vishnevskaya, Galina, 88–90, 91–93, 103–4
Vivaldi, Antonio
  Concerto Grosso in D minor, Op. 3, No. 11, 17
Voisin, Roger, 12
Volkonsky, Andrei, 190–92
  Lamentations of Shchaza, 191
Vosgerchian, Luise, 9–10

Wager, Michael, 445, 447
Wagner, Richard
  Flying Dutchman, 133, 435
  Götterdämmerung, 58, 118, 148–49
  and Israel, 365–66
  Lohengrin, 78–79, 81, 82–83, 563–65
  recordings, 194–95, 435, 447–48, 451, 453
  Ring cycle, 83, 142, 194–95, 447, 451, 453
  Tannhäuser, 69, 422, 426, 446
  Tristan und Isolde, 154, 193–95, 308, 423, 435
  Die Walküre, 118, 194, 453
  Wesendonck Songs, 346, 435
Wallace, Barbara, 212, 416–17
Walt, Sherman, 17, 50, 77, 248, 469
Walter, Bruno, 167, 377, 489
Walton, William
  The Bear, 514–15
  Portsmouth Point Overture, 129
Warsaw Festival, 191
Watson, Chester, 12, 51–52
Watts, André, 187, 349, 411–12
Watts, Helen, 283
Wayland, Newton, 514n.11
Weber, Carl Maria von
  Oberon Overture, 66
  Piano Sonata No. 2 in A-flat, 8–9
Webern, Anton, 116–17, 570–71
  Three Pieces for Cello and Piano, Op. 11, 117
  Four Songs, Op. 13, 474
  Five Movements, Op. 5, 130–31
  Five Pieces for Orchestra, 148–49, 344
  Bagatelles for String Quartet, Op. 9, 117, 141
  Cantata No. 2, Op. 31, 149
  as conductor, 40
  death of, 150
  early works, 148
  festival, 147–50
  Kinderstück for piano, 139, 148
  Movement for String Trio, 139
  Passacaglia, Op. 1, 30, 505
  Piano Variations, Op. 27, 117, 288
  and Schoenberg, 140–43, 148
  Schubert Lieder orchestrations, 148
  songs, 148–49
  String Quartet, Op. 28, 117
Webster, Margaret, 544
Weigel, Helene, 125–26
Weilerstein, Donald, 480
Weill, Kurt, 123–26
  Threepenny Opera, 123–25
Weinberg, Henry
  String Quartet No. 2, 145
Weingarden, Louis
  Triptych, 289–90, 465
Westerman, Gerhard von, 454
Wexler, Peter, 327–28
White, Lawrence, 60, 61–62
White, Robert, 517
Whitman, Walt, 18, 555–58
Whitney, Robert, 73
Wiene, Robert, 507–8
Williams, Emlyn, 47–48
Williams, Jan, 139
Wilson, Charles, 299, 399–400
Windgassen, Wolfgang, 193–94
Winship, Thomas, xx
Wolf, Hugo, 188–89, 219, 307
Wolfe, Lawrence, 542–43
Wolff, Beverly, 101, 146
Wolpe, Stefan
  Form, 265–66
World Youth Orchestra, 520–21
Wright, Elisabeth, 565–66
Wright, Harold, 134, 363–64
Wunderlich, Fritz, 128, 166–67
Wyner, Susan Davenny, 575
Wyner, Yehudi
  Cadenza for Clarinet and Harpsichord, 302–3
Wyss, Nikolaus, 574

Yale Symphony, 508
Yancich, Charles, 13, 408

Zagortsev, Vladimir
  Dimensions, 190–92
Zander, Benjamin, 474–75
Zbinden, Julien-François, 542
Zeitlin, Ralph, 533
Zorina, Vera, 522
Zukofsky, Paul, 72–73, 364